SEIZING THE LIGHT

A HISTORY OF PHOTOGRAPHY

SEIZING THE LIGHT

A HISTORY OF PHOTOGRAPHY

ROBERT HIRSCH

Art Faculty, State University of New York at Buffalo.

McGraw
Hill

Boston   Burr Ridge, IL   Dubuque, IA   Madison, WI   New York   San Francisco   St. Louis
Bangkok   Bogotá   Caracas   Lisbon   London   Madrid
Mexico City   Milan   New Delhi   Seoul   Singapore   Sydney   Taipei   Toronto

McGraw-Hill Higher Education

A Division of **The McGraw-Hill** Companies

Seizing the Light: A History of Photography

Front cover: Carrie Mae Weems. *The Shape of Things,* 1993. From *The African Series,* one of three panels, right print. 20 × 20 inches. Platinum print. Courtesy PPOW. Back Cover: William Henry Fox Talbot. *The Open Door,* 1843. Salted paper print from a calotype negative. Plate VI of *The Pencil of Nature* (London, 1844). Courtesy The Science Museum and Society Picture Library.

This book is printed on acid-free paper.

11 12 13 VNH/VNH 0 9 8 7

ISBN: 978-0-697-14361-7

Editorial director: *Phillip A. Butcher*
Executive editor: *Cynthia Ward*
Developmental editor: *Allison McNamara*
Marketing manager: *David Patterson*
Senior project manager: *Mary Conzachi*
Senior production supervisor: *Lori Koetters*
Senior designer: *Kiera Cunningham*
Senior photo research coordinator: *Keri Johnson*
Compositor: *GTS Graphics, Inc.*
Typeface: *10/12 Times Roman*
Printer: *Von Hoffmann Press, Inc.*

Library of Congress Cataloging-in-Publication Data

Hirsch, Robert.
    Seizing the light : a history of photography / Robert Hirsch.
        p.   cm.
    Includes bibliographical references and index.
    ISBN 0-697-14361-9
        1. Photography—History.   I. Title.
    TR15.H557   2000
    770'.9—DC21   99-16019

http://www.mhhe.com

To my wife, Adele Henderson, my mother Muriel Hirsch, and my father, Edwin Hirsch, for their support and love; and to photographers, past and present, who have made this project so enlightening.

"I have found a way of fixing the images of the camera! I have seized the fleeting light and imprisoned it! I have forced the sun to paint pictures for me!"

—L. J. M. Daguerre to Charles Chevalier at his Paris optical shop

Daguerre's excited words—the inspiration for our title—reflect the driving desire to make permanent images through the action of light. In these pages I hope to convey the fascination surrounding this process we call photography throughout its development over the last two centuries. *Seizing the Light* offers a new resource for history of photography courses while providing an introduction to the photographic arts for the general reader.

I had several goals when I embarked upon this project. As a teacher, I felt the need for a discerning chronological account of Western photography from an American perspective, rather than an encyclopedic world survey. As a curator, I wanted a book that would convey the diversity of contemporary makers, issues, and applications. As a director of photographic arts organizations, I sought to present intriguing images that would inspire people to go and visit galleries and museums. And as a photographer, I wanted to explore the artistic, critical, and social aspects of the creative process that motivates people to make, look at, and interpret images. The knowledge I gained from researching this project has deepened my understanding of photographic practice; it is my hope that others will find the result to be an accessible starting point for open inquiry and discussion.

In these pages, photography is represented within the context of the artistic, cultural, scientific, technological, and utilitarian forces that have shaped Western society. *Seizing the Light* examines how photography developed from centuries of Western imagemaking and how photographers have struggled to discover the medium's own visual syntax. The book also examines how capitalism and market forces have shaped photographic practices by standardizing equipment, materials, and procedures, as well as how public applications, desires, expectations, and demands affect our understanding of images. It offers an initial site for thinking about why we have so embraced photography as a medium, and why and how we make, view, and decipher billions and billions of photo-based images every year.

Seizing the Light does not attempt to be an exhaustive survey; instead it provides a coherent view of selected people, events, processes, and movements that define the extensive roles and meanings of photography throughout its history. In addition, a variety of topics have been given in-depth coverage. These topics, which provide a fuller understanding of how photography can play with the meaning of cultural images, include the portrait, the landscape, the body, urban life, time and space, and typologies.

Technology has always had an effect on how information is shaped, transmitted, and understood; today's digital technology is no exception. The book looks at how digital technology has changed our notions about photographic truth and how it might change our conception of galleries and museums as image presenters and repositories. In addition, this may be the first history of photography written with research assistance from people all over the world through email, listserves, and Internet sites.

I gratefully acknowledge and seek to represent the canon of photographic history composed of luminary figures such as Julia Margaret Cameron, Alfred Stieglitz, and Edward Weston. However, *Seizing the Light* also aims for comprehensive coverage of the past five decades of photography. This has been a time of explosive growth in the number of people working within the photo-related arts, and it demands greater study if we are to understand its diversity and richness. Attention is given to contemporary artists who are expanding the practice of photography and bringing their works to a broader audience, as well as to important women and minority photographers throughout photographic history. In addition, I have tried to move beyond the canon in focusing on certain overlooked vernacular genres of historic practice such as stereographs and snapshots.

Readers need to bear in mind that all reproductions are just approximations of the work—interested viewers should make the effort to see actual pieces in their own local galleries and museums. It is my wish that the images chosen to represent a particular artist or movement will stimulate readers to go beyond those few pictures and kindle a passion for our abundant photographic heritage.

I want to thank the publisher's readers, who provided guidance and feedback at various stages of draft: William Allen, Arkansas State University; Donald R. Anderson, University of Louisville; Thomas Barrow, University of New Mexico; Kathleen Campbell, Appalachian State University; Richard Colburn, University of Northern Iowa; David L. DeVries, California State University, Fullerton; Gregory T. Moore, Kent State University; Tom Patton, University of Missouri; Paul S. Sternberger, Columbia University; Stan Strembicki, Washington University; Brian Taylor, San Jose State University; and Rene West, Tarrant County Junior College.

At McGraw-Hill, I wish to thank sponsoring editor Cynthia Ward, development editor Allison McNamara, project manager Mary Conzachi, production supervisor Lori Koetters, marketing manager David Patterson, marketing coordinator Anne Sachs, and editorial assistant Heather McCabe. I am grateful for the assistance of Margaret Manos, whose close and sympathetic reading of the manuscript was just what was needed to make the manuscript ready for publication. Nancy D'Antonio, photo researcher, managed a myriad of details to get us the right images.

At the George Eastman House, Rochester, New York, I am grateful to Dr. Anthony Bannon, Director; Jim Enyeart, former director; David Wooters, Print Archivist; Janice Madhu, Assistant Archivist; Joseph Struble, Assistant Archivist; Rachel Stuhlman, Librarian; Becky Simmons, Associate Librarian; and Barbara Galasso, Photographic Services Supervisor.

At the Visual Studies Workshop, also in Rochester, my thanks go to Bill Johnson, Coordinator of the Research Center; and John Rudy, former Coordinator of the Research Center.

At CEPA Gallery, Buffalo, New York, I wish to acknowledge the support of Lawrence Brose, Executive Director; Gail Nicholson, former Associate Director; John Valentino, former Education Curator; Kathleen Kearnan, Associate Director; Michael Bosworth, former Gallery and Digital Lab Manager; Nathaniel Brockmann, former Webmaster and Digital Advisor; and Sue O'Donnell, former Designer and Co-Webmaster.

At Light Work, Syracuse, New York, my appreciation goes to Jeffrey Hoone, Director; Gary Hesse, Associate Director; John Freyer, Lab Manager; and Mary Lee Hodgens, Administrative Specialist, for supporting my residency, which allowed me to proof this manuscript and make new images.

Special thanks to Marie Antonella Pelizzari, Assistant Curator Canadian Center for Architecture, Montreal, Canada; the former members of the History of Photography discussion group (PHOTOHST@ASU.EDU; Richard Pearce-Moses, former owner) who were generous in answering numerous queries; William F. Stapp, photographic historian, Washington, D.C.; Andri Gunthert, photographic historian and editor-in-chief of *études photographiques;* Marin Dacos, University of Lyon (Centre Pierre Léon) and University of Avignon.

Robert Hirsch
Buffalo, New York

CONTENTS

CHAPTER TEN

Modernism: Industrial Beauty   213

CHAPTER ELEVEN

The New Culture of Light   237

CHAPTER TWELVE

Social Documents   267

CHAPTER EIGHTEEN

Thinking About Photography   431

SEIZING THE LIGHT

A HISTORY OF PHOTOGRAPHY

CHAPTER ONE

Advancing Toward Photography

The Birth of Modernity

A Desire for Visual Representation

The idea of photography existed long before the camera was invented. A primary function of visual arts originated in the desire to create a likeness of someone or something that was deemed worth commemorating. The human urge to make pictures that augment the faculty of memory by capturing time is at the conceptual base of photography. Since ancient times, artists and inventors have searched for ways to expedite the picturemaking process, eventually concentrating on how to automatically capture an image directly formed by light.

As early as the fifth century B.C.E., the Chinese philosopher Mo Ti discovered that light reflecting from an illuminated object and passing through a pinhole into a darkened area would form an exact, but inverted, image of that object, offering a prototype of the pinhole (lensless)

The first illustration of a camera obscura used to observe a solar eclipse was published in 1544 by Dutch physician and mathematician Reinerius Gemma-Frisius. Courtesy Gernsheim Collection, Humanities Research Center, University of Texas, Austin, TX.

camera. In the West, the first recorded description of the pinhole was made by the Greek philosopher Aristotle [384–322 B.C.E.], who in circa 330 B.C.E. observed the crescent-shaped image of the sun, during a partial eclipse, projected through a small opening between the leaves of a tree onto the ground. When these observations were first formalized into a camera remains uncertain, but by the tenth century C.E., the Arabian mathematician Alhazen (Ibn Al-Haitham) demonstrated how a pinhole could be an instrument and that images formed through an aperture became sharper when the opening was made smaller. Although Roger Bacon's treatise, *Perspectiva* and *De multiplicatione specierum* (ca. 1267), does not specially mention the camera, it indicates he used the optical principles to contrive an arrangement of mirrors in order to project images of eclipses as well as interior views of his house and street scenes. In *Perspectiva communis* (1279), John Peckham, the Archbishop of Canterbury and a probable student of Bacon, remarked about observing a solar eclipse through a pinhole in a dark place.

During the Renaissance the evolution of the camera can be linked to a new Western concentration on science. The fifteenth-century Renaissance scientist, with arguments founded on experiment and observation, meant people no longer had to accept the authorities' unproved word for what was real, but could look to an open process that was not predicated on belief and magic. Besides praying for their invisible souls to be accepted into a theoretical heaven, scientifically minded people built large ocean-going sailing ships and complex machines to carry their physical bodies out of the Old World and into a new material world. Educated society started shifting toward objective, documentable, repeatable facts; science was offering an alternative to faith.

Perspective

Perspective drawing allows artists to depict a three-dimensional space on a flat surface. Although a system of perspective was known to the Romans, Filippo Brunelleschi of Italy invented the linear perspective we are accustomed to around 1413.[1] In this system objects are foreshortened as they recede into space and lines converge to a vanishing point that corresponds to the spectator's viewpoint. Leon Battista Alberti's treatise, *On Painting* (1435), was dedicated to Brunelleschi and provides descriptions for using geometrical linear perspective in picturemaking. Alberti compared the picture plane to a window:

> Let me tell you what I do when I am painting. First of all, on the surface which I am going to paint I draw a quadrangle of right angles of whichever size I want, which I regard as an open window through which the subject to be painted is seen.[2]

Other artists soon converted Alberti's theoretical window into a real window by drawing on a vertical piece of glass while looking through an eyepiece located opposite the center of the pane, establishing the visual convention of constructing a scene by viewing it through one eye at one place at one time. This artificial window was subsequently replicated when light was passed through a pinhole onto a vertical plane to form an image in the manner noted by Mo Ti.

Improvements in mapmaking during the fifteenth century reduced three-dimensional space into two-dimensional guides, producing geometrically consistent maps and changes in pictorial description. For the first time, mapmakers began to refrain from looking through opaque surfaces, veering around corners, or adjusting the size and position of a site according to its cultural significance. Such improvements, made possible by scientific thinking, coincided with the advent of printed, illustrated books and meant that identical, mass-produced, visual information reached a wider audience.

Thinking of Photography

In 1490, Leonardo da Vinci [1452–1519] wrote the earliest surviving description of the *camera obscura* (dark chamber), a device designed to reproduce linear perspective.[3] The camera obscura, the prototype of the photographic camera, was a large dark room that an artist physically entered. Light entered through a small hole in one of the walls and projected a distinct, but inverted, color image onto the opposite wall that could then be traced. Art historian Kenneth Clark stated that before Leonardo "Alberti invented a device which seems to have been a sort of camera obscura, the images of which he called 'miracles of painting.'"[4] German artist Albrecht Dürer [1471–1528] was one of the first to ingeniously adapt these camera-based principles of perspective and proportion to his drawings.[5] In 1558, Giovanni Battista della Porta published his treatise, *Magiae naturalis (Natural Magic)*, describing the camera obscura and how it could make drawing easier:

> The manner in which one can perceive in the dark the things which on the outside are illuminated by the sun, and with their colors . . . will make possible for anyone ignorant of the art of painting to draw with a pencil or pen the image [made by a camera obscura] of any object whatsoever.[6]

In 1589 della Porta discussed the use of a mirror to reverse the image that was reflected backward in the camera obscura; this is the basis of the modern-day single-lens-reflex camera. He also told of using the camera obscura to stage nighttime, torch-light dramas, accompanied by live music, that were viewed on a screen inside his house, demonstrating that the camera could be used for narrative purposes.

Girolamo Cardano's *De Subtilitate* (1550) mentioned

1.1   ATHANASIUS KIRCHER.   Large Portable Camera Obscura, 1646. Engraving.   Courtesy Gernsheim Collection, Humanities Research Center, University of Texas, Austin, TX.

attaching a biconvex lens (a lens curved on both sides so it is thickest in the middle) to a camera obscura, making its image brighter and sharper. Daniele Barbaro's treatise, *La Practica della perspettiva* (1568), described how fitting a diaphragm to the biconvex lens allowed the amount of light passing through the lens to be controlled, enhancing *depth-of-field,* the range in front of and behind a focused subject in which detail appears sharp, and forming a sharper image. By 1611, Johannes Kepler had built a proto-portable camera: a human-size tent that could be dismantled and transported to make drawing easier. By the mid-seventeenth century, Kepler's camera had been modified and scaled down so one did not have to enter into the camera but could remain outside of it and view an image projected onto a translucent window, a forerunner to the first truly portable cameras.

By the end of the seventeenth century lens aberrations had been corrected to give better resolution. They were also made to produce images of different sizes based on the specific needs of portrait and landscape artists. Image size is proportional to a lens' *focal length,* the distance from the lens to the point of sharp focus. The longer the focal length, the greater the magnification of the image. Instruction manuals for matching lenses with cameras and situations appeared. The optics of the camera obscura were simultaneously ideal and natural, reflecting the empirical, scientific, and humanitarian trends of the Enlightenment. Drawing shifted from the private act of a highly trained individual, to a broader commercial enterprise that incorporated ideas of mass production and standardization as seen in rationalistic works such as Denis Diderot's *Encyclopédie.*

By the close of the eighteenth century the camera had been tailored along the lines of Renaissance pictorial standards to help fulfill a cultural demand to make drawing easier and quicker.

Camera Vision

Although they were organized by machines — cameras — early photographs resembled drawings and paintings because they depicted the world according to linear perspective. The camera obscura was popular with artists because it automatically modified a scene by compressing form and emphasizing tonal mass according to pictorial standards. The camera was not designed as a radical device to unleash a new way of seeing, but evolved to produce a predefined look. The camera took into consideration formulas and procedures such as composition, angle and point of view, quality of light, and selection of subject matter. "What" was being represented remained unchanged. This does not diminish the camera's importance in defining an image. As with most inventions, unintentional side effects create unforeseen changes. As imagemakers became more sophisticated they routinely used specific cameras and lenses to shape an image, and critical viewers can often trace the connections between the camera/lens and the resulting picture.

Scholars have debated whether the idea of photography grew from a need for new images reflecting a profound cultural transformation, from a fabrication of Western pictorial traditions, from an increasing desire to make pictures of what is personally important, as an offshoot of the discoveries of chemists and opticians, or from a combination of these happenings. A discussion surrounding the rise of *camera vision,* how a camera visually organizes a scene, often focuses on Dutch painter Jan Vermeer [1632–1675]. Adroit artists like Vermeer,

1.2   ROBERT HOOKE.   Portable camera obscura,
1694.   Courtesy George Eastman House.

who most likely used a camera, did not need it to physically produce their pictures. The camera did act as a
gathering device of fresh approaches for composing
space, observing light, and portraying cultural models in
innovative ways.[7] Vermeer's uncanny domestic interi-
ors possess qualities now considered photographic: very
tight use of space, "unbalanced" compositions, unexpected points of view, exact descriptions of light at specific times of day, concentration on what is happening
on the edges of the frame, attention given to detail, use
of points of focus, and representation, through stillness,
of time.[8] Vermeer's work demonstrates how the camera
doesn't merely capture nature or reflect existing beauty
but originates entire new ways of visualizing the world.

The Demand for
Picturemaking Systems

In the eighteenth century, a rising commercial class
wanted to purchase the status of being commemorated
in the same pictorial style as the rich. Inventors had

commercial incentives to harness the camera to portrait
making, as less training would decrease the cost of making a picture. Machine-based systems for producing multiple copies of objects were on the threshold of overtak-
ing handmade methods. One such picturemaking
machine was the *physionotrace*. Invented by Gilles
Louis Chrétien in 1786, it combined two inexpensive
methods of portraiture, the cutout silhouette and the engraving. An operator could trace a profile onto glass using a stylus connected to an engraving tool that duplicated the gestures of the stylus onto a copper plate at a
reduced scale. A tracing could be done in about a minute,
and multiple copies of the image could be made from the
plate. Although it was not a camera, the physionotrace
reduced portrait making to a mechanical operation that
required moderate hand-eye coordination. It expanded
the portrait market to the middle class while imitating the
style of the miniaturist painters. The physionotrace satisfied a desire for an accurate visual description of one's
presence and social status. The mechanical/scientific nature of the process gave the physionotrace a power of authenticity. This made it a prototype for an entity like photography, which possessed a key characteristic of what
society wanted: a system for the multiple reproduction of
a directly transcribed truth, to be developed.

The start of the nineteenth century saw the introduc-

1.3   CAMERA LUCIDA.   From *Chambre Claire*.
Courtesy George Eastman House.

tion of Aloys Senefelder's 1796 invention of *lithography* that provided a more cost effective means for the mass production and distribution of printed pictures.[9] About this time wood engraving was also revitalized to meet the demand for multiple pictures. Other devices to facilitate personal picturemaking followed. The *camera lucida*, invented in 1807 by the English scientist William Hyde Wollaston [1766–1828], was an optical instrument (not a camera) supposed to help one overcome a lack of drawing skill. The camera lucida consisted of a glass prism, held at eye level by a brass rod attached to a flat, portable drawing board. One looked into a peephole at the center of the prism and simultaneously saw both the subject and the drawing surface. The idea was to let one's pencil be guided by the "virtual" image and to trace that image onto a sheet of paper attached to a drawing board. In practice it was difficult to operate, and frustration with this machine led a later photographic pioneer, William Henry Fox Talbot, to find an automatic way to record a scene without lifting his pencil.

Proto-Photographers: Chemical Action of Light

As alchemy, the precursor of science whose central notion is that buried minerals are in the process of developing into gold, evolved into modern chemistry in the sev-

enteenth century, manufacturing industries were now able to produce and supply experimenters with reliable chemicals and equipment. By 1614 Angelo Sala had recorded the darkening effects of silver nitrate on exposure to sunlight. In the 1700s, various salts of silver, especially silver nitrate, were known to dye feathers, furs, and leather permanently black. Each new discovery and invention suggested that combining the camera and optical systems with the chemical action of light could produce an automatic image directly from life.

In 1727, Johann Heinrich Schulze [1687–1744] set out to repeat an alchemist experiment to make a luminescent substance he called phosphorous. One of the ingredients Schulze used, aqua regia (nitric acid), was impure; it contained silver. When he mixed it with calcium carbonate (chalk), Schulze accidentally created calcium nitrate and silver carbonate, which to his surprise turned a deep purple on exposure to sunlight. Schulze repeated the experiment using heat from a fire and observed no change, deducing that this chemical reaction was caused by light, not heat. Schulze wrote:

> I covered most of the glass with dark material, exposing a little part for the free entry of light. Thus I often wrote names and whole sentences on paper and carefully cut away the inked parts with a sharp knife. I struck the paper thus perforated on the glass with wax. It was not long before the sun's rays, where they hit the glass through the cut-out parts of the paper, wrote each word or sentence on the chalk precipitate so exactly and distinctly that many who were curious about the experiment but ignorant of its nature took occasion to attribute the thing to some sort of trick.[10]

Schulze had uncovered a new method of representing an image—ironically, of text—by the action of light in conjunction with silver. By the 1760s, the prediction that something on the order of photography would be generated as the result of information accrued through scientific inquiries into chemistry, color, and light appeared in Norman Tiphaigne de La Roche's allegorical novel, *Giphantie* (1760). (English translation is *Giphantia*, 1761). Tiphaigne equated a large hall to a camera obscura, whose walls carried a "painting" that precisely traced a storm at sea. He then imagined "elementary spirits" that "fix these passing images" on material soaked in a "very subtle substance," making a permanent image "much more precious than anyone can produce, and so perfect that time cannot destroy it."[11]

In *With a View to a New Art of Dying and Painting* (1794), Elizabeth Fulhame suggested that maps could be made using silver imprinted by the action of light. Her work demonstrated that the chemistry to make

1.4   ARTIST USING A CAMERA OBSCURA.
This Victorian-era engraving depicts an artist using a
table-top camera obscura to trace a scene from life. The
insert is a cut-away that reveals the mirrors and the
path (broken lines with arrows) that the projected image took inside the camera to the flat surface on which
the artist drew the image.   Courtesy Corbis/Bettmann
Archive.

chemist Humphry Davy [1778–1829] in the *Journals
of the Royal Institution* for 1802:

> White paper or white leather, moistened with solution of ni-
> trate of silver, undergoes no change when kept in a dark
> place; but, on being exposed to day light, it speedily changes
> colour, and, after passing through different shades of grey and
> brown, becomes at length nearly black. . . .When the shadow
> of any figure is throw upon the prepared surface, the part con-
> cealed by it remains white, and the other parts speedily be-
> come dark.[12]

a photographic process was in place; what was needed
was the motivation to combine the components into
a new form. The character of the thing called photography was not found at a single source. Hindsight reveals protophotographers had multiple purposes and
destinations.

At the opening of the nineteenth century, Thomas
Wedgwood [1771–1805] experimented with placing
flat objects and painted transparencies on top of white
leather and paper sensitized with silver nitrate. His experiments verified the feasibility of chemically trans-
ferring images of objects and pictures through the
agency of light. His work was described by the British

The paradoxical problem with these profiles, an-
tecedents of photograms (cameraless photographic images) was that the light that created them and was
needed to view them also brought about their destruction. Wedgwood could not stop the action of additional
light from causing an image to darken until it diasp-
peared into blackness. Consequently, Wedgwood could
only show his profiles by candlelight. But Wedgwood's
underlying concept was vital, which according to Davy
was to "copy" images of the camera obscura "by the
agency of light upon nitrate of silver" instead of hand
tracing. Although he did not achieve this goal, the rationale suited the emerging tenets of the modern era by

substituting mechanical work for human labor. Wedgwood's profiles point toward the invention of a photographic system that brings together the direct action of light to chemically record an image constructed by a camera.

Modernity: New Visual Realities

The nineteenth century ushered in the urban, industrial-based movement known as modernity. The modern era unleashed vast new resources in finance, management, science, and technology, leading to self-sustaining capitalist growth that swept away the foundations of ancient European regimes. These economic, political, and demographic changes, without precedent in scale and significance, were accompanied by potent new directions in the arts, philosophy, and science. Such fundamental displacements produced ruptures in the societal framework that allowed the camera and its optics to be recast.

The new expanding capitalist economy and its urban labor force demanded more visual information. Daily life was accelerating and changing as never before. Machines, such as the railroad, the steamship, the telegraph, and the iron printing press, were moving people and information at paces once considered impossible. With the advent of state-subsidized education in England and France, literacy was on the rise. The more people learned, the more information they wanted. Newspapers and the penny presses increased circulation, their pages filled with new human interest stories and illustrated by engravings. Publishers learned that pictures helped sell their product, and by 1842 the world's first picture weekly, the *Illustrated London News,* was circulating. *Realism,* depiction without distortion or stylization, was on the rise in literature and in painting. People wanted to know exactly what their world looked like, and the photographic image arrived at the right moment with the type of proof people had been prepared to accept.

The classical view of nature as a perpetual, immobile entity had begun to shift with the dynamics of industrial revolution. Pre-photography thinkers like Johann Wolfgang von Goethe [1749–1832], Georg Wilhelm Friedrich Hegel [1770–1831], and Immanuel Kant [1724–1804] were transforming nature into an active, living, and tumultuous organism that shifted form and appearance depending on who was observing it. In Paris and London in the 1770s, Philippe Jacques de Loutherbourg combined magic lanterns (a predecessor of the slide projector), automatas with clock drives (that is, mechanical toys), and painted transparencies to create a new form of visual entertainment. The invention in 1784 of the *Argand Oil Lamp,* the first modern lighting system, made it possible for a concentrated beam of light to project images onto a screen, giving Loutherbourg the idea for his *eidophusikon.* The eidophusikon was a protean television, consisting of a miniature theater with a stage 6 feet high, 10 feet wide, and 8 feet deep. Colored glass slides, illuminated by concealed Argand lights, produced a multitude of colors. Sound and weather effects were created by revolving cylinders filled with shells and stones and thin sheets of copper, and a harpsichord provided music. Loutherbourg's financial success allowed him to create a visual show based on Captain Cook's voyages, which the *Daily Universal Register* (later *The Times*) in 1788 hailed as "the most magnificent [spectacle] that modern times has produced. . . . bring[ing] into living action the customs and manners of distant nations—to see exact representations of their buildings, marine vessels, arms, manufactures, sacrifices and dresses."[13]

In Paris in 1800, Etienne Robert and Paul de Philipstal unveiled the *phantasmagoria* (see Figure 1.5). Illuminated by the Argand Oil Lamp, the phantasmagoria was an advanced magic lantern that created rear-screen image projections of ghosts, skeletons, and celebrities in a semidarkened theater. Special effects of lightning, thunder, and smoke enhanced the eerie atmosphere. One popular scene, "Dance of the Witched," used multiple light sources to create moving projections that appeared to advance on the audience, only to vanish just as they seemed ready to leap off the screen. A group of magic lanterns with comblike shutters focused on the same spot on the screen, so that one image could blend into the next, making viewers less conscious of the mechanics and more likely to be swept away by the visual illusions.

In 1826 the Drummond Light, popularly called *limelight,*[14] replaced the Argand light. Limelight not only transformed the look of stage productions, it permitted magic lanterns to project a more powerful and accurate beam of light, increasing the audience for projected images. The acceptance of the camera-projected image as fact changed the perception of the magic lantern from a toy of amusement to a tool for education and social change. These innovative devices typify how the science-based, industrial revolution was transforming how the world was viewed, altering public desires, and signaling an emergence of new forms of representation in the visual arts.

Gothic horror was what the public came to see in these live productions, but these new devices utilized in popular theater also retrained people in what they would accept and expect in a system of visual representation. As the demand for beauty and truth was thus reshaped, many minds set out to satisfy the new hunger. Artists, realizing verisimilitude was an avenue to acceptance and financial success, felt the pressure to get the details right. Various visual presenting systems, such as the Cosmorama, Goerama, Neorama, and Uranorama, were

1.5   PHANTASMAGORIA.   Front piece of *Memoires* by James Robertson.   Courtesy George Eastman House.

tried, but the one that captured the public's imagination as being visually authentic was the *panorama*.

The panorama was a picture on a cylindrical surface, with the spectator in the center, or else a picture that unrolled in front of the viewer to reveal its parts in sequence. In 1794, the painter Robert Barker built a circular exhibition space in London's Leicester Square and presented a 1,479-square-foot painted canvas of the city. Barker's multi-sheet, bird's-eye view situated the audience in the center of London. It was a commercial hit and the idea was widely imitated in other countries, including the United States.

In 1815, **Louis Jacques Mandé Daguerre** [1787–1851] was considered Paris's leading scene designer. His *trompe l'œil* (deceives the eye) theatrical effects were particularly successful. Trompe-l'œil refers to the illusion that one is seeing an actual subject and not a two-dimensional representation of it. In 1822, Daguerre opened his first 350-seat *diorama*. The diorama consisted of a dark circular chamber in which large painted scenes on translucent linen were represented. Each picture was seen through a 2,800-square-foot calico window that was painted half opaque. The opaque portion was frontally lit and the translucent part was illuminated from behind, producing an illusion that the picture emitted a radiant light and was not on a flat surface. The color, brightness, and direction of the light

was controlled through a system of cords, pulleys, shutters, and slides, and its pictorial effects soon included real animals, stage props, and sound effects.[15] The diorama was an immediate success and Daguerre later built an elaborate 200-seat amphitheater in London, capable of pivoting viewers from scene to scene.

Daguerre's dioramas altered the way the public experienced a picture. The moving diorama is a harbinger of how mechanical devices can control human behavior. In it viewers gave up their autonomy and became part of a machine that determined how much time they would spend looking at a scene. Daguerre's dioramas also collapsed the single point-of-view perspective that painting had built up over centuries. All this happened without audiences objecting to giving up their familiar way of seeing. In fact, originality was sought out as amusement. Associating the "new" with being creative and good became a hallmark of modernity. Other early nineteenth century visual phenomena, such as *anamorphic drawings* (distorted drawings or projections that when viewed from a specific point, or where reflected by a special mirror, make the image appear visually correct), reveal a fascination with and demand for systems that reorder visual information.

Optical Devices

A burgeoning middle class, concerned with appearances that would convey its ideas of status, was eager to consume new images of reality. New visual thinking, based on ideas from machines, altered cultural con-

" All things *by turns.*"

1.6   THAUMATROPE.   In *Philosophy in Sport made Science in Earnest* (1839) by John Ayrton.   Courtesy George Eastman House.

structs and perception while retraining public expectations of how the world was represented. The kaleidoscope, invented by Sir David Brewster [1781–1868] in 1815, mechanically re-formed visual experience through repetition and symmetry. The kaleidoscope exemplifies how science and technology give a subject the appearance of simultaneously being repeated and fragmented, challenging the traditional narrative framework of the visual arts.[16]

The optical phenomenon of retinal *afterimage*, the presence of a visual sensation in the absence of a visual stimulus, as discussed by Goethe in the *Theory of Colors* (1810), began to affect how science observed the world.[17] Goethe stated that whatever a healthy eye saw was "optical truth," that there was no such thing as optical illusion. The eye was a model of autonomous vision: The optical experience is produced by and within the person. Goethe's theory challenged the Aristotelian truthfulness of optical perception by tethering the act of observation with the body, fusing time and vision.[18] Additional empirical studies of Goethe's ideas were carried out in Germany during the early 1820s by Jan Purkinje, who was able to time how long it took the eye to become fatigued and how long for the pupil to contract and dilate.

Such studies gave rise to scientific optical devices that were transformed into popular entertainment. The *thaumatrope*, or "wonder-turner," was manufactured in 1825 as an optical toy based on after-image research. It consisted of a disk, about two inches in diameter, with a drawing on each side and strings attached through

holes drilled at opposite ends of the circle. One side of the disk might picture a bald-headed man, the other side a wig. When the disk was spun, the man would appear to have hair on his head. The wonder-turner proved that perception was not instantaneous and demonstrated the contrived and delusionary nature of image formation. Such devices demonstrated the fracture between perception and the subject being perceived.

Joseph Plateau's afterimage experiments in the late 1820s defined the theory of *persistence of vision*. The theory states that if several objects that differ sequentially in form and position are rapidly viewed one after another, the impression they produce on the retina is of a single object that's changing its form and position. Since an image impression lingers for a fraction of a second, individual images appear to be in continuous motion, as in a flip-book. Devices like this and the *zoetrope*, a rotating cylinder with slits, through which one or more people could see sequential, simulated action drawings of acrobats, boxers, dancers, and jugglers, permitted an immobile viewer to have a machine-generated visual experience unfold over time.

Images Through Light: A Struggle for Permanence

As a new scientific and technological order emerged in the nineteenth century, the old ways began to wobble and fail from the pressure of new experiences, and innovative theories were needed to contain them. The invention of photography resulted from the application of quantifiable knowledge to fulfill a capitalistic cultural demand for a practical, automatic picturemaking system, based on light and optics. Its invention marked the establishment of aesthetic, professional, and social practices governing how these pictures would be made, used, understood, and accepted.

Joseph Nicéphore Niépce [1765–1833] developed the first system for making permanent images through the action of light. Niépce (pronounced Nee-epps) was enthralled with lithography, but he lacked the drawing skills the process required. Originally, Niépce sought to automatically transfer an image to a lithography stone without having to draw it. In 1814, Niépce and his elder brother, Claude, shifted direction and undertook experiments to "spontaneously" create original pictures through the camera instead of copying previous existing images. This makes Niépce the first to actively pursue a process of making a permanent camera image.

By 1816 the major technical elements for the invention of photography were present in Niépce's experiments. Niépce was able to precisely describe to his brother Claude his first photographic procedures, with the use of cameras, biconvex lens, and diaphragm. These experiments, on paper sensitized with "muriate d'argent" (silver chloride), were abandoned by Niépce only because he obtained negatives. Niépce could temporarily "fix" the prints by washing them and was able to send some of these "epreuves" (prints) to Claude. Photographic historian Andre Gunthert remarks: "What is a print on sensitized paper, from an outdoor view, realized into a camera obscura, that could be sent by post and observed by a distant viewer, some days later, if not a photographic picture?"[19] If we accept this proposal, then 1816 can mark the beginning of what people would call photography. In 1822, Niépce discovered that bitumen of Judea, a lithographer's material made from asphaltum (a natural tar pitch), was sensitive to light. Niépce knew bitumen of Judea was soluble in lavender oil and would harden when exposed to light. His vital discovery was that bitumen of Judea loses its solubility in lavender oil after exposure to light. Niépce was able to take a paper engraving, place it in contact with the treated lithography stone, and expose it to sunlight for about two hours. He then "developed" it in a solution of petroleum and lavender oil, realizing the cultural dream of an "automatic" picture (although it was not camera-based). Today we would say that Niépce made a latent (unseen) image, that when developed formed a negative (reversed) image of the original.

As early as 1824, Niépce used this process to make his first actual camera image from nature on a lithographer's stone, which he referred to as a *point de vue*. There is still disagreement among historians as to when Niépce first made a permanent view from nature with a camera. Some state it was as early as 1822, others say it was 1824, and still other groups claim it was 1826 or even 1827. A book written by Niépce's son Isidore in 1841 indicates 1824 was the first time Niépce "achieved definitive fixing of images from the camera obscura onto his screen. Although these marvelous products were still imperfect, the problem had been resolved."[20] This remains a fluid situation, based on evidence and semantics, and this date may change. Niépce refined the process, coating a piece of pewter with bitumen of Judea dissolved in lavender oil, placing the plate into his camera obscura, and making an extended daylight exposure.[21] The improvements resulted in what is believed to be the oldest surviving photographically based camera made picture. The image is difficult to recognize; nevertheless, this picture (see Figure 1.7) can still convey its original sense of magical wonderment. Niépce wrote to his brother Claude:

> I succeeded in obtaining a *point de vue*. . . . from my workroom in Gras using my C[amera] O[bscura] and my largest stone. The image of the objects is represented with a clarity, an astonishing fidelity, complete with myriad details and with nuances of extreme delicacy. To get the effect, one must look at the stone from an oblique angle . . . and I must say my dear friend, this effect is truly something magical.[22]

By the late 1820s, Niépce had revised his working techniques to use silver-surfaced copper plates to deliver a problematic, one-of-a-kind positive image that lacked a full tonal range, had excessive contrast, was hard to see, and required extensive time to make. Because Niépce's camera images were not able to withstand the chemical treatment he devised to produce prints in ink, a process he named *héliogravures*,[23] he reconceptualized them as unique images, which he called *héliographs*. However, Niépce realized his process needed crucial revisions to be productive.

In 1825 Daguerre wrote to Niépce proposing they collaborate.[24] Daguerre's enormous diorama paintings were made in a realistic picturesque style by Daguerre and the artist Jean Boulton and took an enormous amount of time to produce. An automatic picturemaking device would save the diorama's creators both time and money. In December of 1829 Niépce and Daguerre agreed to share all knowledge, honor, and profit from their collaboration. Daguerre's assets included funding for research, determination, energy, experience in gauging public taste, friends in prominent places, and credibility and recognition as an artist with public acclaim. The pair worked separately and corresponded in coded letters. In the summer of 1833, with success still eluding them, Niépce died of a stroke. His son, Isidore Niépce [1805–1868], replaced him in the partnership, but he did not offer much new research. Daguerre, with the benefit of Niépce's knowledge, continued on his own.

By 1831, Daguerre had been taking highly polished, silvered plates, sensitizing them in the dark with heated iodine crystals vapor (forming silver iodine), and immediately placing them in the camera and making one-hour exposures in bright sunlight. This process deliv-

1.7   JOSEPH NICÉPHORE NIÉPCE. *View from His Window at Le Gras,* ca. 1826–27. Heliograph.
Courtesy Gernsheim Collection, Humanities Research Center, University of Texas, Austin, TX.

ered, without development, a highly detailed negative image. A breakthrough came in late 1834, when Daguerre sensitized the plates *after* the exposure with heated mercury vapor. Although Daguerre claimed he discovered the usefulness of mercury accidentally, chemical ingredients like mercury have their roots in alchemical texts. Mercury was considered to be the dissolver, the active principal of things, making it a logical choice for experiments.[25] A whitish amalgam of silver and mercury formed on the plate where it had been exposed to light, making a fragile but incredibly detailed, camera-recorded image. When the shiny, mirror-like surface reflected a dark background, the picture was positive. When the background was bright or light-colored the picture appeared as a washed-out negative image. The mercury development had the beneficial side effect of reducing exposures to 20 minutes in bright sunlight. By late 1837, Daguerre was able to make the image stable by treating it in a strong bath of sodium chloride (table salt).

Daguerre and Isidore Niépce tried to market their secret process by subscription in 1838, which proved difficult; the effort was soon abandoned. Daguerre knew the acceptance of his invention depended not only on its merits but on shrewd promotion, and he recruited the ideal advocate, Count Francois Arago.[26] In January 1839, Arago put together a cunning accord with the French government that awarded lifetime pensions to Daguerre and Niépce. In return the French government would freely present the invention to the world (excluding France's arch-rival, England, where a licensing fee was required). The news of the invention, without any details, was out.

In February 1839, upon learning of the work, England's **Sir John Fredrick William Herschel** [1792–1871], an astronomer and chemist, informed Daguerre of his own discovery that hyposulphite of soda ("hypo") would "fix" his camera pictures and make them permanent. With this technical problem solved, Daguerre turned to the conceptual dilemma of whether his process actively made an image of nature or simply made it possible for nature to "imprint" an image of herself. Daguerre neatly addressed the issue by writing: ". . . the DAGUERREOTYPE is not merely an instrument which serves to draw Nature; on the contrary it is a chemical and physical process which gives her the power to reproduce herself."[27]

1.8   Attributed to LOUIS JACQUES MANDÉ
DAGUERRE.   Unidentified Man, 1837. 2¼ × 1¾
inches. Daguerreotype. Collection of Marc Pagneux,
Paris. Courtesy Société Francaise de Photographie, Paris.
This primitive, low–contrast daguerreotype, supposedly
made two years before the official announcement of the
daguerreotype process, could be the earliest example of a
photographic portrait.[28] For reasons yet unknown, Daguerre kept his portrait experiments secret when he publicly announced his process and only referred to them in
his private correspondence. While investigations and debate continue about the authenticity of this claim, it reveals that history is not a fixed entity but a changing and
flowing process. It serves as a reminder that there is still
much research to be done and that history is often filled
with surprises.

On August 19, 1839, amid rhapsodic promises of
"economic advantages, immense service to art, [and
how it would] excel the works of the most accomplished painters, in fidelity of detail and true reproduction of the local atmosphere,"[29] Count Arago described
Daguerre's process before an overflowing and electri-
fied joint session of the Académie des Sciences and the
Académie des Beaux-Arts. Despite the expensive
equipment and supplies, "Daguerréotypomanie" struck
with force, hitting educated, upper-class society and its
growing voracity for realistic images.[30]

Daguerre published a manual and arranged for the
manufacture and sale of lenses and wooden cameras,
but his interest in daguerreotypes rapidly subsided and
he made very few after 1839. Daguerre moved to the
country, revamped his gardens, and made illusionist
paintings. Was Daguerre exhausted, was he satisfied

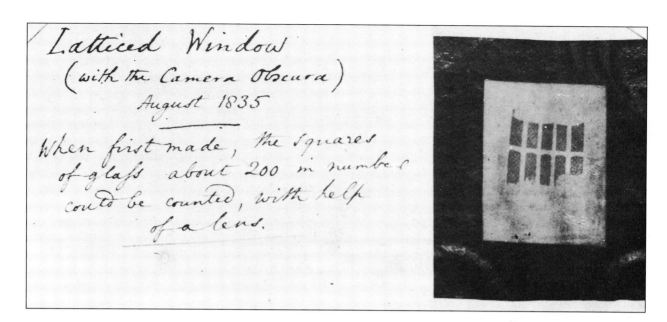

Latticed Window
(with the Camera Obscura)
August 1835

When first made, the squares
of glass about 200 in number
could be counted, with help
of a lens.

1.9   WILLIAM HENRY FOX TALBOT.   *Latticed Window at Lacock Abbey,* 1835. Photogenic drawing. Courtesy NMPFT/Science & Society Picture Library, London, England.

with his accomplishments? Did the fire of 1839 that destroyed his diorama along with most of his works and papers leave him unable to work, or did he not wish to compete with the rest of the world on improving his process? He died in 1851, in relative obscurity and without much money.

The news from across the Channel in January 1839 must have shocked **William Henry Fox Talbot** [1800–1877]. Talbot was an English gentleman (he inherited Lacock Abbey estate), scientist (he was elected to the Royal Society in 1832), and scholar (he earned a Master of Arts degree from Cambridge), who had independently devised a camera-based imaging process in 1834, using the light-sensitivity of silver salts. In Talbot's time, a well-educated person was expected to possess numerous skills, including the ability to draw. Talbot did not draw well and depended on optical devices for assistance. He later recounted his frustration with drawing, using the camera lucida and the camera obscura, during his honeymoon at picturesque Lake Como, Italy:

> And this led me to reflect on the inimitable beauty of the pictures of nature's paintings which the glass lens of the Camera throws upon the paper in its focus—fairy pictures, creatures of a moment, and destined as rapidly to fade away. . . . It was during these thoughts that the idea occurred to me . . . how charming it would be if it were possible to cause these natural images to imprint themselves durably, and remain fixed upon the paper![31]

In 1834, Talbot invented the *salted paper print*, a *printing-out process* that allowed him to make cameraless images of botanical specimens (see Figure 1.10), engravings, pieces of lace, and even solar photomicro-

graphs.[32] For his first salted paper prints Talbot coated sheets of ordinary writing paper with sodium chloride, permitted them to dry, and then recoated them with silver nitrate, forming silver chloride. He had discovered that silver chloride was more sensitive to light than silver nitrate, which reduced exposure time. In Talbot's method the image and the paper became one, as there was no separation between the emulsion and its support.[33] In the printing-out process, the sensitized paper darkened swiftly when exposed to light. The image appeared spontaneously during exposure without chemical development. Once the image was complete, it was fixed, removing or inactivating the unexposed silver chloride. Talbot, like his predecessors, had difficulty fixing the image, eventually stabilizing prints with a strong solution of salt or potassium iodide. These images were negatives, and Talbot wanted direct positives. He solved the reversal problem by taking the negative image and reprinting it in direct contact with an unexposed, treated piece of paper, establishing a nascent negative/positive photographic method. Although he had a successful conceptual solution, Talbot's materials did not make a negative dense enough to produce a positive print with acceptable contrast and detail.

To increase the sensitivity of the paper, Talbot repeatedly brushed it with alternating coats of salted water and silver nitrate, then commenced to make his first camera negatives. Talbot used tiny cameras that his wife Constance, who also took and developed images, making her the first woman photographer,[34] referred to as "little mouse traps." These little instruments enabled the lens to focus the light onto a very small concentrated area, reducing exposure times to an hour or two. Talbot had set aside this work when the news of Daguerre's process jolted him back into action. In January 1839, Talbot hurriedly sent some of his work to England's Royal Society, stating:

I obtained [with a tiny camera] very perfect, but extremely small [negative] pictures; such as without great stretch of the imagination might be supposed to be the work of some Lilliputian artist. They require indeed examination with a lens to discover all their minutiae. In the summer of 1835 I made in this way a great number of representations of my house in the country [Lacock Abbey]. . . . And this building I believe to be the first that was ever yet known *to have drawn its own picture.*[35]

Photogenic drawing, the term Talbot used to describe this early salted paper process, is the archetype for the silver printing-out papers of the nineteenth century. As it incorporated the textural imprint of the paper into the picture, it produced a broad tonal range that favored volume and shape over detail. Talbot's exposure times were excessive and the process appeared overly complex, involving a second series of steps to produce a finished image. The photogenic drawings also did not compete with the verisimilitude of the daguerreotype. When the two processes were first compared, the future seemed to lie with the daguerreotype; it met the aesthetic expectations of how a picture was supposed to look by supplying an easily recognizable trace of the subject.

Daguerre, who came from the tradition of optical entertainment, was an experienced businessman who knew how to commercially promote his process. Talbot was a scientist and an intellectual with interests in astronomy, linguistics, literature, mathematics, and optics. His earliest photography publication, *Some Account of the Art of Photogenic Drawing* (January 1839),[36] indicates an awareness that the temporal premise of his process was different from other tracing methods; it brought together transitory and permanent elements. Talbot wrote that it took no more time or effort to record a simple subject than it did a complex subject. For Talbot photography's purpose was to depict a subject in a fixed compositional order from a lived moment, making time itself the ultimate subject of all photographs.

Talbot's regard for learning led him to devise a new procedure, *iodized paper*,[37] for making negatives. Talbot's breakthrough came accidentally. Having made an exposure that revealed no visible image, Talbot set it aside. When he looked at it later, an image had been formed. Talbot deduced that the gallic acid he brushed the paper with prior to exposure had acted as a developer, causing an invisible latent image (encoded by light) to appear. Talbot called his new method *calotype*, from the Greek words *kalos* and *tupos*, meaning "beautiful print." Calotype involved taking an exposed sheet of iodized paper into the darkroom and brushing it with gallic acid until a potent negative was developed. This negative was contact-printed onto unexposed, salted paper in sunlight to form a positive. The procedure formalized photography as a two-step process beginning with one tonally reversed (negative) image from which an infinite number of tonally correct positive copies could be produced. This concept formed the foundation for the silver-based photographic system still in use today: A camera with a lens was used to record an unseen image on light-sensitive material and chemically developed out to make a photograph.

Herschel had discovered in 1819 that hyposulphite of soda would dissolve silver salts. Learning of the work of Daguerre and Talbot, Herschel launched his own research into the light-sensitive properties of various silver halides and other chemicals. He made a negative image on paper, through a telescope, which he made permanent by treating with hypo. By freely sharing this information with the early pioneers, Herschel provided the missing link in all their processes, of how to make images permanent. Herschel, with a volatile, soaring imagination, is an ideal of learning: He set aside nationalism; openly shared knowledge; did not patent his findings; and did not commercially exploit his discoveries. Although Herschel never considered himself a photographer, his contributions shaped the founding concepts of photographic practice. He helped to establish basic terminology by consistently using the broader terms "photography" and "to photograph,"[38] instead of the individualistic descriptions of heliography and photogenic drawing, creating a sense of unity where there had been none. Herschel also introduced the terms "negative" and "positive" (based on the study of magnetism with which Talbot was also familiar) and "emulsion," helping institute a common nomenclature.

In 1839, Herschel told Talbot that waxing the paper negative after processing would make it more transparent and easier to print.[39] By the end of 1839, Herschel had invented a method of sensitizing a glass plate with silver halides and proceeded to photograph his father's telescope, making the first glass-plate negative, from which he made prints on paper. Next, he invented a method of making direct positive images on paper. Then, he prefigured the ambrotype by demonstrating how his glass negative could be backed with black opaque material to produce a positive image. He discovered silver bromide was the most light-sensitive of the known silver halides, pointing the direction for reduced exposure times that would make portraiture practical. He was able to record, but not fix, a natural color image of the spectrum, without the use of dyes or colorants, on silver chloride material, promoting the possibility of full-color photographs.

In 1842, Herschel invented the *anthotype,* a paper process sensitized with various plant juices that formed the final image by removing the unwanted parts of the emulsion through a bleach-out method, a forerunner of the silver-dye-destruction processes, such as IL-FOCHROME, often used to make prints from transparencies. He rounded out the year with the *cyanotype* (blueprint) process, which he devised to make fast

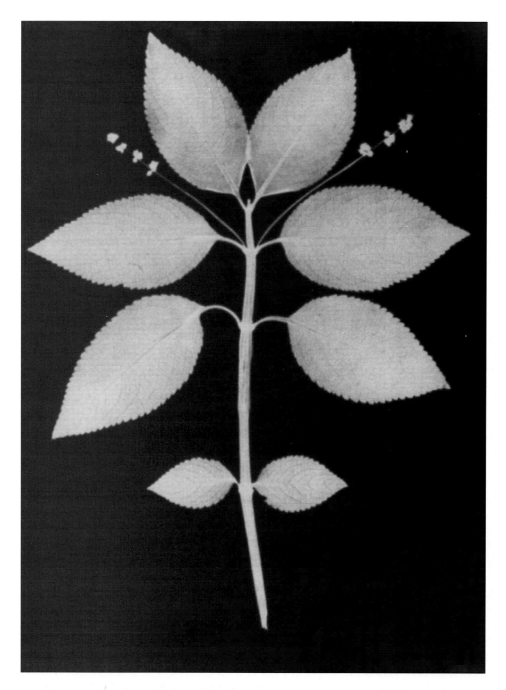

1.10   WILLIAM HENRY FOX TALBOT.   *Botanical Specimen,* 1839. Photogenic drawing.   Courtesy University of Leiden, print room. The Netherlands.

copies of his notes, foreshadowing the electrostatic copier. In the cyanotype process iron salts were absorbed into the paper that was exposed to sunlight in contact with a negative or a drawing on tracing paper, producing an image in Prussian Blue which was fixed by washing in water (see Mungo Ponton's shadowgraphs on page 19). Cyanotype was used by amateurs after the introduction of small, flexible, roll film cameras, adopted by shipbuilders to copy their working plans, and used to copy line-based documents. In 1853 Herschel described methods to reduce images to microscopic size for easier storage and preservation and then enlarge them again when needed.

Anna Atkins's [1799–1871] *British Algae: Cyanotype Impressions,* privately published and distributed, was the first book to be printed and fully illustrated by Herschel's cyanotype.[40] Her effort was the earliest to use photo-based technology for producing cameraless photo-based pictures for scientific investigation, "predating by several months any of Talbot's commercially published camera-based photographic books."[41] Although artistic expression was not her main intent, the works show a strong aesthetic sense

1.11   ANNA ATKINS.   *Lycopodium Flagellatum*
(Algae), 1840s–50s. Cyanotype.   Courtesy Gernsheim
Collection, Humanities Research Center, University of Texas,
Austin, TX.

for translating three-dimensional forms into two-dimensional space. Her influence was limited to a tiny
audience, due to the book's subject matter and the restricted means of production. In the introduction to
her book, Atkins described her intent: "the difficulty
of making accurate drawing of objects as minute as
the Algae and Conferva, has induced me to avail myself to Sir John Herschel's beautiful process of Cyanotype, to obtain impressions of the plants themselves,
which I have much pleasure in offering to my botanical friends."[42]

Other Distinct Originators

Niépce, Daguerre, and Talbot were not alone in their
quest to make pictures directly by the action of light. In
March 1839, **Hippolyte Bayard** [1801–1887], a French
civil servant, independently obtained his first direct positives on paper in the camera. In May he showed examples to Count Arago, unaware that Arago was championing Daguerre's cause. Arago pressured Bayard not to
publish, thus guaranteeing that Daguerre's process
would receive all the attention. Bayard exhibited 30 pictures in Paris in June 1839 and was presented with a
small cash award by the French government. However,
by the time Bayard made the details of his process public, in February 1840, it was old news.[43] Bayard expressed his disappointment with a mini-series of self-

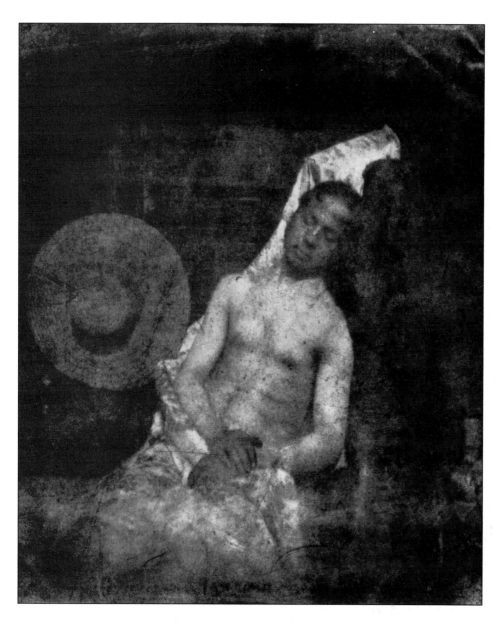

1.12 HIPPOLYTE BAYARD. *Self-Portrait as a Drowned Man,* 1840. Direct paper positive.   © Société Française de Photographie, Paris.

portraits and accompanying "suicide" text, opening a discourse on photography's relationship to death, the use of text to control meaning, and the medium's ability to commingle fact and fiction. On the back of one print the martyred Bayard, an early photographic casualty, returns from the dead with this message:

> The corpse you see is that of M. Bayard. . . . The Academy, the King, and all those who have seen his pictures admired them, just as you do. . . . This has brought him prestige, but not a sou [penny]. The government, which has supported M. Daguerre more than is necessary, declared it could do nothing for M. Bayard, and the unhappy man drowned himself. . . . he has been at the morgue for several days, and no-one has recognized or claimed him. Ladies and Gentlemen, you'd better pass along for fear of offending your sense of smell, for as you can observe, the face and hands of the gentleman are beginning to decay [Bayard's hands and face were sunburnt from working in his garden].[44]

Word of these discoveries circulated, and the eagerness to photograph became apparent as people from across the Western world, Brazil, Germany, Spain, Switzerland, stepped forward with claims that they too had invented a photographic process.[45] Creating a spin-off method based on Talbot's process, Scotsman **Mungo Ponton** [1801–1880] sensitized paper with potassium bichromate (potassium dichromate) instead of silver salt to produce cameraless *shadowgraphs.* He made them by placing objects on top of the paper and exposing his set-up to sunlight. The image was processed by washing with water. The areas affected by light did not dissolve during washing, but the unexposed coating under the object did. Since all the unexposed bichromate was removed, the washing operation

1.13   ANTOINE HÉRCULES ROMUALD
FLORENCE.   Illustrations of Florence's photography
equipment. 8¹/₁₆ × 7½ inches. Pencil drawing from Florence's manuscript *L'Ami des arts livré à luimême ou
Récherches et décourvertes sur différents sujets nouveaux*,
São Carlos (Campinas) 1837. Kossoy explains: "That the
left upper corner shows Florence's diagram of his
homemade camera obscura. The illustration in the upper right shows the adjustable wooden frame he used to
make sunlight contact prints. The bottom figure shows a
platform Florence used as a support for the plate (made
of glass) where you can see the master drawing. In the
middle of this frame (painted in black) and the glass
plate (which functioned as the negative) Florence placed
his sensitized paper.[46]   Courtesy Tereza Cristina Florence
Goedhart.

also served to fix the image. The final result was a white
silhouette of the object on an orange background. The
process showed that the solubility of potassium bichromate was proportional to the amount of light it received.
The process was also cheaper and easier than Talbot's
method. Ponton demonstrated his technique to the Society of Arts of Scotland on May 25, 1839, and correctly
predicted that it would be an important aid to lithogra-

phy. Although he never developed the
process, it was the basis for a number of
nonsilver processes and for most of the photomechanical reproduction methods of the
nineteenth century.

The notion of *simultaneous consciousness*, that an idea can independently occur to
different people, in different places, and at the
same time, is evidenced in the experiments of
Antoine Hércules Romuald Florence
[1804–1879], a French artist who resided in
Brazil. Florence's surviving notebooks, written between 1829 and 1837, record his early
imagemaking with a camera obscura and silver nitrate in January 1833. Florence altered
the conceptual direction of his experiments
from making images with a camera to concentrate on what would become a fundamental application of all such photochemical discoveries: Using a master image to produce
copies. According to Professor Boris Kossoy:

> Florence used master glass plates coated with a
> mixture of gum arabic and soot. He outlined his de-
> signs and texts with a burin, then copied them
> through sunlight exposure on paper sensitized with
> silver chloride or, preferably, gold chloride, thus ob-
> taining printout images. In testing chemical prepa-
> rations that would prevent his gold-chloride copies
> from being altered when again exposed to light, he
> first used a solution of urine (for the ammonia in its
> composition) and water. Later he used caustic am-
> monia (ammonium hydroxide) as a fixer for the
> copies prepared with silver chloride.[47]

What is also astounding is that a detailed examination of his manuscripts by the Conservation Laboratory
of Rochester Institute of Technology in 1976 confirmed
that Florence used the word "photographie" to describe
his endeavors in 1833, five years before Herschel recommended "photography" to Talbot and the word photographer in 1834. Although none of Florence's camera
images have survived, his contact prints of a diploma
and labels for pharmaceutical bottles made before 1837
are in the possession of his descendants.

The formation of a process to address divergent picturemaking desires seemed to converge everywhere, all
at once. Today we can point to notions that photography
worked the borders of reality and representation, culture and nature, objectivity and subjectivity, permanence and transience, and speculate that early imagemakers were striving to show that these boundaries
were false. But such contemporary thinking bypasses
what photography is fundamentally about: empowering
people with the means to make a visual representation
of their reality, a model capable of tracing a subject's
presence. Daguerre summed up the desire best:

> I have found a way of fixing the images of the camera! I have
> seized the fleeting light and imprisoned it! I have forced the
> sun to paint pictures for me![48]

Endnotes

1 Martin Kemp, *The Science of Art: Optical themes in western art from Brunelleschi to Seurat* (New Haven: Yale University Press, 1990), 9–15, 344–45.

2 Leon Battista Alberti, *On Painting and on Sculpture*, ed. and translated by Cecil Grayson (London: Phaidon Press, Ltd., 1972), 55.

3 For a fictional, philosophical account linking the camera obscura from Mo Ti to the present, see David Knowles, *The Secrets of the Camera Obscura* (San Francisco: Chronicle Books, 1994).

4 Kenneth Clark, *Landscape into Art*, new edition (New York: Harper & Row, Publishers, 1986), 44.

5 Kemp, 53–60.

6 Georges Potonniée, *The History of the Discovery of Photography*, translated by Edward Epstean (New York: Arno Press, 1973), 11. Trans. *Histoire de la découverte de la photographie*. (Paris, 1925). First English edition, New York: Tennant and Ward, 1936.

7 Vermeer's vision is the result of constructing images from things seen in the natural world and things seen in his mind: Vermeer transcended the camera. It is the act of seeing and thinking, rather than the limited focus on what is seen and how it is ordered, that enables such an artist to suggest an intricate inner world.

8 Some of Vermeer's later work, such as *A Girl Asleep* (1656), when reproduced in a small black-and-white format can at first be mistaken for a late nineteenth-century snapshot.

9 Lithography is a method of printing based on the aversion of grease and water. A drawing is made with a crayon, pencil, or ink that contains grease and pigment and is chemically fixed to the top of a limestone or a smooth metal surface. This surface is wetted and rolled with oily ink, which adheres only to the greasy drawing; the rest of the surface, being damp, repels the ink. Prints are made in multiple copies, referred to as *editions*, on paper in a press.

10 Johann Heinrich Schulze, "Scotophorous [bringer of darkness] Discovered Instead of Phosphorous; or, A Noteworthy Experiment of the Action of the Sun's Rays." A translation can be found in R. B. Litchfield, *Tom Wedgwood, the First Photographer* (London: Duckworth & Co., 1903), 218–24.

11 Norman Tiphaigne de La Roche, *Giphantia* (London, 1761), printed for Robert Horsfield, original in French, 95–97. Reproduced in Georges Potonniée, *The History of the Discovery of Photography*, trans. Edward Epstean (New York: Tennant and Ward, 1936), 44.

12 Humphry Davy, "An Account of a method of copying Painting upon Glass, and making profiles, by the agency of Light upon Nitrate of Silver. Invented by T. Wedgwood, Esq. with Observations by H Davy," *Journals of the Royal Institution*, vol. 1 (1802), 170–74.

13 R. D. Altick: *The Shows of London* (Cambridge, MA: Belknap Press, 1978), 120–21.

14 In 1826 Thomas Drummond applied a mixture of oxygen and hydrogen to small balls of lime to produce a powerful and steady source of illumination for coastal lighthouses. The entertainment business quickly adapted the Drummond Light, renaming it *limelight*, as a replacement for the Argand light.

15 See H. and A. Gernsheim, *L. J. M. Daguerre, The History of the Diorama and of the Daguerreotype*. Reprint. (New York: Dover Publications, 1968), 14–47.

16 See Sir David Brewster, *The Kaleidoscope: Its History, Theory, and Construction* (1819; reprinted London, 1858).

17 Johann Wolfgang von Goethe, *Theory of Colours*, translated by Charles Eastlake [1840] (Cambridge, MA: MIT Press, 1970).

18 Jonathan Crary, *Techniques of the Observer on Vision and Modernity in the Nineteenth Century* (Cambridge, MA: MIT Press, 1990), 98.

19 Andre Gunthert, email discussion with author, December 17, 1998.

20 Isidore Niépce, *History of the discovery improperly called daguerreotype* (Paris: Astier, August 1841), 17.

21 Most previous publications have indicated an exposure time of about eight hours. However, according to Jean-Louis Marignier and Michel Ellenberger, "L'invention retrouvée de la photographie," *Pour la science*, No. 232, Feb., 1997, 42; Niépce never indicated the precise exposure time he used. The authors, using a similiar type of lens and emulsion that Niépce used, found that their summer daylight exposure times varied between 40 to 60 hours.

22 Letter from Joseph to Claude Niépce dated 16.7bre [September] 1824, in *Dokumenty po istorii izobreteniya fotografii*, T. P. Kravits, ed. (Moscow: Academy of Sciences of the USSR, 1949), 148–49 [*Documents in the History of the Invention of Photography*, The Correspondences of J. N. Niépce, L. J. M. Daguerre, and Others]. Note that Niépce apparently photographed this scene numerous times over many years, adding to the difficulty in dating the surviving example.

23 An early outgrowth of Niépce's research was the first photomechanical process, the héliogravure, an elementary version of photogravure. After the treated plate was exposed and developed it was placed in an acid bath. The acid etched out the unprotected areas, leaving an intaglio plate that could be inked and printed. The process worked when used to make traditional prints, but not with camera-made images that depended on midtone values to be effective. Later Niépce's nephew, Claude Abel Niépce de Saint-Victor, refined the process to include a broader range of midtones.

24 Daguerre learned of Niépce's work from Charles Chevalier, son of the Paris optician, from whom both bought equipment. In 1828, Niépce's brother Claude

died in London while trying to raise funds for the picturemaking system. The loss of his co-experimenter brother and his need for money made Niépce amenable to a partnership.

25   See Hugh W. Salzberg, *From Caveman to Chemist: Circumstances and Achievements*, American Chemical Society, Washington, D.C., 1991, 38, 44–45.

26   Count Francois Arago (1786–1853), the former Minister of War and Director of the Paris Observatory, was a recognized physicist and an astute politician who served as the secretary of the French Académie des Sciences and as a member of the Chamber of Deputies.

27   Daguerre, as quoted in Helmut and Alison Gernsheim, *L. J. M. Daguerre* (New York: Dover, 1968), 81.

28   For details about this claim see: André Gunthert, "Daguerre ou la promptitude. Archéologie de la réduction du temps de pose" in *Etudes photographiques,* No. 5 (November 1998), 5–25.

29   For a detailed account of the events of 1839 see Gernsheim, *L. J. M. Daguerre*, 79–97.

30   For a detailed description of the era in which the daguerreotype was introduced see Rachel Stuhlman, "Luxury, Novelty, Fidelity: Madame Foa's Daguerreian Tale," *Image*, vol. 40, nos. 1–4, (1997).

31   William Henry Fox Talbot, *The Pencil of Nature* (London: Longman, Brown, Green & Longmans, 1844). Facsimiles, New York: Da Capo Press, 1969; and New York: H. P. Kraus, 1989. Unp.

32   An early microscope fitted into a wall so as to collect sunlight and project it through a specimen into a darkened room where the enlarged image was viewed on a screen.

33   Salted paper prints became the mainstay of silver printing-out papers until they were superseded in the 1850s by albumen paper. Salted paper prints produce a reddish-brown image tonality. They are stable to light when properly processed, but the unprotected silver image is extremely susceptible to airborne pollutants, which cause yellow fading.

34   See H. J. P. Arnold, *William Henry Fox Talbot: Pioneer of photography and Man of Science* (London: Hutchinson Benham, Ltd., 1977), 119–20.

35   William Henry Fox Talbot, *Some Account of the Art of Photogenic Drawing* (London, 1839). Reprinted in Beaumont Newhall, *Photography: Essays & Images* (New York: The Museum of Modern Art, 1980), 28.

36   Ibid.

37   Talbot made iodized paper by brushing potassium iodide and silver nitrate (the same active ingredient as in the daguerreotype) onto high-quality writing paper. Prior to camera exposure, the paper was brushed with "gallo-nitrate of silver" (a solution of silver nitrate, acetic, and gallic acid usually referred to as gallic acid) and put into the camera while still moist. This cut exposure times from minutes to 10 to 60 seconds in direct sunlight.

38   The first printed use of the word can be found in an article on Talbot's invention by the German astronomer Johann H. von Madler in the *Vossische Zeitung* of February 1839. Herschel used it in print in a paper to the Royal Society on March 14, 1839.

39   Waxing increased the apparent resolution, as the wax made the negative more translucent and diminished the visibility of the paper's fibrous structure. The process was popular with European amateurs for architectural and landscape work until it was supplanted by the distinctly different *waxed paper process* and the wet collodion process in the 1850s.

40   In October 1843, Atkins began publishing *British Algae: Cyanotype Impressions.* The illustrations were photogenic drawings produced by the cyanotype process. The text and captions were photographic copies of Atkins' handwriting. In 1850, she began to issue massive volumes, completing the publication of three volumes in 1853, which were designed to have 14 pages of text and 389 plates.

41   Larry J. Schaaf, *Sun Gardens: Victorian Photographs by Anna Atkins* (New York: Aperture, 1985).

42   A. A. [Anna Atkins], *British Algae: Cyanotype Impressions.* 3 volumes. Halstead Place, Sevenoaks: privately published, 1843–53. As cited in Larry J. Schaaf.

43   Bayard treated paper with silver chloride and exposed it to light until it turned dark. Then he bathed the paper in potassium iodide and exposed it in his camera. The light bleached the paper in direct proportion to its intensity, forming a unique direct positive picture and solving the problem that had confounded Niépce and Daguerre. Bayard also used Herschel's hypo to fix his images.

44   Collection of the Société de Photographie; reproduced in Lo Duca, *Bayard* (Paris: Prisma, 1943), 22–23.

45   For a list of those who came forward after Daguerre's announcement claiming to be the inventor of photography see Geoffrey Batchen, *Burning with Desire: The Conception of Photography* (Cambridge, MA: MIT Press, 1997), 35 and 50.

46   Boris Kossoy in email correspondence with the author, May 25, 1999.

47   Boris Kossoy, "Photography in Nineteenth-Century Latin America: The European Experience and The Exotic Experience" in Wendy Waitriss and Lois Parkinson Zamora (eds) *Image and Memory: Photography From Latin America 1866–1994* (Austin: University of Texas Press in association with FotoFest, Inc., 1998) 23. Complete references to Kossoy's writing on Florence can also be found in this text.

48   Daguerre, quoted in Helmut and Alison Gernsheim *L. J. M. Daguerre: The History of the Diorama and the Daguerreotype*, second revised edition (New York: Dover Publications, 1968), 49.

CHAPTER TWO

The Daguerreotype
Image and Object

Daguerreotypes reigned from 1839 through the 1850s. In this first period of picturemaking millions of daguerreotypes, from street corner scenes to the Acropolis, were made of almost any subject on which light would shine. All the major cities and tourist destinations were daguerreotyped, but the new process had its most revolutionary impact in portraiture. Before the nineteenth century, only the wealthy had the means to act on the desire to commemorate their likenesses. Industrial-age products, like the physionotrace and the camera lucida, had begun to expand the picturemaking process. But the daguerreotype was the great equalizer, providing ordinary people with access to pictures of themselves and their loved ones. Before the daguerreotype, it is unlikely that tradespeople—say, vegetable sellers—could have acted on the desire to commemorate themselves and their occupations in a portrait (see Figure 2.1). Virtually everyone could now make their own visual history, collecting images that said, "This is *mine*—

UNKNOWN PHOTOGRAPHER. *Maungwudaus* (Chief of the Ojebway Tribe), ca. 1845. Quarter plate daguerreotype with applied color. Courtesy George Eastman House.

2.1   CARL FERDINAND STELZNER.   *Mother Albers, The Family Vegetable Woman*, ca. 1845. 5⅖ × 4⅖ inches. Daguerreotype.   © Museum für Kunst und Gewerbe, Hamburg.

my family, my house, my dog, my trip to Niagara Falls." Commercial, industrial, and scientific applications rapidly followed. By the 1850s a new information age was underway as millions of daguerreotype portraits and views, as outdoor scenes were called, gained circulation.

2.2   Construction of a daguerreotype: hinged, velvet-lined case, plate, frame, matte, and glass.   Courtesy George Eastman House.

What Is a Daguerreotype?

In the winter of 1838–39, American inventor and painter **Samuel F. B. Morse** [1791–1872] was in Paris to demonstrate his electric telegraph and arranged a meeting with Daguerre.[1] After seeing Daguerre's process Morse wrote to his brother that daguerreotypes "resemble aquatint engraving; for they are in simple chiarooscuro [sic], and not in colors, but the exquisite minuteness of the delineation cannot be conceived. No painting or engraving ever approached it. . . . The impressions of interior views are Rembrandt perfected."[2]

The daguerreotype is a physical container of information, having the properties of both a two-dimensional image and a three-dimensional object. The daguerreotype does not look or feel like a photograph, nor is it made like a photograph. Its image rests on highly polished copper plate and its brilliant mirror-like silver surface provides unparalleled visual depth—this attribute also makes viewing problematic. A daguerreotype must be viewed from a specific angle or its image will appear as a negative, that is, tonally reversed. Above all, each image is unique. The daguerreotype's greatest technical advantage is its ability to render incredible detail. Its shimmering surface is physically luxurious; and it can beautify an ordinary subject by anointing it with a sense of visual splendor. As the image can seem to rise from the surface, the daguerreotype can give a sense of a subject's three-dimensionality. The daguerreotype's subtle perfection and ephemeral personality, its sparkling, gemlike quality, lend it a sense of magical realism.

A daguerreotype's mirrored surface includes a viewer in the image. One can adjust the viewing distance so that the viewer's face and the face of the sitter in the portrait synchronize. As the eyes of viewer and subject overlap, one can experience a sense of traveling backward and forward in time and space. The daguerreotype's delicate surface is protected in a small, closed case, making the viewing experience intimate and private. Designed to be held in one's hand, not seen on a wall, a daguerreotype can create a beguiling sense of tension as it flickers between the positive and the negative surface image. It can simultaneously convey two views of a person, providing an extra dimension into the character of the sitter.

Details of the daguerreotype process spread swiftly after Arago's public announcement, but its long exposure times meant that its finest initial

2.3 THÉODORE MAURISSET. *Fantasies: La Da-guerreotypomanie*, December 1839. 9⅖ × 14⅛ inches. Hand-colored lithograph.   Courtesy George Eastman House.

subjects were immobile. Daguerreotyping was not a spontaneous act. A daguerreotype was planned and *made* rather than casually *taken*. Early daguerreotypes recorded premeditated poses constructed over many minutes of exposure time. This built-in sense of time was evident in the daguerreotype and encouraged viewers to linger, to study, and to think about the image.

The daguerreotype immediately revealed the potential for photographic processes to replace hand-done procedures carried out by skilled artisans. Within days of its public announcement, *Le Lithographe* printed a lithograph of the Cathedral of Notre Dame in Paris drawn from a daguerreotype view, forging a new alliance between photography and printmaking. Young America was especially eager for views of historical European sites, and an immediate market developed for cultural icons. Daguerreotype views of famous places in Europe, the Middle East, and America were traced

and transferred onto copper plates by the *aquatint process*[3] and published in Paris between 1841 and 1843 as *Excursions Daguerriennes: Vues et Monuments les plus remarquables du globe*. Within a few years, most major natural formations, such as Niagara Falls, and man-made monuments, including the Kremlin, had been daguerreotyped.

The Daguerreotype Comes to America

On September 20, 1839, Daguerre's instruction manual for his process arrived in the United States, and a week later Samuel Morse exhibited his own view of New York's Unitarian Church (now lost). Within two weeks the first American portraits, with the sitter's eyes shut to diminish movement caused by blinking during the long exposures, had been made. John W. Draper [1811–1882], a chemistry professor at New York University, dusted his sister's face with white flour (to increase light reflectance and reduce the exposure time), made her daguerreotype, and sent it to Sir John Herschel in England. Draper wrote: "I believe I was the

2.4   JOHN DRAPER.   *Miss Dorothy Catherine Draper,* ca. 1840. Daguerreotype. Original ruined. Collotype from a daguerreotype. This early daguerreotype portrait, believed to have been made in July 1840, was destroyed in 1933 during an attempt to clean the plate. This facsimile was made from a copy negative of the original.   Courtesy National Museum of American History, Smithsonian, photo no. 82–11970.

first person here [America] who succeeded in obtaining portraits from the life."[4] (see Figure 2.4.) Despite its difficulties, other daguerreotypists quickly followed, furthering the process of democratizing visual representation by challenging the conventions of who did the depicting, what was depicted, and what the depiction revealed about the subject, and establishing a new basis for portraiture.

The Early Practitioners

Early American daguerreotypists, mostly men without formal arts training, were refugees from other lines of work. The late 1830s saw America's first modern economic depression. Ironically, the daguerreotype, on the verge of destabilizing the business of picturemaking, offered some unemployed and entrepreneurs an opportunity to live the *American Dream* of the second chance. This ideology grew out of the European "New World" myth that saw America as a land of Eden where one could be restored through will power and hard work.[5] The newness of the daguerreotype appealed to the youthful country's frontier mentality and its infatuation with machines that made tasks easier to perform.

Most daguerreotypists were self-taught, learning their skills through apprenticeship or by taking a few lessons. Nathaniel Hawthorne's daguerreotypist in *The House of the Seven Gables* (1851) sets the tone for how people viewed the profession. By the age of twenty-two Holgrave, the hero, had been a schoolmaster, a salesman, a political editor, a peddler of Cologne water, a dentist, a supernumerary official aboard a packet-ship, a public lecturer on Mesmerism,[6] and a daguerreotypist. The narrator describes what many people thought of daguerreotypists:

> His present phase, as a Daguerreotypist, was of no more importance in his own view, nor likely to be more permanent, than any of the preceding ones. It had been taken up with the careless alacrity of an adventurer, who had his bread to earn; it would be thrown aside as carelessly, whenever he should choose to earn his bread by some other equally digressive means.[7]

These itinerant daguerreotypists, oblivious to the academic rules of painting, introduced to portraiture the idea that anything was possible. Daguerreotypists were free to decide what was important and how to record it, making up their own hierarchy. They brought a fresh, uncomplicated sense of ordering and the freedom to document the vernacular, emphasizing the surface appearance of everyday subject matter. The lack of European formality in America allowed pictorial space to be arranged in a more informal, intuitive, and naturalistic manner. This sense of playfulness foreshadows the arrival of the snapshot and can also be seen in other works such as Walt Whitman's *Leaves of Grass* (1855). Whitman's free verse celebrations of individual freedom and dignity, democracy, and brotherhood are part of the same spirit that was captured in many daguerreotypes.

Early Daguerreian Portrait Making

Alexander S. Wolcott [1804–1844] and John Johnson opened what the March 4, 1840, New York *Sun* exclaimed was "the first daguerreotype gallery for portraits." People having their daguerreotypes made at this studio were in for a few surprises. A sitter was arranged in a posing chair with his or her head held stationary by an iron clamp on back of the chair.[8] Two large mirrors, hanging over the street from the third floor, directed light into the studio. Sunlight bounced from the lower mirror onto the upper mirror and was then reflected through a rack of glass bottles, filled with a blue solution of copper sulphate to soften the quality of the light,

2.5 UNKNOWN PHOTOGRAPHER. *Portrait of an Unidentified African-American Woman*, ca. 1850. Sixth plate daguerreotype with applied color. Courtesy George Eastman House.

2.6 HENRY FITZ, JR. *Self-Portrait with Eyes Closed*, ca. November 1839/January 1840. Ninth plate daguerreotype.   In October 1839, Wolcott and Johnson built a miniature camera (4 × 2 inches) that utilized a concave mirror instead of a lens to focus the light. Johnson sat for five minutes in full sunlight to make what he called a profile portrait that was not quite ⅜ inch square. With the assistance of the telescope maker Henry Fitz, Jr., the two built a bigger concave mirror camera and commenced working with 2 × 2½-inch plates. Wolcott patented the camera in 1840. This corpselike self-portrait made by Fitz, with his eyes closed, is believed to be from those first trials. Courtesy Smithsonian Institution, photo no. 44215.A.

directly onto the face of the sitter, who was staring so hard into the light that tears became a regular part of the process. Initially, portraits were usually undertaken only on sunny days, when exposures could be made in about one minute. On cloudy days exposures could last eight minutes or longer, making it impossible for people to remain still enough to get a sharp likeness. The camera did not have a shutter; the exposure was made by removing the lens cap for a period of time, tracked by a pocket watch, that varied according to the intensity of the light. Since daguerreotypists prepared their own plates, exposure time was based on the operator's previous experience. One sitter recalled the tribulation:

[He sat] for eight minutes, with strong sunlight shining on his face and tears trickling down his cheeks while . . . the operator promenaded the room with watch in hand, calling out the time every five seconds, till the fountains of his eyes were dry.[9]

2.7   UNKNOWN PHOTOGRAPHER.   *Post-Mortem Portrait, Woman Holding Baby*, ca. 1855. Sixth plate daguerreotype with applied color.   Courtesy George Eastman House.

Some people, including the French novelist Honoré de Balzac, considered the daguerreian portrait perilous for metaphysical reasons. Balzac believed that physical bodies were made up of an infinite number of leaflike skins and that every time one's daguerreotype was taken, one of these layers was removed from the body and transferred to the image. Each exposure meant the irreplaceable loss of another ghostly layer, the very essence of life.[10]

Most people had more concrete reasons for dreading the daguerreotypist. Lengthy exposures could make the daguerreian portrait an ordeal. Operators, as daguerreotypists were called, were judged for their ability to be quick and painless. The practice of painting faces white and dusting hair with white powder didn't make the occasion any more pleasant or the result particularly natural. It is not surprising that today's viewers of daguerreian portraits comment on how unnatural or serious people appear. One story tells of an operator who:

> had tried all sorts of suasions [to keep his sitter quiet], when it occurred to him that the strongest of all human motives is fear. As soon as he had completed his adjustments, he suddenly draws a revolver, and leveling it at the sitter's head, he explains in a voice and with a look suggestive of lead and gunpowder: "Dare to move a muscle and I'll blow your brains out."[11]

Another operator printed business cards proclaiming: "Photography in all styles without pain." He proposed to use gas on his sitters; once they were rendered unconscious, he would make the exposure.[12] A third suggested: "A good dose (of laudanum [opium]) will

2.8   RICHARD BEARD.   *Portrait of a Young Man Seated at Table*, ca. 1852. Ninth plate daguerreotype with applied color.   Courtesy J. Paul Getty Museum, Los Angeles.

effectively prevent the sitters from being conscious of themselves, or the camera, or anything else. They become most delightfully tractable, and you can do anything with them under such circumstances . . . the procedure entails a certain loss of animation."[13]

The emphasis, clearly, was on getting a physical "likeness" as opposed to probing a sitter's inner state of being. Poses were typically 3/4 length against a neutral background with the sitter gazing straight toward the camera. What the camera saw is what was delivered; there was no retouching. People accustomed to hand-drawn portraits that flattered the sitter were startled by the camera's direct representation. Long exposures necessitated stationary poses that produced experiences like the one Ralph Waldo Emerson related:

> In your zeal not to blur the image, did you keep every finger in its place with such energy that your hands became clenched as for fight or despair, and in your resolution to keep your face still, did you feel every muscle becoming every moment more rigid; the brows contracted into a Tartarean frown, and the eyes fixed in a fit, in madness, or in death? And when, at last you were relieved of your duties, did you find the curtain drawn perfectly, and the hands true, clenched for combat, and the shape of the face or head?— but, unhappily, the total expression escaped from the face and the portrait of a mask instead of a man? Could you not by grasping it very tight hold the stream of a river, or of a small brook, and prevent it from flowing?"[14]

Post-Mortem Portraits

The daguerreian portrait permitted everyone to join the immortals by leaving their image for the future. Even death could be cheated as those who had not found the time in life for a daguerreotype could be memorialized in death. Often considered morbid by contemporary audiences, post-mortem images (see Figure 2.7) were commonplace in the nineteenth century, where death occurred in the home and was an ordinary part of life.

Funerary pictures can fascinate and provoke questions about the effect of photographs. Do funerary images preserve the 'presence' of the dead or do they make us more aware of their absence? Do photographs that picture someone who no longer exists recall death or life? Are *all* photographs funerary in the sense that they show us something from the past that will never be that way again?

Technical Improvements

In 1840 Richard Beard [1802–1885] bought the patent rights to the daguerreotype process in England and hired John Frederick Goddard to increase the plate's light sensitivity, which would reduce exposure times and make portraiture more practical. Goddard refumed the iodized surface of the plate with bromide, and his accelerator, known as *quickstuff,* could increase the speed 5 to 10 times, reducing a 10-minute exposure to 1 minute.[15] Antoine Francois Jean Claudet [1798–1867], a competitor of Beard, also invented a chlorine and iodine vapor accelerator in 1841 for the same purpose.[16] At the same time, Armand Hippolyte Louis Fizeau invented a technique called *gilding*[17] to improve the plate's contrast and make it less susceptible to abrasion and oxidation, thus increasing its life expectancy. These improvements enabled Beard to open the first high-quality daguerreotype portrait studio in London, and probably in Europe, in March 1841. The need for improvements was related by photographer Thomas Sutton's pre-accelerator experience at Claudet's studio, which opened shortly after Beard's:

> [Claudet] informed me, with the utmost gravity, that to achieve anything like success or eminence in it (daguerreotyping) required the chemical knowledge of Faraday, the optical knowledge of Herschel, the artistic talent of a Reynolds or a Rembrandt, and the indomitable pluck and energy of a Hannibal; and under these circumstances he strongly dissuaded anyone from taking it up as an amusement.[18]

In the United States, where Americans embraced the daguerreotype as if it was their own invention, a series of technical improvements, known as the *American Process*, took American daguerreotypes to the highest level of excellence.[19] The American Process included

2.9 Voigtländer camera and lens.   Peter Friedrich Voigtländer of Germany built an all-metal camera that made images 2½ inches in diameter and featured the fastest (f/3.6) and best corrected portrait lens available. Designed by Josef Petzval, this lens was 22 times faster than the original f/17 Chevalier lens supplied with the Giroux daguerreotype camera and 4 times faster than Wolcott's mirror camera. Since it allowed more light to enter, it greatly reduced exposure times, making portraits easier to accomplish. The Petzval lens was outrageously expensive, and the marketplace responded by counterfeiting. Crooked distributors forged Voigtländer's signature on "tubes" (early lenses were often called tubes) of their own manufacture.   Courtesy George Eastman House.

plates re-silvered by electrotyping and polished with power-driven buffers. Cheaper and more compact cameras, with the first accordionlike bellows, were used, and materials were standardized through mass-produced equipment (see list below). A finished plate was often put into what was called a Union Case, marking the first industrial use of thermoplastic in 1853.

Daguerreotype plates were first commercially produced by silversmiths in various sizes that became internationally standardized.

Whole plate: 6½ × 8½ inches

Three-quarter plate: 5½ × 7⅛ inches

Half plate: 4½ × 5½ inches

Quarter plate: 3¼ × 4¼ inches

Sixth plate: 2¾ × 3¼ inches

Ninth plate: 2 × 2½ inches

Expanding U.S. Portrait Studios

Yankee mechanical ingenuity propelled the expansion of American portrait studios. In 1841, **John Plumbe, Jr.** [1809–1857] established the United States Photographic Institute in Boston as a commercial enterprise, taking portraits (see Figure 2.10), selling apparatus and materials, and providing instruction. By 1843 Plumbe was advertising his ability to make a "color" portrait by electroplating portions of the finished plate, fueling a demand for colored images. The first colored daguerreotypes were hand-painted after processing. For an extra fee, the operator made notes about the color of the sitter's clothes. Color was hand-applied, based on these notations, directly onto the finished plate.

Plumbe's national studio network advanced the concept, started by galleries in New York, of collecting celebrity portraits. He had the unique images copied and published as lithographs in *The National Plumbeotype Gallery*. By 1845 Plumbe had a chain of fourteen galleries from New York to Dubuque, Iowa, that eventually offered daguerreotypes for as little as one dollar, all stamped "Plumbe." The daguerreotypist was not credited, establishing a precedent that other chain studios followed, thus making it difficult to attribute a daguerreotype to an individual operator. Most large studio owners managed and promoted their business and rarely worked as operators, yet all the work carried the studio's credit-line. The operator was generally considered a skilled production worker who performed a repetitive, machine-like task. The poses were standardized into ritual formulas still on view in countless yearbooks and in the display cases of chain studios from J.C. Penney to Olan Mills.

In 1844, **Albert Sands Southworth** [1811–1894] took **Josiah Johnson Hawes** [1808–1901] as a partner in his Boston daguerreotype studio. Two years later, Hawes married Southworth's sister, Nancy, who had been working at the gallery coloring plates. Later, another sister, Asa Southworth, also worked as an operator. This family unit produced exceptional work and became a model daguerreian portrait studio. Although individuals at Southworth and Hawes had specific tasks to perform, the collaborative nature of the portrait stu-

2.10   JOHN PLUMBE, JR.   *Portrait of a Man Reading a Newspaper*, ca. 1842. Sixth plate daguerreotype. Courtesy J. Paul Getty Museum, Los Angeles.

Mathew B. Brady [1823–1896] helped pioneer the celebrity portrait. He opened his first Daguerrean Miniature Gallery in New York in 1844 and became an expert at utilizing daguerreotypes in public relations. Brady sent his daguerreian celebrity portraits and the interior views of his fashionable gallery to the new picture papers, where they were converted into wood-engraved illustrations for publication. This free publicity not only promoted his portrait business but signaled the role daguerreotypes would play in the budding mass communications arena by increasing the number and type of images in public circulation. Brady undertook his first historical project in 1845 by making daguerreotypes of American public figures and having a selection of images reproduced in *Frank Leslie's Illustrated Newspaper* so they could be seen by a wide audience. In 1850 Brady continued to unite portraiture, history, and publishing through his *Gallery of Illustrious Americans*, a collection of 12 lithographs, based on his portraits, that included Daniel Webster, John Calhoun, Henry Clay (see Figure 2.12), and John James Audubon. *Humphrey's Journal of the Daguerreotype*, June 15, 1853, describes the atmosphere of manufactured elegance at Brady's Broadway studio where, for a modest fee, one could fabricate a vision:

> The floors are carpeted with superior velvet tapestry, highly colored. . . . The walls are covered with satin and gold paper. The ceiling frescoed, and in the center is suspended a six-light gilt and enameled chandelier. . . . The harmony is not the least disturbed by the superb rosewood furniture—tête-à-têtes, reception and easy chairs, and marble-top tables, all of which are multiplied by mirrors from ceiling to floor. Suspended on the walls, we find Daguerreotypes of Presidents, Generals, Kings, Queens, Noblemen—and *more nobler men*—men and women of all nations and professions.

dio makes it difficult to determine who was responsible for many aesthetic and technical improvements. A side effect of this method of working was to rupture the concept of a single author who directed, supervised, and took credit for the work produced in a studio setting.

Under a skylight studio referred to as the "operating room," the Southworth and Hawes group created bold and direct portraits of Boston's cultural élite (see Figure 2.11.) Ignoring stereotypical poses, they demonstrated how a daguerreian portrait could be more than a detailed physiographic map and could speak in its own physically rich and often sensual language. Southworth commented:

> It is required of and should be the aim of the artist-photographer to produce in the likeness the best possible character and finest expression of which that particular face or figure could ever have been capable. But in the result there is to be no departure from truth in the delineation and representation of beauty, and expression, and character.[20]

The Art of the Daguerreian Portrait

Before the daguerreotype most portraiture was done by artists specializing in hand-size miniatures. Many artists, afraid the daguerreotype would destroy their livelihood, mocked the new form as third rate and its practitioners as untalented. This fear voiced itself in one of photography's most frequently quoted aphorisms, that of the artist Paul Delaroche who has been

2.11 SOUTHWORTH AND HAWES. *Rollin Heber Neal* (Pastor of the First Baptist Church, Boston), ca. 1850. 8½ × 6½ inches. Whole plate daguerreotype.   Courtesy George Eastman House.

misquoted in numerous texts as stating upon seeing his first daguerreotype that painting was "dead."[21] J. J. J. Grandville's *Scenes from the Private and Public Life of Animals* (1842) lampooned this anxious outlook with the tale of a budding portrait painter turned daguerreotypist. The story tells of a talented monkey studying painting in Paris, who discovers that creativity, rather than imitation, is needed to be an artist. To overcome his lack of imagination, the monkey buys a daguerreo-

type outfit and returns to his native Brazil to open the first daguerreian portrait gallery. He becomes fashionable when all of the jungle society come to have their pictures made. At the pinnacle of success, he is ruined by the narcissism of a king and in despair throws himself into the Amazon River.

Despite the mockery, portrait miniaturists saw their sales plummet. Some, such as Carl Stelzner [1805–1894] of Germany, became daguerreotypists; the French painter J. Mansion joined Antoine Claudet's London studio, where he colored and retouched daguerreotypes. Many artists who continued to make miniatures incorporated the photographic process into their working methods. Instead of drawing a portrait by

2.12   MATHEW B. BRADY GALLERY.   *Henry Clay*, before 1852. Copy on a collodion plate of a daguerreotype.   Courtesy The Library of Congress, Washington, D.C.

hand, they painted directly on top of a daguerreotype image. Other portrait painters used daguerreotypes in lieu of their subject to lessen the misery of having a person sit for a portrait, but by 1860, miniature painting was defunct.

Since there was no formal school or aesthetic of photography, the "art" was passed from one practitioner to the next. As the primary studio agenda was to make money, technique rather than aesthetics was stressed. Individuals like Morse were important because they taught others, including Southworth, Brady, and Edward Anthony, who then played key roles in establishing an American photographic practice. Sophisticated studios, especially Brady's, wanted to fashion poses that revealed more than the outer facade of a sitter. Brady and other studio owners looked for inspiration in such publications as Johann Kaspar Lavater's *Essays on Physiognomy* (1789), which encouraged artists to discover "the interior of Man by his exterior—of perceiving by certain natural signs, what does not immediately attract the senses."[22]

2.13   UNKNOWN PHOTOGRAPHER.   *Butterfly Collector*, ca. 1850. 2¾ × 3¼ inches. Sixth plate daguerreotype.   Courtesy George Eastman House.

Most mass market studios, like Plumbe's, combined capitalism and democratic experience: Everyone got the same product, leading the public to think the photographic process was *automatic*. An operator's job was simply to allow each sitter's portrait to be directly recorded by the action of light, giving authorship to the sitter and not the operator. Such daguerreotype studios chronicled ordinary faces, which added up to a synthesized national personality. After viewing hundreds of daguerreian portraits one is struck by the plain ordinariness of the sitter's faces rather than their exceptional beauty. A new portrait genre appeared emphasizing everydayness as its theme, with tradespeople such as cobblers and seamstresses commemorating their labors and the middle class often showing off their possessions (see Figure 2.13).

Daguerreian Portrait Galleries and Picture Factories

In 1853, it was estimated that 1,000 New Yorkers, including women and children, were working in the photographic trade. There were only a few women operators, but many were engaged behind the scenes, especially in hand-coloring plates. Thirty-seven of New York's reported 86 daguerreian studios were located on a single stretch of Broadway. People strolling down Broadway would have seen studio banners and display cases tempting them to walk up the stairs to have their portrait made. Many of the galleries followed the lead of Edward Anthony's *National Daguerreotype Miniature Gallery* and displayed celebrity portraits, to give people the chance to see popular figures—and to encourage them to buy a duplicate portrait or have one made of themselves (see Fig-

2.14 UNKNOWN PHOTOGRAPHER.   *Frederick Douglass*, ca. 1847. Sixth plate daguerreotype.   Courtesy National Portrait Gallery, Smithsonian Institution.

ure 2.14). The implication was that one could have one's portrait made at the same studio that catered to the luminaries. In reality, most of these portraits had been appropriated from other galleries, copied, and displayed without crediting the original maker.

At the time, a skilled laborer earned about $1.50 per day, a common laborer $1.00 a day or less.[23] To meet the needs of working people *picture factories,* with wooden benches and bare walls instead of overstuffed stairs and chandeliers, made portraits for 50 cents. Picture factories were criticized for their sloppy work practices, but the real fear was that their price-cutting methods would take business away from the ornate galleries. The standards of the 50-cent galleries were often not up to par. The most frequent complaint, "blue bosom," resulted when white articles of clothing appeared with a Prussian blue cast. This was due to sloppy working methods that induced the Sabattier effect (a.k.a. solarization), causing a reversal effect which rendered the white highlight areas as blue. In the picture factories the goal was not fantasy, but resemblance. These "50-cent men" were considered unprofessional and were roundly attacked by reputable studio operators in the press:

> Their rooms are frequently the resort of the low and depraved, and they delight in nothing more than desecrating the Sabbath by daguerreotyping these characters in the most obscene positions.[24]

In fact, the frankness and voyeuristic quality of the camera image allowed it to take over the underground market of erotic art. Among the Broadway operators,

2.15   UNKNOWN FRENCH PHOTOGRA-
PHER.   *Two Nude Women Embracing*, ca. 1848. Half
plate daguerreotype with applied color.   Courtesy J. Paul
Getty Museum, Los Angeles.

rumors circulated about unscrupulous individuals making illegal pornographic daguerreotypes after hours and
on Sundays. The realism of the daguerreotype added to
the licentiousness of such imagery. The difficulties of
reproducing daguerreotypes kept the audience for these
secretive pictures limited.

Picture factories prospered due to management
practices that promoted aggressive advertising, used
smaller-sized plates to cut expenses, relied on a division of labor to speed up the operation, and encouraged a relaxed attitude towards aesthetic and technical
standards. Broadway's Reese & Company used an assembly-line approach, with each employee performing a specialized task. Operators followed rigid posing formulas. A customer purchased tickets for the
desired number of sittings and an operator made a corresponding number of plates. The plates were prepared by a polisher and a coater and were brought to
the operator who did the posing. The exposed plates
were passed to a "mercurializer" who developed the
plates by fuming them with mercury. A gilder toned
them, and, for an extra fee, an artist would hand-tint
them. The plates were set into individual cases and
could be delivered in as little as 15 minutes. Generally, the camera operator never saw the finished pictures. Sitters kept the ones they wanted and disposed
of the rest; no refunds or reshoots were given. Abraham Bogardus recalled a customer who protested that,
"My picture looks like the *Devil.*" The Broadway portraitist responded, "I had never seen that personage
and could not say as to the resemblance, but sometimes a likeness ran all through families."[25]

African–American Operators

African-Americans were in the business as well, building a wealth of images in a community where it previously did not exist. Jules Lion is credited with inaugu-
rating the daguerreotype in New Orleans. Augustus

2.16 AUGUSTUS WASHINGTON. *John Brown*, ca. 1847. Quarter plate daguerreotype.   This daguerreotype of abolitionist John Brown was taken by African-American photographer Augustus Washington twelve years before Brown led his aborted slave insurrection in Harpers Ferry, WV. Before the daguerreotype, it is unlikely that a working man like Brown would have left his image for future generations to ponder.   Courtesy National Portrait Gallery, Smithsonian Institution.

Washington operated daguerrean studios in Hartford, CT (from 1843 to 1853), and Berthe Wehnert ran a calotype studio in New York.

James Presley Ball [1825–ca.1904], a free black man, became an itinerant operator after meeting John B. Bailey, an African-American daguerreotypist in Boston (see Figure 2.17). In 1849 he opened "Ball's Great Daguerrean Gallery of the West" in Cincinnati, and he became active in the anti-slavery movement, publishing a pamphlet, *Ball's Splendid Mammoth Pictorial Tour of the United States Comprising Views of the African Slave Trade . . .* (1855).[26] This work also served as guidebook for a 600-yard panorama, on view in Ball's Gallery, depicting the horrors of slavery from capture to bondage. In 1860 his gallery was destroyed by a tornado. His friends helped re-outfit the gallery, which would gain the reputation as 'the finest photographic gallery west of the Allegheny Mountains'[27] and draw prominent sitters like Frederick Douglass and Ulysses S. Grant. Ball later opened studios in Minneapolis, Helena, MT, and Seattle. It was in Helena in 1896 that Ball made his best-known series, of the execution of William Biggerstaff, who was hanged for the murder of another man. A group of cabinet cards show Biggerstaff first sitting pensively in a chair, then hooded and suspended from the hangman's noose, and finally stiffly laid out in his coffin.

2.17   J. P. BALL.   *Portrait of a Bearded Gentleman*, ca. early 1850s. 2⅝ × 2⅛ inches. Sixth plate daguerreotype with applied color.   Courtesy George Eastman House.

Rural Practice

Most Americans in the mid-1800s lived in rural areas, and resourceful daguerreotypists saw they could make money by bringing portraits to smaller communities that lacked studios. The most enterprising traveled in specially made horse-drawn wagons, called "Daguerreotype Saloons." The typical traveling daguerreotypist would come to town, rent a few rooms, pass out handbills or place an ad in the local paper, and wait for customers. If the pictures proved satisfactory, word-of-mouth kept business lively, and when demand dropped off, the daguerreotypist moved on. Rural fam-

ilies, like their urban counterparts, dressed up to present an idealized image that reinforced societal notions about who made up a "normal" family and how they should look (see Figure 2.18).

The Daguerreotype and the Landscape

American daguerreotypists quickly found new uses for daguerreotypes outside of portraiture. James Renwick, who headed a U.S. government survey of the disputed northeast boundary between the United States and Canada, invited Edward Anthony to make daguerreotypes of the area.[28] In 1842, these plates were submitted to a joint commission and reportedly influenced its decision, thus setting a precedent for the use of photographic images as topographical evidence.

2.18 UNKNOWN PHOTOGRAPHER. *George James Webb, Mrs. Webb, and daughters Mary Isabella and Caroline Elizabeth*, ca. 1845. 6⁹⁄₁₆ × 8½ inches. Whole plate daguerreotype.   Courtesy George Eastman House.

John Charles Frémont, who unsuccessfully attempted to make daguerreotypes on his first expedition to the Oregon Trail in 1842, hired Solomon N. Carvalho to make pictures of his fifth Rocky Mountain crossing in 1853—a trip that turned into an ordeal when the group nearly perished in the snowy mountains of Utah. Carvalho later recounted:

> I succeeded beyond my utmost expectation in producing good results and effects by the Daguerreotype process, on the summits of the highest peaks of the Rocky Mountains with the thermometer at times from 20 degrees to 30 degrees below zero, often standing to my waist in snow, buffing, coating, and mercurializing plates in the open air.[29]

Carvalho's daguerreotypes and copy negatives were later destroyed in a fire. (Fires were not uncommon during the early studio era due the use of volatile chemicals in unsafe working conditions and a general lack of concern about safety measures.) However, during the late 1850s photographic apparatus began to be included in western expeditions. American daguerreotypists were now documenting such faraway places as Hawaii, Mexico, the Philippines, and South America. They were also often the first to introduce photography to Central and South America, building large-scale portrait practices that established a working model for local people to follow.

The desire to see nature's wonders, and the railroad's ability to inexpensively transport people to previously inaccessible areas, converted natural sites into tourist attractions. The most popular nineteenth-century North American tourist destination was Niagara Falls.[30] The first daguerreotypes were made by the Langenheim Brothers and Southworth and Hawes in 1845. By 1853, Platt D. Babbitt had obtained a monopoly for making daguerreotypes on the American side. Babbitt's method, of showing tourists taking in the view and becoming a part of the scene, became a formula, fostering a new bourgeois visual pastime: the vacation picture (see Figure 2.19).

The Daguerreotype and Science

By the mid-1800s, optical devices like the telescope and the microscope had altered how the world was conceived, revealing an immense, systematic cosmos

2.19   PLATT D. BABBITT.   *Tourists Viewing Niagara Falls from Prospect Point*, ca. 1855. Whole plate daguerreotype with applied color.   Courtesy George Eastman House.

behind the visible appearance of nature. Aesthetic attitudes towards nature shifted with those of science. The daguerreotype, with its built-in wealth of detail and geometric perspective, was quickly accepted as a reliable scientific witness that also conditioned viewers to embrace photographic representation as the normal appearance of things. This acceptance allowed photographs to be used for study purposes instead of actual subjects. As William M. Ivins, Jr., [1881–1961] stated, it would be "through photography that art and science have had their most striking effect upon the thought of the average man of today."[31] This phenomenon also shows how that even for artists and scientists truth can be just another word for conformity. As early as 1840, William H. Goode of Yale University was making daguerreotypes from a (solar) microscope,[32] setting the precedent for the miniaturization of data. By 1840 Goode and Benjamin Silliman were attempting to make daguerreotypes with artificial light. In 1850, using fifty pairs of Bunsen's carbon batteries, Silliman reported his success and its future importance:

In the United States, where fine sunlight may be obtained almost any day . . . these trials may be considered of minor importance. . . . But in the dark and murky atmosphere of London, it may become an important auxiliary in the art.[33]

The Daguerreian Journal,[34] the world's first photographic magazine, reported in July 1851 that **John Adams Whipple** [1822–1891] had brought together science and daguerreotyping in his Boston studio. He used a steam engine to clean his plates, heat his chemicals, distill his water, and fan his clients in the summer.

Whipple's scientific background as a chemist and his mechanical inventiveness gave him the credentials to realize the Harvard astronomers desire to make a daguerreotype of the moon (see Figure 2.20). Such activity was indicative of the appetite for photographic images of other natural occurrences. About this same time, T. M. Easterly of St. Louis and Alexander Hesler of Chicago both made daguerreotypes of lightning. Whipple began his experiments in December 1849 at what was then the world's largest telescope. In July 1850 he made the first clear daguerreotype of a star (except for the sun). In March 1851 Whipple made the first successful daguerreotype of the moon through a telescope. The image won him a medal at the Great Exhibition in London that same year. The immediate ramifications of this event were recorded in a report by members of the American Philosophical Society who

2.20.   JOHN WHIPPLE.   *The Moon*, 1852. Quarter plate daguerreotype.   Courtesy Harvard College Observatory.

had viewed two of Whipple's daguerreotypes of the moon:

> Hitherto any attempt to portray the scenery of the moon by drawing, has been entirely unsatisfactory in conveying a true impression of its diversified appearance through a telescope; but he now hoped, from the constant improvement in the art of daguerreotyping, that an enlarged picture of the moon's disc may be obtained from which engraved maps might be made, so that selenography of our satellite may be studied in our schools, in conjunction with the geography of our planet.[35]

Whipple copied one of his moon plates with his own *crystalotype process* (his glass-plate negative process that used egg white to hold the light-sensitive emulsion in place) to produce paper prints, which were tipped (glued) into the July 1853 issue of the *Photographic Art-Journal*. Previously only a few people had seen the surface of the moon. The daguerreotype dispersed new knowledge to a large audience, offering fresh ways of knowing the universe. The nineteenth century, which had opened with people believing that what was rea-

sonable was true, would conclude with photography encouraging people to believe that what they saw was true. By the end of the twentieth century, with photography acting as a prime mover, people would realize that what could be seen was not always true.

At the start of the 1850s the daguerreotype appeared to be reigning triumphant, but the expanding picture market demanded cheaper, easier, and faster methods of reproduction than the daguerreotype could provide. By 1854 the daguerreotype was in decline as influential studios turned to the new collodion method. By 1857, the flow of daguerreotypes had slowed to a trickle, with more portraits and views being made in the collodion process than by all others combined.[36] The era of unique daguerreotypes was about to be toppled by William Henry Fox Talbot's concept of a repeatable, negative/positive system of "photography." But the speed at which the daguerreotype had been accepted and disseminated clearly demonstrated that it was an archetypal invention that fulfilled the desire for realistic commemoration that the world had been waiting to receive. While also modifying society's sense of how time and space were visually represented.

Endnotes

1   On March 8, 1839, while visiting with Morse to inspect the telegraph, Daguerre's diorama burnt to the ground.

2   This letter was published in *The Observer* (New York), April 20, 1839.

3   Aquatint is an etching method characterized by extensive tonal graduations, from pale gray to velvety black, and possessing a granular visual effect. The name derives from its resemblance to works done with watercolor washes, and it was often used to make color prints.

4   Marcus A. Root. *The Camera and the Pencil.* (Philadelphia: M. A. Root, etc., 1864), 342. This is America's first photographic history book.

5   For more on this theme, see Leo Marx, *The Machine in the Garden: Technology and the Pastoral Ideal in America* (Oxford: Oxford University Press, 1964).

6   Mesmerism, also known as animal-magnetism or hypnotism, was popularized by the Austrian doctor, Franz Anton Mesmer (1734–1815).

7   Nathaniel Hawthorne, *The House of the Seven Gables* (Oxford & New York: Oxford University Press, 1991), 176–77. Edited with introduction by Michael Davitt Bell.

8   The headrest was not invented for daguerreotype portraits but was already in use by portrait painters. The daguerreotype transformed it into a vernacular object by removing it from its painterly context.

9   Letter signed "G" discussing his visit to Wolcott's studio in New York City in 1840, where Wolcott was setting up a room for making daguerreotype portraits, *American Journal of Photography,* 1861, 42.

10   See Nadar, *My Life as a Photographer* (Balzac and the Daguerreotype), Thomas Repensek (trans.), in *October: The First Decade, 1976–1986,* Annette Michelson, et al (ed.), (Cambridge: MIT Press, 1987), 19.

11   "Talk in the Studio/How to Take a Fidgety Sitter." *American Journal of Photography,* 1861. Reprinted in *The Photographic News,* vol. 5, no. 125, January 25, 1861, 48.

12   "Talk in the Studio/Painless Photography," *Western Photographic News.* As quoted in *The Photographic News,* May 7, 1875, 228.

13   *The Amateur Photographer,* February 22, 1915, 4 (supplement).

14   Ralph Waldo Emerson, *Journals, 1841–1844* (Boston: Houghton Mifflin Company, 1911), 100–01.

15   Goddard published repeatable results in December of 1840. Other daguerreotypists refined the method so that exposures could be made within a 20- to 40-second range. When coupled with the Petzval lens, exposure times could be reduced to 10 seconds or less, opening the profitable gates of the portrait market.

16   Claudet's active mind led him to make numerous contributions to the field, including using a red "safe" light to see in the darkroom; designing painted backgrounds for pictorial effect in portrait making (1841); building a camera with a red safelight window so the plate could be developed inside the camera, thereby eliminating the need to always have a darkroom; making improvements in the hand-coloring of plates (1845); building the first light meter (1848); building a "dynactinometer" to compare the speed of different lenses (1850); and developing a shutter-type device that created the illusion of movement (1853).

17   Gilding was performed after the daguerreotype was fixed. The plate was heated over a low flame and a solution of gold chloride was poured over it. This produced a warm brown tone, adding detail to the highlight areas and improving the contrast. The gold coating helped to render the fragile surface of the plate less susceptible to abrasion, increasing life expectancy of the plate. Since gold is more stable than silver, gilding helped to protect the image from oxidation and tarnishing. After its introduction in 1840, gilding became a standard part of the process.

18   "Reminiscences of an Old Photographer," by Thomas Sutton, *The British Journal of Photography,* vol. XIV, no. 382, August 30, 1867, 413.

19   The high quality of the American images became a source of national pride in international competitions, like the Crystal Palace Exposition in London (1851), where American mechanical products—axes, clocks, hoes, nails, ploughs, screws—were hailed for their ingenuity. Horace Greeley, who founded (1841) and edited the New York Tribune, wrote of the London exhibition that in "Daguerreotypes . . .we [Americans] beat the world."

20   *British Journal of Photography,* XVIII (1871), 583.

21   Delaroche was one of the first important painters to publicly endorse the use of photography by artists. There is no evidence that Delaroche ever made any such an apocalyptic statement.

22   Johann Kaspar Lavater, *Essays on Physiognomy* (1789), quoted in Elizabeth Anne McCauley, *Likenesses: Portrait Photography in Europe, 1850–1870* (Albuquerque: Art Museum, University of New Mexico, 1980). The theory that character could be determined by one's facial characteristics and profile was reflected in silhouette portraits. Lavater's simple theories on aesthetics and posing appeared in photographic journals and manuals and were used in professional practice. They later found a sinister use by providing a basis for ethnic and racial stereotyping.

23   *Historical Statistics of the United States* (Washington, D.C.: Bureau of the Census, 1975), Part 1, 164-65.

24   *The Photographic Fine Art-Journal,* Old Series, VIII, New Series V. 2, (1855), 76.

25   *Anthony's Photographic Bulletin,* vol. XV (1884), 63.

26   See: Deborah Willis (ed.) *J. P. Ball: Daguerrean and Studio Photographer* (New York: Garland Press, 1993) for complete reproduction of *Ball's Splendid Mammoth Pictorial Tour of the United States Comprising Views of the African Slave Trade; of Northern and Southern Cities; of Cotton and Sugar Plantations; of the Mississippi, Ohio and Susquehanna Rivers, Niagara Falls, &C* (1855) and a visual inventory of Ball's known images.

27   George W. Williams, *History of the Negro Race in America from 1619 to 1880: Negroes as Slaves, as Soldiers and Citizens 2* (New York: G. P. Putnam's Son's, 1883), 141. Quoted in Willis, J. P. Ball, xvii.

28   The United States claimed there were highlands on the border while the British denied their existence. Anthony's daguerreotypes (now lost) apparently showed these highlands.

29   *The Photographic and Fine Art Journal,* Old Series, vol. V., New Series Volume 2, Number 8, 124–25 (1855).

30   The opening of the Erie Canal, from New York to Buffalo, NY, in 1825 saw a marked rise in public transportation. Railroads soon followed the same route, spurring the growth of the tourist industry.

31   William Ivins, *Prints and Visual Communication* (London: Routledge & Kegan Paul Ltd., 1953). Excerpt in *Photography in Print: Writing from 1816 to the Present.* 387–88.

32   Microdaguerreotypes, reducing printed material to Lilliputian size for reading under magnification, were reported in 1843 when an experimenter copied a Boston newspaper on a plate just 1 × 1½ inches, which could be read with a twelve-power microscope.

33   *American Journal of Science and Arts,* vol. 11, (May 1851), 418.

34   *The Daguerreian Journal* was edited by S. D. Humphrey of New York. It began publication on November 1, 1850, and continued under various other mastheads until 1870. Another important publication, *The Photographic Art Journal,* was edited by H. H. Snelling of New York. The first issue was dated January 1851 and it also materialized under a series of different titles before ceasing publication in 1860. Both were important assets for the American daguerreotypist, providing a national forum on the latest technical improvements and lively debates about current practice and setting the stage for future publications.

35   *Proceedings of the American Philosophical Society* (July–December 1851), 208.

36   "The Collodion Process—its Use and Abuse," *Humphrey's Journal,* vol. 7, no. 18 (January 15, 1856), 281–82.

CHAPTER THREE

Calotype Rising
The Arrival of Photography

The Calotype

The introduction and acceptance of new mechanically-based devices of visual representation, began to alter the viewing content and expectations of imagemakers and the public. Lithography, mezzotint,[1] and wood engraving fueled the remunerative market for the mass production of prints. Daguerre's one-step, direct-positive image-making method was an ideal fit for these visual conceptions. The possibility that Talbot's two-step, negative/positive print system was a more advantageous process was not at first seriously considered. Daguerre's necromancy had mesmerized viewers with its detailed, miniature, monochrome reflections of the world. Even Talbot's friend Herschel stated that "Certainly they [daguerreotypes] surpass anything I could have conceived as within the bounds of reasonable expectation."[2] Daguerre also held the economic and political advantage, as the British government offered Talbot neither a pension nor honors

T. B. JOHNSON.
Wattie Mure, ca. 1855. 7 × 5⁵⁄₁₆ inches. Salted paper print.
Courtesy George Eastman House.

3.1 WILLIAM HENRY FOX TALBOT (or one of his circle). *The Game Keeper,* ca. 1843. 7⅛ × 5¾ inches. Salted paper print from a waxed calotype negative. Although this image has been attributed to Talbot, ascertaining the identity of who actually made many early photographs can be difficult. Dr. Larry Schaaf, a Talbot scholar who has cataloged some 15,000 Talbot and Talbot-related photographs, doubts that this image was made by Talbot.[3] Regardless of who made this image, its distinctive format and style (not present in Talbot's known work) reveals the versatility of the calotype process and how well it could be used to produce artistic *effect.* Courtesy Smithsonian Institution, National Museum of American History, Division of Photographic History, photo no. 81–10262.

use to those few with capital to invest.[4] Later in 1841, Talbot contracted with Antoine Claudet, who had opened a London daguerreotype studio in June, to offer calotype portraits, but his success was negligible. The calotype process was extremely slow, impure chemicals gave uncertain results, prints often faded, and the highly visible paper fibers produced a soft and grainy look that many found objectionable. The process was considered unreliable, and as a consequence nobody wanted calotype portraits. Nevertheless, the limitations of the daguerreotype, especially in terms of reproducibility, started to become apparent. Upon reconsideration, people realized that Talbot's linkage of light and paper furnished a conceptual and technical vault that united printmaking and science. This in turn provided an engine for mass-produced pictures that Europeans had been developing since the Renaissance, making art more "accurate" and accessible and causing the daguerreotype to finally become obsolete.

The initially perceived "faults" of Talbot's negative/positive system gave it a versatility that proved to be its strength. The calotype's visual softness neutralizes singular detail in favor of the universal. Its matte surface image, with a limited tonal range, makes contrast and mass, and not sharp line, the major visual impulse. In nineteenth-century academic art theory, the intense detail of the daguerreotype was considered detrimental to *effect.* The calotype excelled in *effect,* the emotional atmosphere created by the artist's handling of *tonal masses* (colored areas) as distinguished from linear elements. As photographers considered the artistic potential of their medium, they adopted these painterly concepts, considering photographic detail a mechanical imprint, and tonality as the hand of artistry.

The calotype's flexibility allowed photographers to manipulate the image before a print was produced. Albumen and iodizing solutions were applied to the paper before exposure to increase its light sensitivity. Waxing the negative with beeswax made the paper more transparent and increased visual detail. Retouching was common; pencil, graphite, and watercolor were used to remove surface defects, to add highlights, and to create points of visual emphasis. India-ink was commonly applied to black out the sky portion of a negative so it would print as a clear blank space. Long exposures did not stop movement, and blurry clouds and/or dense and uneven skies gave a mottled effect. Blacking out the sky also hid the imperfections of the paper matrix that

for his discovery. Talbot had to advocate his own cause, patenting his process in February 1841 and demanding a high license fee, which added to its production cost. His patents not only proved unprofitable, but they also had the deleterious side effect of inhibiting the growth of photography in England by confining its commercial

3.2.   WILLIAM HENRY FOX TALBOT.   *The Open Door,* 1843. Salted paper print from a calotype negative. Plate VI of *The Pencil of Nature* (London, 1844–46).   Courtesy Science Museum and Society Picture Library, London, England.

were visible in areas that had a uniform appearance. India-ink was also used to eliminate some parts of the camera-made image and to add others, such as mountains on a flat horizon.

The calotype was grounded in the Romantic aesthetics of its generation, which was at its zenith in 1800, the year of Talbot's birth. Romanticism prized emotional experience; it was a reaction against the established state, Church, and rational Enlightenment thought and a manifestation of the political spirit of the American and French revolutions.[5] The pictorial concepts of the beautiful and the sublime grew to include the picturesque landscape.

The *sublime,* like a storm on the ocean, can trace its origins to awe, terror, and vastness, while the *beautiful,* a calm harbor sunset, situates its lineage within the organization of society, making them opposite concepts that cannot commingle. Characteristics of the sublime include astonishment, darkness, infinity, solitude, and vastness. It features intense directional light and a dynamic interaction between highlights and shadows. The beautiful is less powerful, being delicate, rounded, smooth, and well-proportioned, and favors a soft, diffused light. It was admirable, but it was not capable of arousing great passion.

The Romantic ideal emphasized the *picturesque* and featured rushing brooks, overgrown foliage, and tumbledown structures. It began in England during the late eighteenth century as a method for examining nature and as a guide for making gardens. It provided a construct for seeing what in nature would make a good picture and gave viewers a prescribed route through the picture. Detail and texture were of prime importance, and people were often incorporated into a picture as a pictorial device to help viewers negotiate the space and find their place in nature. Talbot's *Sun Pictures in Scotland* (1845) are a pictorial tribute to Sir Walter Scott's Romantic concepts of the gothic and picturesque, featuring disintegrating structures, dramatic use of light emphasizing highlight and shadow areas, secluded settings, and serpentine, undisturbed vistas. Their warm, luxurious tones and soft delineation of form naturally express Romantic pictorialism.

3.3   Talbot's photographic printing establishment at
Reading, ca. 1845.   Courtesy Gernsheim Collection,
Humanities Research Center, University of Texas, Austin, TX.

Early Calotype Activity

Talbot photographed the daily activities of his estate,
family, and servants, providing a model for future back-
yard snapshooters. During his travels in Britain and Europe during the early 1840s, Talbot made as many as
twenty calotypes a day, showing his enthusiasm as well
as the ease with which calotypes could be made. The
negative material could be prepared the evening before,
freeing the calotypist from needing a darkroom for
every exposure. While traveling on business, Talbot
would develop his paper negatives each evening and
mail the results to Lacock Abbey. There they were
printed by Constance Talbot, making her the first
woman photographic processor, and Nicolaas Henneman, Talbot's Dutch valet, photographic assistant, and
business manager.

Talbot's *The Pencil of Nature* was the first book to be
fully illustrated by calotypes (earlier he had issued a
pamphlet with a calotype on the cover).[6] It was published by subscription, with fewer than 300 copies released in six installments between June 1844 and April
1846. *The Pencil of Nature* realized Talbot's dream of
"every man being his own printer and publisher" and of
"poor authors [making] facsimiles of their works in their
own handwriting."[7] *The Pencil of Nature,* the progenitor

of the photographically illustrated book, promoted Talbot's calotype and provided the first commentary by the
inventor of photography on the aesthetics of the
medium. The introduction to *The Pencil of Nature* traces
the invention of the process, and the succeeding twenty-
four sections illustrate and discuss its possible applications, including artistic expression, documentary uses,
art duplication, scientific illustration, and study and
teaching assistance. The book's calotypes feature architectural studies, still-life compositions, and works of art
alongside a page or two of text discussing the purpose of
each image, setting a precedent, derived from printmaking, for pairing photographic images with words. Talbot
chose not to make only a picture book, but used words
to provide the image with a directed context, indicating
an awareness of how an image's meaning can be affected by the text accompanying it.

Talbot's image selections illustrate his belief that subject matter is "subordinate to the exploration of space
and light."[8] Three plates show that the calotype excelled
in such explorations while securing the ethereal nuances
of light reflected by objects. In the two plates of *The Bust
of Patroclus,* Talbot shows the medium's pictorial possibilities and creative control involving choice of angle of
view, type of light, and scale. In the text to *The Open
Door* (see Figure 3.2), Talbot compares vernacular photographic realism, the forerunner of the snapshot, to
Dutch genre painting, and reveals his allegiance to the
Romantic picturesque landscape conventions:

> We have sufficient authority in the Dutch school of art for tak-
> ing as subjects of representation scenes of daily and familiar
> occurrence. A painter's eye will often be arrested where ordi-

nary people see nothing remarkable. A casual gleam of sunshine, or a shadow thrown across his path, a time-withered oak, or a moss-covered stone may awaken a train of thoughts and feelings, and picturesque imaginings.[9]

Other pictures reveal the calotype's ability to trap "a multitude of minute details which add to the truth and reality of the representation,"[10] that may have even gone unobserved by the photographer. His book also foreshadows the future strength of photographic image-making in its ability to produce multiple (positive) prints from a camera-made matrix (negative).

Talbot founded his own photographic printing factory (the first photo finishing lab), The Talbotype Establishment, in Reading in the fall of 1843. It was a multipurpose facility, producing prints for books and reproducing prints of art objects and valuable documents that were sold through retail outlets. Here paper negatives were placed in contact frames with unexposed silver chloride printing-out paper and exposed, for a couple of minutes to over an hour, in direct sunlight until an image appeared. Afterwards the prints were fixed, washed, and dried. As production procedures were refined, Talbot was able to make thousands of original prints, which were tipped-in (pasted) to illustrate *The Pencil of Nature*.

Here one could also have a portrait made, take lessons, purchase a license to practice, buy equipment and materials, and make arrangements to use the printing and distribution network. These services, plus systematic distribution methods, created standards of practice, bringing together aesthetic ideas and technical inventions that had defied standardization.

However, the high cost of producing a limited edition calotype album or book doomed the calotype in the new, congested domain of commercial printmaking.[11] The search for a photo-based process capable of reproducing editions of hand-created art at affordable prices led to the invention of numerous processes, the first being the *cliché-verre*. The cliché-verre was devised shortly after Talbot announced his method by three English artists and engravers, John and William Havell and J. T. Wilmore, who exhibited prints from their method in March 1839. The cliché-verre combines the handwork of drawing with the action of light-sensitive photographic materials to make an image. Originally a piece of glass was covered with a dark varnish and permitted to dry. A needle was utilized to etch through the varnish to the glass. The glass was used as a negative and was contact-printed onto photographic paper. The process was later modified by Adalbert Cuvelier, using the wet-plate process.

High costs and technical difficulties prevented Talbot from receiving any economic benefits from his discoveries. The first prosperous artistic and economic fusion of the calotype was achieved through the collaboration of painter **David Octavius Hill** [1802– 1870] and chemist **Robert Adamson** [1821–1848] in Scotland, where Talbot did not patent his method. Hill was commissioned to paint a portrait of the Church of Scotland's members, but he did not know how to obtain the likeness of these 474 people who would be in Edinburgh only for a brief period. Sir David Brewster introduced Hill to young Adamson, who was instructing Brewster in the calotype process. The intersection of diverse ages, backgrounds,

3.4   DAVID OCTAVIUS HILL AND ROBERT ADAMSON.   *Lady Elizabeth Eastlake* (Miss Rigby), ca. 1845. 7⅞ × 6 inches. Salted paper print from a calotype negative.   Courtesy George Eastman House.

and interests produced a blend of aesthetic and technological abilities that made Hill and Adamson's calotype portrait studies for Hill's painting among the finest ever done. Hill's giant painting, *Disruption,* not completed until 1866, used the eye of the camera to replace the eye and hand of the artist in making preparatory sketches for a major painting. But its unprocessed agglomeration of figures reflects the difficulty of translating the unique physical effects of the photographic medium into paint.

Their calotype portraits, made under Hill's direction, reflect the artistic and stylistic concerns of Dutch genre and Scottish portrait painting. Generally, the compositions are direct and simple, with each person posed alone, outside, in daylight.[12] Hill diffused the deep shadows that the summer sunlight produced by bouncing light into the scene with a concave mirror, which made for dramatic *chiaroscuro* lighting (a pictorial treatment favoring the play between light and shadow). Hill and Adamson understood that the calotype was matchless at revealing a subject's interaction with the surrounding space and that the lack of specific detail could amplify a subject's specific characteristics. In a letter written in 1848 Hill said:

3.5   PHILIP H. DELAMOTTE.   *Building Up the Colossi of Aboo Simbel* (London, 1855). Salted paper print from a calotype negative. Plate #95, Volume II of Photographic Views of the Progress of the Crystal Palace, Sydenham.   Courtesy Collection of the Juliette K. and Leonard S. Rakow Research Library of the Corning Museum of Glass, Corning, NY.

The rough surface, and unequal texture throughout of the paper is the main cause of the Calotype failing in details, before the process of Daguerreotypy—and this is the very life of it. They look like the imperfect work of a man—and not the much diminished perfect work of God.[13]

Hill and Adamson expanded their efforts and soon were doing general portraiture in their outdoor studio and among the monuments of the Greyfriars cemetery, producing some 1,500 works. They also flawlessly

3.6   SIR WILLIAM JOHN NEWTON.   *Burnham Beeches,* ca. 1855. 6⅝ × 8¹³⁄₁₆ inches. From Album: Pictures of the Photographic Exchange Club. Albumen silver print from calotype negative.   Courtesy George Eastman House.

composed a series of seemingly casual portraits of the fishing people in nearby Newhaven before Adamson suddenly died in 1848.

In the George Eastman House collection of Hill and Adamson's work, the fingerprints of the creators can be seen along the edges of many of their prints, along with the watermark of the J. Whatman "Turkey Mill" paper.[14] The softness of the calotype, juxtaposed with the hard-line quality of the daguerreotype, invites a subjective reading of the image. Since the calotype portrait is two-dimensional, one does not have the sensation of merging with the subject in the picture that is possible with a three-dimensional daguerreotype. A viewer becomes detached, more of a witness than an active participant. Hill and Adamson made the calotype's suppression of detail an asset. There is a feeling of intimacy and subtle beauty in their tight expressionistic compositions, along with an overwhelming sense of atmosphere as light itself becomes a subject. Hill and

Adamson realized that the person in front of the lens was not always the only subject of the picture.[15] They knew that good photographs were the result of conscientious photographers, of what modern photographers call *previsualization,* the awareness that one cannot just point the camera at a subject and expect a miraculous representation to come forth. A good calotype was the result of controlling the process, being acutely aware of the light, constructing a vision, and knowing how it would look photographed. Hill and Adamson understood the subjective nature and the limitations of the calotype. While their images are dependent on established styles, their thoughtful, shadowy pictures are alive and speak directly of the inner, as opposed to the outer, characteristics of their subjects.

London's Crystal Palace Exhibition of 1851 featured the international splendors of artistic, scientific, and technical progress (see Figure 3.5). It included about 700 camera images from six countries, which proved jarring to the small British photographic community. The Americans took the top honors in daguerreotypes, and the French were making such high-quality calotypes that Hill and Adamson received only an honorable mention. This was intolerable to Britain's gentlemen-amateur calotypists, many of whom knew Talbot. In 1852, the presidents

3.7   THOMAS KEITH.   *Edinburgh: Skyline and Rooftops*, ca. 1856. Salted paper print from calotype negative.   Courtesy Gernsheim Collection, Humanities Research Center, University of Texas, Austin, TX.

of the Royal Academy and the Royal Society, Sir Charles Eastlake and Lord Rosse, sent Talbot a letter affably stating that "the French are unquestionably making more rapid process than we are [and] some judicious alteration of the patent restrictions would give great satisfaction, and be the means of rapidly improving this beautiful art."[16] Talbot, realizing that even his friends no longer supported his efforts to profit from his calotype process, relaxed his rights over amateur work. However, he continued to retain patent rights in professional portraiture.

A massive four-volume series of books printed at the conclusion of the Exhibition summarized the best of everything shown.[17] These volumes reveal the Victorian appetite for identifying, categorizing, and labeling all the new products of the industrial age. They also make clear the underlying belief that society could be made better by enlightened technical advancement. This optimistic 'can-do, we are right, and we will make the world better' British attitude is exemplified in the series' factual celebration of the new machine-based culture in which the camera now played a major role as an automatic conveyor of the type and style of information that was in demand. The volumes included salted paper prints of the products that were deemed truly worthy by the Victorians: large blocks of coal (which had been placed outside the exhibit hall and numbered); marine and locomotive engines; a turbine; a steam hammer; an electro-magnetic apparatus; an Indian Rubber boat and pontoons; and a model house for working-class families promoted by Prince Albert (the photograph is credited to the prince, an amateur photographer) to "place within the reach . . . those comforts most conducive to health, to habits of cleanliness and decency, hitherto been enjoyed as luxuries only by the few."[18]

Finally able to make calotypes without a license, British calotypists experienced a brief (1852–1857) golden period. In January 1853 the Photographic Society of London (called the Royal Photographic Society of Great Britain after 1894) was created with Sir Eastlake as president.[19] The Photographic Society commenced publishing the *Journal of the Photographic Society* in March 1853 to facilitate the exchange of information.

A paper, "Upon Photography in an Artistic View," was presented at the group's first meeting by **Sir William Newton** [1787–1869] and published in the *Journal of the*

3.8   UNKNOWN PHOTOGRAPHER.   Unidenti-
fied Landscape, ca. 1851–55. 10 × 7⅖ inches. From:
Blanquart-Evrard/Cahier 5 No. 11. Salted paper print.
Courtesy George Eastman House.

Photographic Society (see Figure 3.6). It touched off a
tempest that has never completely settled.[20] Newton, a
miniaturist painter who took up photography, advised
photographers making photographs intended as studies
for painting to put their subject "a little *out of focus,*
thereby giving a greater breadth of effect, and consequently more *suggestive* of the true character of nature."
Newton also advocated the process of altering the negative "by a chemical or other process" to achieve a "picturesque effect," emphasizing areas of light and shade

while downplaying detail or to make up for defects that
occurred in the process. Newton did say that "When photography is applied to buildings for *architectural* purposes, then every effort should be exerted to get all the detail as sharp and clean as possible." However, his interest
lay in how photography could best serve the painter by
"applying photography as an assistant to the Fine Arts,"
not in how it might function as an independent art.

Newton's paper set the terms of the ongoing debate
between those who believe that photography's heart
lies in its ability to provide "exactitude of delineation
which completely sets at nought the exertions of *manual* ingenuity," and those who believe that artistic effect
takes precedence over precision. As in the parlor game
of "telephone," Newton's statements became distorted
as they were repeated. Over time people allied "artis-

3.9   MAXIME DU CAMP.   *Egypte Moyenne, Le Sphinx,* from album *Egypte, Nubie, Palestine et Syrie,* 1852. 6³⁄₁₆ × 8⅛ inches. Salted paper print (Blanquart-Evrard).   Courtesy George Eastman House.

tic" photographs with unsharp photographs, forgetting that Newton was only referring to photographs made for use by artists. At a later meeting Newton reiterated, to no effect, his belief that when making "record" photographs the focus should be as sharp as possible.

Newton's paper also opened the continuing discussion on the qualities a photograph must have to be considered art. One side, the realists, claimed then as now that photography's intrinsic quality is its ability to provide a precise representation of reality. They believe that this straightforward, objective characteristic makes photography a unique art form, and that it should be held sacred. The other side, the expressionists, believe the photographic process to be a series of manipulations of reality, postulating that additional reworking is justified to introduce the imagemaker's subjective concerns and to remove the photograph from the realm of mechanical reproduction. As the medium grew these questions would expand into a larger controversy as to whether photography was capable of being an independent art form.

Thomas Keith [1827–1885], an Edinburgh physician, was an upper-class amateur who practiced the waxed-paper calotype from 1851–56. Keith was a friend of Hill's who admired and collected some of his calotypes. Keith made penetrating factual architectural studies of the Edinburgh environs (see Figure 3.7), including the Greyfriars Cemetery. He was fastidious in his materials preparation and only made images before seven in the morning or after four in the afternoon, when atmospheric pollution (caused by burning coal and wood) was minimal and the angle of light was low enough to best reveal surface detail and texture. His city views revel in an atmopshere of Romanticism and ignore the new machine age constructs, lamenting the loss of a place that has been altered by the effects of industrialization.

Calotypists Establish a Practice

The calotype was widely and richly practiced in France. Without Talbot's patent restrictions the calotype was cheaper to make, easier to use, and provided countless positive prints, giving daguerreotypists

3.10   THOMAS SUTTON.   *Jersey*, 1856. 4⁵⁄₁₆ × 5⁵⁄₈
inches. Salted paper print from calotype negative.
Courtesy George Eastman House.

numerous reasons to take up the process. One of the
most accomplished calotypists was **Louis-Désiré
Blanquart-Evrard** [1802–1872], who in 1847 discovered that soaking the paper in the emulsion, rather
than brushing it, made the paper more sensitive, eliminated streaking, and produced a longer and more continuous tonal scale. This generated more radiant highlights and greater detail in the shadows, making
calotype less ephemeral and more representational
(see Figure 3.8). He also devised a practical method of
reducing exposure time by chemically developing-out
the invisible (latent) image, which became the model
for future negative and positive systems.

In 1850, Blanquart-Evrard introduced his albumen-
coated paper, whose emulsion layer was applied *after* it
was coated with egg white, which gave a print more detail and contrast. This solved a major public aesthetic
barrier, for the image no longer rested *in* the paper but
above it, on a separate, glossy, smooth surface. The
downside was that the glossy surface reduced the visual
intricacy the paper fibers provided and diminished a
sense of depth, as the picture floated ever so slightly
aloft from its support base. Prints made from this
process are known as *albumen silver prints,* and they
became the principal medium for photographic printing
until the end of the nineteenth century, when they were
superseded by gelatin silver prints.

The biggest technical obstacle facing the commercial use of the calotype was the problem of fading. In
England, the Photographic Society formed a Committee on Fading to investigate.[21] The Committee discovered that the major culprit of fading was improper fixing that left a residue of hyposulfite of soda in the
paper fibers. Blanquart-Evrard's prints, however, were
so uniform in quality that they did not suffer from fading as Talbot's did, and Blanquart-Evrard's technical
improvements enticed people to use the calotype.
Blanquart-Evrard opened a printing enterprise at Lille
in September 1851. He devised a method of increasing
the number of prints made from a single negative from
3 or 4 a day to 200 or 300, then expanded production
up to 5,000 prints a day, lowering the cost of making
books with tipped-in photographs. The Lille facility
was an assembly-line operation, employing up to 40
people in a division of labor in which procedures were
individualized and carried out in special rooms. The
paper was sensitized in one room and exposed in another. Each employee produced an isolated piece of the
process, without ever being involved in the creation of
a unified product, demonstrating that the process could
be standardized and industrialized just like the daguerreotype. His printing enterprise had an immense
impact on French calotype production and spurred a
number of imitators, but it was not financially successful and closed in 1856. British calotypist Thomas Sutton convinced Blanquart-Evrard to collaborate with
him in Jersey (1855–57), bringing the British and
French photographic communities closer together.
This endeavor too was doomed as the public taste had

3.11   GUSTAVE LE GRAY.   *The Sun at Zenith, Normandy,* ca. 1855. 12¾ × 16⅜ inches. Albumen print from paper negative.   In addition to being fast enough to stop action like breaking waves, the practicality and reproducibility of Le Gray's process also made it excellent for making architectural views and was used by many of the photographers who documented France's endangered national historical sites.   Courtesy George Eastman House.

switched to albumen prints, which were made from glass plate negatives and eliminated the defects of the paper negative.

However, these early printing companies established the photographic print as a vehicle capable of providing an accurate representation in a mass communication setting. The French printing firms produced calotypes in a wide range of colors, from slate-gray, to purple-black, to a series of red tones ranging from pale rose to a dark oxblood, to an occasional yellow print. The range of colors produced by the French printing firms matched the look of lithographs and mezzotints familiar to the public, placing the calotype in an established visual system. Through their circulation the public became acquainted with convenient, inexpensive, and practical photographic prints.

Blanquart-Evrard's Lille printing establishment produced the prints for three important archeological books: Maxime du Camp's *Eqypte, Nubie, Palestine et Syrie* (1852) (see Figure 3.9), J. B. Greene's *Le Nil* (1854), and Auguste Salzmann's *Jerusalem* (1856). Blanquart-Evrard also edited and published a series of albums, including *Mélanges photographiques and Galerie photo-graphique,* featuring photographs of architecture and works of art, and provided printing services for other photographers.

Thomas Sutton [1819–1875] learned the calotype process when he moved to the pastoral island of Jersey in 1850. He was so astonished by Blanquart-Evrard's printing improvements that he had Blanquart-Evrard print his album, *Souvenir de Jersey* (1854), and embarked on a series of experiments to equal Blanquart-Evrard's methods. Sutton actively promoted the calotype by writing books, including *A Handbook to Photography on Paper* (1855); running a Photographic Institute in Jersey where lessons and photographic outfits were available; and publishing a journal, *Photographic Notes* (1856–67), to express his ideas on calotype aesthetics. Sutton considered the prints of Blanquart-Evrard superior to other calotypes and comparable to any "chaste works of art."[22] Sutton recalled how Blanquart-Evrard's prints first visually affected him:

> Nobody's printing . . . safisfied me. . . . I fell in love at first sight with its [Blanquart-Evrard's] rich, deep velvety tones, to which nothing in pictorial art seems to approach, and compared with which prints upon albumenised paper seemed intolerably vulgar.[23]

Sutton applied the visual criterion of lithography to the calotype, favoring prints that looked like "proofs on India paper." He did not care for the practice of using a hypo-toning bath that gave a yellow-green color, and he disliked the glossiness of albumenized paper. Sutton devised a whey-coated paper, rather than salt, utilizing a developing-out process that relied on a gold-toning bath before the fixer to achieve its visual richness and permanence.[24] He had a repugnance for the deadness of prints produced from negatives in which the sky had been blacked out.[25] Sutton dealt with movement in his pictures by making his views of the Jersey harbor at low tide, when the boats were securely anchored (see

3.12   CHARLES NÈGRE.   *Chimney Sweeps Walking,* 1851. 6 × 7⅛ inches. Salted paper print.   Courtesy National Gallery of Canada, Ottawa.

Figure 3.10). Sutton's drive to resolve issues of permanence and improve the calotype's printmaking aesthetic assisted photographers in discovering their own compositional structure and set photography on the road to becoming a recognized art form.

Four important calotypists, Roger Fenton, Charles Nègre, Henri Le Secq, and **Gustave Le Gray** [1820–1882] took up photography after studying painting at Paul Delaroche's atelier, demonstrating the active interchange of ideas among a close circle of practitioners. Like Blanquart-Evrard, Le Gray's refinements got more people interested in the calotype.

Le Gray improved the waxing of calotype negatives. In *Le Gray's process*[26] the negative was waxed *before* it was sensitized (in Talbot's it was waxed after processing). Le Gray's method allowed the paper to be prepared in advance, provided greater retention of detail, and reduced exposure times that permitted moving subjects like the ocean to be recorded (see Figure 3.11). Le Gray used the process for his *Forest of Fontainebleau*

series in which he tackled the calotypist's nightmare of moving foliage. Moving foliage had been such a problem that other practitioners, such as Newton, favored making images of trees when they didn't have any leaves. Le Gray was able to retain the velvety, ethereal shimmer of rich foliage, permitting viewers to move into the deep space of a forest setting. The original bronze-colored prints reflect the concerns of the Barbizon School of landscape painters, who rendered their subjects from direct observation of nature. This straightforward, anticlassical style fit with how the camera was being used. The attitude of academically trained painters towards the calotype was summed up by Le Gray in his introduction to one of his books on photographic technique:

> The artistic beauty of a photographic print consists almost always in the sacrifice of certain details, in such a manner as to produce *une mise à l'effet* which sometimes reaches the sublime of art.[27]

Charles Nègre [1820–1880] learned the waxed-paper process from Le Gray in order to make studies for his genre paintings. Unlike most historical painters, who only saw photography as a visual dictionary, Nègre rethought the position of the photograph and by 1851

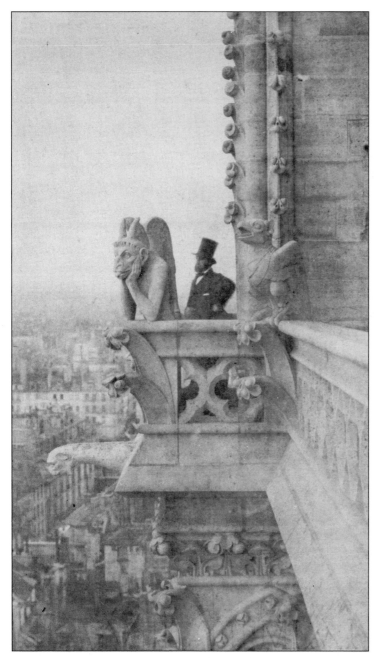

3.13 CHARLES NÈGRE. *The Vampire* (Henri Le Secq at Notre Dame Cathedral, Paris), 1853. 33 × 23.4 cm. Salted paper print. Courtesy National Gallery of Canada, Ottawa.

was making finished work as a painter and photographer. Nègre is a model for the artist/photographer who used observation and reason to produce highly selected, subjective renditions of what he saw through the camera.

His *The Little Ragpicker* (1851), which was regarded as being "no longer a photograph" but rather a consciously envisioned act of art,[28] signaled his readiness to photographically explore genre scenes of Parisian street life (see Figure 3.12). This marked another turn in the "who" being pictured, expanding what was important to be "saved" for the future. Imagemakers no longer had to concentrate only on subjects endowed with upper-class substance and began to represent the ordinary scenes of daily life. To satisfy this pre-snapshot impulse for instantaneous street pictures, Nègre fabricated a "fast" lens, with increased *lens speed*,[29] that could stop most action, giving them the spontaneous quality of a snapshot. These concerns culminate in Nègre's last major photographic commission, of the Vincennes Imperial Asylum for disabled workmen. Working inside with available light, Nègre made remarkable environmental portraits of the personnel and the patients engaged in their everyday routines. Nègre also knew how to calotype architecture so that it retained a strong physical and emotional presence. He often printed his paper negatives on salted paper, which allowed him to emphasize form and tonal mass, to give a sense of pictorial depth while letting go of optical clarity.[30] Commenting on his work at Chartres, Nègre said:

I have sacrificed a few details, when necessary, in favor of an imposing effect of a kind that would give a monument its real character and would also preserve the poetic charm that surrounded it.[31]

One of Nègre's remarkable visions is *The Vampire* (1851), made from the balustrade above the Grande Galerie of Notre Dame. It juxtaposes monumental shapes with differentiating light and dark sectors to produce a magnetic force across the picture surface. The visual, directional thrusts come together on the platform where a man in a top hat, Nègre's friend Henri Le Secq, stands out against the white sky. Exercising aesthetic control, Nègre opaqued the negative for emphasis and used pencil shading to accentuate highlight areas of the vampire gargoyle, the floral design on the top of the balustrade, the building below, and aerial perspective. The compressed tonal range of the salted paper print provides warmth and a strong tactile sense of the stone surfaces of the church. The space becomes self-animated, possessing a vibrant glowing quality of movement.

Calotype and Architecture: Missions Héliographiques

The calotype's field serviceability and ability to provide numerous copies was important in the early 1850s in a series of architectural and archeological documentary projects. In 1851, the *Missions Héliographiques* was

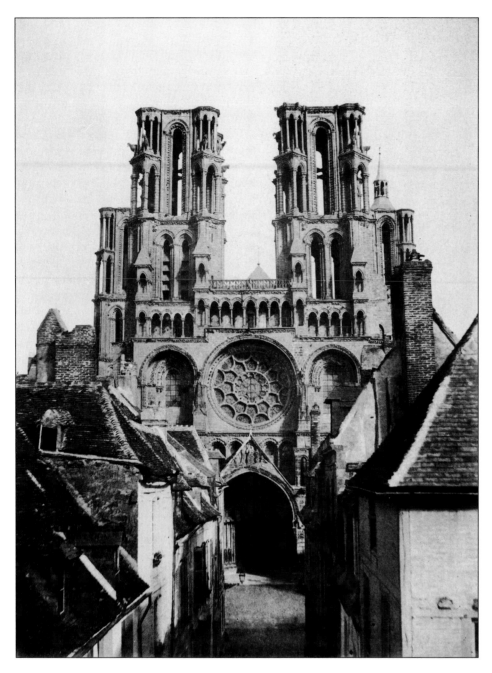

3.14   HENRI LE SECQ.   *Cathedral at Laon, France*
(View between houses to Cathedral Portal), 1851.
12 × 8⅝ inches. Calotype.   Courtesy George Eastman
House.

formed to record France's important monuments, which
were endangered by deterioration and indifference. Five
photographers, Édouard Baldus, Hippolyte Bayard,
Gustave Le Gray, Henri Le Secq, and O. Mestral (whose
first name has been lost), were hired and assigned to different regions, marking the first government sponsor-
ship of a major photographic project. The project was
fraught with the problems artists face when they accept
state patronage: the risk of becoming agents of national
policy and compromising their own standards of purpose and quality. Yet aesthetically this survey set a standard for future governmental projects and began a
worldwide trend of documenting historical sites.

A core group of the Missions Héliographiques photographers was instrumental in forming the Société
Hélio-graphique, the world's first photography association, predating London's Photographic Society by about
two years. The Société was organized in 1851 to dissem-
inate information, professionalize the practice, provide a
forum for practitioners, and publish Europe's first photographic journal, *La Lumière* (1851–60). Such early journals, on both sides of the Atlantic, were major sources of
photographic information and provided forums for readers to discuss and advertise practices and products.

3.15 ÉDOUARD BALDUS. *The Louvre, Colbert Pavilion*, ca. 1857–58. 17⁵⁄₁₆ × 13⁷⁄₁₆ inches. Albumen silver print from glass plate negative?   Courtesy George Eastman House.

Henri Le Secq [1818–82] learned the calotype process from Gustave Le Gray and made a series of architectural investigations for the Missions project. His work revealed a new structural strategy of formal, frontal composition that concentrated on the relationship between the building and the angle of the camera. To Le Secq, the visual order of the cathedrals and monuments corresponded to the structure imposed by the camera on the photographer (see Figure 3.14). The perspective of the camera, as well as the photogra-

pher's sense of composition, determined how best to photograph an architectural site. At each site, Le Secq typically made a general view emphasizing the organization and symmetry of the structural mass and a series of details revealing the intricacies of sculptural minutia (he collected ironwork). His images show an ordered approach of a person in control of the medium, relying on the repetition of line to form a powerful flow of upward, directional movement, representing the spiritual quality of geometry. His final project, before he gave up photography in 1856, was a deft series of still lifes.

Édouard Baldus [1813–1882], a painter of portraits and religious subjects, got interested in photography in 1849 and became the "official" photographer

3.16 CHARLES MARVILLE.   *La Porte Rogue, Notre Dame de Paris.* 8⅛ × 6⅛ inches. Salted paper print. Plate 46 of the album *Mélanges photographiques* (Paris, 1851), Blanquart–Evrard, editor.   Courtesy George Eastman House.

of his generation, completing numerous government and private commissions between 1851 and 1859. He photographed the monuments of Paris and areas south of it, including Fontainebleau, Burgundy, the Rhone Valley down to Arles, and Nîmes, for the Commission des Monuments Historiques. He photographed the Midi under a commission by the Ministry of the Interior. Some of his other commissions included the architectural motifs and sculpture of the Louvre's new facade (see Figure 3.15); the building of Baron James de Rothchild's railroad; the flooding of the Rhone; and the new railroad line from Paris to Lyon. Baldus recognized the importance of choosing a vantage point that illuminated the three-dimensional nature of the subject. In addition to the traditional frontal views of his contemporaries, he often favored oblique points of view. His compositions rely on balancing competing planes of pictorial space through the use of horizontal and vertical counterpoints, eliminating distractions, and concentrating the viewer's focus within the pictorial organization of his frame.

Baldus, an expert printer, regularly retouched his prints with ink and pencil. He relied on three print-making methods to create *effect*. First, he used the softness of the salted paper to tone down the hard-edged effects of retouching and to provide a lithographic texture. Second, he favored salted paper that was albumenized after printing to supply a surface sheen that resembled a varnished oil painting. Lastly, Baldus counted on the albumen paper to deliver unrivaled detail and tonality. Even when Baldus switched to the wet-collodion glass-plate process in the mid-1850s, he used a printing style that allowed him to retain the visual character and artistic effect of the paper negative. His exquisitely sharp, open, yet poetic printing style favored full highlight detail while retaining an airy translucency in the shadows, communicating a tremendous amount of visual information. The degree of visual organization, compositional tension, and a full, rich printing style that accented relief helped establish standards of documentary practice. Baldus continued to make new images until about 1874, after which he devoted his energies to publishing photogravures of his views.

Charles Marville [1816–c.1879] was an engraver, lithographer, and painter before taking up photography in 1850. His early landscapes and architectural photographs began to appear in Blanquart-Evrard's folio collections in 1851 (see Figure 3.16). Beginning in 1852, and continuing for almost 20 years, Marville methodically recorded the cobbled, medieval Paris neighborhoods that were being destroyed in Napoleon III's massive urban renewal project. Marville photographed all phases of the project: the old structures, their demolition, and the new site construction. His early work was done in calotypes, but sometime in the latter 1850s he switched to collodion glass plates. Marville set a precise standard for the seemingly artless mapping of an urban area that other photographers, such as Eugène Atget, later expanded. His balanced city compositions, often devoid of people, reveal an eye for detail. Marville's romantic style favored chiaroscuro, allowing the separate parts of a scene to achieve autonomy from the general site.

The End of the Calotype and the Future of Photography

The calotype never found its place in the American consciousness, which appeared immune to its merits. Americans overwhelming favored the brilliant, dazzling detail of the daguerreotype, and with the ideals of the American Revolution not that distant, the idea of paying a commercial licensing fee to a British aristocrat was not very popular. William [1807–1874] and Frederick [1809–1879] Langenheim made a deal in 1849 with Talbot for the American rights to his process in hopes of promoting their Philadelphia studio, but a year later they had not sold a single license. In any case, the 1850s saw the refinement of a practical method of making glass negatives with a wet-collodion process on albumen paper, bringing the calotype as well as the daguerreotype era to an end and ushering in a new system for making photographs.

Nevertheless, the calotype shaped photography's future. Technical improvements to the calotype in terms of delineation of detail, expanded tonal range, print permanence, and mass-production methods placed photography in a position to succeed as an international print medium. The printing establishments, by publishing the work of early photographers, animated the vital role that photography would carry out in the mass communication of visual information. Aesthetically, the calotype offered important new interpretive controls to assist the young medium in finding its own visual language. The negative/positive printmaking system gave the photograph the intense power of chiaroscuro and the means, through retouching, to alter a camera image after exposure. These key conceptual steps were necessary for photography to become an independent medium rather than a robotic hand-maiden to the other arts. The molding of these characteristics by outstanding calotypists demonstrated that the camera could be an instrument of individual artistic expression.

Endnotes

1   Mezzotint is an engraving method on copper or steel accomplished by burnishing or scraping away a uniformly roughened surface. This technique of reverse relief printing produces form in tonal areas rather than in line. It was widely used for color reproductions of paintings in the eighteenth and nineteenth centuries and became obsolete with the introduction of photoengraving and photogravure.

2   Beaumont Newhall, *Latent Image: The Discovery of Photography* (Garden City, NY: Doubleday & Company, 1967), 84.

3   Email correspondence between Dr. Larry Schaaf and the author on November 15 and 16, 1998.

4   See H. J. P. Arnold, *William Henry Fox Talbot: Pioneer of photography and man of science* (London: Hutchinson Benham Ltd., 1977), 175-216.

5   Educated and visually literate, Talbot was familiar with these concerns. He valued Classical art, enjoyed his Uncle William Fox-Strangway's collection of Italian Renaissance paintings, and had seen European art collections. He knew the work of the foremost seventeenth century landscape artist Claude Lorrain, who used lyrical variations of light to dissolve detail for *effect* much like the calotype. This last concern can be seen in Talbot's investigations of light and space, which subordinate the subject.

6   Talbot later produced *The Talbotype Applied to Hieroglyphics* (1846) and *Annals of the Artists of Spain* (1847).

7   Letter of March 21, 1839. Herschel Collection. The Royal Society, London.

8   Gail Buckland, *Fox Talbot and the Invention of Photography* (Boston: David R. Godine, 1980), 15.

9   Henry Fox Talbot, *The Pencil of Nature* (London, 1844–46), reprint (New York: Da Capo Press, 1969), Unp.

10   Ibid.

11   Talbot was not able to commercially establish any of his photographic print-making methods. By 1846 Talbot had sharply reduced his license fee, yet even this failed to improve his market share. The following year the printing factory went out of business, so Talbot had Henneman open a portrait studio, which also failed.

12   The long exposure times, starting at about 10 seconds and often running into minutes, provide a sense of movement within time. The sitter is not frozen for examination, as in a daguerreotype, but is often blurred and appears alive and fidgeting before the camera. When the figures are still, they can lose their individual identity and take on an archetypal presence. This could be due to the direct, contrasty lighting style that causes a loss of detail in the shadow areas of the print that would reveal human attributes, such as the eyes, placing further emphasis on form and shape.

13   David Octavius Hill to Mr. Bicknell, January 17, 1848, George Eastman House, Rochester, NY.

14   In some instances the fading adds to the sensation of a hand-produced image. To the contemporary eye, its dapple-like effects seem impressionistic. In other prints, the now yellow/brown color gives a nostalgic sense of time past, while stains and other blemishes show the chaotic, transitory nature of existence.

15   The competition between the light and dark areas of Hill and Adamson's compositions are strikingly similar to those of the Dutch masters such as Rembrandt. The dark, uncluttered backgrounds provoke an atmosphere of mystery that enables the face and hands to be compositionally paramount. Many of the male sitters wore white shirts and black ties, producing an internal contrast that drew the viewer's eye first to the face and then to the hands.

16   The Eastlake-Rosse letter and Talbot's response were printed in the London *Times*, August 13, 1852. The Eastlake-Rosse letter is reprinted in Gernsheim, *History*, 180–81.

17   *Great Exhibition of the Works of Industry of All Nations, 1851* Reports by the Juries in Four Volumes (London: W. Clowes and Sons Printers, 1852).

18   Ibid. Vol. 2, 439.

19   It replaced the Calotype Society, an elite club of about a dozen English gentlemen founded in 1847, whose members adhered to the Victorian principle of amateurism, in which the educated upper class was expected to adequately perform in the arts and sciences for the sheer joy of it (part of the Anglo/American tradition of volunteering for the public good).

20   All quotes in this section are from Sir William Newton, Upon Photography in an Artistic View, and Its Relation to the Arts, *Journal of the Photographic Society*, vol. 1 (March 3, 1853), 6–7.

21   The committee announced that the use of gelatine as a mounting substance and sulphur in the atmosphere contributed to fading. Their first findings were published in the *Journal of the Photographic Society* II, 36 (November 21, 1855), 251-2.

22   See *Journal of the Photographic Society* II, 31, June 21, 1855, 178–80.

23   "Reminiscences of an Old Photographer," Thomas Sutton, *British Journal of Photography*, Vol. XIV, No. 382 (August 30, 1867), 414.

24   In the developing-out process an invisible (latent) image is chemically developed to completion. Available from the 1840s on, the developing-out process was infrequently used as the contrast was hard to control and the public was not familiar with the neutral black color of the developed prints. In Talbot's printing-out process the image was visible, which had the advantage of stopping the printing process at any time. However, the long, sunlight exposures limited the number of prints that could be produced.

25   See *Journal of the Photographic Society* II, 23, October 21, 1854, 53–54.

26   For details on Le Gray's process, see J. Towler, M. D., *The Silver Sunbeam* (Hastings-on-Hudson, NY: Morgan & Morgan, 1969), 175–76. Facsimile 1864 edition with an introduction by Beaumont Newhall.

27   Gustave Le Gray, *Photographie—Traité nouveau sur papier et sur verre* (Paris: Lerebours et Secretain, 1852), 2.

28   Francis Wey, "Album de la Sociétéz Héliographique," *La Lumière* I, No. 5 (May 18, 1851), 58.

29   Lens speed is the measure of the maximum light-transmitting power of a lens, usually taken as the *f*-number of the lens's largest aperture, such as $f/1.4$.

30   Nègre's knowledge may have resulted from the ébauche technique taught by the nineteenth century ateliers. The ébauche method consists of a broad laying-in of the forms and masses in a final painting to aid as an underpainting to the picture, helping to suggest the effect of light and shade. Since it was generally monochromatic, its relationship in representing tonal mass could be correlated to the calotype. This type of training makes it apparent how Sir William Newton would accept a calotype that was manipulated to reduce detail and enhance a broad pictorial effect.

31   Charles Nègre, *Le Midi de la France photographié*, 1854–55, unpublished MS, c.1854, National Archives, Paris. Cited in James Borcoman, *Charles Nègre as Photographer* (Ottawa: National Gallery of Canada, 1976), 34.

CHAPTER FOUR

Pictures on Glass
The Wet-Plate Process
The Albumen Process

The 1840s saw the cornerstones of modernity, capitalism and science, applied to photography, as inventors searched for a low-cost, easy-to-use process that would combine the detail of the daguerreotype with the reproducibility of the calotype. Activity centered on making glass negatives, as it was an ideal emulsion support base, cheaper than a silvered plate, and free from the drawbacks of the paper process. The chief obstacle in devising an efficient glass process was finding a way to keep the silver salts from dissolving or floating off the glass during processing. In 1847 Claude Félix Abel Niépce de Saint-Victor, a cousin of Nicéphore Niépce, discovered that albumen (egg white) provided an excellent binder for silver salts on glass plates. This breakthrough blended the desired attributes of the daguerreotype and the calotype, but the process's five-minute minimum sunlight exposure time was not conducive to making portraits.

UNKNOWN PHOTOGRAPHER (Manila). *(Anthropological Cabinet of Natives)* ca. 1873. 4 × 2½ inches. Carte-de-visite. Courtesy George Eastman House.

4.1   FREDERICK SCOTT ARCHER.   Sparrow's House, Ipswich, Suffock, 1857. 8½ × 6⅞ inches. Albumen print.   Courtesy George Eastman House.

In 1849 **Frederick Scott Archer** [1813–1857], who had learned the calotype process as a visual aid for his portrait bust business, turned his "attention to collodion as a substitute for paper, with the hope that by its means a surer and more delicate medium might be produced to work upon than paper was ever likely to be."[1] Archer coated a glass plate with iodized collodion and exposed it while it was wet. This proved to be the recipe for success, as previous investigators had used collodion as a dry base to which iodide of silver was applied.[2] The so-called collodion process provided a finely detailed negative, one that was endlessly reproducible and required less exposure time than Niépce's method.

Archer did not patent his method, but Talbot claimed that Archer's process, wherein a latent image was imprinted on a light-sensitive surface that had to be developed out and fixed, was an infringement on his own calotype patent. Talbot announced that he would prosecute any commercial portrait photographers who used the collodion process without his license. In December 1853, Silvester Laroche resisted an injunction issued by Talbot against his Oxford Street studio. The case went to trial and on December 20, 1854, a jury declared Laroche not guilty, freeing England at last from Talbot's threats and patents. Talbot did not appeal or renew his calotype patent (Daguerre's English patent had

expired in 1853), allowing England's professional photographers to use any process without paying a licensing fee.

The *collodion process* became known as the wet-plate process because all the procedures had to be carried out while the plate was damp, since the ether in the collodion rapidly evaporated. The coating procedure required speed, on-the-spot darkroom access, and the ability to follow preparation directions that read like a cookbook. Before making an exposure it was necessary to pour the collodion, with potassium iodide, a mixture of alcohol, ether, and nitrated cellulose (known as gun-cotton due to its explosive nature), onto a clean prepared glass plate under darkroom conditions (see Figure 4.2). The photographer had to tilt the plate back and forth to ensure an even coat or the pour marks would be visible in the negative. Next, the plate was dipped into a sensitizing bath of silver nitrate and immediately placed into the camera and exposed (sensitivity dropped greatly as the collodion dried). As soon as the exposure was made, the plate was developed in pyrogallic acid and fixed with sodium hyposulphite (hypo).

Photographers were willing to put up with these difficulties as the collodion's increased light sensitivity meant that small, highly detailed portraits could be made in as little as two seconds. Also, glass plate negatives printed faster than paper negatives, prints could be produced more quickly and cheaply. Collodion's raw materials were inexpensive and once mastered tended to be more constant and predictable than the paper processes. By 1855 the majority of commercial photographers had added collodion to their repertoire. Collodion ushered in a period of growth and good fortune for the budding commercial photographic community. It would eventually dethrone the albumen, calotype, and daguerreotype processes and reign until the introduction of the gelatin dry plate in the 1880s.

The New Transparent Look

The introduction of the collodion process solved a series of technical problems and heralded a new aesthetic ideal as well. Photographers had been dissatisfied with "the imperfections of paper photography" and wanted a negative capable of delivering "fineness of surface [and] transparency."[3] They desired a negative/positive process capable of rendering a consistent tonal range with ample density and detail in the highlight and shadow areas. Collodion's transparent glass support solved these difficulties and resolved the aesthetic concerns of clarity, chiaroscuro, and resolution, signaling the demise of what D. O. Hill saw as the artistic virtues of the calotype—its rough and unequal texture.

"Transparency" referred to a direct translation of reality in which subjects were not "suggested," as in the calotype, but were clearly stated and defined without

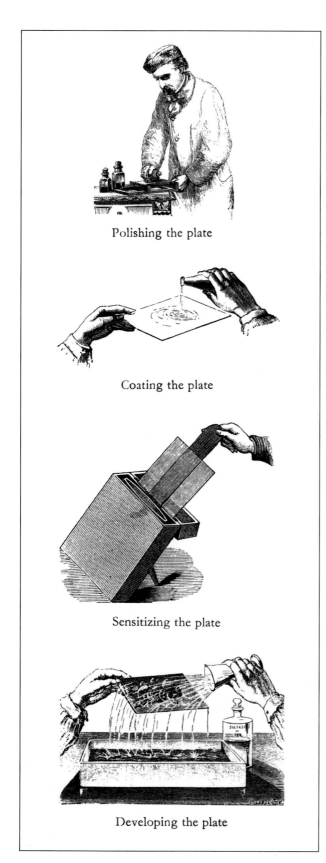

Polishing the plate

Coating the plate

Sensitizing the plate

Developing the plate

4.2   Preparing and processing a collodion wet-plate. From Gaston Tissandier, *A History and Handbook of Photography* edited by John Thomson, 1878.

overt intervention, as in the daguerreotype. *Naturalism* began to be the benchmark of photographic practice. Its goal was not to interpret or interact but to concretely represent the world, naturally, with previously unmatched depth of clarity, capable of preserving enormous amounts of visual information. The glass support of the collodion replaced the obscure shadow areas of the calotype with a clear, distinct, and unobstructed view. The idea of naturalism would lead to a decline in retouching the negative for serious artistic effect, and indirectly supported the notion that photography was an authorless process in which the subject imposed its presence onto a plate. Such an uncompromised *natural* image was thought to be "truer," easier to see and understand than anything previously obtainable.

A new printing paper was essential to retain the detail and sharpness of the glass negative. The first practical *albumen paper,* with a smooth and glossy surface, was designed by Blanquart-Evrard in 1850 and rapidly supplanted the matte surface of the calotype, remaining in use until the end of the nineteenth century. Photographers could make their own albumen paper. According to J. Towler's 1864 edition of *The Silver Sunbeam,* one was supposed to use only fresh eggs and then get "the white of egg, entirely freed from the germ and yolk, and beat the egg up well with a wooden spatula until it is completely converted into froth. This operation must be performed in a place as perfectly free from dust as possible; and then the albuminous mixture is covered with a clean sheet of paper and put aside to settle for a number of hours." Fortunately, albumen paper could be purchased already prepared, spawning the beginning of the manufacture of presensitized paper.

The laborious steps in the albumen paper process included beating the mass of egg white; allowing it to froth in earthenware vats; fermenting it in tall glass jars; filtering it, beating it again, refiltering it, and salting it with chlorides; and dying it pink, mauve, or blue. Then paper, such as Rives B. F. K., was floated by hand in the mixture. Next, the paper was dried and stored for three to six months, so the albumen could completely harden, and then it was coated again and hung up to dry in the reverse direction to equalize the unevenness of the first coating.

Albumen paper gave a new look and consistency to photographic printmaking, allowing *editions,* where the first to the last images all look the same, to be produced. Such consistency had not been possible with the calotype, where differences in the surface and texture of the paper support and the hand-applied emulsion produced noticeable changes when multiple prints were made. This new found consistency diminished the distinctive differences of the individual print, causing it to lose its uniqueness and reducing its market value as an artistic object. People did not give the photographic print the

4.3   UNKNOWN ARTIST.   *Traveling photographer's collodion wet-plate darkroom tent,* ca. 1865.   Courtesy Gernsheim Collection. Humanities Research Center, University of Texas, Austin, TX.

respect they had given the daguerreotype. A damaged albumen print was not considered a catastrophe, as another print could be made; replaceability was a major attribute of the paper print.

This idea of the replaceability of photographs was encouraged as the photograph became synonymous with other machine-produced objects of the industrial culture. Photography became commercially viable, as more of its components could be carried out by a division of labor that allowed a few skilled managers to control an operation of unskilled employees. Assembly-line production attitudes and techniques replaced those of a personally crafted object. By 1894, the Dresden Albumenizing Company's staff of 180 opened 60,000 eggs daily for the production of double-albumenized paper.[4] Repeatability had substituted for the calotype's distinctive atmosphere and character, as easy replication became the order of photographic business by the end of the 1850s.

The collodion process produced a tremendous demand for albumen paper. The new paper not only provided more detail than a salted paper print, but it changed the surface look of the paper photograph. The albumen's glossy surface sheen gave photo-based images a novel appearance. This glossiness was considered very modern and machine-like and was accepted

as part of the new system of representation. It also further removed the photographic print from traditional printmaking, where shininess was an undesirable characteristic. In collodion's early days, practitioners diluted their albumen with salt water to reduce the gloss to a luster. As the wet plate's popularity grew, photographers used undiluted albumen to reveal the abundant detail of their glass negatives, raise the contrast level, and provide a greater luster to the print. By the 1860s double-coating of the paper with albumen became a standard practice, giving prints a truly glossy appearance.

The base color of the paper, once the dominion of each photographer, became standardized as commercially prepared papers, with a limited range of colors, achieved market domination. These new surface changes provided unmistakable evidence that the image originated from a photo-based process. Albumen prints were *gold-toned* to make the print more stable and alter their intense red-brick color to a more acceptable warm purplish-brown or even a blue-black hue.

The Ambrotype

The rapid commercial adoption of the collodion process and the immediate invention of a series of spin-off processes—the ambrotype, the tintype, and the carte-de-visite—insured collodion's rapid domination of the field. The *ambrotype* was a collodion, positive-looking image on glass that when first introduced was

4.4   UNKNOWN PHOTOGRAPHER (AMERI-
CAN).   *Untitled Portrait*, ca. 1858. Ambrotype with
half the backing removed to show positive and negative
effect.   Courtesy Gernsheim Collection, Humanities Research
Center, University of Texas, Austin, TX.

referred to as a "collodion positive." The name ambrotype was devised by the Philadelphia daguerreotypist Marcus A. Root in 1855, from a Greek word
meaning "imperishable." When first shown in the
United States, in December 1854, they were called daguerreotypes on glass and were often mistaken to be
daguerreotypes because they are laterally reversed,
one-of-a-kind objects, often hand-colored, made in the
same-size formats, and put into similar cases. In Europe
ambrotypes were generally referred to as *amphitypes*.

The ambrotype lacked the highly reflective surface of a
daguerreotype and appeared somewhat dull in comparison, but it was less expensive to make. Frederick
Archer and other calotypists discovered that the density
of a collodion negative could be varied through a
bleaching process. When such a bleached image was
viewed by reflected light against a dark background, it
appeared as a positive. This effect can be observed with
any negative, even without using a bleaching process.
In practice, most photographers underdeveloped or underexposed the glass plate to achieve the same effect.
After processing, the plate was lacquered with an
opaque black on its backside or placed against black
paper or velvet. It is often possible to identify an ambrotype because its backing has deteriorated. When the
black varnish starts to crack the image can give a visual

4.5 UNKNOWN PHOTOGRAPHER. *Unidentified Family*, ca. 1858. 5¼ × 3⅝ inches. Ambrotypes: two ninth plates, three sixteenth plates in a single case.
Courtesy George Eastman House.

sense of separation and physical relief (fake 3-D) as well as a ghostly effect of being able to see through parts of the image.

Ambrotypes were set in elaborately designed, molded, and hinged cases called *Union Cases*. Introduced in 1854, Union Cases marked the beginning of thermoplastic molding in the United States and were produced in hundreds of designs featuring scenes derived from classical works of art and popular culture concerning history, nature, patriotism, and religion. Often the photographer's name and hometown were imprinted on the gold-colored interior frame to let the viewer know where to obtain one. The case gave the ambrotype a physical weight. The closed, hinged case introduced the element of surprise, a sense of drama as one held it in one's hands, wondering what was going to be pictured inside. As the case was opened this sense of theater became part of the viewing experience.

Ambrotypes were generally used in portraiture. The posing was usually intimate, featuring tight head and shoulder shots, which worked well with the small format. The glass surface of the ambrotype could reflect a viewer's image into the scene, though not as intensely as

4.6 UNKNOWN PHOTOGRAPHER. *Fireman,* ca. 1865. Quarter plate. Tintype. Courtesy George Eastman House.

the daguerreotype. A negative image could be produced by holding the ambrotype at different angles to the light, but it was still much easier to view than a daguerreotype. Unlike most American daguerreotypes, some ambrotype cases had hooks on the back for wall hanging, and others had pop-up legs to allow the picture to stand upright in its frame. By the mid-1850s the ambrotype had surpassed the daguerreotype as the portrait medium.

In July 1854, James Ambrose Cutting [1814–1867] tried to profit from the American portrait business by patenting a method for sealing collodion images in their cases.[5] Outraged over Cutting's "ambrotype patent," American photographers banded together for the first time, eventually forming the National Photographic Convention, to fight what they considered to be an illegal patent. The patent was reversed in 1868 thanks to this organized effort and to the rising popularity of new imaging systems such as the stereograph and the carte-de-visite. By 1861, however, the ambrotype was on the way out and the making of collodion pictures on paper was in.[6]

Pictures On Tin

A second collodion spin-off method was the *ferrotype,* that was first described by French photographer Adolphe Alexandre Martin in 1853. The name fer-

rotype (Latin *ferrum* is *iron*) was orginally used by Robert Hunt in the mid-1840s for a paper negative process (Energiatype) that utilized an iron-compound developer. The ferrotype was basically an ambrotype made on a thin piece of sheet iron, instead of glass, that was enameled black or brown-black and coated with collodion and sensitized just before an exposure was made. The ferrotype process was patented in February 1856 by Hamilton L. Smith, who assigned his patent rights to his collaborator Peter Neff. The patent only covered how to produce what Neff advertised as *melainotypes.* Neff attempted to exploit the process's commercial potential by building a tinplate factory, sending out teachers to instruct daguerreotype operators in the new method, and giving away a 53-page manual, *The Melainotype Process, Complete.* Tintypes, as they were known in America, were made in a variety of sizes, the most common being 2¼ × 3½ inches (the same size as the carte-de-visite), and were often hand-colored. The name, *tintype,* evolved from popular usage. The tintype never achieved a high level of market influence, but it did find a niche and outlasted all the wet-plate processes (a dry tintype process was introduced in 1891). It was used by itinerant and street photographers until it was replaced by the Polaroid process in the 1950s.

Tintypes were the visual currency of soldiers and their families during the American Civil War because they were cheap, lightweight, and durable. Tintypists, generally unskilled in other photographic processes, were the least significant people in the photographic hierarchy. In fact, big city studio photographers considered tintypes to be low-class pictures practiced by "cheapjacks" who were only interested in making quick money, who knew nothing about photography, and whose deceitful practices diminished the profession's reputation. Tintypists often traveled from town to town, working on the street, out of a wagon, or in a rented room, using a modified camera that doubled as a tiny darkroom and allowed all the processing to take place inside the camera. Such cameras had slotted bottoms to hold canisters of developer and fixer for processing. After fixing, the plate was given a quick rinse in a bucket of water, waved through the air to speed drying, and handed to the customer. It was considered an instant process since it could be done in about a minute. The tintype was never as popular in Europe, where it was used almost exclusively by street and seaside photographers. Today its practitioners are the largely forgotten and unnamed photographers referred to as "anonymous" or "unknown photographer."

The tintype's image did not jump out at the viewer but lay flat as if it were rolled onto the tin surface. The tintype's tonal range appeared uniform because its black backing absorbed a great deal of light, and it did not possess the mirrorlike sheen of the daguerreotype

4.7   ANDRÉ DISDÉRI.   *Paul Legrand (clown in white face)*, CA 1860–65 Uncut carte-de-visite, 7⅞ × 9½ inches. Albumen print.   Courtesy George Eastman House.

or the glass depth of the ambrotype to enhance contrast. However, what the tintype lacked in aesthetic qualities it made up in social significance: Citizens could have their likeness recorded for as little as twenty-five cents, further democratizing the process of commemoration. The tintype's universal affordability also spoke to the nineteenth-century American notion that societal position was not solely predetermined by one's birth status, visually denoting the American Dream of possible upward mobility. Democracy not only gave the industrial classes a taste for the arts and letters, it also brought a technological spirit to the arts.

The tintype's lower price, its practitioners' lack of formal artistic training, and its immediacy reduced the specialness surrounding the act of having a picture made. Pictures became less serious, more spur-of-the-moment affairs. The idea of casual pictures for amusement started when tintypists introduced humorous background scenes of painted canvas with cutouts

through which sitters could insert their heads. People's "camera attitude" shifted as they played and acted informally for the camera. This type of unpremeditated silliness and lack of respect had not been previously pictured. Discounting any technical limitations due to long exposures, smiles had been considered inappropriate for an occasion that was seen as making a social statement about the sitter. The spontaneous tintype spirit of picturing the vernacular was the precursor of the snapshot sensibility.

The Carte-de-Visite and the Photo Album

The third spin-off from collodion was the *carte-de-visite*, or visiting card. A number of photographers claimed credit for introducing the carte-de-visite, but the idea was patented by **André Disdéri** [1819–1890] and introduced to the public in Paris in 1854.

The concept of using photographs on documents such as licenses, passports, permits, and visiting cards was proposed by Louis Dodero of Marseilles in 1851.

The carte-de-visite, or *carte,* was a 2¼ × 3½-inch photograph, usually a full- or bust-length portrait, attached to a 2½ × 4-inch paper card. A number of exposures were made with a multilens camera on a single collodion wet-plate and were contact-printed onto albumen paper. Individual exposures were cut apart and mounted on cards. The multilens, referred to as *tubes,* could be uncovered (there were no shutters), making it possible to vary the poses on the plate. The intent was to take the time and expense needed to make one print and divide it by many prints, reducing the cost of each print. Numbers were the deciding factors; the more cartes people had made, the greater the photographer's profit. Enhanced savings were also realized since retouching was not needed, as many defects were not noticeable in the small prints, and the processing procedures could still be performed by unskilled labor. Daguerreotypists like Abraham Bogardus initially dismissed the carte. Bogardus recalled his first impressions of the carte as "a little thing; a man standing by a fluted column, full length, the head about twice the size of the head of a pin. I laughed at that, little thinking I should at a day not far distant be making them at the rate of a thousand a day."[7]

After a slow start the carte became a hit in May 1859 when Napoleon III, leading his army out of Paris on a military campaign against Austria, stopped to have a publicity portrait made at Disdéri's studio. It proved a successful public relations tactic for both men as people flocked to have their carte made at the same place as the emperor. Disdéri became a celebrity and was appointed Court Photographer. In 1860 Disdéri redecorated his studio, the "Palace of Photography," in the ornate Second Empire style with portraits of della Porta, Niépce, Daguerre, and Talbot along with allegorical statues signifying Chemistry, Painting, Physics, and Sculpture. The Apotheosis of Light was painted on the ceiling. By 1861 Disdéri was reported to be the richest photographer in the world, eventually opening branch studios in London, Madrid, and Toulon. His Paris studio had a staff of 90, could make thousands of prints a day, and promised 48-hour delivery.

The carte did not become chic in England until August 1860, when **John Jabez Edwin Mayall** [1810–1901], an expatriate American daguerreotypist who had become one of London's most elegant photographers, published his *Royal Album,* consisting of fourteen carte portraits of the royal family (see Figure 4.8). Hundreds of thousands of cartes of Queen Victoria and Prince Albert were sold, leading to an explosion of celebrity photographs. Photographers courted personalities to sit for them, often paying a fee to the sitter and/or royalties based on sales. The practice of collecting and exchanging photographs and placing them in embellished, manufactured albums began with the *Royal Album* cartes. Mayall's carte business

reportedly generated more income than any other English photographer's, with his studio turning out half a million cartes a year. Mayall also patented the *Ivorytype* in 1855, a method in which a photographic image was printed on artificial ivory that had been sensitized with either albumen or collodion. This imitation effect was popular as it played off the association of ivory as a valuable object reserved for the power elite.

The royal family itself was keen on photography. Queen Victoria was said to have over 100 photo albums, many arranged and inscribed by Prince Albert. The Queen enjoyed giving and sending photographs. The royal family not only consented to the sale of their cartes but commissioned numerous portraits, bought (collected) contemporary photographs, were patrons of The Photographic Society, and even had a darkroom installed at Windsor Castle for their private use, increasing interest in photography and giving it status and credibility.

The carte was a formula picture; no particular effort was made to reveal the sitter's character. Even though posing equipment was still required, shorter exposure times allowed more naturalistic styles to evolve, and people appeared less rigid and stern. In various poses controlled by the photographer, from vignetted heads whose undefined edges merged into the background to full-length images, the sitter could look either directly at the camera or gaze off to one side. The backgrounds could be neutral, or they could be elaborate painted settings. Most scenes included props, such as fancy upholstered chairs, balustrades, columns, drapery, and furniture. People often wore clothes or held objects that revealed their status or their aspirations. Cartes were personal, handheld portraits made to be preserved in albums and stir memories: "This is what I look like, this is what I do, this is who I am."

Cartes of current events, politicians, royalty, actors, and people in the news were widely circulated. In 1861, The Chicago & Milwaukee Railroad Co. issued identity cartes for their season-ticket holders. Abraham Lincoln credited his election to his Cooper Union speech and to his carte made by Mathew Brady. Stage figures, such as Jenny Lind, became cult personalities in the United States through the publicity supplied by their cartes. Besides celebrities there was a market among the educated for cartes of authors, such as Charles Dickens, George Sand, and Victor Hugo. In addition, leaders of reform movements, including the American abolitionists Frederick Douglass and Harriet Beecher Stowe, were in demand.

Cartes catered to the armchair traveler with views of moated castles and foreign lands, to the sophisticated with works of art, to the believers of "Manifest Destiny" with bare-breasted female natives who could be both ogled and looked down on, and to the morose with

4.8   JOHN MAYALL.   *Death of Prince Albert* (Montage of Royal Album). 4 × 2½ inches. Carte-de-visite. Courtesy George Eastman House.

"freaks of nature" like the woman with no arms who could write with her feet (see chapter opener). Cartes provided the realistic images the public now expected at affordable prices and furthered the picturing of more diverse subjects.

As the carte could be carried around and handed to others, text, both printed and handwritten, was often added to supply the appropriate context. The public, accustomed to mechanical reproductions with accompanying text, readily accepted this practice. Typically, the front of the carte had the photographer's signature

WHITNEY,   CUT NOSE,   ST.PAUL.
Who in the Massacre of 1862, in Minnesota, murdered
18 Women and Children and 5 Men.

Entered according to Act of Congress, by J. E. Whitney, in the year 1862
in the Clerk's Office of the U.S. District Court for Minnesota.

4.9 J. E. Whitney Studio, St. Paul, MN. *Cut Nose,*
1862. Carte-de-visite. If the information on this carte is
true, it raises a macabre point about social behavior—
why would a person purchase an image of a murderer?
Today electronic media has taken this phenomena to
levels unimaginable in the nineteenth century with
videos like the Lives of Serial Killers and websites that
contain outright lies about history and promote hate
against minority groups. Courtesy Visual Studies Workshop, Rochester, NY.

printed below the image and a caption below the picture. Many had advertisements
printed on the backside of the carte. Typically, the photographer's and publisher's
name and address were given. The back-
knotes reminded the public that the carte
was reproducible with pronouncements
such as: "Negatives preserved, Duplicates
can be had at any time." A carte of three
small children stated that

> The copies are sold in furtherance of the Na-
> tional Sabbath School effort to found in Penn-
> sylvania an Asylum for dependent Orphans of
> Soldiers; in memorial of our Perpetuated
> Union. This picture is private property, and
> can not be copied without wronging the Sol-
> dier's Orphans for whom it is published.

J. E. Whitney's *Cut Nose* carte shows
how words attached to a picture not only
supply meaning but raise critical issues concerning accuracy. Photographers strategi-
cally titled their cartes. As allegorical subjects gained popularity in the mid-1850s,
many photographers titled their portraits
with the names of Greek deities so that
viewers could bring their formal knowledge
to bear. Such practice was exclusionary,
closing out the less educated. Photographers who did not wish for this type of interchange or who wanted to be more ambiguous and less directional referred to their
work as "untitled." Such an open-ended
viewing situation made it the viewer's responsibility to supply the meaning.

As cartes were not deemed inviolable
objects, the public joined the titling
process, adding inscriptions to the backside, or verso, of the cartes. A carte of a
dapper young man asked: "Please acknowledge the receipt of this by returning
one of yours. J. Crane." A middle-aged
man thought his image was worth many cartes: "Aunt
Susan, you must be sure and send me some of *all* of you
as soon as you can. Me." Others provided factual information about the sitter: "Ma when 16." Others offered
commentary: "The arch traitor Jeff Davis." A woman in
a long dress, holding a straw hat, wondered whether it
was really possible to be known through one's carte. On
the verso she wrote: "Do you know me?" A piercing example of the reality of war can be seen in a Civil War
portrait album that contains brief penciled comments
recording each person's name and what happened to
him: "killed at . . . , wounded at . . . , lost leg, died of
wound, eye shot out at . . . , lost arm." A portrait of four
soldiers in uniform, with devil-may-care looks, was inscribed: "All killed in battle."

4.10 UNKNOWN PHOTOGRAPHER. *Portrait of Four Civil War Soldiers.* 4 × 2½ inches. Carte-de-visite. The juxtaposition of the faces in the portrait and the description of what became of them provokes feelings of melancholia and loss. Through the play between pictures and words, the horrors of war and life exist not on a battlefield, but in the mind of the viewer.
Courtesy George Eastman House.

The Cabinet Photograph: The Picture Gets Bigger

The carte fad peaked about 1866, and as the fad began to decline photographers such as Edward Wilson bemoaned the change and searched for something else to reinvigorate declining sales:

> The adoption of a new size is what is wanted. In our experience, we have found that fashion rules in photography as well as in mantua-making and millinery, and if photographers

4.11 MATHEW BRADY STUDIO. *Abraham Lincoln*, ca. 1863. 3⅓ × 2³⁄₁₆ inches. Albumen Cabinet Card.   Courtesy George Eastman House.

would thrive, they must come into some of the tricks of those whose continual study it is to create fashion, and then cater to its tastes and demands.[8]

The answer to this dilemma came in the cabinet photograph, essentially an enlarged carte designed for portrait work. The name predates photography and may reference the fifteenth and sixteenth century Augsburg cabinets that were produced for well-to-do bourgeois to hold collectible items or the small cabinet canvases made by the Dutch and Flemish painters for merchants' houses. The cabinet card format was introduced in 1862 by Marion & Co. with the publication of a series of 6¾ × 4½-inch views by G.W. Wilson. The format gained popularity when F.R. Window's London studio applied it to making portraits in 1865–66. The increased image size showed more detail and was considered more aesthetically gratifying than the smaller carte. By the late 1860s, the cabinet had swept the portrait field, and photographic suppliers began to make new card mounts and albums as the collecting mania that had faded with the carte craze began anew.

Cabinet pictures were made in a method similar to the carte. The glass plate for the negative was first coated with a thin layer of albumen and the collodion was flowed on. Next, the plate was sensitized in a silver nitrate bath. It was exposed while still moist and was immediately developed in an acetic-acid-iron-sulfate solution that also contained alcohol, silver nitrate, and nitric acid, and was fixed with potassium cyanide. The completed negative was often varnished to prevent the thin collodion film from being scratched. Prints were made on albumenized stock that was commercially available in several surface finishes. The paper too had to be sensitized before printing by floating it, albumen side down, in a bath of silver nitrate. The paper was sometimes fumed with ammonia after being sensitized, in order to increase its speed. The negative and paper were placed in a printing frame and exposed in sunlight. Next the paper was toned with gold chloride to give it a brown appearance and was fixed in hypo, washed, and dried. The cabinet was offered in three sizes: No. 1, 5¼ × 4 inches (the most popular); No. 2, 5¾ × 4 inches; and Special, 6 × 4¼ inches. All were mounted on a 6½ × 4¼-inch card. The cabinet was supplanted by the postcard format around 1900 and disappeared by the end of World War I.

The cabinet created a demand for larger pictures.[9] The increase in image size changed the photographic viewing experience from an intimate affair to a public display on a mantle or wall. The bigger sizes provided photographers with more space to orchestrate, and new aesthetic possibilities could be realized as light and pose were used to reveal a sitter's character. As the image's size and cost increased, the public paid closer attention to what was happening within the frame.

4.12   ANDRÉ DISDÉRI.   *Suppliciés* (Louis Napoleon Album, Heads of Executed Men), ca. 1850s. 4 × 2½ inches. Carte-de-visite.   Courtesy George Eastman House.

These changes in turn encouraged photographers to push the boundaries of the portrait to express each sitter's character.

The cabinet style peaked with the collecting of stage personalities in the 1880s. Its decline began at the turn of the twentieth century as folding cameras, with which people could make their own postcard-size pictures, gained popularity. By World War I the cabinet had just about vanished from the commercial scene.

Since photography was young and still not considered an independent medium, many developments in the field stemmed from market demands. *What* was pictured continued to expand, with the addition of pet portraits, still lifes, and more reproductions of art, reflecting the idea of the camera as an all-seeing gatherer of information. The larger image area of the cabinet encouraged more photographers to try their hand at the rudimentary art of *montage,* cutting apart photographs, pasting selected pieces onto a board, and rephotographing them to form a new context and viewing experience. Like combination printing, montage was devised to overcome aesthetic and technical limitations. The concept of removing a photograph from its original context and placing it into a new one has had

profound effects on the viewer's willingness to accept as "real" visual information supplied by the photograph. Montage broke the rules about representing perspective, point of view, space, and time, yet people were willing to accept it as long as it remained photographically based.

The Studio Tradition

The affordability of the collodion processes led to the rapid expansion of portrait making. In 1841 there were only three portrait firms in London; in 1851 there were less than a dozen, but in 1861 there were over 200.[10] Skilled posing, lighting, and retouching allowed photographers to push the boundaries of portraiture, expanding the enterprise of studio photography.

One of the most highly skilled studio portrait makers was Gaspard Félix Tournachon [1820–1910], who first achieved acclaim as a caricaturist. Becoming a photographer was a natural extension of his talent for recording a subject's essential characteristics. His ability to create stinging caricatures earned him the nickname "Tourne à dard" (one who stings), which he shortened to "Nadard" and eventually to "**Nadar**."[11] Nadar's studio was a meeting place for Paris's intelligentsia, and he produced portraits of his guests: Charles Baudelaire, Alexandre Dumas, Gustave Flaubert, Victor Hugo, Franz Liszt and George Sand.

4.13 NADAR. *George Sand,* ca. 1860. From *Galerie Contemporaine,* 1877. 9⅛ × 7⅜ inches. Woodburytype. Courtesy George Eastman House.

Nadar was an artistic director: He posed his best-known clients but relied on his staff to carry out the actual work. This arrangement was taken for granted and typifies the actual teamwork that went into the making of the majority of images attributed solely to most well-regarded studio photographers.[12]

Nadar's approach was direct and simple, making use of plain dark backgrounds and, when possible, full natural light. Later, through the aid of reflectors, screens, veils, and mirrors, he made considerable use of side lighting to model the features of the face. Nadar favored three-quarter views, using poses that often hid the sitter's hands in order to emphasize the facial expression and the body. Nadar may have been influenced by his friend, Adam-Salomon (see page 86), whose lighting methods were considered unusual and who learned posing methods from his painter associates. Nadar was able to organize his subject around recognizable gestures and looks that revealed the character's essence while breaking down the sense of distance between the subject and the photographer. Sitters were encouraged to discover their own poses with a minimal use of props. Nadar knew his sitters, and the intimacy of the portraits, and his understanding of their often familiar human fragility, record the bonds of friendship and remembrance of shared events. Although Nadar was a comrade, he was not necessarily reverent: He did not flatter his sitters, but often seemed on the verge of revealing one of their secrets.

The subjects in many of Nadar's portraits seem to have been participating in the act of photography rather than just undergoing it. Spontaneity was in play, often revealing a part of the sitter's inner psychological being. Nadar understood the wet-plate's ability to render detail, but he was not obsessed with it. He knew how to suppress detail and sharpness, moving sitters through different levels of focus to bring out their essence. In his work, the sitter's clothes were an important element of personality, used to build an atmosphere of class, ethnic, and social character previously unachieved in photography. These qualities, combined with his talent as a caricaturist, enabled Nadar to go after the "moral intelligence" of the sitter and expand the boundaries of the social portrait.

Nadar was an experimenter who in 1858 made the first aerial photographs, coating his wet-plate while in a hot-air balloon. In 1861 he made photographs with artificial light, using Bunsen batteries in the catacombs of Paris. The failure of the revolutionary Commune of Paris financially ruined Nadar, and in 1871 he turned the business over to his son Paul (1856–1939), who continued on as a fashionable commercial portraitist through the turn of the twentieth century. In 1856, Nadar observed:

> Photography is a marvelous discovery, a science that has attracted the greatest intellects, an art that excites the most astute minds—and one that can be practiced by any imbecile. . . . Photographic theory can be taught in an hour, the basic technique in a day. But, what cannot be taught is the feeling for light. . . . It is how light lies on the face that you as artist must capture. Nor can one be taught how to grasp the personality of the sitter. To produce an intimate likeness rather than a banal portrait, the result of mere chance, you must put yourself at once in communion with the sitter, size up his thoughts and his very character.[13]

Nadar's restrained portraits of French novelist George Sand unobtrusively convey her dominating personality as a literary talent and nonconformist who protested the unequal treatment of women by openly wearing trousers, smoking cigars, and taking lovers like a man.

Camille Silvy [n/d, active 1857–69] was a French aristocratic and amateur photographer who ran a lavish London portrait studio. Silvy's style was the antithesis of Nadar's. He favored intricate sets of his own design, with painted backdrops creating the proper atmosphere for his upscale clients. Silvy specialized in posing the fashionable in front of mirrors, to soften the light and to manufacture a luxurious glow that accented the sitter's attire and hairstyle. Known for his exemplary taste and understanding of how to pose women, Silvy cultivated his reputation by publishing a series of cartes called *The Beauties of England,* which were acclaimed for their elegance, refinement, and vivacity. Silvy closed his studio, which employed 40 people, when the carte fad fizzled. Silvy's photographic career, lasting just over a decade, was cut short due to health problems—associated, perhaps, with the collodion process. (In fact, Silvy's death was probably hastened by his exposure to photographic chemicals. Numerous reports tell of early photographers being made ill or poisoned by improper handling of photographic chemicals.)

Antoine Samuel Adam-Salomon [1811–1881] was a Parisian sculptor who took up photography part time in 1858. Using his knowledge of modeling clay, Adam-Salomon was able to bring forth the *plastic,* three-dimensional effects of his two-dimensional subjects. He introduced what was called *Rembrandt Lighting,* the use of high side light to achieve distinct visual projection of a sitter's face after the style of the Dutch painter (see Figure 4.14). Greater facial contour enhanced the characterization of the sitter. Adam-Salomon, whose prints were known for their rich range of luxurious tones, also paid homage to painting by draping his sitters in velvet and posing them in the style of the Old Masters. Since his work venerated the traditions of painting it was appreciated by critics who believed the insemination of classic artistic ideas was necessary to elevate photography from a means of mechanical reproduction to an art. Adam-Salomon's work was also criticized for downplaying the individual attributes of subjects in favor of making them part of a formal configuration. In 1867–68 he became embroiled in controversy when he was accused of achieving his effects by retouching (a microscopic examination revealed that he did retouch his prints).

Napoleon Sarony [1821–1896], born in Quebec the year Napoleon Bonaparte died, opened his first New York studio in 1864. No taller than his namesake, Sarony was referred to as "the Napoleon of Photography" because of his flamboyant and volatile approach to making portraits. A natural actor, Sarony enjoyed parading down Broadway in an astrakhan cap, a calfskin waistcoat (hairy side out), with his pants tucked into highly polished cavalry boots.

Sarony's studio was equally flamboyant. His Wunderkammer or *wonder room,* as it was called, took up an entire building and featured a hydraulic elevator, an Egyptian mummy, stuffed birds, Russian sleighs, Chinese gods, armor, statues, musical instruments, bamboo umbrellas, chests, Indian pottery, a maze of pictures, and a crocodile suspended from the ceiling. The forerunner of the modern museum in the sixteenth and seventeenth centuries, the wonder room was a place where the nobility and the wealthy kept their collections of diverse objects for the purpose of celebrating the strange and marvelous. The contents were selected solely according to the owner's fancy and were presented unsystematically, in a way designed to astonish and amaze.

4.14 ANTOINE SAMUEL ADAM-SOLOMON.
Alphonse Karr from *Galerie Contemporaine,* 1877. 9⁵⁄₁₆ ×
7⁷⁄₁₆ inches. Woodburytype.   Courtesy George Eastman
House.

Sarony was an early photographic specialist, concentrating on theater personalities (supposedly making
40,000 portraits of the members of the theatrical profession) and developing this concentration into a market. Sarony was skilled at retouching and used it to
achieve "effect" and to satisfy the vanity of his clients.
As a photographer he was the equivalent of a modern-
day director, cajoling, parodying, and even intimidating
his sitters to elicit dramatic and expressive representations. To overcome the difficulties of 5- to 60-second
exposures, Sarony used a mechanical "posing machine" that allowed a sitter to maintain a more flexible
and natural position. This device enabled him to capture the emotional energy of the fictional roles of his actor clients, freeing them from conventional portrait
poses. Sarony had no interest in the mechanics of photography and worked with his cameraman, Benjamin
Richardson, to whom he gave credit, to make the pictures he desired. Sarony positioned the sitter as
Richardson deftly captured his vision. Richardson offered this account of Sarony's technique:

> When he photographed Jim Mace, the pugilist, on his first
> visit to this country, he danced around him, slapping him on
> the chest and in the ribs in a way which fairly astonished the
> champion, who enjoyed it hugely.[14]

4.15 NAPOLEON SARONY.   Ahah Isaacs Menkin as Mazeppa, 1866. 2³⁄₁₆ × 3³⁄₁₆ inches. Albumen carte-de-visite.   Courtesy George Eastman House.

Sarony was one of the first photographers to display the *copyright notice* on his card mounts.[15] Sarony sued a lithography firm for copyright violation over his portrait of Oscar Wilde and not only won the suit, but established the legal precedent that photography could be an art.[16]

Retouching and Enlargements

Although hand-coloring of images was widely practiced, photographers often balked at retouching, for it was time consuming and expensive, and many considered it fraudulent. Hence, anything that Sarony or Adam-Solomon achieved by retouching was of no value to those who believed that making revisions to the negative was blasphemous, which showed how quickly the negative achieved the status of an inviolable container of truth.

However, the new larger-sized cabinet prints revealed characteristics many sitters did not find flattering. Customers demanded that the camera image be softened and facial imperfections eliminated. Photographers thus began to offer sitters the option of having an idealized portrait made, marking the beginnings of *image* (fantasy) taking precedence over reality. As pho-

tographers became more proficient in their use of light, pose, and retouching, they could now modify human appearance and offer illusionary beings as role models, triggering new standards for looks and fashion. Problems surfaced as people forgot that these images were constructions and began to use them as yardsticks to measure their own appearance and came up lacking. This conflict between reality and how that reality is pictured generates the question: Do photographs show how things are or how they look photographed?

Before the collodion era, almost all photographic images were the size of the original camera exposure. John Draper experimented with enlarging daguerreotypes in 1840, and in 1843, Alexander Wolcott patented an enlarging device that permitted a daguerreotype to be rephotographed onto a larger plate or a piece of calotype paper. Others, including Talbot, conducted enlarging experiments, but the process was impractical and rarely done. In the early 1850s, however, photographers began to make enlargements with cameras that used reflectors and a copying lens to transmit sunlight through a glass plate negative onto a bigger piece of albumen paper. The first utilitarian *solar enlarger,* designed to make enlargements onto canvas that would later be painted over, was patented in 1857 by David A. Woodward. The solar enlarger, based on the solar microscope in use since 1740, was a horizontal device that used a mirror to relay sunlight to a condenser lens the same size as the negative. This light passed through the negative to a copy lens that focused the image onto an easel where the albumen paper was placed for exposures of 45 to 60 minutes. By the mid-1860s, solar en-

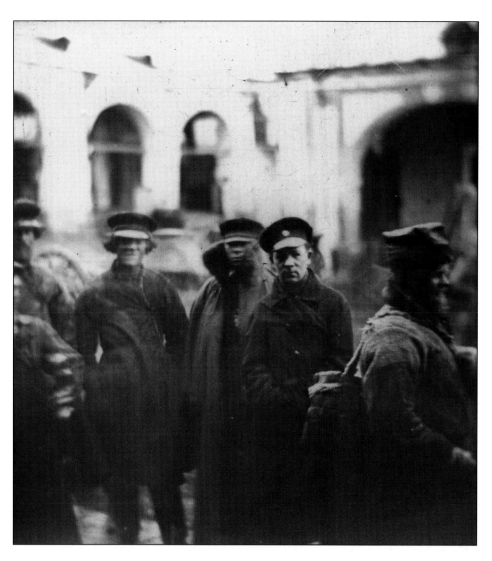

4.16   CHARLES PIAZZI SMYTH.   *Novgorod Street Scene,* 1859. Smyth's pictures, taken with the understanding that they would be enlarged, are antithetical to the wet-plate's contemplative nature and tap into the urge that would shortly bubble up to make candid pictures.   Reproduced by permission of the Royal Society of Edinburgh from the Royal Society of Edinburgh Piazzi Smyth Archive, held on deposit at the Royal Observatory, Edinburgh.

largers could be seen on the roofs and in the windows of major photographic establishments, and, with improvements, they continued in use until the 1890s. The first vertical enlarger was designed by Achille Quinet of Paris in 1852. In 1858, J. F. Campbell implemented this idea by placing a camera in an opening he had made in his studio roof so he could make enlargements on a table below. Campbell continued to refine his device until it came to resemble our modern-day enlarger. Adolphe Bertsch's *megascope* (1860) was the first solar enlarger specifically designed to be used with a miniature camera; Bertsch's camera made 2¼-inch square negatives.

Larger images increased the demand for more photographs, which led to more companies producing manufactured photographic goods and services, thus imposing standardization on the practice. Retouching and spotting became everyday procedures, as small defects were now noticeable. As bigger pictures were hung on walls instead of being placed in albums, photographs became more directly related to drawing and painting, causing confusion as to the aesthetic criteria needed to evaluate a photograph.

The concept of *enlarging* meant that a print did not have to adhere to the original construction of the negative, but could act as raw material for the postcamera operations that defined the final image. This was a radical departure from how pictures were previously put together, and it came to shape much of twentieth-century practice. Thomas Skaife's single-lens miniature camera, the *Pistolgraph* (1858), took instantaneous 'shots' by means of a spring shutter that was operated by rubber bands when its trigger was fired. (Skaife was almost arrested for "shooting" Queen Victoria with his "pistol." The image was lost when Skaife had to open his camera

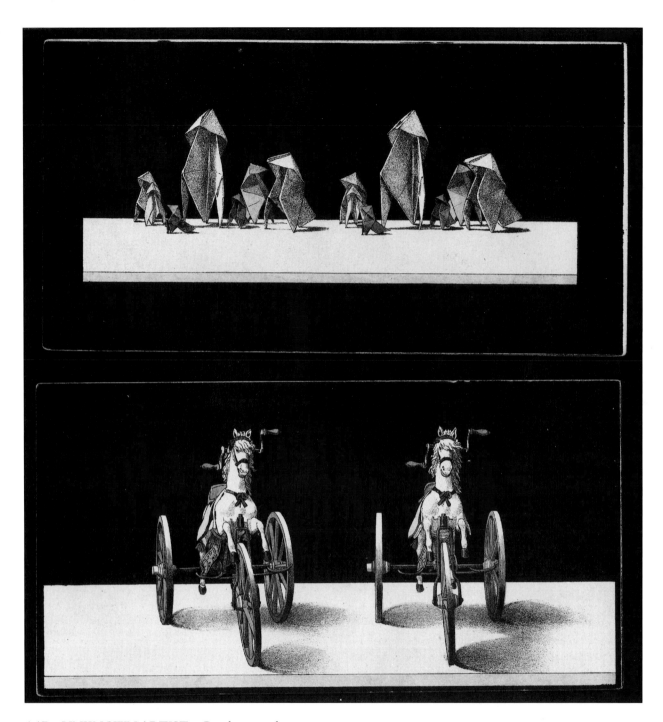

4.17 UNKNOWN ARTIST. Prephotography
stereo cards, ca. 1840. 3³⁄₁₆ × 7 inches. Stereograph
lithographs.   Courtesy George Eastman House.

to convince police he was not an assassin.) The tiny
plates, 1½ inches in diameter, were "hand-enlarged,"
that is, the processed negatives were projected to their
chosen size, but the image was hand-traced onto a piece
of paper rather than transferred by photographic means.

Charles Piazzi Smyth [1819–1900], Astronomer
Royal for Scotland, devised a miniature camera that
made 1-inch-square negatives, which he used to
capture unrehearsed street scenes during a visit to Rus-

sia. In 1865, Smyth used his tiny camera to make photographs of the Great Pyramid's interior with magnesium light. During a lecture at the Edinburgh Photographic Society in 1869, where Smyth exhibited
enlargements from these negatives, Smyth told why his
"poor man's" technique was superior to that of the
"London wealth" whose servants made contact prints
directly from large negatives:

> the poor man, with his little box of very little negatives
> brought home modestly in his waistcoat pocket . . . sits him
> down at a table, having a compound achromatic microscope
> . . . and . . . wanders . . . over the various parts of each picture
> . . . and . . . decides whether a positive copy should be shaped

4.18   ANTOINE CLAUDET.   *Portrait of Claudet Family*, ca. 1855.   3³⁄₁₆ × 7 inches. Daguerreotype stereo view with applied color.   Courtesy George Eastman House.

as a long, i.e. horizontal, rectangle, or as a tall, i.e. vertical, rectangle . . . or whether some special scientific purpose may not be better served by extracting one little subject . . . and making a very highly magnified picture of that one item.[17]

The Stereoscope

The phenomenon of stereo, based on *binocular vision*—the fusion by the brain of the two slightly dissimilar images as seen by our eyes (the distance between our eyes is about 2½ inches) into a single image—was observed as early as 280 B.C.E. by Euclid. In his *Treatise on Painting,* Leonardo calls attention to the topic and regrets that painting cannot render volume as persuasively as the eye can perceive it. Regardless of how well chiaroscuro and perspective are used to create the illusion of depth, they rarely overcome the obstacle of surface flatness. The invention of photography offered a practical way to create and view convincing stereo scenes.

In 1832, Sir **Charles Wheatstone's** [1802–1875] experiments led to the discovery that the illusion of depth could be created by looking at two slightly different drawings of a subject side by side through a binocular device (see Figure 4.17). Wheatstone built a device, which he called a *stereoscope,* that allowed only the right eye to view the right image and the left eye the left image. When the brain combined the two separate images, a person got the visual sensation of 3-D.

When Daguerre and Talbot announced their new methods in 1839, Wheatstone had stereographs made in both daguerreotypes and calotypes. The daguerreotypes produced reflections, and the calotype proved too slow for portraits and did not hold up well under close inspection. Stereo pictures designed for Wheatstone's elaborate and expensive reflecting stereoscope were sold in London during the 1840s, but did not receive much notice.

However, the process was nurtured by Sir David Brewster's [1781–1868] *refracting stereoscope,* a greatly simplified version of Wheatstone's cumbersome design, which Brewster first exhibited in 1849. It duplicated the 2½ inch separation between the eyes by placing a pair of lenses, side by side, in a small box with a small door on the side to admit light (the center points of the two pictures were also 2½ inches apart). A slot on the bottom allowed the insertion of a mounted pair of stereoscopic pictures. The base was made of frosted glass to allow the viewing of transparencies by refracted light. During the Great Exhibition of 1851 Queen Victoria became captivated by this stereoscope. When a special one was made for her, 250,000 stereoscopes and millions of stereo cards were sold in London and Paris within three months. Due to this royal boost, London's top daguerreotypists, Beard, W. E. Kilburn [n.d, active 1825–1871], T. R. Williams [1825–1871], Mayall, and Claudet, began hotly making stereoscopic views at the Crystal Palace site of the exhibition.

The meteoric rise of stereoscopic views touched off lawsuits and feuds. Jules Duboscq, the optician who made Brewster's device, patented the stereoscope in 1852 and seized the stereo apparatuses and images of

4.19   WILLIAM ENGLAND.   *Views of Switzerland #30: Glacier Supérieur et Caverne à Grindenwald, Suisse.* 3³⁄₁₆ × 7 inches. Albumen stereo card. The transparency of the albumen-on-glass process further spread the authority of photography by allowing simultaneous group viewing by means of magic-lantern and stereoscopic slides.[18]   Courtesy George Eastman House.

his chief competitors until his patent was declared void in 1857. Brewster published *The Stereoscope* (1856) and followed that with a series of letters to the London *Times,* in which he challenged Wheatstone's claim to have invented the stereoscope and contradicted as well his claim of having discovered the principle on which the stereoscope effect works (Brewster's claims were all unfounded).

Claudet, using two cameras set up side by side, was able to make successful group portraits and became a devotee to the process. Claudet patented a folding pocket stereoscope designed for daguerreotypes in 1853 and an improved viewer in 1855, one with the lenses set in adjustable tubes and a giant stereoscope capable of holding 100 stereoscopic slides for viewing. Claudet also experimented with "moving photographic figures" that linked the zoetrope with the stereoscope to create three-dimensional moving pictures. The quality of his own work set significant standards for others to follow.

The Stereo Craze

By 1856 the London Stereoscopic Company, whose motto was "No home without a stereoscope," had sold an estimated 500,000 inexpensive stereo viewers. The ease of reproducing collodion images insured cheap paper stereo cards. Mass production allowed the "optical wonder of the age" to find its way into middle and upper economic level homes, and made the stereo craze photography's biggest nineteenth-century bonanza, remaining enormously popular until 1910. The company's staff of photographers, under the guidance of William England [n.d.–d. 1896], traveled the world and compiled a stock of 100,000 views.

The stereograph was introduced to America by the Langenheim Brothers. In 1854 the brothers' American Stereoscopic Company began to sell scenic stereo views (on glass as transparencies and on paper as card-mounted prints) of American scenery recorded as *hyalotypes.* Hyalotypes (from the Greek *hualos,* meaning glass) were clones of Niépce de Saint-Victor's process that used albumen to bind a silver salt emulsion to a glass plate. They were almost identical to John Adams Whipple's previously patented crystalotype albumen plates. The brothers used the hyalotypes to produce magic lantern slides, making the first photographically based images designed for projection. This forerunner of the present-day slide show proved so profitable that by the start of the Civil War all their efforts were directed at producing glass lantern slides.

Stereo pictures became a sensation because they provided affordable home entertainment. Their small size (3½ × 7 inches) made them convenient to handle, and there was a magical quality to the illusion. No matter how often one looked at them, a sense of wonderment remained as the two flat images came together and offered a visual sense of depth that transcended the physical size of the picture. Stereo cards made it possible to be amused, to travel, and to expand one's knowledge without leaving home. Claudet wrote:

It [the stereo card] introduces to us scenes known only from imperfect relations of travelers, it leads us before the ruins of antique architecture, illustrating the historical records of

4.20 UNKNOWN PHOTOGRAPHER. *Rainy Day Sports.* 3³⁄₁₆ × 7 inches. Albumen stereo card. As the stereo craze spread, it crossed class and cultural boundaries. Even the ruling elite were caught up with recording daily life. The February 19, 1886, issue of *The British Journal of Photography* reported that "When the [Russian] Czar catches sight of his aunt, or a courtier, a fowl, a sentinel, or a baby, he has out his [stereo] photographic apparatus in a moment. The Nihilists will soon be frightened to come near him." Courtesy George Eastman House.

former and lost civilizations; the genius, taste and power of past ages, with which we have become familiarized as if we had visited them. By our fireside we have the advantage of examining them, without being exposed to the fatigue, privation, and risks of the daring and enterprising artists who, for our gratification and instruction, have traversed lands and seas, crossed rivers and valleys, ascended rocks and mountains with their heavy and cumbrous photographic baggage.[19]

The American physician and writer, **Oliver Wendell Holmes** [1809–1894], was frustrated by Brewster's viewing device, which gave him headaches. In 1861 Holmes and Joseph L. Bates designed a hand-held viewer with a sliding T-bar that allowed the viewing distance to be individually adjusted. The Holmes-Bates Stereoscope made viewing of paper stereo cards less strenuous, and was lighter weight, easier to handle, and less expensive than any previous device. Since neither man patented the improvement, their device became the standard viewing appliance, adding to the growing popularity of stereoscopic work.

Photographers courted the mass market by making pictures of scenes people wanted in the style people recognized and understood. Although the viewing experience of the stereoscope was radical, the subject matter was conservative and did not push the bound-

aries of the visually acceptable. The vast majority of stereo work recorded views or group scenes, as individual portraits did not provide a dramatic sense of visual depth; views offered a distinct foreground, middleground, and background, enhancing the three-dimensional effect. Also, although an individual might order a dozen stereo portraits, a photographer could sell more copies of a single view. Printed text was often linked with a card to anchor the image's context according to the maker's wishes.

Many of the top photographers did not respect the stereo card. It was small, and its illusion of depth was considered too close to reality to be aesthetically gratifying. Serious photographers were brought up with the notion that picturemaking was a matter of translating three-dimensional space to a flat surface. Many considered stereo a betrayal of this tradition and stereo photographers charlatans. As a consequence, top photographers only took stereo views after they had made their "real" picture, with a monocular camera, and they only did it to enhance their profits. Photographer J. Craig Annan [1864–1946] offered this criticism:

The stereoscopic effect is an endeavor to imitate nature, while the object of an ordinary photograph, or drawing is only to reproduce an impression of nature. The failure of the stereoscope in its greater aim is more marked than the less ambitious but more practical endeavor to reproduce on a flat surface an impression of what we see.[20]

Photographers worked by visiting a locale and making stereo views of the important structures. The majority of stereo cards are direct, straight-forward tracings of the world that reflect the viewer's expectation for an informational map, rather than artistic expression. The stereo image's small size did not require retouching, and no effort was expended to discover the unique qualities of one town's courthouse over the next. The way to make money was to rapidly cover a market and move on to the next before the competition got there. Except for photographers who published their own stereo cards, most stereo cards did not carry a credit line. A typical stereo card had the publisher's name, address, name of the series, sometimes the photographer's name, and possibly a caption printed on the front. Occasionally the backside provided a printed list of other available views. Stereo views were mainly printed on albumenized paper; hand-coloring was prevalent. Unlike cartes, stereo cards were rarely personalized with greeting, messages, and inscriptions.

The stereo card became the home encyclopedia for the eye, providing an authoritative and comprehensive reference of facts that was a consummate manifestation of the empiricism of the Enlightenment. In the Age of Reason, the empirical mindset depended on direct experience and/or observation. The camera, with its seemingly neutral recording, could represent the naive, ideal, and rational. If an encyclopedia is a source where data is collected, then anyone with a camera could collect evidence. The concept that one could be educated through the use of photographs and that history could be recorded and learned by means of photography got a lift from the stereo card.

Since each stereo image was no bigger than 3 × 3 inches the lens for the stereo camera could be of a shorter (wide angle) *focal length* than the lenses used in portrait work. The focal length of a lens establishes its angle of view, magnification, and the exact point at which a sharp image of a distant object will be formed. Think of the light that forms an image as a lever bar. As the light passes through the lens it rotates in a circular motion until a complete image is formed. If there is movement at one end of this imaginary lever bar, the image being formed at the other end will also move. The shorter the arm of the lever bar behind the lens, whose distance is set by the focal length of the lens, the less an image will move.

A short focal length lens reduces the amount of perceptible movement, permitting live-action scenes to be recorded without ghostly blurs while delivering a sharp image at larger apertures, thereby reducing exposure time. It offers more depth of field at any given aperture than a longer focal length lens, adding visual information to the view. Instantaneous stereo cards freed photographers from the anchor of static subject matter and permitted the picturing of transitory moments.

Stereo cards may not have been noted for artistic effect, but they did provide a plenitude of representations, and people clamored to see anything they couldn't see for themselves. Holmes proposed creating a comprehensive stereographic library, "where all men can find

the special forms they particularly desire to see as artists, or as scholars, or as mechanics, or in any other capacity."[21] E. & H. T. Anthony of New York met the demand by issuing metropolitan views of Broadway, the elevated railroad, Coney Island, and the Vanderbilt mansions, as well as a series on Niagara Falls. Travel views promoted tourism, which further increased the demand for pictures. Comic, idealized, and sentimental images of domestic life, like *The Happy Homes of England* series, became common fare. Religious edification was met with *Scenes in the Life of Christ,* twenty different cards portraying Christ under a giant halo, being beaten by Roman soldiers. Everyday activities—men drinking beer, families having dinner, a hometown band playing—appeared as a presnapshot innovation.

The financial crash of 1873 put many photographers out of business and caused others to cease making new views. Pirating views was a common way to cut expenses, but it also lowered quality, which disrupted the stereo illusion. The 1880s saw Underwood and Underwood deploying college students door-to-door selling cards. Mass production and marketing doomed the small independent operators, allowing corporate publishers to gain control over how and what was pictured. In the 1920s, by concentrating on the educational sector, Keystone View Company dominated the market. Keystone survived the Great Depression of the 1930s, the rise of pictorial magazines, and the expansion of motion pictures and radio, and continued making stereo views until 1964, when it succumbed to color television. Inexpensive plastic View-Master 3D viewers and their companion Stereo Reels, featuring 14 color transparencies (that provide 7 separate views) in a circular paper mount that rotates through the viewer by pushing a finger operated lever, can still be found at major tourist destinations and toy stores.[22]

The popularity of stereo cards, made possible by the collodion process, demonstrated that people not only wanted images of themselves and their loved ones but also of their world. This reveals what most people considered the primary function of the typical nineteenth century photographer: To find and record people and scenes from the flow of real-world time for future contemplation. This photographic act of remembrance evolved into an *aesthetic of finding*. The influence of this ritual can later be seen in the rethinking of the definition of art that inspired artists to incorporate actual objects and representations into their work. It also affected ordinary people who developed an appetite for collecting items from the material world. This desire for visual information, and the profits that could potentially be made by supplying it, led photographers into situations that had previously been thought unpictureable.

Endnotes

1   Frederick Scott Archer, *The Collodion Process on Glass,* second edition, enlarged (London: Printed for the author, 1854) 10.

2   Archer credited Gustave Le Gray's pamphlet of 1850 as the first published account of collodion and its possible use, but he pointed out that Le Gray never provided the details that would qualify him to call it a photographic method. Archer released the first account of his process in the March 1851 issue of *The Chemist* and followed it up with his self-published *Manual of the Collodion Photographic Process* (1851).

3   Frederick Scott Archer. "The Use of Collodion in Photography," *The Chemist,* no. 2 (March 1851), 257.

4   *The Photogram,* vol. I, 1894, 159.

5   Cutting and Isaac Rehn, his friend and business partner, both took out patents covering several photographic ideas that were not their own. Nevertheless, the U.S. Patent Office gave Cutting the legal right to sell licenses for the use of collodion photography. He hired agents in several areas of the country to sell permits ($100 per town of 5,000 people) and bring legal proceeding against photographers who were making collodion pictures without a license.

6   In 1862 Cutting was committed to the Worcester, MA, Insane Asylum and remained there until his death in 1867. The administrator of Cutting's estate filed for an extension of his patent. Some of America's most influential photographers, including Mathew Brady, Abraham Bogardus, John Carbutt, Alexander Hesler, and John Whipple, met on April 7, 1868, at the Cooper Institute in New York to form the National Photographic Convention for the purpose of establishing America's first national photographic organization and to fight the ambrotype patent.

7   *Anthony's Photographic Bulletin,* vol. 15 (1884), 65.

8   *The Philadelphia Photographer,* vol. 3, 311–13.

9   New sizes featured the Promenade, 7½ × 3¾ inches; the Boudoir, 8¼ × 5 inches; the Imperial, 10 × 7 inches; and the Panel, 13 × 8 inches.

10   Helmut Gernsheim, *The Rise of Photography 1850–1880: The Age of Collodion* (New York: Thames and Hudson, 1988), 23.

11   Helmut and Alison Gernsheim, *The History of Photography, 1685–1914,* (New York: McGraw-Hill, 1969), 306–07.

12   Many of Nadar's works were reproduced in the *Galerie Contemporaine,* a series of 241 portraits by 28 photographers of artistic, literary, and political figures in France, which was published in Paris between 1876 and 1894.

13   Translated from Jean Prinet and Antoinette Dilasser, *Nadar* (Paris: Armand Colin, 1966), 115–16 (Nadar's testimony in a lawsuit).

14   *Wilson's Photographic Magazine,* vol. 34, no. 482 (February 1897), 69.

15   Copyright protection was extended to photographs in 1865, but it took several years before most photographers started to claim copyright.

16   "Sarony v. Burrow-Giles Lithographic Company," *Federal Reporter,* vol. 17, no. 600, (1883) as quoted in *Photography in Nineteenth Century America,* "The Portrait Studio and the Celebrity" by Barbara McCandless (Amon Carter Museum, Fort Worth, TX and Harry Abrams, NY, 1991), 69–70.

17   Charles Piazzi Smyth, *A Poor Man's Photography at the Great Pyramid in the Year 1865* (London: Henry Greenwood, 1870), 14.

18   The Langenheim brothers made their first *Hyalotypes* (lantern slides) in 1849, while A. and C. M. Ferrier of Paris began, in 1851, to produce albumen transparencies for use with Brewster's stereo viewer.

19   A. Claudet, "Photography in its Relations to the Fine Arts," *The Photographic Journal,* vol. VI, June 15, 1860.

20   *The Amateur Photographer,* vol. 15 (1892), 328.

21   Oliver Wendell Holmes, "The Stereoscope and the Stereograph," *Atlantic Monthly,* vol. 8, June 1859, 728.

22   A few contemporary makers continue to work with the traditional stereo method. A notable example was Jim Pomeroy's [1945–1992] installation/exhibition *Stereo Views* (1988) that was produced by Light Work and also shown at CEPA Gallery. The project featured a publication that included a View-Master and three custom stereo reels that provided 21 stereo views of his work.

CHAPTER FIVE

Prevailing Events/Picturing Calamity

Once life was primarily rural and local events had the greatest impact on people's lives. As Western society became industrialized and urban, events outside of the immediate surroundings began to have a pronounced influence on daily existence. Improvements in communications and transportation during the nineteenth century narrowed distances between peoples and reduced isolation. People were curious and wanted more information about the world outside their village community. As seeing was equated with knowing, the more people saw, the more they could feel they possessed knowledge of the world. The photograph was conceptually positioned to fulfill this desire, and people took the opportunity to try and make a profit. The photograph faced technical obstacles; the process couldn't stop action, and there was no cost-effective way to immediately get news photographs to large audiences. However, the

UNKNOWN PHOTOGRAPHER. *Soldiers' Photographs at United States Post Office Dead Letter Office,* 1861–65. Albumen silver prints and tintypes. Courtesy George Eastman House.

An unusual grouping of soldier portraits was assembled at the U.S. Post Office's dead letter office and displayed to see if anyone would claim them. Someone took the undeliverable cards and laid them out in a grid, attached them to a board with brass brads, and gave each image a number. This homemade display visually raises the question of the fate of all the men pictured and indirectly references the essential maleness of war, as women are rarely seen in any Civil War imagery.

5.1   GEORGE N. BARNARD.   *Fire in the Ames Mills, Oswego, NY,* 1853. 2¾ × 3¼ inches. Sixth plate daguerreotype with applied color. The smallness of Barnard's hand-tinted, sixth plate daguerreotype, one of the earliest American action news pictures, reduces the tragedy to a compact, illusory event.   Courtesy George Eastman House.

premise of the photograph as a container of information and carrier of cultural values was established and accepted by society at large.

Working from the notion of photographic "transparency," the job of a good wet-plate photographer was to make "everyperson" views, that is, to give people the impression that the photograph was what they would have seen had they been there themselves. This working mode also demanded an impeccable technical performance, one that allowed the subject to reveal itself with the utmost clarity. Truth and accuracy were believed best served by showing the "wholeness" of a scene. This was done by making broad views with an abundance of visual information for the viewer to sort through and decide what was important. Typically photographers would position themselves some distance from the subject, place the camera at eye level, and aim straight ahead. Close-ups of three feet or less, isolating a subject from its surroundings, were rare, as *more* information was thought to be *better* information. It was unusual for a photographer to impose an unconventional vantage point or idiosyncratic perspective. As an authentic photographic syntax was just evolving, pho-

tographers relied on the painter's vocabulary[1] and on picturesque lithographs to determine how and what was being pictured in photographs. Religion with its notion that art should be instructive and morally uplifting also played a role. Since a photograph's form was driven by its subject, the frame was left *open,* encouraging viewers to meander within its confines to decide what was meaningful. Sometimes this distancing defeated the possibility of obtaining important visual information. Consequently, contemporary viewers, facing images that have *deteriorated,*[2] lacking the context of the times, and accustomed to seeing action close-ups, find that early nineteenth-century images possess a static sameness.[3]

Current Events

Although unsuitable for reportage, it was a daguerreotype overview by Carl Ferdinand Stelzner [1805–1894] of the incinerated ruins of Hamburg, Germany, after the fire of 1842 that is one of the first camera renditions of a current event. Because the early methods could not stop motion, the action was always somewhere else, forcing photographers to make pictures before, after, or surrounding an event. Artifacts from the scene and views of the site or of the area were considered worthy subjects. Photographers involved with this type of work can be compared to police photographers arriving at the scene after the crime has been committed. They depicted what had occurred, but they never caught the

5.2 ROGER FENTON. *Railroad Yard Balaclava #2,* 1855. Albumen silver print. Instantaneous views were not possible. Typical exposure times for Fenton's large plate cameras (12 × 16 inches and 14 × 18 inches) ranged from 10 to 20 seconds. Under ideal conditions his small 6 × 8 inch camera could deliver a 3-second exposure. Fenton had to wait for a lull in the action, set up a scene that would give the impression of being a natural occurrence, or accept ghostly blurs.   Courtesy George Eastman House.

actual happening. Today these images would not be considered news photographs, but at the time they were regarded as dynamic, factual, and timely.

Early War Coverage

Daguerreotypes were attempted of every possible subject, and reportage was considered crucial to photography's future. People wanted to see how the camera reported current events. People believed photography was a part of the new scientific method. This belief helped to legitimize the role of the arts as a vehicle that would encourage the growth of knowledge and promote moral progress.

War was an ancient ritual whose deadly effects were felt worldwide, yet its depiction was often abstract and idealistic. Photography was about to change that by recording and circulating pictures of actual events that in turn instituted new patterns for the vital utilization of the medium. The earliest surviving images of a military campaign are from the Mexican War (1846–48) between the United States and Mexico over the annexation of Texas. A deteriorated image, now in the Amon Carter Museum, made by an unidentified daguerreotypist (Mexican?), shows General Wool and his staff posing on their horses in the town of Saltillo, Mexico, during the winter of 1846–47. It is not exactly a war scene by today's standards, but it was well within the expectations of visual accuracy and interest of that time.

The Crimean War (1853–56) was the first major conflict to be covered by newspaper reporters, artists, and photographers. The war was unpopular in England, and during the winter of 1854–55 William Howard Russell, a reporter for the London *Times,* sent back dispatches detailing the horrifying conditions under which the soldiers lived. **Roger Fenton** [1819–1869] left England in February 1855 to photograph the war zone. Fenton was financed by Thomas Agnew, a Manchester publisher, who intended to profit by selling pictures of historical interest to an upper-class market. Fenton's expedition was made under royal patronage with assistance from the Secretary of State for War, who sought to boost public support for the campaign. These factors provide the context surrounding the type of images Fenton produced. None dealt directly with the havoc, death, or human suffering brought on by the mismanagement and lack of medical facilities reported in the press that forced the government to resign.

5.3   ROGER FENTON.   *The Valley of the Shadow of Death,* 1855. Salted paper print. Fenton attempted photographs under battle conditions, but the vast, horizontal desert landscape made his van an easy target. Fenton wrote: "The Russians fired constantly. . . . The ground here is covered with cannon balls. . . . I could hear by the whir and thud that the balls were coming up the ravine on each side. . . . The 68-pounders especially almost burst the ears. . . . The awful clangour as if hell had broken loose and legions of Lucifer were fighting in the air."[4] Here the barren and rocky landscape, littered with cannon balls, tells the terror and fieriness of battle without violating the dictums of his backers or their Victorian sensibilities.   Courtesy Gernsheim Collection, Humanities Research Center, The University of Texas, Austin, TX.

Fenton, an experienced documentary photographer who had traveled abroad, was the ideal candidate for the Crimean assignment. In the early 1840s he had studied in Paris at the atelier of Paul Delaroche along with Gustave Le Gray, Charles Nègre, and Henri Le Secq. In 1844 he returned to England to study law and later practiced as a solicitor. As a member of the elite Calotype Club he proposed a photographic group modeled after the Société Héliographique, which led to the formation of the Photographic Society in 1853. In 1852 he went to Russia to photograph the construction of a suspension bridge at Kiev and the architecture of Moscow and St. Petersburg. Trained as an artist, Fenton knew how to arrange compositions that invoked classical beauty and its related Victorian moralistic values.

He was connected with influential people in the government and was aware of their public positions. Fenton's upper-class connections and sympathies made it unlikely he would disturb the artistic or political status quo. Understanding that the basis of camera vision is subtractive composition, Fenton knew what to exclude, but in some instances he may have subtley subverted his backers' interests.

Fenton arrived at Balaclava on March 8, 1855, with a wagon, a driver, and a photographic assistant. The wagon, with "photographic van" painted on its sides, had been modified for darkroom work, cooking, and sleeping. Fenton's outfit consisted of five cameras, 700 glass plates, chemicals, all the necessary darkroom paraphernalia, a tent, tools, and tinned food. By April Fenton's working conditions had become dreadful due to heat, dust, and flies. He reported that "When my van door is closed before the plate is prepared, perspiration is running down my face, and dropping like tears. . . . The developing water is so hot I can hardly bear my hands in it."[5]

By June Fenton was making portraits at 4 AM to avoid the glare of the sun; it was so intense that by 10 AM Fenton's subjects could hardly keep their eyes open. The harshness of the light created contrast problems, which caused a loss of detail in his negatives, a major flaw in a working mode where clarity and detail were gauges of success. Fenton's backers wanted morally instructive and uplifting pictures that would reinforce their war propaganda. Fenton thus made staged portraits of officers, generals on horseback in full regalia, the staff at headquarters, and pashas and their attendants, while complaining that ordinary soldiers

5.4 FELICE A. BEATO. *Interior of Fort Talsu in North China Immediately after Capture,* 1860. 9⅗ × 12⅜ inches. Albumen silver print.   Courtesy George Eastman House.

pestered him to take their pictures to send back home. Fenton's pictures of the accessories of war, from the harbor clogged with ships to mortar batteries, formed the descriptive stylistic basis for photographers during the American Civil War.

Fenton did not picture a single dead body. Instead, an image of a man with a perfectly wrapped, pristine head bandage seated beside a nurse implied that the atrocious hospital conditions reported in the press had been alleviated. If seeing is believing, then Fenton's pictures proved that getting wounded was nothing to worry about. If it did happen, though, a nurse would take care of you and dress your wound heroically. However, the image is subversive: It demonstrates that people do get wounded.

At the end of June, after a large Allied attack on Sevastopol failed, Fenton, suffering from cholera, returned to England, where he secured royal support to publish his prints. Although the photographs present the British military positively, they are not the usual depictions of wartime valor that people were accustomed to seeing in paintings. Fenton castigated such pictures for their "total want of likeness to reality."[6] His photographs produced no public heroes, but they did introduce a new photographic standard of depicting reality, one that began to debunk the romantic war fantasies

promoted by painters and sketch artists. With the emergence of this new standard, photographs were getting the nod as being the most *real*.

Fenton's backers did not reap financial rewards, but their idea that photographs could be propaganda was given a field trial. Fenton's underwriters had hoped his photographs would override the written journalistic accounts of the war. This was not the case, because the war ended before the photographs were published, but time has shown the underwriters' aim to be an effective strategy. The idea has been refined in the late twentieth century, where images have a tremendous impact on political opinion. While today's audience is more visually sophisticated about how images are constructed, it continues to wish to accept the photograph as a custodian of reality.

James Robertson [n.d., active 1852–1865], the British superintendent and chief engraver of the Imperial Mint at Constantinople, and **Felice A. Beato** [1830–1906], his assistant, worked together making views in Constantinople, Athens, Malta, Cairo, and Palestine. Their Crimean series, made with a different set of intentions and standards than Fenton's, picks up the story where his pictures left off. Their images continue and complete Fenton's Crimean documentation with coverage of the ruins of Sevastopol after its capture by the Allies. Their work concentrates on the landscape, presenting a vista of the aftermath of the siege, but by the time their work was exhibited and used for illustrations in the London press, the war had ended and people were not interested in the pictures. In hindsight it points out that the effectiveness and

5.5 ALEXANDER GARDNER. *Home of the Rebel Sharpshooter, Gettysburg,* 1863 (from *Gardner's Photographic Sketch Book of the War*). 6⅞ × 8⅞ inches. Albumen silver print. Gardner's *Sketch Book* offers us a window into the adage that it is the winners who write history. The text with this image reported "that his suffering must have been intense. What visions, of loved ones far away, may have hovered about his stony pillow!" The text then skips ahead four months and transmits the ultimate fate of a Rebel: "The skeleton of the soldier lay undisturbed within a mouldering uniform . . . . None of those who went up and down the fields to bury the fallen, has found him. 'Missing,' was all that could have been known of him at home, and some mother may yet be patiently watching for the return of her boy, whose bones lie bleaching, unrecognized and alone, between the rocks at Gettysburg."[7] Courtesy George Eastman House.

profitability of war images depend on immediately getting the pictures to the intended audience, for once the conflict ends most people want to forget it. At the war's conclusion Robertson and Beato traveled to India to cover the aftermath of the Indian Mutiny of 1857–58.

Beato, a naturalized British subject from Venice, was fascinated by the British army's colonialist campaigns. His photographs of the capture of Fort Taku near Tientsin by the British and French fleets in 1860, at the conclusion of the Second Opium War, unflinchingly show battle dead (see Figure 5.4). Beato covered the fighting in the Simonaki Straits of Japan in 1862, providing early European views of this closed society. In 1870, Beato returned to China to record massacres resulting from renewed anti-foreign sentiment. His war work concluded with the British campaign of 1884–85 during the siege of Khartoum.

Beato was an outsider with inside connections, looking in twice: Once as a foreigner who had adopted the British outlook, and again as a witness from the occupying military force who could see things that born insiders took for granted. His meticulous work has been referred to as aloof, dispassionate, even ghoulish. Although Beato does present the colonial view of "underdeveloped natives" as curiosities, he was the first to photographically show the horrific, unglamorous side of war to the British public. The precise coolness of Beato's work reveals his underlying belief that the unmanipulated photograph possessed the power of truth. Beato's urge to categorize, define, and label typifies the Enlightenment belief that understanding is achieved through description. From this perspective, Beato's work represents the quintessential nineteenth-century documentary photograph.

The American Civil War

The American Civil War began on April 12, 1861. The North was swiftly evolving into urban, capitalistic, industrial centers that were organized around factories, mass production, and a free, diverse, and skilled labor force. Northerners believed that the war would be short, and photographers expected it to generate a demand for

5.6 JOHN REEKIE. *A Burial Party, Cold Harbor, VA*, 1865 (from *Gardner's Photographic Sketch Book of the War*). 7 × 9 inches. Albumen silver print.   Courtesy George Eastman House.

souvenir pictures of dashing, uniformed men who would slay the dragon in an afternoon and be home for dinner that night. As it turned out, the war lasted four years, saw 2.9 million men in uniform, and produced as many casualties—over one million, including at least 623,000 deaths—as all the other American wars, from the Revolution to Kuwait, combined.[8] By the war's end, the demand for images had diminished; people were exhausted from the events and did not want any more war mementos. Nevertheless, the war offered photographers new opportunities to hone their craft, try new methods, improve their aesthetics, link images with text, and get photographs before more people's eyes than ever before.

To profit from an audience anticipating a quick victory, portrait studio photographer **Mathew Brady** quickly organized a group of field photographers to make photographs under actual wartime conditions. On July 21, 1861, three months after the start of the Civil War, Brady and his cameraman Timothy O'Sullivan parked their photographic wagon on a bluff overlooking the Bull Run battlefield. The anticipated great Union victory turned into a calamitous retreat. Brady claimed to have made views of the battle and to have lost them in the chaotic flight.[9] Although his deteriorating eyesight is often cited as the reason he made few battlefield pho-

tographs, after Bull Run Brady rarely went to the front. Instead, he spent the war managing his New York studio and supervising 20 units of field photographers who amassed at least 7,000 negatives, the most complete coverage of a major event to date. Brady's approach supports traditional images of national identity etched in our consciousness by heroic narrative painting such as Emanuel Leutze's *Washington Crossing the Delaware* (1851). Brady's collection continues to capture our imagination, showing that the notion of freedom that became emblematic of the Union cause still persists in our culture in photographic exhibitions, books, and television and film portrayals of the Civil War.

Because the war lasted so long and casualties were so high, nobody wanted souvenir pictures after the struggle ended; they wanted to forget. Brady was financially ruined, though eventually the government awarded him $25,000 in recognition of his unique historical endeavor. Brady continued to make portraits in a small Washington, D.C., studio until the early 1890s, and he died in the poor ward of a New York hospital in 1896, partially blind and indigent, after being run over by a delivery wagon.

Alexander Gardner [1821–1882], a self-taught master of the wet-plate process, was in charge of Brady's Washington studio in 1861. With war imminent, he arranged for E. and H. T. Anthony & Company, the country's biggest dealer in photographic goods, to print and distribute pictures of officers and soldiers with the inscription "Brady's National Photographic Art Gallery." The mechanism for producing war hero pictures was thus set up before the fighting even started. Preparations

Execution of Lincoln Assassination Conspirators.

5.7   ALEXANDER GARDNER.   *The Four Condemned Conspirators (Surratt, Payne, Herold, Atzerodt) with Officers and Others on the Scaffold; Guards on the Wall, Washington, D.C.,* July 7, 1865. 6½ × 9⁷⁄₁₆ inches. From Album: "The Lincoln Conspiracy," 1865. Albumen silver print.   Courtesy George Eastman House.

for the war around Washington, D.C., were documented by the Brady team and published as part of a series called *Incidents of the War* that carried the credit line, "Photograph by Brady." These images were not considered to be news pictures due to the time lag between when they were taken and when they were seen. However, they were considered to be collectable, visual references.

Gardner joined General George McClellan's staff as a civilian photographer and made his first battle pictures of the carnage at Antietam in September 1862. These first photographs of battle corpses removed the society's prohibition against picturing actual war dead. Nobody in America had ever seen such unromantic war pictures. These inescapable records destroyed the myth of the beautiful battlefield death. Dead, bloated, broken, distorted, and decomposing bodies offer visceral

proof that war is not glorious. Whether by collusion or societal pressure, such disturbing death scenes were reproduced on only about six occasions in the illustrated press.[10] Oliver Wendell Holmes's response to Gardner's Antietam pictures explains why:

> It was so nearly like visiting the battlefield to look over these views, that all the emotions excited by the actual sight of the stained and sordid scene, strewed with rags and wrecks, came back to us, and we buried them in the recesses of our cabinet as we would have buried the mutilated remains of the dead they too vividly represented. Yet war and battles should have truth for their delineator.[11]

When Gardner's Antietam work was shown at Brady's New York Gallery, written about in the newspapers, and reproduced in *Harper's Weekly,* it was identified as Brady's, even though Gardner held the copyright. This custom, common in the early photographic studios, was frustrating to talented portrait photographers and infuriating for photographers who bore the dangers and hardships of the Civil War. By extensively publishing such images under his own name, Brady formed an association between his name and Civil War photography that endures to this day.

5.8   TIMOTHY O'SULLIVAN.   *A Harvest of Death, Gettysburg, PA,* 1863 (from *Gardner's Photographic Sketch Book of the War*). 6¼ × 7¹³⁄₁₆ inches. Albumen silver print. The *Sketch Book* removes the veneer of war pageantry and matter-of-factly reports: "The rebels represented in the photograph are without shoes. These were always removed from the feet of the dead on account of the pressing need of the survivors. The pockets are turned inside out also show that appropriation did not cease with the coverings of the feet. Around is scattered the litter of the battle-field, accountrements, ammunitions, rags, cups and canteens, crackers, haversacks, and letters that may tell the name of the owner, although the majority will surely be buried unknown by strangers, and in a strange land . . . they paid with life the price of their treason, and when the wicked strife was finished, found nameless graves, far from home kindred."[12]   Courtesy George Eastman House.

Asserting his independence from Brady, Gardner opened his own Washington studio in 1863. The majority of Brady's finest photographers, Timothy O'Sullivan, Egbert Fowx, T. C. Roche, and D. B. Woodbury, went to work for Gardner, who credited the maker of any picture he published. Gardner's practice acknowledged that photographic vision was not generic and that photographers did have a personal vision. Declaring that the photographic image was worthy of a signature elevated photography's status and declared that photographers should receive the same treatment as other visual artists.

The decisive land battle of the war was fought at Gettysburg from July 1 to July 3, 1863. It generated 51,000 casualties—dead, wounded, captured, or missing. Gardner, O'Sullivan, and James Gibson arrived at the battlefield on July 5 to photograph the bodies being gathered and moved for burial. Gardner constructed the photograph, *Home of a Rebel Sharpshooter,* for artistic effect (see Figure 5.5). He moved the body of a Confederate infantryman about forty yards and added a Springfield musket (not a sharpshooter's rifle) to the scene, and turned the corpse's face toward the camera, thus forcing the viewers to gaze directly into the tragedy of a violent and premature death.

Civil War photographers expanded the definition of photographic documentation. Technical limitations and thick battlefield smoke enforced a standard of accuracy different from today's. Photographic truthfulness was not only a question of picturing what chance placed before the camera, but of depicting the experience of war. Creating a field representation, rather than accepting only what could be recorded as it happened in front of the camera, was an inventive act. If a studio photographer's duty was to arrange the sitter for a specific effect, and if the resulting image was considered reality, then where were the boundaries of truthfulness when a photographer went outside the studio?

Nobody questioned Gardner's right to rebuild the scene for the camera. It was accepted as an accurate overall representation of that situation. This established a silent compact between the viewer and the photographer, giving the photographer license to adjust a

5.9   GEORGE BARNARD.   *Destruction of Hood's Ordinance Train, Atlanta*, 1864. 10 × 14 inches. Albumen silver print. Barnard's photograph is composed so that the track and wheels create a dynamic 45-degree angle, leading our eyes through the destruction into a sky whose clouds have been delicately printed in. This produces a paradox: the ethereal lightness of the clouds plays against the darker and starkly graphic landscape of annihilation.   Courtesy George Eastman House.

situation to deliver a truer, more complete sense of a subject. The "liberties" Gardner took reflected the upheavals within American society over truth and righteousness. Since the dawn of civilization, the concept of slavery had been accepted by most cultures, including America's. Lincoln's Gettysburg Address, in just 272 words, remade America by introducing the idea of equality, which is not actually stated in the U.S. Constitution. His speech—"That this nation under God shall have a new birth of freedom—and that government of the people by the people for the people shall not perish from the earth"—not only changed the direction of the Union cause, but altered the nation's political future by calling into question previously unchallenged concepts pertaining to individual freedom.

After 1863, Gardner rarely went into the field, acting instead as a producer for other photographers covering the war. At the conclusion of the war Gardner wrote, produced, and published a significant photographic chronicle of the conflict, *Gardner's Photographic Sketch Book of the War* (1866). Gardner's title, "sketch book," implies an artist's spontaneous reaction to selected subjects, not an exhaustive visual record. The book presents 100 pictures (from about 3,000 made by Gardner and his colleagues) together with interpretive text designed to provide a Northern, moralistic overview, characteristic of the entire conflict that speak of the cataclysmic repercussions of taking on an allegiance to an immoral crusade. It is the first extensive, thematic photo-essay, offering an astute, emotional view of the war, with the battle of Gettysburg as its nucleus. It was an expensive ($150) limited edition (200 copies), containing actual prints, designed to be sold to an elite audience.

The arrangement of the images and text reflected the feeling of many in the North. The blockade of Southern ports and the Confederacy's general economic straits greatly restricted the number of photographs made from the Southern perspective, giving the Union the historic advantage of having most of the surviving Civil War images represent a Northern point of view. Gardner inter-

5.10   ANDREW RUSSELL.   *Stone Wall, Rear of Fredericksburg, with Rebel Dead,* May 3, 1863. 9¹⁹⁄₃₂ × 13⅛ inches. Salt print. In this view we are confronted with the bloody face of a dead soldier, lying on his back in a shallow ditch, next to his rifle. Our sight line leads us down the ditch of crumpled, dead soldiers, compositionally reinforced by a parallel stone wall as far as we can see, suggesting an endless line of wrecked manhood.   Courtesy J. Paul Getty Museum, Los Angeles.

prets and manipulates the viewer's response with such words as "devilish," "distorted dead," "buried unknown by strangers, in a strange land," and "they paid with life the price of their treason" when referring to the Confederates. The parable of Old Testament justice for the insurgents can be seen in his descriptions of the Union dead as having "passed away in the act of prayer," with "a smile on their faces," "having friendly hands . . . prepared them for burial," and "appealing to heaven." The *Sketch Book* demonstrates that photography has never been impartial and that the history it presents is in part a construct of the photographer's imagination. The *Sketch Book* is as much an ethical literary allegory as it is historical documentation, relying on image sequencing and text to elucidate and supply meaning.

One of the last images in the *Sketch Book* is John Reekie's *A Burial Party*, Cold Harbor, VA, 1865, which pictures a group of freed slaves performing the grisly job of gathering up the remains of Union troops (see Figure 5.6). Reekie's focus is on the foreground, where a man sits next to a hospital litter that bears five skulls and a leg with a boot on top of a disgusting mix of decaying battle-ruined clothes and, ironically, a canteen. The postwar public did not have the stomach for such legend-breaking images and until recently this picture was not widely reproduced. In spite of its social importance, American painters rarely dealt with the Civil War. Audiences expected art to provide a remedy for the shadowy side of life and did not want to look at scenes of ghastly suffering. Photographic work like the *Sketch Book* broke down such notions by providing a ringside view of a fratricidal horror show.

The *Sketch Book* text reminds readers about the moral failings of the entire rebel cause; one that did not bury the dead. "It speaks ill of the residents of that part of Virginia, that they allowed even the remains of those they considered enemies, to decay unnoticed where they fell."[13]

Gardner also made portraits of President Lincoln and prison studies of Lincoln's assassination conspirators (*The Lincoln Conspiracy Album*). For their executions

5.11   WILLIAM BELL (OR STAFF).   *Gunshot Wound Middle Third of Left Femur,* 1866. 8 × 6⅞₁₆ inches. Albumen silver print.   Courtesy Gilman Paper Company.

Gardner set his camera on a roof overlooking the gallows and made a series of seven exposures (see Figure 5.7). This sequence is considered the first photographic picture story of an event that unfolds over actual time. It took on the dual photographic role of picturing the news and acting as a document. It also provides evidence of the vital function sequential photographs would perform in future news reporting. Gardner went on to photograph the Union Pacific Railroad, the Great Plains Indians and the Indian delegates to Congress, and a rogues gallery for the Washington, D.C., police before contracting tuberculosis and dying in 1882.

Timothy O'Sullivan [1840–1882] worked at Brady's Washington studio under Gardner's supervision before joining Gardner's staff in 1862. Civil War photographs, powerful as they may be, tend to have a sense of sameness about them. Their level, straight-on, maximum depth-of-field view, made at a genteel distance

from the subject, discourages us from thinking of a photographer as having personal impressions that direct our concentration to specific facets of a site. In the aftermath of Antietam and Gettysburg, O'Sullivan began breaking this precedent by incorporating intrinsically photographic forms, like selective focus, into compositions to elicit powerful corporeal responses. Gardner recognized O'Sullivan as sophisticated imagemaker and used forty-four of O'Sullivan's images in his *Sketch Book.*

In one such image, *A Harvest of Death* (see Figure 5.8), O'Sullivan presents sharply focused bloated bodies in the middleground while the foreground and background are explicitly out of focus. This uncommon practice has the macabre effect of centralizing our attention on a corpse whose mouth is open in an apparent death-scream. The visual rhythm of the arched corpses produces a sense of trepidation that visually echoes into the surrounding landscape. The highly expressionistic selective focus actively manipulates our concentration to re-experience O'Sullivan's sense of amazement, horror, and motionlessness. Such methods encourage the audience to fasten onto subjective sensations rather than concentrating on analytical facts.

O'Sullivan executed the same selective focus technique in *Field Where General Reynolds Fell,* in which the swollen corpses are not only the subject of the composition but are the only objects in critical focus. This view and the title inform us that the field where General Reynolds was killed is significant and worthy of depiction. In terms of social status it is noteworthy that General Reynolds's body is nowhere to be seen, as he was no doubt given a prompt and proper burial. As for the five ballooning bodies so sharply pictured in the frame, they are the classic unknown soldiers. The image questions the notion of the romantic last hurrah by showing us the anonymous, undignified deaths of the everyday soldiers, buried where they fell with their stories untold.

George N. Barnard [1819–1902] opened his first studio in Oswego, NY, in 1846 and moved to New York City about 1859 to make stereographic views for E. & H. T. Anthony and to work in Brady's portrait studios. When the war broke out Barnard began to make views for Brady and later for Gardner, often working with James F. Gibson. In 1864 he became a Union army photographer in a division commanded by General William Tecumseh Sherman and recorded the destruction of Atlanta by Federal troops (see Figure 5.9). In November 1866 Barnard issued his *Photographic Views of*

5.12 A. J. RIDDLE. *Manner in Which Dead Were Buried at Andersonville Prison, GA.* 7⅜ × 4⁷⁄₁₆ inches. 19th century copy print. One of the most dreadful albums was made by A. J. Riddle at the Andersonville, GA, prison for captured Union soldiers. This image shows a group of men with Captain Wirz, the camp commander in the center, standing alongside a four-foot-deep trench lined with bodies, laid side by side. The caption informs us that this was the manner in which the dead were buried at Andersonville. The Andersonville album appears as a premonition of Nazi concentration camps and conjures up the inhumane conditions that led to the camp commander's trial, conviction, and hanging as a war criminal. The execution was photographed by A. J. Russell.   Courtesy George Eastman House.

Sherman's Campaign, a limited-edition book (about 100 copies) of 61 original 10 × 14-inch prints that sold for $100.

Barnard's images possess a serenity that projects a sense of sadness and loss. After the soldiers left the battle sites, Barnard often returned to the empty fields to record their sense of tranquility that, paradoxically, evoked the tempestuous nature of the fray. The ferociousness of battle is vicariously experienced in *The Hell Hole, New Hope Church, GA,* picturing trees that were shot down during combat. The tormented landscape replaces the mutilated soldiers' bodies, expressing the social rupture of war. The credit line ironically reads: "Photograph from nature by G. N. Barnard." This sense of calm after the passing tempest can also be seen in *Ruins in Charleston, SC,* as two men, one with a pipe, sit seemingly contemplating the rubble that was once the city.

Barnard relied on symbolic devices and pictorial effect for emotional impact. In *Scene of General McPherson's Death,* a horse's skull, human bones, and pieces of explosive shot were arranged, depicting death in a more allegorical manner than Gardner's *Home of a Rebel Sharpshooter.* Barnard's use of combination printing—making separate cloud negatives and printing them into the sky portion of the original landscape — indicates that his photographs were not meant to be read as war news, but as personal, artistic statements about the war. In *Rebel Works in Front of Atlanta,* the clouds are heavily printed into a depopulated view. They blend into the tops of the moving trees (blurred due to the long exposure time) and feel as though their celestial forms dare not get any closer or risk being punctured by the rows of *chevaux-de-frise* (logs with fixed sharpened wooden stakes) that form the trench lines and palisades of hell.

Andrew Joseph Russell [1830–1902] was a Union captain assigned to document the work of Herman Haupt, an innovative engineer known for his experiments in transporting troops and for the construction, repair, and destruction of railroads and bridges. Russell was an experienced artist and photographer, who emphasized pictorial qualities even when making didactic pictures.[14] As Russell's audience was the officers of the Corps of Engineers, he had no commercial restraints, and he was able to make stereo views from unusually low angles and some battlefield photographs featuring atypical close-ups of dead soldier's faces (see Figure 5.10).

1865   The War For the Union.   1861
1861   Photographic War History.   1865

2594.   A Group of "Contrabands."
[FOR DESCRIPTION OF THIS VIEW SEE THE OTHER SIDE OF THIS CARD.]

5.13 UNKNOWN PHOTOGRAPHER. *Contrabands.* 6⅝ × 8⅞ inches. Albumen silver stereo card. In conjunction with their text, stereo views provide a contextual window for understanding prevailing social attitudes. Northern racial stereotypes are on view in *Contrabands* as seven black men, all wearing hats and tattered clothes, are pictured standing in front of a shanty. The text reads: "The negroes who ran away from slavery and came into the union lines, were employed by the government as teamsters, laborers, and c[ontrabands]. They were happy, good-natured fellows, and made lots of fun for the soldiers." Courtesy George Eastman House.

The number of Civil War casualties created an unparalleled demand for medical care in an era when diseases were little understood and surgical procedures primitive. To increase medical effectiveness the Surgeon General established the Army Medical Museum in 1862 to analyze military medicine. Photography played a new role, as the Museum established its own photographic department headed by **William Bell** (active 1861–1872). The editor of the *Philadelphia Photographer* gave this account of Bell's activities:

> [T]he principal work of the photographer is to photograph shattered bones, broken skulls, and living subjects, before and after surgical operations have been performed on them. . . . We saw a picture of one poor fellow as he came from the field, with his face almost torn asunder by a shell. After surgery had exercised its skill upon him, he was again photographed, and looked much better than any one could be expected to look with his lower jaw gone.[15]

The Museum's photographers re-photographed patients whose conditions were being monitored, in one of the first such projects. These images are different than the war views. They are often close-up, extremely deadpan examinations of broken bodies against a neutral background (see Figure 5.11). The pictures document injuries with cool detachment and label them with baffling professional jargon that does not provide the layperson with any context to understand what has happened. The combination separates cause and effect, removing the ruined bodies from their warfare context. When we look at these grim pictures there is no correlation between the shattered men and the war that caused their condition. This distancing effect reinforces the fact that the bodies are no longer sites of beauty, fashion, joy, or pleasure, but of disfigurement, ugliness, suffering, and pain.

How Photographs Were Circulated

Carte portraits of individual soldiers were much in demand and made up the bulk of photographic work during the war years. These inexpensive cards were not intended as artistic portraits, but to impartially preserve the likeness of a soldier going off to war. War scene cartes, sold by subscription and collected in albums, established a precedent for marketing future disasters, from the Johnstown flood of 1889 to the San Francisco earthquake and fire of 1906. By the war's end, the pop-

5.14 UNKNOWN PHOTOGRAPHER. *Dead Union Soldier on Field at Gettysburg Showing Effect of a Shell,* 1863. 12 × 9⁹⁄₁₆ inches. Albumen silver print. "Authentic" Civil War photographs were constructed, often with text, to justify the maker's point of view, producing a prototypical, matter-of-fact American style of strict, unadorned plainness that killed off the heroic ideal of military painting. Courtesy George Eastman House.

ularity of these paper prints had finished the ambrotype, which was too fragile to be sent through the mail. The mailing of cartes was so common that the Federal government imposed a tax stamp, requiring a two-cent stamp for card-size photographs sent through the mail, between September 1, 1864 and August 1, 1866.

The majority of field views were made with stereographic cameras, as they were lighter than view cameras and used smaller plates, which were easier to prepare, thus allowing operators to work more quickly and make more photographs. The first true combat photographs were stereoviews taken in Fort Sumter by Southern photographer George S. Cook.[16] The selling of Civil War stereo cards was a big business fraught with unauthorized copying.[17] By the war's end, Ed-

ward Anthony's catalog listed more than 1,400 stereo views selling at $4.50 a dozen. Along with ambrotypes, tintypes, and photographically derived wood engravings in popular magazines, such as *Harper's Weekly* and *Leslie's Illustrated,* the endless, inexpensive supply of paper prints made the Civil War the first conflict to be brought directly into people's parlors.

What does the sum of these wartime experiences add up to? Did the photographers believe that their war pictures might reduce the chance of its recurrence? There is not much photographic evidence that they had such feelings. A line of text that accompanies O'Sullivan's *A Harvest of Death* in Gardner's *Sketch Book* is an exception. It reads: "Here are the dreadful details! Let them aid in preventing such another calamity falling upon the nation."[18] In general, photographers seem to have accepted war as part of life. The war photographs are not so much evidence of history as they are themselves history. They reveal that the camera is not an impartial observer, but a human-guided tool that makes contrived and coded images that need to be interpreted. They show us how photographs are in flux, their meanings constantly reinvented and used for contrasting purposes depending on what the photographer wants to represent. The Civil War moved photography out of the studio and into the field, demonstrating that photographs could perform other functions in addition to making portraits. The formation of private, for-profit, photographic corps gave photographers rigorous, hands-on training for the government surveying expeditions of the uncharted territories between the Great Plains and the Pacific Coast that resumed after the war.

Although the demand for portraits was very high, public exposure to war views remained limited, as there was yet no direct way to reproduce a photographic image in a newspaper or magazine. The images that were published had to be translated through woodcuts, which significantly altered them. The depicted horrors of warfare were thus only truly seen by a few people at the time, so that in all likelihood they had little impact on public sentiment. Their power and influence built up over time in their use as historical documents for future generations of viewers.

Endnotes

1   John Burnet's *A Treatise on Painting: In Four Parts . . .* (1822), had an impact on early photographic picturemaking. It remained in print through W.W. I.

2   See James M. Reilly, *Care and Identification of 19th Century Photographic Prints* (Rochester, NY: Eastman Kodak Publication No. G-25, 1986).

3   Problems of image deterioration affect today's viewers of nineteenth-century prints. Albumen prints are predisposed to *yellowing,* which occurs in direct proportion to the thickness of the albumen layer, and to *foxing,* a type of paper staining characterized by blotchy, reddish-brown patches, often circular or irregular in shape. These conditions alter the aesthetic quality of the print and can affect the quantity and quality of discernible information.

4   Quoted in Helmut and Alison Gernsheim, *Roger Fenton: Photographer of the Crimean War* (London: Secker & Warburg, 1954), 64–65.

5   Quoted in Lena R. Fenton, "The First Photographer at the Crimea in 1855," *Illustrated London News,* vol. 92 (1941), 590.

6   Roger Fenton to William Agnew, April 19, 1855; Ibid, 62.

7   Alexander Gardner, *Gardner's Photographic Sketch Book of the Civil War* (New York: Dover Publications, 1959), unp. (Plate 41). Reprint that combines volume 1 and volume 2 of the original and adds the word "Civil" to the title for purposes of clarification.

8   E. B. Long with Barbara Long, *The Civil War Day By Day: An Almanac 1861–1865* (New York: Doubleday and Co., 1971; reprint (New York: Da Capo Press, 1985), 705–12.

9   See William F. Stapp, "Subjects of Strange . . . and of Fearful Interest," in Marianne Fulton, *Eyes of Time* (Boston, Toronto, and London: Little, Brown and Company, 1988), 16.

10   William A. Frassanito, *Grant and Lee: The Virginia Campaigns 1864–1865* (New York: Charles Scribner's Sons, 1983), 342–43.

11   Oliver Wendell Holmes, "Doing of the Sunbeam," *The Atlantic Monthly* 12 (July 1863), 1–15. As reprinted in Beaumont Newhall, *Photography: Essays & Images* (New York: Museum of Modern Art, 1980), 73.

12   Gardner, unp. (Plate 36).

13   Gardner, unp. (Plate 94).

14   Haupt distributed thousands of Russell's photographs to political and military leaders to secure continued support for his work. A limited edition album was put together for engineers and generals to instruct and promote ingenious solutions to complex, practical, technological problems.

15   *Philadelphia Photographer,* vol., 3, n. 31 (July 1866), 214.

16   Bob Zeller, *The Civil War in Depth: History in 3-D* (San Francisco: Chronicle Books, 1997), 65–67.

17   The backside of Brady's Album Gallery war cards carried this admonition: "The photographs of this series were taken directly from nature, at considerable cost. Warning is therefore given that legal proceeding will be at once instituted against any party infringing the copyright."

18   Gardner, unp. (Plate 36).

CHAPTER SIX

A New Medium of Communication

Art or Industry?

The introduction of the wet-plate process and the relaxation of Talbot's patent restrictions led to an explosive increase in the number of people making their living in photography.[2] During the 1850s, some of England's most notable photographers, including Roger Fenton, Robert Howlett, and Henry Peach Robinson, abandoned their amateur status and turned professional. Photography had become a business with a widening division of purpose between amateurs and professionals. The professionals were motivated by market forces to produce salable products. The amateurs pursued their personal inclinations and claimed the moral high ground of art, beauty, and truth, relegating the professionals to the corner of crass commercialism. The professionals perceived the amateurs as elitists who ignored the basic photographic needs of the majority of people. Amateur groups, such as the Royal Photographic Society of London,

JULIA MARGARET CAMERON. *Sir John Herschel,* 1867. 12 × 9½ inches. Albumen silver print. Courtesy George Eastman House.

"When I have such men before my camera my whole soul has endeavored to do its duty towards them in recording faithfully the greatness of the inner as well as the features of the outer man. The photograph thus taken has been almost the embodiment of prayer."[1]

6.1   HONORÉ DAUMIER.   *Nadar Raising Photography to the Height of Art*, 1862. 5³⁄₁₆ × 4 inches. Lithograph.   Courtesy George Eastman House.

championed their role as keepers-of-the-flame whose duty was to pursue photography for the sake of photography. The publication of Sir William Newton's article, "Upon Photography in an Artistic View" (1853), brought to a boil the issues surrounding the purpose of photography (see Chapter 3). Was photography the handmaiden of art or could it be an art unto itself? Was it a technical process or did it possess its own syntax that set it apart from other mediums? Was photography's purpose to objectively reproduce what was before the camera or could it be controlled for artistic concerns?

Some well-educated people viewed photography as an upstart whose popularity and commercialization threatened the position of high art. They believed photographers were failed artists who were mere slaves to reproducing the natural appearance of their subjects, and doubted whether the process could be manipulated to create works based on inner feelings and thoughts. Charles Baudelaire [1821–1867], the French symbolist poet who claimed to hate having his picture made (but

had it made anyway by a number of photographers), summed up this position in a diatribe on the role of photography in the arts and society and the public's lack of imagination—its failure to critically think and question the world in which it lives—a situation that he blamed on the ascendance of science and mechanical inventions. Baudelaire wrote:

> Since photography gives us every guarantee of exactitude that we could desire (they really believe that, the mad fools!), then photography and Art are the same thing. From that moment our squalid society rushed, Narcissus to a man, to gaze at its trivial image on a scrap of metal. As the photographic industry was the refuge of every would-be painter, every painter too ill-endowed or too lazy to complete his studies, this universal infatuation bore not only the mark of a blindness, an imbecility, but had also the air of a vengeance. . . . It is time, then, for it to return to its true duty, which is to be the servant of the sciences and the arts—but a very humble servant, like printing or shorthand which have neither created nor supplemented literature. . . . let it be the secretary and clerk of whoever needs an absolute factual exactitude in his profession. . . . But if it be allowed to encroach upon the domain of the impalpable and the imaginary, upon anything whose value depends solely upon the addition of something of a man's soul, then it will be so much the worse for us![3]

Not everyone thought photography was bound up by its technical limits. **Lady Elizabeth Eastlake** [1809–1893], married to Sir Charles Eastlake [1793–1865], the Director of the National Gallery of Art in London and first president of the Photographic Society of London, published an early, unsigned history of photography, offering an astute appraisal of the medium's position in relation to art. After indexing photography's inadequacies when compared with painting, she dismissed the position taken by critics like Baudelaire as "mistaken" and described photography's future as an autonomous "new medium of communication," Eastlake wrote:

> The broader the ground which the machine may occupy, the higher will that of the intelligent agent be found to stand. If, therefore, the time should ever come when art is sought, as it ought to be, mainly for its own sake, our artists and our patrons will be of a far more elevated order than now: and if anything can bring about so desirable a climax, it will be the introduction of Photography.[4]

A turning point in photography's quest to be recognized as an independent medium occurred in 1861 when the French studio of Mayer and Pierson accused another studio, Betbeder and Schwabbe, of unauthorized copying, claiming their celebrity photographs were protected under French copyright laws that

6.2 EUGÈNE DURIEU. *Reclining Nude,* ca, 1855.
6⅞ × 9⅜ inches. Salted paper print. Some painters, including Dante Gabriel Rossetti, made use of photography without publicly acknowledging its influence.[5]
Others, such as Eugène Delacroix [1798–1863], saw
photography as advantageous to drawing and painting.
Delacroix was a leader of the *Romantic Movement* that
rejected classical formalism and emphasized artistic
imagination featuring the dramatic, emotional, and personal, often through the use of historic and/or exotic
subject matter. Delacroix posed nude models for Eugène Durieu to photograph and then enthusiastically
used these photographs as source material. Delacroix
claimed that looking at photographs provided him a
greater understanding about the human body than the
inventions of any "scribbler."[6] Courtesy George Eastman
House.

satirist Honoré Daumier released *Nadar Raising
Photography to the Height of Art,* a lithograph featuring
Nadar in his balloon, taking pictures above Paris, in
which every building was labeled with the word "Photography" (see Figure 6.1). A group of artists, fearful of
the effects this decision would have on their profession,
signed a petition objecting to the appeal court's decision, which the court rejected. Photography was held to
be the product of thought and spirit, of taste and intelligence, and to bear the imprint of the individual personality; therefore, it could legally be considered a legitimate art. Mayer and Pierson published *La photographie* (1862), a book on aesthetics and technique that
proclaimed the importance of the photograph. That
same year André Disderi brought out *L'Art de la Photographie,* in which he discussed the artistic controls
available to photographers and compared his studio
methods to those of contemporary painters, proclaiming the camera could be controlled like a painter's
brush. The joining of photographic form to the arts was
officially underway.

applied to the arts. To be covered under these laws,
photography had to first be declared an art. In early
1862, the court ruled against Mayer and Pierson. Later
that year, however, the court declared on appeal that
photography was indeed an art and entitled to legal protection. After the second decision, the artist and social

As Lady Eastlake noted, one of the major obstacles
blocking the recognition of photography as art was
the wet plate's insensitivity to all parts of the spectrum except blue and ultraviolet radiation, which

6.3   WILLIAM LAKE PRICE.   *Don Quixote in His Study,* ca. 1855. Albumen silver print. The simplest way for photography to appear artistic was to take on the trappings of painting. William Lake Price [1810–1896], a watercolor painter, took this literal approach by dressing up his subjects in the style of the Royal Academicians. The problem with this imitative manner is that it did not go past the surface appearance and explore photography's innate language.   Courtesy Gernsheim Collection, Humanities Research Center, University of Texas at Austin.

gave colors an inaccurate translation into black-and-white tones.[7] Red or green subjects were not properly recorded and appeared in prints as black. Exposures, calculated to record detail in the land, overexposed the sky. The amount of overexposure was not even and produced areas of low density in the negative. When the negative was printed these sections appeared gray and mottled, an effect not suitable for picturesque landscapes.

There were two ways to correct the problem. The first was to outline the horizon area of a negative with opaque paint and cut a mat to cover the sky portion of the negative. This resulted in a print with an open, solid white sky that was still unpicturesque. The artistic solution was to make a *combination print* that was complicated, time-consuming, and expensive. It involved making two separate negatives, one for the ground and a second for the sky. After processing they were masked, with the land's features printed in from the first negative and the sky's from the second. Landscape photographers often made a stock collection of sky negatives, which were used in printing future views. Gustave Le Gray's seascapes were considered spectac-

6.4   UNKNOWN PHOTOGRAPHER.   *Untitled,*
[Girl in a black dress holding a small white dog], ca.
1850s. Calotype.   Courtesy George Eastman House.

ular for not only stopping the action of waves but for
their dramatic cloud formations, achieved from separately made cloud negatives. Le Gray's work demonstrated that photographers could translate feelings into
their work and control their medium just as other artists
did. Oscar G. Rejlander's allegorical work, *Two Ways
of Life* (see Figure 6.9), so clearly verified the artistic
potential of combination printing that it became an accepted practice.

The practice of hand-applying color overcame photography's lack of color. Alfred H. Wall promoted the
practice in his *Manual of artistic colouring as applied
to photographs* (1861). Wall, a former miniature and
portrait painter, said that painting over a photograph
was no more unacceptable than painters such as
Leonardo and Titian painting over the *abbozzo*.[8] Wall
complained that artists repudiated colored photographs
because they were not paintings and that photographers
rejected them because they were not true photographs.
He saw no reason for censuring work that combined
"the truth of the one with the loveliness of the other."
Composite and hand-colored images took time and deft
handwork. The additional time was seen as a way to
make photography less mechanical and more artistic.
This in turn increased a photograph's value and encouraged photographers to portray subjects previously reserved for painters.

6.5   UNKNOWN PHOTOGRAPHER (British).
Windsor Park, Virginia Waters. ca. 1865. 8⁵⁄₁₆ × 10¹⁄₁₆
inches. Albumen silver print. The orderly picturing of
nature was a prominent topic in Exchange Club work.
Windsor Park, Virginia Waters shows an idyllic English
country scene. The elegant suburban park presents life
as a "view." The river, the waterfalls, the lawn, the boat,
and the stylishly dressed women give the impression
that nature has been subdued. The tall, sharply focused
trees on the left side of the composition are juxtaposed
against the blurry trees in the background. The calm
hills offer a sense of aerial perspective. The lavish presentation of lights and darks, the balance between spa-
cious effect and detail, provide the sense of a romantic
painting.   Courtesy George Eastman House.

Discovering a
Photographic Language

During the mid-nineteenth century *realism* became
a force in the arts.[9] Realism sought to counter the idealized subject matter of Romantic and Neoclassical
painting with direct and frank views of everyday life.
The first Realist exhibition was organized by Gustave
Courbet [1819–1877], who used the camera for nude
studies in paintings, in protest against the rejection of
his works by the Academy. As the public became acquainted with photography's veracity and ability to
give significance to everyday experiences, their expectations about how reality should be represented
and what subjects were worthy of depiction changed.
Confusingly, photographs were considered more
artistic when they looked less photographic, and retouching methods were developed that made a photograph resemble a painting. Paintings, on the other
hand, were thought to be more artistic if they featured

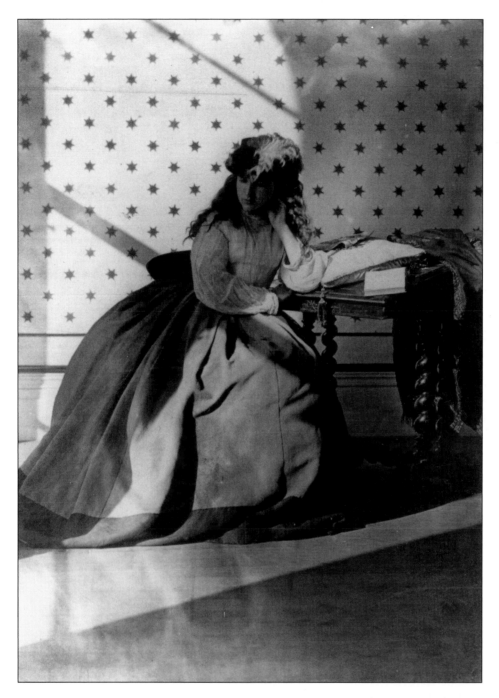

6.6   LADY CLEMENTINA HAWARDEN.
Photographic Study, early 1860s. 7⅞ × 5⅝ inches. Albumen silver print. Courtesy Gilman Paper Company Collection, N.Y.

"photographic" detail. This paradox resulted in neither medium being valued for its own inherent characteristics.

To enhance the artistic value of their work, educated photographers looked to the painterly style of the *symbolic, narrative allegory,* the figurative treatment of one subject under the appearance of another. Their subjects often appeared as representations of abstract moral and/or spiritual qualities, related as a fable or parable. The *Pre-Raphaelites,* a brotherhood of English painters and poets founded by Dante Gabriel Rossetti in 1848 to protest the low standards of British art, reacted against the material world of industrializing England and embraced the beauty and simplicity of the medieval world through symbolism; they were a major influence on photographers with artistic aspirations. This initial process of imitating accepted artistic styles put photographers on track to discovering their medium's own bona fide artistic characteristics.

Amateur calotypists realized that the calotype's inherent "imperfections" also provided a key to unlock its innate strengths. This reinforced the discoveries of Hill

6.7   LADY FILMER.   *Untitled*, circa 1864. 11¼ × 9
inches. Watercolor with collaged photographs.   Courtesy University Art Museum, University of New Mexico, Albuquerque, NM.

and Adamson's genre work that connected a subject
with the space around it and amplified its distinct identity. With the inclination, time, and resources to experiment, amateur calotypists saw that the beauty and
power of their calotypes came from their broad, soft,
grainy portrayals, where the human figure can be perceived as form and mass. The professionals favored the
detail that the wet-plate system offered even though it
required methodical planning that discouraged spontaneity. The calotypist could make a negative in ten
minutes, whereas the wet-plate maker needed an hour,

reducing the likelihood the wet-plate photographer
would serendipitously make pictures. A wet plate was
also more expensive, and if a plate did not deliver the
expected result, a photographer would scrape the
emulsion off and reuse the glass. Calotypists, in contrast, were stuck with their mistakes because the paper
negative was not reusable, which gave them time to reflect on these accidental happenings. Many such accidental negatives were printed to see what the photographic process had revealed. These fresh and unique
camera-regulated ways of seeing that also incorporated
unexpected, chance occurrences into the visual outcome, offered an alternative to natural vision and Renaissance models for portraying the world.

A homemade portrait album from the 1850s by an
unidentified photographer (probably English) shows us
the family pictures of a well-to-do amateur who seemed

6.8   LEWIS CARROLL.   *Irene MacDonald*, 1863. Albumen silver print. 5⅝ × 7½ inches   Courtesy Gernsheim Collection, Humanities Research Center, University of Texas at Austin.

aware of posing strategies used by other calotypists, including Talbot. Mixed in with the formalistic concerns of composition and light is an unmistakable *snapshot impulse*. We see what has become the traditional snapshot subject matter of family and home: a slightly blurry, smiling little girl with her doll, looking directly into the camera; a mother and her baby; a mother with her son and his grandmother; a close-up portrait of the family dog; a group portrait of mother, father, and six children. One photograph (see Figure 6.4) is of a girl in a black dress holding her small, moving white dog, which has turned into a multiplasmic ghost. Such early family albums capture and relay a sense of everydayness and commemorate these previously undepicted scenes.

The structure already existed in Europe for clubs of upper-class amateurs that provided a sense of community, organization, and common purpose. (American photographers had to rely on photographic magazines to communicate as photo clubs did not evolve in the States until the advent of the hand camera in the 1880s.) The

British *Exchange Club* membership featured prominent practitioners such as Roger Fenton, Oscar Rejlander, William Lake Price, and William Newton, and women such as Lady Caroline Nevill, Lady Augusta Mostyn, and Mary E. Lynn. A jury would select picturesque landscapes, still lifes, genre scenes, exotic foreign subjects, historic sites, and allegorical compositions from the membership for an annual album.[10] To meet the increasing demand to learn photography, King's College, the University of London, became the first site of higher learning to offer photography in December 1856. By the start of the 1860s, there were at least twenty-four different photographic societies in Great Britain. Some, such as the Amateur Photographic Association (1861–1905), mounted exhibits of up to a thousand photographs. The images, often in ornate frames, were squeezed onto the wall from the floor to the ceiling, forcing viewers to assume an "all fours" position to see some of the pictures. This dense-pack style of presentation continued through the end of the century.

Amateurs pushed the boundaries of accepted practice and explored a more personal style of expression than the commercial studios. Rejecting the genteel and preordained poses of the commercial studio in favor of a more active image, they pictured a wider range of

6.9   OSCAR G. REJLANDER.   *Two Ways of Life,*
1857. 16 × 31 inches. Albumen silver print.   Courtesy
Royal Photographic Society, Bath, England.

facial expressions and postures. One such amateur,
Lady Clementina Hawarden [1822–1865], working
with family and friends, provides glimpses into the dynamics of the intimate female world of the well-to-do
Victorians where passion is kept hidden. Through the
languor that surrounds Hawarden's restrained subjects,
viewers search the frame for a trace of desire.

Another amateur, **Lady Filmer** [1840–1903], made
early collages that combined carte-de-visite portraits
with watercolor designs of butterflies and floral
arrangements (see Figure 6.7). These pieces, with their
occasional sexual allusions, reveal a pre-Freudian spirit
of *unconscious association,* aspects of mental life not
subject to recall at will, that could only be expressed in
pictures—the language for such a discussion did not
exist at the time. Photographic montage allowed people
of various levels of artistic skill to take everyday events
and reorient them in time and space. This positioned
photography as a medium that invited artists to delve in
the free association, cut and paste world of dreams, enabling the unconscious, repressed residue of socially
unacceptable desires and experiences to come to conscious recognition.

Lewis Carroll, the pseudonym of Reverend Charles
Lutwidge Dodgson [1832–1898], began making photographs in 1856 that mirror the concerns he wrote
about in his Victorian fantasy novels *Alice's Adventures
in Wonderland* (1865) and *Through the Looking Glass*
(1872). Carroll's adroitness in the company of prepubescent girls enabled him to compose images revealing

their natural sense of dexterity and intuitive spontaneity. Influenced by the Pre-Raphaelites ideals of feminine innocence and virgin beauty, Carroll's images
probed beneath the surface of the sitter, and have come
to play a role in creating our conception of Victorian
childhood. Carroll's preference for moralizing works
also led him to endow his childhood sitters with his
own adult, melancholic emotional and sexual dilemmas
(see Figure 6.8). Criticized for photographing young
girls in the nude (Victorians rarely made the distinction
between poetic representations and pornography), Carroll destroyed those negatives that he said "so utterly
defied convention."

Oscar Gustave Rejlander [1813–1875] learned the
basics of photography one afternoon in 1853 in order to
make studies for his paintings. Within two years he had
opened a photographic portrait studio. In 1857 the influential Manchester Art Treasures Exhibition allowed
photographs to be displayed alongside painting, drawing, sculpture, and engraving for the first time, signaling
an acceptance of artistic photographs. This was a breakthrough, as photography was often shown in segregated
categories under industrial, scientific, and technical
headings. Victorians regarded the camera as a machine,
with its own diagnostic and interpretive capabilities,
and its practitioners as scientists and technicians first,
artists second (if artists at all). As the standards for artistic photography were based on painting, the sharp, mechanical literalness of the photograph was considered a
hindrance in achieving high art. To overcome this obstacle photographers began to use second-rate optics,
smear their lens, or kick the tripod during exposure to
suppress photographic sharpness. Finally, in order to
compete with allegorical painting, photographers' work

6.10 OSCAR G. REJLANDER. *The Bachelor's Dream*, 1860. 5⁸⁄₁₆ × 7⁷⁄₁₆ inches. Albumen silver print. Is this image a parody of the hoop craze, a moralistic allegory on the fruitlessness of striving, or is it a pre-Freudian blending of the masculine and feminine selves? Could the climbing figures represent the different levels of the mind? Are the two upside-down figures celebrating, or have they "fallen" after reaching the pinnacle? Do we climb to the top only to discover that "it" can't be understood with the rational mind?
Courtesy George Eastman House.

had to be morally uplifting and instructive. This was accomplished by constructing complex *tableaux,* an arrangement of persons and/or objects to form a scene. This style of working allowed photographers to overcome photography's mechanical status and circumvent the technical limits of the wet plate. Rejlander set out to create a photograph requiring "the same operations of mind, the same artistic treatment and careful manipulation"[11] as works done in crayon or paint.

Rejlander produced an elaborate allegorical piece contrasting Philosophy and Science. *The Two Ways of Life* is a marvel of combination printing. During a six-week period Rejlander did sketches, hired models, and made thirty separate negatives which he masked, printed on two pieces of paper, and connected. This work was rephotographed, and editions were reproduced. The photograph's unusually large size, 16 × 31 inches, made people stop and notice, enabling it to hold its own on a gallery wall. *The Two Ways* represents "a venerable sage introducing two young men into life—the one, calm and placid, turns towards Religion, Charity and Industry, and the other virtues, while the other rushes madly from his guide into the pleasures of the world, typified by various figures, representing Gambling, Wine, Licentiousness and other vices; ending in Suicide, Insanity and Death. The center of the picture, in front, between two parties, is a splendid figure symbolizing Repentance, with the emblem of Hope."[12]

Two Ways did not sell well and provoked debate on the ethics of combining negatives to manufacture an image that never existed, marking an early instance of critical thinking about the medium. The picture's detractors claimed it was a violation of the "true nature" of photography; works of "high art" could not be accomplished by "mechanical contrivances."[13] In the Victorian age, when piano legs were costumed with pantaloons, the photographic nudity of *Two Ways* was shocking.[14] The process of combination printing led to the first photographic montages designed for a public audience, providing a

as a necromancer

6.11   R. C. LUCAS.   *A Necromancer,* from *Studies of Expression.* Albumen silver print. Following the lead of British artist and sculptor R. C. Lucas who made a series of role-playing self-portraits, Rejlander used himself to catalog human emotional responses before the camera in *Studies of Expression* (1865). These became well-known when they appeared as illustrations in Charles Darwin's *The Expression of the Emotions in Man and Animals* (1872). Rejlander also made children's portraits, attracting the notice of Lewis Carroll and Julia Margaret Cameron.   Courtesy George Eastman House.

prove artistic eloquence and public taste, and that "what makes an artist is not the process but the feeling."[15]

Photography as a fine art also faced resistance from art dealers who saw photography as a threat to their investments and sought to keep photographs out of their galleries. Rejlander complained that "picture-dealers are, or have been, from interested motives, the greatest opponents to photography."[16] But even as photography was being denounced, the very fact that important minds, such as Baudelaire's, were critically discussing the medium increased its credibility, importance, and visibility. The rise of photography as an art form would transform art's traditional function of portraying reality. This encouraged artists to explore new directions that eventually included *abstraction,* in which the concept of art as imitation of nature was abandoned. Rejlander's efforts have been criticized as being "imitations," yet they were a necessary step in expanding the boundaries of photographic practice, inspiring others to enlarge photography's dialogue and role. The artistic criticism and financial hardships took their toll on Rejlander, however, who only made a few more combination prints; none of them approached the polemic nature and scale of *The Two Ways.*

Rejlander produced numerous formula-driven portraits, but he also created other images that broke with accepted working practice. *Hard Times* (1860) made conscious use of double exposure, converting an error into an authentic photographic form, one not based on painting's prescriptions. In *The Bachelor's Dream* (Figure 6.10), which resembles no other photograph from that time, Rejlander grapples with visualizing a mental impression by incorporating the fashionable woman's skirt hoop into the composition. Its phantomlike qualities blend fantasy and reality, raising questions and providing no answers. The photograph invites viewers to interpret it, challenging the audience to think about and question whether photography can convey complex intellectual thoughts.

Henry Peach Robinson [1830–1901] was a painter who took up photography in 1852 and opened a photographic portrait studio five years later. Rejlander's *The Two Ways of Life* inspired Robinson to undertake combination printing. In 1858, Robinson exhibited *Fading Away* (see Figure 6.12), made from five negatives, showing a young girl on her deathbed with her grieving mother, sister, and fiancé. By Victorian standards this sorrowful scene was scandalously morbid as it did not conform to accepted ideas about what photography

refreshing set of representational possibilities. Since it questioned established viewing rules, many felt threatened and rejected the new way of picturemaking. The concept that art was a matter of ideas and not limited to specific practices was given voice by the French naturalist Louis Figuier, who believed photography could im-

6.12   HENRY PEACH ROBINSON.   *Fading Away*,
1858. 9⅝ × 15⅛ inches. Albumen silver print.   Courtesy George Eastman House.

should picture. Far more distressful scenes were
painted, but because *Fading Away* was a photograph
people perceived it as a literal representation. In an age
when death was not hidden away, most people were familiar with such scenes. After Robinson revealed that
his primary model "was a fine healthy girl of about
fourteen, and the picture was done to see how near
death she could be made to look,"[17] the work was criticized for being manufactured.

The combination prints of Rejlander and Robinson
challenged the belief that painters alone had the right to
create scenes while photographers could never be more
than mere mechanical extensions of their equipment.
For photography to make its way in the art world it had
to debunk such limiting ideas. Robinson championed
combination printing as Prince Albert purchased *Fading Away* and gave Robinson a standing order for every
pictorial image he created. Once audiences overcame
the shock of the combination print, they accepted it, realizing that Robinson's fundamental ideology embraced their notions of art. This made Robinson the
most popular, emulated, and well-to-do photographer
of the second half of the nineteenth century. Robinson's
books and articles energetically articulated his position
and influenced the development of future photographers. His *Pictorial Effect in Photography* (1869),

which advocated the basic canons of painting, "composition and chiaroscuro," as the "guiding laws" of an art
photograph,[18] was the most widely read photography
textbook of the nineteenth century.[19]

Robinson sought methods for uniting the rational
with the subjective, to allow photographers to achieve
the picturesque. He believed that combination printing
gave "much greater liberty to the photographer and
much greater facilities for representing the nature of nature."[20] Critics were outraged by Robinson's constructed images for violating their sense of photographic veracity. Combination printing was acceptable
in landscapes as the public was conditioned by painting
to expect idealized renditions, but when it came to portraying humans viewers associated photography with
unarranged truth. Robinson was able to expand photography's reach and get the public to embrace his combinations as expressing the accepted allegorical ideals
and standards of the day. Robinson's work possesses a
duality common to educated practitioners born before
the invention of photography who thought like painters.
Although Robinson's representations broke no new
ground, he showed that photography could achieve the
same artistic goals as painting, thus allowing the next
generation to explore photography's own morphology.

In the short term his work had the opposite effect.
Robinson's allegorical ideas, magical theatrical techniques, and moralizing sentiment were so successful
that they dominated photographic discourse and stifled
other ways of thinking photographically until the
1880s. Robinson's striving for a literary image,

6.13   JULIA MARGARET CAMERON. *Kathy Kuhn and Her Father,* 1864, from the *Watts Album.* 8⅛ × 6⅜ inches. Albumen silver print. Nathan Lyons observed that Cameron's "portraits represent a radical departure in thinking about photographic portraiture. . . . The work possessed movement, a type of direct confrontation, and a scale of the head within the frame that had nothing to do with other works being made photographically at that time. Her excitement about what she saw on the ground-glass did not depend upon the subject she was photographing, but on her subjective response."[21]   Courtesy George Eastman House.

self the collodion process. Her goal was to make romantic, allegorical photographs capable of expressing the ideals of the Pre-Raphaelites, who saw evil in industrialization and wanted the return of heroes who believed in God, honor, and morality. Cameron wrote: "My aspirations are to ennoble Photography and to secure for it the character and uses of High Art by combining the real & Ideal and sacrificing nothing of Truth by all possible devotion to Poetry and beauty."[22] Toward these ends, Cameron turned a coal-house into a darkroom; a glass-roofed chicken-house became her studio, where maids and family modeled. Cameron's status as an aristocratic amateur, who did not have to make a living with her photography, enabled her to embark on series of portraits that were uniquely photographic in nature. Cameron tossed aside many standard working practices in order to photographically record the spiritual essence of her sitter. The spontaneous quality of her earliest work, such as *Kathy Kuhn and Her Father,* reveals a proto-snapshot sensibility.

Cameron brought her camera close to her subjects, fashioning a close-up portrait that brought to the forefront the subject's distinctive intellectual and psychological qualities. Her head portraits (see chapter opener) were made on large plates (about 11 × 14 inches) with a giant 30-inch focal length lens! They were so unusual Cameron would sometimes write below the print: "From Life Not Enlarged." Cameron's use of directional light rendered the features and modeling of each sitter. Although Cameron's exposures averaged about five minutes, she did not use a headrest, instead allowing the sitter's natural motion to add spiritual life to the picture. The idea that the blur could be used as a strategy was a conceptual break from the portrait ideal in which a sitter was rendered absolutely still and part of the viewing pleasure was in examining idiosyncratic detail. Cameron played down photographic veracity in favor of a subjective response that included bodily sensations, merging the rational and immaterial levels of reality.

Cameron's most innovative work involved capturing a sitter's spiritual qualities. Her blurry image of Herschel (see chapter opener), with its competing areas of light and dark and its tracts of absolute black, is more about atmosphere than it is a portrait of a man. The head, surrounded by darkness, radiates a metaphysical endowment as exactitude loses all consequence. Cameron was not ignorant of standard methods, but she chose to go her own way, making what others considered blunders part of her style. Cameron's *Sappho* (circa 1866) had a big crack in the lower left portion of plate, and rather than discarding it she printed it.[23] Casting against

reminiscent of nineteenth-century painting, has been in critical eclipse for most of the twentieth century. Yet today Robinson's practices look like progenitors of the postmodern photographers who stage tableaux before the camera and digitally manipulate their materials.

Julia Margaret Cameron [1815–1879] lived in India as a member of the socially privileged British-Indian colonial system before returning with her family to England in 1848, where their home became a meeting place for people in arts and letters. When Cameron was forty-nine, her daughter gave her a camera and she taught her-

6.14   UNKNOWN PHOTOGRAPHER.   *The Ghost of Milton.* 3½ × 7 inches. Albumen silver stereograph. Ghosts were created when a veiled figure entered the scene for a portion of the exposure, producing a transparent phantom. To maintain believability, less scrupulous operators concealed their methods from the public and used ploys such as: a plate with a previously recorded ghost image, a transparency of a ghost image placed in front of the lens, a miniature ghost transparency placed behind the lens, or a ghost image reflected into the lens during exposure.   Courtesy George Eastman House.

type and selecting a heavy featured, middle-aged woman for Sappho, Cameron's rendition of the Greek lyrical poet from the island of Lesbos also succeeds. Rather than concealing the nature of the photographic process, Cameron exults in it, even allowing processing drips to remain visible in the final image, thereby establishing a direct visual connection between the process and the product. She let the viewers know that what she accomplished was done through the agency of photography, paving the way for the formation of an inherent, rather than imitative, photographic language.

Cameron also disobeyed the rules of focus to create fresh visual forms and points of emphasis. She was influenced by the photographic work of the English painter David Wilkie Wynfield, with whom she took photography lessons, who pictured his friends dressed-up in Renaissance costumes. A critic had this to say about Wynfield's work and its relationship to the boundaries of photographic portrayal:

> A photographer's grand aim is get everything into an "artificial focus," which is widely different from that of the human eye. . . . Mr. Wynfield—has actually produced a set of photographs which are intentionally and confessedly "out of focus" . . . they ought to revolutionize photographic portraiture.[24]

The issue of focus was critical in defining serious nineteenth-century artistic practice. During the 1860s, Cameron's work helped establish the issue of selective focus as a criterion of peerless practice. The making of "out of focus" photographs was considered an expressive remedy that shifted the artificial, machine-focus of a camera towards a more natural vision. Cameron stated that "my first successes in my out-of-focus pictures were a fluke. That is to say, that when focusing and coming to something which, to my eye, was very beautiful, I stopped there instead of screwing on the lens to the more definite focus which all other photographers insist upon."[25] As the aesthetics of practice changed in the early 1870s, coming to rely on the transparent exactitude of the wet-plate as the photographic standard, Cameron shifted too and made "in focus" pictures.

Cameron's roots were those of a family photographer who celebrated the lives and values of those closest to her, establishing transcendental principles still being pictured by millions of family snapshooters. Inspired by her friendship with allegorical artist George Watts, Cameron's idealized, mythical pieces picture women in marriage and motherhood, and illustrious women from history, literature, and religion. Cameron was the first photographer to stress the power and significance of women's roles.[26]

Americans and the Art of Nature

Americans approached the spiritual image not through the religious icons of Italian master painters but through nature, in an optimistic movement known as *transcendentalism.* Espoused by Thomas Carlyle, Ralph Waldo Emerson, and Henry David Thoreau in the mid-1800s,

6.15 DR. HUGH WELCH DIAMOND. *Mental Patient,* 1855. Lightly albumenized salt print. Photography seemed to be a mechanism that could produce faithful records whose authenticity could be certified by the institutions of power and control from which they arose. As the British medical journal *Lancet* proclaimed: "Photography is so essentially the Art of Truth—and representative of Truth in Art—that it would seem to be the essential means of reproducing all forms and structures of which science seeks for delineation."[27] Courtesy Royal Photographic Society, Bath, England.

transcendentalism emphasized individualism, self-reliance, the rejection of authority, and the mystical unity of nature. Transcendentalism was a reaction against scientific rationalism that relied on intuition as the way to understand reality and stressed that redemption is only to be found in one's own intuition and soul. Its ideas also affected the viewing of images. The transcendentalists believed that sight was related to insight, or a kind of hypervision, suggesting that clear perception is a precursor to understanding. Thus a focused viewer became a *seer.*

In *Nature* (1836), Emerson describes this mystical state of intense perception as becoming a "transparent eyeball; I am nothing; I see all; the currents of the Universal Being circulate through me; I am part or parcel of God."[28]

A segment of this movement was *spiritualism,* founded in Rochester, NY, in 1848 by the medium Margaret Fox and her sisters, who later admitted their activities were fraudulent. Spiritualists believed that the human personality survived death and could communicate with the living through a medium who was sensitive to the spirit's vibrations. This gave rise to so-called spirit photography, which purported to make visual records of ectoplasmic manifestations of persons in a state beyond death. William Mumler, who ran a spirit photograph studio in New York in the early 1860s, was eventually arrested as a swindler, though the charges were eventually dismissed because trickery was not proved.[29] Nevertheless, spirit photographs attracted a large audience of predisposed believers who paid no attention when it was demonstrated that spirit photographs were produced by double exposure or multiple printing. Other photographers used these techniques and got into this commercially viable escapade without making any supernatural claims. To help sell his stereoscope, Sir David Brewster suggested making "ghost" stereo cards for fun; they quickly became a fad (see Figure 6.14). Although Americans did not get involved with allegorical combination printing, spirit pictures encouraged experimentation with multiple exposure and acceptance of this style of depiction. Even though ghost cards were known to be fabricated, the fact that they were done photographically gave the appearance of truth. Spirit photography spread to Europe during the mid-1870s and again in the 1890s. These were times of recession for portrait studios, and ghosts were good for business. Spirit photographers also experienced a resurrection following World Wars I and II, as grief-stricken survivors attempted to maintain their access to the dead through photography.

Positivism

While a small fellowship of amateurs struggled to represent photography as art, the majority were interested in the photograph's ability to commemorate people, places, and things. During this time the philosophy of *positivism,* as put forth by Auguste Comte, was in

6.16 DR. THOMAS JOHN BARNARDO. *No. 27, Once a Little Vagrant,* and *No. 28, Now a Little Workman,* ca. 1875. Cartes-des-Visites. Tactics used by Dr. Thomas John Barnardo caused contemporary critics, such as John Tagg, to express concern with how photography had been deployed as "a means of surveillance." Tagg wrote: "We have begun to see a repetitive pattern: the body isolated; the narrow space; the subjection to an unreturnable gaze; the scrutiny of gestures, faces and features; the clarity of illumination and sharpness of focus; the names and number boards. These are the traces of power, repeated countless times, whenever the photographer prepared an exposure, in police cell, prison, consultation room, asylum, Home or school."[30] Courtesy Barnardo Photographic Archive, Essex, England.

vogue. Positivism stated that social progress and human knowledge were dependent on precise ordered observation, classification, and comparison of external events. Positivism accepted the technical exactitude of science and the machine over the relativity of human perception. Positivism declared that reality, the physical facts, are precisely what we perceive. Its followers were opposed to metaphysics, the supernatural, and earlier pseudoscientific ideas. According to Dennis Grady:

> Comte relies upon science to find relationships among facts—laws—thus leading to the ability to make predictions. In applying this idea to human behavior Comte became the founder of sociology. Positivistic politics . . . has the goal of finding the social order most attuned to man's happiness and progress. . . . Eventually, photographers became aware of the power of photography to effect social change . . . to use the photographic documents to improve the lot of mankind.[31]

In terms of art, photographers were trying to make pictures that would find acceptance and credibility in the academic establishment. The *Realist movement,* typifying the positivistic spirit, believed that unaffected authenticity and naturalness would reveal truth. In its quest for approval, art photography embraced the old-fashioned values of *metaphysical idealism* and not those of Realism, which was snubbed by the Academy and not considered to be High Art. Metaphysical idealism proposes that reality has an ultimate nature that sense impressions do not reveal, that knowledge of that ultimate reality is attainable through reason and intuition, and that people are not mere physical matter but spiritual beings. The differences between metaphysical idealism and positivism represent the division between two Western ways of looking at the world: "Is Truth a-priori, apart from and above man and sensation—or simply material nature as seen by the human eye?"[32]

During the second half of the nineteenth century, positivist philosophy was applied in social institutions, including law enforcement and hospitals, that were given more centralized power to control individual behavior. The positivists put their ideas into practice with the perfect positivistic tool—the photograph. Beginning in the 1840s, police began making identification pictures that led to the use of photographs as court room evidence. **Dr. Hugh Welch Diamond** [1809–1886], the superintendent of the Female Department of the Surrey County Lunatic Asylum and founding member of the Royal Photographic Society, combined positivism, aesthetics, photography, psychiatry, and physiognomy in a new institutional order. Using an unadorned background and frontal posing, Dr. Diamond made portraits of his patients that direct attention to the face and hands of the sitter. Diamond claimed clinical photography aided his patient's treatment, provided a record for medical guidance and physiognomic analysis, and offered a means of identification. Diamond saw photography as a method of securing "with unerring accuracy the external phenomena of each passion."[33]

Photography began to be incorporated into the activities of institutions concerned with observing and controlling behavior. **Thomas John Barnardo** [1845–1905], who in 1871 founded the "Home for Destitute Lads," established a photographic department in 1874 which produced some 55,000 isolated portraits between 1874 and 1905 in order "to obtain and retain an exact likeness of each child and enable them, when it is attached to his history, to trace the child's career."[34] Individual dossiers containing a portrait, personal history, and statistics were prepared for each child. Albums were made up to show to parents, police, and visitors.

Before-and-after pictures were commissioned, purporting to show children arriving in a motley state and then cleaned and industrious under the guidance of the Home. Barnardo was brought to court on charges of capitalizing on the children by putting them into fictitious settings and altering their appearance to benefit his fund-raising operations. Nowadays charities regularly send out appeals for contributions in which picture/text combinations are used that convert the bodies of those being observed into advertising commodities.

This push for cataloging and standardizing society along the scientific model, through the tenets of positivism, found a willing partner in photography's encyclopedic impulse. The idea of truth in the optical and chemical processes of photography was often in direct contradiction with the ideal of photographers who sought to discover artistic truth beneath the veneer of reality. The jockeying for position between these two practices continues to divide the profession and the public over photography's role in society.

Endnotes

1   Julia Margaret Cameron, "The Annals of My Glass House," 1874, *Photo Beacon* (Chicago) 2 (1890), 157–60. Reprinted in Beaumont Newhall, ed. *Photography: Essays & Images* (New York: Museum of Modern Art, 1980), 137.

2   *The Photographic News*, vol. 5, no. 152, (August 1861), 370, reported that the 1841 census did not list photography as a profession. Ten years later, 51 photographers were recorded; by 1861 there were 2,879. In 1851, a Miss Wigley was the only woman professional; ten years later there were 204 women. In 1861, no fewer than 33,000 Parisians claimed to make their living from photography.

3   Charles Baudelaire, "The Salon of 1859," translated by Jonathan Mayne, *The Mirror of Art: Critical Studies by Charles Baudelaire* (London: Phaidon Press, 1955). Reprinted in Beaumont Newhall, *Photography: Essays & Images* (New York: The Museum of Modern Art, 1980), 112–13.

4   Elizabeth Eastlake, "Photography," *Quarterly Review* [London], April 1857, 442–68. Reprinted in Newhall, *Essays & Images*, 81–95. This quote appears on pp. 94–95.

5   See Van Deren Coke, *The Painter and the Photograph: From Delacroix to Warhol* (Albuquerque: University of New Mexico Press, revised and enlarged edition, 1972).

6   *Correspondence*, vol. III, 195–96. Cited in Coke, *The Painter and the Photograph: From Delacroix to Warhol*, 9.

7   *Photography: Essays & Images Illustrated Readings in the History of Photography*, Beamont Newhall, ed. (New York: The Museum of Modern Art, 1980), 90.

8   *Abbozzo* is Italian for sketch. In painting, it refers to the first outline or drawing on the canvas; also to the first underpainting.

9   See Aaron Scharf, *Art and Photography* (London: Allen Lane, 1968), 131–34.

10   The photographers who had work selected sent the negative and the club printed an edition. The elaborate, polished leather bound albums contained lustrously printed images on albumen paper, as there was not an effective way to print the photographs on an ink press.

11   O. G. Rejlander, "On Photographic Composition with a Description of Two Ways of Life," *The Photographic Journal*, vol. IV, no. 65, April 21, 1858, 191–96.

12   *Humphrey's Journal of Photography*, vol. 9, no. 6, July 15, 1857, 92–93.

13   Unknown author, "Fifth Annual Photographic Exhibition," *Art Journal*, April 1, 1858, 120–21.

14   When The Photographic Society of Scotland showed the work, they draped the unrespectable part of the composition.

15   Louis Figuier, *La photographie au salon de 1859* (Paris, 1860), 14.

16   *Photography in Print: Writing from 1816 to the Present*, Vicki Goldberg, editor , (Albuquerque: University of New Mexico Press reprint 1988), 146.

17   Henry Peach Robinson, *The Elements of Pictorial Photography* (Bradford, England: Percy Lund & Co., Ltd., 1896), 102.

18   See Henry Peach Robinson, *Pictorial Effect in Photography*, Preface, unp. Reprinted by Helios, Pawlet, VT, 1971, second impression 1972.

19   Henry Peach Robinson, *Pictorial Effect in Photography* (London: Piper & Carter, 1869). This book's publication record indicates the significance and acceptance of its concepts. British editions in 1869, 1879, 1881, 1893; American: 1881, 1892; French: 1885; German: 1886. The text was based on the art education system of the Royal Academy and relied on Joshua Reynold's eighteenth century *Discourses on Art* and John Burnet's *Treatise on Painting* (1822). Unlike earlier texts, such as Disdéri's *L'art de la photographie* (1862) and Marcus A. Root's *The Camera and the Pencil* (1864), Robinson devoted most of his discussion to handling the figure in landscape rather than to the making of studio portraits.

20   Robinson, 198.

21   Robert Hirsch, "Nathan Lyons on the Snapshot," *CEPA Journal,* Winter 1992–93, 6–7.

22   Julia Margaret Cameron to Sir John Herschel, December 31, 1864, collection of the Royal Society of London, quoted in full in Colin Ford, *The Cameron Collection: An Album of Photographs by Julia Margaret Cameron* (London: Van Nostrand Reinhold with the National Portrait Gallery, 1975), 140–41.

23   Cameron printed on albumen paper, toned in a gold chloride solution to alter its reddish-brown color to a cooler purplish-brown. The toning made the image more stable and increased the apparent contrast by making the highlight details easier to see. These prints do not look the same as when they were created. Deterioration produces *yellowing,* a loss of detail in the highlight areas, and color shifts to a warm reddish-brown. Although these effects can be aesthetically pleasing, this was not the original intent.

24   Unknown author, "Fine Arts," *Illustrated London News* 44 (March 19, 1864), 275.

25   Cameron, "The Annals of My Glass House" as reprinted in Newhall, *Photography: Essays & Images,* 136.

26   See Joanne Lukitsh, *Cameron: Her Work and Career* (Rochester: International Museum of Photography at George Eastman House, 1986), 29.

27   *Lancet,* 22 January 1859, 89, quoted in S. L. Gilman, ed., "Hugh W. Diamond and Psychiatric Photography," *The Face of Madness* (Secaucus, NJ: Brunner-Mazel, 1976), 5.

28   Brooks Atkinson, ed., *The Selected Writing of Ralph Waldo Emerson* (New York: Modern Library, 1940), 6.

29   Stories later surfaced that Mumler hired a man to remove photographs of deceased relatives from homes, bring them to Mumler to be copied, and then return the pictures. This agent then directed the relatives to Mumler's studio, where through a combination of double exposure and manipulation Mumler produced the desired results—a spirit image of their dead loved one. Many people thought Mumler was legitimate. Mary Todd Lincoln visited Mumler's studio and came away with a photograph of a ghostlike Lincoln standing behind his widow, his hands upon her shoulders.

30   John Tagg, *The Burden of Representation: Essays on Photographies and Histories* "A Means of Surveillance," (Minneapolis: University of Minnesota Press, 1993), 87.

31   Dennis P. Grady, "Philosophy and Photography in the Nineteenth Century," Thomas F. Barrow, Shelley Armitage, William E. Tyeman (eds.), *Reading into Photography: Collected Essays 1959–1980* (Albuquerque: University of New Mexico Press, 1982), 151–52, 157. Reprinted from *Exposure,* February 1977.

32   Thomas Barrow, et al., *Reading into Photography: Selected Essays, 1959–1980* (Albuquerque: University of New Mexico Press, 1982), 153.

33   *The Photographic Journal,* vol. 3, no. 44, July 21, 1856, 88–89. Summary of Diamond's paper "On the Application of Photography to Physiognomic and Mental Phenomena of Insanity."

34   Quoted in Valerie Lloyd and Gillian Wagner, *The Camera and Dr. Barnardo* (Hertford: Barnardo School of Printing, 1974), 14.

CHAPTER SEVEN

Standardizing
the Practice
A Transparent Truth
Mechanical Photography

During the age of Western industrial development and colonial expansion, with its railroads, steamships, and pocket watches changing society's sense of time and space, people believed that the machine's ability to accurately perform repetitive tasks held the key to a better life. Photographers recognized the demand for accurate pictures of historic sites, and the latest technical improvement to the photographic repertoire, transparent collodion materials, was a way to meet this need. The collodion process's increased sensitivity, retention of detail, and ease of reproduction made it and paper prints the new professional standard. As the Pre-Raphaelite painters struggled for photographic accuracy, people took pleasure in a photograph's ability to let them count every brick in a wall. In *Modern Painters* (5 volumes, 1843–60), John Ruskin [1819–1900], reveled in photography's ability to preserve evidence:

TIMOTHY O'SULLIVAN. *Steamboat Springs,* Washoe, Nev., 1867. 8⁵⁄₁₆ × 11 inches. Albumen silver print. Courtesy George Eastman House.

Viewers looking at *Steamboat Springs* and the faint appearing/disappearing figure standing on barren desert, in the smoke of the fissure vent, knew this was not a European landscape but an unfamiliar place of natural power, freshly presented.

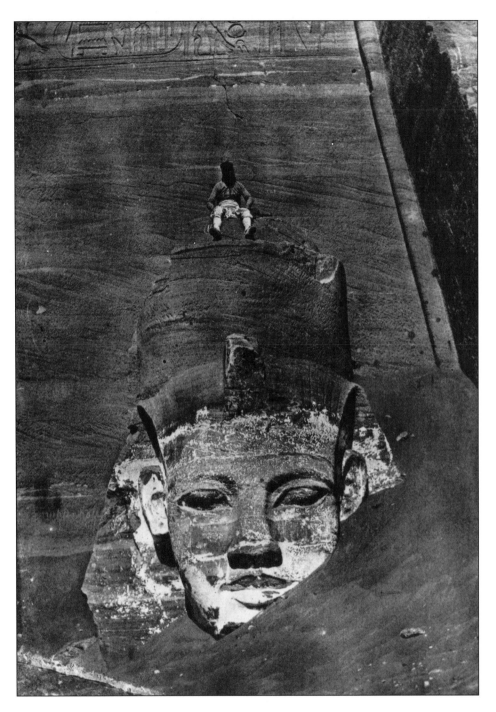

7.1 MAXIME DU CAMP. *The Colossus of Abu-Simbel, Nubia,* 1850. 8⅞ × 6⁵⁄₁₆ inches. Salted paper print from a calotype negative by L. D. Blanquart-Evrard. Plate 107 of the album *Égypte, Nubia, Palestine et Syrie* (Paris, 1852).   Du Camp's work was published in several volumes by Blanquart-Evrard. One of the first and most profusely photographically illustrated books issued in France, *Egypte, Nubie, Palestine et Syrie* (1852), contained 122 calotypes. Du Camp later founded the *Revue de Paris,* which featured works such as Flaubert's *Madame Bovary* (1857).   Courtesy George Eastman House.

My drawings are truth to the very letter—too literal perhaps; so says my father, so says not the daguerreotype, for it beats me grievously. I have allied myself with it. . . . It is certainly the most marvelous invention of the century; given us just in time to save some evidence from the great public of wreckers.[1]

The idea of seeing it all had immense appeal. This verbatim style of representation was labeled "mechanical-photography" by C. Jabez Hughes to distinguish it from art photography, whose purpose was aesthetic and personal. Hughes specified:

7.2   JOHN BEASLY GREENE.   *Bank of Nile at Thebes*, 1854. 9¹⁄₁₆ × 10⅞ inches. Salted paper print. In this ambiguous landscape Greene sacrifices information for pictorial effect. Nothing is clearly defined; everything is suggested. Greene's work was also published by Blanquart-Evrard in an album *Le Nil: Monuments, paysages, explorations photographiques* (1854).   Courtesy George Eastman House.

I do not mean the term *mechanical* to be understood depreciatingly. On the contrary, I mean that everything that is to be depicted exactly as it is, and where all the parts are to be equally sharp and perfect, is to be included under this head. I might have used the term *literal* photography, but think the former better. This branch, for obvious reasons, will always be the most practised; and where the literal unchallenged truth is required, is the only one allowable.[2]

By the mid-1850s, the practice of commercial photography was established to satisfy the demand for architectural wonders, works of engineering and industry, and scenic views. This new class of photographers specialized in the mechanical style, one that required a virtuoso technical performance featuring maximum detail and sharpness. Accurate and affordable pictorial records were now available in a manner unimaginable fifteen years before.

The Traveling Camera

Taking the wet-plate out of the studio was not an impromptu affair as its complicated preparation made field work problematic. Small stereographic cameras were utilized to make stereo cards, but exhibition prints were done with large, wooden folding cameras. Cameras with flexible, corrugated leather bellows that formed a light-tight passageway between the lens and the film plate were slow to be adopted and often were not steady enough for long, windy, outdoor exposures. As enlarging was not yet feasible, a large picture meant

7.3   AUGUSTE SALZMANN.   *Jerusalem.* 9¼ × 13 inches. Salted paper print. Salzmann's general views of Jerusalem's ancient monuments rely on picturesque landscape models, favoring asymmetrical compositions that document the massive walls of the city. The soft, pencil-like quality of the salted-paper prints link the city with the site. Blanquart-Evrard published this work as *Jerusalem, époques judaïque, romanine, chrétienne, arabe, explorations photographiques par A. Salzmann* (1854). Courtesy George Eastman House.

a glass plate of 10 × 12 or 12 × 16 inches had to be exposed in order to make a contact print of the same size. A Scottish photographer recalled the ordeal of taking a large-format camera into the field:

> I reached the railway station with a cabload consisting of the following items: A 9″ × 11″ brass-bound camera weighing 21 lbs. A water-tight glass bath in wooden case holding over 90 ozs. of solution [silver nitrate] and weighing 12 lbs. A plate box with a dozen 9″ × 11″ [glass] plates weighing almost as many pounds. A box 24″ × 18″ × 12″ inches into which were packed lenses, chemicals, and all the hundred-and-one articles [scale, measures, funnels, trays, fixer, and a pail for water] necessary for a hard days work, and weighing something like 28 lbs. The advent of folding tripods had not come [circa 1857], . . . and so I had perforce to encumber myself with one that when closed looked like an Alpine-stock over 5 ft. in length. It weighed about 5 lbs. Lastly, there was the tent, that made a most convenient darkroom, about 40″ × 40″ inches and 6½ ft. high, with ample table accommodation; the whole packed into a leather case and weighed over 40 lb. . . . We did not care to walk far.[3]

Three approaches to making travel pictures were established: amateur, official, and commercial. Talbot set the precedent for amateur travel pictures with his excursions to popular tourist destinations like Lake Como. Such images, embryonic snapshots, were done for personal satisfaction. Governments employed photographers to document official sites of interest. These images, of everything from historic monuments to railroad bridges, were seen by small, elite audiences and sometimes offered for sale in limited-edition albums of original prints. Finally, commercial photographers produced sellable images, such as the pyramids, as quickly and cheaply as possible. To get to out-of-the-way locations, they outfitted wagons as traveling darkrooms, but they still needed dark-tents for pictures that were not being made close to the wagon. In the field, photographers relied on one-person tents, where they coated and processed the plates at folding tables in odorous and stifling conditions. Water, if it was not readily available, had to be hauled. Since the wet-plate lost sensitivity as it dried, it was inadvisable to pitch the dark-tent more than

7.4   JOHN SHAW SMITH.   *Untitled (Temples of Nubia)*, 1851. 6¹³⁄₁₆ × 8¹³⁄₁₆ inches. Calotype negative. In *Temple Ruins* Shaw retained a double exposure (probably accidental) and substantially reworked it with ink. The inadvertent overlapping is striking, communicating the complexity of the ruins in a way particular to the camera. It also reveals how photographers can straddle the boundary between the enchantment of photographic objectivity and the frustration of having to accept what the mechanics of the camera provides.
Courtesy George Eastman House.

a three-minute walk or run from where the camera was set up. To make six successful exposures a day required hard work, skill, and luck and quick exposures from multiple vantage points were rare. The amount of energy needed to make a view drove photographers to select sites they knew would appeal to accepted notions of picture composition and subject matter, rather than try to discover innovative ways of depiction. Under these circumstances, the first photographic travels were launched.

A fascination with Egypt led French journalist **Maxime Du Camp** [1822–1894] on an extended photographic assignment to the Middle East from 1849 to 1852.[4] Trained by Le Gray in the waxed calotype process for its field versatility, Du Camp took advantage of its improved clarity and made calotypes at the hours when the angle of light revealed the form and texture of the monuments. Du Camp favored including a human figure in his compositions as a scale reference (see Figure 7.1).

John Beasly Greene [1832–1856], an amateur archeologist from Boston, used the calotype to record his explorations. Greene's calotypes along the Nile interpret the desert environs by emphasizing space, often by allowing the sky to dominate the composition. With the calotype's granular look, this strategy unified the space, giving the sky and water the same organization as the desert sands, reinforcing a feeling of dislocation and timelessness (see Figure 7.2). In other photographs the subjects are composed to accentuate, rather than command, the extended horizon line.

In the spirit of documenting historical sites, the French Ministry of Public Instruction commissioned **Auguste Salzmann** [1824–1872] to photograph the remaining monuments of the Crusades erected by the Knights of the Order of St. John in Crete, Cyprus,

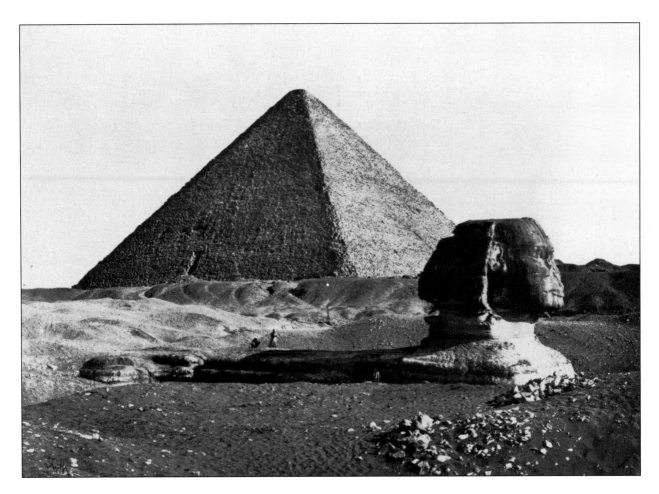

7.5 FRANCIS FRITH.   *The Sphinx and Great Pyramid Geezeh.* 6⁵⁄₁₆ × 9 inches. Albumen silver print. The sheer amount of visual information available on the hard, smooth surface of Frith's contact print, with its staggering shadow detail and creamy warm eggshell highlights, gives us hope that the mysteries of the pyramids can be solved. In his publications like *Lower Egypt, Thebes and the Pyramids* (ca. 1862), Frith also provides hard facts—the largest pyramid has a base of 746 feet, is 450 feet high, and covers about 12 acres—as if they would somehow give insight into these enigmatic structures. Then Frith reveals the conflict the Sphynx creates for his picturesque ideals: "The profile, as given in my view, is truly hideous. I fancy that I have read of its beautiful calm, majestic features; let my reader look at it, and say if he does not agree with me, that it can scarcely have been, even in its palmiest days, otherwise than exceeding ugly."   Courtesy George Eastman House.

Jerusalem (see Figure 7.3), and Rhodes. While carrying out this work, Salzmann also photographed monuments of disputed attribution for the archeologist Louis-Félicien-Joseph Caignart de Saulcy. In 1853 Salzmann made waxed calotype negatives in support of de Saulcy's theory that Jerusalem's ancient monuments could be correctly re-dated by their physical construction. Done in the instructional style of archeological illustration, Salzmann's images go beyond the draftsman's model, meditating on patterns created by the play of light and shadow. Most of the details are tightly composed from a centered, frontal point of view, relying on directional light to accent texture and focus attention on the masonry construction used to date most of the monuments. The unrelenting frontality solved the problems of depth-of-field associated with view cameras of the time, that lacked the proper controls to adjust the front and back standards—swings and tilts—to make perspective corrections, flattening the image and emphasizing line, mass, and pattern. This photographic way of seeing simplified and abstracted the close-up view while conveying a sense of the heaviness of the stone structures. The calotype's graininess and lack of shadow detail added a dark, foreboding atmosphere of mystery. The contrasty prints of this series gave the visual sensation of contradiction, providing viewers with an unresolvable riddle that stated that the information pertinent to when these monuments were built was not what was really important to know about them.

John Shaw Smith [1811–1873], an Irish amateur calotypist, took an extended grand tour of the Mediterranean, Egypt, and the Holy Land between 1850 and

7.6 ROBERT MACPHERSON. *Biga* (Statue of Horses and Chariot), ca. 1863. 8⅞ × 14⅞ inches. Albumen silver print. MacPherson's precise delineation and feeling for chiaroscuro elaborate the majesty of the ancient ruins and provide an experience of the place, leading the *Art Journal* to say: "You are struck with surprise at seeing so much that you never saw before. . . . In the light and shade of these ruins there is a sentiment which, with the stern truth of the photograph, affects the mind more deeply than a qualified essay in painting."[5]   Courtesy George Eastman House.

1852. Exposing his paper negatives while they were damp, Smith's visual souvenirs show his understanding of the historic legends of these foreign locales.[6] While mindful of the rules of conventional pictorial practice, Smith experimented with sequential viewpoints, such as circling St. Peter's Square with his camera to create a panoramic effect. Smith blackened the sky portion of the negative with Japanese ink so that it printed clear, without the calotype's characteristic mottled effect. Smith also altered the photographic truth by outlining objects along the horizon with ink on the negative or with pencil on the print, making them stand out against the sky. In other cases he eliminated unwanted objects, and sometimes he added clouds. Shaw was willing to use the camera as a point of departure for his own interpretations, leaving visual evidence of an enterprising amateur spirit that helped define early practice (see Figure 7.4).

By applying the latest wet-plate methods to the landscape, **Francis Frith** [1822–1899] became a major publisher of English and European views, eventually boasting a stock of one million images sold in more than 2,000 shops. Frith's picturesque views satisfied Victorian curiosity and reconfirmed the positivist belief that knowledge was a collection of facts. Frith traveled to the Near East, boating through the dangerous white waters of the Nile, fighting off wild dogs, battling bandits, encountering desert princes "blazing with jewelled-hilted swords and gold-mounted firearms,"[7] and watching his collodion boil when he poured it onto his glass plate. Frith pioneered comprehensive coverage, often systematically photographing from a distance and then, from different angles, closer up, allowing the viewer to reconstruct the scene. Frith's trademark composition was to juxtapose human figures with giant statues, which provided a sense of mass and scale (see Figure 7.5). Frith's status came from his numerous books, illustrated with mounted photographs and accompanied by descriptions and dialogue. In *Sinai and Palestine* (ca. 1862), each large albumen print was accompanied by facts and commentary to coach the viewer to the same conclusions as the maker. The text accompanying *The Sphynx and Great Pyramid, Geezeh* reads:

> The day and hour in a man's life upon which he first obtains a view of "The Pyramids," is a time to date from for many a year to come; he is approaching, as it were, the presence of an immortality which has mingled vaguely with his thoughts from very childhood, and has been to him unconsciously an essential beautiful *form*, and the most majestic mystery ever created by man.

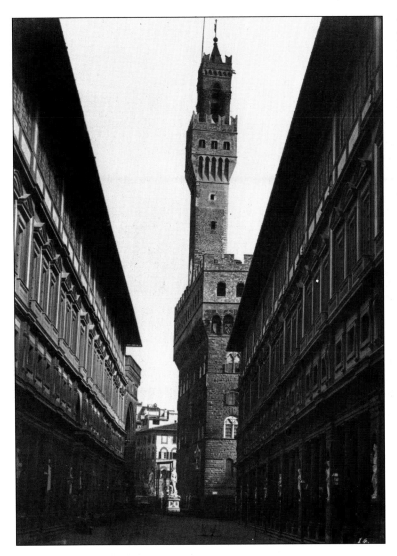

7.7 FRATELLI ALINARI (Giuseppe and Leopoldo). *Il Portico Degli Uffizi E Il Palazzo Vecchio,* ca. 1860. 13½ × 9⅞ inches. Albumen silver print. The practice of organizing groups of photographs around a theme reflects the narrative tradition that expects pictures to tell stories, a practice reinforced by picture magazines. The Alinaris understood these expectations and capitalized on them in creating their catalog of Italy, founded on their desire to portray "Bella Italia." The company is still a major photographic publisher of illustrative material with an archive of over 200,000 negatives.   Courtesy George Eastman House.

In an era before mass-produced picture book production, Frith's books stand out for allowing the subject to control the format. *Cairo, Sinai, Jerusalem and the Pyramids of Egypt* (ca. 1860) had 16 × 20-inch views on 21 × 29-inch pages; they conveyed a grand sense of contrast, space, and texture. *Upper Egypt and Ethiopia* (1863), with its oversized pages, leather binding, gold leafing, and marblized endpapers, is an *objêt d'art.* Af-

ter Frith completed his Near East tours, he hired photographers to make views of Europe, Great Britain, and America, utilizing the principles of industrial standardization to produce workmanlike, topographical portfolios. These images reflected the new photographic axiom that to see all was to know all. This industrious output sums up the ideal of "mechanical picturesque" photography as F. Frith & Co. became England's largest supplier of architectural views, landscapes, and *postcards.*[8] Frith & Co. continued to operate and sell postcards until 1971.

Robert MacPherson [1811–1872] took up photography in 1851 to sell tourists views of classical Roman sites. In 1856 MacPherson began making carefully composed, large wet-plates (from 12 × 16 inches to 18 × 22 inches) of cultural emblems from his travels around Italy. These refined views culminated in the publication of a Vatican guidebook in 1863, illustrated with MacPherson's photographs of over 300 sculptures (see Figure 7.6). Commercial photographers like MacPherson had an extensive, well-organized, and ongoing dialogue with tourists; MacPherson delivered the views tourists were expecting to take home to share with their friends.

While a small band struggled to win a place for photography in the art world, its topographic applications had the greatest impact on visual literary. European commercial photographers, such as **James Anderson** [1813–1877], realized that accurate reproduction of art work could increase the circulation of culturally significant subjects and be profitable as well. In the 1850s, photographers commenced publishing photographic prints of Western art masterpieces, establishing the photograph's role as the provider of visual artifacts. Even those who said photography was not art heralded its use for chronicling art works: It made people familiar with masterworks that could inspire their spirit, cultivate their taste, and assist in daily aesthetic decision making.

Leopoldo Alinari [1832–1865] opened his first studio in 1859 and was joined two years later by his brothers Giuseppe [1836–1890] and Romualdo [1830–1891] to form "**Fratelli Alinari**, Fotografi Editori." Relying on standard straightforward rules of composition, the Alinari brothers made unequivocal documents of Italian architecture, art, and landscape, conveying the Romantic look and myth of Italy. The Alinaris understood the public's visual expectations and supplied the market with art reproductions and stereocards. In the 1870s, they hired photographers to follow the firm's prescribed practices

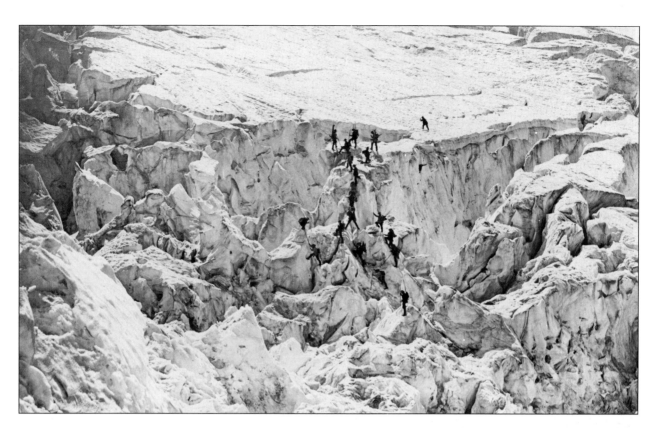

7.8 AUGUST-ROSALIE BISSON (BISSON FRÈRES). *Ascension of Mont-Blanc,* from the album *Haute-Savoie, Le Mont Blanc et Ses Glaciers: Souvenir du Voyage de M.M. L'Imperatrice* (Paris, 1860). 11¼ × 14⅛ inches. Albumen silver print. The Bisson Brothers' alpine accomplishments resulted in a 24-photograph album, dedicated to the Emperor and Empress of France, featuring majestic views of crevasses, ice, snowfields, and mountain tops. *Ascension au Mont Blanc* provides a sense of the sublime as the humans making their way through the snowfield appear as insects in this landscape.   Courtesy George Eastman House.

for chronicling the cities and art treasures of Italy. Thus photographic style began to move from the idiosyncratic characteristics of individual photographers to an industrial/corporate model that insisted on standardization. It is from this corporate model of hiring people to work as instructed that the Alinaris drew their effectiveness—the strength of numbers, with tourists being able to order views from a catalog. They were a team with a collective point of view, whose patterned images were most effective when seen in organized sets.

Louis-Auguste Bisson [1814–1876] opened a daguerrean portrait studio in Paris in 1841 with his brother, Auguste-Rosalie Bisson [1826–1900], after being introduced to the process by Daguerre himself. For over a decade the **Bisson Brothers** produced craftsmanlike portraits of artists and political figures tailored to meet public demand. In 1851, they switched

to the wet-plate and expanded their subject range. Since people wanted to see the Alps, but few could afford the trip, the Bisson Brothers used photography to vicariously fulfill this arduous desire. The brothers failed in their ascent of Mont Blanc in 1860, but the following year Auguste Bisson made a second attempt, using a guide and 25 porters to haul his gear. On the third day, after a difficult and frigid climb, they conquered the 16,000-foot peak. A darkroom tent was set up and three 8 × 10-inch plates were coated and exposed.[9]

Picturing Industrialization

The industrialization of society posed problems for romantically trained photographers, who attempted to impose picturesque ideals onto man-made landscapes. As photographers gained experience, new treatments for photographing industrial settings evolved. Relying on the transparent negative and its companion glossy paper, the notion of suggestion was abandoned in favor of a strategy in which everything is specified, shifting the budding, individualistic documentary style from allusion to machinelike utilitarianism.

Philip Henry Delamotte [1820–1889] commemorated the reconstruction of the temporary Crystal Palace of London at Sydenham. Delamotte photographed the site weekly for three years (1851–1854), from its inception through the installation of exhibits, eventually publishing an album, *Photographic Views of the Progress of the Crystal Palace* (1855). At a site dedicated to new

7.9   PHILIP H. DELAMOTTE. *Stuffed Animals and Ethnographic Figures.* Plate #100, vol. II of Photographic Views of the Progress of the Crystal Palace, Sydenham (London, 1855). The colonial attitude about "white man's burden" is represented amidst models of unindustrialized, half-naked people and wild animals. The endless high-technology geometric iron columns and frames imply that the wilds are confined and under control.   Courtesy Collection of the Juliette K. and Leonard S. Rakow Research Library of the Corning Museum of Glass.

commercial products, Delamotte juxtaposed the repetition of the iron against the geometric rhythms of the arched roof frame (see Figure 3.5). This sense of sameness was a exemplary metaphor for the Iron Age, venerating engineering feats in ironic duality. Within the recreation, the divergence between the old, heavy-handed, stone construction and the new modern, light, delicate, and airy machine methods of glass and iron are apparent.

During the 1850s, the camera was used to chronicle feats of mechanization. **Robert Howlett** [ca. 1830–1858] and his partner **Joseph Cundall** [1818–1895] photographed the building of a huge coal-driven steamship, the *Great Eastern*.[10] Cundall, who favored compositions showing the entire ship, did most of the early construction photographs, including two-plate panoramas that reveal a giant, ugly, hulking shape. Howlett covered the remaining stages of production by photographing what he saw, rather than contriving situations. Instead of showing the entire boat, Howlett made tighter compositions that em-

phasized the ship's imposing proportions (see Figure 7.10). Through his fresh approaches to daily industrial activities, Howlett raised the issue of which approach should be the standard for documentary camera work: one that presents as much of a subject as possible or one that only shows a selected portion.

Nineteenth-century photographers like Howlett attempted to resolve the issue of where the perimeters of their composition lay, to decide what could be subtracted from the scene while maintaining pictorial integrity. Portrait photographers used neutral backdrops, vignettes, and oval-shaped overmats to obliterate everyday detritus and offer an artistic setting for the sitter to materialize within. Landscape photographers borrowed the painterly device of using deep shadows along the periphery to keep the eye from wandering outside the frame. Architectural photographers established points of view from a distance, making a structure appear to be naturally incorporated into its surroundings. Many workaday commercial photographers nonchalantly placed their subject in the middle of the frame and let the edges fall where they may, accounting for much of the perfunctory architectural and travel work of the 1860s and 1870s.

The precise orderliness of the railroads and their industrial paraphernalia altered the landscape, making them sites for photography's developing documentary style. **Edouard Baldus's** visual affidavits, such as the album *Chemin de Fer du Nord, ligne de Paris à Boulogne,* celebrate the building of Baron James de

7.10 ROBERT HOWLETT. *Leviathan* (The Great
Eastern), *Side View of Hull,* ca. 1857. 11¼ × 14⅛
inches. Albumen Silver Print. In this composition the
bulk of the vessel is cut off and the camera is positioned
upward so that the hull towers over us. Backlighting
causes the two figures on the bow to almost vaporize,
giving the sensation that the humans are inconsequential. Howlett's tight framing utilizes the edges of the
frame, leaving the impression that the ship goes on in-
definitely.   Courtesy George Eastman House.

Rothschild's railway lines in France in 1855 and 1859.
Images like *Viaduc de S. Chamas* (see Figure 7.11) use
the apparent rational, visual logic of the wet-plate
process to ponder the illusion of symmetry produced by
the repetition of industrial shapes. Baldus's depictions
transcend their utilitarian origins and furnish visual
gratification in a formal pictorial poetry of light, line,
and shape. Most of the early railroad views explore a
fascination with the regulated, geometric design elements that made up these machined constructions, focusing on the product and not on the human conditions
surrounding their construction.

Leisure time expanded in the nineteenth-century industrial society. **Camille Silvy's** *River Scene, France*
(see Figure 7.12), presents people relaxing at a place
where urban and country values intersect—the river.
Constructed from two negatives, one for the land and
another for the sky, and reworked with ink and pencil
for pictorial effect, Silvy printed a number of renditions, some dark and moody, others light and open. The
success of Silvy's picturesque composition lies in its binary nature. From top to bottom, the river mirrors the
sky and makes an affable connection. From left to right,
an affluent couple can be seen in a boat, commanding
the water, juxtaposed with the landbound working people who admire the water from the bank. The scene in-
structs us on Romantic aspirations concerning beauty,
its rejuvenating benefits, and the moral uplift possible
from the natural world.

One of the ways people used their newfound leisure
time was by looking at sites they were unable to visit.
Western interest in the British colony of India led to an
outpouring of photographically illustrated albums and
books in the 1860s and 1870s (see Figure 7.14).
Samuel Bourne [1834–1912] arrived in Simla, India
in 1863 and swiftly formed a partnership with Charles

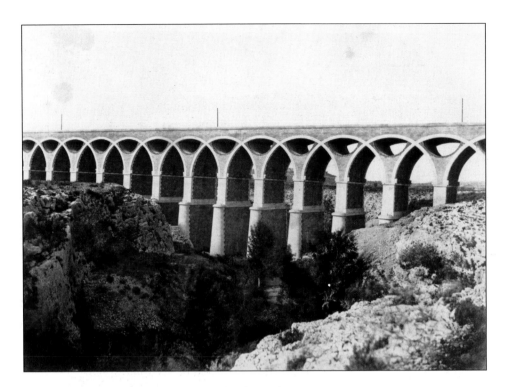

7.11   EDOUARD BALDUS.   *Viaduc de S. Chamas,* from the album *Chemin de fer de Paris à Lyon et à la Méditerraneé,* ca. 1861. 15³⁄₁₆ × 21⁵⁄₁₆ inches. Albumen silver print.   Courtesy George Eastman House.

Shepherd, the owner of the oldest Anglo-Indian photographic firm and leading provider of Indian views. Bourne was a tireless traveler who journeyed in India, Burma, Ceylon, and Kashmir (see Figure 7.13). His daring undertakings culminated in 1868 with views made in the Himalayas at 18,600 feet. Bourne, a former banker, made meticulous images in regions where no Europeans had previously gone, during trips that lasted up to nine months (in 1864) or required up to sixty bearers (in 1868) to transport his gear.[11]

Urban Life

John Thomson [1837–1921] moved to the Far East in 1862 and commenced ten years of photographing China, Cambodia, Formosa, Siam, and Vietnam. Thomson's topographic and ethnographic studies of native cultures, published as albums, recorded a vanishing civilization and made him a progenitor of early social documentation and travel. Thomson embarked into remote tropical areas of the Orient to survey "principal antiquities" like the temple at Angkor Wat, resulting in his first album, *The Antiquities of Cambodia* (1867). His Asian voyages culminated in the four-volume work *Illustrations of China and its People* (1873–74), which contained 200 tipped-in albumen prints. Thomson selected subjects of colonial interest

by spotlighting social customs and distinctive types of people who fit into recognizable Victorian social types. These photographs were accompanied by text that was often based on *phrenology,* a pseudoscience that alleged a person's character could be determined by examining the outer surface of the head. (For an overview of this subject see Michel Frizot "Body of Evidence: The Ethnophotography of Difference" in *A New History of Photography* Michel Frizot, ed. English edition [Cologne: Könemann, 1998], 258–271.) In his introduction Thomson wrote that he "frequently enjoyed the reputation of being a dangerous geomancer, and my camera was held to be a dark mysterious instrument, which combined with my naturally, or supernaturally, intensified eyesight gave me power to see through rocks and mountains, to pierce the very souls of the natives." His encyclopedic drive helped formulate a Western style of typecasting and foreshadowed his later work, *Street Life in London* (1877).

Thomson's *Street Life in London* (1877),[12] made with writer Adolphe Smith, harnesses the photograph to social reform. The introduction states: "The unquestionable accuracy of this testimony will enable us to present true types of the London Poor and shield us from the accusation of either underrating or exaggerating individual peculiarities of appearance."[13] Thomson's previous experiences taught him how to pose people in an unrehearsed manner, to picture trades practiced by working people: street doctor, flower seller, public disinfector. *Street Life,* issued in serial form, contains thirty-six *Woodburytypes*[14] from photographs Thomson made to illustrate Smith's dramatic and moralistic text. This format helped establish the so-

7.12 CAMILLE SILVY. *River Scene, la Vallée de l'Huisne, France,* 1858 (print: 1860s). 10⅛ × 14 inches. Albumen silver print. Courtesy J. Paul Getty Museum, Los Angeles.

cial documentation practice of linking image and text to present a desired meaning. Smith wanted the episodes to increase middle-class sensitivity to the dilemmas of the urban poor and make them more willing to improve working-class living conditions (see Figure 7.15). The project had at least one tangible result, the construction of an embankment to stop the flooding on the Thames River that had been plaguing London's poor.

As urban renewal projects got underway in Paris, London, and Glasgow, photographic surveys were organized to record the doomed historical architecture (see Chapter 4). In 1868 and again in 1877, the Glasgow Improvement Trust commissioned the Scottish photographer **Thomas Annan** [1829–1887] to document the buildings and streets of the city.[15] The first part of his assignment appeared as albumen prints in 1868 and later as photogravures in *Old Closes* [unsavory, narrow passageways between multistoried buildings] *and Streets of Glasgow* (1900). Annan's images "afford a peep into dark and dismal dens unvisited by

the great purifying agencies of sun and wind, and in surveying them, we instinctively feel that human life born, bred, or led within their shades is sorely handicapped, and that the day of their extinction is more than due."[16] Although Annan did not concentrate on people and the project's aim was romantic and sentimental rather than reformist, his attention to light reveals the dark tactile sensations of dampness and slime that make up the unhealthy character of the buildings inhabited by the working poor (see Figure 7.16). Annan's gloomy, realistic depiction of inner city slums, rarely encountered in British art, can be seen as a reflection of a God-fearing capitalist's obligation to care for those who labor for society. The work helped to establish an urban documentary style and can be linked with John Thomson and the later work of Jacob Riis and Eugène Atget.

The Other

Picture/text combinations, as in Figure 7.17, allow us to more accurately decipher how photographers contextualize their subjects. Critics today, such as Edward W. Said (*Orientalism,* 1978), argue that Western cultures have systematically misrepresented non-Western

7.13 SAMUEL BOURNE. *The Viceroy's Elephants*, ca. 1866–67. 9¼ × 11¼ inches. Albumen silver print. Photographs like *The Viceroy's Elephants* portray the exotic and powerful trappings of the British Imperial Administration (the raj) who took over the Indian government from the East India Company. Pax Britannia was maintained by a large military and a minimum of mixing with the native peoples. Bourne's work maintained a Western appreciation for the subcontinent's splendors and cultures without questioning the whites-only social policies. Courtesy George Eastman House.

peoples as exotically *the Other* in order to achieve political and economic dominance (see Figure 7.18). The concept of *the Other* refers to groups including women, people of color, inhabitants of the Third World, and gays and lesbians, that have traditionally been denied economic, political, and social power. Psychoanalysis has expanded into loose designation to include those mental constructs that do not fit into mainstream thinking. Western depictions often fail to grant *the Other* the same humanity and psychological complexity as their male European counterparts. *Others* are viewed as static objects rather than active subjects who possess the same desires and needs as the viewer. Adherence to these traditions make up the foundation of Western prejudice and its psychic armament against understanding anyone who is different from the mainstream culture. Control of production and distribution allow dominant societies to regulate history and its interpretation. In *Culture and Imperialism* (1993) Said critiques the Western military along with media and consumer cultures that have been used to erase native values. Said maintains such policies are counterproductive because they give rise to virulent forms of anti-imperialism, including fundamentalism, nativism, terrorism, and ethnic identity politics.

The American West: The Narrative and the Sublime

At the end of the Civil War, America's attention shifted from pessimistic devastation to the optimistic development of its Western frontier regions. The American West, unlike Europe, was not a fixed culture. Its perceived attraction was that no culture, group, or government was seen as having hegemony over others. The West was an escape from enclosure to a wide-open space without history. It was a dynamic force of physical and transcendental freedom, waiting for someone to act upon. The American spirit was not housed in a

7.14   LÁLÁ DEEN DAYAL.   *Water Palace Deeg,*
1893, from *Indian Ancient Architecture Album.* 7⅝ ×
10⁹⁄₁₆ inches. Albumen silver print. Indian photographer Lálá Deen Dayal [1844–1910], started working
about 1870, becoming the official photographer to the
viceroy and later to the nizain (ruler) of Hyderabad. At
the turn of the century he made before-and-after images of starving children who were fed by the nizam to
provide evidence of his government's relief programs.
In his *Indian Ancient Architecture Album* (1893), symmet-
rical landscape compositions and effective use of light,
as in *Water Palace Deeg,* create a sense of timelessness.
Dayal's photography business is still run by his descendants today.   Courtesy George Eastman House.

cathedral but within people who believed that spiritual
growth necessitated breaking free from society's con-
strictions and moving instead toward purifying solitude, toward nature, toward Walden. "I go and come
with a strange liberty in nature,"[17] said Thoreau. The
West combined these mythic ideals of American *ex-
ceptionalism,* a contract with nature that distrusted authority and strove for dignity through performance. In
the West, the easterner was a dude, a comic character
encumbered with useless knowledge who was too
bogged down by theory to act. The completion of the

transcontinental railroad, connecting the east and west
coasts in 1869, made the West an economic site for
government-planned programs of expansion and settlement that outwardly manifested the restless American spirit. The railroads hired artists, photographers,
and writers to produce narrative, informational stories
(propaganda, in fact), designed to excite would-be settlers, travelers, investors, and the public about the region's potential. They were assigned to replace the va-
cancy of the Great American Desert with promotional
images of an Eden-like farmland that would get viewers to commit their families and savings, sight unseen,
to a landscape pictured in a book.[18] These storytellers
relied on the *Manifest Destiny* theme, the duty and the
right of the United States to expand its territory and influence throughout North America, reflecting a can-do
spirit in a time of increasing population and recession.
Manifest Destiny provided a rationalization for dominating this intercultural contact zone, for conquering
the wilderness, its native peoples, and the westward
expansion of American civilization. It all occurred in
front of a backdrop of romanticism that portrayed the
sublime grandeur of nature, particularly the mountains, as evidence of the role a supreme deity played in
the Creation. Public curiosity and tall tales about the
West fueled demand for photographic documents that

7.15   JOHN THOMSON.   *The Crawlers*, ca.
1876–77, from *Street Life in London*, 1877. 4½ × 3⁷⁄₁₆
inches. Woodburytype. The crawlers "are old women
reduced by vice and poverty to that degree of
wretchedness which destroys even the energy to
beg."[19] They were so feeble from hunger and lack of
sleep that they crawled on their hands and knees to get
their primary form of sustenance, bread and hot water
for tea. The crawler in this photograph was keeping a
baby while its mother worked in a coffee shop.   Courtesy George Eastman House.

constructed an emblematic narrative landscape of accomplishment; gorges bridged, mountains tunneled,
and nature subjugated (see Figure 7.19).

Photography had to compete with the size, symbols,
and dramatic license of artists who were the principal
Western storytellers to a public expecting to be enter-
tained and informed. George Catlin [1796–1872] put
on theatrical presentations of his Indian paintings in the
1830s and followed then with his "Indian Gallery," designed for European audiences, which featured artifacts
and live Indians. During the 1850s, magic lantern
shows accompanied by narrative dialogue became popular. Words enabled storytellers to take even inconsequential photographs and make them part of a larger

7.16   THOMAS ANNAN.   *Close, No. 31 Saltmarket,* from *Old Closes and Streets of Glasgow,* 1868–1877. 10⅞ × 9 inches. Albumen print. The lack of detail in the man standing against the wall in shadow takes away his human individuality. The long exposure produced a ghostly three-legged child, seeming to say that this environment can distort life. The broken windows, laundry hanging from buildings, and waste water running in an open sewer ditch convey a depressing, claustrophobic feeling of a worn, medieval stone city.   Courtesy George Eastman House.

tale. In the spirit of entertainment, information, and theater, painted panoramas, incorporating music and spoken narratives, became fashionable. The panorama's sequential linear format was spatially suited for celebrating and documenting the expansive growth and prosperity of America's vast, horizontal, western space.

Clarence King's [1842–1901] motives were not commercial but scientific and theological when he participated in and led geological and topographical expeditions in the American West. King was interested in the relationship between God and geology and rejected the prevailing belief, *uniformitarianism,* that all geo-

logical functions took place slowly and evenly over time. King believed that periods of calm were interrupted by catastrophic intervals of what he called Divine Creation that compelled life forms to alter or perish. For King geology offered a way to use scientific knowledge to confirm the Old Testament's account of God's violent creation of the world. As a supporter of John Ruskin's belief in the symmetry of art and science, King believed artists should blend their capability to communicate with scientific observations about nature to transcend specific situations and make universal statements. Much of nineteenth-century American landscape imagery was formulated on the model of the picturesque, the sublime, and the beautiful, dealing with the virtues of nature and its transcendental ramifications (see Chapter 3). The American West was the place where the hand of God could be cherished in its authentic splendor. Expressions of these beliefs are disclosed in the images of the photographers with whom King worked, including Carleton Watkins and Timothy O'Sullivan.

After apprenticing with California photographic pioneers James Ford and Robert Vance and photographing mines and the Mission Santa Clara, **Carleton E. Watkins** [1829–1916] undertook his series of Yosemite views. Yosemite, the sublime dream place of romantic painters, was discovered by white settlers in the early 1850s and was an organized tourist site by 1856. Following Ruskin's precepts, Yosemite was considered to be a finished, natural work of art, and beginning with C. L. Weed in 1859, photographers confronted Yosemite with deliberate discretion and impeccable technique. Often using a mammoth plate camera (18 × 21 inches), Watkins initiated the cardinal construct of American landscape photography: God was in the details, a concept that was brought to a climax a hundred years later by Ansel Adams. His large, toned albumen prints emphasize the abundant richness of highlight detail and embellish the dark shadows and black tones, while adding contrast that makes the mountains appear to rise out of the background. Watkins dealt with the wet-plate's blue light sensitivity by creating layered compositions that increase the illusion of depth. Utilizing compositional devices, especially water, Watkins leads the eye upward towards mountain peaks, adding to an image's three-dimensionality. Watkins favored dome-topped prints (rounded on the top corners) to hold the eye at the crest of the print (see Figure 7.20). Aside from studying the established subject matter of painters, Watkins found a

7.17   THOMAS M. EASTERLY.   *Na-che-ninga,*
Chief of the Iowas, 1849. Daguerreotype. Numerous
photographers undertook ethnological studies, mostly
to satisfy curiosity, but few were designed like *Street Life*
to reach an audience that could influence decisions. In
America, daguerreotypists such as Thomas Easterly (active 1840s), applied a straight-ahead portrait approach
to Native American sitters, giving them the same grave
demeanor as everyone else who sat for a daguerreotype. Later stereographs, made by expedition photographers who used the camera to reaffirm their
stereotypical beliefs, became the popular method of
distributing studies of Native American groups to
white society.   Courtesy Missouri Historical Society, St.
Louis.

formal voice for the Western landscape and its sense of
space directly from natural sources, formulating a sophisticated practice that personified the artistic and societal values America was searching to affirm.

In 1867, Timothy O'Sullivan became the photographer for Clarence King's Geological Explorations of
the Fortieth Parallel. O'Sullivan's views mark a departure from representing nature as a place of salvation.
O'Sullivan saw the West with "eastern" eyes, as a hostile place where one must struggle to survive (see Figure 7.21). Whether this vision was influenced by the
horrors he had witnessed during the Civil War or by
campfire talks with Clarence King, O'Sullivan presented the West in the ancient spirit of the sublime, as a
place that is astonishing, demanding, and terrifying
(see chapter opener). Since the main purpose of the

7.18   MR. OSCANYAN (?).   *Turkish Lady of Rank.* Plate #4 from *Oriental Album.* 4 × 2½ inches. Carte-de-visite. This *Oriental Album* contains carte-de-visites of Turkish women with text that extols the exotic and forbidden: "The Ladies of the East are very fond of a listless state of repose as they lounge on their silken couches and smoke their long and graceful *chibouks,* or puff the fumes of *tombeky* to the gurgling music of the *nargilleh* or water pipe. Thus hours are often passed in delightful revery, the monotony of which is only broken by occasional glances in the enameled hand-mirror . . . or by giving vent to their pleasurable emotions in some of their wild native melodies."[21]   Courtesy George Eastman House.

photographs was scientific O'Sullivan did not have to be overly concerned with the paying public or with sticking to conventional straight presentations, and it is now known that he tilted his camera to make formations appear more menacing.[20]

In 1870, O'Sullivan was hired as the photographer for the Darien survey that was attempting to determine a route for a canal across the Panamanian Isthmus. In 1871, he commenced working with Lieutenant George Montague Wheeler's survey, which ascended the Colorado River through the Grand Canyon. He spent 1872 back with King's survey and did his final field work again with Wheeler during the 1873 and 1874 seasons. Since the majority of O'Sullivan's images were only seen by a handful of people as original prints in albums, they did not have a big influence on public perception or on the practice. In late 1880, O'Sullivan was appointed chief photographer for the U.S. Treasury Department. He succumbed to tuberculosis in early 1882.

After serving in the Union Army, **William Henry Jackson** [1843–1942] opened a photographic studio in Omaha, NE, in 1868, doing portraits and documenting the building of the Union Pacific Railroad. In 1870, Ferdinand V. Hayden, the director for the U.S. Geological and Geographical Survey of the Territories, made Jackson the official photographer of his survey team, enabling him to spend most of the summers between 1870 to 1879 making photographs. In 1871, the Hayden team began to explore the bubbling mud pots, steaming geysers, exotically colored hot springs, and rushing waterfalls of Yellowstone. Using a mule named "Hypo" and an ambulance to haul his equipment and 400 glass plates, Jackson worked with the survey's landscape painter, Thomas Moran, to "solve many problems of composition."[22] Jackson's vision tempered the sublime with the picturesque, representing the West as a classically beautiful milieu while providing mythical publicity images for Hayden's project. Jackson's dramatic narrative context provided an official voice, giving a face to a restless society's search for its national character while answering fables about the West. His famous image of *Old Faithful in Eruption* was instrumental in Yellowstone's development as a tourist attraction. Hayden placed Jackson's images in an album, *Yellowstone's Scenic Wonders* (1872), and circulated it among prominent Washington officials, helping persuade Congress to pass legislation making Yellowstone the country's

7.19   ANDREW J. RUSSELL.   *Trestle Work, Promontory Point, Salt Lake Valley,* ca. 1868–69, from *Sun Pictures of Rocky Mountain Scenery,* 1870. 6 × 8 inches. Albumen silver print. Andrew J. Russell painted panoramas before documenting the Civil War and the construction of the Union Pacific Railroad during 1868–70. Russell replicated the panorama's narrative, linear approach in his railroad pictures, accounting for one section of track after the next, hardly getting out of sight of the rails. The photographers accompanying the government surveys, traveling along invisible meridian and parallel lines, labeled their prints with their precise locations. Russell not only documented the joining of the rails but also the engineering accomplishments of a multinational work crew made up largely of Chinese immigrants. The appendages of the steam locomotive, tracks, trestles, and water towers added new elements into the natural landscape and became popular subjects in literature and painting.   Courtesy George Eastman House.

first national park. In 1874, Jackson and Ernest Ingersoll of the New York *Tribune* became the first white people to rediscover and document the Rio San Juan cliff dwelling ruins (ca. 800s) in what is now Mesa Verde National Park. Ironically, these first white explorers seemed to realize that their descriptions would change these pristine areas, which would require government protection in order to survive.

Jackson's most famous image was *The Mountain of the Holy Cross* (1873) (see Figure 7.22). Since the time of the Spanish explorers there were rumors about a mountain with a snow-filled cross. Jackson wrote how he and two companions carried his photographic equipment up Notch Mountain, across the ravine from the Holy Cross, where Jackson made eight exposures as "the long flamelike shadows on Holy Cross were rapidly sweeping down into the valley. Since 1873 I have been back four or five times. I have used the best cameras and the most sensitive emulsions on the market. I have snapped my shutter morning, noon, and afternoon. I have never come close to matching those first plates."[23]

In early 1879, Congress curtailed all survey activities. Jackson moved to Denver and became a prominent industrial photographer, opening his photographic and publishing business, which he ran until 1898. Western

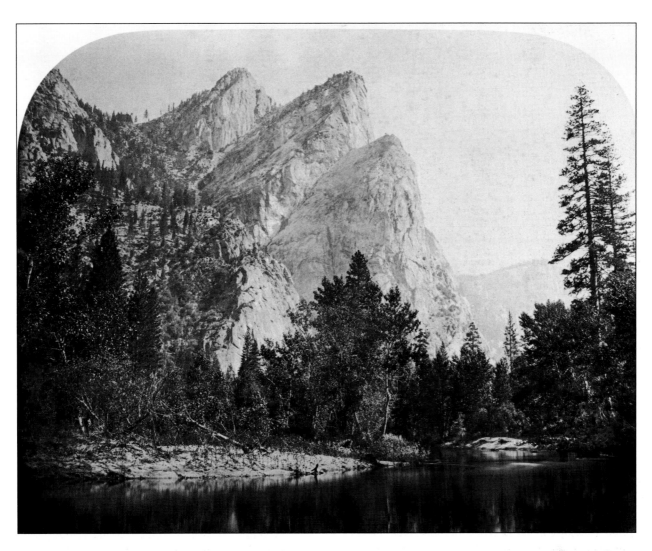

7.20 CARLETON E. WATKINS. *El-Eachas* or *Three Brothers,* ca. 1861. 16³⁄₁₆ × 20¹⁰⁄₁₆ inches. Albumen silver print. Watkins's huge plates capture the detail and awe-inspiring scale and sublime potency of Yosemite, enabling photographers to compete with monumental landscape painters such as Albert Bierstadt, Frederick Church, and Thomas Moran. Watkins's images helped to photographically establish the mountain landscape as an emblem of transcendental idealism by accentuating the energetic attributes of these formations.   Courtesy George Eastman House.

railroads commissioned him to photograph their operations, opulent accommodations, and spectacular scenery to encourage commerce and travel. As railroads ran by measured clock time they promoted corporeal rather than geological time that linked capitalism and technological achievements to present a public image of an imaginary future of boundless progress. The railroads wanted images that depicted a tamed and organized landscape that could be converted from a phenomenon of contemplation into a commodity of profit.

As the frontier closed, Jackson made a business arrangement with the Detroit Photographic Company (1898–1924) to convert his images into postcards and *chromolithographs,* colored prints made by lithography, using a separate stone or plate for each color. The postcard was an ideal medium to distribute the commissioned views of tourist interest for the railroads and related businesses like the Fred Harvey company that ran hotels and restaurants.[24] Jackson's business acumen got his images into the hands of the public, extensively influencing how the nation saw the West. Jackson remained vigorous into his nineties, taking credit for over 80,000 pictures[25] and writing his autobiography, *Time Exposure* (1940). His images cast the American West as a stupendous, pristine, and generous Valhalla, permeated with astonishing phenomena and remaining ever benevolent.

Eadweard Muybridge [1830–1904] began life in England as Edward James Muggeridge, but he changed his name and went to America in 1852. He worked for Carleton Watkins in the early 1860s, before publishing his own views of Yosemite. These and subsequent "examples of the perfection to which photography can

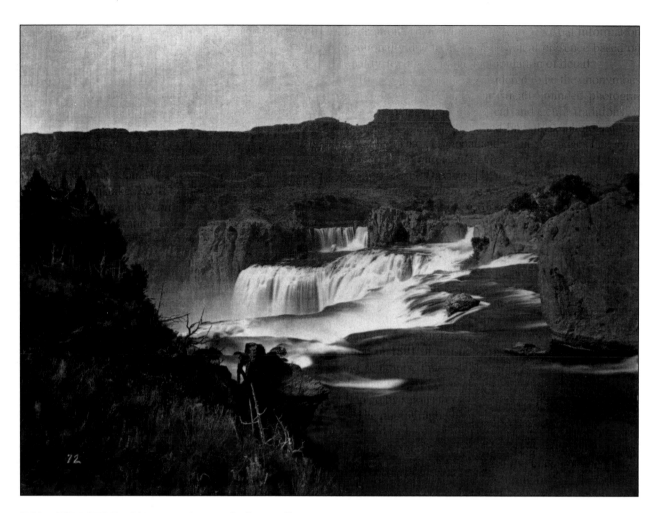

7.21   TIMOTHY O'SULLIVAN.   *Shoshone Falls,*
Idaho, 1868. 7¾ × 10⅝ inches. Albumen silver print.
O'Sullivan's views at the Falls of Soshone speak of danger and the power of nature. His views of the vastness
of the West embrace themes of isolation, silence, and
solitude. O'Sullivan's views point out the insignificance
of people and are reflective of Clarence King's writing:
"No sheltering pine or mountain distance of uppiled
[sic] Sierras guard the approach to the Shoshone. You
ride upon a waste—the pale earth stretched in desola-
tion. Suddenly, you stand upon a brink. As if the earth
has yawned, black walls flank the abyss. . . . You turn
from the brink as from a frightful glimpse of the In-
ferno, and when you have gone a mile the earth seems
to have closed again. Every trace of the cañon has vanished, and the stillness of the desert reigns."[26]   Courtesy
George Eastman House.

attain in the delineation of sublime and beautiful
scenery"[27] brought Muybridge an international reputation. The full plate views, about 6 × 8 inches when
trimmed, were distinguished by splendid cloud effects
(see Figure 7.23). Muybridge devised a "sky shade," a
shutterlike device permitting various exposures to be
made on a single plate, to compensate for the wet-

plate's over-sensitivity to blue light. This let Muybridge
make a single negative, instead of the combination
printer's two, and more accurately portray a range of
tones. To position himself squarely within the grand
landscape tradition, Muybridge returned to Yosemite
Valley in 1872 with a mammoth-plate camera (20 × 24
inches) that yielded 18 × 22-inch prints. During this
time Muybridge was associated with the landscape
painter Albert Bierstadt, who reportedly made on-site
consultations and acted as a patron. The lengths that
Muybridge would go to make his views were reported
in the *Alta California*:

> he has waited several days in the neighborhood to get the
> proper conditions of atmosphere for some of his views; he
> has cut down trees by the score that interfered with the cam-
> eras from the best point of sight; he had himself lowered by
> ropes down precipices to establish his instruments in places
> where the full beauty of the object to be photographed could
> be transferred to the negative; he has gone to points where his
> packers refused to follow him, and he has carried the appara-
> tus himself rather than to forego the picture on which he has
> set his mind.[28]

Numerous photographers covered the West between
1865 and 1880 (see Figure 7.24). William Bell (see
Chapter 5) became the photographer for Lieutenant
George M. Wheeler's 1872 expedition in Arizona and

106. MOUNTAIN OF THE HOLY-CROSS

7.22   WILLIAM HENRY JACKSON.   *The Mountain of the Holy Cross*, 1873. 10¼ × 13¼ inches. Albumen silver print.   Numerous photographers have tried to duplicate Jackson's image without success.[29] Today the picture is a curiosity, but to the viewers of that time, besieged by theories of positivism and Darwinian evolution, the image was widely viewed as a concrete symbol of Christian faith and a solid manifestation of God's law.   Courtesy George Eastman House.

Utah. **Frank Jay Haynes** [1860–1920], who obtained the first official photographic concessionaire lease at Yellowstone, followed the formal compositional artifice of the times, but his pictures often revealed how intruding humans were changing unsullied nature. Improvements in reproduction technology reduced the demand for original views, shifting the marketing and distribution of photographs from individual photographers to national companies. Haynes arranged with Photochrom Company,[30] the postcard branch of the Detroit Photographic Company, to reproduce his work. Postcards increased image production but diminished the scale of landscape and altered it through the inclusion of text. Coloring techniques softened photographic description through abstraction and sensualization, manufacturing romantic and impressionistic notions about the West.

The 1880s saw the closing of the frontier. Commercial interests demanded the West be made safe for development. In this burgeoning climate of commercial travel, **Isaiah West Taber** (1830–1912) issued *View Album and Business Guide of San Francisco* (see Figure 7.25), a protean Yellow Pages of local businesses whose purpose was to "combine art and advertising . . . for businessmen . . . in hotels and mail steamers of America, England, and Australia [that] will be able to relieve the tedium of travel on industries and products of California, and gain some idea, or renew their acquaintance with, its beautiful scenery. . . . **TREAT THIS BOOK KINDLY.**"[31]

The fragmentation of the Indian alliance and the use of industrial technology by the whites, including firearms, telegraph, and railroads, and the byproducts of clashing cultures, such as smallpox and the slaughter of the buffalo, insured European control of the Western lands and its indigenous peoples. As curiosity about the West diminished, so did the demand for views, forcing photographers to develop new markets.

Breakthroughs in vision and technology redefined and reorganized cultural ideals. The new concepts of scientific and mechanical time and space enabled European culture to control the means of distribution and monopolize the practice of representation. The

7.23. EADWEARD MUYBRIDGE. *Clouds Rest,* Valley of the Yosemite, ca. 1870 (print ca. 1874). 16⅞ × 21⁷⁄₁₆ inches. Albumen silver print. Muybridge's views of Yosemite demonstate young America's nature worship and nationalism. Muybridge did not include people; his pictures are of unadulterated wilderness, giving visual form to the notion that God created this abundance for a new chosen people. Here was paradise regained, the proof of Manifest Destiny—that it was God's wish for Americans to transfigure the uncultivated land into a useful Garden of Eden. The dark side of this concept can be seen in Muybridge's Modoc War (1872–73) stereocards,[32] which pictured racial stereotypes and were produced for a white audience who used them as proof that their prejudices could be documented by the camera.   Courtesy George Eastman House.

wet-plate's transparency clouded the issues surrounding its so-called empirical sense of genuineness. By dominating the mechanical structuring of space within the frame, photographers determined not only what was represented but *how* it was represented. The consumers of such images were likely to identify with the structure and aims of a viewmaker who reaffirmed their beliefs. People curious to see what they had never seen before, but naive about how these documents were formulated, were vulnerable to a viewmaker's scheme. This vulnerability allowed the values behind the views to be absorbed by viewers and shape their thoughts about what they were seeing. People had not yet learned to actively question the motivations driving the creation of photographs. The lesson that photographic truth is as transparent and changeable as any good negative had yet to be formulated.

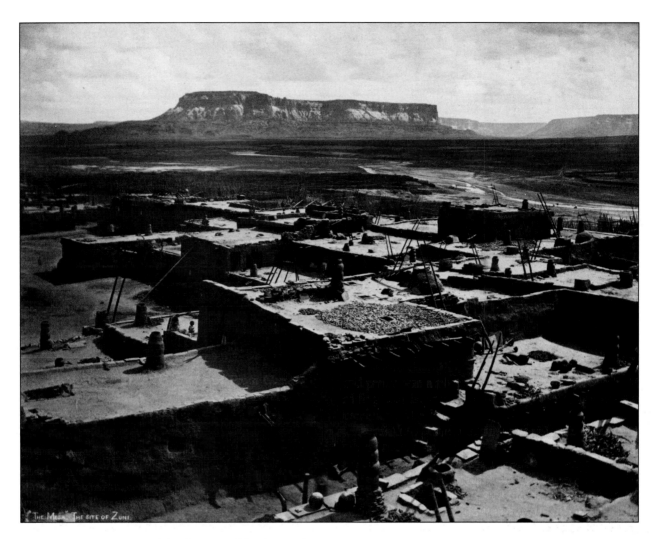

7.24.   JOHN K. HILLERS. *Captains of the Cañon,* De Chelley Cañon, AZ, ca. 1875. 13 × 9⅝ inches. Albumen silver print.   Courtesy George Eastman House.

John Wesley Powell [1834–1902] was a geologist and ethnologist who surveyed the Colorado River in 1869, becoming the first white person to pass through the Grand Canyon by boat—a feat for a man who had lost an arm in the Civil War. **John K. Hillers** [1843–1925], originally an oarsman, became the group's photographer, producing some bold compositions that captured a sense of place and the quality of light while making ethnological studies of the indigenous peoples (see Figure 7.24). Hillers remained Powell's photographer from 1873–79, when he was appointed Chief Photographer for the newly established U.S. Geological Survey, which Powell was instrumental in creating and headed from 1881–1894.

7.25.   ISAIAH WEST TABER. *Pacific Saw Manufacturing Co.*, ca. 1880. From *View Album and Business Guide of San Francisco*, 1884. 7⁵⁄₁₆ × 9¼ inches. Albumen silver print.   Courtesy George Eastman House.

Endnotes

1   John Ruskin, *Works,* eds. E. T. Cook and A. Wedderburn (London, 1906), vol. 3, 210. Letter to W. H. Harrison, August 12, 1846.

2   C. Jabez Hughes, "On Art Photography," *American Journal of Photography,* new series vol. 3, no. 17, February 1, 1861, 261–63.

3   Dr. John Nicol, "Photography in the Field," *The British Journal of Photography,* vol. XXXIV, no. 1403, March 25, 1887, 184–86.

4   Du Camp's traveling companion for the French Ministry of Education commission, Gustave Flaubert, provides a connection between topographical photography and the realistic novel. Flaubert was known for his efforts to find the exact word (*le mot juste*) and for his aim for complete objectivity. Flaubert, who assisted Du Camp, began working on *Madame Bovary* (1857) upon his return from this voyage. For an intriguing interpretation of this journey, see Francis Steegmuller, *Flaubert in Egypt: A Sensibility on Tour* (Boston: Little, Brown & Co., 1972).

5   *The Art Journal,* New Series I, November 1862, 227.

6   Maria Antonella Pelizzari, *John Shaw Smith, An Irish Traveler with the Calotype Process (1849–1852).* An unpublished paper presented at the University of New Mexico, Spring Symposium, 1993.

7   Bill Jay, *Victorian Cameraman; Francis Frith's Views of Rural England 1850–1898* (Newton Abbott, David and Charles, 1973), 17.

8   The postcard appeared as a hybrid of the mass-produced albumen print and the carte-de-visite in Europe about 1869. Its straightforward approach filled the void for imagery of historical and tourist sites, making it popular as a collectible, low-cost method of communication. When coupled with new photomechanical processes, it helped elevate the level of visual literacy. The postcard imparted the value of the straight-on stare and the appreciation of the vernacular.

9   See "Photography on Mont Blanc," *The Photographic News,* vol. V, no. 155, August 23, 1861, 401–02.

10   *Great Eastern,* three years in the making and capable of transporting 4,000 passengers plus a crew of 400, was a symbol of imperialist pride. It was launched in 1858 and laid the first transatlantic cable.

11   See Samuel Bourne, "Narrative of a Photographic Trip to Kashmir and Adjacent Districts," *British Journal of Photography,* vol. XIII, no. 335, October 5, 1866, 474–75. This article was published in 9 installments running through vol. XIV, no. 353, February 2, 1867, 63–64.

12   *Street Life in London* was modeled on Henry Mayhew's *London Labour and London Poor* (1850), which was illustrated by wood engravings based in part on daguerreotypes made under the direction of Richard Beard and "cleaned-up" by the engravers. The engraving process separated the subjects from their surrounding, causing them to lose their veracity. Mayhew's combining of interviews and photographs of London's urban poor became the model for legitimate sociological documentation.

13   John Thomson and Adolphe Smith, *Street Life in London* (London: Sampson Low, Marston, Searle and Rivington, 1877), preface.

14   The Woodburytype was a photomechanical process, patented by Walter B. Woodbury in 1865, in which a negative was exposed to bichromated gelatin to produce a shallow relief mold, following the contours of the image, that was placed in contact with a block of lead. The block was coated with pigmented gelatinous ink and transferred to paper by means of a hydraulic press. The Woodbury print often displays a visible relief, but reveals no structural grain, thus possessing all the tonal delicacy of the original photograph. They were widely used for book illustrations in the 1870s and 1880s.

15   Annan operated studios that did portraits, architecture, art reproductions, and landscapes and was the father of photog-

rapher J. Craig Annan (1864–1946), who was active in the Pictorialist movement.

16   William Young, introduction to Thomas Annan, *The Old Closes and Streets of Glasgow* (Glasgow: James MacLehose & Sons, 1900), 22.

17   Henry David Thoreau, *Walden,* or *Life in the Woods* (New York: Library of America, 1985), 425.

18   See Jonathan Raban, *Bad Land: An American Romance* (New York: Pantheon Books, 1996).

19   John Thomson and Adolphe Smith, *Street Life in London,* 81–84.

20   See *Second View: The Rephotographic Survey Project* essay by Paul Berger; Mark Klett, chief photographer; Ellen Manchester, project director; JoAnn Verburg, project coordinator (Albuquerque: University of New Mexico Press, 1984), 17, 20–21.

21   Mr. Oscanyan (?), *Oriental Album,* carte-de-visites with printed text. No additional information. Opening text pictures Mr. Oscanyan, the Oriental lecturer in citizen's costume. "He is the first Oriental educated in the U.S. He received his education at New York University after which he returned home."

22   *Time Exposure: The Autobiography of William Henry Jackson,* intro. Ferenc M. Szasz (Albuquerque: University of New Mexico Press, 1986). Reprint. Originally published: New York: Van Rees Press, 1940.

23   Ibid., 218.

24   See Edward Buscombe, "Inventing Monument Valley: Nineteenth Century Landscape Photography and Western Film" in Patrice Petro ed., *Fugitive Images: From Photography to Video* (Bloomington: Indiana University Press, 1995), 101–02.

25   The Colorado Historical Society has 53,879 glass plate negatives made west of the Mississippi River and the Library of Congress has 30,000 negatives associated with the east and with foreign countries. Some of the negatives were

acquired or made by associates, but unlike Mathew Brady, Jackson produced the lion's share.

26   Clarence King, "The Falls of the Shoshone," *The Overland Monthly,* vol. 5, no. 4 (October 1870), 379–85.

27   From Muybridge's 1868 brochure cited in Mary V. Jessup Hood and Robert Bartlett Haas, "Eadweard Muybridge's Yosemite Valley Photographers 1867–1872," California Historical Society Quarterly, vol. XLII, no. I (March 1963), 10.

28   Ibid, 18.

29 Some critics claimed Jackson retouched the snowy cross portion of the image. Handwork does appear in the shadowy stream (lower right center) leading up to the cross, but not in the area around the cross itself. There is nothing unusual about this practice, as wet-plate photographers relied on handwork for effect as well as to correct for deficiencies in the process. It is probable that erosion has caused the arm to retain less snow.

30   Photochrom was a Swiss-developed photolithographic process for making a continuous-tone color rendition of a black-and-white photograph using multiple impressions from color-inked lithographic stones.

31   Isaiah West Taber, Introduction to *View Album and Business Guide of San Francisco,* ca. 1884.

32   The Modoc Indians lived in northern California and southwest Oregon. They violently clashed with early white settlers and were forced onto a reservation in 1864. Their chief, Captain Jack, led a band of rebels back to California, triggering the Modoc War of 1872–73 that finally divided the tribe, who now live mainly in Oregon.

CHAPTER EIGHT

New Ways of Visualizing Time and Space

The Inadequacy of Human Vision

ETIENNE-JULES MAREY.
Chronophotographic study of Man Pole Vaulting. 1890–1891. 2¹²⁄₁₆ × 4³⁄₁₆ inches. Albumen silver print. Courtesy George Eastman House.

Marey's picturing of the "all at oneness" of time, its flow as a progression of events, broke with the traditional Renaissance representation of a still, solidified moment. Marey's work was indicative of how art and science were combining to change the way people saw the world.

The technical innovations of the nineteenth century altered and expanded the perimeters of human vision in art and science. As early as 1834, Sir Charles Wheatstone observed that an object painted on a revolving disc appeared to be stationary when illuminated by intense electric light. He also noticed that flying insects seemed to be fixed in mid-air by the same means. In 1851, Henry Fox Talbot attached a page of the London *Times* to a swiftly revolving wheel in a darkened room, uncapped the lens of his camera, and made an exposure of about 1/100,000 of a second by means of an electric spark, sharply freezing the action of the moving paper. Talbot concluded that pictures of moving objects could be made by illuminating them with a sudden electric flash. By the 1860s, as we have learned, photographers were making instantaneous stereoscopic views that arrested the action of

8.1   EADWEARD MUYBRIDGE.   *Galloping Horse, Motion Study—Sallie Gardner,* owned by Leland Stanford, running at a 1.40 gait over the Palo Alto track, June 19, 1878. 9³⁄₁₆ × 12 inches. Collotype. Courtesy George Eastman House.

Locomotion

people walking on the street. In 1887 Ernst Mach, an Austrian scientist, used an electric spark (the precursor of flash) as a lighting source to make postage-sized, stop-action images of projectiles moving at about 765 miles per hour. By the mid-1890s, spark exposures of one-millionth of a second were being made by scientists such as Lord Rayleigh and Théodore Lullin (who photographed dripping tap water) and A. M. Worthington (who photographed splashing milk), providing the first images of previously unseeable occurrences. What these photographs depicted was often startlingly different from earlier visual depictions, making it obvious that human vision was unreliable for detecting events that unfolded in fractions of a second. New methods developed that affected the look and content of photographs and further altered society's sense of how time and space were visually represented.

In 1872 Leland Stanford, a builder of the Central Pacific Railroad, former governor of California, and horse enthusiast, hired **Eadweard Muybridge** to photographically prove that a running horse had all four feet off the ground.[1] The slow wet-plate process gave inconclusive results. Before additional experiments could be carried out, Muybridge went on trial for killing his wife's lover. Although a jury acquitted him in 1874, he left the country and didn't return to San Francisco until 1877. When he resumed the work for Stanford, he used a *ripen emulsion,* one aged for several days at 90°F to increase its sensitivity. It produced underexposed negatives of a silhouetted horse with all four hooves off the ground. Because Muybridge had retouched the pictures "for the purpose of giving a better effect to the details,"[2] however, their authenticity was challenged. To alleviate doubts, the experiment was redone and expanded from a single camera to a battery of cameras.

Under radiant California sunshine, against a white background on a limed track, Muybridge arranged twenty-four cameras at right angles to the line of motion. Threads, connected to electric switches, were strung

8.2   THOMAS EAKINS.   *Jesse Godley,* 1884.
Chronophotograph taken with a single-disk, Marey-
wheel camera.   Courtesy Philadelphia Museum of Art: Gift
of Charles Bregler.

across the track. The horse raced by, breaking the
threads, firing each shutter at about 1/2000 of a second.
These silhouetted images confirmed that the horse had
all four feet off the ground. What was surprising was that
all four feet left the ground only when the horse had its
feet tucked under its abdomen. People were astounded
because none of the photographs showed the horse in a
painterly hobbyhorse pose, with its front and back legs
fully extended. The photographs were considered preposterous because they did not match the accepted
modes of representation. Realizing the importance of
such pictures, Stanford commissioned Muybridge to
photograph additional animals and people in motion.[3]

Muybridge used photographic images and the phenomenon of *persistence of vision,* the sensation that images are continuous, to show an audience moving pictures. Eighteen drawings from the horse series were
reproduced in the October 19, 1878, issue of the *Scientific
American.* Readers were instructed to cut and paste the
images onto paper strips that were then placed (image
side out) into the interior compartment of a *zoetrope.*
Based on the principle of persistence of vision, a zoetrope
is a simple hand-held rotating drum with an open top that
blends the sequential pictures when viewed through a
series of slits in the side of the drum to produce the illusion of motion. Muybridge began a lecture tour of America and Europe and illustrated his talks with his *zooprax-
iscope,* a modified zoetrope in which transparencies of the
images were mounted on a rotating circular glass and pro-

jected by a magic lantern. The visual uncertainty in Muybridge's presentation can be likened to the sensation of
sitting in a train at a station as a train on the next track is
pulling out. A passenger looking out the window of the
stationary train may perceive that the still train is moving.

While lecturing in Philadelphia in 1883, Muybridge
met realist painter **Thomas Eakins** [1844–1916], who
used the horse pictures as visual source material in his
own paintings and incorporated the camera in his teaching. Eakins suggested Muybridge include a measurement scale in the background of future photographs so
artists could easily copy them. Eakins convinced the
University of Pennsylvania to underwrite Muybridge's
plan for a vastly expanded photographic study of animal
locomotion. Muybridge commenced working in a specially built outdoor studio in June 1884 and concluded
the next summer. The resulting project used animals
from the local zoo and was published by subscription in
eleven volumes in 1887 as *Animal Locomotion,* 781 collotype plates compiled from 19,347 individual photographs. Eakins worked alongside Muybridge during
the first part of the summer, using a *wheel* or *disk camera*[4] to record the successive phases of movement on
one plate. Each facet of the action in an Eakins photograph could be analyzed to give viewers a more accurate
visual analysis of the spatial relationships of the animal's anatomy as it moved through time.

Muybridge continued to use multiple cameras
whose shutters were controlled by an electromagnetic
device, enabling them to be fired at selected intervals,
but he switched to gelatin dry plates, which were easier
to use. His models were photographed against a black
background, which was divided by white threads into a
grid of squares that provided a conceptual Renaissance

8.3   EADWEARD MUYBRIDGE. *Toilet; Stooping, Throwing Wrap Around Shoulders* (Miss Louise, July 23, 1885). 6⅞ × 16½ inches. Collotype.   Courtesy George Eastman House.

device so that the images could be more effortlessly analyzed and drawn. He used a variety of camera arrangements, typically in groups of twelve, to make his images. The first group of cameras was stationed parallel to the subject and the other two groups were set up at angles of sixty and ninety degrees. By the end of the summer of 1885, Muybridge adopted a single camera with a row of twelve shooting lenses and a thirteenth for viewing, allowing all the images to be made on a single plate. This multilens camera could be substituted for one of the batteries of twelve cameras. He photographed men and women, nude and draped, wrestling and hopping, as well as more horses and zoo animals.

Muybridge wanted to formulate a visual dictionary of human and animal locomotion for artists. Muybridge was an artist, not a scientist; he was concerned with "how" subjects in motion looked. He took single images and arranged (collaged) them to form an assemblage that was rephotographed and printed to produce the illusion of movement. His sequencing techniques used persistence of vision to encourage the belief that the action was continuous when it was not. Muybridge chose artistic pictorial effect over making a scientifically accurate and complete recording of movement; to that end, he even altered the numbering system of his negatives to construct a sequence whose individual elements came from different sessions.[5] Muybridge took fragments and individual images and built elaborate narrative sequences in which tiny stories unfolded. While Muybridge's constructions may not be verifiably scientific for the analysis of locomotion, his cinematic montages impacted artists interested in redefining the vocabulary of motion that lay beyond the visual threshold.

Muybridge's work can also be examined for its gender commentary. In his photographs men perform bricklaying and carpentry while women do the sweeping and washing. Under a pseudoscientific guise, Muybridge made visible what was hidden by social convention—a masculine, voyeuristic, erotic fantasy. Muybridge made more plates of nude women than of any other subject, covering a variety of sexual proclivities. His small action sequences of women kissing, taking each other's clothes off, pouring water down each other's throats, dumping water over each other, and smoking in the nude as well as his naked men pole vaulting, wrestling, throwing a discus, and batting a baseball invite viewers to join in these provocative constructions.

Muybridge used the authority of the camera to convince viewers that what they were seeing was accurate, even if it did not conform to anything they had previously seen. Each camera image enclosed a slice of time and space in which formerly invisible aspects of motion were contained. This new reality disturbed the thinking of artists who relied on "being true to nature" as their guiding force. It was clear that what was true could not always be seen and that what could be seen was not always true. Muybridge demonstrated that for many artists *truth* was just another word for conformity. Some artists adjusted their work to make it conform with Muybridge's results, but others saw their interests collide with the alleged veracity of the photograph. The sculptor Auguste Rodin said:

> It is the artist who is truthful and it is photography which lies, for in reality time does not stop, and if the artist succeeds in producing the impression of a movement which takes several moments for accomplishment, his work is certainly less conventional than the scientific image, where time is abruptly suspended.[6]

Unlike Muybridge, **Etienne-Jules Marey** [1830–1904] was a scientist who wanted to make an unseen world visible in an objective manner. A physiologist,

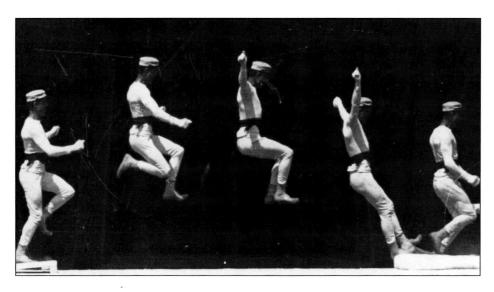

8.4   ETIENNE-JULES MAREY.   *Schenkel, High Jump,* July 1886. Chronophotograph.   Courtesy Cinémathèque Française.

grounded in the tenets of positivism that sought knowledge by describing a phenomenon, Marey wanted hard, measurable facts to analyze animal and human movement. In the late 1850s, Marey built mechanical and pneumatic devices that were directly attached to his subject; they activated a pen resting on a band of moving paper, which recorded the unobservable movements that make up human locomotion. Marey was interested in *how* animals and humans moved as opposed to what they *looked like* while in motion. Marey's search for a technique that would simultaneously display the relationship of all the bodies' moving parts in time and space led him to photography. Marey's quest was to picture a body's "all at oneness"—to picture time as a progression of events in which patterns blend and circulate together and can be simultaneously observed. This thinking was a break with the Renaissance representation of the still frame. It indicated a rupture in the Western perception of time, formed in the fourteenth century with the introduction of clocks that gave a consistent, universal, two-dimensional representation to the previously invisible. Marey was curious about subjective, individual time that flowed at irregular intervals and could not be measured by the uniform rhythm of a clock. He wanted to portray the formation of the new modern instant of "now" in which "moments" were realized as a collection of events that needed to be comprehended all at once. This evolving notion of simultaneous time formed what is now known as *stream of consciousness* and helped to steer a new course in Western art and science in the twentieth century.

Marey's interest in locomotion led him to invent graph methods of recording skeletal and muscle movements. Marey designed the *fusil photographique* (the

photographic gun), a camera with a rotating plate capable of taking a rapid sequence of separate images, to provide an accurate, schematic diagram of muscular movement. Concluding that he would get more factual information if the sequential movements appeared on the same plate, Marey made systematic, multiple exposures on a single plate, *chronophotographs,* using a rotating slit shutter. To eliminate unwanted details, Marey had his models dress in black, with bright metal bands attached to the sides of their arms and legs, and move in front of a black backdrop, thus producing a white, linear graph of geometric movement.

Marey also devised a method to accurately photograph the free flight of birds, which was of interest to early aviators such as the Wright Brothers. Although he never made moving pictures, Marey's method of recording a subject with one camera from a single vantage point was precinematic in concept, and he created a film projector (1892) to analyze his motion studies. In essence Marey reinvented the camera, taking it from a machine of a single moment to one of a flow of moments. This new way of making pictures re-educated the eye, expanded the visual syntax, and revolutionized the representation of the passage of time. Marey's descriptions of human locomotion were applied to physical training programs. His techniques were used to recast how people performed industrial work on assembly lines. His cinema camera would become a cornerstone of the motion picture industry. Artists studied Marey's and Muybridge's images to represent humans and animals in motion, and their works were echoed by the avant-garde.[7] Unfortunately for Marey, he was unable to commercially develop his research and his accomplishments were not widely recognized.

Marey's overlapping images offer an industrialized sense of motion, speed, and time. His images visually link the concepts put forth by Charles Lyell in

8.5   OTTOMAR ANSCHÜTZ.   *Storks*, 1884. 3¾
× 5½ inches. Albumen silver prints.   © Rheinisches
Bildarchiv. Museum Ludwig/Agfa Foto-Historama Köln.

Principles of Geology (1830) and Charles Darwin in
On the Origin of Species (1859) that the earth is not a
static environment, governed by a biblical clock, but a
continuum of time. Marey also influenced the French
philosopher Henri Bergson [1859–1941], whose *Matter and Memory* (1896) argued that time is not made up
of individual, measurable pieces but is a continuous
and indivisible movement. In place of static values
Bergson substituted those of change and motion ("I am
a thing which continues"). Bergson's thinking was popular among artists of the early twentieth century and affected writers such as Marcel Proust (*Remembrance of
Things Past,* 1913–27) and James Joyce (*Ulysses,*
1914–21). Paradoxically, Marey's analytical chrono-
graphs were eventually used by others to undermine
positivism and launch new methods of seeing and
thinking about time and space. Initially, however, the
repetitious rhythms and compressed space of Marey's
chronophotography can be seen in works such as
Georges Seurat's [1859–1891] last study for *Chahut*
(1889) and later in the overlays of Edgar Degas's
[1834–1917] *Frieze of Dancers* (ca. 1895). The dis-

placement of static time into an endless flow of movement altered the artist's rendition of time and space in
such depictions as Marcel Duchamp's *Nude Descending a Staircase* (1912). Its role in the development of
futurism can be seen in Giacomo Balla's *Dynamism of
a Dog on a Leash* (1912).

In 1882, the German photographer **Ottomar Anschütz's** [1846–1907] animal-motion studies led him
to develop a folding hand camera with a *focal-plane
shutter,*[8] considered the prototype of the folding bellows, flatbed-type press camera, which allowed exposures to be made at 1/1000 of a second. His pictures of
nesting storks, featuring detailed images of the birds in
flight, amazed the photographic and scientific communities in 1884. Starting in 1886, Anschütz improved
Muybridge's multiple camera system to allow faster sequential human and animal locomotion studies. His
tachyscope, a modified zoetrope with a vertical rotating
drum instead of a horizontal one, allowed these studies
to be seen in motion. Anschütz's *electrotachyscope,* in
which transparencies were placed on a revolving disk
and illuminated from behind by an electric spark, let a
few people view the image at one time (the images
were not projected). Following the lead of Ernst Mach,
Anschütz also made electric spark photographs of projectiles in flight at the Krupps weapons plant.

8.6   UNKNOWN PHOTOGRAPHER   *Untitled*
[Boy on dock pointing to dog standing on his hind legs], ca. 1890. 2½-inch diameter, (Kodak #1 snapshot). Albumen silver print.   Courtesy George Eastman House.

Transforming Aesthetics: Technical Breakthroughs

Although the wet-plate process was universally adopted, it was difficult and cumbersome. The first collodion dry plates were formulated by French scientist J. M. Taupenot and produced in limited quantity in England in 1860. They were more manageable, but they required exposure times six times longer than wet collodion, making them useful only for static subjects. In 1864, B. J. Sayce [1837–1895] and William Blanchard Bolton [1848–1899] improved the speed with *collodiobromide* dry plates that needed only three times the exposure of a wet-plate. A major breakthrough was made by physician and amateur photographer Richard Leach Maddox [1816–1902], who substituted gelatin for collodion. This greatly simplified the picturemaking process, permitting plates to be sensitized in advance and developed at a later time, thereby encouraging photographers to make pictures that were less conventional in their content and construction. The dry plate disposed of all the equipment and procedures needed to prepare a wet-plate and eliminated the dangerous and odorous alcohol and ether fumes associated with the process—fumes that aggravated chronic health conditions in practitioners like Maddox. Maddox published his finding in the *British Journal of Photography.*[9] Stating that his medical practice did not allow him time to refine his work, he urged others to further the effort.

Improvements in Maddox's method led to the manufacturing of the first practical dry plates in 1878, in which a glass plate was coated with a silver bromide emulsion that had been prepared with a special gelatin binder. These plates were less contrasty and about ten times as sensitive as the wet-plates they were supplanting. Initially, their increased sensitivity was a problem for photographers accustomed to the wet-plate; they overexposed the new gelatin plates and then complained about their poor quality. During the 1880s, the glass was replaced with celluloid. The dry plates freed photographers from having to be their own platemakers, allowing fieldwork without a portable darkroom. Dry plates remained sensitive for months and did not have to be processed immediately. Ripening increased the emulsion's sensitivity, permitting daylight exposure times of a fraction of a second. These breakthroughs opened stop-action images to all photographers, allowing subjects to be represented in ways that were previously not possible, astounding and changing people's perceptions of their world. Edward L. Wilson, editor of *The Philadelphia Photographer,* took gelatin dry plates on a 22,000-mile voyage and developed them upon his return, eight months later. He proclaimed: "It has been the salvation of photography. . . . Blessed then be the dry plate!"[10] The gelatin emulsion changed photographic practice, encouraging photographers to make their lives easier by accepting the commercial standardization of materials, equipment, and processes. Visually, the gelatin emulsion advanced the investigation of motion by providing material access to more practitioners. Scientifically, it encouraged research that extended the emulsion's sensitivity into the green, yellow, orange, and red bands of the spectrum.

Early photographic materials were sensitive only to the blue-violet and ultraviolet portions of the spectrum. In 1873, German photochemist Hermann Wilhelm Vogel [1834–1898] discovered that the addition of certain dyes to an emulsion made it sensitive to the spectral region that was absorbed by the dye, opening up the field of dye sensitization of emulsions. Preoccupation with the introduction of the gelatin process prevented Vogel's discovery from being actively pursued. However, in 1884 Vogel, along with Johann Obernetter, formulated the first truly commercial orthochromatic (sensitive to all parts of the visible spectrum except red) gelatin silver dry plate (a gelatin binder that contained the light-sensitive silver emulsion). Although it suffered from fog (unwanted density not produced by camera exposure) and loss of sensitivity, pictorially it provided a more accurate

8.7   UNKNOWN PHOTOGRAPHER.   *Untitled*
[Cow with collar and chain standing in front of a
wooden fence], ca. 1890s. 2½-inch diameter, (Kodak
#1 snapshot). Gelatin silver print.   Courtesy George East-
man House.

black-and-white tonal translation of a subject than the
wet-plate, delivering a wider range of gray print tones.
As the first professor of photography at the Institute of
Technology in Berlin, Vogel published an important
textbook, the *Handbook of Photography* (1867); his
students developed the first *panchromatic* emulsions
(sensitive to all wavelengths in the visible spectrum)
and, with them, color photography (see this chapter's
section on color).

Meanwhile, British scientists and amateur photographers Vero Charles Driffield [1848–1915] and Ferdinand Hurter [1844–1889] found it "intolerable to practice an art whose principles were so little understood."[11]
They devised scientific methods to study and measure
development, exposure, and sensitivity to light, leading
to the formation of *sensitometry*—the process of determining the response of photographic materials to light
and processing. Driffield and Hurter asserted that: "The
production of a perfect picture by means of photography
is an art; the production of a technically perfect negative
is a science"[12] Their discoveries permitted photographers to make exposures and process film based on scientific study instead of experience and luck. Driffield
and Hurter showed that an emulsion could be developed
for a predetermined amount of time at an exact temper-

ature to obtain specific levels of tonal contrast instead of
by visual inspection under a safelight. Emulsions
processed in total darkness could be made sensitive to
all parts of the spectrum and safely developed without
safelight fog. Increases in emulsion speed and expanded
spectrum range, on the other hand, necessitated developing a precision shutter mechanism to control discrete
segments of time, the most common being the *between-
the-lens shutter,* placed between the lenses' elements.

Refinements in lens design, such as *anastigmat* lenses
(1886), solved basic lens aberrations, especially that of
astigmatism, which causes an object being imaged to
blur around the edges. Previously, photographers had to
stop-down their lens to small apertures to avoid this
problem and be content with a narrow field of sharpness
(about twenty-five degrees). The widespread use of
anastigmat lenses at the beginning of the twentieth century improved overall image sharpness, provided larger
(faster) useful working apertures for low light and action
situations, and let photographers show more of a scene
by sharply covering a wider field of view (70 degrees).

By the 1890s new printing materials were impacting
how the image was made and seen. *Gaslight paper*[13] allowed photographers to make prints without the sunlight usually required to expose printing-out papers. It
also freed the photographer from using an expensive,
ventilated gas safelight with the new and much faster
bromide papers. These papers caused the albumen papers to become extinct by the start of the new century;
they were obsolete themselves by 1920, except for
making portrait proofs.

The Hand-Held Camera and the Snapshot

Up until the late 1880s, the expense, difficulty, and physical size of the equipment had kept people from making
their own photographs. Technical advances during the
late nineteenth century enabled designers to make the
camera a hand-held instrument, freeing it from the tripod. The market responded with cheap, mass-produced,
simple-to-use cameras with names like Compact, Hawk-
Eye, and Instantograp, referencing their size and concepts of vision and speed. Some used a *magazine,* a rigid,
lighttight, often reloadable container for holding up to a
dozen plates, enabling quick, stealthlike exposures, earning these machines the nickname of "detective cameras."

One camera is mythically associated with amateur
photography—the "Kodak," introduced by George Eastman [1854–1932], a banker from Rochester, N.Y., in
1888. The first Kodak was a simple 3¼ × 3¾ × 6½-
inch box camera, weighing 22 ounces, with a 27 mm, f/9,
fixed focus lens and a barrel shutter that could make 100,
2½-inch in diameter, circular negatives (see Figure 8.6).
The Kodak came already loaded with paper, "American

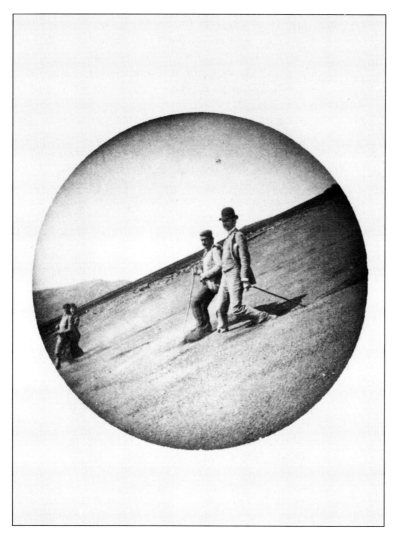

8.8   R. K. ALBRIGHT.   *Descending Vesuvius*, ca. 1880. 2⅔-inch diameter, (Kodak #1 snapshot). Albumen silver print. Courtesy George Eastman House.

film," that had to be sent back to the Eastman factory for processing and printing. "Transparent film," released in 1891, allowed the photographer to do the processing.

Eastman's conceptual breakthrough was to separate the photographic act of exposure (seeing) from the need to know the precise details of the mechanics of the camera and the chemical steps of the process. In essence, Eastman's system could deliver a photograph of anything one could see (and even things one could not). This strategy enabled Eastman to market the Kodak to people who had never taken a photograph or owned a camera. The Kodak rethought the boundaries of photographic practice, providing an industrial support system capable of producing standardized materials to maintain it. The Kodak's simplicity transformed a decentralized practice into a mass retail market of goods and services. Eastman launched the photofinishing industry in 1891 with daylight loading film and the antielitist motto, "You press the button, we do the rest," making the cam-

era part of American life. For $25 (still a luxury item) a customer purchased a loaded Kodak, pointed it at a subject, released the shutter button, wound the film to the next frame, recocked the shutter, and was ready to make ninety-nine more exposures. When the roll was completed the camera was shipped back to the Eastman factory where a contact print was made from each negative and mounted on a gilt-edged chocolate-brown card. The camera was reloaded with film and returned to the customer with the prints. The Kodak enabled a broader cross-section of the population to actively become part of the process, making images of their own choosing whenever they wished, without any special training (see Figure 8.7). Its existence contradicted the proclamations of artists and scientists that special equipment and training were needed, making photography a middle-class hobby. The Kodak initiated a new dialogue between the viewer and the subject, continuing photography's ability to level hierarchy and creating a sense of visual democracy. Eastman referred to the Kodak as:

A photographic notebook. Photography is thus brought within the reach of every human being who desires to preserve a record of what he sees. Such a photographic notebook is an enduring record of many things seen only once in a lifetime and enables the fortunate possessor to go back by the light of his own fireside to scenes which would otherwise fade from memory and be lost.[14]

The images made with a hand-held camera became known as "snapshots," adopted from the hunting term meaning to shoot instinctively without taking aim. Sir John Herschel anticipated the concept and mechanism of snapshooting in 1860:

I take for granted nothing more tihan the possibil:ty of taking a photograph, as it were, by a snap-shot—of securing a picture in a tenth of a second of time; and . . . that a mechanism is possible . . . by which a prepared plate may be presented, focussed, impressed, displaced, numbered, secured in the dark, and replaced by another within two or three tenths of a second.[15]

The snapshot is based on vernacular (colloquial) attitudes rather than the trained sensibilities of Western European art. The classical aesthetic criteria of content, form, and technique did not apply, as the typical hand-held camera user was not schooled in picturemaking strategies or in the proper use of equipment and materials. The attitude of the snapshooter was direct, spontaneous, and matter-of-fact, casually exploring the pleasures of everyday life rather than the subject of photography. Typically, the hand-held camera acted as a democratic collector of memories, and the combination of the snapshot and its accompanying album functioned as a visual diary of

8.9 ÉMILE ZOLA. *The Universal Exposition, Taken from the Eiffel Tower, Paris,* 1900. Zola's image, taken from an unusual vantage point, foreshadows the concerns of photographers in the 1910s and 1920s who would more fully investigate the enigmatic spatial arrangements of the new machine age. © The Museum Association of Émile Zola, Médan, France.

the familiar. The snapshooter's interest was almost exclusively personal and the values presented were life-affirming. This uninhibited and unpretentious outlook had a deceptively simple sensory freshness capable of changing the attitude of an observer toward a subject.

The snapshot genre was not the invention of an individual but an extended collaborative process of exploring the prosaic that relied on idiomatic consensus to establish meaning. The will of the individual was set aside in favor of community consent, with a partiality for familiar moments positioned in the center of the frame with little thought to what was occurring in the rest of the scene. The snapshot's proliferation meant professionals were no longer needed to make basic record pictures, forcing them to become proficient in highly specialized applications, such as *gum printing,* in which the image-receiving paper was brushed with a pigmented solution of gum bichromate emulsion, that were beyond the scope of hobbyists. The hand-held cameras renewed interest in making prints that were larger than the original negative, encouraging enlarging and its accompanying aesthetics to become universal practice.

The snapshot personified a natural desire to recreate what we think we believe, know, or have seen. The circular image of the early Kodak was revised into a rectangle to conform with the standards of how a picture

was supposed to look. But the snapshot led a dualistic existence. The ease of producing a snapshot encouraged people to take chances just to see what would "come out." The sheer number of photographs being taken increased the impact of chance, leading George Bernard Shaw to say: "The photographer is like the cod which produces a million eggs in order that one may reach maturity."[16] Through its million incarnations, the snapshot altered the visual arts. While meeting certain pictorial expectations, the snapshot invited the unexpected. This element of surprise could reveal a subject without adornment, covering another or a different kind of truth. The snapshot attitude became provocative when gaffes, previously eliminated by professionals, were adopted as working methods by serious imagemakers of other mediums like painting. What were initially accidents, such as informal framing, unexpected cropping, unbalanced compositions, skewed horizon lines (see Figure 8.8), unusual angles, weird perspectives, banal subject matter, extremes in lighting, out-of-focus subjects, blurring, double exposures, extended time exposures, and poor quality optics, grew into conscious design. These ideas and ways of seeing transformed pictorial convention, influencing modern art movements, including surrealism and dadaism, that set themselves in opposition to the ideals of the classical, empirical scientific models of thinking.

The explosion of snapshooters changed the societal relationship between photographers and their subjects. Before the hand-held camera, the act of making a photograph required the cooperation of both parties. Now the hand-held camera made it possible to surreptitiously photograph without a subject's consent. Not only hunting terminology but also hunting strategies were incorporated into how people used the miniature camera, including

8.10   EDGAR DEGAS.   *Portrait of his Brother Rene at His Writing Table,* ca. 1895. The artist Edgar Degas (1834–1917) became interested in the photograph's ability to seize and suspend motion and made numerous drawings using Muybridge's horse studies as inspiration. He also made his own photographs, favoring interior studies illuminated by artificial light. His ordered compositions lend intrigue to dramaless household situations. His photographic vision may have also influenced his drawing, daring compositional innovations incorporating "accidental" cutoff views, off-center framing, and unusual angles.   Courtesy Bibliotheque Nationale, Paris.

stealthily stalking and shooting a subject before it could protect itself. The number of amateurs "kodaking" everything everywhere were considered a social annoyance and were ridiculed as camera fiends. The expansion of subject matter by the snapshooters collided with society's restrictions about decency and good taste. Without a subject's consent, photographers faced an ethical dilemma of whether or not to take a picture. On August 20, 1884, *The New York Times* ran a story about "The Camera Epidemic," equating it to cholera and labeling it a "national scourge." The article related how healthy people were being harassed by those who had contracted the camera disease. It complained no one could walk down the street or sit in the woods with a young lady without a dozen or more cameras trained on them by "camera lunatics." As amateurs became bolder the public became more resentful, as this response indicates:

> There is but one remedy for the amateur photographer. Put a brick through his camera whenever you suspect he has taken

you unawares. And if there is any doubt, give the benefit to the brick, not the camera. The rights of private property, personal liberty, and personal security—birthrights, all of them, of American citizens—are distinctly inconsistent with the unlicensed use of the instantaneous process.[17]

The situation got so bad that there were calls for laws against public photography in America and Europe (none were passed). Camera magazines published proposed rules for snapshooting in public. *Punch* lampooned the topic with its own "Regulations for Camera-Fiends" which included:

> 8. Biograph [film] operators who attack a large assemblage of persons with a wide-angle lens in broad daylight shall be liable to three years' imprisonment in a dark room.

Although hand-held cameras were still too expensive to be used universally, they expanded the ranks of the snapshooters that made up half of the middle-class population—women—who were no less enthusiastic than the men.[18] At one point, during a trip to America, Prince George of Greece was "pursued by 150 ladies who persisted in photographing him, despite his protests."[19]

The clandestine use of hand-held cameras made the ethics of street photography a controversial matter. How could the subject's rights of personal privacy be reconciled with the photographer's freedom of expression and the public's right to know? *The Amateur Photographer* sarcastically observed that "Our moral character dwindles as our instruments get smaller."[20] The snapshot, by breaking aesthetic and societal rules, altered how we see and what we are allowed to picture.

Camera clubs and their publications grew to meet amateur photographers' demands for guidance and exhibition opportunities. In turn of the century America a

8.11   PAUL NADAR.   *The Art of Living a Hundred Years,* 1886. Each image is 5¾ × 4 inches. Photogravures.   Courtesy George Eastman House.

dozen illustrated magazines, with photographic illustrations, were in regular circulation. Many publications acted as the official voices of amateur clubs, from those that met in living rooms to large, full-service organizations that offered programming and darkrooms. Big societies, such as the New York Camera Club and the Camera Club of London, had "advanced" members whose ideas and work would come to influence the entire practice of photography (see Chapter 9). Besides offering visual stimulus, the clubs were educational, providing how-to-do articles, exhibition reviews, roundups of photo-related happenings, product advertisements, and advice columns with tips like the one from C. W. Davis of Athens, Georgia. Davis trained a canary to sing on signal so that "The sitter forgets all about the head-rest, the trying light, the wearisomeness of keeping a fixed position. . . . A pleasant and unconscious expression on the face of the sitter is the result of the little bird's melody."[21] Soon photographers were able to buy a mechanical bird that chirped when a pneumatic bulb was squeezed—and "watch the birdie" became a command at portrait sessions.

Writers and artists who had no intention of becoming professional photographers were infatuated with the snapshot and used the camera as an adjunct to their other aesthetic activities. Émile Zola [1840–1902], author of highly detailed novels about French society, took up photography late in his career. As the leading exemplar of *naturalism,* a style based on the accurate depiction of people, places, and things, Zola believed that the novelist, like the scientist, should observe and

record dispassionately. Given his interest in everyday subjects, the camera seemed to be the ideal instrument for accurate depiction. Zola remarked: "In my opinion, you cannot say you have thoroughly seen anything until you have got a photograph of it, revealing a lot of points which otherwise would be unnoticed, and which in most cases could not be distinguished."[22] Zola made observant snapshots of family, friends, and architectural subjects (see Figure 8.9). This style of photography can be seen as a response to Baudelaire's plea for art (although he was antagonistic towards photography as an art) that would take the "heroism of modern life" as its subject.

Time and Motion as an Extended Continuum

Up until the 1880s, most people considered photography to consist of single images that depicted and made a subject known to the viewer. The work of Marey, Muybridge, and others opened the possibility of learning more about a subject through a series of photographs that occurred over time. These new ways of conceptualizing time and motion shifted society's understanding of the present moment as a singular instant to that of a temporally extended continuum. This profound transformation in understanding and experiencing time encouraged photographers like Nadar to experiment in the portrait studio with extending the amount of visual time a viewer had to know a subject by presenting an extended collection of moments. In 1886 Nadar published a photo-interview, *The Art of Living a Hundred Years,* based on a series of twenty-

Alexander Black [1859–1914] used the halftone process in conjunction with the concept of the *tableau vivant* (living picture, a representation of a scene by suitably costumed and posed people) to reproduce a sequence of still images to illustrate his short story, "Miss Jerry," for *Scribner's Magazine* in 1895. Black wanted the tableaux vivants to act progressively, so that the illusion of reality would be created not by suspending action in isolated pictures but by visually fusing many images together.[23] Sir John Herschel had anticipated these events in 1860 when he discussed the possibility of taking a series of *snapshots* and showing them in a *phenakistoscope,* an apparatus comparable to a zoetrope used to present animated drawings:

> What I have to purpose may appear a dream, . . . by snap-shot . . . the representation of scenes in action—the vivid and lifelike reproduction and handing down to the latest posterity of any transaction in real life . . . where any matter of interest is enacted within a reasonably short time, which may be seen from a single point of view.[24]

Moving Pictures

By the 1890s, a cluster of autonomous inventors was simultaneously bringing Herschel's vision to fruition. The first continuous-film motion picture viewing machine to gain public acceptance was developed and marketed by Thomas Alva Edison [1847– 1931]. The *kineto-scope* was designed for Edison by William Kennedy Laurie Dickson. It was a 1½-minute peepshow. An individual peered through an eyepiece at a continuous, 50-foot loop of 35mm positive film, permanently threaded through rollers. As the crank was turned, the film moved past an electric light bulb and a whirling slotted disk (an intermittent shutter) that interrupted the light as each frame changed at the rate of 46 frames per second. To make certain the film moved at a constant rate without slipping, Dickson perforated the edges of the film so it could be driven by toothed sprocket wheels with the same design as the Kineto-scope. Edison contracted George Eastman to make this film, establishing the 35mm format as the *motion*

8.12 An advertising poster for moving pictures made for and viewed with Edison's stereo-projecting Kinetoscope that allowed the images to be seen by a group of people on a screen, 1902. Courtesy Corbis/Bettmann.

one exposures made by his son Paul Nadar [1856–1939] as Nadar conversed with the French scientist Michel-Eugène Chevreul on his 100th birthday (see Figure 8.11). Chevreul's commentary formed the captions to the photographs, which were reproduced via the new halftone process that allowed photographs and text to be simultaneously printed together. The serial use of sequential photographs combined with an interview resulted in the first photo-essay.

8.13   LEVI L. HILL.   *Landscape with Farmhouse,*
1851. Hillotype. Until his death in 1865, Hill still
claimed to have made color photographs, but he con-
fessed that he had managed it by accident. He revealed
that he had spent the last fifteen years of his life attempting to repeat the accidental combination without
success. Recently new scientific evidence has suggested
that Hill may have indeed stumbled onto a direct color
process.[25]   Courtesy Division of Photographic History, Natural Museum of American History, Smithsonian Institution.

picture standard. Little thought was given to subject
matter. The first Kinetoscope Parlor, with ten machines, opened in New York in April 1894, and featured snapshots in motion. In June machines were
shipped to San Francisco, and by September they were
in London and Paris.

The problem with the Kinetoscope was that its small
image size allowed only one person at a time to view its
pictures. Using the magic lantern shows as a model, numerous inventors set about to design a machine that
would enlarge the image onto a screen. The breakthrough occurred on December 28, 1895, when Auguste [1862–1954] and Louis [1864–1948] Lumière
projected very short films of vernacular subject matter
(such as a train coming into a station) to a Parisian audience by means of the *Cinématographe.* The Cinématographe projector, constructed by Jules Carpentier,
used a clawlike device to pull the perforated 35mm celluloid film at the required intermittent speed. Similar

devices were invented almost simultaneously by
William Friese-Greene and Birt Acres in England and
by Charles Francis Jenkins and Dickson, Edison's designer, in America. Edison and the Lumière family
were able to link science and business to make cinema
commercially viable. Through the corporate research
laboratories of Edison's Kinetoscope and the Lumière's
Cinématographe, teams of people, rather than a solitary
inventor, marketed their inventions through mass-
production and distribution. By the close of 1896, moving pictures were being projected regularly throughout
Europe and America (see Figure 8.12).

These simple moving snapshots rapidly evolved a
new visual vocabulary based on juxtaposing nonsuc-
cessive events, altering the Renaissance tradition of using a continuous, single point of view to represent time
and space. The editing methods that developed in early
films, such as *The Great Train Robbery* (1903), proved
people could conceptually leap through time and space
and link together discontinuous events. Grounded in
scientific thought and industrial technology, moving
pictures became a reality.

Color

Since photography's inception, people complained
about its lack of color. In 1840, Sir John Herschel reported recording, but not fixing, blue, green, and red on
silver chloride-coated paper, suggesting that color photographs could be made directly from the action of light

8.14 JAMES CLERK MAXWELL. *Tartan Ribbon,* 1861. Reproduction by Vivex process, a three-color method. Maxwell's demonstration not only proved the additive color theory but provided a method, known as the triple projection process, for producing photographic color images.   Courtesy National Museum of Photography, Film and Television/Science and Society Picture Library, London.

on a chemically sensitive surface. Other experimenters, including Edmond Becquerel in the late 1840s and early 1850s and Niépce de Saint-Victor in the 1850s and 1860s, recorded colors directly on daguerreotypes, but they were unable to make them permanent. In early 1851 Levi Hill, a Baptist minister from Westkill, New York, announced a secret, permanent, direct color process. When Hill's *A Treatise on Heliochromy* was finally published in 1856, it did not contain any workable instructions for his process and was dismissed as a hoax (see Figure 8.13).

The first true color photograph was made in 1861 by James Clerk Maxwell, a Scottish scientist, based on the *additive color theory* developed by Thomas Young and refined by Hermann Helmholtz. The theory held that all colors of light can be mixed optically by combining in different proportions of the three primary colors of the spectrum: red, green, and blue. Maxwell made three separate black-and-white positives of a tartan plaid ribbon through three separate blue-violet, green, and red

filters. When all three positives were simultaneously projected, the result was a projected color image (not a photograph) of the multicolored ribbon (see Figure 8.14). In 1891, Gabriel Lippman used the additive theory in his *interference* method, making full-color plates by means of interference between wavelengths of light without the use of colorants or dyes. The plate resembled a negative in transmitted light but turned into a brilliant, iridescent positive when viewed by placing the emulsion against a mirror and shining light into it at the proper angle. Though Lippman received the 1908 Nobel Prize for this work, it was not commercially viable; since the emulsion was about 100,000 times slower than that of ordinary film, the process was extremely complex, and the plates were difficult to view.

In *Photography in Color* (1869), Louis Ducos du Hauron, a French scientist, proposed that the additive theory could be used to make color photographs more simply. He speculated that a screen ruled with fine lines in the primary colors of red, yellow, and blue would act as a filter, producing a color photograph with a single exposure instead of the three Maxwell required. In 1894 John Joly, a Dublin physicist, patented the first line-screen process for additive color photographs, but it was not commercially practical. A major breakthrough in the making of additive screen color photographs was patented in 1904 by the Lumière brothers, with manufacture beginning in 1907. In their *Autochrome* system, a glass plate was dusted

8.15   CHARLES C. ZOLLER.   *World War I Support Parade, Red Cross Nurses and Uncle Sam,* ca. 1918. 3¼ × 4 inches. Autochrome.   Courtesy George Eastman House.

with microscopic grains of potato starch that had been dyed with orange, green, and blue-violet. A fine powder of carbon black was used to fill in any spaces that would allow unfiltered light to pass through this filter screen, eliminating the need for colored lines to act as filters. A newly developed panchromatic emulsion, which greatly extended the accurate recording of the full visible spectrum, was then applied to the plate. The exposure was made through the back of the plate, with the dyed potato starch acting as tiny filters. The plate was then developed, re-exposed to light, and fi-nally redeveloped to form a positive transparency made up of tiny dots of the primary colors. Autochrome could be used in any regular plate camera, giving serious amateurs and professionals access to color. Autochrome was the first color process to get beyond the novelty stage and become commercially successful. It cracked a major aesthetic barrier and was taken seriously for its picturemaking potentiali-ties, enabling professional and amateur photographers to explore the visual possibilities of color. By the end of World War I, magazines like *National Geographic* were using Autochromes to make color reproductions. Autochrome provided the missing layers of believ-ability and realism for the system that would conduct most future forms of public representation.

CHAPTER NINE

Suggesting
the Subject
The Evolution of Pictorialism

Roots of Pictorialism

By the 1880s, public fascination with photographic reality was losing its luster as hordes of snapshooters could now make their own photographs. People were questioning the previously semimagical position of professional photographers and the level of intelligence, sensitivity, and skill required to make photographs. The photographer's status as a shaman suffered a body blow. The professional portrait business declined as amateurs made more photographs of people. The photography studios needed something to restore their authority and their business.

In response, organizations such as the Photographers Association of America formed (1880) to "reach out beyond the chemistry, optics, art, and mechanics of our art-science, and take hold of the morals of the craft, [and encourage all in the profession to] respect themselves more, and the

P. H. EMERSON.
Furze-Cutting on the Suffolk Common, 1886. $9\frac{3}{16} \times 11\frac{3}{8}$ inches. Platinum print. Courtesy George Eastman House.

public to honor us in a larger degree than they have."[1] Schools, like the Chicago College of Photography (1881), validated a photographer's skills by offering certificate courses in photography. A graduate would presumably "possess the art, character, and tone" of a knowledgeable professional and thus command "a higher money value . . . for his work."[2]

At the time, artists, disenchanted with claims of the omnipotence of scientific observation and deduction, were searching for ways to express abstract and subjective viewpoints. This also could be good for the photographic profession. If the role of a trained photographer switched from depicting an objective likeness to portraying subjective conditions that reveal an inner state of the subject, then the expressive abilities of the individual photographer took on significance, becoming as important as the subject before the lens. This elevated the stature of the maker of the photograph over the taker of the snapshot, making the name of the photographer a viable commodity, someone who provided the customer with a unique vision.

Throughout the arts, a loss of faith in science and technology was communicated by the banishment of literalness and scientific objectivism. This led to the rise of *symbolism,* a revolt against realism and its minute descriptions of an objective, external reality. The symbolists turned inward to express the shifting, subtle state of the human psyche, using symbols and metaphors to evoke and suggest subjective emotions. Instead of positivism, they allowed spiritualism and the role of dreams to be their guide. Symbolist artists and writers such as Charles Baudelaire, whose subtle poems spoke of the world as a magical "forest of symbols," believed allusion and suggestion, rather than delineation and description, evoked the imagination and raised their work above the mechanics of objective description. As long as photography was thought to be based only on reality, the photograph was expected to be sharp and precise, for this was science; but if the offering of ideas in a photograph had a basis in the arts, then the photograph had the prerogative of being elusive and suggestive.

Pictorialism and Naturalism

During the 1880s amateurs, influenced by the ideas of Henry Peach Robinson, and technologists, concerned with process, dominated photography, and artistic practice slid into the doldrums. **Peter Henry Emerson** [1856–1936] reacted to the combination printers and the incoming tidal wave of amateur work in March 1886 with a lecture at the Camera Club in London, "Photography, A Pictorial Art,"[3] attacking the self-conscious, painting-derived compositions favored by the chief arbiters of artistic and photographic taste, John Ruskin and H. P. Robinson. Emer-

son saw photography as an independent medium combining art and science and the photographer as the one who determined the camera's own intrinsic attributes. Emerson's promotion of the photograph to the status of art became the goal of a movement known as *pictorialism*. Pictorialism was founded on the premise that camera images could engage the feeling and senses in the manner expressed by Emerson's notions of *naturalism*. Naturalism explains all phenomena by natural categories instead of the supernatural. It looks for causes as opposed to reasons. When applied to the arts, naturalism infers that the artist, like the scientist, should observe and record dispassionately. According to Emerson's naturalistic theory of photography, enduring art is made directly from nature; the artist's role is to imitate these effects on the eye. Emerson believed photography had shortcomings, but "in capable hands" it could be "a work of Art." Emerson's method was to photograph his subjects within their natural environment, without so-called artificial manipulations, relying on the selection of subject, lighting, framing, and selective focusing to make an artistic camera image (see chapter opener).

Emerson followed up his lecture with *Life and Landscape on the Norfolk Broads,* a limited folio edition of forty platinum prints that demonstrated his ideas by portraying the amphibious life of the marsh dwellers of East Anglia.[4] The *platinum process* is a contact printing process in which the image is partially printed out with ultraviolet radiation. After exposure the image is chemically developed out to completion.[5] These "straight"—that is, containing no post-camera manipulation of the photographic materials—formally composed photographs recorded the customs and manners of Fenland people.

The prints were accompanied by text written by Emerson and the painter T. F. Goodall, his guide and friend. The text described the landscape and documented the disappearing customs of these working rural people, often in their own voice. Made on location, the prints' feeling of immediacy was in unswerving opposition to Robinson's strictures for constructed pictures. Emerson released six more books on the Norfolk Broads, illustrated with *photogravures*, or photo-etchings, a photomechanical process invented by Fox Talbot that became commercially viable around 1880. To make a photogravure, an original negative is etched into a metal plate, inked, and printed in an etching press. Often regarded as a direct photographic printing method, photogravure was popular with many pictorialists in the 1890s and 1900s for its ability to maintain subtle tonal variations and delicate luminosity. It also alleviated the problem of making thousands of platinum prints while delivering a softer and more artistic rendition, proving that photography required the same creative energies and skills as painting.

9.1   P. H. EMERSON.   *Throwing the Cast Net. Norfolk Broads,* ca. 1886. 9⅞ × 11½ inches. Platinum print. To situate his subjects within their environment, Emerson often made low-angle views that incorporated the foreground. Visually, he presented the elemental forces of nature as all-encompassing while simultaneously leading the viewer to the main figures of the composition.   Courtesy George Eastman House.

In *Naturalistic Photography for Students of the Art* (1889), Emerson counseled developing negatives the day they were taken, while the experience was still fresh, and scorned the hand-held camera, enlarging, and retouching in favor of the delicate detail of a contact print made in platinum or photogravure. While Emerson's choices in printing processes were appreciated, his theory of *differential focus,* loosely derived from the numerous optical discoveries made by Hermann von Helmholtz about the structure and action of the eye, caused consternation. Emerson believed that only the central portion of the human field of vision is sharp and that the borders are "only roughly sketched in." Emerson stated:

Nothing in nature has a hard outline, but everything is seen against something else, and its outlines fade gently into that something else, often so subtly that you cannot quite distinguish where one ends and the other begins. In this mingled decision and indecision, this lost and found, lies all the charm and mystery of nature.[6]

To reproduce this effect, Emerson instructed photographers to make images slightly out of focus, so the subject would be "just as sharp as the eye sees it and no sharper," while all other parts of the picture would be "subdued." These recommendations, which combine bits of science and mysticism, renewed debate about how to create "art" photographs. Emerson's working style proved difficult in the hands of the less sensitive or skilled and his focusing methods, developed in moist, light-scattering English air, did not take into account different climates. Emerson's statement, combined with the continued misinterpretation of Sir William Newton's "Upon Photography in an Artistic View . . ." (1853) led many amateurs to confuse out of focus with "art." Many applied numerous techniques to manufacture a "look," referred to as "fuzzygraphs," without the content.

Emerson engaged in heated editorial battles with those who disagreed with his ideas until January 1891, when he suddenly recanted his position in letters to major photographic magazines, addressed "TO ALL PHOTOGRAPHERS," requesting forgiveness from his supporters and from those he had attacked. Emerson said that he had misinterpreted Hurter and Driffield's study of exposure, development, and speed of materials (see Chapter 8) and had therefore failed to understand how tonal values could be manipulated through exposure.[7] This mistake led Emerson to incorrectly conclude that photography could not be controlled by the maker, that photographers could not be artists, and that the medium "must always rank the lowest of all arts."[8] Emerson's retraction was shortly reprinted (probably in February) in a pamphlet, *The Death of Naturalistic Photography.* After this episode, Emerson quit publicly campaigning for photography as an independent art form. However, he continued, until the turn of the century, to make and publish photographs that reflected his belief that photographic art resulted from the direct recording of natural subjects in their surroundings. Emerson's ideas marked the beginnings of a modernist aesthetic philosophy, modeled on human vision instead of the mechanical objectivity of the camera, that would guide photography into a dialogue with modern art movements such as Impressionism, that were also influenced by optical theories.

The Development of Pictorial Effect

The pictorialist movement thrived between 1889 and the start of World War I by stressing beauty over fact. Optical sharpness and exact replication of subjects were seen as inhibitors of individual expression. The movement broke with Emerson and other purists as many of its practitioners embraced the hand-manipulation of the print as a meaningful aspect of self-expression. The pictorialists asserted that artistic photographs were the equivalent of works in other media and should receive equal treatment by the art establishment.

The 1890s saw the evolution of "pictorial effect" based on the methods of the painters from the *Barbizon School,* such as Jean-François Millet [1814–1875], whose softened brushwork created atmospheric effects. Pictorialists wanted unique images that relied on post-camera techniques, linking their work with the public's expectations of a one-of-a-kind masterpiece. The pictorialists favored processes like carbon, gum-bichromate, platinum, and later *bromoil*[9] that allowed considerable leeway for interpreting the negative. They preferred printing on hand-coated artist paper for its expressive implications and tactile suggestiveness, thus asserting control over their craft during a time of commercial standardization. Their prints convey their visual information emotionally due to a strong physical presence based on tonality, texture, and the manipulation of detail.

To counter what they considered to be the anonymous qualities of photography, artistically minded photographers embraced the allegorical and genre traditions of painting. Relying on light and line, these photographers sought to make emotional and intuitive images that symbolically communicated what could not be stated in words. **George Davison** [1856–1930] advocated *photographic impressionism,* the renouncing of objectivity and realistic representation, as in Impressionistic painting, in favor of transitory visual impressions. To create a monochromatic image directly from nature, Davison substituted a pinhole for the lens on his camera (see Figure 9.2). Davison's stylistic synthesis of naturalistic subject matter and impressionistic strategies that concentrated on effect rather than the naturalistic truths of the land and its inhabitants influenced others. His ideas induced the Vienna Club der Amateur-Photographen to mount a major exhibition in 1891 of artistic photographs juried by painters and sculptors, thus establishing a model for exhibiting photographs based on their aesthetic qualities that was adopted by salons throughout Europe.

The photographer's ability to suppress unwanted detail, add colors, alter the tonal range, and synthesize negatives showed that photography could be an art, subject to the will and hand of the maker. If the photograph was not limited to presenting reality, then the relationship between the photographer, the subject, and the viewer was up for grabs. By defying expectations, the pictorialists created a breach between photography and science, cleaving artist/photographers from amateurs, professionals, scientists, and technicians. For pictorialists, what was important was not the subject in front of the lens but how the artist manipulated images to express ideas. By separating photography from its scientific history, the pictorialists broke the link between the photograph and reality, challenging photography's machinelike authenticity.

Although much of pictorialism never rose above the imitation of graphic art, the movement increased the discussion about the aesthetic character of photography, enhanced awareness of the medium's specific attributes, and encouraged contemplation of photography's relationship to the modern world.

The Secession Movement and the Rise of Photography Clubs

The early 1890s saw the commercial and scientific values of earlier photographic (and art) societies challenged by supporters of the new aesthetics. The

9.2 GEORGE DAVISON. *The Onion Field*, 1889. 6⅛ × 8 inches. Photogravure. George Davison's *The Onion Field* visually embodies the painterly principles of photographic impressionism that emphasized mood. The concept was controversial with those who felt it was an imitative process that betrayed the true nature of photography. Emerson was a severe critic: "photographic impressionism indeed!—a term consecrated to charlatans and especially to photographic imposters [sic], pickpockets, parasites, and vanity-intoxicated amateurs."[10]   Courtesy George Eastman House.

Secession movement reflected the disenchantment of younger artists with the practices and exhibition policies of established Western art societies and led to the formation of alternative institutions in Berlin, Munich, and Vienna, among other places. In photography it led to the creation of the Wiener Kamera Klub in 1891, the Linked Ring in London in 1892, the Photo-Club de Paris in 1894, and the Photo-Secession in New York in 1902.

The Brotherhood of the Linked Ring, a loose group of photographers disenchanted with the Photographic Society of London's exhibition practices, was one of the most influential secession groups. The "Links"

found alternative venues to display and promote photography as an independent medium whose works could be evaluated in their own context and terms rather than by their ability to imitate other media. This privileged club (membership by invitation only) was founded by educated men including Emerson, Robinson, Alfred Maskell, George Davis, and Alfred Horsley Hinton, the editor of *The Amateur Photographer*, begun in 1884 as the first magazine to cater to amateurs. Their first exhibition of some 300 prints in 1893, generated a stir for being mindfully hung, asymmetrically, breaking with the Photographic Society's Victorian tradition of cramming pictures of different sizes and subject matter frame to frame from the floor to the ceiling. The Links wanted more stringent exhibition standards: They were fed up with all types of photographs on a gallery wall, awarding medals to mediocre formula pictures, and using non-photographers to jury show entries. They adopted a motto: "no medals and rigid selection." The Links wanted to separate utilitarian work, whose goal was to record facts, from aesthetic photographs, whose goal was to express beauty. They sought "complete emancipation of pictorial photography . . . from the retarding . . . bondage of that which was purely scientific or technical [so it could pursue] its development as an independent art."[11] Their annual Salon of Pictorial Photography continued to be an important exhibition site until the group dissolved in 1910.

In 1893, Alfred Lichtwark [1852–1914], the director of the Kunsthalle Museum in Hamburg, Germany, put together the "First International Exhibition of Amateur Photographs" in a museum setting. Believing that only amateurs had the economic freedom and time for experimentation, Lichtwark displayed 6,000 amateur photographs in hopes of revitalizing the art of photographic portraiture, which he felt had become artificial and formally constrained. Lichtwark wanted to use artistic amateur photography to infuse portrait painting and commercial illustration with innovative concepts and heightened aesthetic standards. An international network of pictorial photographers evolved to promote pictorial concepts and exhibit and publish each other's work, thereby spreading their personal influence and recognition. Even though this network possessed the reciprocal nature of an "old boys" club, other photographers looked to these groups for direction and began the compliment of imitation.

Photo clubs and publications mushroomed. In 1880 there were about ten camera clubs or societies in the United States composed of people with professional connections to the field. By 1895, there were over 150 such groups, made up largely of white upper middle-class amateurs who could afford the equipment, supplies, and annual membership dues. Women were active in these groups, which often asserted that a woman's place was in the home, leading some women to challenge their limited opportunities and the unequal treatment they often endured. As an early proponent for women in photography Catharine Weed Barnes Ward (1851–1913) wrote, "Why Ladies Should be Admitted to Membership in Photographic Societies," (1889) that called on photographic establishments "to give us a fair field and no favor . . . [as] the day is coming . . . when only one question will be asked as to any photographic work—'Is it well done?'"[12] Many clubs did not permit professionals to join either, fearing they would use the club to promote their own work and inventions. The club members' amateur status gave them financial autonomy and aesthetic independence from commercial interests, and they insinuated that the professionals' aesthetic sense could not be trusted as their values had been compromised by the exchange of money. Such attitudes widened the gulf within the field between amateurs and professionals.

The Aesthetic Club Movement

Reformist aesthetic notions gained popularity during the 1890s under the *Art Nouveau* movement (1880– 1914). Art Nouveau rejected the academic painting of historical events and scenes from legends and literature and advocated a withdrawal from the uniform, mechanical vulgarity of the industrial age by promoting the arts as an indispensable part of daily life. This was done through aesthetic self-improvement clubs that encouraged the procuring of splendid objects and the pursuit of music, poetry, and picturemaking. Photography offered members of this new "Aesthetic Club Movement" a way to bring art into their lives by becoming picturemakers without years of training. These clubs and movements filled a power vacuum of their own making, creating their own local authorities to bestow the status of art in a picture, changing the amateur movement into a "high art" undertaking with its own social network, aesthetic, exhibitions, publications, writers, and critics.

One of the effects of the Industrial Revolution was the rise of the bourgeoisie and a larger audience for the arts, one with ready capital and leisure time. The photographic industry, recognizing that amateur artistic ambitions could translate into increased sales of equipment and supplies, began to advertise in amateur publications and to sponsor shows featuring serious amateur photographers. The aim was to imply that anyone could make photographic art by investing in the proper equipment and materials. Publications recommended their advertisers' goods. Product ads sometimes headlined the endorsement of a well-known photographer. Commercial support added credibility to the small artistic movement and amplified its message. The January 1905 issue of *Camera Work* contained a full-page editorial announcement: "The reader of *Camera Work* who does not buy through these pages does himself an injustice — good photography depends much upon good material and up-to-date methods."

Working Pictorially: A Variety of Approaches

Robert Demachy [1859–1937], was a wealthy European amateur who took up photography in 1880, championing the pictorialist cause in Paris with an outpouring of prints and articles. Demachy was a founding member of the Photo-Club de Paris, and with his English cohort, Alfred Maskell [ca. 1857–, active 1890s], he exhibited prints made with the *gum-bichromate process* at the group's first show, the French Photographic Salon. In the gum bichromate process a contact-size negative is placed over a support material that has been coated with gum arabic containing a pigment (watercolor or tempera) and with a light-sensitive chemical (ammonium or potassium dichromate). The negative is then exposed to UV radiation. Gum arabic is hardened by such exposure and made insoluble in direct proportion to the density of the negative. The areas that are not hardened remain water soluble and are

9.3 ROBERT DEMACHY. *Speed*. From *Camera Work* #7 July 1904. 4⅞ × 7 inches. Photogravure.
Courtesy George Eastman House.

washed away, along with the unneeded pigment, during development. The hardened areas are left intact and bond the pigment to the support. Control of the final image can be exercised through choice of paper and pigment, by localized development, by recoating the support with a different color, or by using different negatives for additional exposures. It can also be combined with other processes, such as platinum, to create greater visual depth. Brushstrokes are often left visible, giving the print a handworked look that can replicate the look of a watercolor painting. The process was created in 1855 by Alphonse Louis Poitevin [1819–1882], but was recast in 1894 by A. Rouillé-Ladévèze [active 1884–1894], from whom Demachy learned the process. Gum printing was popularized by the pictorialists under the name Photo-Aquatint and was used from the 1890s through the 1920s. The process was inexpensive, as it contained no silver metal salts, and was very permanent. It experienced a revival in the late 1960s as part of a resurgence in alternative processes.

After making its debut in the pictorial arena, gum printing was embraced for the controls it provided in constructing a print for pictorial effect. The promoting of the pictorial cause led to Demachy's election to the Linked Ring in 1895. Maskell, a founding member of the Links, collaborated with Demachy on *Photo Aquatint, or The Gum Bichromate Process* (1897), a guide for pictorial imagemakers. Opponents dismissed their work as "fakery," but both men defended gum printing by pointing out how the alteration of negatives

and prints was a photographic tradition in the form of adding clouds, vignettes, and posing portraits against handpainted backdrops.

Demachy's prints, ranging from portraits to nudes to urban landscapes, often reverberated with the impressionistic style and always revealed the hand of their maker. Technically brilliant, Demachy was disdainful of the clarity of detail and the automatic trace of reality of the "straight," unmanipulated print and defended the painterly image:

> A straight print may be beautiful, and it may prove superabundantly that its author is an artist; but it cannot be a work of art. . . . A work of art must be a transcription, not a copy of nature. . . . there is not a particle of art in the most beautiful scene of nature. The art is man's alone, it is subjective not objective. If a man slavishly copies nature, no matter if it is with hand and pencil or through a photographic lens, he may be a supreme artist all the while, but that particular work of his cannot be called a work of art.[13]

The "Trifolium" of the Vienna Kamera-Club, formed in 1896 and active until 1903, was a collective made up of **Heinrich Kühn** [1866–1944], Hugo Henneberg [1863–1918], and Hans Watzek [1848–1903]. They adopted Demachy's gum process and exhibited under the collective known as *Das Kleeblatt* (Cloverleaf) and were a driving force of the Austro-German secession/pictorialist movement. Kühn, an amateur since 1879 and a member of the Linked Ring, made multilayered landscapes and portraits in gum and, later, oil-pigment printing (a variation of the bromoil process). His characteristic style featured bold, emblematic compositions on textured paper, printed in inviting brown or blue hues. His approach, to sometimes photograph from above eye level, broke with the stagnant habits of professional portraitists and began a

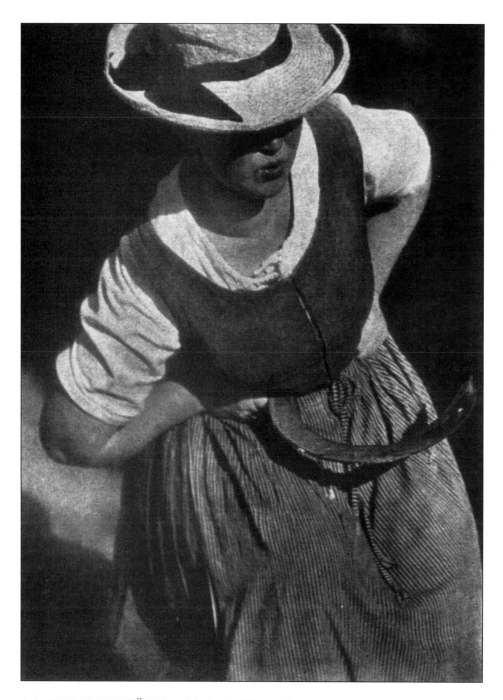

9.4   HEINRICH KÜHN.   *Schnitterin (Harvester),* ca.
1925. 11⁵⁄₁₆ × 8¼ inches. Photogravure.   Courtesy
George Eastman House.

progressive photographic movement in Germany that
reflected the concerns of similar pictorial groups that
sprang up worldwide.

Pictorialism was not exclusively about manual alteration of negatives and prints. During the early 1880s another amateur, **Frederick H. Evans** [1853–1943], studied photography with George Smith, a specialist in
microphotography (scientific photography involving a
microscope) and a "purist" zealot who believed that
"any artistic effect desired can be faithfully done by

pure photography without any retouching whatever."[14]
Evans absorbed Smith's lessons and championed
straight-from-the-camera photography.[15] Evans's aesthetic concepts were rooted in the *Arts and Craft Movement* that stressed the dignity of work, the beauty of fine
materials, and the spiritual importance of the preindus-
trial life. In 1895, Evans began a photographic meditation on medieval cathedrals in England and France. He
mastered tight compositions, often through the use of
repeating lines, capturing a strong sense of chiaroscuro.
His exquisite sense of space and volume gave his interior views, laden with physical texture, a sensation of
uplift. His exterior cathedral prints could transcend
earthbound architectural detail and give the viewer a vi-

9.5   FREDERICK H. EVANS.   *Kelmscott Manor, Attics,* ca. 1897. 6⅛ × 8 inches. Platinum print. Evans counseled photographers to "Try for a record of emotion rather than a piece of topography. Wait till the building makes you feel intensely . . . then try and analyse what gives you that feeling, see if it is due to the isolation of some particular aspect or effect, and then see what your camera can do towards reproducing that effect, that subject."[16]   Courtesy George Eastman House.

sual sense of a spiraling medieval spirit reaching up to the heavens. In this series Evans favored the early morning light and used neutral density filters to extend exposure times and give the impression that the images were made when a cathedral was first erected. If something entered his field of view that "dated" the image, Evans capped his lens, waited for the unwanted object to leave, then uncapped the lens and continued the exposure, purging evidence of the contemporary world, leaving only the beautiful and the eternal. His Kelmscott Attic pictures transform a utilitarian space into a sacred site much like a cathedral and are unprecedented in their luxurious delicacy, detail, and subtle brilliance.

Elected to the Linked Ring in 1900, Evans hung the group's 1902 Salon in an extraordinary fashion. After covering the walls with canvas, Evans used two-inch-wide battens to make vertical divisions, suspended white cloth beneath the skylight to diffuse the light, and grouped pictures on the vertical panels without regard to authorship. The care manifested by the presentation indicated that the photographs were works of art. One critic wrote, "Each section of the wall is itself a sermon in massing and composition."[17] Evans hung the next three Salons, initiating a re-evaluation about how photographs were presented in galleries.

Another major influence on pictorialism was Japanese art, referred to as *Japonism,* which came to Europe after the opening of Japan by Commodore Perry in 1854. Western artists incorporated the Japanese printmakers' use of clear and vibrant color, forceful outline, foreshortened and aerial perspectives, and asymmetrical and cropped compositions at the same time many of these devices were also being discovered through photography. Many of these attributes can be seen in work by **Pierre Dubreuil** [1872–1944], a wealthy amateur known at the turn of the century for his soft-focus, impressionist, *oil-pigment prints*[18] with the Photo-Club de Paris and later as a "Link." Around 1908, Dubreuil's

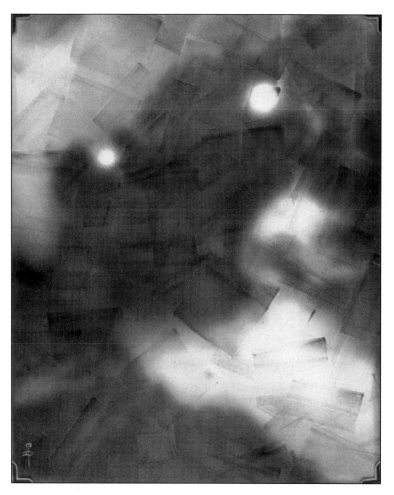

9.6   PIERRE DUBREUIL. *Interpretation Picasso: The Railway*, 1911.   Courtesy Centre George Pompidou, Paris.

compositions began to emphasize the two-dimensional flatness of the image by sharply focusing on nonessential objects, making them stand out, while placing the main subject in the background and out of focus, destroying traditional visual hierarchies. Between 1908 and 1912, Dubreuil experimented with abstraction by using his camera to fragment key subjects within the scene, as in his *Interpretation Picasso: The Railway* (1911). Here Dubreuil diagonally printed a negative of a locomotive and repeatedly effaced the surface of the print with a rectangular form, producing a transparent overlapping of geometric planes. This projection of the rectangular form introduced abstraction of the subject and provided one of the critical ingredients—the other being the return to sharp focus—that would re-define modernism in photography around 1916.

American Perspectives

While the battle for photography as an independent art was being waged in Europe, American photographers continued to improve commercial photography, leaving the culturally high-minded still looking towards Europe for inspiration. In 1881, **Alfred Stieglitz** [1864–1946] went to Berlin to study mechanical engineering and met Hermann Wilhelm Vogel, whose experiments with orthochromatic emulsions and active role in photographic societies convinced Stieglitz to pursue photography. Under Vogel Stieglitz became a master technician and learned about pictorial photography. Returning to America in 1890, Stieglitz decided to pursue a life in photography that would take him to the forefront of the crusade for photography's acceptance as an independent medium.

The fight for the independence of photography in the New World held special appeal for a first American-born son of a Jewish immigrant like Stieglitz who wanted to leave behind many customs of the old country. Although Stieglitz did not practice Judaism one can speculate how Jewish culture might have influenced him. Since Judaism is based on the word and not the image, Stieglitz's making of photographs could be interpreted as an act of rebellion against the authority of the Old Testament, a rejection of Judaism's fear of the eye, saying NO to the taboo on graven images.[19] By indirect mechanical means, the camera allowed Stieglitz to break this prohibition and embrace Christian pictorialism (without endorsing its history of church-sponsored art) on a new, wide-open playing field. This enabled Stieglitz to fulfill a role as a "chosen one," guiding his people out of the slavery of old practices. Stieglitz could be a rabbi (teacher), leading services of a new monotheistic, aesthetic order. Instead of studying the Torah and writing expositions, Stieglitz would polemicize and publish the order of modernism from the position of the persecuted outsider. Instead of being tormented by anti-Semites, Stieglitz was harassed by uncultured barbarians.

As editor of *The American Amateur Photographer* Stieglitz promoted the handheld camera when most practitioners believed it a plaything. Stieglitz shocked readers by stating that it was acceptable to use only a portion of the original negative. According to Stieglitz, serious imagemaking could occur after the shutter was pressed, and he demonstrated it by using less than half his plate to produce *Winter on Fifth Avenue* (1892) (see Figure 9.7). Stieglitz joined together the "proper moment" in front of the camera with post-camera strategies in the darkroom. He showed that weather conditions did not have to be a deterrent in making pictures and that chance operations could be incorporated into the process. Stieglitz gained a reputation for using a hand camera to capture unretouched, precisely observed moments from real time, whether at night (*Re-*

9.7 ALFRED STIEGLITZ. *Winter on Fifth Avenue,* 1892. 15¾ × 12⅞ inches. Gelatin silver print. "My picture, *Fifth Avenue, Winter,* is the result of a three hours' stand during a fierce snow-storm on February 22nd, 1893, awaiting the proper moment. . . . the result contained an element of chance. . . . I remember how upon having developed the negative of the picture I showed it to some of my colleagues. They smiled and advised me to throw away such rot. . . . when the finished picture was shown to these same gentlemen it proved to them conclusively that there was other photographic work open to them during the "bad season". . . This incident also goes to prove that the making of the negative alone is not the making of the picture. . . . My experience has taught me that the prints from the direct negatives have but little value as such."[20] The two broken lines on the left and the right sides of the full plate show the portions that Stieglitz cropped to form the final image in the central picture area, converting the original horizontal into a vertical photograph.
Courtesy George Eastman House.

flections, Night, 1896), in the rain (*A Wet Day on the Boulevard,* 1894), or under difficult lighting conditions (*Sunlight and Shadows, Paula,* Berlin, 1889). These aesthetic revelations that Stieglitz called "snapshots" broke with the attitudes of the painted image, furthering photography's quest to define itself based on its intrinsic elements. Ironically, the proponent of using hand cameras, which almost anyone could operate, was not interested in the democratic aspects of the process; Stieglitz believed that only inspired artists could make fine images.

In 1896, the Society of Amateur Photographers and the New York Camera Club merged to form the Camera Club of New York. Stieglitz recast its journal, *Camera Notes* (1897–1903), into a high-quality international quarterly that presented America's first concrete claim for photography as a fine art. *Camera Notes* featured splendid reproductions, perceptive articles, and critical reviews, representing Stieglitz's standards of aesthetic excellence that other photographers could look to for aesthetic guidance.[21]

Camera Notes portrayed the emerging style of the American pictorial movement, which was typified by subjects that steered clear of topical issues, placing importance on how a subject was handled rather than the subject itself. Soft focus was used to evoke mystery

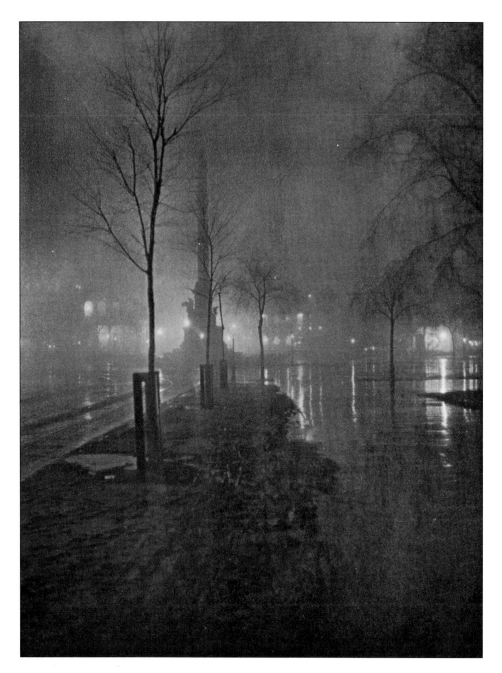

9.8   WILLIAM FRASER.   *A Wet Night, Columbus
Circle, NY,* ca. 1897–98. From *Camera Notes,* Vol. 2,
No. 3. 1899. 6½ × 4¹³⁄₁₆ inches. Photogravure. William
Fraser (1840–1925) responded to the modern beauty
of the electric light that transformed the urban night.
Working in moist conditions favorable to pictorial effect, Fraser produced an atmospheric, luminously detailed poem, synthesizing a dreamy impression with a
technical tour de force that viscerally elicited a sense of
the nocturnal.   Courtesy George Eastman House.

and de-emphasize photography's connection with reality. Simplified compositions, manually manipulated to
eliminate extraneous elements, removed images from
their dependence on the real world and fitted them into
a new definition of what constituted art. Stieglitz challenged his readers to do more than impersonate another
medium's achievements and to discover their own photographic medium's visual models.

Stieglitz desired to produce a major exhibition reflecting the principal pictorialist concerns that stressed
elaborate printing processes, post-camera manipulations, atmospheric effects, and the tonal values of the
image over the subject matter. Such a show would
demonstrate that photography was a tool, like a paintbrush, for achieving aesthetic effect. Stieglitz was un-

9.9   FRED HOLLAND DAY.   *An Ethiopian Chief,*
ca. 1898. From *Camera Notes* Vol. 1. No. 2. 1897. 4⅝ ×
4⅝ inches. Photogravure.   Courtesy George Eastman
House.

able to make this exhibition happen at the Camera
Club. Instead, John G. Bullock [1854–1939] and
Robert S. Redfield [1849–1923] of the Photographic
Society of Philadelphia produced a show under the patronage of the Pennsylvania Academy of Fine Arts in
1898. According to the catalogue, the purpose of the
Philadelphia Salon was to present work with "distinct
evidence of individual artistic feeling and execution."
That same year, the Munich Secession group hung photographs alongside paintings in an effort to inject new
concepts and vigor into German art. Other groups soon
followed suit.

In early 1901, a political coup at the Photography
Society of Philadelphia toppled the leadership, replacing it with a group who believed there was "a little too
much art" in photography and who wanted to "popularize" the Salon, which led to its demise. Stieglitz, realizing that camera clubs could no longer support the standards he valued, opened his first independent exhibition

space. As he solicited work, Stieglitz was forming a
new group of photographers that would be known as
the Photo-Secession.

The Photo-Secession

The *Photo-Secession* was founded on February 17,
1902 to "loosely to hold together those Americans devoted to pictorial photography in their endeavor to
compel its recognition, not as a handmaiden of art, but
as a distinctive medium of individual expression."[22]
The group was made up of American pictorial photographers who shared the same philosophies as the
Linked Ring, the Photo-Club de Paris, and the German
secession movements that had rebelled against academic authorities and organized their own exhibitions.
The founders included Stieglitz, as director of the
Council, John Bullock, Frank Eugene, Gertrude Käsebier, Joseph Keiley, Robert Redfield, Eva Watson-
Schütze, Eduard Steichen, and Clarence White.

Stieglitz resigned as editor of *Camera Notes* in 1902
and immediately launched a new quarterly, *Camera
Work,* assisted by Joseph T. Keiley [1869–1914], who
had worked with him as an associate editor for *Camera*

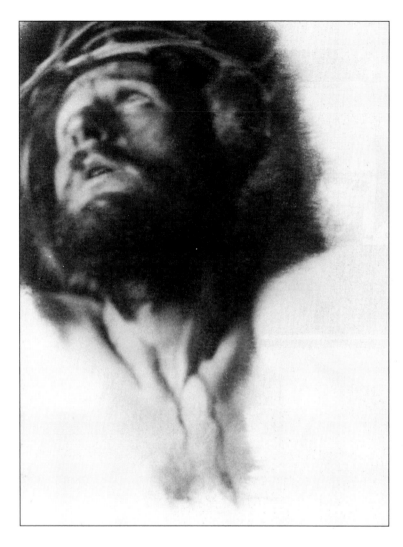

9.10   FRED HOLLAND DAY.   *The Crucifixion, #4*
"My God, My God, Why hast thou forsaken me?" 1898.
Printed by F. Evans, 1912. 7⅞ × 6 inches. Platinum
print.   Courtesy George Eastman House.

Is itself a work of art: the lover's touch having
been lavished on every aspect of its form and
content. . . . Many of the reproductions are actual pulls from photogravure plates made directly from the original negatives; and all are
printed in the spirit of the original pictures and
retain their intrinsic qualities. They are actually original stamps.[24]

Camera Work spotlighted monographs
of the Photo-Secessionists and leading
European practitioners, along with the
historic works of David Octavius Hill,
Robert Adamson, and Julia Margaret
Cameron. Articles by noted critics, such
as Charles Caffin (*Photography as a Fine
Art*, 1901) and Sadakichi Hartman (*The
History of American Art*, 1901), and by
authors such as George Bernard Shaw and
Gertrude Stein raised the level of critical
discussion.[25] *Camera Work* had a decidedly intellectual appeal, claiming to be
"published for those who know or want to
know."[26] In 1905, Stieglitz took out a
lease at 291 Fifth Avenue, giving the
group a permanent exhibition and operations center. Later known as "291," the
gallery featured the leading pictorialists
of America and Europe. During its later
years, from 1911 to 1917, "291" was the
only place in America that steadily presented modern artists and engaged in a dialogue of their ideas.

Notes. Keiley was also a member of the Linked Ring
and, as a founding member of the Photo-Secession, became its historian. Fifty issues of *Camera Work,* with a
press run of only 1,000 copies, were published between
1903 and 1917.[23] Stieglitz covered the evolution of the
pictorial movement through the new hard-edged modernism and introduced the new art movements of Fau-
vism, Cubism, and Futurism (see Chapter 10). Stieglitz
was conscious of how a medium's physical nature affects the information it carries, and great care was taken
with the reproductions. Stieglitz favored presenting individual artist portfolios by means of photogravure on
thin Japanese paper, tipping the pictures in on brown or
gray submounts. The quality of these reproductions
often gave them a delicacy and depth absent in the original, showing what the mechanical printing process was
capable of (printers were given credit lines). Paul
Rosenfeld wrote that *Camera Work:*

The Decadent Movement and Tonalism

Fred Holland Day [1864–1933], a wealthy biblio-
phile, became the third American member of the
Linked Ring. As cofounder of the publishing firm
Copeland & Day (1888), he produced noncommercial
titles such as those illustrated by Aubrey Beardsley.
George Davison brought Day's work to the notice of
Stieglitz in 1895, and Stieglitz featured Day's images in
Camera Notes in 1897 and gave him a one-person show
at the Camera Club. Day was influenced by the *Decadent Movement* (a.k.a. dandyism) and was friends with
Oscar Wilde and William Morris of the Arts and Craft
Movement. In the manner of Beau Brummell, artists of
the Decadent Movement (at its height towards the end
of the nineteenth century) were fashionably dressed
and displayed exquisite manners. Their value system
prized artificiality, self-consciousness, and a disdain for
bourgeois values, expressed through intellectual skepticism, humor, and a withdrawal from conventional society. They rejected the notion that art should imitate na-

9.11   ALVIN LANGDON COBURN.   *The Temple of Ohm (Grand Canyon),* 1911. 16 × 12⅝ inches. Gelatin silver print.   Courtesy George Eastman House.

ture and emphasized amorality, play, and relief from the mounting social and spiritual problems caused by untethered industrialism. Decadent Movement artists often saw themselves as extensions of their work, and Day enjoyed dressing in exotic costumes. Day posed his models in unconventional dress in historical and mythological settings, often eliciting an idyllic homoerotic sense of ancient Greece or an atmosphere of Orientalism (Africa and the Middle East).[27]

Day used the subjects before his camera to raise significant issues dealing with sex, religion, race, and the physical perfection of youth. He created a stir by making images of adult full-frontal female and male nudity. In separating the nude from the lewd, pictorialists had stylistically photographed women to stress beauty rather than sensuality: Sexual details such as nipples and pubic hair were suppressed. With its ability to confront the body, photography helped end the tradition of concealing the female nude in an allegorical setting, letting the body be seen as a sensuous, aesthetic form. However, the undraped male body was considered too sexual for mixed audiences. Journal articles suggested using young boys, believing their bodies would be less sexually titillating than a woman's.[28] Photographers like **Frank Meadow Sutcliffe** [1853–1941] and Kühn portrayed nude boys in down-to-earth, Barbizon-type settings, such as swimming in the sea, to give the body a sense of spontaneity. These depictions were considered immoral, however; Sutcliffe was excommunicated from the Roman Catholic Church for depraving women and children after his

9.12   ANNE BRIGMAN   *The Bubble,* 1907. 6⁵⁄₁₆ ×
9⁵⁄₁₆ inches. Photogravure. **Anne Brigman** [1869–
1950], actress, photographer, and champion of woman's
rights, separated from her husband to "work out my
destiny." Brigman received acclaim and notoriety for
her innovative interpretations of the female figure in
nature, often inhabiting the landscape with her own
nude body. Brigman's interpretation of the landscape
removed the female body from the gaze of a clothed
man in the confines of his studio.   Courtesy George Eastman House.

picture, *Water Rats,* featuring nude boys swimming, was
exhibited. Day's images directly acknowledged the
beauty and sensuality of the adult male body, implying a
forbidden homosexual lifestyle and demonstrating how
photography can hint at the secret life.

Day was condemned for the double sin of judi-
ciously portraying a nude black man. The model was
Day's chauffeur and confidant, whom he photographed
for years. The images were shocking because Day cast
them against type. Nudes were supposed to be female,
not male, and white society was comfortable with images of blacks in clinical studies or in subservient positions, not as individuals and certainly not as equals.
Day forged new ground by portraying his sitter as a fellow human being (see Figure 9.9).

During the summer of 1898, Day caused a sensation
in Boston by making hundreds of exposures on the
theme of Christ's last days. Day starved himself and
grew his hair down to his shoulders so he could model
as Christ, a role he also wanted to play as the artistic
leader of photography (see Figure 9.10). Day sought to
affirm that photographs could reveal the same spiritual
sensations as paintings with religious themes. By casting himself as artist and savior, Day projected the romantic belief that fine culture and sacred beliefs can be
revived through an understanding of the arts.

A fervent competition developed between Stieglitz
and Day to be the first to prove that photography could
hold its own in the art world. In 1900, Day organized an
exhibition of 300 prints by the New School of American
Photography and offered it to the Linked Ring. Stieglitz
saw Day stealing his thunder and intervened, and the
show was refused. Day got the Royal Photographic Society to take the exhibition instead and then traveled it to the
Photo-Club de Paris in early 1901. The exhibition was a
critical success, helping establish photography's place in
the art world and boosting the reputation of American pictorialists in a hostile environment in which the old-guard
photographic societies resisted aesthetic change.

Day's strong character and independence of thought
fostered a rivalry with Stieglitz for leadership of the
American pictorialist movement, but it was a struggle
that he was not temperamentally suited to win. Stieglitz

9.13   GERTRUDE KÄSEBIER.   *Turner Family*, Woburn, Mass., ca. 1912. 4⁵⁄₁₆ × 9¼ inches. Platinum print.   Courtesy George Eastman House.

was better connected and possessed the appropriate mixture of charisma and intellectual prowess that enabled him to maintain a following of major talent. Day made very few photographs after 1904, when a fire destroyed his studio and most of his work. In 1917, Day took to his bed and remained secluded until his death in 1933.

The connecting of European and American pictorial movements received an assist from **Alvin Langdon Coburn** [1882–1966]. In 1900 Coburn helped his cousin, Fred Holland Day, organize Day's *New American School Exhibition* in Europe. Coburn was a founding member of the Photo-Secession and was elected to the Linked Ring. His early work was influenced by *tonalism,* a turn of the twentieth century, American artistic movement in painting and photography that was typified by an idealized, often melancholic, mysterious, personal, romantic interpretation that favored muted color and mood. In 1910 and 1911 Coburn traveled through the American West, pursuing the tonalist's favorite subject—the natural landscape. At the Grand Canyon, Coburn's series of poetic representations reflected the nature-based spiritualism of Thoreau and the transcendental harmony of Ralph Waldo Emerson. The series tackled the difficulty of conveying the Grand Canyon's sense of scale. Coburn's tightly composed serial views concentrated on specific aspects of the Canyon instead of trying to portray it in a single image (see Figure 9.11). The work has a sequential logic and is most effective when seen as a set. Coburn's textured, gritty prints render a visual playback of the canyon's shale landscape. The soft-focus, sometimes almost blurry effect adds an other-worldly feeling to the scene. It also distorts the sense of distance by manufacturing a near *bas-*

relief[29] effect of physical relief in the background. In other views the visual sense of distance is collapsed and perspective is diminished. This creates spatially flat images that rely on the abstracting of atmospheric patterns to bond the composition together. Both styles generate a visual paradox, making the images appear solid yet unattainable while conveying an awareness of the eternal. The prints feel old and give viewers a sense of historical time. Coburn's use of chiaroscuro adds a dramatic, emotionally uplifting grandeur to the land. Other views incorporate atmospheric effects, such as aerial perspective, to provide a sense of distance.

Women Pictorialists

Feminists in the late 1890s began actively crusading for equal rights and greater opportunities in all areas of life. Women were admitted as members to the major camera clubs in New York, Buffalo, Chicago, Boston, San Francisco, and Los Angeles. Women came to reject the idea of receiving separate segregated awards and agitated for genderless categories. Catharine Weed Barnes Ward summed up the position: "Good work is good work, whether it be by man or woman, and poor is poor by the same rule."[30] Although the majority of the 105 members of the Photo-Secession were East Coast men, 21 were women. Alice Boughton, Anne W. Brigman (see Figure 9.12), Sarah C. Sears, Eva Watson-Schütze, and Gertrude Käsebier played active roles as artists. They also served the movement's symbolic foundation as archetypal nurturing mothers and primal forces of nature, both major themes of the pictorialists.[31]

Gertrude Käsebier (pronounced KAY-za-beer) [1852–1934], apprenticed herself to a chemist and later worked for a portrait photographer before opening her

9.14   ALICE BOUGHTON   *Nude* (children). From *Camera Work* #26. April 1909. 8⅝ × 5¼ inches. Photogravure.   Courtesy George Eastman House.

own studio in New York in 1897. Käsebier's work was recognized at the first Philadelphia Salon of 1898, followed by a solo show at the New York Camera Club in 1899. She was elected the first American woman in the Linked Ring in 1900. Käsebier's images were included in Day's *New School of American Pictorial Photography* exhibition and she was a founding member of the Photo-Secession. Stieglitz featured her work in the first and subsequent issues of *Camera Work* as well as in shows he organized at "291" and elsewhere. Käsebier went on to help found the Pictorial Photographers of America in 1916.

Up until World War II, women photographers often specialized in portraits, flowers, and child and baby work. Such work could be done from the home, thus preserving the traditional family hierarchy, and was appreciated by critics. And, because women were trained and expected to be more sensitive to the needs of others, such work seemed a natural specialization. Käsebier is known for her unconventionally composed scenes that depict the subtle complexities of mother-child relations and evoke a tranquil sense of intimacy. Käsebier reformed pictorialist practice by ridding scenes of idealized, middle-class domestic life of their Victorian backdrops and emphasizing the individuality of the subjects as they would be found in their everyday settings. Käsebier's goal was to "make likenesses that are biographies, to bring out in each photograph, the essential personality that is variously called temperament, soul, humanity."[32]

Alice Boughton (1865-1943) was among the women pictorialists who not only celebrated the beauty of young women, but also wrote about the qualities required to produce images of people:

> He [the photographer] must have tact, the social instinct and infinite patience. In doing children, for instance, he must amuse, watch for the right moment, be constantly and continually alert, and work for the unconsciousness which is one of their charms.[33]

A Kodak ad in *Camera Work* #26 (April 1909), in which Boughton's images appear, shows two women going into a darkroom to develop film with the new Eastman Plate Tank (a daylight developing tank). The caption reads: "Where the tank enters, the dark room worries end." While the ad implies that even a woman can use the Kodak tank, it also recognizes the involvement of women in photography and as potential customers. At a time when women in the United States still did not have the right to vote, such ads reveal the photographic industry's awareness that women's relationship to photography was changing from being the ones depicted to being the ones doing the depicting.[34]

The Pictorial Epoch/ The Stieglitz Group

Stieglitz was able to assemble a core group of photographers that played key roles in developing and expressing the pictorial aesthetic. In 1900, en route to Eu-

9.15   EDWARD STEICHEN.   *Auguste Rodin*, 1903.
8½ × 6⁵⁄₁₆ inches. Photogravure.   Reprinted with permission of Joanna T. Steichen, Carousel Research.

rope, **Edward Jean Steichen** [1879–1973] visited Stieglitz, who bought three of his photographs for five dollars each. In 1901, Day included Steichen's prints in his *New School of American Photography* exhibition. Steichen was also elected to the Linked Ring and began a friendship with the sculptor Auguste Rodin, of whom he would make numerous portraits.

In 1902 Steichen returned to New York from Europe to become a founding member of the Photo-Secession and take studio space at 291 Fifth Avenue. During his European trip of 1906 Steichen sent Stieglitz works by practitioners who would later be featured in *Camera Work* and at "291." Steichen's aesthetic sensitivity, combined with enormous and diverse productivity and technical virtuosity, made him one of the most extensively published and critically examined members of the Secession. Steichen's prints met the avant-garde requirement of what art was supposed to be: A subjective response to the visible world, forcing

an acknowledgment that a photograph could be an expressive statement. His gum prints and use of copy negatives in combination with other alternative photographic printing processes reflect the late nineteenth century propensity for moody, meditative fantasy. The subject, reinforced through the controls of gum printing and soft focus, demonstrated Steichen's emotional fascination with photography's prime mover: light. In prints like *Moonlight: The Pond* (see Figure 9.16), Steichen created a dark, enigmatic atmosphere of nostalgia and sensuality that initiated a visual dialogue between the transitory archetypal powers of light and shadow. Steichen's prints sum up the Secessionist aesthetic of suggestiveness, of evoking the mystery of an echo rather than a replica of the original, that takes one beyond the visible experience.

Baron **Adolf de Meyer** [1886–1946], a European involved with the issues of pictorial photography, corresponded with Stieglitz, had his first exhibition in the Photo-Secession Galleries in 1907, and in 1908 had his images published in *Camera Work* and was listed as Fellow of the Council of the Photo-Secession. In 1903 Meyer began to use a specially constructed *soft-*

9.16   EDWARD STEICHEN.   *Moonlight: The Pond,*
1906. 6⅜ × 8 inches. Photogravure.   Reprinted with
permission of Joanna T. Steichen, Carousel Research.

focus lens[35] to control the sharpness in his large-scale
portraits and still lifes. De Meyer's still life set-ups of
glass containers on a glass tabletop use transparency
to produce visual ambiguity between the subject and
the background. He employed artificial lights to make
a high-key sparkle and even "blinded" his lens by
shooting into the light for effect (see Figure 9.17). De
Meyer circulated with and photographed the stylishly
wealthy. When World War I broke out, de Meyer came
to the United States as a photographer for *Vogue* and
Vanity Fair. In this capacity he produced high-key,
soft-focus, idealized portraits of American celebrities
in elegant settings throughout the 1920s, expressing a
range of feeling from joy to ennui. With the coming of
the Great Depression and a shift towards social realism de Meyer's work fell out of favor and has been
largely forgotten.

Frank Eugene (Smith) [1865–1936], a painter
who evolved into a photographer, was a member of the
Linked Ring and a founder of the Photo-Secession. His
approach to making negatives with optically corrected
lenses was atypical of the Secessionists. Rather than
relying on printing methods to introduce subjective interpretation, Eugene hand-altered his negatives by
scratching on the emulsion with an etching needle (see
Figure 9.18). He maintained the photographic character of his subject while adding a painterly physical
presence, permitting a subjective postcamera investigation into the psychological nature of his subject. His
working methods were viewed with horror, even by
some of the Secessionists, for violating the sacred surface of the negative, but Stieglitz supported the work
through publication and exhibition.

Clarence Hudson White [1871–1925] was a self-
taught photographer whose work in the 1898 Philadelphia Salon came to the attention of Stieglitz. Eventually White and Stieglitz collaborated on a series of
nude studies and, later, with the autochrome process.

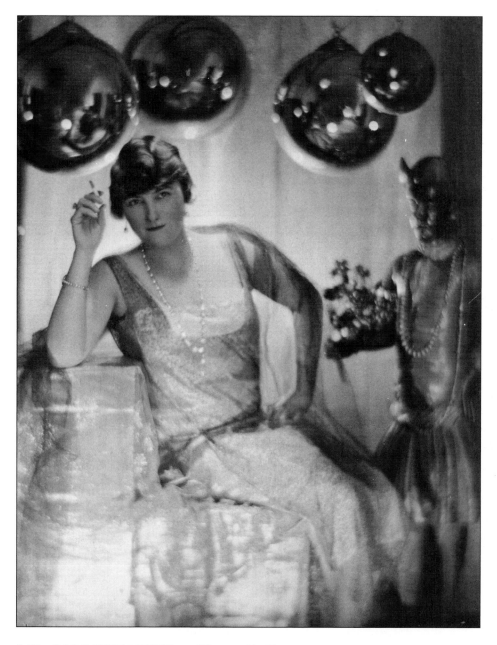

9.17 BARON DE MEYER. *Woman with Cigarette Case*. 9⁷⁄₁₆ × 7½ inches. Platinum print. Courtesy George Eastman House.

White's simple early compositions of family and friends, featured common, middle-class settings and relied on his use of natural light to inject emotion (see Figure 9.19). Favoring soft, early morning light, White used backlighting to bring forth accepted romantic notions of midwestern domesticity and commonplace portrayals of feminine home endeavors, from ring toss to reclining on a daybed. White began an influential teaching career in photography at Columbia University in 1906. In 1912, White broke with Stieglitz after a feud and in 1914 founded the Clarence White School of Photography, which was instrumen-

tal in the development of the next generation of photographers (see Chapter 11). In 1916 White helped establish the Pictorial Photographers of America, whose membership wanted to continue to promote the pictorial ideas that Stieglitz was abandoning. White's teaching, a monetary necessity criticized by Stieglitz (who could afford not to mix photography and business), reduced White's artistic output and development. White's situation exemplifies the continuing dilemma facing artists of how to earn a living in a society that offers little support to artists while remaining artistically vital. White died while leading a group of photography students in Mexico.

In November 1910, the Albright Art Gallery (now the Albright-Knox) in Buffalo, N.Y., presented the *International Exhibition of Pictorial Photography*,

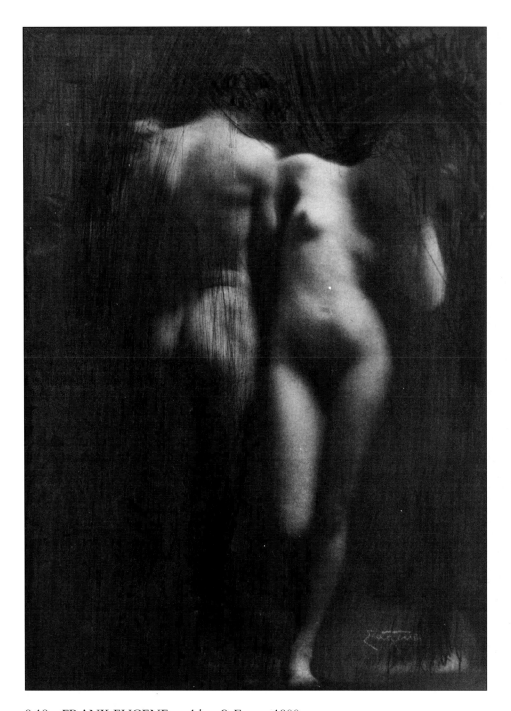

9.18   FRANK EUGENE.   *Adam & Eve*, ca. 1900.
7 × 5 inches. Photogravure.   Courtesy George Eastman
House.

organized by Stieglitz to sum up pictorial photography. The Albright's purchase of twelve prints linked
the pictorialists with the Pre-Raphaelites (see Figure
9.20), who broke away from the traditional avenues of
aristocratic, church, and government art patronage
and actively framed the idea of the modern gallery
system, with its dealers, collectors, and high prices for
art works. These modern conceptions about gallery
sales, collections, and connoisseurship made up a key
ingredient of the Western art scene during the twentieth century. The Buffalo Exhibition marked the culmi-
nation of the pictorial movement by "the most beautiful gallery in America." It was a recognition and
sanctioning of photographers as artists and photography's ability to compete with traditional art mediums.
Because the pictorialists changed the status of their
photographs through the investment of time in their
handwork, people were now willing to purchase photographs for display on their walls instead of just in
their private albums. Pictorialist methods removed the
photographic process from the machine, elevating the
image and its maker to the plane of art and artist.

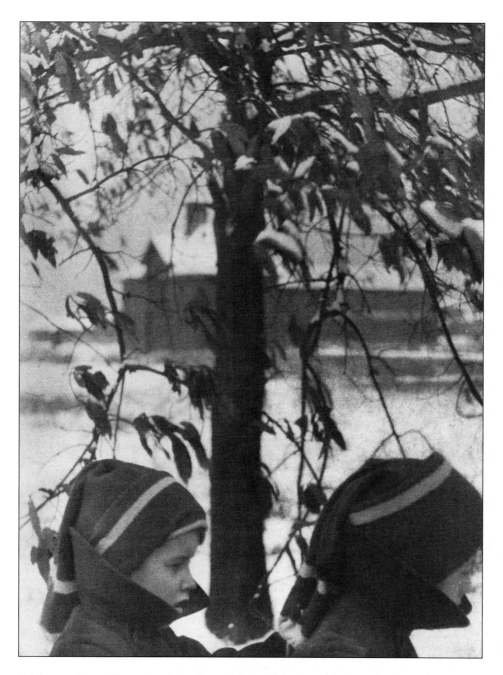

9.19   CLARENCE WHITE.   *Boys Going to School,*
1903. 8⅟₁₆ × 6⅛ inches. Photogravure. Working as a
bookkeeper taught White to concentrate on detail and
planning. He favored the familiar, using the same subjects over again in the belief that it furthered his understanding of their inner emotions, creating compositions
suggested by the subject. Formations, such as *Boys Going to School,* use ordering and limited depth of field to
heighten the beauty of form and texture in everyday
events.   Courtesy George Eastman House.

The Decline of Pictorialism

The success of the pictorialists resulted in numerous
uninformed imitators interested only in achieving a pictorial look and led to a tarring of the movement. Leading practitioners, such as Demachy, recognized that
"many pictorialists will meddle with their prints in the
fond belief that any alteration, however bungling, is the
touchstone of art."[36] As pictorialism became a recognized style, others assumed the trappings without the
context, resulting in pictures that appear affected. With
the original impetus gone, the emulators' work became
synonymous with vapid, strained, and worn-out formu-
lae. Eventually, even images in *Camera Work* seemed

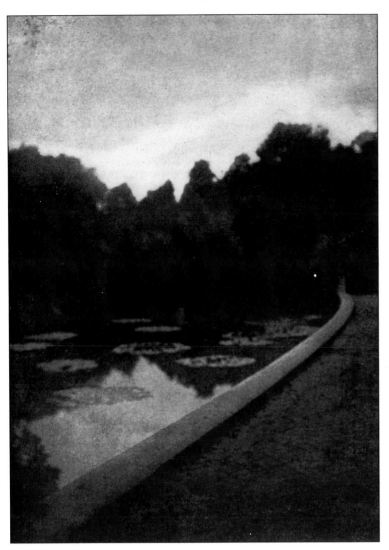

9.20   JOSEPH T. KEILEY.   *Garden of Dreams*, 1899.
From *Camera Work* #17 January 1907. 7½ × 5½ inches.
Photogravure. One of the twelve prints purchased by
the Albright Art Gallery from the *International Exhibition of Pictorial Photography* (1910) in Buffalo, New York.
Courtesy George Eastman House.

As art is an evolutionary process, rooted in people's experiences, it is always in flux. The process of interchange and crossing boundaries confirms how "realism" is continually being reinvented. It verifies that reality in art is artificial and has to be recreated if the art is going to be more than an illustration. When a society agrees that something is real, it indicates that a comparison with reality has confirmed the observation. When we look at a work of art and are moved by it, we do not make such a comparison because it is the power of the work, not its imitation, that speaks to us. This is what artists, including the pictorialists, traditionally strive to achieve. Photography released painters from their societal compact to make realistic representation, pointing artists toward the pursuit of personal and abstract concerns while supplying examples of a new, and previously unseen reality. Artists were influenced by the contemporary look and subject matter of the photographic image and photographic effects such as *halation*. Halation is the luminous halo, with a diffused outer edge, that occurs when an exposure is made into a bright source of light (backlighting). Early films were prone to halation and would exaggerate the effect. Impressionists picked up on such effects and incorporated them into their visual vocabulary.

Aesthetically, pictorialism demonstrated that photography was an elastic medium and could be used to interpret life with the same aesthetic impulses used in making paintings. In turn, photography freed artists to expand the boundaries of representation, making impressionistic and other modern explorations possible. Theoretically, pictorialism established photography as an art by assimilating it to various styles and theories of art. Once photography was established as an interpretive medium, its own photographic art theory was free to emerge. The pictorial movement was a big stride in the direction of photographers investigating their own medium and establishing their place in the art world. With these changes underway, some of the foremost pictorialists, especially Stieglitz, reconsidered photography's position, not as it related to painting but on its own inherent characteristics.

overwrought because everyone, including Stieglitz, was struggling to discover where the boundaries of the practice lay. What is evident is that even gifted artists make bad art; their genuine ability is in not being afraid to take chances and risk failure. By the time of the Buffalo exhibition, the group Stieglitz had founded and the style it championed had ceased to interest him and was disintegrating. Stieglitz turned his attention to modern art which he began to present in *Camera Work*, and he only presented one photography show, of Paul Strand (1916) during the last four years of "291." Many excesses were committed in the name of pictorialism, but the Photo-Secession helped photography realize its place as an artistic medium.

Endnotes

1   "Society Gossip," *Philadelphia Photographer,* vol. 17, no. 195 (March 1880), 98.

2   "Photographers' Association of America," *Philadelphia Photographer,* vol. 17, no. 201 (September 1880), 275.

3   Peter Henry Emerson, "Photography, A Pictorial Art," *The Amateur Photographer,* vol. 3, no. 76 (March 19, 1886), 138–39.

4   The photographs were influenced by Joseph Mallord William Turner (1775–1851), an English romantic landscape painter concerned with portraying the elemental forces of nature, James McNeill Whistler (1834–1903); and the French Impressionists.

5   Like all printing-out processes, platinum's self-masking abilities allow subtle highlight details to be retained without the shadow areas becoming "buried." The images have a matte surface and are permanent, as platinum is more stable than silver. The platinum process was patented in 1873 by William Willis, who marketed it in 1879 as the Platinotype. Its high cost caused it to disappear from the commercial market by 1937, though it reappeared again in the mid-1980s through alternative sources.

6   Peter Henry Emerson, *Naturalist Photography for Students of the Arts* (London: Sampson, Low, Marston, Searle and Rivington, 1889), 150.

7   Although trained as a physician, neither Emerson nor other photographers of the time grasped the potential creative mastery that the understanding of the H & D curve could provide. It was not until 1941, when Ansel Adams translated sensitometry into aesthetics through his Zone System, that photographers had a reliable method of accurately depicting tonal relationships as they "previsualized" them.

8   Peter Henry Emerson, *The Death of Naturalistic Photography* (privately published, 1890). Reprint edition (New York: Arno Press, 1973) from the back of *Naturalistic Photography,* 3rd ed. (New York: The Scovill and Adams Co., 1899).

9   Bromoil was introduced in 1907 and allowed the option of making an enlargement from a small negative. In the bromoil process a gelatin silver bromide print was bleached and redeveloped in pigment, allowing color, tonal effects, and the diffusion of detail to be controlled by hand. Multiple impressions could be made with different colored inks. Bromoil's latitude and painterly appearance gave it a following among expressive printmakers through the 1940s.

10   Emerson, *The Death of Naturalistic Photography* (privately published, 1890).

11   Joseph T. Keiley, "The Linked Ring," *Camera Notes,* vol. 5, no. 2 (October 1901), 113.

12   Catharine Weed Barnes Ward, "Why Ladies Should be Admitted to Membership in Photographic Societies," *American Amateur Photographer,* vol. 1, no. 6 (December 1889), 224. For a reprint of this short piece and seven of her other essays see Peter E. Palmquist, *Catharine Weed Barnes Ward: Pioneer Advocate for Women in Photography* (Arcata, CA: Peter E. Palmquist, 1992), 35–83.

13   Robert Demachy, "On the Straight Print," *Camera Work* 19 (July 1907), 21–24.

14   George Smith, "Lantern Slides," *British Journal of Photography,* vol. 33, no. 33 (1886), 20–21.

15   An energetic writer, Evans explained his ideas in articles for popular journals. He wrote a series of twelve instructional lessons for *The Photogram* in 1904 and was a regular contributor to *Camera Work,* becoming the first English photographer to gain recognition in America.

16   F. H. Evans, "Some Notes on Interior Work," *The Amateur Photographer,* May 12, 1904, 372.

17   Ward Muir, *The Amateur Photographer,* October 2, 1902, 273.

18   Oil-pigment printing was a contact process in which a gelatin-coated paper sensitized with potassium bichromate could absorb hand-applied inks or pigments. Known for its limited granular resolution and broad, slightly uneven tonal effects, it was revived in 1904 by G. E. H. Rawlins and remained popular through World War I.

19   The Second Commandment, the Prophets' battles with idolatry, the teaching of the rabbis, and the cultural and economic traditions of the Jews militated against the visual arts. The only reference to painting in the Old Testament is in the context of lewdness and whoredom. *Ezekiel* 23:13-16.

20   Alfred Stieglitz, "The Hand Camera—Its Present Importance," *The American Annual of Photography,* 1897, 18–27. This article contained fourteen "snapshots" by Stieglitz.

21   For reproductions of all of *Camera Notes*'s images see Christian A. Peterson, *Alfred Stiegliz's Camera Notes* (Minneapolis: The Minneapolis Institute of Arts in association with W. W. Norton & Co., New York, 1993).

22   Alfred Stieglitz, *Camera Work* 6 (April 1904), 53.

23   See Simone Philippi, Ute Kieseyer, *Alfred Stieglitz Camera Work: The Complete Illustrations 1903–1917* (Köln: Benedikt Taschen Verlag GmbH, 1997).

24   Paul Rosenfeld, "The Boys in the Darkroom," *America and Alfred Stieglitz,* Waldo Frank, Lewis Mumford, Dorothy Norman, Paul Rosenfeld, Harold Rogg (eds.) (New York: Doubleday, Doran & Co., Inc., 1934), 82.

25   See Jonathan Green, *Camera Work: A Critical Anthology* (Millerton, NY: Aperture, 1973).

26   Ads, *Camera Work* 42–43 (April–July 1913), unp.

27   See James Crump, *F. Holland Day: Suffering the Ideal* (Santa Fe: Twin Palms Publishers, 1995), 23.

28   J. M. B. W., "A Note on some Open-Air Nude Studies," *The Amateur Photographer and Photographic News,* vol. 52, no. 1344 (July 5, 1910), 20–21.

29   The bas-relief effect is achieved by making a contact positive transparency from a negative, placing the two pieces of film together slightly out of register, and printing from the combination.

30   Catharine Weed Barnes Ward, "Photography from a Woman's Standpoint" (paper read before the Society of Professional Women, December 10, 1889), *American Amateur Photographer*, vol. 2 (January 1890), 10.

31   See Barbara L. Michaels, *Gertrude Käsebier: The Photographer and Her Photographs* (New York: Harry N. Abrams, 1992), 17–18.

32   Giles Edgerton [pseudo. of Mary Fanton Roberts], "Photography as an Emotional Art: A Study of the Work of Gertrude Käsebier," *The Craftsman,* vol. 12 (April–September 1907), 88.

33   Alice Boughton, "Photography, A Medium of Experience," *Camera Work* 26 (April 1909), 33–36.

34   This indicates how industrialization transformed women's roles in the economy of the northeast. In 1800, only one woman in twenty worked outside her home, but within a hundred years in cities such as Boston, one woman in three derived income outside the home. The work experience had a significant cultural effect, fostering new attitudes and relationships. Women who worked in mills, shoe manufacturing, domestic service, or teaching tended to stay in the city, marry urban men, and have fewer babies than their rural counterparts.

35   With a soft-focus lens, no correction is made for spherical aberration. The result is that no part of the image is sharp. Special soft-focus portrait lenses allow the degree of diffusion to be controlled. Images produced from soft-focus lenses possess an exaggerated degree of brilliance in the highlight areas.

36   Robert Demachy, "On the Straight Print," *Camera Work* 19 (July 1907), 21–24. Also reprinted in Peter E. Palmquist *Catharine Weed Barnes Ward: Pioneer Advocate for Women in Photography*, 39–42.

CHAPTER TEN

Modernism
Industrial Beauty

A new set of Western artistic, cultural, and spiritual precepts evolved during the early modernistic period (1880–1920), based on the new urban, industrial, and secular order. Modernist artists abandoned historical subject matter and Renaissance *illusionism,* the convincing depiction of nature, in favor of portraying contemporary events and experimental representation. The decline of aristocratic, church, and state patronage in the nineteenth century meant artists were no longer beholden to these powers and their values. In the new fledgling capitalist art market, where the probability of sales was small, artists were freer to experiment with appearance and content, and even ridicule the ruling powers. *Aesthetic formalism,* emphasizing form over content, emerged in part from an ecumenical belief that pure forms could transcend differences implicit in content and become as important as subject matter. Modernists also believed that meaning is inherently placed in an art work by the artist and read by the viewer. The positivist

ALVIN LANGDON COBURN. *Vortograph.* 1917. 10½ × 8 inches. Gelatin silver print. Courtesy George Eastman House.

belief in progress was applied to art and photography, as new styles were continually promoted on the heels of others. Without a rudder to steer art towards collective societal goals, the modern artists and photographers distinguished themselves by being unique. There was a reward for being "first," as new and different became values unto themselves. During this period there was a growing sense of moral instability that was related to the apparent crumbling of religious belief. "Art for art's sake" described personal art without social or religious sanction. A touchstone of modernism was individual freedom over social authority. With it came the side effect of alienation, the separation and estrangement from the usual societal positions. Once an affliction, alienation became a prized accessory of art. Dissenting artists created an ambiguous environment of detachment and uncertainty, making them major themes of twentieth-century art that have continued to isolate artists and their art from mainstream society.

In addition to his economic theories, Karl Marx [1818–1883] believed that art is part of a shared social reality and must be integrated into daily life. As the social function of art shifted from the public to the private, Marxist critics assailed the presumption that the purpose of art was aesthetic and individualistic. Marxists contended that art should scrutinize political and social reality, getting behind appearance to elucidate social relationships. Marxists insisted that art must not divorce itself from the realities of everyday people, as this weakened its ability to pinpoint problems and bring about social change. For art to be vital, Marxists said, it must operate in society and reach a large and diverse audience—a goal for which photo-based processes were ideal. The divergence of capitalist and Marxist positions marked a split in Western cultural values: whether culture should express private beliefs or group values.

The increased speed at which technology changed fundamental societal guideposts about industry, religion, and science produced a corresponding loss in traditional cultural values. The machine revolutionized social experience by shifting the balance of population growth from rural to urban areas. The velocity at which culture reinvented itself through technology between 1875 to 1905 had been unthinkable a generation before, and many were optimistic that technology's benefits were endlessly bountiful.[1]

Cubism

Rapid changes in the modern world stimulated and challenged artists to reflect the immense shifts in human consciousness caused by the new technological landscape, including photography. Inspired by the work of painter Paul Cézanne, the *cubists*—Pablo Picasso, George Braque, Fernand Léger, Juan Gris—attempted to parallel the dynamism of the machine age by means

of Enlightenment ideals that extolled analysis and reason. Active in Paris from 1907 through the 1920s, the cubists abandoned the Renaissance system of one-point perspective and its accompanying geometrical system for depicting reality. They developed their own analytical system in which three-dimensional subjects were fragmented and redefined from various points of view simultaneously. Cézanne was engrossed with the way visual relationships shifted every time he moved his head. This process of seeing, the making of choices, how each turn of our head offered up a new truth, was what Cézanne sought to paint. This way of seeing is often used to organize a photograph. Photographers can hold a camera to their eye, making exposures (choices) as the camera is moved with each turn of the head through the scene. Cézanne's use of broken outlines took viewers through a neverending process of visual change. In cubist paintings the making of choices is relative to one's physical and mental position, making doubt a major subject of their work.

During cubism's first period called the *analytic* phase (1907–12), Picasso and Braque demonstrated their belief that knowledge of a subject is the sum of all its possible points of view. They compressed their inspection, which takes time for a viewer to comprehend, into a single view to show that the multiplicity of a subject was the governing element of reality. Cubism was a fresh visual language, fragmented, simultaneously dissolving and re-forming. It can be seen as a visual analogue for Einstein's discoveries of the molecular interrelationship of space and time.[2] Picasso and Braque regarded their work as realistic, emotionally and intellectually true, and did not consider complete abstraction a viable way to visually communicate contemporaneous experience. Their work offered a new definition of what constituted "authentic" visual reality. Both artists paid attention to photography's ability to create unusual juxtapositions, flatten and equalize space, exaggerate proportions, alter scale, and disrupt time. Picasso made and manipulated his own photographs during his cubist period. Earlier, he was formally influenced by a group of postcards made between 1905 and 1906 by **Edmond Fortier** (see Figure 10.1), a photographer based in Dakar in Senegal.[3] As the limits of analytic cubism were reached in muted oval canvases of almost indiscernible subject matter, Picasso and Braque vastly enriched their visual vocabulary with *synthetic cubism* (1912–14). It featured vibrant color, and assemblage and collage techniques, such as stenciling in letters and physically incorporating pieces of newspaper type and sand into their paintings. Cubism became an international movement, prevailing in the avant-garde art realm until World War I.

Society's acceptance of photographic veracity allowed painters to explore new boundaries of representation. If painters were no longer needed to create one-point Renaissance perspective views of their subjects because photography could do it more quickly and

Afrique occidentale Française
1072. SOUDAN - Types de Femmes

Collection Fortier, Dakar

10.1 EDMOND FORTIER. *Type of Women, West Africa*, 1906. Collotype postcard. Pablo Picasso had a collection of some 40 colonial photographic postcards made by Edmond Fortier. The visual correlations between Fortier's "studies" and Picasso's paintings of 1906–1907, culminating in *Les Demoiselles d'Avignon* (1907), suggest that photographic African source material helped Picasso redefine his pictorial language and was a critical factor in the development of analytic cubism.   Courtesy Musee Picasso, Reunion des Musees Nationaux, Paris.

inexpensively, then they were free to make paintings that did not look like paintings of the past. With photography usurping art's traditional function as the mirror of nature, artists had to leave imitation behind and discover a new rationale for their profession. Art was forced to become smarter. This latitude in turn permitted photographers to consider how photography could address the same modernist concepts that had altered painting's sense of representation and ask: What was a photograph supposed to look like? Photographers no longer had to rely solely on the aesthetics of painting and could concentrate on the instinctive qualities of the photographic process. A few photographers shed the romantic approach that had influenced the pictorialists of extolling emotion and idealism through spirituality. They explored modernism, steering photography back to its roots in the principles of the Enlightenment.

As analytic cubism emerged, Alfred Stieglitz, who was still championing pre-modernist pictorialism, underwent a transformation in his aesthetic thinking. In 1907, Stieglitz decided that for photography to grow it had to stop mimicking other mediums and return to its original "straight" foundation: the direct, unmanipulated, camera-made view. With "purity of use" as a guide, the automatic and hence accurate recording of reality by a camera that placed a premium on clarity of detail would be essential points in judging the value of a photograph. By 1908, Stieglitz began to move away from pictorial photography; at "291" he showed the works of highly modernistic painters like Henri Matisse, Cézanne, Picasso, Braque, Constantin Brancusi, Jean Renoir, and unknown American painters such as John Marin, Arthur Dove, Marsden Hartley, and Max Weber. Stieglitz's change in visual thinking can be seen in his photograph *The Steerage* (Figure 10.2).

In *The Steerage,* Stieglitz no longer waited for everything to arrange itself (as in *Winter on Fifth Avenue*); instead, he recognized the hand camera's potential for instantaneously framing situations from life. The resulting negative was printed without cropping.[4] Using the full frame became a badge of honor, an announcement that the finished piece had been visualized before the shutter was released. The composition stood on its innate structure and did not rely on any postvisualization methods. The full frame said that a photograph should look like a photograph and not like an etching or a painting. It inferred that the pictorialists'

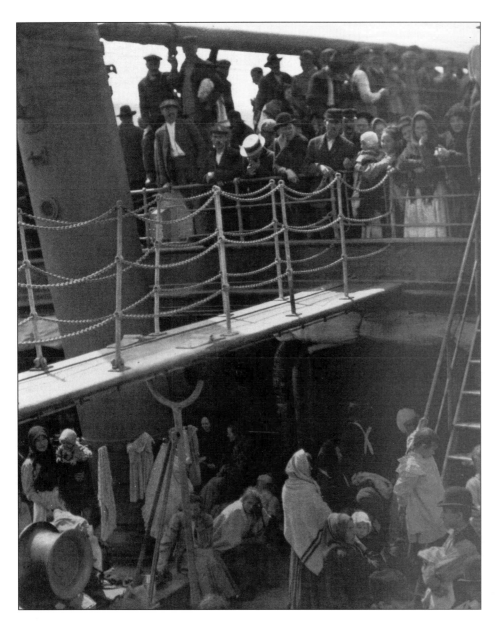

10.2   ALFRED STIEGLITZ.   *The Steerage,* 1907.
13⅛ × 10⁷⁄₁₆ inches. Photogravure print. While walking
the first-class deck on a large steamer bound for Europe,
Stieglitz looked down onto the lower level of the steerage and saw a young man in a straw hat gazing over the
rail at the group below. Stieglitz ran and got his camera.
The scene had not changed, and Stieglitz made his photograph. He later told how: "I saw shapes related to one
another—a picture of shapes, and underlying it, a new
vision that held me."[5]   Courtesy George Eastman House.

vision was weak, relying on artificial devices to construct an impure picture. These "straight" ideals would
eventually dominate artistic photographic practice and
become the dogmatic fetish of "proper technique."

In 1913, the newly organized Association of American Painters and Sculptors staged the International Exhibition of Modern Art at the Armory of the 69th Regi-
ment in New York, introducing photographs, and cubist, expressionist, and post-impressionist art to a new
audience. Stieglitz urged people to see the Armory
show and mounted an exhibition of his own work at
"291," the first in fourteen years, to see how it compared with the work at the Armory. The Armory show
jolted American art from its provincial slumber and left
the public bewildered as the show's work dismantled
their visual gauges for measuring and responding to art.
The public's confusion and interest can be seen in the
reaction to Marcel Duchamp's [1887–1968] *Nude Descending a Staircase No. 2* (1912), a painting about the
idea of movement. Based on Marey's sequential photographs, Duchamp's figure in the continuous action of
coming down a staircase became a canonical image of
modernism and was lampooned as "an explosion in a
shingle factory." People waited in line to get a glimpse
of this somber painting totally without prurient interest.
As Calvin Tomkins has noted, "the painting seemed to

sum up everything that was arbitrary, irrational, and incomprehensible in the new art from Europe."[6] Initially, the exhibition's only effect was the opening of a few new commercial galleries geared toward investment collectors. Stieglitz was saddened that so little attention was paid to the American artists he admired, and he wondered how America could expect to produce first-rate creative figures without societal support.[7] Later Duchamp would comment that Stieglitz "abandoned the worldly conception of art. . . . He believed passionately that America should have its own artists. He felt his influence could force the issue."[8] During his career, Stieglitz's galleries would remain lonely outposts of modernism in an American society reluctant to fund contemporary arts. This lack of support assured the rise and dominance of self-sustaining popular culture throughout the twentieth century.[9]

High and Low Art

As leisure time spread to the urban working class during the nineteenth century, demand rose for entertaining art forms that were more accessible than academic paintings, classical music, literature, opera, and traditional theater. These "high art" forms were considered elitist by the public: They had evolved in Europe for the aristocracy and required an education to be understood. Popular or "low" culture, often thought of as an American phenomenon, grew out of a multitude of everyday forms of communication—advertising, the comics, detective and romance novels, illustrated newspapers, popular music, nightclub scenes, and, later, movies and television.[10] During the first half of the twentieth century, an abyss stretched between high art and popular culture. As the lack of sales at the Armory show demonstrated, many modernist artists were considered revolutionary, making their work difficult to sell and uncoupling them from the capitalist engine of commerce. The makers of popular culture took a diametric stance, attempting to reach the broadest audience and defining success by business standards of profitability.

While Stieglitz's *Camera Work* reached only a few, albeit influential, readers, photomechanical reproduction in the form of the postcard was accessible to all. Between 1905 and 1918, the "low art" form of the postcard was the major method for circulating photographs thanks to three factors: The U.S. Postal Service cut the cost of mailing postcards by half; Kodak in 1906 offered to print images on postcard stock at no extra charge; and reproducing photographs in newspapers continued to be difficult. Professionals used the postcard to record county fairs and disasters and to make portraits. Amateurs mailed their snapshots out into the world. The anonymous postcard subject taught the beauty of the plain, straight-ahead stare and an appreciation of the vernacular.

Stieglitz continued to photograph the expanding urban experience, with "high art" images of ferry boats, flying machines, railroad yards, and skyscrapers. He also turned inward by making portraits of the people close to him at "291," expecting his sitters to wait until the "living moment" revealed itself.[11] Konard Cramer, a painter turned photographer, described a session with Stieglitz in 1911:

He used an 8 × 10 view camera, its sagging bellows held up by pieces of string and adhesive tape. The lens was Steinheil, no shutter. The portraits were made in the smaller of the two rooms at "291" beneath a small skylight. He used Hammer plates with about three second exposures. During the exposure, Stieglitz manipulated a large white reflector to balance the overhead light. He made about nine such exposures and we then retired to the wash room which doubled as a darkroom. The plates were developed singly in a tray. From the two best negatives he made four platinum contact prints, exposing the frame on the fire escape. He would tend his prints with more care than a cook does her biscuits. The finished print finally received a coat of wax for added gloss and protection (the shift to a glossy surface, previously considered "unartistic," was a major change in Stieglitz's visual thinking).[12]

Futurism

A few European artists reacted to technology's rapid changes to the urban scene with a manifesto on *futurism* in 1909.[13] Futurism was promoted by Milanese poet Filippo Tommaso Marinetti [1876–1944]. Referring to himself as "the caffeine of Europe," Marinetti believed that every aspect of human behavior could be seen as art, making him the godfather of later happening and performance pieces that began with the dadaists after World War I. Marinetti was anti-historical and saw the past as an enemy to be destroyed.[14] In its place he wanted to use the power of the machine to create a new type of man. Futurism acclaimed a new modern industrial-age beauty: "the beauty of speed." The futurists used the vocabulary of cubism to show multiple and simultaneous points of view. Futurists were interested in Marey's photographic work showing the successive positions of a figure on a single plate because it introduced the notion of continuous time into a fixed space.

Influenced by futurism, the brothers **Anton Giulio Bragaglia** [1890–1960] and **Arturo Bragaglia** [1893–1962], made photographs of moving figures that blurred the intermediate phases of the motion by having their subjects move while the camera lens remained open (see Figure 10.3). The Bragaglias' blurry depictions connected the science of positivism with transcendental idealism, suggesting that beyond the visible lay a recordable dynamic of continuous movement at play. Their photographic tracings of physical gestures that normally happened too quickly to be observed expressed the energy of modernity and linked the Bragaglias with futurist painters such as Giacomo Balla, Umberto Boccioni, and Gino Severini. Despite this, the

10.3   ANTON BRAGAGLIA.   *Self Portrait, Changing Position*, 1911. 5 × 7 inches. Gold-toned gelatin silver photograph. In *Fotodinamismo futurista*, Anton Bragaglia raged against rational empiricism: "With photodynamism we have freed photography from the indecency of its brutal realism, and from the craziness of instantaneity, which, considered to be scientific fact only because it was a mechanical product, was accepted as absolutely correct."[15] Courtesy Anton Giulio Bragaglia, Gilman Paper Company Collection.

futurist painters maintained the art hierarchy against photography and excluded the Bragaglias from being welcomed into their movement. Even so, the camera would become the definitive futurist tool, a machine proficient at catching the sensation of speed.

Time, Movement, and the Machine

In the mechanized era of factory work, management searched for ways to make the worker fit the machine. Fredrick Winslow Taylor, a proponent of "scientific management," created a stir in labor relations by measuring the time it took the fastest worker to perform a task in order to show management how to increase productivity. Instead of a stopwatch, **Frank B. Gilbreth** [1868–1924] and **Lillian M. Gilbreth** [1878–1972] used a motion picture camera to analyze job sites and uncover "the one best way to do work." Like the futurists, the Gilbreths wanted to harness the power of the machine to formulate a new type of individual. Based on their visual findings, they would redesign job sites so that workers were in the right position to perform most efficiently. They discovered that stereo photographs delivered the most useful information and developed the "stereo chronocyclegraph," in which tiny lights were attached to the subject to give a visual indication of the physical action.[16] The stereo effect made it easy to see which motions were needed to perform a task with the least amount of exertion (see Figures 10.4 and 10.5). Each task was photographed, and the chronocyclegraph provided the pattern for each employee to imitate the "one best way to do work."

The Gilbreths' work, like Etienne-Jules Marey's, alluded to the entire history of an action. The continuous light dashes in their chronocyclegraphs suggested the immediate past and future of the action, allowing for the action to be interpreted within the environment in

10.4 and 10.5   FRANK B. AND LILLIAN M.
GILBRETH. *Photograph of inefficient work operation,* ca.
1935. 3³⁄₁₆ × 2½ inches each on 3½ × 7 inch mount.
Gelatin silver stereograph. And *Photograph of efficient
work operation,* ca. 1935. Gelatin silver stereograph.
According to a letter written by Lillian Gilbreth to
Beamont Newhall on July 9, 1957, these chronocycle-
graphs were taken for the Eastman Kodak Company.
Courtesy George Eastman House.

which it was taking place. The Gilbreths' style seemed
to present facts, but their interpretation favored Big
Business. Their photographs had an immediate financial and social effect: They helped businesses make
their employees more machinelike, resulting in greater
profitability. Although the Gilbreths claimed concern
for a worker's "right to happiness," others saw their
photographs as a vision of the corporate terror of continuous production, a loss of personal identity, and the
standardization of life. It was science coupled to a
process that brought with it a sense of alienation and
psychological anxiety, as later satirized by Charlie
Chaplin in his film *Modern Times* (1936).

10.6   ALVIN COBURN.   *The Octopus,* 1912 (direct overhead view, ca. 1957). 8 × 10½ inches. Gelatin silver print.   Courtesy George Eastman House.

Toward a Modern Practice: Distilling Form

For Alvin Coburn pictorialism had run its course. He was ready to push his work forward by combining modern notions of personal freedom and futurist attitudes about the dynamic character of the early twentieth century to move towards abstraction. Coburn made pictures of New York skyscrapers by pointing his camera down at the subject and sometimes replacing the camera lens with various sized pinholes to modify sharpness. The aerial perspective of *The Octopus* (1912), made after a fresh, white snowfall, eliminated unwanted detail and banished the familiar. Coburn abolished the horizon line, flattened perspective, and abstracted shapes, producing a startlingly different point of view. One exposure made from almost directly overhead was so abstract and therefore unfamiliar that Coburn did not print it for decades. His methods invited viewers to celebrate formalistic beauty rather than the photographic impulse to identify and name subjects. Such work attested to photographers' readiness to make pure form the content of their image. Technological wonders like the skyscraper dominated the urban experience, making the human form less significant. As moving pictures, telephones, and automobiles entered daily culture and altered the landscape as well as societal perceptions of time and space, artists began to make machines the subjects of their work.

10.7 ALVIN LANGDON COBURN. *Vortograph* (Ezra Pound), 1917. 8 × 6¹⁄₁₆ inches. Gelatin silver print. Is this dynamically composed, robotlike image a golem that protects its master, or does it portray the lost belief in the goodness of the machine? Even though the print is not sharp, this angular machine-age image seems to possess an inhuman sense of strength capable of uncircumspect destruction. Ezra Pound's head is disembodied and appears to be almost sticking on a pike. There is also a hint of a swastika foreshadowing Pound's later embrace of facism. Courtesy George Eastman House.

Coburn vaulted towards abstraction in 1916 with his kaleidoscopic portraits of the poet Ezra Pound, called *vortographs* after Pound's *vorticism* movement [1914–15], a British offshoot of futurism. Vorticism rejected the cool placidity of cubism and emphasized abstraction and movement. Coburn used a prism in front of the lens to distort, flatten, multiply, and transform his subject into two-dimensional form. In Coburn's most radical work of this period, he arranged geometric objects on glass to achieve a cubistlike appearance that fractured the realism of subject content and single point perspective. The vortographs' rejection of nature as subject was received with such disapproval that Coburn abandoned his investigations. Nevertheless, the vortographs represented what critic Marius De Zayas articulated as photography's quest within the modernist movement to find a way of "being equally subjective and objective."

Visual experiments like Coburn's moved photographic practice towards the modernist concern with form. While Coburn was experimenting with abstraction, Marius De Zayas, a caricaturist and essayist on modern and African art, saw photography shifting from recording the outside world to penetrating the inner world. This shift reflected the modernist belief that rational scientific values, as understood by the process of distilling form, could be the new basis for life and culture. De Zayas saw a split opening between the objective and the subjective approaches as represented by Steichen and Stieglitz and wrote:

> The work of Steichen brought to its highest expression the aim of the realistic painting of Form. In his photographs he has succeeded in expressing the perfect fusion of the subject and the object. He has carried to its highest point the expression of a system of representation: the realistic one. . . . Stieglitz has begun with the elimination of the subject in represented Form to search for the pure expression of the object. . . . one is the means by which man fuses his idea with the natural expression of Form, while the other is the means by which man tries to bring the natural expression of Form to the cognition of his mind.[17]

This fundamental difference has continued to affect the practice of photography throughout the twentieth century. One continues to be based on objective science and the other subjectively based on natural/spiritual ideals. This difference also caused a division between those who thought the purpose of photography was informational and those who wanted to push beyond the concerns of realism. In a 1913 issue of *Camera Work,* Stieglitz reproduced work by Steichen and displayed his own modernist stance with a boxed announcement:

> Are you interested in the deeper meaning of Photography?
>
> Are you interested in the evolution of Photography as a medium of expression?
>
> Are you interested in the meaning of "Modern Art?"
>
> Are you interested in the Development and Exposition of a living idea?
>
> Are you interested in the Freedom of Thought and Freedom of Expression?
>
> Camera Work is published for those who know or want to know.[18]

By 1917, Stieglitz and Paul Strand (see below) would become proponents of "straight" photography, whose essence and limitation lay in its unqualified objectivity and whose power was dependent on its purity of use. Others pursued "antiphotographic" pictorial strategies, but Stieglitz's views dominated the practice until the 1960s.

Paul Strand [1890–1976] became interested in photography at the Ethical Culture High School in New York, where he studied under the art critic Charles Caffin and took a photography course from Lewis Hine, who sent his class to Stieglitz's "291" gallery. After completing his studies and establishing himself as a commercial photographer, Strand was encouraged by Stieglitz to relinquish pictorial effects and experiment with the principles of cubism that led to his breakout images of 1916. The first of these hand camera images, *Wall Street* (Figure 10.8), showing the insect-sized human figure within the monumental concreteness of the metropolis, was reproduced in the October 1916 issue of *Camera Work*. In the final issue of *Camera Work* (June 1917), Stieglitz presented a sequence of eleven Strand photogravures that moved from pictorialist notions into modernistic ideologies. Stieglitz's awareness of how the physical nature of a medium helps form the information the viewer receives led him to alter the way in which *Camera Work* was printed, eliminating his use of tissue proofs to make Strand's reproductions more effective. Stieglitz comments:

> These photographs are the direct expression of today. We have cut out the use of Japan tissue for these reproductions, not because of economy, but because the tissue proofs we made destroyed the directness of Mr. Strand's expression. In their presentation we have intentionally emphasized the spirit of their brutal directness.[19]

The powerfully edited series, which contained remnants of his earlier soft-focus style, presented emotionally charged images, such as *Man, Five Points Square, New York* (1916), an extreme close-up of a man's hopeless desperation. Another image, *New York,* moved towards abstraction with the tilted angle of the figures and their shadows on the street. In 1916, images like *Abstraction* accentuated geometric form, sharper focus, and getting closer to the subject. By concentrating on important characteristics that could be understood in a concentrated structure, Strand informed viewers that these were not documents but abstract representations, making Strand not Stieglitz's protégé but one who was able to link modern art and photography.[20]

Dada

At the beginning of the twentieth century many people looked to modern machine technology to make life easier and better. However, World War I unleashed an era of

10.8   PAUL STRAND.   *Wall Street,* 1916. From
Camera Work, October 1916. 7⅛ × 4½ inches. Photogravure. Strand said: "I was trying to re-create the abstract movement of people moving in a city; what that
kind of movement really feels like and is like. . . . They
[the photographs] required a technique which could
only be described as a snapshot . . . it is a snapshot
when it becomes necessary to stop movement. . . .
Thoreau said years ago, 'You can't say more than you
see.' No matter what lens you use, no matter what the
speed of the film is, no matter how you develop it, no
matter how you print it, you cannot say more than you
see."[21]   ©1971, Aperture Foundation Inc., Paul Strand Archive.

industrialized death that nullified most people's faith in
the benevolence of technology and radically altered
Western culture. The hand-held camera and faster emulsions allowed photographers to make such distressing
images of World War I that governments often banned
or censored frontline photographs. Many artists were
killed, fled to neutral cities, or emigrated to America. In
New York Stieglitz offered artists, such as Francis Picabia [1879–1953], who helped establish a typographi-

cally emancipated arts journal, *291,* a cultural refuge.
World War I marked the collapse of Europe as the center of Western civilization and the ascendancy of America as the driving cultural force of the twentieth century.

After World War I, a mass disillusion with the myth
of the future based on the machine set in. Cosmopolitan
European artists reacted to the war by launching an assault on the society that had unleashed such terror. Novels like James Joyce's *Ulysses* (1914–21) ripped at the
logic of language by destroying customary grammar
and syntax. Visual artists dismantled what was left of
Renaissance perspective and abandoned the precise
rendition of heroic subjects in favor of works that relied
on chance and irrationality. This collection of exiled
artists called themselves *dadaists.*

Nobody knows who invented the name dada, but
filmmaker Hans Richter believed it had a relation to the
joyous Slavonic phrase, "Da, da" meaning "yes, yes" to
life. Dada was never a style and did not have a didactic
political or social agenda. Dada claimed the freedom to
experiment, declaring play the preeminent human activity and using chance as its agent. Dadaists took art out
of the studio and into the streets, creating early

10.9   CHRISTIAN SCHAD. *Schadograph,* No. 10, 1919. 3⅛ × 2⅜ inches. Printing-out paper. Christian Schad, influenced by his dadaist friends, without any apparent prior knowledge of the work of Niépce or Talbot "reinvented" the photogram as art in 1919. Working with ordinary objects and often cutting the paper into nontraditional shapes, Schad constructed tiny lightworks by arranging discarded articles to illuminate a condition of gemlike elegance. His photograms were appreciated by dadaists because they ridiculed the idea of using photography to make recognizable images. Dadaist Tristan Tzara named them schadography, a play on Schad's name and the penumbralike character of the process.   Courtesy The Museum of Fine Arts, Houston, TX. Museum purchase with funds provided by Isabell and Max Herstein.

photomontage. Their aggressive assault on bourgeois values, including the definition of what is art, enraged the public and led to dadaist works being labeled anti-art.

Marcel Duchamp, a member of the dada group, invented the idea of the *readymade,* common manufactured objects that he promoted to art by selecting and signing them. One readymade was a urinal entitled *Fountain* (1917). The point was to create "a new thought for that object," to demystify art by proclaiming that there were so many interesting things in the world there was no need to make more objects. Duchamp's approach was conceptual, making the mental act of choice, not the physical act of the hand, the center of creation. Readymades were Duchamp's antidote to what he called "retinal art," art that pleased the eye, because they put the idea before the visual example. Duchamp also separated himself from the traditions of retinal art through his "assisted" readymade *LHOOQ* (1919), in which he added secondary male sexual characteristics—a black-penciled mustache and goatee—to a postcard of the "Mona Lisa." The uncouth French schoolboy title meant, for which *LHOOQ* was an abbreviation: "She's got a hot ass." This dada gesture satirized not only the cult of the masterpiece but the then forbidden subject of Leonardo's homosexuality and Duchamp's own curiosity and confusion concerning sexual roles. Along with Picabia, Duchamp influenced artists like Man Ray, who would bring dadaist concepts to photography. In view of the audience, the artistic stage was being struck of its traditional props and the reigning rules of beauty were being reformatted.

Exploring Space and Time: The Return of the Photogram

Albert Einstein's [1879–1955] special theory of relativity (1905) changed the view of the universe more than any scientist since Isaac Newton. Artists were not mathematicians or philosophers, but their concerns were interwoven with those of an industrial world. Even without understanding the details of $E = mc^2$, some artists realized that the rules for ordering everyday life were faltering under the pressure of a multitude of new experiences and that innovative forms were needed to contain them.

"happenings." Dadaist art was produced unconventionally and took unorthodox forms. Jean Arp dropped torn paper, "arranged according to the laws of chance," to form collages. Kurt Schwitters made collages out of garbage. Raoul Hausmann, Man Ray, and Morton Schamberg formed sinister assemblages out of everyday objects. Hannah Höch and John Heartfield reinvented

10.10   MAN RAY.   *Untitled* (Gun with Alphabet Squares), 1924. 11⅝ × 9¼ inches. Gelatin silver print. Courtesy John Paul Getty Museum, Los Angeles.

Post–World War I artists reinvented the nineteenth-century *photogram* as a pictorial method of reinvestigating time and space. A photogram was made in a darkroom by placing an object on top of a photosensitive surface, exposing it to light, and processing it. A photogram could take an everyday object and transform it into something the human eye would not normally see, proving that human vision could not be trusted. Although photograms comply with optical laws and their processing can be controlled by normal methods, the results were unforeseeable and unique. Photographically faithful, yet liberated from Renaissance perspective, the photogram seemed able to instinctively express its own rules for representation. The photogram appeared to be a "natural," automatic process, bypassing the pitfalls of representational systems.

Man Ray (Emmanuel Radnitsky) [1890–1976], a painter and member of the New York dada group led by Duchamp and Picabia, had become acquainted with the modern art Stieglitz was presenting at "291" in 1910. In 1915, Man Ray learned photography in order to document his painting, but he was soon experimenting with the machine motifs that fascinated his friends. Duchamp's cerebral skepticism about the emotional values of painting found an active, sensually poetic voice in Man Ray. Placing objects on white paper, Man Ray airbrushed paint around them, producing white forms on a colored ground similar in concept to the photogram. Man Ray also "reinvented" the photogram in

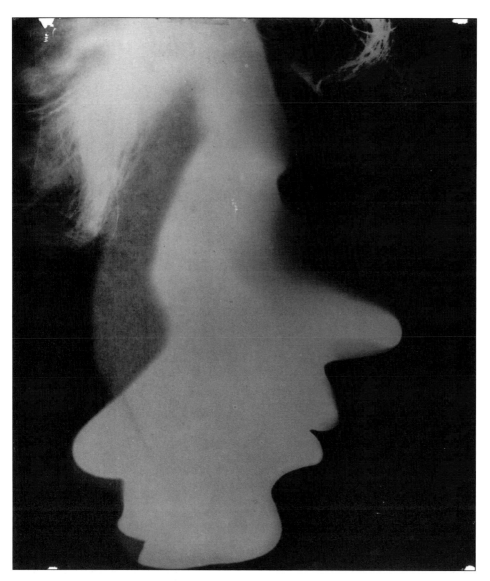

10.11   LÁSZLÓ MOHOLY-NAGY.   *Untitled,*
12¹⁄₁₆ × 10¾ inches. Gelatin silver print. Moholy-Nagy
stated: "The photogram . . . is the real key to photography. It allows us to capture the patterned interplay of
light on a sheet of sensitized paper without recourse to
any apparatus. The photogram opens up perspectives of
a hitherto wholly unknown morphosis governed by
optical laws peculiar to itself. It is the most completely
dematerialized medium which the new vision commands."[22]   ©1999 Artists Rights Society (ARS), New York.

1922. He later characterized his discovery as an unconscious, "automatic" darkroom happening that occurred
in his tiny bathroom/darkroom when he "placed a small
glass funnel, the graduate and the thermometer in the
tray on the wetted paper and turned on the light."[23]

Immodestly, Ray called these cameraless images
"rayographs." The enigmatic quality of the white shadows of the partially revealed everyday objects appealed
to the dadaist love for the unexpected and pictorial belief in ordinary items. By moving his light source during the exposure and by shifting the objects in space
above the paper, Ray extended the amount of time contained within the image and wreaked havoc with perspective. The technique also added depth and expanded
the tonal range, making the work more gestural and dynamic. Ray continued these experiments for decades,
selecting objects for their ability to invoke associations,
feelings, and memories. The rayogram reopened the
definition of a photograph by liberating it from the
camera image, returning photography to its basic concept of creating an image through the agency of light.

Man Ray was a significant painter, sculptor, and filmmaker. He participated in the first international dada exhibition in Paris, joined the surrealist movement in 1924,
and exhibited in the first surrealist show in Paris in 1925.
Ray was an avid experimenter who combined diverse
techniques, such as the Sabattier effect (or solarization)
and the use of negative prints, to create "disturbing ob-

jects" that could extend awareness of the interior working of the mind (see Chapter 11). His ideas were also disseminated by his assistants, who included photographers Berenice Abbott, Bill Brandt, and Lee Miller. Arturo Schwarz wrote that "Man Ray never loved or felt admiration for the camera—to his students he would say, 'if you wish to make photographs throw your camera away!' Duchamp observed, 'It was his achievement to treat the camera as he treated the painter brush, as a mere instrument at the service of the mind.' "[24]

László Moholy-Nagy [1895–1946] was the third reinventor of the technique he called the *photogram*,[25] based on an analogy with the telegram. With Einstein working in Berlin and describing the world as a four-dimensional space-time continuum, it follows that the Berlin avant-garde would find new positions for observing the world. In Berlin, Moholy-Nagy sought to make images without transmitting the sentimental values of the hand and brush. In a search for a medium that retained its spiritual purity by "painting" itself, Moholy became interested in portraying the dynamics of light and space.

Moholy came from a *constructivist* background. Constructivism covered a period from 1913 through the 1920s during which Russian avant-garde artists rejected easel painting and the idea of "art for art's sake" in favor of utilitarian designs intended for mass production. Photography was an ideal constructivist medium: It was considered the antithesis of painting by many traditional artists and offered a way to make images in quantity. Moholy looked at photography as a means by which light, instead of paint, could sketch itself on a photosensitive surface. The obstacle in the direct link he sought was the camera lens. The photogram eliminated the lens, allowing pure light to directly picture itself as an organic element. The photogram permitted Moholy to retain the constructivist principle of "truth to materials" and reflect the constructivist celebration of scientific rationality and technology. Moholy's photogram of a face shows us an artist who uses his or her "head" to shape the constantly changing flow of light in time (during the photogram's production), space, and volume (see Figure 10.11). His later photograms moved away from identifiable objects to what Moholy referred to as "light modulators," allowing the experiments to concentrate on form and light as the source of content.

The photogram, as Talbot had first realized, was a "light paradox" that reversed the nineteenth century's trust in photographic description and narrative content. It inverted the values of the subject and produced a "negative" rendering with no narrative format. Without using mechanical darkroom equipment a photogram, unlike a normal photograph, revealed only what was blocked by the light, not what was illuminated by it. Like x-rays, photograms divulged unforeseen facets of reality. By banishing of linear perspective, the pho-

togram liberated photography from its role as the literal depictor of nature. These differences demonstrated the relativity of the viewing experience and even challenged the visually educated by denying viewers easy entry into the work. Moholy, who in 1929 called for "light studios to replace outdated painters' academies," situated the photogram as a fundamental photographic form capable of opening other doors of perception.

Surrealism

Surrealism emerged after World War I from symbolism and dadaism. Surrealism, a term coined by the French poet and critic Guillaume Apollinaire [1880–1918] in 1917, was a state of mind rather than a style. Begun as a European literary movement influenced by psychoanalytic thinking, surrealism helped to popularize Freudian notions about dreams, sex, the unconscious, and free association through methods, such as automatic writing, that liberated one from conscious reason and convention. The movement was defined by French poet André Breton [1896–1966] in his first "Manifesto of Surrealism" (1924) as:

> Psychic automatism in its pure state by which one proposes to express—verbally, by means of the written word, or in any other manner—the actual functioning of thought. Dictated by thought, in the absence of any control exercised by reason, exempt from any aesthetic or moral concern. . . . Surrealism is based on the belief in the superior reality of certain forms of previously neglected associations, in the omnipotence of dream, in the disinterested play of thought.[26]

Celebrating the dream as a method of problem solving, Breton looked towards "madness"—hallucination and illusions—as a pathway capable of freeing oneself from "the reign of logic." Breton described "the realistic attitude, inspired by positivism . . . [as] hostile to any intellectual or moral advancement . . . for it is made up of mediocrity, hate, and dull conceit . . . by flattering the lowest tastes."[27] People began to accept, in the 1930s, the notion that dreams could mirror repressed emotions and fantasies. Dream interpretation became in vogue, and photographers responded by devising images that evoked the prevailing look of the dream world.

Collage

The collage works of **Max Ernst** [1891–1976] were an enigmatic group of fantasy images arranged in a dreamlike chance-encounter format. Based on readymade images, cut from catalogues and magazines, they offered up a dread-filled parallel universe that defied bourgeois explanation. Ernst's collage-novels took revenge on the late Victorian world of his youth by irrationally attacking and subverting its authoritarian underpinnings.

10.12   MAX ERNST.   *Mr. Knife, Miss Fork*, 1931.
9⁵⁄₁₆ × 7½ inches. Cliché-verre.   © 1999 Artists Rights
Society (ARS), New York/ADAGP, Paris.

Ernst wrested improbable meaning from images by using *frottage* (rubbing) and cliché-verre to illustrate books, such as *Mr. Knife, Miss Fork*, 1931.

Raoul Hausmann [1886–1971] was one of the Berlin dadaists who created avant-garde *photographic collages* out of cut-up photographs during the summer of 1918, based on a practice used in advertising since the nineteenth century. A photographic collage was produced when cut and/or torn pieces from one or more photographs were combined on a common support material. An expanded definition may include images from magazines and newspapers; combinations of colored papers, wallpaper, or fabric; natural materials such as flow-ers, leaves, and sand; and three-dimensional objects. There was no attempt to deny that the image was made up from a variety of source materials. It was not rephotographed and was itself presented as the final image.

Hausmann, along with other German dadaists George Grosz [1893–1959], Helmut Herzfelde or **John Heartfield** [1891–1968], and **Hannah Höch** [1889–1978], pushed the idea of using mass-printed source material by inventing the *photomontage* in which pieces of photographs were combined into new compositions. A photographic montage follows the guidelines of collage, but the completed work is photographed so that the final image is converted back into a photographic print. This gives the option of using photographic methods to hide the sources of the work's various images and materials to create a new, seamless representation from which additional copies may be reproduced. Digital imaging tools have now eliminated intricate and laborious handwork.

They called their approach montage, meaning "assembly line," and termed the maker "monteur," or "engineer/mechanic," indicating that the picture was "engineered," not "created." World War I and the era's cultural and scientific revolutions affected the German dadaists' syntax with the cut and torn refuse of urban life acting as a metaphor for the divided and fragmented society of the Weimar Republic. Combining found photographs and text enabled the dadaists to alter the original content and attack the bourgeois with images from their own publications. Höch's work offered insight into the *new woman*, the official redefinition of women's roles going on in German society. The increase in mass print media, Höch's raw material, supplied her with fresh images of women's changing identity—working, using appliances, and modeling in advertisements. Höch explored the intersection of avant-garde photomontage and the splintered experience of daily life in Weimar Germany. Her work deployed allegory, caricature, the grotesque, and irony, reflecting the dadaist concern with alienation (*Verfremdung*) and estrangement, taking the familiar and making it unfamiliar, and refashioning photo-based images into photomontages. Höch's disruptive, emotionally and sexually charged work played on tensions between anger/violence and pleasure/beauty to investigate issues of femininity and identity.[28] Some of Höch's other montages, like *Strange Beauty* (1929),

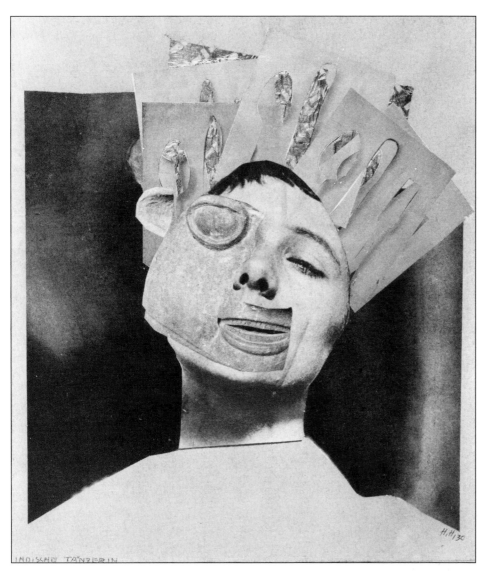

10.13 HANNAH HÖCH. *Indian Female Dancer (From an Ethnographic Museum)*, 1930. 10⅛ × 8⅞ inches. Collage of cut and pasted papers and photographs on paper. © 1998 The Museum of Modern Art, New York. Francis Keech Fund.

also fused Western and tribal imagery, thus dissolving the hierarchy that had defined their cultural relationship. Höch worked with montage throughout her life. Her cataloguing and reconfiguring of signs of modernism reflected the upheaval and uncertainty of the post–World War I Weimar period. Viewers saw the shattering and rearranging of traditional women's roles, involving children, kitchen, and church, as one more frightening aspect of the change that led many to embrace national socialism.

In the 1920s and 1930s photomontage penetrated art and mass media in Germany, the Soviet Union, and the United States. It visualized common cultural themes in a new system of representation that ruptured the narrative format and Renaissance window frame. Montage broke out of "straight" photography's encasements and replaced it with reassembled images that conveyed a multifaceted sense of reality. It collapsed multiple points of views—discontinuous subjects, in different locations, and at various times—into a single, often unexpected, view. These newly created juxtapositions extended the concept of publicly acceptable reality by linking subjects that in turn formed new relationships that were not previously visible. This encouraged viewers to rethink their previous ideas about the subjects and formulate new opinions.

Suprematism

Aleksandr Rodchenko [1891–1956] came from a *suprematism* background that gave artists permission to depart from the objective illustration of the world. Suprematism (1915–1923) was a Russian avant-garde movement to reduce painting to pure geometric

В постели она, она лежит, —
Он.
На столе телефон.

10.14 ALEKSANDR RODCHENKO. *She is on the bed, She's lying/He/The telephone is on the table,* 1923. From *Pro-Eto.* 6⅝ × 4⅞ inches. Offset lithograph. Rodchenko wrote: "In photography there is the old point of view, the angle of vision of a man who stands on the ground and looks straight ahead or, as I call it, makes "bellybutton" shots. . . . I fight this point of view, and will fight it, along with my colleagues in the new photography. The most interesting angle shots today are those "down from above" and "up from below," and their diagonals."[29]   Courtesy Howard Schickler Gallery, New York.

abstraction by purging conspicuous allusions to the real world. It was the high-water mark for diverse artistic experiments affiliated with Russia's successful Bolshevik Revolution. Tracing its roots back to cubism and futurism, Kazimir Malevich defined the movement as "the supremacy of pure feeling." Suprematist ideas influenced constructivism and spread to the Bauhaus (see below) when they entered into the discourse of modern art.

A leader of the constructivists and a supporter of the Russian Revolution, Rodchenko viewed these new systems of seeing as a way to reshape society. In 1920,

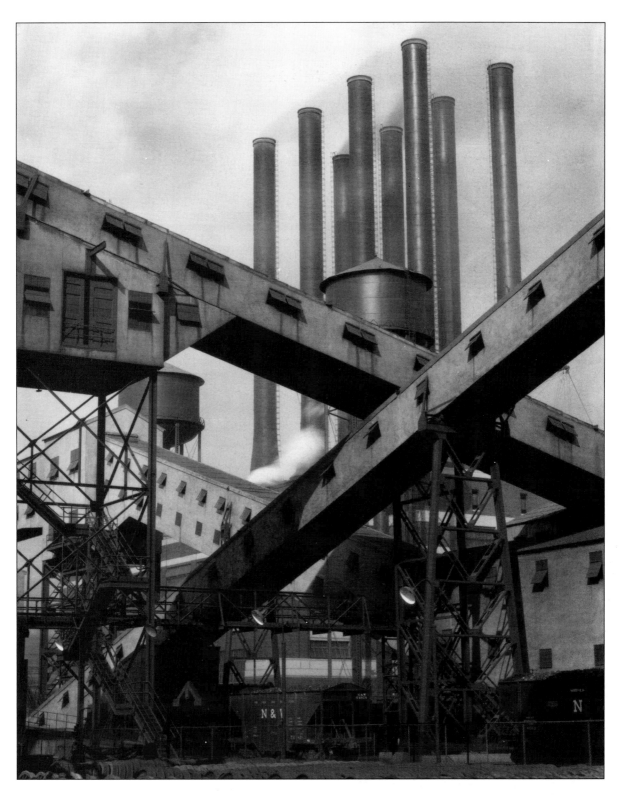

10.15   CHARLES SHEELER.   *Criss-Crossed Conveyors—Ford Plant,* 1927. 10 × 8 inches. Gelatin silver print. Sheeler summed up his analytical picture-making method by stating: "I favor the picture that is planned and executed with the same consideration for its parts—within the complete design as is necessary in the building of a watch or an aeroplane."[30]   The Lane Collection: Courtesy, Museum of Fine Arts, Boston. © 1999. All rights reserved.

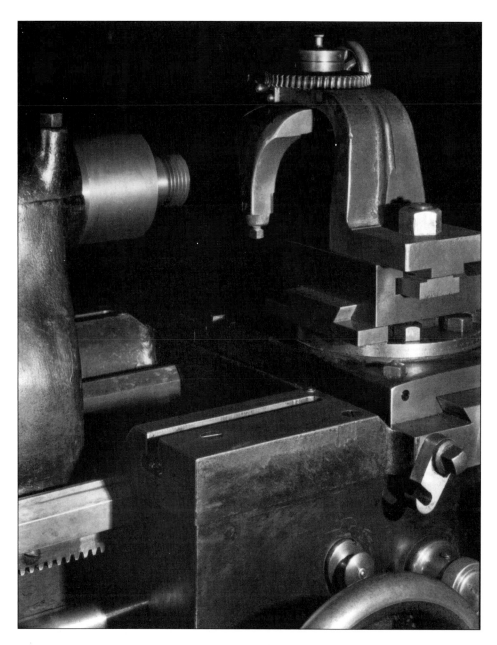

10.16 PAUL STRAND. *The Lathe,* 1923. 9¾ × 7½ inches. Gelatin silver print. ©1985, Aperture Foundation Inc., Paul Strand Archive.

Rodchenko joined Inkhuk (the Institute of Artistic Culture), whose mission was to integrate art into everyday life. Abandoning painting for graphic design, Rodchenko designed some of the most original political posters in a Russian culture where the poster was a primary form of mass communication. About 1923, Rodchenko came under the influence of El Lissitzky and Moholy-Nagy and commenced making photomontages (see Figure 10.14). El Lissitzky (Eliezer Markovich) [1880–1941], an innovative typographical designer, wed abstract form to social use. For Rodchenko photography was the ideal socialist medium: It was inexpensive, quick, and repeatable. Photography, according

to Rodchenko, would furnish the monuments of the future: "What ought to remain of Lenin: an art bronze, oil portraits, etchings, watercolours, his secretary's diary, his friend's memoirs—or—a file of photographs taken of him at work and rest . . . ? I don't think there's a choice. Art has no place in modern life. . . . Every cultured modern man must wage war against art. . . . Photograph and be photographed!"[31]

By 1924, Rodchenko was using a small hand camera to make photographs of people and ordinary scenes that explored unconventional points of view. His pictures disturbed rules of composition and subject hierarchy, setting atypical priorities of visual importance. Seeing as the camera sees, Rodchenko developed an unusual sense of space by tilting the camera and shooting from above or below the subject, using the instantaneous sense of the snapshot to create a sense of activity. These often diagonal compositions were compositionally reinforced by a rhythmic sense of contrast between the highlight and shadow areas, delivering psychological retorts and factual information about the times. During an era when most Soviet photographers followed the party line and documented revolutionary acts by the customary means, Rodchenko defined a socially relevant photograph as one that destabilized an audience by portraying everyday scenes from unfamiliar angles.

Art, Technology, and a New Faith

While some imagemakers were disassembling the narrative and looking for ways to visualize inner psychological experiences, others challenged the idea of content through their investigations of form based on the new technology. The most influential spot for these investigations was the *Bauhaus* school of art, craft, and design, founded in 1919 by architect Walter Gropius in the hyperinflationary economy of Weimar Germany. The Bauhaus, roughly meaning "building house," had its lineage in the socialist notions of the arts and crafts movement. Its curriculum was designed to synthesize architecture, painting, and sculpture into a single way of thinking and creating. In its effort to revitalize crafts, the Bauhaus, unlike the arts and crafts movement, sanctioned industrial technology. It sought to unite constructivist concern for modern materials with the emotional content of expressionism and the higher consciousness of spiritualism. Its faculty included Josef Albers, Herbert Bayer, Theo van Doesburg, Wassily Kandinsky, Paul Klee, El Lissitzky, and László Moholy-Nagy.

Under its credo, "Art and Technology, a new unity," the Bauhaus concentrated on functional craftsmanship as applied to the problems of mass production, producing revolutionary designs in tubular steel furniture, typography, and ceramics as well as experiments in abstract film, photography, dance, theater, and sculpture. Hitler closed the school in 1932, forcing most of the faculty to emigrate. Moholy-Nagy founded the New Bauhaus (now the Institute of Design of the Illinois Institute of Technology) in Chicago in 1937, which introduced new concepts about photographic process in the United States and established a precedent of teaching photography on the graduate level.

Philosopher Friedrich Nietzsche's proclamation about the death of God in 1882 was based on his observation that the rapid expansion of technology produced social change that caused traditional beliefs to crumble. Nietzsche wanted to create a new heroic morality, set in place by a breed of supermen whose "will to power" was needed to lead this new society. Others, out of this sense of anxiety, searched for this missing "essence" in nontraditional belief systems, from *theosophy,* a blend of American transcendentalism and Hinduism, to *swendenborgianism,* in which individual free will allows for profound communication with God. Scientific discoveries like Einstein's seemed to indicate that the world could not be trusted to be rational. For some, the pursuit of science offered hope of uncovering the essence of life.

In the heyday of American economic growth following World War I, American painters like Charles Demuth, Georgia O'Keeffe, Charles Scheeler, and Morton Schamberg took a more formalistic and highly materialistic approach to replacing their loss of faith and embraced the strong, self-evident precepts of *precisionism.* Precisionism (1918–1930) incorporated the streamlined design of cubism while retaining recognizable subject matter, reflecting American society's antagonism towards dematerialization and complete abstraction. Its spatially flattened formations celebrated the down-to-earth, solid geometric forms of the technologically rooted industrial and architectural landscape of concrete and steel, such as factories, grain elevators, machines, and skyscrapers, with directness and simplicity.

The work of **Morton Schamberg** [1881–1918] and **Charles Sheeler** [1883–1965] exemplified what Strand considered to be "the very essence of photography," the camera's "absolute unqualified objectivity,"[32] to replace American faith in ephemeral spiritualism with something physical, an essence one could believe in regardless of what science discovered next. Schamberg's death in the flu epidemic of 1918 prematurely ended his work of placing abstracted machine parts into paintings and making cubist-derived, geometric urban photographs. In 1914, Sheeler initiated a series celebrating the "straight" American style of form and texture as found in Pennsylvania barns. Soon he was photographing the details of the unadorned interior of the stone farmhouse he shared with Schamberg, a house styled on necessity and Puritan self-denial. This recognition of the plain design strength of line found its way into the modernist compositions that were fascinated with revealing the "soul" of machines. In 1923, Steichen hired Sheeler for *Vogue* and *Vanity Fair.* In 1927, Sheeler was commissioned to photograph the Ford Motor Works at River Rogue, site of Henry Ford's effort to manufacture a universal automobile through industrial standardization. Sheeler's concern for structure slimmed down the industrial compositions to a skeleton, delivering interacting, geometric forms without any trace of disorderly humanity. In his pictures, mechanical perfection reined, allowing viewers to believe that the industrial landscape could lead to a logical utopia. These machine-based images served Sheeler as models for drawings and paintings that also celebrated the machine as heroic and stalwart subject matter (see Figure 10.15).

Paul Strand and Straight Photography: Purity of Use

Writing in the final issue of *Camera Work,* Strand helped plot the course of "straight" photography for the next few generations:

> Photography . . . finds its raison d'être, like all media, in a complete uniqueness of means. This is an absolute unqualified objectivity. . . . The full potential power of every medium is dependent upon the purity of its use. . . . This means a real respect for the thing in front of him, expressed in terms of chiaroscuro. . . . The fullest realization of this accomplished without tricks of process or manipulation, through the use of straight photographic methods.[33]

After serving as an x-ray technician during World War I, Strand teamed up with Charles Sheeler to make a short film, *Mannahatta* (1921), combining confident, geometric visions of urban New York's skyscrapers with fragments of Walt Whitman's poems. In 1922, Strand purchased an Akeley motion picture camera and for the next seven years made his living doing film work.

In his article "Photography and the New God" (1922), Strand narrated the union of a fictional inventor and a scientist who created a "new Trinity: God the Machine, Materialistic Empiricism the Son, and Science the Holy Ghost." This fable aptly symbolized the new secular era whose deity was the machine. In a decade when Karel Câpek introduced the term "robot" in his play *R.U.R.* (1921) and the first American science-fiction magazine, *Amazing Stories,* hit the stands (1926), Strand looked for ways to have his photographs embody this machine-conscious period (see Figure 10.16). Strand's formalistic and scientific outlook, on view in his machine images, opposed the emotional and irrational. These images would lay the groundwork for the mainline modernistic aesthetic values of photographic practice for nearly six decades, serving as visual indicators of a widening gulf between science and art.

Endnotes

1   During this period the world witnessed the invention of the phonograph (1877), the incandescent filament lightbulb (1879), the recoil-operated machine gun (1882), synthetic fiber (1883), the steam turbine (1884), the electric motor and pneumatic tire (1888), the Diesel engine (1892), the Ford automobile (1894), and the gramophone disk (1894). As the century drew to a close the pace became even more frenzied with the discovery of x-rays, the principles of rocket propulsion, and the publication of Freud's studies on hysteria (1895), and the opening of the Niagara Falls hydroelectric plant (1896). These were followed by the discovery of radium (1898), the magnetic recording of sound (1899), the first voice radio transmissions (1900), the Wright Brothers' first flight (1903), the digging of the Panama Canal (1904), and Albert Einstein's formulation of the *special theory of relativity* (1905), the photon theory of light (precursor of quantum theory), and his law of mass-energy equivalence, $E = mc^2$, the harbinger of the nuclear age.

2   Einstein discovered that as time expands, space contracts, annihilating Euclid's concept of space and time as separate phenomena. The popular understanding of this theory is expressed by the space traveler who comes back to earth almost unaged when compared to those who stayed on the planet.

3   See Anne Baldassari, *Picasso and Photography: The Dark Mirror* (Paris: Flammarion, 1997), 45–61.

4   It is not clear when Stieglitz first printed *The Steerage* as he didn't publish it for four years after making the negative. Some critics claim his account of taking *The Steerage,* which was written much later, acts as a self-serving retrospective effort to cover the fact that he didn't recognize the significance of the image until later. Nevertheless, *The Steerage* is emblematic of the new "straight" aesthetic.

5   Dorothy Norman, *Alfred Stieglitz: An American Seer* (New York: Random House, 1973), 76.

6   Calvin Tomkins, *Duchamp: A Biography* (New York: Henry Holt & Co., 1996), 117.

7   Norman, 76.

8   Ibid., 128.

9   Continued evidence of this lack of support can be witnessed in the funding of the National Endowment for the Arts, which was not established until 1965; its budget remains one of the smallest of any industrial nation.

10   See Kirk Varnedoe and Adam Gopnik, eds., *Modern Art and Popular Culture: Reading in High & Low* (New York: Harry N. Abrams and The Museum of Modern Art, 1990).

11   Norman, 121.

12   Ibid., 212.

13   F. T. Marinetti, "The Founding and Manifesto of Futurism 1909"; reprinted in *Futurist Manifestos,* ed. Umbro Apollonio, The Documents of 20th Century Art (New York: Viking Press, 1973), 19–24.

14   Acting as an agent-provocateur for modern art, Marinetti called for the destruction of libraries and museums as "mausoleums" and glorified speed, violence, and war as "the world's only hygiene." The futurist worship of the machine and the belief that technology would allow humans to solve all their social ills, was supported by many of Europe's avant-garde. The futurists welcomed the start of World War I as the end of nineteenth-century civilization, but it had the side effect of killing some of the group's most talented members. After the war, the surviving futurists were assimilated into fascism.

15   Anton Giulio Bragaglia, *Fotodinamismo futurista* (Rome: Nalato, 1913; reprint with critical essays, 2nd ed., Turin: Einaudi, 1980), 18. Quoted in Marta Braun, *Picturing Time* (Chicago: The University of Chicago Press, 1992), 299.

16   During this procedure, tiny electric lights, blinking twenty times a second, were secured to a worker's wrists and a single sequence of the subject's motions were recorded in a darkened space called the "betterment room." The direction of the hand movements was easy to see as the photographic plate saw the light tracings as discrete, white, pearl-shaped increments. Distance was gauged through the use of a background grid. Time was measured by including a clock. The distance between the light fragments indicated pauses and variations in speed.

17   Marius De Zayas. "Photography and Artistic-Photography," *Camera Work,* 42/43 (April/July 1913), 13–14.

18   *Camera Work* 42/43 (April/July 1913), unp.

19   Alfred Stieglitz, *Camera Work,* 49/50, June 1917, 36.

20   See Maria Morris Hambourg, *Paul Strand Circa 1916* (New York: The Metropolitan Museum of Art, 1998).

21   Paul Strand in *The Snapshot,* Jonathan Green, ed., *Aperture,* vol. 19, no. 1, 48–49, also as a book 1974.

22   Moholy-Nagy, "A New Instrument of Vision," *Telehor* (Brno, 1936); reprinted in Richard Kostelanetz, ed. *Moholy-Nagy* (New York: Praeger, 1970), 50.

23   See Arturo Schwarz, *Man Ray: The Rigour of Imagination* (New York: Rizzoli, 1977), 236.

24   Schwartz, 230.

25   Moholy-Nagy first introduced the term photogram in his *Malerei Fotografie Film* (Munich, 1925), Bauhaus Book no. 8.

26   Jean-Jacques Pauvert, ed., *André Breton: Manifestoes of Surrealism,* translated by Richard Seaver and Helen R. Lane (Ann Arbor: The University of Michigan Press, 1972), 26.

27   Ibid., 6.

28   See Maud Lavin, *Cut with the Kitchen Knife: The Weimar Photomontages of Hannah Höch* (New Haven: Yale University Press, 1993).

29   Beaumont Newhall, *The History of Photography,* 1982, 201.

30   Archives of American Art, Charles Sheeler Papers, 4 pp., n.d., Reel NSH–1. Quoted in Merrill Schleier. *The Skyscraper in American Art, 1890–1931* (New York: Da Capo Press, republication, 1986), 80.

31   Robert Hughes, *The Shock of the New,* (New York: Alfred A. Knopf, 1981) 95.

32   Paul Strand, "Photography," *The Seven Arts,* vol. 2, no. 10 (August 1917), 524.

33   Paul Strand, "Photography," *Camera Work* nos. 49/50, June 1917, 3.

CHAPTER ELEVEN

The New Culture of Light

Teaching Modernism: The American Impulse

The chaos of post–World War I Europe gave Americans the opportunity to assume a leadership role as a cultural center with New York as its capital. Between the end of World War I in 1918 and the Wall Street stock market crash of 1929, American photographers actively shaped Western artistic practice. America did not have a tradition of cathedrals, frescoes, and monumental sculpture. It was precisely this lack of history that gave American photographers the freedom to turn to their own native cultural strengths— Puritan simplicity, mechanical ingenuity, and the building materials of an industrial society—for the basis of their approach. The adventurous left behind the moody, soft, moist air look of pictorialism in favor of a harder and more direct approach. It almost seemed as if the spiritual quality of light in the new world was cleaner, clearer, and sharper than the refined atmosphere of the old world. The American approach to light

MAN RAY. *elevage de Poussiere* from *The Green Box*, 1934 aka *Dust Breeding* (on Duchamp's *Large Glass)*, 1920. 7⅞ × 10¼ inches. Gelatin silver print. Courtesy Philadelphia Museum of Art: The Louise and Walter Arensberg Archives.

11.1 PAUL OUTERBRIDGE. *Crankshaft Silhouetted Against Car,* 1923. 1⁷⁄₁₆ × 4¹⁄₁₆ inches. Platinum print. Inspired by Strand's Akeley movie camera series, Outerbridge photographed machine parts as if they were sculptures, converting the ordinary into the remarkable. His work unfolded from Outerbridge's belief that "to appreciate photography one must dissociate it from other forms of art expression. Instead of holding a preconceived idea of art, founded on painting, it must be considered as a distinct medium of expression—a medium capable of doing certain things which can be accomplished no other way."[1]   Courtesy San Francisco Museum of Modern Art.

gave spiritual significance to the ordinary subjects of a material culture dedicated to finding better, faster, more affordable ways of performing tasks in order to make goods affordable to all. Instead of building another Chartres, Americans like Henry Ford built automobile assembly lines, manufacturing an entire culture around a mass-produced item that promised personal freedom.

In addition to the activities at "291," Clarence White's School of Photography (1914–1942), which offered classes in New York, Maine, and Connecticut, was a site for the modernist aesthetic, especially through the design theories of Arthur Wesley Dow, which emphasized simplified geometric design as the basic structure of art.[2] While photography in Europe continued to be taught as a commercial craft in an apprenticeship system, White's School applied the artistic principles of modernism to training a generation of professionals, including Paul Outerbridge, Anton Bruehl [1900–1983], Ralph Steiner, Laura Gilpin, Margaret Bourke-White, Dorothea Lange, Karl Struss [1886–1981], and Doris Ulmann [1884–1934]. White's school was the only school in the United States devoted exclusively to the instruction of art photography, and it set a precedent for American leadership of photographic education in the twentieth century.

Paul Outerbridge [1896–1958], a White School alumnus, influenced the commercial field by combining the new "direct" aesthetic and the celebration of technologically derived objects, like an automotive camshaft, as heroic subject matter. Ralph Steiner's [1899–1986] close-up of typewriter keys, a machine for making words, used Arthur Dow's ideas about controlling highlights and shadows to accentuate the abstract harmony within his vernacular subject matter, providing them with a spiritual base in fact. After completing her studies with White, Laura Gilpin [1891–1979] returned to the Southwest and opened a commercial portrait studio, but she continued to emphasize design and the unity of geometric pattern through her recording of indigenous American cultures that often related the native architectural forms to the landscape. **Margaret Bourke-White** [1904–1971], a student of White's at Columbia University, emerged in the late twenties with an industrial series on the Otis Steel Mills in Ohio, whose products went into the making of automobiles and skyscrapers (see Figure 11.2). This work, especially the active interior views, came to the notice of Henry Luce, who hired Bourke-White for his new publication, *Fortune* (1930), as her work echoed *Fortune's* editorial penchant for finance and technology.

Stieglitz's "Equivalents"

After a decade of facilitating the work of others, **Alfred Stieglitz** returned to making images. In 1918, he embarked on a decade-long, cumulative psychological portrait series of his wife-to-be, painter Georgia O'Keeffe [1887–1986]. The intimate-sized contact prints portray O'Keeffe abstractly, heroically, and personally. This extended portrait is a collaboration, an intellectual dialogue, that challenged, enriched, and melded the ambitions, drives, and talents of both artists.

In 1922, Stieglitz continued to explore this inner psychological theme, but he returned one last time to nature and symbolist theory and isolated the sky as a

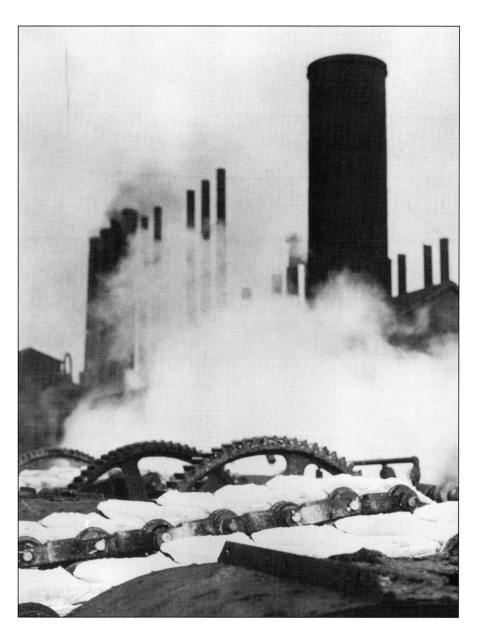

11.2　MARGARET BOURKE-WHITE. *Hot Pigs,* Otis Steel Mills, Cleveland, 1928. 18¼ × 14¹⁄₁₆ inches. Gelatin silver print. Bourke-White's romantic admiration of functional architecture can be seen in her later pictures for *Fortune* and *Life* magazines. Bourke-White wrote: "To me ... industrial forms were all the more beautiful because they were never designed to be beautiful. They had a simplicity of line that came from their direct application of purpose. Industry ... had evolved an unconscious beauty—often a hidden beauty that was waiting to be discovered."[3]　© Margaret Bourke-White Estate.

surrogate heart. Excluding all traces of land, clouds became Stieglitz's abstract, metaphoric equations of his emotions and psychological states, a personal testament that the universe is a comprehensible component of the self. The "Equivalents" demonstrated Stieglitz's symbolic power to recast the everyday with spiritual significance in the midst of the post–World War I atmosphere of nihilism. His idea of an equivalent world applied an aesthetic sensibility to be applied to any subject regardless of its external context and use in daily life. This not only freed his subject matter from literal interpretation, but it also freed Stieglitz from the confines of his print's edges and allowed his images to take on a much larger mental stance that no longer relied on the physical attributes of the picture (see Figure 11.3).

During the 1920s, Stieglitz responded to the culture of the machine by making pictures from his Manhattan apartment window of the new steel skyscrapers arising amid the old brownstones (see Figure 11.4). The post–World War I building boom propelled the skyscraper into the American topography and psyche as its image proliferated throughout the arts. Stieglitz saw there was a social price attached to the skyscraper mania, and his images paradoxically juxtaposed

11.3   ALFRED STIEGLITZ.   *Equivalent*, 1930. 6⅝ × 4⅝ inches. Gelatin silver print. For his "Equivalents," Stieglitz photographed around Lake George in upstate New York with a 4 × 5-inch Graflex camera and made only contact prints on gelatin silver paper. Stieglitz presented his goals as a visual riddle: "My aim is increasingly to make my photographs look so much like photographs that unless one has eyes and sees, they won't be seen—and still everyone will never forget them having once looked at them."[4]   Courtesy George Eastman House.

symbols of progress with their accompanying alienation. Human scale lost its significance among the long black shadows cast by the shiny techno-mega-structures that crowded out the past. Stieglitz was no longer concerned with spreading his ideas via the graphic arts. With age, Stieglitz was increasingly con-cerned with presenting his cabalistic conclusions about modernistic art and photography in a majestic, patrician manner. Stieglitz remained active as a New York City impresario, promoting modern painters and a few photographers at the Anderson Galleries from 1917 through 1925. Between 1925 and 1929, Stieglitz ran the Intimate Gallery, then he operated An American Place until his death in 1946.

Steichen Goes Commercial

In 1911, the year following the International Exhibition of Pictorial Photography in Buffalo, NY, **Edward Steichen** made his first fashion photographs. Steichen applied his artistic principles to commercial photography, which led to his falling out with Stieglitz. Never having to earn a living through his photography,

11.4   ALFRED STIEGLITZ.   *New York, From My Window at Shelton, West,* 1931. 7⅝ × 5¾ inches. Gelatin silver print.   Courtesy George Eastman House.

Form as Essence

Stieglitz had complex and unrealistic attitudes about the activities that artists could do for money without selling their artistic souls to the devil. During World War I, Steichen was commander of the photographic division of the Army Expeditionary Forces, in charge of aerial photography. Discovering beauty in these high-definition pictures led Steichen to reject his soft-focus gum prints and burn his paintings. To reinvent himself, Steichen devised visual exercises, such as lighting and photographing a white tea cup on a black background a thousand different ways. Steichen became chief photographer for Condé Nast Publications in 1923, translating his newly learned visual data onto the printed pages of popular magazines (see Figure 11.5).

Edward Henry Weston [1886–1958] received his first camera in 1902 and by 1906 was working as a door-to-door photographer. After attending the Illinois College of Photography, Weston ran a successful portrait studio in Glendale, CA from 1911 to 1922, where he was known for his soft-focus, pictorial style. During this period, under the influence of his studio partner, Margrethe Mather, [1885–1952] and his apprentice and friend, Johan Hagemeyer [1884–1962], Weston awakened to the modernist directions in art and reevaluated his own work.

In 1922, Weston traveled to New York to meet the leaders of the modernist photography movement, Alfred Stieglitz, Paul Strand, Charles Sheeler, and Clarence White. On this journey Weston stopped in

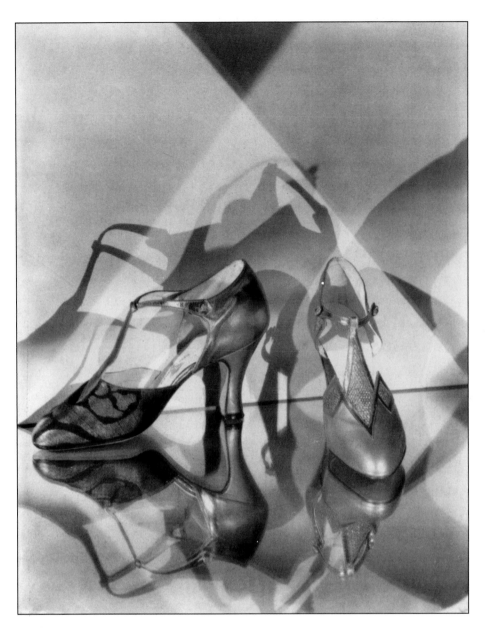

11.5 EDWARD STEICHEN. *Shoes,* ca. 1929.
7⅞ × 7½ inches. Photogravure. Publishing regularly in
Vogue and *Vanity Fair* for fifteen years, Steichen introduced the notion of modernism to a cosmopolitan audience interested in fashionably adorning itself. His
product shots and his celebrity portraits of Charles
Chaplin, Greta Garbo, and Gloria Swanson, among
others, bring out the personality of each subject or
product within the confines of a precisely designed and
lit set.   Reprinted with permission of Joanna T. Steichen,
Carousel Research.

Ohio to photograph the American Rolling Mill
(Armco) steelworks. These precise, straightforward images honor industrial architecture and technology while
displaying Weston's ability to visually sort complex
subjects into simplified semi-abstract form, marking a
distinctive break with his pictorial origins.

In 1923, Weston moved to Mexico City and opened
a studio with his lover and apprentice, Tina Modotti
[1896–1942]. Through Modotti, Weston became acquainted with members of the Mexican Renaissance,
such as the mural painter Diego Rivera [1886–1957],
whose dynamic social and political works had heroic
intonations. During this period of self-analysis Weston
began his *Daybooks,*[5] notebooks in which for the next
twenty years he detailed his artistic struggles, emotional anxieties, and financial dilemmas. He wrote:

> the camera should be used for a recording of *life,* for render-
> ing the very substance and quintessence of the *thing itself,*
> whether it be polished steel or palpitating flesh. . . . I feel def-
> inite in my belief that the approach to photography is through
> realism—and its most difficult approach.[6]

Weston's work was about what lies beyond the subject and its form. For Weston, "the thing itself" was not
the recording of what was in front of the camera, but a

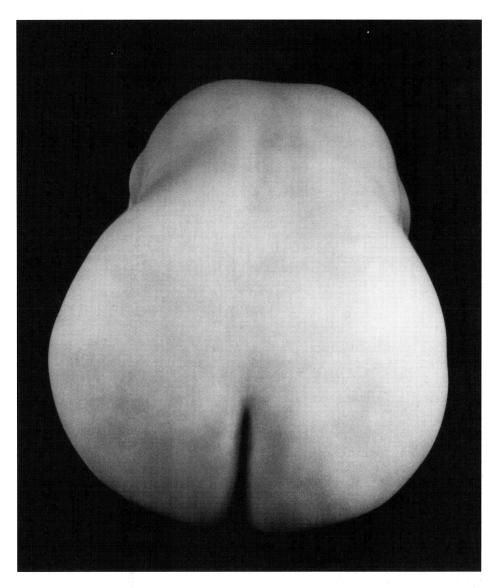

11.6 EDWARD WESTON. *Nude,* 1926. 8½ × 7½ inches. Gelatin silver print. Weston's sensual and sexual energy can be seen in over one hundred nude female studies made between 1918 and 1945. Unlike Stieglitz, Weston's approach was less romantic and more modern, not commemorating an individual but gazing at the female body with a coolness that eluded him in his private life. Weston's photographs acknowledge the beauty of the female body, and he later makes this appeal eternal by linking it with other organic life forms such as shells. ©1981 Center for Creative Photography, Arizona Board of Regents.

search for what the popular philosopher Henri Bergson called "life force," the pure essence of existence.[7] Hence Weston wrote of the "seeing of parts—fragments—as universal symbols"[8] that are interchangeable. Through this transformative process of reducing the subject to its fundamental structure, Weston worked to reunite rational thought and subjective feeling. The ground glass became a site for harmonizing the technology and science of photography with a spiritual quest for knowledge of nature's most basic extract—the underlying unity of life forms. To obtain this Bergsonian vision, Weston changed his approach to make his method one with his aesthetic through his concept of *previsualization,* the ability to see one's finished print on the ground glass in all its desired qualities and values before exposure.[9]

To achieve explicitness of form, Weston put aside his soft-focus lens for a sharp focusing Rapid-Rectilinear. "The shutter stops down to 256 [the modern equivalent is f/64]; this should satisfy my craving for more depth of focus,"[10] he wrote. He began giving up the soft, subtle tonal range of the platinum paper for the sharper, more punchy tones of the gelatin silver paper. Weston's compositions grew tighter, excluding nonessentials and repudiating the fashionable studio portrait to prove the unimportance of subject matter. He simplified his darkroom, eliminating enlarging and using only a light bulb to make detail-packed contact prints. For two weeks Weston studied and

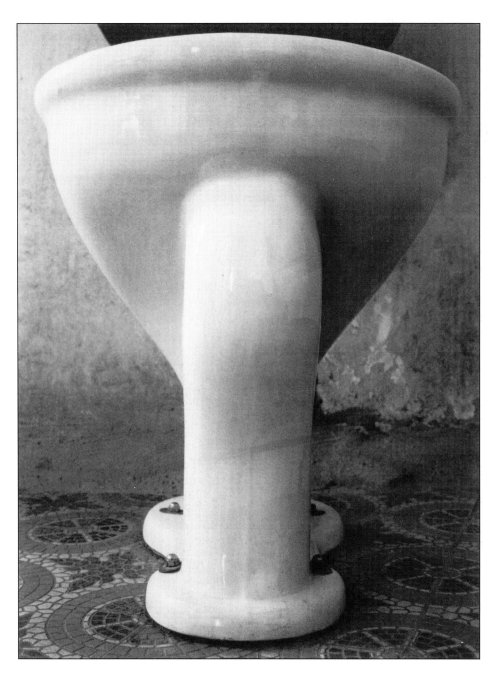

11.7   EDWARD WESTON.   *Excusado,* 1925. 9½ ×
7¼ inches. Platinum print. As Weston searched to find a
new way of seeing he experimented with different versions of this subject as both platinum and gelatin silver
prints. Weston wrote in his *Daybooks:* "My excitement
was absolute aesthetic response to form. For long I have
considered photo-graphing this useful and elegant accessory to modern hygienic life, but not until I actually
contemplated its image on my ground glass did I realize
the possibilities before me. I was thrilled!—here was
every sensuous curve of the "human form divine" but
minus imperfections . . . Never did the Greeks reach a
more significant consummation to their culture."[11]
©1981 Center for Creative Photography, Arizona Board of
Regents.

photographed a toilet, turning the modernist axiom of
"form follows function" inside out by removing the
form from its function and comparing it to a smooth-
flowing, sensual shape.

In 1927, Weston moved to Carmel, CA, applying his
lessons in abstraction to making close-up images of organic objects. Fruits and vegetables were isolated in a
wash basin, photographed in natural light, and then
eaten, satisfying Weston's physical and metaphysical
hunger (see Figure 11.8). Later Weston applied the
same abstract approach within the landscape, altering
and disguising scale so that organic matter turned into
architectural form. By the early 1940s, Weston was re-
versing the process so that industrial sites could be
viewed as organic shapes.

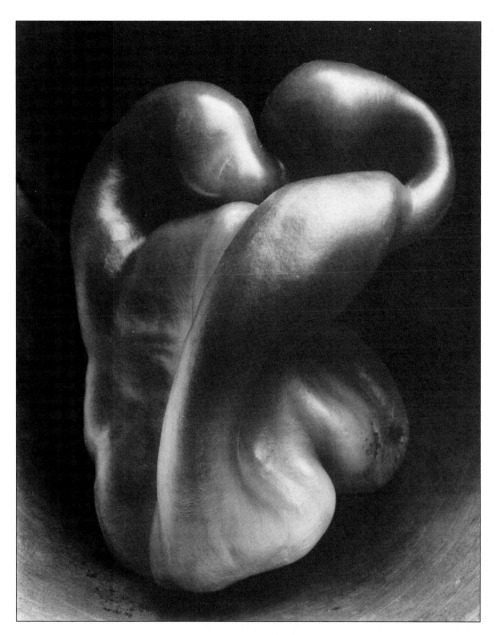

11.8   EDWARD WESTON.   *Pepper #30,* 1930. 9⅜ × 7½ inches. Gelatin silver print. "Life is a coherent whole: rocks, clouds, trees, shells, torsos, smokestacks, peppers, are interrelated, interdependent parts of the whole. Rhythm from one become symbols of all. The creative force in man feels and records these rhythms, these forms, with the medium most suitable to him."[12] ©1981 Center for Creative Photography, Arizona Board of Regents.

In 1937 and again in 1938, Weston became the first photographer to receive a John Guggenheim Memorial Foundation Fellowship, easing his financial stress and leading to the publication of *California and the West* (1940).[13] The Guggenheim gave Weston freedom and time to combine what he had learned about reducing a subject to its essential form into the Western landscape. The result can be seen in his meditative desert sand dune images where the vastness of the landscape overwhelms human scale and emptiness is everything. The sensual, textural beauty of the dunes supplants the human figure; the earth itself is presented as a nude. The minimalism of the scene is maximized to reveal its spiritual essence within its apparent nothingness. Often working with his son Brett Weston [1911–1993], Weston's last Point Lobos, CA, images, made with spare, pristine working methods, give concrete form to his belief that "one must feel definitely, fully, before the exposure [is made]."[14]

Straight, Modernistic Photography

Group f/64 (1932–35), founded in Oakland, CA, was a loose band of seven photographers—Edward Weston, Ansel Adams, Imogen Cunningham, Willard

11.9   ANSEL ADAMS.   *Mono Lake Reflections, CA,* ca. 1947. 9⁵⁄₁₆ × 12 inches. Gelatin silver print. Adams believed that photography was about interaction. He often compared the negative to a musical score and the print to its performance. It was Adams's view that: "The picture we make is never made for us alone; it is, and should be a communication—to reach as many people as possible without dilution of quality or intensity.... To the complaint 'There are no people in these photographs,' I respond, There are always two people, the photographer and the viewer."[15]   Courtesy Corbis/Ansel Adams Publishing Rights Trust.

Van Dyke [1906–1986], Sonya Noskowiak [1900–1986], John Paul Edwards [1883–1968], and Henry Swift [1890–1960]—who promoted straight, modernistic photography. With their aesthetic stance based in precisionism, they named themselves after the smallest aperture on the camera lens, expressing their allegiance to sharply focused images printed on glossy gelatin silver papers without any signs of pictorial "handwork" and mounted on white board. Favoring natural forms and found objects, they offered an alternative to Stieglitz's disdainful urban bias against the naturalistic West Coast artists and the California pictorialist style.

In the 1920s, **Ansel Adams** [1902–1984] split his time between taking photographs for the Sierra Club and playing music, but after seeing some of Paul Strand's negatives he decided to devote himself to photography. The public came to see his images as the absolute pictorial testimony of the American Western landscape, a site of inspiration and redemptive power that must be preserved. Adams's visual understanding came from being in tune with the changing nature of light and how it moves within the landscape. To be able to record the visual sensations of a specific quality of light, at a precise location, and at an exact moment, Adams, with the help of Fred Archer [1888–1963], developed the *Zone System* in the late 1930s.

The Zone System takes the conceptual basis of Group f/64 and gives photographers a practical, yet scientifically grounded, method to implement their vision by controlling exposure, development, and printing, incisively translating detail, scale, texture, and tone into the final image. A *zone* represents the relationship of a subject's brightness to its density in the

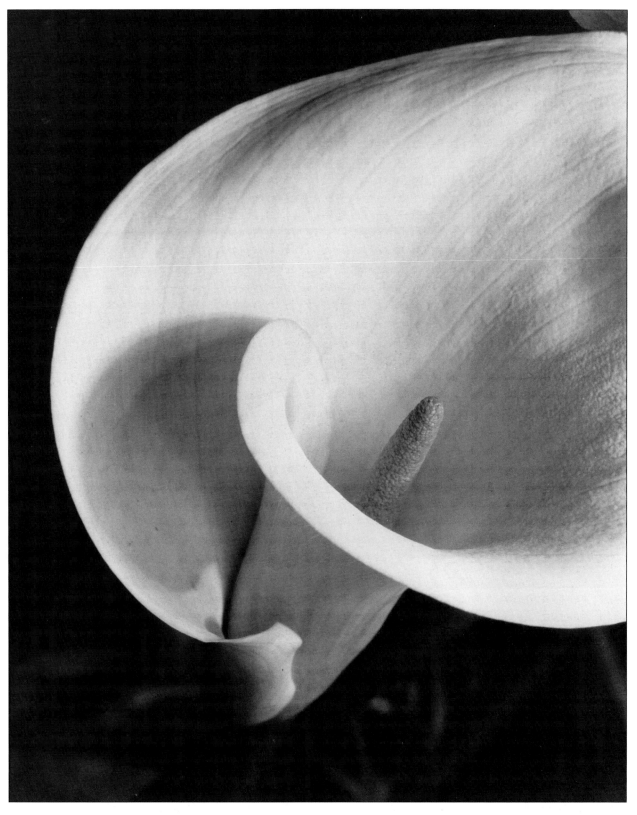

11.10 IMOGEN CUNNINGHAM. *Calla,* ca. 1925. 11 × 9½ inches. Gelatin silver print. While caring for her young children, Cunningham condensed her domestic landscape into still life. Her tightly rendered plant studies present nature with machine precision or as sexual allusion, drawing sensual parallels to the female form that she explored through her long career. Although the picture is a faithful rendering of a plant, Cunningham's concern was not the subject itself but what the subject could become under special circumstances controlled by the photographer. Courtesy Imogen Cunningham. © The Imogen Cunningham Trust.

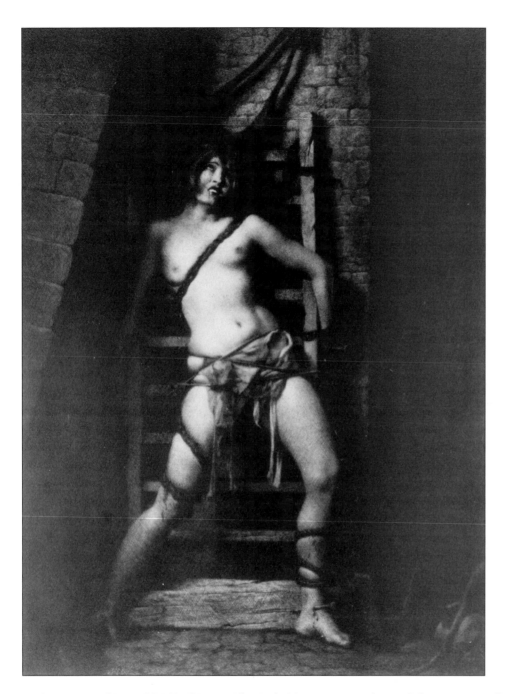

11.11   WILLIAM MORTENSEN.   *The Spider Tor-
ture.* 7⅝ × 5¾ inches. In his essay, "Fallacies of 'Pure
Photo-graphy,'" Mortensen challenged the assumptions
of Group f/64 by stating: "Purists and puritans alike
have been marked by a crusading devotion to self-de-
fined fundamentals, by a tendency to sweeping condemnation of all who over-step the boundaries they
have set up, and by grim disapproval of the more pleasing and graceful things in life."[16]   Courtesy George Eastman House.

negative and the corresponding tone in the final print.
Adams took the grayscale of a full-tone black-and-
white print and refined it into eleven different zones,
from Zone 0, maximum black, to Zone X, pure white.
Adams identified the zones with Roman numerals to
avoid confusion with other numerical combinations
used in photography. Each zone is the equivalent to
one f/stop difference in subject brightness and negative
exposure. The zone system is designed to eliminate
guesswork and give photographers repeatable control
over their materials so that the outcome can be predicted (that is, previsualized).

Through Adams's writing, publications, and workshops, the Zone System became so popular with serious imagemakers for its ability to scientifically offer

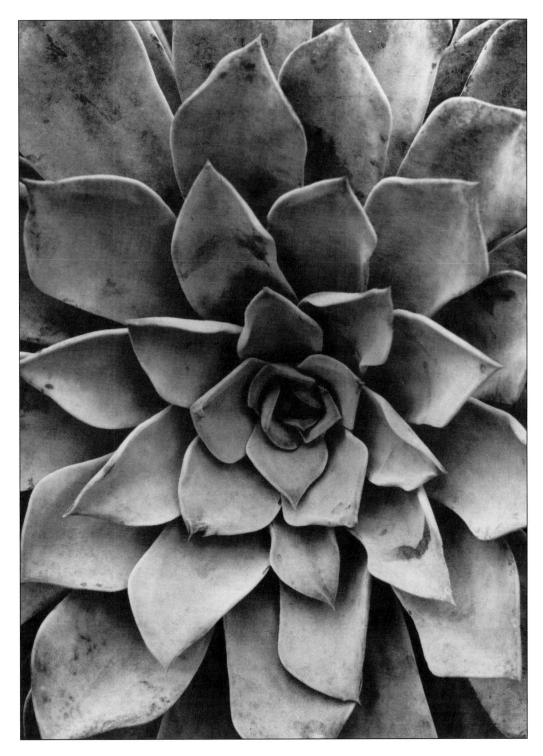

11.12 ALBERT RENGER-PATZSCH. *Echeoeria,* 1922. 15 × 11 inches. Gelatin silver print. ©1999 Artists Rights Society (ARS), New York/VG Blld-Kunst, Bonn, Germany.

artistic control of the photographic process that it eclipsed other forms of printmaking. As with any method, the Zone System has been abused by the unthinking, who have turned it into aesthetic dogma, which was never Adams's intent. Images like *Mono Lake Reflections, CA* (see Figure 11.9), reveal how

Adams's interpretations fused seemingly competing concerns. The foreground and background are razor sharp and utterly still while the middleground moves. Dark shadows compete with bright highlights. The image uses the straight nature of photography not to report but to interpret and recite silvery poetry. It is accessible without pandering. The view is not overly dramatic or romantic but possesses subtleties that will be yielded on serious viewing. It is mythological, conveying a sense of optimism about the open Western

11.13   KARL BLOSSFELDT. *Blumenbachia Hieronymi* (Loasacea) Nette Closed Seed Capsule enlarged 14.94 times. 10¼ × 8⅛ inches. Gelatin silver print.
Courtesy Center for Creative Photography.

space. It says that there are still uncovered possibilities in America and that our society can push on into the future. These transcendental qualities allow the work to escape the "thingness" that can be so stifling and evoke a sense of essence about a place. By the 1960s, the accessibility of Adams's images, the respect for his technical brilliance, and the ability of his work to command higher prices gained photography entrance into a broader range of arenas, including mass media, galleries, and museums.

Imogen Cunningham [1883–1976] took up photography in 1901 after seeing the work of Gertrude Käsebier. By 1910 she had opened her own studio. As with the other members of Group f/64, Cunningham was a romantic pictorialist who took up modernism with the zeal of a convert. Cunningham's allegiance was clearly with Group f/64's credo that the "greatest aesthetic beauty, the fullest power of expression, the real worth of the medium lies in its pure form rather than in its superficial modifications."[17] The changes in Cunningham's work, from soft-focus pictorialism to sharply focused, geometric compositions (see Figure 11.10), parallel the economic collapse that led modernism into the documentary realism of the 1930s. As the fascination with technology was replaced by the im-

11.14 EUGÈNE ATGET. *Fête du Trône de Géant,*
1925. 7 × 9 inches. Printing out paper, gold toned.
Courtesy George Eastman House.

mediate need to find solutions to Depression-era social
problems, questions about the proper function of art
and the correct use of materials replaced disputes over
style, and abstraction gave way to straight descriptions
of everyday culture.

The antithesis of Group f/64's philosophy can be
seen in **William Mortensen's** [1897–1975] prolific
output of melodramatic tableaux, instructional books,
and classes. His work was so at odds with Group
f/64's fundamental beliefs that Ansel Adams once referred to Mortensen as the "antichrist." Mortensen's
manipulated work portrayed women under the control
of male power, in male fantasies of domination (see
Figure 11.11). Mortensen's work rejected as mechanistic the doctrine of the straight print, seeing it only
as a gateway for expression. Mortensen thought
Group f/64's stance was hypocritical in allowing manipulation of tonality for "emotional" effect yet labeling other forms of manipulation unacceptable. As far
as Mortensen was concerned, "If tone is granted to be

subject to control, why not line, also, which has equal
emotional significance? And if line, why not shapes
and forms? . . . And if all these things are allowed,
what becomes of the "record of actuality"? . . . sunk
without a trace."[18]

Film und Foto and New Objectivity

Europeans continued to push the boundaries of the conceptual practices of photography with projects like the
1929 international exhibition, *Film und Foto,* organized in Stuttgart by the Deutscher Werkbund, a professional organization of artists, craftspeople, and manu-
facturers. At *Film und Foto,* the precisionist American
and the conceptually adventurous European ideas about
modern photography commingled. Weston selected
Cunningham's unromantic work along with the images
of Berenice Abbott, Paul Outerbridge, Edward Steichen, Charles Sheeler, and his own for the exhibition.
Bauhaus master László Moholy-Nagy put together a
blend of advertising, artistic, journalistic, and scientific
images, disregarding their original context, to promote

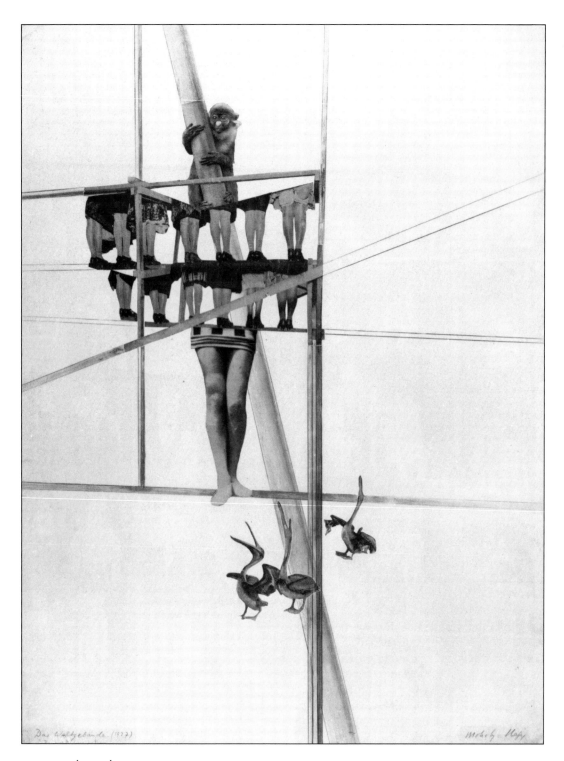

11.15 LÁSZLÓ MOHOLY-NAGY. *The Structure of the World,* 1927. 25½ × 19⅜ inches. Photomechanical offset, rotogravure, pencil.   ©1999 Artists Rights Society, (ARS), New York/ADAGP, Paris, France.

photography as a flexible medium of communication. To promote his ideas about geometric form, light, and space, Moholy included his own works and those of Albert Renger-Patzsch, Herbert Bayer, John Heartfield, Florence Henri, André Kertész, El Lissitsky, Man Ray, and Alexander Rodchenko. *Film und Foto* also linked the most daring film and photography of the modernist movement, screening Sergei Eisenstein's *Potemkin* (1925), Dziga Vertov's *Man With a Movie Camera* (1928), and Man Ray's *L'Etoile de Mer* (1928).

11.16 LÁSZLÓ MOHOLY-NAGY. *Chairs at Margate,* 1935. 14½ × 11⅝ inches each. Gelatin silver print diptych.   ©1999 Artists Rights Society, (ARS), New York.

Albert Renger-Patzsch's [1897–1966] *Die Welt ist schön* (*The World Is Beautiful*), 1928, exemplified the concern for order in modernist German photography. The book alternated tight shots of animals, landscapes, and plants with factories and industrial equipment; there was no text on the picture pages. The concept showed the interrelationship between natural forms and machine-made objects, demonstrating the formal structure of all things. Renger-Patzsch relied on photography to impose order on subjects cut from the tumultuous Weimar Republic. Whether the subject was industrial or natural, Renger-Patzsch applied a narrow clinical template of unyielding visual precision that removed and isolated the subject from its worldly context for viewer scrutiny. For instance, Renger-Patzsch chose a flower not for its softness or sensuality but for its sharp, repetitive features that did not invite intimacy or sentimentality (see Figure 11.12). For Renger-Patzsch, photography was a tool of natural science, encouraging viewers to ignore the individuality of the subject and see it analytically as a specimen to be categorized, labeled, and filed, and therefore known and safe to handle.

Renger-Patzsch's belief in "photographic photography," allowing "a fragment to symbolize the whole" and the "sharpness of photographic seeing [to] conjure

up the fantastic in everyday nature,"[19] formed the underpinnings of *neue Sachlichkeit* (*New Objectivity*), as straight photography was known in Germany during the 1920s. The director of *Film und Foto*, Gustaf Stotz, observed the effect of this quest for structural order:

> We see things differently now, without painterly intent in the impressionistic sense. Today things are important that earlier were hardly noticed: for example shoe lasts, gutters, spools of thread, fabrics, machine, etc. They interest us for their material substance, for the simple quality of the thing-in-itself; they interest us as means of creating space-form surfaces.[20]

The close-up became one of the main compositional devices in the New Objectivity. **Karl Blossfeldt's** [1865–1932] book *Urformen der Kunst* (*Art Forms in Nature*, 1928; 1932 English translation) used macro- and microscopic photography to present the "artistic" organizing patterns in nature. Such extreme views were intended to eliminate all atmospheric effects and personal reactions and to reveal a subject's basic design: "Nature is our best teacher,"[21] said Blossfeldt. By enlarging discrete portions of a subject—the characteristics, details, patterns, and textures that would otherwise go unobserved by human vision or in normal-range photography—Blossfeldt made the imperceptible perceptible (see Figure 11.13).

The close-up has long been a source of essential information in the medical, scientific, and technical communities. Using the camera to enlarge and isolate the subject has been the most logical and scientific method.

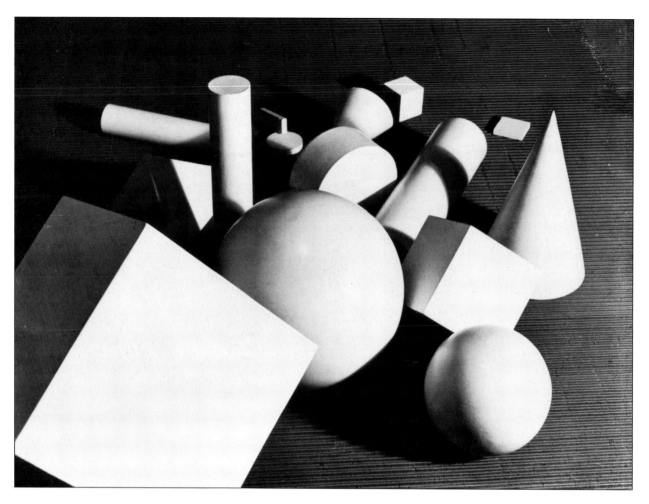

11.17   HERBERT BAYER.   *Untitled,* geometric
shapes on white corrugated cardboard, ca. 1930s. 9 ×
12¹³/₁₆ inches. Gelatin silver print. **Herbert Bayer**
[1900–1985] was a graphic designer, trained at the
Bauhaus with Moholy, who incorporated photographs,
rather than drawings and paintings, into his work. Bayer
constructed highly geometric studio compositions with
a deep sense of plastic (three-dimensional) space, rather
than linear space, that relates to Moholy's idea of fotoplastik.   © Galleria Martini & Renehetti, Genoa, Italy.

By eliminating all nonessentials and dispensing with
recreating a psychological mood or a social relationship, the close-up seems to confirm that art and nature
are "intimately bound up as to be inseparable."[22] In his
images of plant forms, Blossfeldt believed that the New
Objectivity revealed the connection between natural
form "governed by some fixed and eternal force"[23] and
art. Other imagemakers used the close-up as an ingenious way of examining ordinary subject matter and to
interject private beliefs and emotions about what was in
front of their camera lens.

   Eugène Atget [1857–1927] turned to photography
at age forty after working as a cabin boy, actor, and
painter. Atget undertook a methodical photographic
survey of the old quarters of Paris and its surrounding
parks. Working in the tradition of Charles Marville and
the *Monuments historiques* project, Atget spent thirty
years making over 10,000 photographs with an outmoded wooden view-camera and tripod, often using a
wide-angle lens that did not match the camera format.
This produced *vignetting,* a darkening of the image towards the corners in the final print. Under his hand-let-
tered sign, "Documents pour artistes," Atget scratched
out living selling contact prints, made from his glass
plate negatives on printing-out paper and toned with
gold chloride. Seemingly resistant to change, Atget
never professed belief in any artistic movement, nor
was he given to technical experimentation. Atget's sa-
vant-like accumulation of empirical observations of a
premodern Paris is as much about the psychological nature of time as it is an extended architectural study. His
work went unnoticed until his neighbor, Man Ray, published some of his images without credit in the official
surrealist journal, *La Révolution Surréaliste,* in 1926.[24]
The surrealists, who gave themselves permission to
find new meaning in a subject or discard the intended
one, saw Atget as a primitive in touch with his unconscious self. For the surrealists Atget's storefront pictures of mannequins, window reflections, and odd jux-

11.18   FLORENCE HENRI.   *Composition No. 12,* ca. 1929. 9³⁄₁₆ × 14¾ inches. Gelatin silver print. *Composition No. 12* embodied what Moholy called a "new space, which was to be produced through the relations of the elemental material of visual expression—a new space created with light directly. . . . The surface becomes a part of the atmospheric background; it sucks up light phenomena produced outside of itself—a vivid contrast to the classical conception of the picture, the illusion of an open window . . . it represents the mastery of the surface, not for atmospheric, but for plastic spatial ends."[25]   Courtesy Gyorgy Kepes.

tapositions of objects could distort time, space, and scale so that they appeared to have emerged from a dream (see Figure 11.14).

Atget's poised, commonplace scenes have a disturbing sense of apprehension and of being removed from the world. The combination enabled Atget's photographs to transcend photography's competing views of documentation and self-expression. His body of work does not evoke a quaint sensation of the past, but provides the materials necessary to analyze the elusive attributes of time. Atget, an avid reader of nineteenth-century French literature, wanted to preserve the Paris of the past by photographing buildings slated for demolition and recording in detail how the ironworks, stone, and vegetation evoked a spirit beyond their physical description. Atget's catalogue of arcades, doorways,

private gardens, public spaces, and ordinary people struggling to earn a living shows a lyrical understanding of the street and a society on the verge of extinction. Atget's seemingly simple photographs have a sense of sorrow for an irreclaimable era. Atget vetoed Man Ray's proposal that he use a hand-held Rolleiflex camera, complaining to him that "le snapshot went faster than he could think. . . . Trop vite, enfin! Too fast."[26] Atget understood that the element of time built into his antiquated style of working allowed him to meditate on what was in front of his camera. Atget's extended study prolonged the photographic moment to reveal how time transforms a subject.

Experimentally Modern

The 1920s was a period of experimentation, and at the forefront, dealing with the "realm of the fantastic," was the Bauhaus master **László Moholy-Nagy.** Moholy-Nagy sought a purely photographic approach independent of all previous forms of representation. Moholy urged investigation into "the new culture of light" so that "the strongest visual experiences that could be granted to man" could be made available through its understanding and use. He wrote: "This century belongs to light. Photography is the first means of giving tangible shape to light, though in a transposed and— perhaps just for that reason—almost abstract form."[27] Unlike the precisionists, Moholy-Nagy wanted to use

11.19   GYORGY KEPES.   *Juliet in Camouflage Jungle*, 1942. 7⅝ × 5⁷⁄₁₆ inches. Gelatin silver print.
Courtesy George Eastman House.

photography to show what the human eye alone could not see. In "Production-Reproduction,"[28] Moholy took the position that mediums primarily used for reproduction, such as photography and film, could be reduced to their most elemental level and then extended on a new, innovative course. For Moholy, "reproduction" stood for imitative or repetitive relationships. "Production" signified the new forms, such as his photograms, appropriate to the world of technology, that make "new, previously unknown relationships . . . between the known and as yet unknown optical."

Moholy and his wife, **Lucia Moholy** [1894–1989], who was his collaborator and darkroom technician as well as a teacher and the author of *A Hundred Years of Photography, 1839–1939,* experimented with these concepts in 1922 by making photograms and pho-

11.20   LOTTE JACOBI.   *Photogenic Drawing,* ca. 1950. 13½ × 5⅝ inches. Gelatin silver print.   Courtesy George Eastman House.

tomontages. Moholy's practice of montage, which he called *fotoplastik,*[29] was based on the surrealist method of recording the unconscious, but without the surrealist attachment to the irrational. Moholy saw his approach as an experimentally disciplined and judicious strategy to achieve an art form that struck a balance between reason and spirit, and between people and their culture. Moholy's photomontages relied on the graphic suprematist forms of the circle, cone, and spiral to create multiperspective compositions. This scheme disturbed Renaissance perspective and its companion formulas for acquiring knowledge through images. Moholy's photomontages juxtaposed contrasting imagery in open compositions, with much of the surrounding space left intentionally blank. The resulting interplay of movement between the fragmented images and the stillness of the unused space applied both optical and psychological pressure on viewers to recreate the same commotion and unstableness they experienced in modern daily life.

New Vision

Much of what is called *New Vision* or Bauhaus photography, based on the aesthetic possibilities of geometric form, is discussed in Moholy's *Malerei Fotografie, Film* (*Painting, Photography, Film*), 1925. New Vision reflected the aesthetic possibilities of geometric form as it related to architecture and the machine. In straight photography it was characterized by the use of geometric compositions, the close-up, the oblique points of view, the inclusion of reflective surfaces to alter perspective, and the hand-held camera to cover sports events and produce action scenes. It permitted any type

of optical manipulation of light, making the medium its own subject. Its underlying premise was that images must be made by photography and must look photographic. During the 1920s this mode of working, without its conceptual base, spread rapidly after being co-opted by the German commercial advertising, marketing, and the popular press.

Moholy's straight photography favored non–eye-level points of view to duplicate the constructivist antiperspective, compositional structure. Moholy also incorporated Theo Van Doesburg's painting theory of "counter-composition," designed to relieve the abstract purity of *De Stijl*[30] compositions, such as those of Mondrian, by rotating his camera and even making double exposures in order to secure a counter-composition that was less rigid and more active. He also made regular use of negative prints, and would juxtapose two images to create an energetic and varied reading of a subject.

After Hitler closed the Bauhaus in 1933, Moholy eventually settled in Chicago and opened the New Bauhaus in 1937. The school closed within a year, during the Great Depression, but Moholy opened his own institution, the School of Design (reorganized in 1944 as the Institute of Design). Graduates of this institution, such as Arthur Siegel and Henry Holmes Smith, spread Moholy's ideas that "a knowledge of photography is just as important as that of the alphabet" and "the illiterate of the future will be ignorant of the uses of camera and pen alike."[31] These beliefs disseminated through American photography as other educators, including Harry Callahan, Aaron Siskind, and their students, continued Moholy's teachings.

Florence Henri [1895–1982] studied with Moholy and the painter Fernand Léger and doubtless had seen Léger's film, *Les Ballets mécaniques* (1923–24), which used light and mirrors to distort, fragment, and multiply images. Henri blended Moholy's and Léger's approaches to formulate a geometric, multiplaned, semi-abstract vision founded on the dematerialization

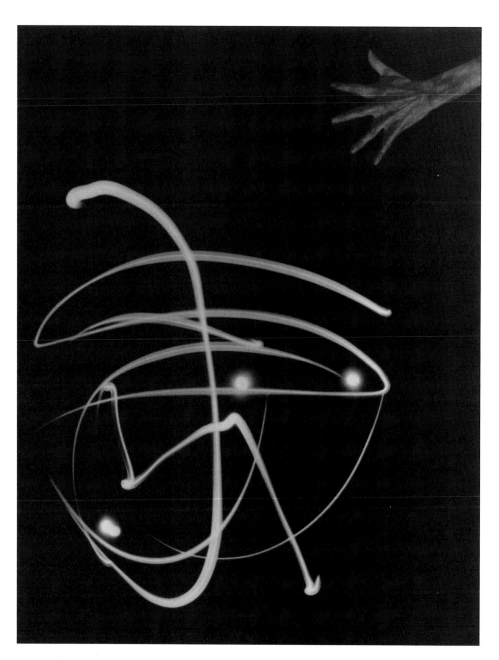

11.21   BARBARA MORGAN.   *Pure Energy and Neurotic Man,* 1941/71. 19¾ × 15¼ inches. Gelatin silver print.   Courtesy Herbert Bayer Estate.

of light. The overlapping space, utilizing reflections and refractions, became enigmatic and permitted meaning to be ambiguous and fluid. On the verso (backside) of *Composition No. 12,* a cataloguer positioned it as a vertical. In Figure 11.17 it is reproduced as a horizontal. Eastman House print archivist David Wooters acknowledged Henri's invitation to interpret the work's position with his comment: "Let the bottom find itself."[32]

Gyorgy Kepes [b. 1906], a close associate of Moholy who became the head of the light department at the New Bauhaus, proclaimed he was not a photographer but an artist "committed to working with light."[33] An avid experimenter, Kepes juxtaposed fragmented light spaces with structured rhythmic patterns of geometric shapes to create visual opposition. This use of opposites, natural forms in a dreamlike field of geometric shapes, was a metaphor of alternating natural and technological realities (see Figure 11.18). Kepes used "to read nature, to learn about nature, and to create patterns which reveal nature."[34] In response to the teaching of Kepes, Carlotta Corpron [1901–1988] embarked on a series of studies utilizing the properties of light, rather than the object, to produce images. **Lotte Jacobi** [1896–1990], known for her stylized portraits, also combined light graphics with camera imagery to produce what she called "photogenic drawings"(see Figure 11.19).

11.22 FRANTIŠEK DRTIKOL. *Composition,*
1929. 8⅝ × 11⁵⁄₁₆ inches. Pigment print.   © Ervina
Bokôvá-Drtikolová.

Pathways of Light:
Time, Space, and Form

Barbara Morgan [1900–1992] combined camera and
cameraless images into the same composition, using
what Moholy referred to as "automatic photomontage."
Her multiple exposures conveyed the complexity of energy, time, and human psychology. Against a black vacuum of nothingness, as in *Pure Energy and Neurotic
Man,* Morgan presented an anxious hand, tentatively
frozen in the act of deciding whether to reach toward or
pull away from a light force (see Figure 11.21).

Morgan's cinematic use of space and time may symbolize an interior dream/thought process, permitting
what Moholy referred to as *mirroring,* sharpening the
"identification of the inside and outside penetrations, to
take place. With this instrument of thought many other
phenomena (dreams for example) can be explained as
space-time articulations. In dreams there is a characteris-

tic blending of independent events into a coherent whole.
Superimposition of photographs, as seen in motion pictures, can be used as the visual representational form of
dreams, and in this way, as a space-time synonym."[35]

František Drtikol [1883–1961] was a Czech pictorialist, grounded in the ideas of symbolism and *Jugend-
stil* (the German art nouveau), who in the 1920s incorporated modernist ideas about geometric form, light,
and space into studies of the female nude. In 1922, he
developed the halftone photolithography process, a
combination of oil printing and lithography.[36] In his
Salome theme nudes, the female body is not individualized but is presented as form and space, integrating the
settings and themes of art deco, symbolism, expressionism, and cubism. The expressionistic shadows become as important as the subject, offering visual depth,
emotional weight, and sensuous mystery in a theatrical
setting of fascination with the nude. In the early 1930s,
before giving up photography, Drtikol replaced live
models with plywood figures, marking a shift towards the abstract. His work and teaching influenced
other Czech photographers including Josef Sudek
[1896–1976] and Jaromír Funke [1896–1945], whose
still-life compositions emphasize abstraction in concert
with light and heavy shadow.

11.23   FRANCIS JOSEPH BRUGUIÈRE.   *Woman on Phone,* ca. 1936/40. 7⁷⁄₁₆ × 9⁷⁄₁₆ inches. Gelatin silver print.   Courtesy George Eastman House.

Francis Joseph Bruguière [1879–1945] studied photography with American pictorialist Frank Eugene and experimented with multiple exposures and printing techniques as early as 1912. Throughout the 1920s, Bruguière made formally abstract photographs, whose principal subject matter was light, by photographing cut and shaped paper designs. These "designs in abstract forms of light"[37] were his way of "apprehending light as an active symbol of consciousness."[38] In the early 1930s, Bruguière inserted elusive figurative components into these experiments, which can be seen in the book *Few Are Chosen* (1931). The intricate interplay of light and shadow produce a visual counterpoint to each other, giving the work kinetic and sculptural attributes. By moving his light source during the exposure to make overlapping shadows, Bruguière's tonally lavish prints take on surreal attributes: The viewer knows such shadows do not occur in nature but may exist in a dream. This sense of multidirectional light is also evident in the

cliché-verres he did during this period. In the later 1930s, Bruguière combined solarization, cut paper, and multiple exposure with a figurative element in a dynamic geometric composition, *Woman on the Phone*. The photograph has a sense of movement and a disquieting energy in a still situation. The solarization results in a surrealistic glimpse of both the exterior and interior reality of the subject. Multiple exposure lets objects take on a dual existence, making it appear as if viewers can look in and look out at the subject simultaneously, bridging the Bauhaus concern with the pathways of light and the surrealistic drive to connect the conscious and unconscious mind.

Surrealistic Themes

During this same era, surrealist artists took yet another approach to defining modernism, announcing that anything could be art if it was observed as art. According to the surrealists, the definition of reality itself was the question that must be answered; photography confirmed that the world was not what it appeared to be. For the surrealists, photography was a witness that gave

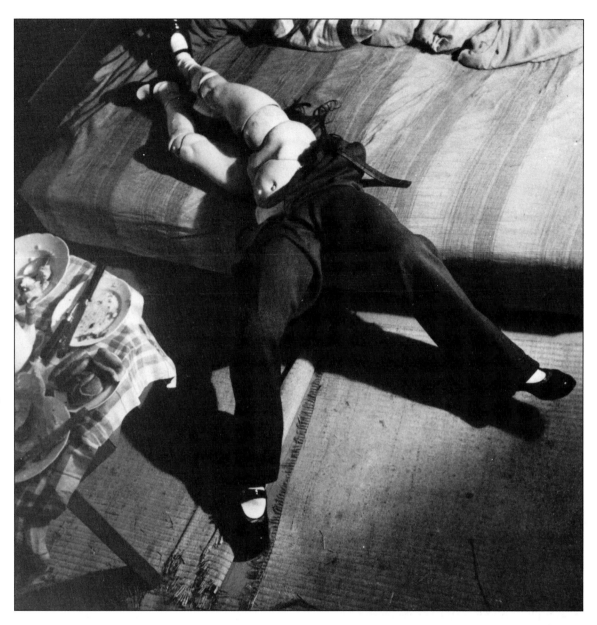

11.24   HANS BELLMER.   *The Doll,* ca. 1934. 5¾ × 5⁷⁄₁₆ inches. Gelatin silver print with applied color. Bellmer's doll images undermined the nostalgic Nazi vision of undisturbed Aryan youth, faithful to family and nation. Bellmer's surrealistic representation of an interior rather than an exterior view made visible the internal terrors of human sexual obsessions and proclivities normally beyond the scope of photographic vision.   ©1999 Artists Rights Society (ARS), New York/ADAGP, Paris, France.

true but conflicting testimony: One version adhered to the facts while the other was a construct of the mind based on a viewing of the facts.[39] In a surreal context, photographs could stop being quotations and could act as conduits for free association. From this belief the surrealist **Hans Bellmer** [1902–1975] used sexually taboo imagery to symbolize decaying German society.

Dolls and mannequins became surrealist fetishes of male sexual desire. Bellmer fabricated a doll, the size of an adolescent girl, held together by ball joints so that its head, breasts, and limbs could be moved, and used it to make ambiguously erotic and jarring tableaus. The doll appeared in a variety of locations, wearing wigs, and little attire except for shoes, stockings, or a flimsy top, creating a pornographic environment. The doll appeared to have been physically abused, eliciting a sympathetic yet voyeuristic response that both attracts and repels. Bellmer hand-colored these photographs to bolster their menacing nature.

In 1935–36, Bellmer made a second doll with a central ball joint that enabled him to compose anatomically impossible configurations of doubled body halves, such as a torso with legs at both ends. Here the body was a prison of dissonance and futility, straining to break free from its own human limits. Many of these synthetically

UN OISEAU
héritier
des
petites passions d'enfant
espère
et conserve sa jeunesse

on ne saurait mieux dire

LE PREMIER DÉCAN DU SCORPION
sous un bloc de pierre
LA CHEVELURE
disent les vendeuses
porte le nom de
la PUBERTE

Frileuse

11.25   GEORGE HUGNET.   *La septième face du dé, Poèmes—découpages,* 1936. 11⁵⁄₁₆ × 8¼ inches. Photomechanical offset.   Estate of the Artist, courtesy Zabriskie Gallery, New York.

colored images were published in *Les Jeux de la poupée,* 1935–36, his limited-edition *artists' book.*[40]

At the age of fourteen, **Georges Hugnet** [1906–1974] met Jean Cocteau, Marcel Duchamp, Max Ernst, and Pablo Picasso and began writing poetry and making artists' books. His early work examines characteristic surrealist topics of sexual violence and unorthodox sexual practices. He uses found images and text to evoke a narrative sense, but maintains an air of mystery that keeps viewers from obtaining enough clues to know what is being conveyed. Hugnet's *La septième face du*

dé, Poèmes—découpages (1936) is a ninety-page offset printing work of twenty chapters. Each unconventionally laid-out page features poetry in a multitude of typefaces with some small appropriated images, against a montage of found images and text. The merging of images and text produces a suggestive serial narrative that contemplates interior pathologies based on the photographic evidence. An erotic fantasy of male supremacy is established through installments revolving around a young girl's sexual life. Bare-breasted women appear in enigmatic situations featuring sadomasochist activities and positions of male conquest and control. Hugnet's ordered montages contain an abundance of open white space and have a shared ancestry with Moholy-Nagy's fotoplastiks. The clarity of Hugnet's constructions can be even more disconcerting than Moholy's as what is actually being

11.26   RAOUL UBAC.   *Maquette for a Wall/Maquette pour un mur*, 1938–39. From the series Battle of Pentheseúa/Le Combat des Penthésilées. 6¾ × 9½ inches. Gelatin silver print.   Courtesy San Francisco Museum of Modern Art.

described, the subconscious netherland of dream and spirit, is not physically evident but comes to fruition in the viewer's mind.

Man Ray, who Cocteau called "the poet of the darkroom,"[41] was a deft experimenter whose compositions contained unexpected juxtapositions based on dada and surreal premises. Man Ray placed no credence in the purity of practice, taking the position that "a certain amount of contempt for the material employed to express an idea is indispensable to the purest realization of this idea."[42] This attitude led him to use the *Sabattier effect,* to question reality and disconnect the subject from the photograph. The Sabattier effect, first documented by French scientist Armand Sabattier in 1862, is the partial reversal of an image caused by exposing it to light during development. Ray called it "solarization," and like the rayograph it was rediscovered in 1929 in Ray's darkroom. Lee Miller, at the time Man Ray's assistant and lover, accidentally turned on the lights while developing film. Ray went with the chance occurrence and printed the negative, discovering that

its partially reversed tones yielded a print that appeared both as a positive and a negative. It became a Man Ray signature technique, kept secret until about 1932 when his relationship with Miller ended.

Under Ray's influence, **Raoul Ubac** [1910–1985], an artist and a poet, found new combinations of photomontage, solarization, bas-relief, and *brûlage* (using direct heat to melt the photographic emulsion) to remove a subject from its original context and place it into a surrealistic dream. Finding Breton's *Surrealist Manifesto* "a revelation and a calling," Ubac sought to disintegrate form, often using the body as a site for these invasions of light that turn representation inside out. In the series *Le Combat des Penthésilées* (*Battle of the Amazons,* 1938–39), Ubac photographed a single female nude in a variety of positions and made prints from which he produced a collage. This image was rephotographed and solarized to embellish and reverse tonal relationships. Then the solarized images were photographed twice and the resulting negatives were sandwiched together, slightly out of register, to produce a *bas-relief* effect. In conventional bas-relief printing an exact positive and negative image of the same scene are combined slightly out of register to create the illusion of relief. Ubac's double positive method produced a print whose sense of low sculptural relief is achieved with only glowing grays, instead of the dark contour lines of regular bas-relief. This allowed what surrealist writer

Georges Bataille called *informe,* to take place; the "unthinking" (the undoing) of all categories, the removing of all boundaries and concepts (or proper forms) used to shape meaning. Informe does not transcend meaning; it transgresses meaning. A notion of formlessness emerges by means of collapse and defilement, allowing new forms and definitions to emerge. Ubac's methods invade the space of the body, destroying its normal boundaries, defying gravity, distorting perspective, and transforming the body into various psychic states from violent disintegration to ecstasy.

Man Ray's solid conceptual base allowed him to find his voice in a variety of mediums, including films, such as *Emak Bakia* (1926), that investigate the fourth dimension through editing that collapsed and restructured time and space. Man Ray understood that photography's mooring in reality let him keep order even in a surrealist squall. Ray did not think that truth could be discovered in the "thing itself" because truth was fluid and was constantly being transformed. Ray's photographing of Duchamp's dadaist work in progress, *Large Glass,* a big piece of glass that had been lying flat on sawhorses collecting dust, demonstrates the celebration of ideas over subject matter (see chapter opener). At the time Duchamp decided this ephemeral act could only be made permanent through photography and called the resulting document *Dust Breeding*

(1920).[43] Man Ray saw a different meaning and published the same image as *View Taken from an Airplane* (1922). These two interpretations of the same image point out the elusive nature of photographic truth. Although the photograph remains the same, it takes on a new existence under different framers and dissimilar interpretations. Conceptually the image discloses the fluid and contradictory nature of the photograph and how the interpretation of the image is dependent on the circumstances of the viewer. Does the viewer see the image as a literal document that is tethered only to itself (the thing)? Or can the image have its own separate identity (that of the mind) that shifts with its surroundings? Both Duchamp and Ray saw artmaking as a process that involved the artist, the art object, and the viewer in an ongoing venture of reciprocal creation and interpretation.

As the older Stieglitz and his progeny now relied on straight photography to uncover eternal truth, dadaists and surrealists, such as Man Ray, steered a different course. For Ray reality was a flux, and like the name he gave himself, Man Ray did not settle for what was already a given for most people, but searched for new ways to visualize life's temporary and evanescent nature. He stated: "Perhaps the final goal desired by the artist is a confusion or merging of all the arts, as things merge in real life."[44]

Endnotes

1   *Paul Outerbridge: A Singular Aesthetic. Photographs and Drawings 1921–1941: A Catalogue Raisonné,* Elaine Dines, ed., in collaboration with Graham Howe (Laguna Beach, CA: Laguna Beach Museum of Art, 1981), 21.

2   See Bonnie Yochelson and Kathleen A. Erwin, Marianne Fulton eds., *Pictorialism into Modernism: The Clarence H. White School of Photography* (New York: Rizzoli, 1996).

3   Margaret Bourke-White, *Portrait of Myself* (New York: Simon and Schuster, 1963), 49.

4   Alfred Stieglitz, "How I Came to Photograph Clouds," *The Amateur Photographer,* vol. 56, no. 1,819 (September 19, 1923), 255.

5   *The Daybooks of Edward Weston:* vol. 1, *Mexico and The Daybooks of Edward Weston:* vol. 2, *California,* Nancy Newhall, ed., (Millerton, NY: Aperture, 1973).

6   *The Daybooks of Edward Weston:* vol. 1, *Mexico,* Nancy Newhall, ed., (Millerton, NY: Aperture, 1973), 55.

7   Henri Bergson (1859–1941), a French philosopher, postulated that the world is made up by two opposing tendencies, the life force and the resistance of matter against that force. Bergson believed that we know the material world through our intellect, but that it is by intuition that we perceive the life force and the reality of time, which is not a unit of measurement but a "duration" of "the persistence of the past in the present" that makes up life experience. These ideas were enthusiastically adopted by artists during the 1920s.

8   Edward Weston, "Photography," 1934, in Peter C. Bunnell, ed., *Edward Weston on Photography* (Salt Lake City: Peregrine Smith Books, 1983), 74.

9   Edward Weston to Frank Roy Fraprie, June 7, 1922, The Center for Cre-

ative Photography, University of Arizona, Tucson. Quoted in Newhall, *The History of Photography,* 1982, 188.

10   Edward Weston. *The Daybooks of Edward Weston,* vol. 1, 80.

11   Nancy Newhall, ed., *The Daybooks of Edward Weston,* 132.

12   Nathan Lyons, "Weston on Photography," in Beaumont Newhall and Conger, eds., *Edward Weston Omnibus* (Salt Lake City: Peregrine Smith Books, 1984), 170.

13   Edward Weston with Charis Wilson Weston, *California and the West* (New York: Duell, Sloan & Pearce, 1940).

14   Edward Weston, "Photography—Not Pictorial," *Camera Craft,* vol. 37, no. 7 (July 1930), 318. Also reprinted in Peter C. Bunnell, ed., *Edward Weston On Photography* (Salt Lake City: Gibbs M. Smith, 1983), 59.

15   Ansel Adams, *Camera and Lens,* Book 1 of the Ansel Adams Basic Photo Series (Hastings-on-Hudson, NY: Morgan and Morgan, 1948), 23.

16   William Mortensen, "Fallacies of 'Pure Photography,'" *Camera Craft,* vol. 41 (June 1934), 260–61.

17   John Paul Edwards, "Group f. 64," *Camera Craft,* vol. 42, no. 3, (March 1935), 107.

18   Mortensen, 257.

19   Carl Georg Heise, "Preface" to Albert Renger-Patzsch, *Die Welt ist schön,* (1928) trans. in "Photography and the Neue Sachlichkeit Movement," David Mellor ed., Germany: *The New Photography, 1927–33* (London: Arts Council of Great Britain, 1978), 10.

20   Gustaf Stotz in Das Kunstblatt (May 1929), trans. in Van Deren Coke, "Introduction," *Avant-Garde Photography in Germany, 1919–1939* (San Francisco: San Francisco Museum of Modern Art, 1980), 18.

21   Karl Blossfeldt, *Art Forms in Nature,* Second Series (New York: E. Weyhe, 1932), Foreword, unp.

22   Karl Nierendorf, "Preface," *Urformen der Kunst,* 1928; trans. in David Mellor, ed., *Germany: The New Photography, 1927–33* (London, 1978), 17.

23   Ibid.

24   Atget's work might have been lost if not for Berenice Abbott, Man Ray's assistant at the time, who raised money to purchase Atget's prints and negatives. Abbott spent years crusading to bring Atget's images to the notice of photographers and collectors. The Museum of Modern Art purchased the collection in 1968 and began to exhibit and publish his work. See John Szarkowski and Maria Morris Hambourg, *The Work of Atget* in four volumes: vol. I, *Old France* (New York: The Museum of Modern Art, 1981); vol. II, *The Art of Old Paris,* 1982; vol. III, *The Ancient Regime,* 1984; and vol. IV, *Modern Times,* 1985.

25   László Moholy-Nagy, *The New Vision* (1928), in *The New Vision and Abstract of an Artist,* trans. by Daphne M. Hoffman, (New York: George Wittenborn, Inc., 1947), 38–39.

26   Julien Levy, *Memory of an Art Gallery* (New York: G. P. Putnam's Sons, 1977), 91.

27   All quotes in this paragraph from László Moholy-Nagy, "Unprecedented Photography," 1927; reprinted in Christopher Phillips, *Photography in the Modern Era: European Documents and Critical Writings, 1913–1940* (New York: The Metropolitan Museum of Art and Aperture, 1989), 83–85.

28   László Moholy-Nagy, "Produktion-Reproduktion," *De Stijl* (Leiden) vol. 5 no. 7 (July 1922) as in Christopher Phillips, *Photography in the Modern Era: European Documents and Critical Writings, 1913–1940* (New York: The Metropolitan Museum of Art and Aperture, 1989), 79–82.

29   Fotoplastik was the term Moholy used to separate his photomontages from the montages of the dadaists. A completed fotoplastik was a finished collage that was photographed by Lucia Moholy and altered in the printing to produce a series of variant images, such as a negative print. The titles, also done with Lucia Moholy, were not intended to be descriptive and were often colloquialisms or made-up words that defy translation.

30   De Stijl ("The Style"), based on the belief that absolute artistic purity is possible, was launched in the Netherlands by Theo van Doesburg and was active from 1917 to 1931. Entirely abstract and aiming towards a purity of vision, De Stijl permitted only the use of the straight line, the right angle, and the three primary colors (red, blue, and yellow), augmented by white, black, and gray.

31   László Moholy-Nagy, "From Pigment to Light," *Telehor,* vol. 1, no. 2, (1936), 32–36 translated and reprinted in Nathan Lyons, ed., *Photographers on Photography* (Englewood Cliffs, NJ: Prentice-Hall, 1966), 80.

32   David Wooters, George Eastman House Print Archivist in conversation with author about Florence Henri's *Composition No. 12,* June 29, 1994.

33   Telephone interview with Diana du Pont, October 24, 1984 in Van Deren Coke with Diana C. du Pont, *Photography: A Facet of Modernism* (New York: Hudson Hills Press in association with the San Francisco Museum of Modern Art, 1986), 58.

34   Ibid.

35   See László Moholy-Nagy, "Space-Time and the Photographer," *American Annual of Photography, 1943* (Boston: American Photographic Publishing, 1942), 7–14.

36   In Drtikol's method an oil print image is transferred onto a litho stone in order to divide tones into half- and quarter-tones, resulting in prints that possess more physical depth than a gelatin silver print and have the light texture of a lithograph. This technique was used to print his book *Les Nus de Drtikol* (1929).

37   Quoted in James Enyeart, *Bruguière: His Photographs and His Life* (New York: Alfred A. Knopf, 1977), 16.

38   Walter Chappell, "Francis Bruguière" *Art in America,* vol. 47, no. 3, (Fall 1959), 59.

39   See Rosalind Krauss et al, eds., *L'Amour fou: Photography and Surrealism* (New York: Abbeville Press, 1985).

40   Artists' books refer to works constructed in a book format, produced in limited editions, and usually only available in art bookstores, galleries, and museums. The term is attributed to Dianne Vanderlip, who arranged the exhibition *Artists Books* at Moore College of Art, Philadelphia, in 1973. Its precursor was work such as William Blake's *The Marriage of Heaven and Hell* (ca. 1790), which he wrote, illustrated, and published with the help of his wife.

41   Neil Baldwin, *Man Ray: American Artist* (Da Capa Press, unabridged republication by arrangement with Clarkson N. Potter, 1988), 139.

42   Arturo Schwarz, *Man Ray: The Rigour of Imagination* (New York: Rizzoli, 1977), 230.

43   After this photograph was made, Duchamp fixed the dust with varnish. The *Large Glass,* eventually evolved into *The Bride Stripped Bare by Her Bachelors, Even* (1915–23).

44   Man Ray, interview, 1951 as quoted in Neil Baldwin, *Man Ray: American Artist,* Chapter 1 opener, unp.

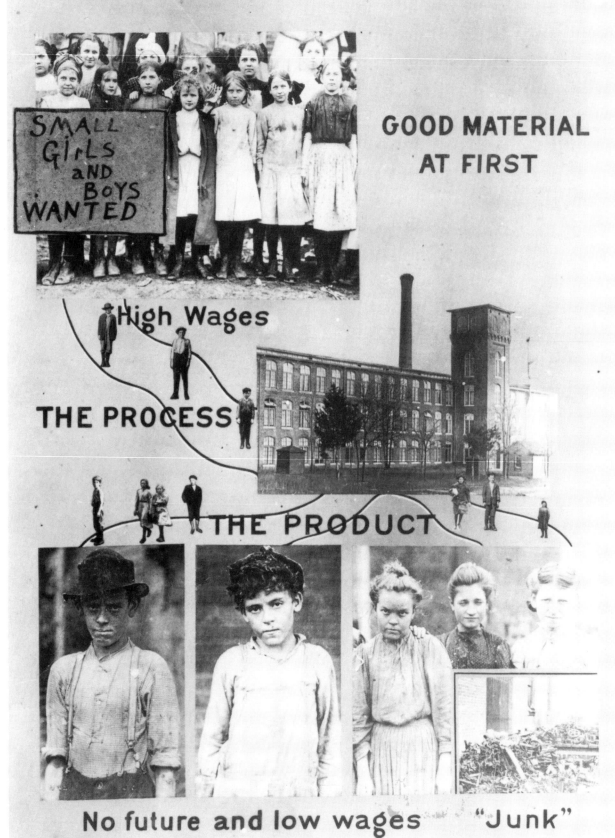

CHAPTER TWELVE

Social Documents

An American Urge: Social Uplift

Millions of European immigrants came to America in the nineteenth century, looking for personal freedom and the opportunity to make a better life. Buffeted by a series of post–Civil War depressions, however, many immigrants were left jobless, hungry, and psychologically beaten down, barely existing in disease-plagued New York City tenements.[1] **Jacob A. Riis** [1849–1914], who came to New York from Denmark in 1870, suffered the degradations of spending more than one night in a police lodging house (for the homeless), tramping the streets in search of work, doing chores for food, and even walking to Philadelphia to look for a job before finding employment with a New York news bureau in 1873. In 1877, Riis became a police reporter in the Mulberry Bend, the East Side's worst slum district. Here more than a million people lived in 37,000 airless, dark, and unhygienic tenement buildings. Forty thousand people a year entered workhouses or asylums,

LEWIS HINE. *Making Human Junk,* poster published in Hine's brochure, "The High Cost of Child Labor," 1915. Courtesy Library of Congress, Prints and Photographs Division.

12.1   JACOB A. RIIS.   *Eldridge Street Police Station Lodger: An Ancient Lodger and the Plank on Which She Slept*, ca. 1888. Gelatin silver print.   Courtesy Jacob A. Riis Collection, © Museum of the City of New York.

thousands of homeless children scavenged for food until they were old enough to join criminal gangs.[2] Reporting on the scandalous conditions as a journalist was not enough for Riis, who wanted to bring about reform: windows in every tenement room, indoor plumbing, tenant rights. Realizing that words did not convey the horrid conditions, Riis turned to photography to document the evidence and used the photographs as weapons for social change. Riis's pioneering efforts at social reform would lead Theodore Roosevelt, then NYC police commissioner, to call Riis "the most useful citizen in New York." The exposing of political and social corruption that Riis and other reformers engaged in became known as *muckraking*.[3]

The hand camera enabled Riis to photograph at night or in low light, in the tenements. Riis used dangerous flashlight powder to illuminate the horrid details of grim poverty: the dirt, the trash, the peeling paint, the starkness of having nothing. The flash cartridges were fired from a

revolver whose explosive discharge would awaken sleepers: Riis set places on fire, ignited his own clothes, and almost blinded himself. He described how he started a fire while photographing a group of blind beggars inside the attic of a tenement: "When the blinding effect of the flash had passed away. . . . I saw the flames creeping up the wall, and my first impulse was to bolt for the street and shout for help. The next was to smother the fire myself, and I did, with a vast deal of trouble."[4] Riis's article for *The Sun* (New York), February 12, 1888, "Flashes from the Slums," illustrated with wood engravings made from photographs, described how his subjects reacted to "the blinding flash . . . the patter of retreating footsteps and the mysterious visitors were gone before they could collect their scattered thoughts and try and find out what it was all about."[5] Riis's hit-and-run strategy can make his images seem dispassionate; he was not concerned, after all, with individuals but with the collective problems of the group. Nevertheless, his images offered a first public glimpse into the unmerciful, claustrophobic life of destitution by someone who had been there too.

Riis was interested in obtaining photographs to illustrate his widely attended reformist lectures, in which he introduced the concept of "social uplift." Riis saw

12.2   *Lunch Hour,* 1949. Poster, from a series, designed by Ernst Halberstadt, based on Lewis Hine's *Breaker Boys in Coal Chutte, South Pittston, Pa.,* 1911. 11 × 28 inches. Photo-mechanical reproduction.   Courtesy George Eastman House.

poverty, crime, ignorance, and vice as the effects, rather than the causes, of poverty. People needed government and private programs to raise themselves out of poverty and to instill middle-class values. Social uplift has been disputed by some who see it as patronizing and others who say it is expensive and ineffective, but food stamps and the Medicaid program are part of the legacy of this crusade. Riis did not see himself as a photographer; photographs were only one component of his social crusade. Riis wanted to make his case as persuasively as possible and toward this end he enlisted Richard Hoe Lawrence and Dr. Henry G. Piffard, members of the Society of Amateur Photographers of New York, to make pictures under his direction. This explains the varying styles of what became known as the Riis photographs, from the stark and confrontational to the near picturesque. In his lectures, Riis presented facts on the tenement problem: population density, death rates, immigration rates, and police statistics. He did not rely on the rational to achieve results, however, but crafted entertaining and emotional lectures, appealing to the heart and the hankie. Riis understood that a photograph's narrative content was fluid and could be directed to create meaning and symbols. By synthesizing music, lights, and lantern slides, Riis played to his audience's family and religious values, pressing for reforms such as razing the worst slums and constructing "pocket" neighborhood parks, settlement houses, and schools.

Although Riis claimed to be a clumsy photographer, uninterested in aesthetics or technique, the images produced under his direction have profoundly influenced social documentary practice. Riis did not idealize, sentimentalize, or arrange his subjects into pleasing compositions to explain the difficulties of industrial transformation. The pictures reveal the problems of explosive urban growth and increased ethnic diversity that were causing major societal upheavals without calling attention to their construction. The randomness of the compositions lends authenticity while the chance recordings of the unexpected add authority. By juxtaposing sympathetic subjects with their dilapidated surroundings, Riis made a case for social response, by insisting that *the other* does not have to live like this.

His book, *How the Other Half Lives* (1890),[6] included seventeen halftone illustrations and nineteen line drawings based on his photographs, along with text calling for action. The halftone process for translating photographs into printer's ink had not been perfected and so the photographs lacked detail and sharpness: even so, the book is a landmark in American social reform.[7] Riis showed how photography in a printed form in combination with text, could direct social activity. Although Riis was not free from prejudice, he was an indefatigable magic lantern lecturer, and his blend of amusement and instruction influenced civic-minded people to act. When Theodore Roosevelt was governor of New York, he worked with Riis to institute reforms. As an early photojournalist reformer, Riis continued to lecture and eventually published over a dozen books, including his autobiography, *The Making of an American* (1901).

As part of this American wave of social reform, **Lewis Wickes Hine** [1874–1940], a sociologist from Columbia University who became interested in artistic photography, began to photograph at Ellis Island in 1904, where 71 percent of all immigrants to America landed between 1892 and 1924.[8] Hine taught camera courses and took his students, such as Paul Strand, to Stieglitz's "291." As a teacher at the Ethical Culture School in New York, a vital setting for the progressive movement, Hine used photography to combat the rampant prejudice against the newly arrived peoples from eastern and southern Europe. Using a 5 × 7-inch camera, Hine revealed the potential of these individuals. Hine's subjects appear to be aware of the camera and cooperative in constructing an image whose structure and use of light is empowering. His sympathetic style challenged accusations that the "new" immigrants, unlike the "old" immigrants from England, Ireland, and northern Europe, were morally and socially depraved and responsible for crime, corruption, labor unrest, political radicalism, and the slums. Hine outlined the beliefs that made his photographs potent weapons for change:

> The picture is the language of all nationalities and all ages. . . . the average person believes implicitly that the photograph cannot falsify. . . . This unbounded faith in the integrity of the photograph is often rudely shaken, for, while photographs may not lie, liars may photograph. It becomes necessary, then, in our revelation of the truth, to see to it that the camera we depend upon contracts no bad habits.[9]

This outlook would separate Hine's work from earlier reportage and formulate his "documentary" style that combined objective facts with subjective emotions into what Cornell Capa would later call the attitude of the "concerned photographer" (see Chapter 14).

Between 1906 and 1918, Hine photographed for the National Child Labor Committee (NCLA). He was assigned to photograph for the *Pittsburgh Survey* (1909), whose massive six-volume report on the city's industrial conditions was a pivotal document of the reform movement. Here Hine learned the methods of case studies, statistics, and surveys that made up the budding discipline of sociology. The NCLA needed facts documenting abuses of children in the workplace in order to pass protective legislation. Hine collected information about the children he photographed, including their name, age, height, weight, nature of their work, how long they had been on the job, and any work-related injuries, so as to "refute those who, either optimistically or hypocritically, spread the news that there is no child labor."[10] The act of naming people and placing them in time transformed Hine's images from the general to specific, making them appear genuine. Decades later, labor unions continued to make use of his images in their "before and after" campaigns to show how they had improved the lives of American children (see Figure 12.2).

Hine, generally an unwanted visitor at industrial sites, developed ingenious ways to make his images, posing as a fire inspector, postcard vendor, Bible salesman, and as an industrial photographer who needed a child standing next to a machine to provide a sense of scale. Working quickly with available light, which necessitated large apertures and limited his depth-of-field, Hine gave up fine art references, recording instead the dirty details of the industrial landscape and its small, forlorn, ill-clad inhabitants. With less artistic stratagem, Hine's pictures had a more immediate impact, a sense of being objective records.

Hine exposed the myth that everyone could pull themselves up by their bootstraps and succeed in America. Moralistic tales, such as Horatio Alger, Jr.'s *Ragged Dick,* encouraged the capitalist rags-to-riches fable that in a "free country poverty in early life is no bar to a man's advancement."[11] Destroying these fictions would discourage the rationalization of child labor as a training camp for junior capitalists. Hine made the process of labor, the people who labored, rather than the products of labor the focal point of his images. He laid open the fable of consumerism, in which people enjoyed mass-produced products without considering their negative repercussions—the sweatshops, the dangerous working conditions, unemployment, and pollution.

Hine produced both visual and written material for exhibition and publication. As early as 1910, Hine was creating picture sequences, forerunners of the photo-essay, for *Survey* magazine. His cropped images have captions to contextualize the meaning of the image, instituting a narrative format that editors would refer to as the "photo story." Hine developed "Time Exposures," a series of photographs of the same subject, from different points of view, collaged with text, offering a descriptive and interpretive analysis that clarified a situation in need of change. Hine also designed didactic collages that portrayed a greedy industry converting healthy children into "Human Junk" (see chapter opener). Hine referred to himself as an "interruptive photographer" who understood the chameleonlike nature of the photograph and realized that a knowledgeable person did not have to just take a picture but could make an image and use text to direct viewers to a predetermined conclusion. "With a picture," Hine stated in 1909, "thus sympathetically interpreted, what a lever we have for the social uplift."[12] Hine's work appeared in books, magazines, pamphlets, slide lectures, and traveling exhibits, helping to mobilize public concern to pass legislation reforming the child labor laws in the 1910s.

In 1930, Hine undertook his last major project: photographs of the men who built the Empire State Building. Following the construction over 102 vertigo-producing steel stories, Hine had himself swung out in midair with his view camera to record the final rivet being installed on the pinnacle of the building. These dangerous efforts celebrate the mythological spirit of labor, not the building, a counterpoint to the growing feeling in American cities that people had become insignificant in the urban landscape. Unlike the work of those interested in the beauty of the machine, Hine's compositions juxtaposed human and machine characteristics (see Figure 12.3). Often emphasizing the faces of the workers, Hine stepped away from the massive and flawless authority of industry to show how humans fit into industrial progress. The resulting innovative photographic picture book, *Men at Work* (1932), contained full-bled pages and unadorned typography.

12.3 LEWIS HINE.   *Steelworker, 85 stories up. Look-ing north to Central Park,* ca. 1931. 6⅝ × 4⅝ inches. Gelatin silver print.   In *Men at Work,* Hine summed up his position on the friction between humans and tech-nology by writing: "Cities do not build themselves, ma-chines cannot make machines. . . . We call this the Machine Age. But the more machines we use the more do we need real men to make and direct them. . . . I will take you into the heart of modern industry . . . where the character of the men is being put into the motors, the airplanes, the dynamos upon which the life and happiness of millions of us depend."[13]   Courtesy George Eastman House.

Ethnological Approaches

During the nineteenth century, photography was placed in the service of numerous ethnological theo-ries as a technically powerful means for imposing positivist classifications on nonindustrial cultures (see Figure 12.4). Photographers made images from their own view, as outsiders, and distributed them; thus they established and controlled another group's visual identity.

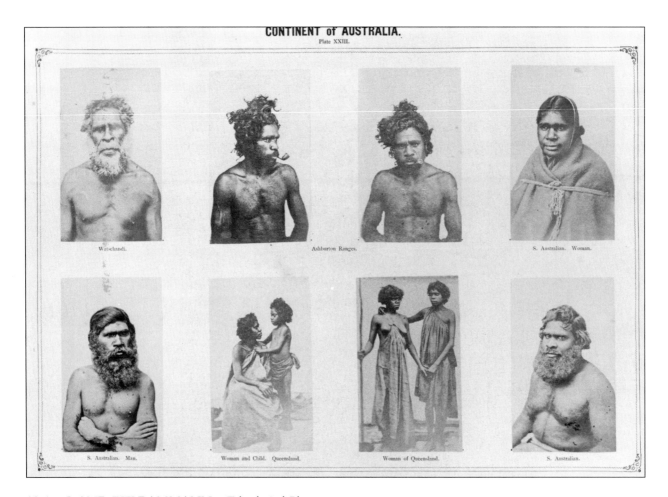

CONTINENT of AUSTRALIA.
Plate XXIII.

Watschandi.   Ashburton Ranges.   S. Australian. Woman.

S. Australian. Man.   Woman and Child. Queensland.   Woman of Queensland.   S. Australian.

12.4   C. AND F. W. DAMMANN   *Ethnological Photographic Gallery of the Various Races of Men,* Plate 23. 12$^{7}/_{16}$ × 15$^{15}/_{16}$ inches. C. and F. W. Dammann's *Ethnological Photographic Gallery of the Various Races of Men* typifies the British colonial attitude as it presents eight carte-sized plates of native people in the "Continent of Australia" section with this accompanying text: "There is a great diversity in the characters of the different tribes; many are intelligent and inoffensive, some are fierce and in a state of the rudest barbarism. There is no doubt that some of the tribes indulge in cannibalism." (Stoke's *Australia*).[14]   Courtesy George Eastman House.

Adam Clark Vroman [1856–1916] was one photographer who took a less invasive approach. Between 1895 and 1904, Vroman photographed Hopi, Navajo, Zuni, Laguna, and Acoma peoples to record a way of life that was rapidly vanishing, bringing the first reports of the Pueblo aesthetic back to cluttered, eastern Victorian homes. Vroman's modernistic portrayals have been considered honest and unpretentious; he did not create a pictorialist, romantic "noble savage" or conceal nontraditional elements. Vroman respected the dignity and privacy of his subjects at a time when tourists were invading holy Native American sites and ignoring restrictions on photographing sacred ceremonies and dances. Disrespectful and insensitive behavior by white pho-

tographers who treated the Hopi snake dance (a sixteen-day rain prayer) as an exotic spectacle of "otherness" eventually led the Hopi to first restrict and then ban all photographers from the dance in the early twentieth century (see Figure 12.5). Vroman spent time in the villages, obtained people's trust, and returned with prints for his sitters to demonstrate good faith. Vroman gave slide lectures to white Americans, helping alter the distorted, stereotypical depiction of Native Americans as subhuman, bloodthirsty savages.

A photographer who made a career of photographing Native Americans was **Edward Sheriff Curtis** [1868–1952]. As a teenager, Curtis built his own camera and taught himself photography, and in the early 1890s he opened a photography and photoengraving business in Seattle. Curtis learned ethnographic methods as the official photographer for the Harriman Expedition to Alaska (1899). Between 1900 and 1906, Curtis and his assistants photographed native Americans of the Northwest, Southwest, and Great Plains. Curtis traveled and lived with Native Americans at a time when the Bureau of Indian Affairs was suppressing native religious ceremonies. In an era when respectable scientists considered native groups as an early phase of evolution and white domination a Darwinian triumph, many native people were willing to reenact scenes of traditional life for posterity.

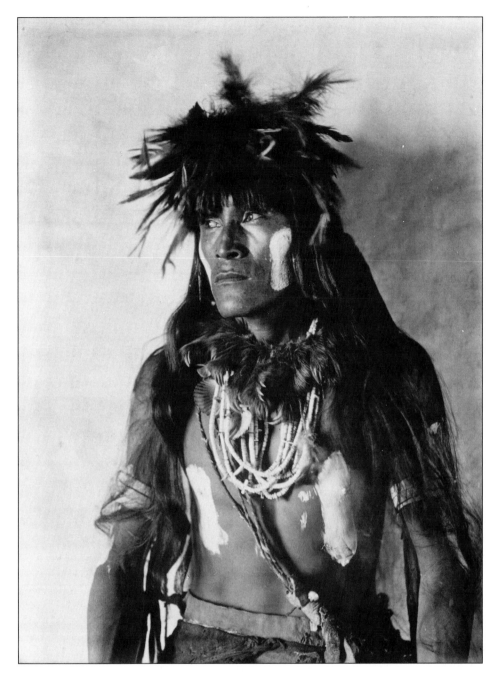

12.5 ADAM VROMAN. *The Snake Priest, Hopi,*
1901. 8¼ × 6³⁄₁₆ inches. Gelatin silver print. Numerous
native groups do not believe in making permanent
records of sacred events out of reverence for the original. The legacy of outside groups, beginning with the
Spanish, suppressing native religious life and forcing
them to carry on their rites in secret, also made them
suspicious of whites who wanted to record their ceremonies, which they feared could be used as evidence
for additional repression.   Courtesy George Eastman
House.

Curtis was not an objective documentarian. His
work applied a white European cultural filter to native
life, combining romantic, soft-focus pictorial methods
with the ethnological to manufacture a nostalgic view
of the vanishing noble savage. Curtis suppressed evidence of assimilation and manipulated his images for
emotional effect. Costumes, wigs, props, and backdrops were transported from one group to another for
picturesque purposes. Sculptural lighting, silhouettes,
touched-up highlights, and print burning and dodging
were used to produce formal, dramatic, and dignified
portraits (see Figure 12.6).

From 1900 to 1930, Curtis worked with about eighty
native groups, producing some 40,000 images. He
wrote four books, supervised sixteen others, made

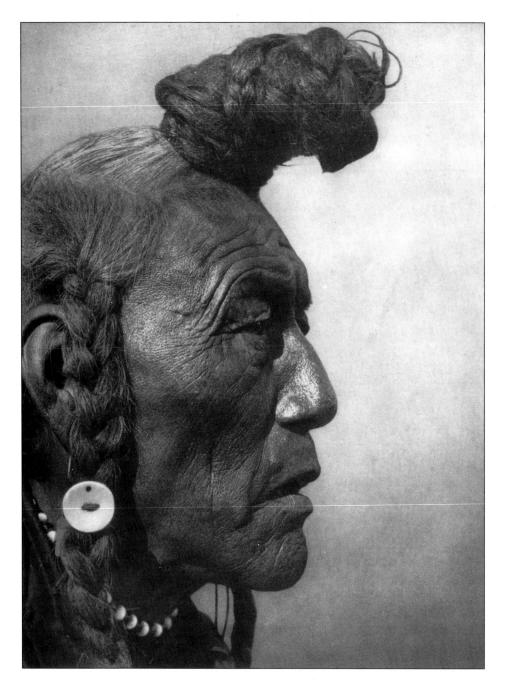

12.6   EDWARD CURTIS.   *Bear Bull—Blackfoot.*
From *The North American Indian,* vol. 18, plate 640, ca.
1926. 15⅝6 × 11⅞6 inches. Photogravure. Curtis manipulated the contents of scenes for pictorial effect and removed or retouched all evidence of the modern world
in an effort to recreate an authentic past that was in the
process of slipping away.   Courtesy George Eastman House.

more than 10,000 recordings of native language and
music, and recreated northwest coast native life on a set
for his silent film, *In the Land of the Headhunters*
(1910–14). His monumental work, *The North American Indian* (1907–30), contains almost 2,200 images,
with twenty volumes of text, each of about 350 pages.
Only 250 editions, printed in photogravure to achieve

brilliant luminous effects and unusual depth, were published. The original plates were rediscovered in 1977
and their partial reprinting brought Curtis's work back
into public attention.

Although it is criticized for its racist attitudes and romantic treatment of native people as exotica, Curtis's fabricated work continues to provide the only evidence of artifacts, costumes, ceremonies, dances, games, legends,
and songs of many tribes' previous existence. There was
no market for the realism of reservation despair, but with
the Native Americans' complicity, Curtis used his narrative skills to recreate idealized symbols of a vanished
time in the West. Made during an era of unrestrained industrialization, Curtis's ennobling treatments continue to
represent the timeless myth of the virtuous primitive.

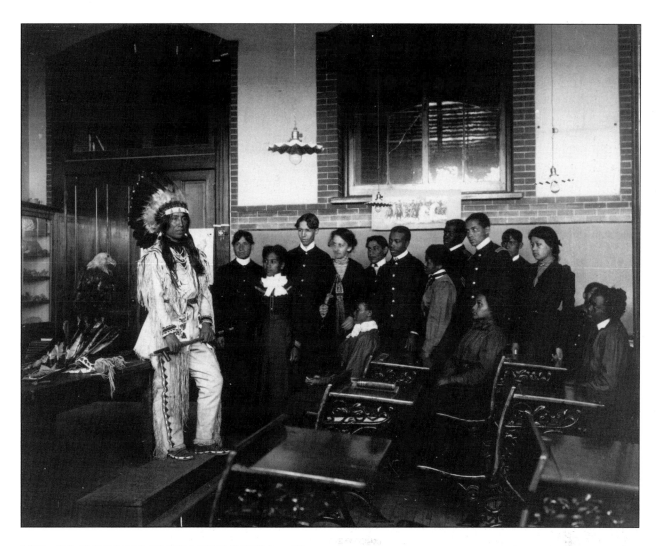

12.7   FRANCES BENJAMIN JOHNSTON.   *Class in American History, 1899.* From the *Hampton Album.* 7½ × 9½ inches. Platinum print.   © 1998 Museum of Modern Art, New York. Gift of Lincoln Kirstein.

Racial exploitation and idealistic myths were also being perpetrated through photographic means in the East. **Frances Benjamin Johnston** [1864–1952] received her first camera from a family friend, George Eastman, and in the early 1890s opened a studio in Washington, D.C. Johnston encouraged women to consider careers in photography by writing articles and arranging shows and publications to serve women photographers. Through her friend Gertrude Käsebier, Johnston experimented with pictorialism and in 1904 became an associate member of the Photo-Secession. Johnston did commercial assignments around the theme of the workplace. Her most widely known images were for a Virginia school, the Hampton Institute, dedicated to the reformist ideal of industrial training to eliminate poverty among rural Native- and African-Americans. At the turn of the nineteenth century, the "Hampton Idea," typified by its most famous graduate, Booker T. Washington [1856–1915],[15] was championed as a remedy for racial troubles by

bringing the "light of civilization" to the nation's "darker races." Johnston's Hampton prints, originally produced for the Paris Exposition of 1900, were later numbered, captioned, and placed in a leather album. During the 1940s, the album was donated to the Museum of Modern Art, where it was eventually exhibited and published in an abridged version as the *Hampton Album* in 1966.

Johnston's tableaus offered a version of the white American Dream with faces of color. Her immaculately constructed, almost sculptural "friezes" dramatize the Hampton philosophy. Viewers get a privileged look at humble students learning the white man's ways. The captions stress that students are receiving a plain, utilitarian education. Images such as *Class in American History*, 1899, can be compared with Rejlander's *Two Ways of Life,* where a person comes to a crossroads and must decide whether to take the hard route of righteousness or the lazy path of wickedness. In Johnston's allegory viewers observe the stereotypical Native American warrior as a specimen of the old (bad) picturesque wild west dramatically juxtaposed with the new (good) examples of Hampton's "specimens." The photographs are proof that the Hampton program could assist Native- and African-Americans to become

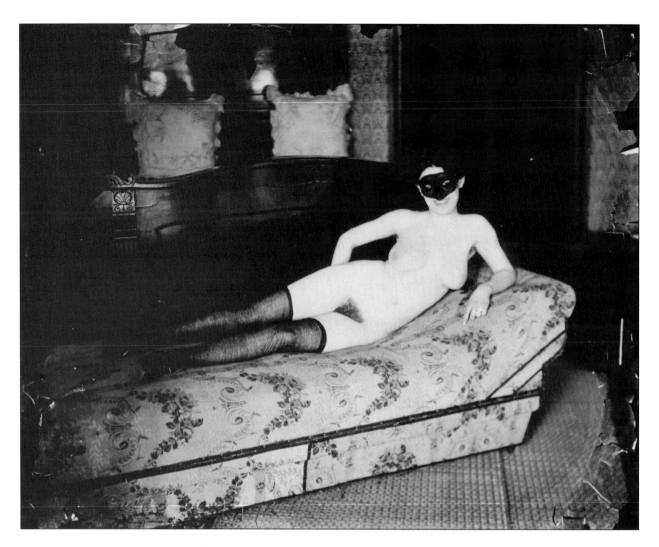

12.8   E. J. BELLOCQ.   *Storeyville Portraits: Untitled, Plate 27 (Reclining Nude with a Mask)*, ca. 1912. 8 × 10 inches. Gelatin silver print.   Courtesy Frankel Gallery, San Francisco.

productive members of civilized, white culture. The participants, including a symbolic stuffed American eagle sitting on a table, appear as a lifeless diorama, celebrating the conservative belief that sheer determination leads to a quick transformation. Nobody is out of position, implying that Hampton students follow orders and maintain discipline. Viewers are free to examine their space and give a blessing without having to participate.

The *Hampton Album* reminds us how difficult it is to critically examine the concepts that influence our thinking. Johnston shows how our beliefs influence how we see, make, and interpret images. Johnston's beguilingly formalistic images continue to deliver racist messages, just as Leni Riefenstahl's *Triumph of the Will* (1935)[16] beautifies the ideals of Hitler's Third Reich. The reformist faith in the American Dream was so deep, however, that it never seemed wrong to impose it on others. By examining the original thinking behind and the con-

text of such documentary work and comparing it with contemporary beliefs, we can gain an understanding of the "truth" of those underlying ideologies that the photographer wanted to convey.

Photography offers photographers a social license to interact with other, nonmainstream people and situations that they may find disturbing, problematic, or unfamiliar, and share their impressions with the curious who wish to vicariously scrutinize these circumstances. **E. J. Bellocq** [1873–1949] was a New Orleans commercial photographer who used photography to explore the forbidden world of prostitutes. Not much is known about the surviving plates made in the Storyville red light district, except that they convey a sense of complicity between the male gaze and the female sitter.[17] Although the atmosphere is a mix of lassitude, resignation, and sexuality, no sexual acts or men are depicted, and some of the photographs offer no clues that the women were prostitutes. Overall, the images wrestle with penetrating the veil of languor and suppressed desire in a way not possible before photography. Even the most explicit, where the woman is presented in dark surroundings as a mysterious sexual

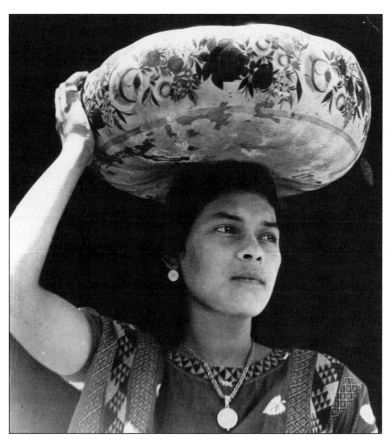

12.9   TINA MODOTTI.   *Woman of Tehuantepec,* ca. 1929. 3¼ × 2¹⁵⁄₁₆ inches. Gelatin silver print. Modotti's strongest iconic images combined the pure formal clarity of Weston, the elegant composition of Vermeer, and the social/political concerns of the Mexicanidad movement into a geometric balance that emphasized the heroic qualities of Mexico's working class people.
Courtesy George Eastman House.

stead of the hard, direct light that Weston used to emphasize mass and texture. Modotti was willing to challenge Weston's purist axioms and would crop or enlarge a negative to make the final image. As a documentarian of Mexican workers, Modotti merged her work into a "place in social production" consistent with the symbols and doctrines of communist *social realism* that favored didactic illustration of political subjects and forbade abstraction.[18] Modotti considered photography as the muralists regarded mural painting: as a democratic art. Unfortunately this led some of her later work, like *Mexican Sombrero with Hammer and Sickle* (1927), and *Bandolier, Corn, Sickle* (1927), which attempt to join art with propaganda, to become preachy clichés. Modotti eventually abandoned photography in favor of overt political activism, stating, "I put too much art in my life—too much energy—and consequently I have not much left to give to art."[19] Her sympathetic treatment of Mexican working people can be seen as part of an embryonic awakening of a new type of ethnic/social consciousness that would change not only how photographs looked but who was making them.

Emerging Ethnic Consciousness

During the first decades of the twentieth century, entrepreneurs of diverse ethnic backgrounds opened photographic businesses to make cultural records within their own communities. Minority photographers, like **Richard Throssel** [1882–1933] faced the challenge of surviving in a commercial world that would not hire them.[20] Their circumstances rarely provided the financial freedom or leisure time to do personal work, and their personal interests had to be consolidated into their daily studio work.

Horace Poolaw [1906–1984] was a Kiowa who became one of the first Native American professional photographers. Poolaw used a straight style to present an insider's view of the difficult relationship between natives and non-natives. Poolaw's best work juxtaposes the traditional and the modern, astutely representing the incongruities and underlying difficulties of forced cultural assimilation (see Figure 12.10). Poolaw's inclusion of "anachronisms," such as six-packs of soda, breaks down what critic Lucy Lipard refers to as "the time-honored distance between Them and Us, the illusion that They

object, is countered by the fantasy of availability in the woman's expression that hints at the pleasures to be had once the masks between the observer and the observed are lifted. Some recently published Bellocq images show scratched-out women's faces, lending the pictures a kind of licentiousness. The aggressive cancellation of their faces by an anonymous hand hints at the vulnerable position of people who offer their bodies for sale and, by proxy, shows how the making of a photograph of any powerless other always places the photographer in the judgment seat.

Tina Modotti [1896–1942] was indicative of a new generation—socially involved artists who saw the camera as a tool for cultural change, balancing formalism with human content. Modotti had an intimate as well as a working relationship with Edward Weston from 1922 to 1930, whose photographs were not made for political or social purpose. Modotti preferred flat light that favored the linear qualities of the subject in-

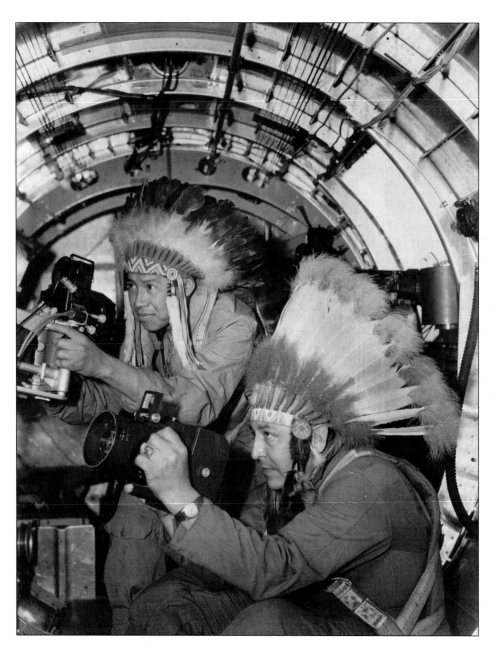

12.10   HORACE POOLAW.   *Horace Poolaw, Aerial Photographer, and Gus Palmer, Gunner, MacDill Air Base, Tampa, FL, ca. 1944.* 12¼ × 9⁹⁄₁₆ inches. Gelatin silver print.   Poolaw's photographs often reveal the contradictions and irony of the Kiowa life-style as it underwent rapid transition during the first half of the twentieth century. After World War II broke out Poolaw enlisted in Army Air Corps (the Kiowa's ancestral enemy) where he trained young men in aerial photography. "Because young Kiowa men were expected to become warriors, many of Poolaw's contemporaries joined the armed forces feeling that this was not only their patriotic duty as Americans, but an opportunity to fulfill traditional roles."[21]   Courtesy Stanford University. Horace Poolaw Photography Project.

live in different times than We do. 'Anachronisms' may also be somewhat threatening to Our peace of mind, recalling how They got There (the Reservation), were put There, in a space that is separated from Us by the barbed wire of "absentee colonialism."[22]

One of the best known studios serving the African-American community was run by **James VanDerZee** [1886–1983], who began an eighty-year career when he bought a mail-order camera and set up a darkroom in his bedroom closet as a teenager.[23] Opening his first Harlem studio in 1916, VanDerZee made portraits of members of the Harlem Renaissance of the 1920s, including religious leader Adam Clayton Powell, Sr., comedian Florence Mills, dancer/actor Bill "Bojangles" Robinson, and activist Marcus Gravey, founder of the Back-to-Africa movement. VanDerZee's romantic representations of the black middle and upper classes provided records of fam-

12.11   JAMES VANDERZEE.   *Future Expectations,*
1925. 8 × 10 inches. Gelatin silver print. Photo by
James VanDerZee. © Donna VanDerZee, New York.

ily and social events while testifying to the private
achievement, aspiration, and elegance of a people beginning their struggle for racial equality. VanDerZee was expert at using light, composition, props, retouching, and
montage to achieve a flattering, positive, sometimes sentimental ambiance of a life seldom seen by outsiders who
were accustomed to viewing degrading images of black
life (see Figure 12.11). Deborah Willis says his work defines "a people in the process of transformation and a culture in transition . . . VanDerZee presented in visual terms
the growing sense of personal, and national identity of his
sitters, underpinning this is the thoroughly modern sensibility with which he confronted the issue of race."[24]

Writer **Eudora Welty** [b. 1909] made "snapshots"
from the position of an outsider who wanted to honestly
represent another group. While working for the Works
Progress Administration (WPA), Welty traveled through
the nation's poorest state, Mississippi, writing articles
about the WPA Projects for local newspapers. On her
own, Welty used a Kodak to picture the people she encountered and upon returning home made prints in her
kitchen at night. The merit of Welty's work is in its human subject matter. Welty's book, *One Time, One Place,*

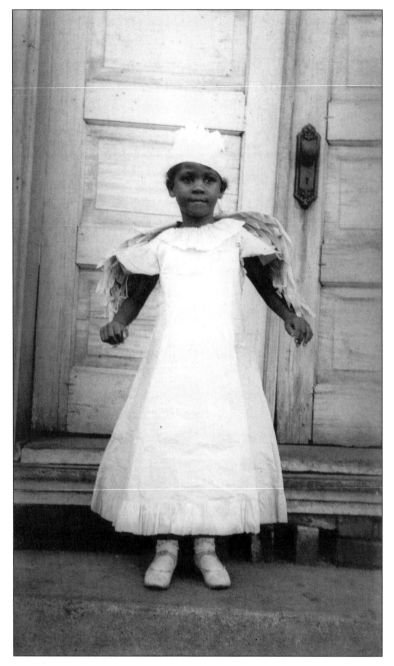

12.12   EUDORA WELTY.   *Baby Bluebird, Bird Pageant, Jackson, MS.* Size varies. Gelatin silver print. Welty learned "a story-writer's truth: the thing to wait on, to reach there in time for, is the moment in which people reveal themselves. . . . Insight doesn't happen often on the click of the moment, like a lucky snapshot, but comes in its own time and more slowly and from nowhere but within. . . . My continuing passion, would be not to point the finger in judgment but to part a curtain, that invisible shadow that falls between people, the veil of indifference to each other's presence, each other's wonder, each other's human plight."[25]   Courtesy Eudora Welty Collection, Mississippi Department of Archives and History, Jackson, MS.

Mississippi in the Depression: A Snapshot Album (1971), is not an anthropological study but "a family album"[26] of individuals with whom she was "well positioned [to photograph], moving through the scene openly and yet invisibly because I was part of it, born into it, taken for granted."[27] Welty noted that many of the people she photographed had never had their picture taken before; by photographing them, she was "able to give something back" to her subjects. Pictures like those of the Bird Pageant (see Figure 12.12) "were made at the invitation, and under the direction, of its originator. . . . I would not have dared to interfere with the poses."[28] Welty was aware of the difficulties of photographing outside one's own group. She stated:

> In taking all these pictures, I was attended . . . by an angel—a presence of trust. In particular, the photographs of black persons by a white person may not testify soon again to such intimacy. It is trust that dates the pictures now, more than the vanished years. . . . I was too busy imagining myself into their lives to be open to any generalities.[29]

The Physiognomic Approach

From photography's earliest days, police had hired daguerreotypists to record criminals' faces. By the 1870s, police mug shots were used for visual identification and in "wanted" posters. French police first used photographs to identify rebels during the revolutionary Commune of Paris uprising of 1871, leading Alphonse Bertillon to standardize the practice and its accompanying data, known as *bertillonage,* in 1872.[30] By the 1880s, Paris police had 90,000 images on file, and the production of photographs for court evidence was standard practice.[31] Photographs were displayed in rogue's galleries and circulated in albums such as Thomas Byrnes' *Professional Criminals of America* (1886), which contained over 200 photographs of important and dangerous criminals along with descriptions of their methods and records.

The use of photography and technology by government to guarantee its own authority and economic interest by isolating and classifying individuals has grown in importance during the twentieth century. Contemporary social critics Michel Foucault,[32] Allan Sekula, and John Tagg all expressed concern about photography's role in controlling people. Tagg linked the modern police force

Copyright, 1884, by Thomas Byrnes.   Heliotype Printing Co., Boston.

THE INSPECTOR'S MODEL.

12.13   THOMAS BYRNES.   *The Inspectors Model,*
1884. From *Professional Criminals of America,* 1886. *Photomechanical reproduction.* Offenders did not always want to
cooperate with police. In *The Inspectors Model* (1884),
four men struggle to hold a prisoner so that his picture
can be taken as Byrnes, the inspector, looks on. Byrnes
described the importance of photographing criminals:
"Deception is their business [and] there are many—
who carry no suggestion of their calling about them . . .
men who lead double lives."[33] Yet Byrnes also comments: "Is physiognomy any guide? A very poor one.
Judge for yourself. Look through the Rogue's Gallery
and see how many rascals you find there who resemble
the best people in the country."[34]

with industrial capitalism's need to protect the means of
production, labor, from which it draws its profit. Tagg
believes police continue to use photography, from
photographing speeders to mounting video cameras on
lamp posts, to intimidate and pacify by using "observa-
tion-domination" techniques to compile "forms of conduct, attitudes, possibilities, suspicions: a permanent account of individual's behaviour."[35]

Control can also be exercised though more insidious
means. For centuries, Europeans had been fascinated by
the *physiognomic* approach that depicted society through
hierarchies of function, position, and trade. Many still believe that body type and facial expression provide a window onto one's inner moral character and that photography offers a truthful method of revealing these facts. The
Western belief in positivism went hand in hand with
physiognomy. In 1912, **August Sander** [1879–1964] began a sociological study of the German people by making
their portraits. He bicycled through the farming country
with his view-camera and tripod looking for new subjects, beginning a systematic approach to "collecting"
people from German society. Sander's straightforward,
unretouched portraits, generally made at eye-level, used a
large lens aperture to convert the landscape into a neutral
setting, similar to a seamless studio backdrop, placing attention on the subject (see Figure 12.14).

His concern for direct representation was shared by
the practitioners of the *new objectivity,* whose rational-
ist beliefs led them to probe beneath the surface in
hopes of uncovering universal knowledge. Although
World War I had annihilated the idea that civilization

12.14   AUGUST SANDER.   *Prize-Winning Choral Club, Westerwald,* 1927. 11¾ × 8¼ inches. Gelatin silver print.   ©Die Photographische Samsung/SK Siftung Kultur–August Sander Archiv, Cologne, ARS, New York, 1999.

was advancing toward a new rational order, the survivors wanted proof that there was an intrinsic natural order waiting to be uncovered. Sander's tactics reflected these concerns as well as the institutionalized, medieval hierarchies that permeated German culture. Through precise attention to the details of dress, environment, expression, and pose and a sense for the sym-

bolic, Sander's "naturalistic" portraits respectfully represent a pictorial sociology of faces that reveal cultural and economic history and the struggle to accept the difference between social position and the person who inhabits that position. Sander printed on glossy paper, normally reserved for architectural and technical illustration, after friends told him it simplified and reduced personal interpretation and made the image more objective.[36] Sander planned to publish a series of books covering his project, "Man in the Twentieth Century," but only the first volume, *Antlitz der Zeit (Face of Our Time)*, appeared in 1929.[37] The Nazis, who used the

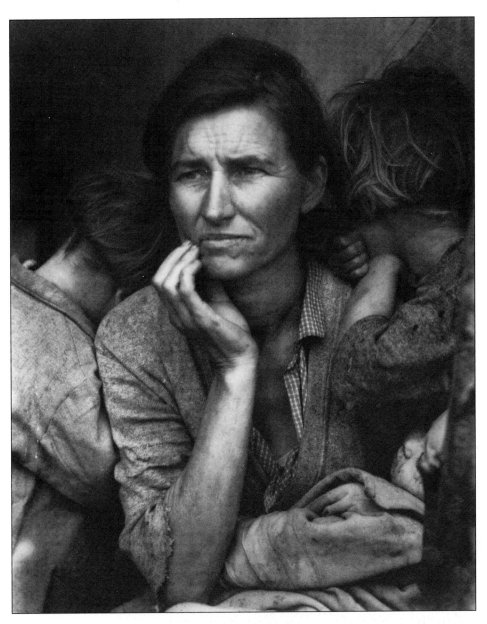

12.15 DOROTHEA LANGE. *Migrant Mother, Nipomo, Cal., 1936.* Gelatin silver print. Stryker called *Migrant Mother*: "*the* picture of Farm Security.... She has all the suffering of mankind in her but all the perseverance too. A restraint and a strange courage. You can see anything you want to in her. She is immortal."[38] The success of this image overshadowed Lange's other accomplishments, especially her humanizing of compositional formalism in a documentary style that was used in other projects with Paul Taylor such as *An American Exodus: A Road of Human Erosion* (1939). Copyright the Dorothea Lange Collection, The Oakland Museum of California, The City of Oakland, Gift of Paul S. Taylor.

same physiognomic approach to spread racial hatred, banned the book in 1934, destroyed the printing plates, and seized the negatives, because it revealed a diversity of physical characteristics that did not match their genetic mythology. Sander then took up landscape and nature photography. He continued working after World War II, modeling an objective approach to a documentary style that viewed photography as an accurate notary with a humane duty to perform.

The Great Depression: The Economics of Photography

In 1935, President Franklin Delano Roosevelt created the Resettlement Administration (RA), headed by former Columbia University economics professor and

12.16   WALKER EVANS.   *Window Display of Photographer's Studio, Birmingham, AL,* 1936. 9½ × 7½ inches. Gelatin silver print. Evans's style builds on the force of specific, familiar details, transforming them into a universally recognized pattern of facts. Evans could see beneath the surface of the ordinary and uncover the extraordinary without commentary, footnotes, or statistics. His deceptively laconic head-on presentation of the facts, just before what feels like a looming collapse, have influenced how imagemakers view vernacular architecture and the American Main Street scene of signs and gas stations.
© Walker Evans Archive, The Metropolitan Museum of Art.

Undersecretary of Agriculture Rexford G. Tugwell. The RA's purpose was to aid poor, rural Americans who were uprooted from their tenant farms during the 1930s Depression and forced to move to urban areas and find industrial jobs. Tugwell appointed his former student and co-worker, Roy E. Stryker [1893–1975], as chief of the historical section. Stryker's job included implementing Tugwell's idea of using photography to showcase the agency's work and American rural life. Stryker was influenced by Lewis Hine, whom he knew from using his photographs to illustrate Tugwell's textbook, *American Economic Life*

12.17   WALKER EVANS.   *Floyd Burroughs, a cotton sharecropper Hale County, AL,* 1936. 9½ × 7½ inches. Gelatin silver print.   © Walker Evans Archive, The Metropolitan Museum of Art.

(1925). Stryker hired photographers like Walker Evans, Dorothea Lange, Carl Mydans [b. 1907], and Arthur Rothstein for the project. Tugwell's goal was to show urban America a desperate situation and enlist popular support for Roosevelt's new programs of grants, loans, and resettlement money to displaced farmers. Depending on funding levels, many other photographers, including Ben Shahn, Russell Lee, Jack Delano [1914–1997], Marion Post Wolcott, John Vachon [1914–1975], John Collier, Jr., Gordon Parks, and Theo Jung [b. 1906], worked on the project. While the group is generally referred to as the Farm

Security Administration (FSA) project, the FSA was not officially organized until 1937, when the Resettlement Administration was absorbed into the Department of Agriculture.[39]

To carry out the mission, Stryker held briefings, gave reading assignments, conducted critiques, and developed shooting scripts for the field assignments, formulating an official FSA documentary style. Stryker established a network of publishing contacts to ensure that the images would reach their intended audiences. In the field, photographers developed their film, wrote captions, and sent materials back to Washington for editing, printing, and publication. Stryker was an unrivaled producer, who maintained the balanced distance between photographers, bureaucrats, media, and public necessary to implement Tugwell's idea: "We

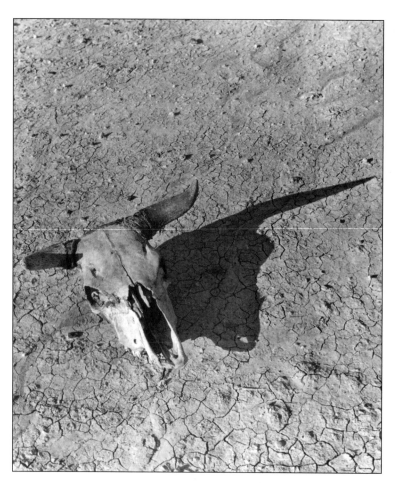

12.18 ARTHUR ROTHSTEIN. *Steer Skull, Bad-lands, SD*, 1936. 12⅝ × 10⁵⁄₁₆ inches. Gelatin silver print. Courtesy George Eastman House.

introduced Americans to Americans."[40] Stryker summed up what he saw as the difference between his strategy and that of the print media:

> Newspictures are the noun and verb; our kind of photography is the adjective and adverb. The newspicture is a single frame; ours a subject viewed in series. The newspicture is dramatic, all subject and action. Ours show what's back of the action.[41]

The middle-class audience, at which these pictures were aimed, was not aware of the stylized approach and considered the images accurate documents. The term "documentary" has been consistently mistakenly applied to informational images, such as identification, legal, police, and scientific pictures, whose purposes are to be neutrally objective by authenticating the existence of specific subjects at a precise place and time. Stryker's intent was to dramatize real subjects in their actual settings, linking them to specific cultural messages so that viewers would formulate a favorable response to the new government programs. Stryker's agenda was to be positive and portray rural people working to improve their predicament. Humor and

irony appeared, but the bizarre and the grotesque were circumvented. Camera angles and distance tended to follow the normal eye-level standards, giving a sense of cooperation and social equality, underlining the idea that these were good people experiencing hard times. Overall, the images are respectful of their subjects, providing a visual counterweight to the negative stereotypes of the mass media, such as Erskine Caldwell's *Tobacco Road* (1932) and *God's Little Acre* (1933), which gave the impression that the rural workers were misfits, loafers, and sex fiends.

Dorothea Lange's [1895–1965] FSA photographs epitomized the human cost of the Depression. Lange studied photography with Clarence White at Columbia University before opening a portrait studio in San Francisco in 1916. The Depression awakened Lange's social consciousness and she began photographing unemployed laborers. A childhood bout with polio left Lange with a permanent limp, possibly increasing her sympathy for circumstances that dramatically alter people's lives over which they have no control. By 1933, Lange had quit her commercial work to make photographs of the "forgotten man," in labor strikes and street demonstrations. A quotation by English philosopher and essayist Francis Bacon, tacked to her darkroom door, was her credo: "The contemplation of things as they are, without substitution or imposture, without error or confusion, is in itself a nobler thing than a whole harvest of invention."[42] Willard Van Dyke, of Group f/64, exhibited her early socially driven work in his Oakland, CA gallery. They were seen by economics professor Paul Taylor, who hired Lange to illustrate a report recommending sanitary camps be built to provide migrant farm families with decent temporary housing. Taylor credited Lange's emotionally compelling photographs with convincing officials to set up the first camps. After seeing the report, Stryker hired Lange for the RA/FSA project, where she made what many considered the quintessential FSA image: *Migrant Mother,* 1936. Echoing the Madonna and child theme, Lange's archetypal image communicates the essence of a situation and its human relationship to history.

Lange took the photograph almost by chance. Speeding home one rainy late winter day after a cold month of photographing migrant workers, Lange drove past a crude sign saying "PEA-PICKERS CAMP." "I didn't want to stop and didn't,"[43] she later said. Twenty miles later she made a U-turn and returned to the camp. Lange wrote:

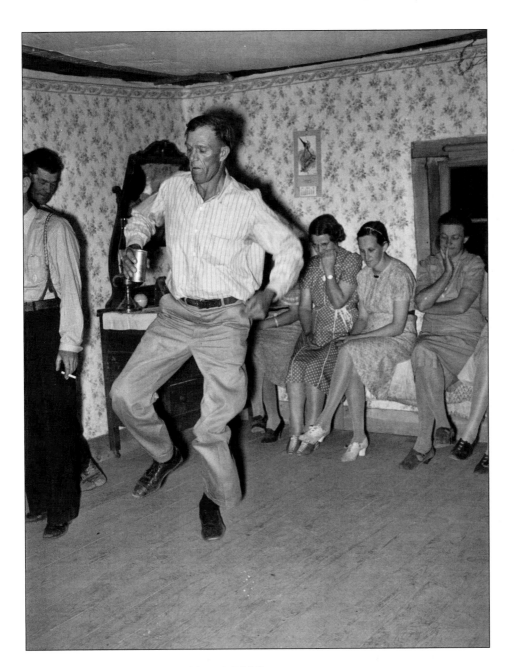

12.19   RUSSELL LEE.   *Pie Town, NM* (*Jigger at Square Dance*), 1940. Gelatin silver print.   Courtesy Library of Congress.

I was following instinct, not reason. . . . I saw and approached the hungry and desperate mother, as if drawn by a magnet . . . she asked no questions. . . . She said they had been living on frozen vegetables from the surrounding fields, and from birds that the children killed. She . . . seemed to know my pictures might help her, and so she helped me. There was sort of equality about it. . . . I knew I had recorded the essence of my assignment.[44]

Lange took these pictures to a newspaper editor who contacted United Press (UP); UP informed the government authorities, who then took action to help. The headline of the March 10, 1936, edition of the *San Francisco News* proclaimed: "FOOD RUSHED TO STARVING FARM COLONY." The article contained two of Lange's images, but not *Migrant Mother*. Within a short time, however, the initially overlooked *Migrant Mother* took on a life of its own, and was reprinted and exhibited to such an extent that Lange later complained that it was making her a one-picture photographer.[45]

After leaving the FSA in 1940, Lange continued to photograph desperate social conditions. Her series on the Japanese-Americans of the Pacific coast who, in the post–Pearl Harbor hysteria that catapulted America into World War II, were interned in camps by the Federal government, revealed a person would also take on unpopular causes. For a number of years, poor health prevented Lange from working, but she was a staff photographer for *Life* in 1954–55. Lange's compassionate project. Disappearing into the South for weeks, Evans, the only FSA photographer consistently using an 8 × 10-inch view camera, returned with unheroic, clinical recordings of ignored scenes from a fading regional American culture. The images, unveiled by sentimentality, are possessed by the photographer's puritanical objectivity mixed with an edge of pessimism. The works' understatement offered a testimony of facts, making viewers believe in the power of the plain photograph. We look at how Evans constructed a scene and nod in agreement: "Yes, this is how it is." Evans's self-effacing style made the relevance of the ordinary undeniable. Evans could ordain a moment from the present with a historical perspective, showing the present as if it was the past (see Figure 12.16).

In the summer of 1936, Evans collaborated with his writer friend James Agee [1909–1955] on an article about three tenant cotton farmers in Hale County, AL for *Fortune*. This unlikely New York journalistic duo spent most of August with one of the families, who under the cotton tenantry system did not own the land, the house, or the mule, and paid the landlord half of the crop. The two defied accepted working methods, each taking his own approach to the story. Evans rejected fairy tales of the rural South and worked with his subjects to directly represent their dignity in the face of hardship. The resulting images are a barebones inspection of the inner resources that enabled these people to survive. The compositional economy of the images make the truth of the situation self-evident (see Figure 12.17).

Fortune rejected the piece. A vastly expanded version was published as *Let Us Now Praise Famous Men* (1941). The book design was remarkable: The first thing a reader encountered was not text but a portfolio of Evans's photographs. Also highly unusual was that the photographs were not illustrations; as Agee said, the images and words were "coequal, mutually independent, and fully collaborative." The critical and public response was indifferent at best; first year sales totaled less than 600 copies.

In the late 1930s, Evans made a series of anonymous New York subway riders, using a hidden camera, that was eventually published as *Many Are Called* (1966). These portraits dispense with the smiling face, revealing each person to be suspended within his or her own universe. The sequencing of the repeating images replaces the individuality of each person with a sense of exhaustion, similar to the monotonous effect of a subway car rumbling along the

12.20   BEN SHAHN.   *Sheriff's Deputy*, 1935. 10¼ × 8 inches. Gelatin silver print.   Courtesy George Eastman House.

concern to make politically and socially driven work ran into difficulty in the narrowness of the photojournalism market of the 1950s, and some of her projects for *Life,* such as *The Public Defender* (1956–57) and *The Last Valley* (1957) essays, were either not used or were distorted by the editors. Lange continued freelancing, often with Paul Taylor, from 1958 to 1965, making vital work that presented the relationship of people to their culture and their connection to the earth.

The FSA photographer whose work most profoundly influenced the field of photography was **Walker Evans** [1903–1975]. Evans's dislike for the materialism of the affluent 1920s led him to cultivate an economy of practice that can be seen in his 1930 series of Victorian and vernacular architecture. His deceptively transparent approach—that this is exactly what the viewer would have been drawn to had he been there himself—uncovers the essence of a place and allows the unexpected beauty of the everyday to reveal itself. In the fall of 1935, Stryker hired Evans for his RA/FSA

12.21 GORDON PARKS. *Emerging Man,* 1952.
14⅞ × 19⅛ inches. Gelatin silver print. *Emerging Man*
visualizes the continuing identity crisis that has affected
generations of African-American men. The image is
based on Ralph Ellison's novel, *Invisible Man* (1952), that
chronicles the story of a nameless African-American
man who lives alone in an underground room as he
searches to find himself in a society that does not want
to acknowledge his existence and insists that he remain
unseen and powerless. This image and three others were
published as "A Man Becomes Invisible," in *Life* (August 25, 1952), 9–11. The article states that with Ellison's help Parks re-created scenes from the novel "to
show the loneliness, the horror and the disillusionment
of a man who has lost faith in himself and the world."
Courtesy of the artist.

track station after station. In 1945, Evans joined the
staff of *Fortune,* where he became an associate editor
before retiring in 1965. His relationship with *Fortune*
was ironic and sad. It marked the end of Evans's willingness to reveal the view from his privileged position. The view had shaped the information influential
businesspeople used to make decisions of enormous
social impact.

One of the FSA's most controversial photographers
was **Arthur Rothstein** [1915–1985], who studied under Stryker at Columbia University and joined the
RA/FSA staff from 1935 to 1940. Rothstein's *Dust
Storm, Cimarron County, OK,* 1936, an image of a
farmer and his two young sons walking against the
wind across a field that is buried to the top of fence
posts with drifting dirt, became the consummate theatrical interpretation of the Dust Bowl—the prairie
states' loss of unprotected topsoil due to winds and improper farming procedures. Unlike Lange's, some of
Rothstein's best work was not "found" but was constructed on-site to make a point. In May of 1936, while
driving through the South Dakota Badlands, Rothstein
spotted a steer skull, a victim of the natural forces responsible for the severe weather, lying on the dry,
cracked earth. Rothstein made some exposures and
then he moved the skull about ten feet and made another exposure. He processed the film and returned it to
Washington to be printed. An Associated Press editor
used one of Rothstein's skull pictures as a symbol for
the drought of 1936 (see Figure 12.18). The image,
with the editor's caption, "skull of a drought-stricken
steer," received national syndication. Spotting an opportunity to discredit Roosevelt's farm policies, a North

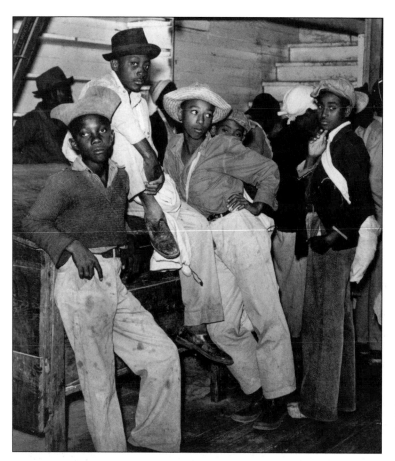

12.22   MARION POST WOLCOTT.   *Young Boys Waiting in the Plantation Store to be Paid off for Picking Cotton, Marcella Plantation, Mileston, MS,* ca. 1939. Gelatin silver print.   © Marion Post Wolcott. Print courtesy Linda Wolcott-Moore Fine Art Photography.

arose when text was added to an image made as a general statement, thus converting it into a particular instance, as in the case of the steer skull (after all how would we know that the steer died of drought?). Rothstein's skull image demonstrates the slipperiness of photographic meaning and how original intent can be shifted without the audience's awareness through the use of text, cropping, and placement within a different context. Rothstein's other "straight" images corroborating the effects of the drought conditions were never questioned. Rothstein went on to help found the American Society of Magazine Photographers in 1941 and spent his life as a working photojournalist for *Look* and *Parade* magazines and as a journalism teacher.

To overcome public relations fiascoes like the steer skull incident, Stryker wanted to present "New Deal" communalism that was beyond the scare tactics of the administration's foes. Stryker found it in Pie Town, NM, an isolated alternative community of about 250 hardworking Dust Bowl homesteaders who cooperated to survive. **Russell Lee** [1903–1986] sought to detail the intimacy of Pie Town as a frontier experience of church dinners and square dances, a town patterned on a belief in the "American character" of family, church, and enterprise. To record the wealth of natural detail and expression inside people's homes, Lee used direct flash. This harsh, unnatural light produced artless images, thus striking a cord of incorruptibility and honesty that visually emphasized the primary subject of the photograph (see Figure 12.19). But even as Lee was constructing this series, he was aware that Pie Town was a fading cultural vestige of pioneer ingenuity and cooperation soon to be overrun by "progress." In his notes, Lee wondered how long these values would last after electricity came and replaced community sings with radios and burros and horses with tractors.[48] In 1941, Lee spent several weeks with his wife, Jean, photographing the environment of urban African-Americans in Chicago as part of an FSA project with the writer Richard Wright, author of *Native Son* (1940). The project resulted in *Twelve Million Black Voices* (1941), illustrated with numerous Lee and other FSA images of black ghetto life.

Ben Shahn [1898–1969] brought the viewpoint of a nonphotographer to the FSA project. Shahn was an artist who learned to use a Leica from his former roommate Walker Evans. Shahn photographed the growing social disruption that was breaking down societal behaviors on the streets of New York. His images found their way into his social protest drawings and lithographs of the 1920s.

Dakota newspaper ran Rothstein's skull image with the headline, "It's A Fake."[46] The story, that Rothstein fabricated the scene, received national coverage. Roosevelt's opponents latched onto the image as proof that the RA program tricked people into accepting socialist experiments. Cartoons appeared showing a photographer (Rothstein) wandering the West with a skull under his arm. Stryker was left with the task of convincing people that the RA did not make a practice of "faking" photographs. Although Stryker encouraged his photographers to find the most compelling way to present their message, the public had different expectations. Newspaper readers expected photographers to act only as objective witnesses in their stead—their job was to report not interpret events. They accepted Lange's images but thought that Rothstein's "aesthetic document" compromised his privileged position as a witness and invalidated the evidence. Rothstein's intent in moving the skull was not to "fake" but to portray, not to make "news" photographs of a specific drought but to characterize the overall drought conditions.[47] The difficulty

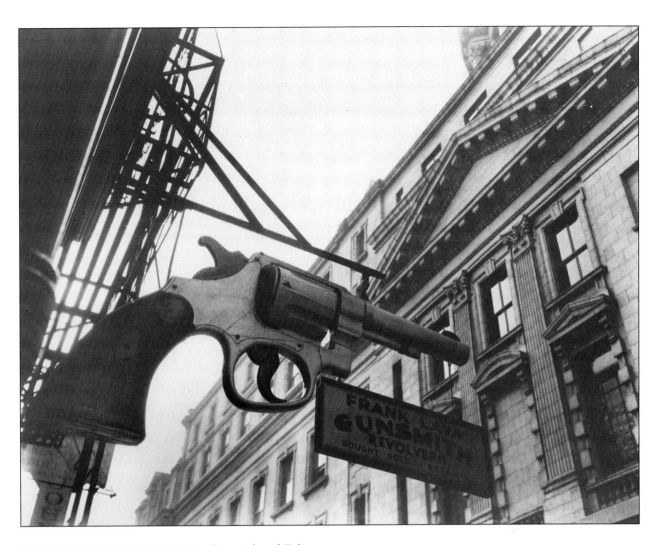

12.23   BERENICE ABBOTT.   *Gunsmith and Police Department, 6 Centre Market Place,* February 4, 1937. 8 × 10 inches. Gelatin silver print.   © Museum of the City of New York, Federal Arts Project, "Changing New York."

Shahn went to work for the Special Skills Department of the RA. His strong opinions on dramatizing social issues helped formulate Stryker's belief that the RA/FSA images needed to go beyond visual artifacts and convey empathetic statements informed by a class, economic, racial, and religious awareness. Shahn's casual approach produced nontraditional asymmetrical compositions with an emphasis on form, and encouraged other RA/FSA photographers to consider the ephemeral genuineness of the *candid* approach. In candid work the subject is supposed to be represented naturally, without interference from the photographer. Shahn cultivated the unposed mode by equipping his camera with a 90-degree right-angle viewfinder so that he could make "snapshots" without the subject's consciousness of the camera affecting the outcome. Shahn also practiced *post-visualization,* cropping his negative to arrive at a satisfactory composition (see Figure 12.20).

At a time when segregation rather than integration was the social norm, Stryker hired African-American **Gordon Parks** [1912] as a photographer for the FSA project (1942–43). Stryker employed Parks again for his Standard Oil Company of New Jersey Project in 1945–48,[49] during which time Parks made some of his most unusual images of white corporate culture. Parks's ability to function in a multitude of social situations led to his hiring as the first black staff photographer for *Life* in 1949. His photo-essays on the black fight for equality brought issues and leaders from a cross-section of the African-American community like Martin Luther King, Jr., the Black Muslims, the Black Panthers, Eldridge Cleaver, and Muhammad Ali into white middle-class living rooms (see Figure 12.21). His film, *Shaft* (1971), crossed over racial differences and influenced Hollywood and American culture.

With the approach of World War II, Stryker shifted the strategy and themes of the FSA to assert the country's sense of physical and spiritual plenty. These transformations are exemplified by the work of **Marion Post Wolcott** [1910–1990]. Wolcott's photographs of the interaction of nature and society consoled viewers,

12.24 ROMAN VISHNIAC. *Granddaughter and Grandfather, Warsaw,* 1938. 16 × 20 inches. Gelatin silver print. The Nazis' rise to power and the accompanying anti-Semitism prompted Roman Vishniac to document the Jewish ghettos of eastern Europe on the eve of the Holocaust. The surviving 5,000 candid images provide evidence of people, places, and traditions that were forcibly erased. Vishniac managed to get out of a French concentration camp and make his way to America in 1941, where he continued his scientific work with his photomicrography and time-lapse cine-mamicrography of small animals, insects, and plants.
© Mara V. Kohn. Copy print © 1999 The Museum of Modern Art, New York. The Ben Schultz Memorial Collection. Gift of the photographer.

tired of seeing people out of work, with scenes where traditional work values were being practiced (see Figure 12.22). This trend of sweeping aside troubling news and concentrating on affirmation would become the hallmark of the 1940s.

War reversed the hardships of the Great Depression. Suddenly, people who might have been in migrant labor camps were in the military, working in war factories, or back on the farm. The FSA expired in 1943, and its photographic activities were absorbed into the Office of War Information, leaving behind an exhaustive public archive: Between 1935 and 1943, some 80,000

prints and 200,000 unprinted negatives were produced and made available to editors and publishers at little or no cost, creating a legacy that has determined the country's vision of the Depression.[50]

The FAP Project: Changing New York

During the 1930s, the documentary approach was the predominant mode for serious American photographers. After working as Man Ray's assistant and securing Atget's photographic estate, **Berenice Abbott** [1898–1991] returned to New York and opened a studio in 1929. Affected by Atget's unadorned realism, Abbott embarked on a photographic record of New York City. She supported this project through magazine work and teaching until 1935 when she gained funding from the Federal Arts Project (FAP) of Works Progress Administration. Abbott sustained one of the few government-sponsored urban documentary projects over four years by fusing the earnestness of Atget with the playfulness of her Parisian modernist experience. Abbott deployed her 8 × 10-inch camera from a multitude of viewpoints and cropped prints in her effort to manifest the chaotic and complex relationships between people and a great city. Her book, *Changing New York* (1939), astringently and humorously contrasts the rela-

12.25 HUMPHREY SPENDER. *Wash on the Lines, Bolton,* 1937. 9¼ × 13½ inches. Gelatin silver print. Unlike the Farm Security Administration project, Mass-Observation was not interested in putting an affirmative face on things. Tom Harrisson thought it was important to include unobserved photography in his methodology because he "distrusted the value of mere words."[51] Humphry Spender had difficulty with this style because it eliminated human interaction between the photographer and the subject.   Courtesy Bolton Metro Museums and Art Gallery, Bolton, England.

tionship of beauty and decay within an urban environment (see Figure 12.23). Abbott also promoted the documentary stance by championing the work of Atget and helping to arrange a retrospective of Hine's work. During the 1930s other photographers like **Roman Vishniac** [1897–1990] made a visual record of a people and their culture that was systematically being destroyed by the Nazis (see Figure 12.24).

Mass-Observation

Another unique project undertaken during the Depression years that incorporated documentary photography, anthropology, socialism, and surrealism was carried out by **Mass-Observation**. Mass-Observation was founded in 1936 by journalist and poet Charles Madge

to study British society from real life in order to learn its true feeling about issues, such as the Abdication Crisis of 1936 when Edward III gave up his kingship to marry American divorcée Wallis Simpson, he felt had been repressed. He was joined by filmmaker Humphrey Jennings and by ornithologist and anthropologist Tom Harrisson [1911–1976], who had studied cannibals in Borneo and wanted to show comparisons between their culture and his own. Among other things, the group was interested in chance occurrences, how the juxtaposition of different types of events could disturb the status quo and how individuals interpreted the same event differently. By the end of 1937 their ethnographic undertaking involved more than 500 people keeping detailed diaries of everything they did on the twelfth day of each month throughout the year. Other volunteers acted as living "subjective cameras," doing "continuous observation" to collect a mass of data for future studies that science would use to "build new hypotheses and theories." They also asked people to make snapshots of their daily lives and send them in with their written diaries. The theme of these activities was a search for identity during the time of the crumbling British Empire in which everyday people reported what society looked like to them. In 1937 photojournalist **Humphry Spender** [b. 1910] joined the group to photograph the working-class cotton mill town of Bolton, England (referred to as Worktown), where Harrisson had moved and disguised himself as a worker in order to become

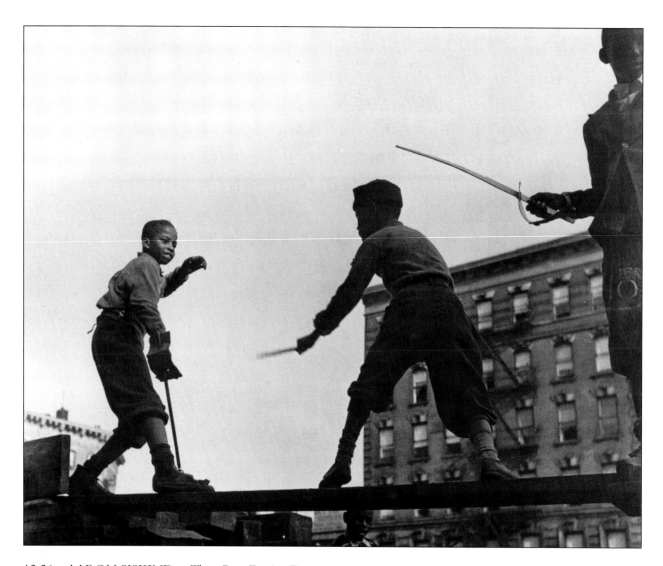

12.26   AARON SISKIND.   *Three Boys Fencing,* From
Series *Most Crowded Block in the World* ca. 1938/39.
4½ × 5⅝ inches. Gelatin silver print.   ©Aaron Siskind
Foundation/Courtesy Robert Mann Gallery.

an inside observer. Harrisson loosely directed Spender
to use hidden 35mm cameras, making him an "unobserved observer," to make secret pictures of people in
public places carrying out various activities so that
things could "speak for themselves": housing conditions, industry, leisure, political, religious, and social
activities. With the outbreak of World War II, Mass-Observation supplied information on home-front morale
to the Ministry of Information and eventually became a
for-profit research center.

The Film and Photo League

The Film and Photo League was originally part of the
cultural propaganda wing of Workers' International Relief, a leftist strikers' aid group in Berlin that supported

Workers' Camera Leagues in European and American
cities. By 1934, the American group had evolved into
the New York Film and Photo League, known for its
propaganda films on social injustice and its documentary film classes. In 1936, the organization's filmmak-
ers split over aesthetic and social issues. The still photographers regrouped under the leadership of **Sidney
Grossman** [1913–1955] and Sol Libsohn [b. 1914] to
recreate a self-supporting Photo League as a meeting
place, gallery, and education site. The Photo League
promoted the sanctity of the straight image and the belief that photography needed to serve a social-political
purpose. During the 1930s, under the direction of
Aaron Siskind [1903–1991], members of the Photo
League's Feature Group spent three years covering
New York's vital black community, producing the
Harlem Document. Disputes with League members
over his growing interest in formal aesthetics led to
Siskind's leaving the organization in 1941. He contin-
ued his contemplative work and eventually joined the
Abstract Expressionist movement (see Chapter 15).

The driving force between 1938 and 1949 for the ideals of the politically conscious Photo League, where the officers, teachers, and speakers donated their time, was Sid Grossman. The League was the site for photography exhibitions at a time when few art museums would show photography. In December 1947, the United States Attorney General's office included the Photo League on its list of "Totalitarian, Fascist, Communist, and Subversive Organizations." Grossman, a member of the Communist Party, was blacklisted. In an effort to save the League, Grossman resigned from the organization. Ironically, by the late 1940s the League was attracting photographic talents without Marxist agendas, including Ansel Adams, Beaumont and Nancy Newhall, Barbara Morgan, Edward Weston, and Richard Avedon. But the blacklist's threat of lost livelihood and the growing public hysteria that accompanied Senator Joseph McCarthy's Communist witch hunts led to the League's collapse in 1951, leaving a spiritual black hole for those who wanted to unite photography and social change. Faced with the repression of intellectual freedom under McCarthyism in the 1950s, many American photographers shifted their position from work that called for social action to a more inner highly personal approach. The Photo League's social activism would not manifest itself again in the photographic community until the civil rights struggles of the 1960s.

The conclusion of World War II with the dropping of two atomic bombs on Japan, the immediate transformation of the U.S.S.R. from an ally to a foe that started the Cold War, and the explosive growth of the postwar economy shifted American concerns from the social issues of the Great Depression to those of materialism and nationalism. With this realignment, the social consciousness documentary practice that had been supported by government funding was replaced by corporate models like *Life* magazine, which tempered cultural needs with its own commercial interests (see Chapter 14).

Endnotes

1   Tenements appeared in New York when old houses were subdivided into small rooms and rented to immigrants. During Riis's time they evolved into four- to six-story apartment houses with tiny, often unventilated, dark rooms. Typically four families occupied a floor, each having one or two dark bedrooms about $6\frac{1}{2} \times 7$ feet, a 10×12-foot living area, and a communal kitchen, hall, and stairway.

2   Charles A. Mason, Preface to the Dover Reprint Edition, Jacob A. Riis, *How The Other Half Lives: Studies Among the Tenements of New York* (New York: Dover, 1971), vi.

3   The term muckrake comes from John Bunyan's *Pilgrims Progress* (1678–84) and was used in a speech by President Theodore Roosevelt in 1906. The name muckrakers was applied to American critics, journalists, and novelists who exposed corruption in business and politics at the turn of the twentieth century and called for social reform. They included Sinclair Lewis, Lincoln Steffens, and Ida Tarbell.

4   Jacob Riis, *How the Other Half Lives: Studies Among the Tenements of New York*, reprint (New York: Dover Publications, 1971), 30.

5   "Flashes from the Slums: Pictures Taken in Dark Places by the Lightning Process," *The Sun* (New York), February 12, 1888. Reprinted in Beaumont Newhall ed., *Photography: Essays and Images,* 1980, 155–57.

6   Jacob A. Riis, *How the Other Half Lives: Studies Among the Tenements of New York* (New York: Charles Scribner's Sons, 1890).

7   The halftones did not do justice to the photographs, causing the work to be neglected until the original plates were rescued by Alexander Allard who made new prints and began exhibiting them in 1947.

8   Pamela Reeves, *Ellis Island: Gateway to the American Dream* (New York: Dorset Press, 1991), 134.

9   Lewis Hine, "Social Photography, How the Camera May Help in the Social Uplift." *Proceedings, National Conference of Charities and Corrections* (June 1909), in Alan Trachtenberg, ed., *Classic Essays on Photography* (New Haven: Leet's Island Books, 1980), 111.

10   Alan Trachtenberg, "Ever—the Human Document," *America and Lewis Hine: Photographs 1904–1940* (Millerton, NY: Aperture, 1977), 133.

11   Horatio Alger, Jr., *Ragged Dick,* 203, quoted in James Guimond, "Lewis Hine and American Industrialism," *American Photography and the American Dream* (Chapel Hill: The University of North Carolina Press, 1991), 74.

12   Hine, 111.

13   Lewis Hine, "The Spirit of Industry," Introduction to *Men at Work* (New York: The Macmillan Co., 1932), unp.

14   C. and F. W. Dammann's *Ethnological Photographic Gallery of the Various Races of Men* (London: Trubner, n.d.), unp.

15   Booker T. Washington was the organizer and director of the Tuskegee Institute (1881), an early black educational institution, and author of *Up from Slavery* (1901).

16   Most of Germany's film community was forced to flee when Hitler was elected chancellor in 1933. Riefenstahl remained and was given carte blanche by Hitler to make a motion picture of the 1934 Nuremberg Party Convention. The result was her brilliant and inflammatory propaganda film, *Triumph of the Will* (1935), banned by the Allies even after the end of World War II.

17   For a discussion about the Storyville work, see John Szarkowski, ed., *E. J. Bellocq: Storyville Portraits: Photographs from the New Orleans Red-Light District,* ca. 1912 (New York: Museum of Modern Art, 1970). Also see revised edition with introduction by Susan Sontag (New York: Random House, 1996) and Janet Malcom, "The Real Thing," *The New Yorker,* vol. XLIV, no. 1 (January 9, 1997), 12, 14–16.

18   Drawn into a cultural movement known as *Mexicanidad,* which realigned Mexico's national identity with its ancient and indigenous cultural rather than its more recent colonial past, Modotti engaged in revolutionary political activities in the early 1920s, joined the Mexican Communist Party in 1927, was deported in 1930, and later went to the Soviet Union.

19   Letter to Weston, July 7, 1925; cited in Amy Stark, ed., *The Letters from Tina Modotti to Edward Weston* (Tucson: Center for Creative Photography, 1986), 39–40.

20   See Peggy Albright, *Crow Indian Photographer: The Work of Richard Throssel* (Albuquerque: University of New Mexico Press, 1997)

21   Lucy R. Lippard, ed., *Partial Recall: Photographs of Native North Americans* (New York: The New Press, 1992), Introduction, 27.

22   Linda Poolaw, *War Bonnets, Tin Lizzies, and Patent Leather Pumps: Kiowa Culture in Transition, 1925–1955. The Photographs of Horace Poolaw, October 5–December 14, 1990.* (Stanford: Stanford University, 1990, 13.

23   Telephone conversation with Donna VanDerZee and author, February 2, 1999.

24   Deborah Willis-Braithwaite, *James VanDerZee, Photographer 1886–1983* (New York: Harry Abrams in association with The National Portrait Gallery, Smithsonian Institution, 1993), 10.

25   Eudora Welty, *One Time, One Place, Mississippi in the Depression: A Snapshot Album* (New York: Random House, 1971), 7–8.

26   Ibid.

27   Ibid., 4.

28   Ibid.

29   Ibid., 6.

30   For additional information on the taxonomic uses of photography, see Allan Sekula, "The Body and the Archive," in *The Contest of Meaning: Critical Histories of Photography,* Richard Bolton, ed. (Cambridge: The MIT Press, 1989), 342–89.

31   Heinz K. Henisch and Bridget A. Henisch, *The Photographic Experience 1839–1914: Images and Attitudes* (University Park: The Pennsylvania State University Press, 1994), 300–3.

32   See Michel Foucault, *Discipline and Punish: Birth of the Prison,* trans. A. Sheridan (Allen Lane: London, 1977).

33   Thomas Byrnes, Professional Criminals of America (New York: Cassell and Company, 1886), 54.

34   Ibid., 55.

35   John Tagg, *The Burden of Representation,* "A Means of Surveillance," (Minneapolis: University of Minnesota Press, 1993), 74.

36   Robert Kramer, *August Sander, Photographs of an Epoch, 1904–1959* (Millerton, NY: Aperture, 1980), 23. The author tells that Sander's use of glossy paper may have occurred when he ran out of his normal portrait stock, but his friend painter Wilhelm "Seiwert was quick to point out that he had in fact made an important aesthetic breakthrough and encouraged Sander to continue with the technique."

37   The complete work was envisioned as forty-five portfolios containing twelve photographs each. Sander wanted to present mankind as a cycle, with a moralistic hierarchy, centering on the roles men and women played in society.

38   Roy Emerson Stryker and Nancy Wood, *In This Proud Land: America 1935–1943 as Seen in the FSA Photographs* (Greenwich, CT: New York Graphic Society, 1973), 73.

39   For a history of the FSA, see F. Jack Hurley, *Portrait of a Decade, Roy Stryker and the Development of Documentary Photography in the Thirties* (Baton Rouge: Louisiana State University Press, 1972).

40   Roy Emerson Stryker and Nancy Wood, 73.

41   Ibid., 8.

42   Lange first used the Bacon quote on a change of address announcement and later on a Christmas card. Quoted in David Travis, "Ephemeral Truths," *On the Art of Fixing a Shadow: One Hundred and Fifty Years of Photography,* Sarah Greenough, et al. (Washington, D.C.: National Gallery of Art, 1989), 248.

43   Dorothea Lange, "The Assignment I'll Never Forget," *Popular Photography,* vol. 46, no. 2 (February 1960), 42, 126. Also reprinted in Newhall, *Photography: Essays and Images* (1980), 262–65 with all six exposures.

44   Ibid.

45   For a chronicle of this image see Vicki Goldberg, *The Power of Photography: How Photographs Changed our Lives* (New York: Abbeville Press, 1991), 136–42.

46   *Fargo Forum* (August 27, 1936) quoted in Forrest Jack Hurley, *Portrait of a Decade, Roy Stryker and the Development of Documentary Photography in the Thirties* (Baton Rouge: Louisiana State University Press, 1972), 88.

47   Conversations between Arthur Rothstein and the author, January 26–28, 1979.

48   As referred to in James Guimond, *American Photography and the American Dream,* 132. These notes are located in Library of Congress, microfilm lot 639M, item no. 36715D.

49   For background information about this project see Steven W. Plattner, *Roy Stryker: USA, 1943–1950: The Standard Oil (New Jersey) Photography Project* (Austin, TX: University of Texas Press, 1983).

50   All the FSA work is owned by the government and inexpensive prints can be ordered from the Library of Congress. Many images are available on their website.

51   As quoted in Deborah Frizzell, *Humphrey Spender's Humanist Landscapes: Photo-Documents, 1932–1942* (New Haven: Yale Center for British Art, 1997), 26.

CHAPTER THIRTEEN

Nabbing Time
Anticipating the Moment

For most of the nineteenth century photographers had worked with extended time exposures that required forethought and the cooperation of the subject. As film sensitivity increased, a shutter capable of isolating units of time in fractions of a second was invented to control brief exposure. By the close of the nineteenth century, changes in artistic, philosophical, and scientific thinking about how time was measured and portrayed, along with technology-based, mass-production methods, made it possible to gauge, see, and think about time in ways that were formerly unimaginable. The actualization of Herschel's notion of the snapshot, by the hand-held camera, allowed all photographers to define previously undetectable moments of life. This change enhanced the democratic nature of the hand-camera by further expanding the range of vernacular subject matter, from loved ones to street cars, that thoughtful photographers like Stieglitz began to incorporate into their visual thinking. The hand-camera cemented the most popularly

DUCOS DU HAURON.
Distorted Self-Portrait, ca. 1890.
$3^{10}/_{16} \times 5^{1}/_{16}$ inches.
Gum bichromate print.
Courtesy George Eastman House.

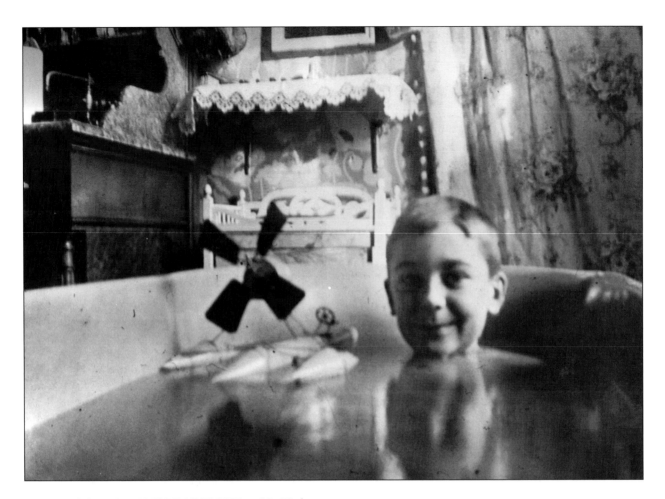

13.1   JACQUES-HENRI LARTIGUE.   *My Hydro-
glider with Propeller,* 1904. 5¼ × 6¹¹⁄₁₆ inches. Gelatin
silver print.   © Ministére de la Culture. Courtesy Association
des Amis de J.H. Lartigue, Paris.

cherished concept of twentieth-century practice: nab-
bing a precise instant from the flow of time. This ability
to rapidly distill complicated activities would define the
majority of practice throughout the twentieth century.

By the start of the twentieth century, the technology
for taking time prisoner was so easy that even a child
like **Jacques-Henri Lartigue** [1894–1988] could use it
to offer his version of life. Lartigue was an affluent amateur, one with the freedom to observe without concern
for posterity or the public, who now had the means to
record life's commonplace details from a personal
point of view. Lartigue's instinctively ebullient images
capture his enchanted childhood, which was a testing
ground for new inventions, including automobiles, bi-
cycles, and airplanes, and show how new technology
quickly altered that existence.

Beginning with a view-camera at age seven, Lartigue soon convinced his father to get him a hand-
camera so he could naturally pursue his child's point
of view, like putting the camera on the floor to record
his toy racing cars. Hand-cameras made it easier and
less financially risky to make conscious experimental

decisions, as when Lartigue balanced his camera on a
plank of wood extended over a bathtub to picture himself and his toy water glider. For Lartigue, photography's new simplicity made it part of childhood play,
"a magic thing with all sorts of mysterious smells, a
bit strange and frightening,"[1] an arena of visual pleasure. During France's cultural renaissance, "La Belle
Epoque," young Lartigue's snapshots collected the
amusements and fragile beauties available to the well-
to-do just before this well-bred world disappeared into
the abyss of World War I.

Lartigue's albums chronicle a fascination with the
motion and speed that was transforming the world and
providing new aesthetics. The ease of the hand-held
camera allowed anybody to embrace the physical act of
seeing subjects as they moved through time. Lartigue
took his camera everywhere, eventually deforming his
shoulder from carrying it. Lartigue's intuitive images
reveal and confirm what serious photographers struggled to discover and master: the expertise of anticipa-
tion. Lartigue's obsession was with capturing the peak
moment of action where critical timing was achieved
through observation and calculation. His most advanced Block Note camera had a top shutter speed of
1/300th of a second, making his decision when to release the shutter crucial. Pushing the shutter at the moment the image was seen was too late, due to the me-

chanical and physiological delay between seeing and exposing. Lartigue compared it to playing tennis—one had to foresee the exact moment beforehand and have the ability and training to act without consciously thinking. As a child Lartigue was an unthreatening spectator, able to glide into situations and uncover unguarded instances of highly complex, fleeting human interrelations. Although he never received any photography training, through practice Lartigue was able to use the camera to organize the random attributes of life with coherent clarity. Lartigue's work did not influence the practice of his time; It remained unknown to the public until it was presented at the Museum of Modern Art in 1963.

Technological breakthroughs in camera design placed an image-making system at the fingertips of any photographer who wanted to take part in the expanded uses and markets of the medium. During the first two decades of the twentieth century, faster films and lenses allowed the Kodak to evolve into a truly miniature camera. By eliminating technical obstacles, the hand-camera permitted photographers to be in the flow of events as they unfolded, trapping moments from time, instead of being outside and having to forge happenings for the sake of the camera. In 1924, designs like the Ernox defined the future of hand-cameras. Renamed the Ermanox and claiming that "What You Can See You Can Photograph," it had shutter speeds up to 1/1000 of a second and a fast f/2 lens but used small, individual sheets of film.

This sheet film camera was shortly supplanted by the quintessential miniature camera, the Leica. Invented by Oscar Barnack of the Leitz Company as an exposure testing device for cinematography in 1913, it was marketed in an improved version using a 24 × 36 mm frame in 1924. It was not only smaller and lighter than other hand-cameras, but it utilized inexpensive standard movie stock, letting a photographer rapidly and unobtrusively make thirty-six exposures without reloading. Faster, high-definition, interchangeable lenses and a built-in coupled rangefinder followed. The built-in *coupled rangefinder,* originally introduced in 1932 on the Zeiss Ikon, let photographers quickly align overlapping images into a single image, insuring sharper images by eliminating the need to guess focusing distance. Evolutionary features, such as Zeiss Contax S's single-lens-reflex (SLR) viewing at eye level, were marketed after World War II.

In 1929, the compact Rolleiflex, producing twelve 2¼-inch square negatives on a single roll of film, revitalized the twin-reflex camera of the 1890s. SLR viewing was added to this design by Victor Hasselblad in 1948. Built-in meters were added to hand-cameras in the 1960s; autofocus became common by the 1980s. The march toward miniaturization continued with the 1996 introduction of the Advanced Photo System (APS) that uses a film cartridge about a third smaller than a conventional 35-mm cassette. APS film has a magnetic coating that captures data about each exposure that photofinishing equipment uses to make print processing more accurate. The miniature camera's ability to allow repeated exposures, stop action with fast shutter speeds, perform in low-light situations, avoid attracting attention, and produce sharp, enlargeable images, altered how photographs were conceived, executed, and seen.

The miniature camera leveled long-standing societal rules about what was private and what was public, disregarding social position and thereby making everyone more or less equal. In 1927, **Erich Salomon** [1886–1944] used a concealed camera to make pictures inside a courtroom during a murder trial in which photography was forbidden. These images aroused enough notice that Salomon quit his job and began to make unposed, available light photographs of celebrities, diplomats, politicians, social gatherings, concerts, and theater presentations with a miniature camera. By 1929, an editor for *The London Graphic* coined the phrase *candid camera/photograph,* in reference to Salomon's ability to capture unguarded moments. Referring to himself as a "historian with a camera,"[2] Salomon brought the camera into social realms where it had been prohibited. By means of silent shutters and cable releases, Salomon's camera (he switched to a Leica in 1932), hidden in his hat, a valise, or a potted plant, informed the general public of cultural events and ways in which the powerful carried out their business beyond public scrutiny. Salomon commented on the adrenaline rush of making such images: "The work of a photojournalist is a constant battle, a battle for the picture, and as in hunting, he gets his game only if he has an obsession for the chase."[3]

A collection of Salomon's candid photographs was published as *Berühmte Zeitgenossen in unbewachte Augenblicken (Celebrated Contemporaries in Unguarded Moments),* 1931. The public demand for these "extraordinary" pictures would, through repetition, lead them to become ordinary. During a period when Germany was newly experiencing democracy, what was striking was how unremarkable these people who made important decisions looked. The small camera showed the human connection between the statesman and the citizen.

The practice of making images without a subject's consent was epitomized by the flash attack style of Italy's *paparazzi,* as portrayed in Federico Fellini's film *La Dolce Vita* (1960), who aggressively "stole" people's images. This strategy of interjecting a camera into strangers' lives during moments of extreme stress has become the staple of numerous television docu-dramas, and continues to blur the line between the public's right to be informed and an individual's right to privacy. The death of British Princess Diana in 1997 while being chased by the tabloid press produced cries for legislation to restrict

13.2   ERIC SALOMON.   *Royal Stables, The Hague,*
1938. 11 × 14 inches. Gelatin silver print.   Dr. Erich
Salomon.

photographers' freedom to photograph a person anyplace, anytime. In 1998 a law was passed in Quebec, Canada forbidding photographers to take pictures of people in public situations without their written permission.

Salomon's images continue to be of historical interest, but they have lost their excitement as their social context has faded. They were designed to function in a print environment with a caption providing supplemental information. Seen today without their captions, many of these images appear mundane, pointing to the transient nature of photographic meaning. The photograph's chameleon-like ability to possess numerous interpretations, instead of a single fixed one, led critic Walter Benjamin to observe:

> The camera will become smaller and smaller, more and more prepared to grasp fleeting, secret images whose shock will bring the mechanism of association in the viewer to a complete halt. At this point captions must begin to function, captions which understand the photography which turns all the relations of life into literature, and without which all photographic construction must remain bound in coincidences. . . . Will not captions become the essential component of pictures?[4]

In 1931, Salomon fled Nazi Germany to Holland. Here he worked with a miniature camera to present a behind-the-scenes look at social activities that were not overtly political. As his interest in celebrities and news value gave way to photographing ordinary people involved with everyday tasks, the subject and caption were no longer crucial, allowing Salomon's photographs to be interpreted in an open manner. Salomon was later betrayed to the Nazis as a Jew and sent to the Auschwitz extermination camp, where he perished. Salomon's images survived because he buried his negatives, which were recovered by his son after World War II. Salomon's small camera methods were slow to be adopted by the American photographic establishment. It would be well into the 1950s before most magazines would routinely allow their photographers to use the miniature camera for many of their assignments.

By the late 1910s, **André Kertész** [1894–1987] was demonstrating the visual language of modernism with asymmetrical compositions, close-ups, distortions, re-

13.3   ANDRÉ KERTÉSZ.   *Duna Haraszt, Hungary,*
1919. $9^{10}/_{16} \times 7^{3}/_{4}$ inches. Gelatin silver print.   Courtesy Jane Corkin Gallery, Toronto.

flections, and unusual points of view. Grainy compositions, involving the bodies of swimmers seen through
the refraction of water, indicated Kertész's willingness
to reshape reality. Ducos du Hauron had produced a series of distorted images in 1888 (see chapter opener),
and in the 1930s Kertész returned to this theme by using a mirror to transform the female body in a manner
similar to Picasso's. Kertész's modernist/surrealist
spirit led him to Paris in 1925. Here he used his Leica to
geometrically order the unexpected moments of everyday life, like children playing in the park or the corner
of Piet Mondrian's studio, in a life-affirming, lyrical,
sometimes sentimental fashion. He joined a small cadre

of photographers making their living as photojournalists in the growing market of the European picture press
(see Chapter 14).

Kertész haunted the streets of Paris in a state of expectation, waiting to examine the unforeseen. Kertész,
like the surrealists, believed the mask of reality could
be decoded by a spontaneous vision that was possible
through accidents in time. Writer Pierre Mac Orlan referred to the work of these freelance photojournalists as
"révélateurs" (developing agents), who by observing
life could apprehend the "right moment," reflecting the
idea that a photograph taken in one moment becomes
history in the next. Mac Orlan wrote:

> The greatest field of [documentary] photography . . . consists
> . . . in its latent power to create . . . death for a single second.
> Any thing or person is, at will, made to die for a moment of
> time so immeasurably small that the return to life is effected
> without consciousness of the great adventure.[5]

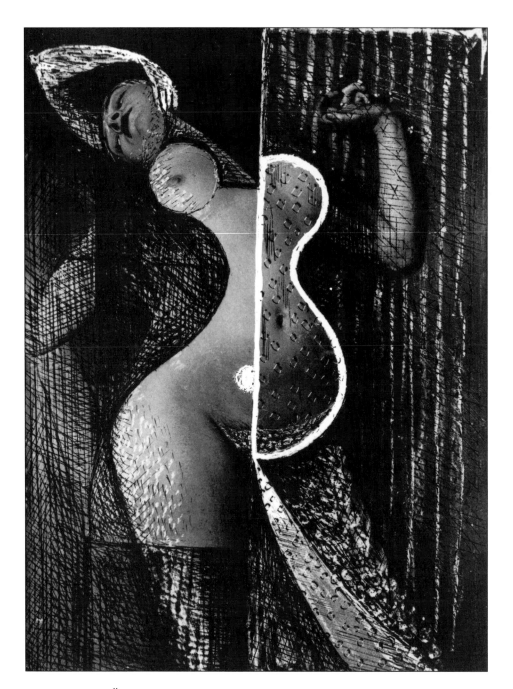

13.4 BRASSAÏ. *Odalisque,* 1934/5. Plate III from
Transmutations album. 9⁷⁄₁₆ × 7 inches. Gelatin silver
print.   © Gilberte Brassel.

Kertész's joyous "Leica spirit," the new small camera mentality, combined the formal design elements of
De Stijl and the Dutch painter Piet Mondrian
[1872–1944] with a natural intuition to extract poetic
"rest-stops" from the flow of time that alter expectations about common occurrences and objects. His work
was inspirational to numerous photojournalists, including Brassaï, Henri Cartier-Bresson, and Robert Capa.
In 1936 Kertész moved to New York, but the American
picture press did not appreciate his distinctive form that

they felt "talked too much." Their lack of support contributed to Kertész's growing sense of disillusionment,
and his later work, relying on urban architecture as a
major theme, was more formal and remote. In 1930
Kertész wrote:

> I am an amateur and intend to remain one my whole life long.
> I attribute to photography the task of recording the real nature
> of things, their interior life. The photographer's art is a contin-
> uous discovery which requires patience and time. A photo-
> graph draws its beauty from the truth with which it is marked.[6]

Not all the new candid work was seized from the
ever moving stream of time. Some photographers constructed images around the notion of suggesting a situation. The relativistic attitude of Einstein's theories, in

which the truth of any situation is determined by one's position in time and space, was a stance adopted by many photographers. Although a photograph may not represent absolute truth, what it did report was something difficult to judge as true or false.

Since its invention, the photograph has acted as an eyewitness, but the rise of the illustrated press demanded more unusual subject matter, leading photographers, such as **Brassaï** [1898–1984], to photograph situations considered forbidden topics for public discourse. Brassaï (Gyula Halász), who took his name from his hometown of Brasso, Transylvania, was an artist motivated by Kertész's work to portray the night life of Paris. A compatriot of the Paris surrealists and of Picasso, Brassaï contrived stylized tableaus in brothels, cafes, and on the streets of this fringe culture that Mac Orlan referred to as the subconscious "social fantastic," where the erotic and dangerous lay outside of mainstream society. Brassaï had his subjects act out their concealed activities as he set up his small plate camera on a tripod, opened the shutter, and fired his flash, recording a theatrical version of a candid moment that demystified and humanized the people from the world of night. Sixty-two identified plates from this series (one photograph per page), minus the most risqué, were published as *Paris de nuit* (*Paris by Night*) in 1933. Brassaï blended reality and fantasy to get beneath the surface, presenting a voyeuristic suggestion of shrouded taboos that only come out in the dark. Brassaï explained:

> For me the photograph must suggest rather than insist or explain; just as a novelist offers his readers only part of his creation—in leaving certain aspects unexpressed—so I think the photograph shouldn't provide superfluous explanations of its subject.[7]

Brassaï's philosophy of suggestion can also be observed in his series of clichés-verre, Transmutations, (see Figure 13.4) for which Brassaï wrote: "I compelled myself here to reveal the hidden figure which lay in each mental picture. . . . The dislocated parts of the photographs reorganized themselves into new combinations. . . . I cut their flesh as one carves a block to break loose the figure which it conceals. . . . The photograph is now and then volatilized. At times some debris has survived: a piece of quivering breast, a foreshortened face, a leg, an arm. Enshrined in graphism this debris gives to our obsessions, to our dreams the flash of the instant, the breath of reality."[8]

The small camera allowed photographers like **Henri Cartier-Bresson** [b. 1908] to blend into situations. Like an alert detective with a camera, Cartier-Bresson did not intrude, but waited for the scene to arrange itself before him. Cartier-Bresson was a consummate surrealist[9] who studied cubist painting and spent a year traveling in Africa before acquiring a Leica in 1932. Cartier-Bresson's photography manifests a form of visual alliteration and rhyme by patiently waiting for the right juxtapositions of coincidence and disparity to occur in real-life situations. The split second that he called the *decisive moment* is not the height of action, but rather that instant when the formal spatial relationships of the subjects reveal their essential meaning. Cartier-Bresson called that moment "the simultaneous recognition, in a fraction of a second, of the significance of an event as well as a precise organization of forms which gave that event its proper expression."[10]

Although he worked for numerous publications, Cartier-Bresson was not a journalist interested in reporting the news, but was concerned with significant moments that had the audacity to surprise us with their own meaning. Such an image is Bresson's *Gestapo Informer Accused. Dessau, Germany,* 1945 in which an enraged, puffed-up woman reaches over and seemingly deflates another woman with her indictment.

Cartier-Bresson's belief in the revelatory moment and his antipathy for prestaged situations defined and shaped the modernist, small-camera aesthetic of intuitively anticipating when a component of life opens and defines itself for an instant. Often utilizing limited depth-of-field, Cartier-Bresson created a shallow stage for his subjects to reveal themselves within. This construct made it simpler to forecast and follow action, removed subjects from their normal environment, and transformed them into portable collage material for surrealistic theater (see Figure 13.5). His *full-frame* aesthetic, a scene completely visualized at the time of exposure, separated the mental act of seeing from the physical craft of photography. Typical of French photographers of the era, Cartier-Bresson did not express himself by making sensitive prints, preferring to employ professional labs to do his processing and printing. His stripped-down photographic grammar shunned fine print adages in favor of a direct application of materials and process. This was ideal for photographers like Cartier-Bresson who traveled and made their living by having their work reproduced in magazines and newspapers and not by selling individual photographs as aesthetic objects. To have more control over his images, Bresson and a small group of likeminded photographers formed *Magnum Photos,* the first cooperative photographic agency (see Chapter 14).

The type of moments that a camera can report are only limited by the visual resources of the photographer. **Bill Brandt** (Hermann Wilhelm Brandt) [1904– 1983] was influenced by the surrealists when he left London to go to Paris in 1929 and became Man Ray's assistant. In the first phase of his career Brandt pictured the divisions of social class in England during the Depression. Returning to London in 1931, Brandt distinctly saw and characterized British types in their cultural context. Using family members and their household servants, Brandt recreated scenarios he had witnessed in the upper-class milieus and in working-class mining towns. These docu-dramas, published in *The English at Home* (1936), *A Night in London* (1938), and *Camera in*

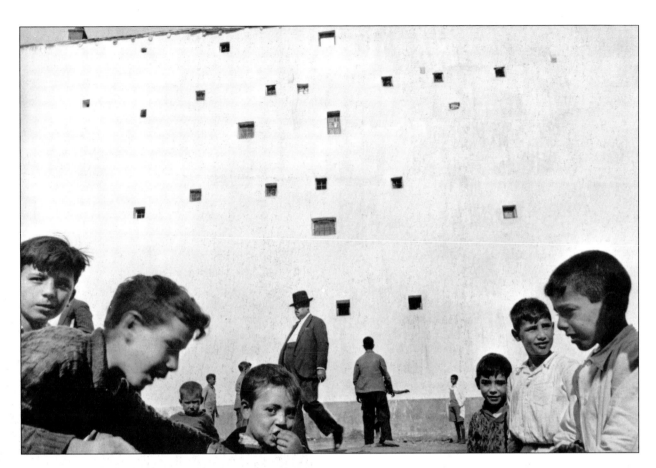

13.5   HENRI CARTIER-BRESSON.   *Untitled, Madrid, Spain,* 1933. Gelatin silver print. In discussing his ideas about composition Cartier-Bresson stated: "We look at and perceive a photograph . . . all in one glance. In a photograph, composition is the result of a simultaneous coalition, the organic co-ordination of elements seen by the eye. Composition must have its own inevitability about it . . . at the moment of shooting it can only come from our intuition. . . . If you start cutting or cropping a good photograph, it means death to the geometrically correct interplay of proportions."[11]
© Cartier-Bresson/Magnum Photos.

London (1948), are expressionistic interpretations rather than reportage. His compositions, based on German Jugendstil/Art Nouveau posters, are graphic, sober and contain an undertow of foreboding. His grainy images are printed *down* (dark), sacrificing shadow detail and mid-tone separation, emphasizing a brooding and ominous psychological state. In the introduction of *The English at Home,* Raymond Mortimer refers to Brandt as an anthropologist who had the "detached curiosity of a man investigating the customs of some remote and unfamiliar tribe."[12]

Brandt's later Cold War work deals with literary figures, landscape, and the female nude. Influenced by Greg Toland's wide-angle photography in *Citizen Kane* (1940), Brandt used a pinhole camera to exaggerate perspective, making statuesque female nudes reminiscent of El Greco that stretch and extend in space while remaining uncomfortably close. The distortion of scale and the displacement of objects produce puzzling optical illusions that free subjects from their surroundings, encouraging the exploration of nonrational meanings. This lack of definitive meaning, the atmosphere of a troubled dream, presents a mysterious and imposing sense of femininity. Working in isolation, Brandt crafted formal, strangely lit, high-contrast prints of figures that glow with an unknown power (see Figure 13.6). These images offer a reflective, inscrutable vision in opposition to the factual, and poetically explore the anxiety of the atomic era (see Chapter 15). In his 1948 book, *Camera in London,* Brandt stated that:

> It is part of the photographer's job to *see* more intensely than most people do. He must have and keep in him something of the receptiveness of the child who looks at the world for the first time or of the traveler who enters a strange country. . . . We are most of us too busy, too worried, too intent on proving ourselves right, too obsessed with ideas to stand and stare. . . . Very rarely are we able to free our minds of thoughts and emotions and just see for the simple pleasure of seeing. And so long as we fail to do this, so long will the essence of things be hidden from us."[13]

The surreal moment of fantasy in collision with social conventions was explored by **Manuel Alvarez Bravo** [b. 1902]. Bravo, the son and grandson of Mexican painters and photographers, was encouraged by Tina

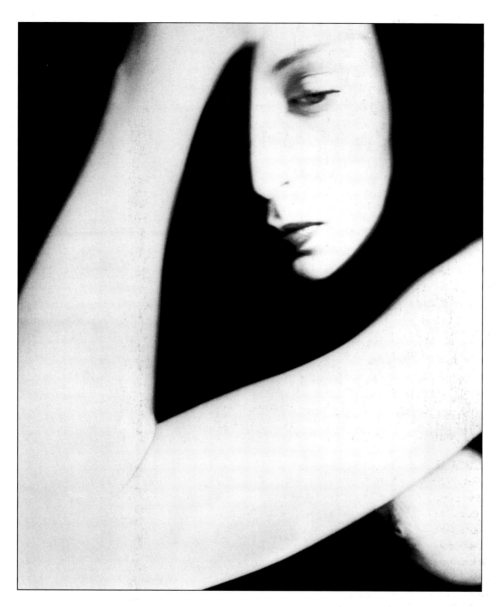

13.6   BILL BRANDT.   *Untitled,* 1961. Gelatin silver print.   © Bill Brandt Archive Ltd.

Modotti and Edward Weston to pursue photography. After meeting André Breton in 1938, Bravo's work took a decidedly surreal turn to include Mexican societal customs and Catholic religious beliefs, featuring peasant life, death, and dreams. In response to Breton's request for a cover image for the *International Surrealist Exhibition* (1940), Bravo photographed a female nude on a rooftop in strong sunlight. A doctor bandaged the model's feet and hips, leaving the model's pubis exposed as she lay on a rough blanket against an adobe wall next to four pieces of thorny cacti. *La buena fama durmiendo* (*Good Reputation Sleeping*), 1939, creates surrealistic sexual tension by contrasting concealment and display with the psychological interaction of seduction, threat, and humor. The enigmatic tableau blends the reality and fantasy of a woman alone, asleep, and vulnerable with

what is private now public. The model does not appear concerned as the cacti stands guard, protecting her against the perils of desire. Due to international censorship forbidding the display of pubic hair, this image was not used on the cover. Bravo constructed images, such as *El Sistema Nerviso del Gran Simpatico* (see Figure 13.7), that take on mythological dimensions as the male and female figures become one. Surrealist sentiments about alteration and confinement are juxtaposed with the differences in how society values men and women—the man is viewed from within (the intellect) while the woman is seen from outside (physical beauty).

Bravo has photographed numerous types of surreal moments as part of his belief that "Philosophy is something that is not as delineated as you might think; it's as ephemeral as life itself. The different chapters in life are influenced by the age in which they are formed. The individual goes on developing without being aware—until the circumstances have passed—that changes

13.7   MANUEL ALVAREZ BRAVO.   *El Sistema Nerviso del Gran Simpatico,* 1929. 9½ × 7¹⁰/₁₆ inches. Gelatin silver print.   Courtesy Colette Urbaltel and Manuel Alvarez Bravo.

have happened to you, that you no longer resemble the individual you once were."[14]

Another surrealist who found the day-to-day points of reality stranger and more compelling than imagined situations was **Lisette Model** [1906–1983]. Trained as a musician and painter in Austria, Model took up photography to earn money during the Nazi rise of the 1930s. After serving a brief apprenticeship with Florence Henri, Model emigrated to New York in 1938. While she was looking for work as a darkroom assistant at the *PM* newspaper, editor Ralph Steiner saw her prints of the wealthy French on the Riviera and the

street people of Nice. He featured them, changing their original context, on the cover of the Sunday *PM's Weekly* magazine with six full-page reproductions.[15] The headline read, "Why France Fell," and each image was accompanied by only a single-word caption: Weariness, Boredom, Underprivileged, Greed, Cynicism, Self-Satisfaction.[16]

The *PM* portfolio intrigued Alexey Brodovitch, art director of *Harper's Bazaar,* who hired Model to photograph for the magazine. Model combined her appreciation of the immediacy of the snapshot and her need to orient herself in a new country by reordering the vitality of New York City into a fresh and challenging vision. Model never showed interest in conventional beauty, but pursued the collecting of the deadly sins. Their expressive impact derived from Model's confrontational and intrusive style of treating her human subjects in a grand and monumental scale. Her use of

13.8   LISETTE MODEL.   *Coney Island, NY* (Large woman on the beach), ca. 1942. 15½ × 19½ inches. Gelatin silver print. Berenice Abbott stated: "She [Model] uses the camera with her entire body as an extension of the eye itself . . . to look at life unblinkingly. . . . Lisette said: "Don't shoot 'till the subject hits you in the pit of your stomach."[17]   Courtesy National Gallery of Canada, Ottawa. Gift of the Estate of Lisette Model, 1990, by direction of Joseph G. Blum, New York, through the American Friends of Canada.

unfamiliar perspectives created the sensation of people bulging forward out of the frame. People become landscape, massive and heroic shapes, that take on roles of exaggerated sardonic allegory. Around 1950, Berenice Abbott encouraged Model to teach photography at the New School for Social Research in New York. Model taught small workshops for the rest of her life, influencing developing photographers such as Diana Arbus (see Chapter 16).

Helen Levitt [b. 1918] looked for direct photographic expressions of her feelings by anticipating moments from life as seen from the street; the city was her motif. Levitt was inspired by Cartier-Bresson to photograph children in Harlem in 1936, and she followed that theme throughout her career. In 1938 she met Walker Evans, who became her mentor and friend, and James Agee. Her collaborations with Agee included two films, *The Quiet One* (1949) and *In the Street* (1952), and a book, *A Way of Seeing,* done in 1946 but not released until 1965.[18] Agee romanticized the work, but the corners of Levitt's spontaneous renderings of New York's neighborhood children engaged in games of fantasy are filled with eerie allusions to an explosive underclass (see Figure 13.9). Working with a Leica and a right-angle prism allowed her to point the camera in one direction while photographing in another, as her friend Ben Shahn had done for his FSA work. Levitt saw the streets of New York as a stage and its people as performers of whom she made visual memorials, capturing the fleeting confluence of chance from the episodic flow of real life. Levitt does not offer a structure of rhetoric, like that of the FSA or Photo League, to contextualize her images. In spite of urban poverty and violence, her photographs are not about despair, and their lack of verbal mooring lets them retain a transitory sense of the fantastic.

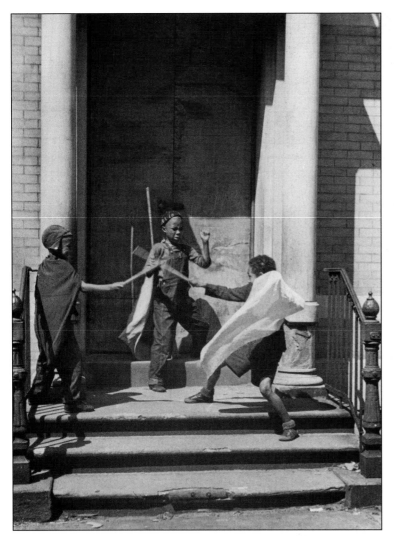

13.9   HELEN LEVITT.   *Untitled, New York,* ca. 1940
(Boys fencing with capes and sticks on stoop). 9³⁄₁₆ ×
6¹³⁄₁₆ inches. Gelatin silver print. In his essay for *A Way
of Seeing* Agee compares Levitt's attitude to Johann
Wolfgang von Goethe's (1749–1832), who combined
sensuous experience with poetic intuition in much of
his work: "It would be mistaken to suppose that any of
the best photography is come at by intellection; it is,
like all art, essentially the result of an intuitive process,
drawing on all that the artist *is* rather than on anything
he thinks, far less theorizes about. . . . Goethe wrote it is
good to think, better to look and think, best to look
without thinking. Such photographs as these can do
much to show us what he meant."[19]   © Helen Levitt.
Courtesy George Eastman House.

Levitt's statement: "All I can say about the work I try to
do, is that the aesthetic is in reality itself,"[20] keeps intel-
lectualization to a minimum and explains nothing about
her mysterious aesthetic decisions except to say that this
is how she saw life. Levitt's open attitude encourages
people to imprint their own attitudes as the photogra-

pher shapes, summarizes, reflects, and allows her experiences to resonate against
our own. In the late 1950s, Levitt investigated the potential of color to expand, intensify, and transform the emotional and
psychological content while continuing to
work the same themes.

Sometimes it takes a person who is
skilled with both pictures and words to create a collection of moments to describe a
place. In *The Inhabitants* (1946) and *The
Home Place* (1948), **Wright Morris**
[1910–1998] examined rural, small-town
midwestern life during the 1930s and
1940s by placing text on one page and an
image on the facing page. For Wright there
was no single moment but a woven tapestry of what he called "photo-texts." In contrast to his novels, the bright Nebraska sun
does not illuminate the skin of people but
only the surfaces of their surrounding artifacts and structures; the people are
nowhere to be seen (see Figure 13.10).
They have vanished and the reader/viewer
is confronted with their relics. The lives of
the visually absent people are described in
his fictional text, a blend of accounts and
impressions that act in concert to present a
community of people and their environs.
This strategy extends the moment as a
reader travels back and forth between the
visual and the verbal, salvaging from the
ruins of the Depression a distilled, affec-
tionate, but unnostalgic collection of a
time, place, and people now vanished. Morris' melding
of words and pictures provided a model for future imagemakers, such as Robert Frank, who thought that a
collection of moments was needed to fully describe a
subject. Morris commented on his multiple presentation and its effect:

> How are we to distinguish between the real and the imitation?
> Few things observed from one point of view only can be con-
> sidered *seen.* The multifaceted aspect of reality has been a
> commonplace since cubism, but we continue to see what we
> will, rather than what is there. Image-making is our prefer-
> ence for what we imagine, to what is there to be seen.[21]

Harold E. Edgerton [1903–1990] had no interest in
moments from urban or rural life. Edgerton did share
some of the same concerns as Hans Felix Siegismund
Baumann, a.k.a. **Felix H. Man** [1893–1985], who used
a tripoded miniature camera to arrest the peak gestures
of musicians and conductors, providing a record and a
physical sense of their performance. Edgerton wanted
to visualize such climactic and unseen instances under
laboratory conditions. Edgerton was an electrical engineer; he devised the modern stroboscope, using light-

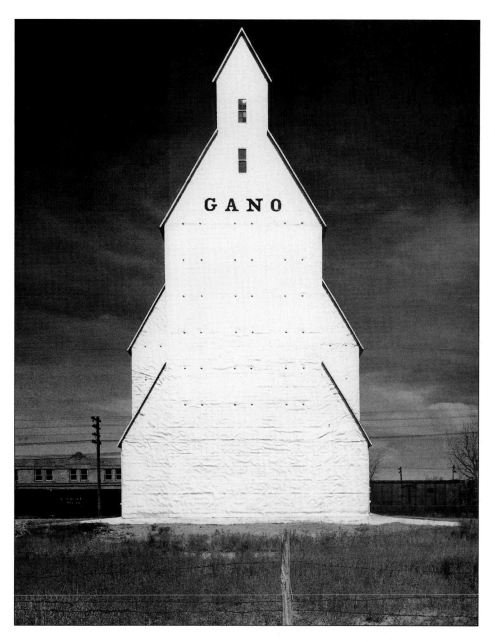

13.10 WRIGHT MORRIS.   Gano Grain Elevator, Western Kansas, 1940. Gelatin silver print.   Morris said: "If there is a common photographic dilemma, it lies in the fact that so much has been seen, so much has been 'taken,' there appears to be less to find. The visible world, vast as it is, through overexposure has been devalued. The planet looks better from space than in a close-up. The photographer feels he must search for, or invent, what was once obvious. This may take the form of photographs free of all pictorial associations. This neutralizing of the visible has the effect of rendering it invisible. In these examples photographic revelation has come full circle, the photograph exposing a reality we no longer see."[22]   Courtesy Mrs. Wright Morris.

emitting gas discharge tubes triggered by high-voltage pulses, in the process of solving a scientific problem. Edgerton's discovery, in the early 1930s, that tubes filled with xenon gas greatly increased light output, provided the foundation for manufacturing electronic flash units in the early 1940s. Edgerton used these findings to make two types of motion studies. One involved a series of repeating flashes, with a predetermined interval of time between them, to make multiple-exposure and motion pictures of subjects as they moved through time in a manner similar to the one pioneered by Marey. The other used only one flash of extremely short duration, as brief as 1/1,000,000 of a second, to make single images that made visible what had been an empty, unseeable, hence unknowable moment in time. Edgerton adapted ordinary cameras, replacing the shutters with electrical illumination that substituted light for the opening and

13.11   HAROLD EDGERTON.   *Firing an Antique (1878) Revolver,* 1936. Gelatin silver print.   Scientific value aside, Edgerton's photographs possess an element of the fantastic not only because they depict a formerly vacant space, but because of their ability to prolong the childhood pleasure of objects violently exploding and breaking—firing pistols, bursting glass, bullets impacting, and bucking horses.   © Harold & Esther Edgerton Foundation, 1999. Courtesy Palm Press, Inc.

closing of a shutter. Edgerton utilized technology to identify and incorporate previously unobserved instances of time into visual vocabulary and public consciousness. His visual evidence, like Atget's, provides data and artistic revelation. James R. Killian, Jr., wrote: "Edgerton is primarily interested in analyses and hitherto undiscovered information. . . . He does not seek a style charged with mystical inner meaning, metaphor, or emotion. . . . Throughout his career he invented new

photographic systems as tools to solve problems. In this work his photography is sometimes secondary to the information he seeks."[23] As the world entered the atomic age, Edgerton was there with his camera to record an early above-ground atomic explosion.[24]

Even though a moment may have been captured by a camera its meaning is never fixed. Today such a moment as Edgerton's atomic blast can be read as a signal marking the end of America's idealistic transcendental myths and the beginning of an embrace of European existential angst. As photographers became aware of the difficulty of holding on to a single meaning, they moved away from the notion that meaning must be controlled by the maker, as in *Life* magazine, in order for the image to be successful. The atomic age unleashed a new generation of artists who made images not only directly from their lives but by recycling previous moments. The images' meaning was intentionally left open to encourage viewers to participate in the process by ascribing their own set of beliefs to the picture.

Endnotes

1   Richard Avedon, ed., *J. H. Lartigue: Diary of a Century* (New York: Viking Press, 1970), unp., 1901 diary entry.

2   Peter Hunter (Salomon), *Erich Salomon* (Millerton: Aperture, 1978), 5.

3   Erich Salomon, *Berühmte Zeitgenossen in unbewachten Augenblicken/Celebrated Contemporaries in Unguarded Moments* (Stuttgart: J. Engelhorns Nachf, 1931). Quoted in Beaumont and Nancy Newhall, *Masters of Photography* (New York: Castle Books, 1958), 134.

4   Walter Benjamin, "A Short History of Photography," 1931, in Alan Trachtenberg, ed., *Classic Essays on Photography* (New Haven: Leete's Island Books, 1980), 215.

5   Pierre Mac Orlan, "La photographie et le fantastique social," *Les Annales* (1 November 1928), 414. Quoted Travis, "Ephemeral Truths" in Sarah Greenough, et al., *On the Art of Fixing a Shadow: One Hundred and Fifty Years of Photography* (Boston: Bulfinch Press, 1989).

6   Cited in Anna Fárová, ed., *André Kertész,* adapted by Robert Sagalyn (New York: Grossman Publishers, 1966), 7–8.

7   Ibid., 12.

8   Brassaï, introduction to *Transmutations,* 1934–5, unp., an album of twelve cliché-verre prints.

9   For information on André Breton's influence, see Peter Galassi, *Henri Cartier-Bresson: The Early Work* (New York: Museum of Modern Art, 1987), 12.

10   Henri Cartier-Bresson, *The Decisive Moment* (New York: Simon & Schuster, 1952), unp.

11   Henri Cartier-Bresson, *The Decisive Moment,* unp.

12   Raymond Mortimer, Intro. to Bill Brandt, *The English at Home* (London: B. T. Batsford, 1936), 4.

13   Bill Brandt, *Camera in London* (London and New York: Focal Press, 1948), 14–15.

14   Manuel Alvarez Bravo, *Revelaciones: The Art of Manuel Alvarez Bravo,* an interview conducted by Isaac Artenstein in MoPA members publication #13 (1990) (Balboa Park, CA: The Museum of Photographic Arts), 6.

15   For Model's account of the *PM* story and her relationship with Brodovitch, see James McQuaid and David Tait, unpublished transcript, "Interview with Lisette Model," January 28–30, 1977 (1978) located at GEH Library, RB TR 140 M52 M26.

16   Lisette Model, "Why France Fell," *PM's Weekly,* Sunday Edition, Section Two, January 19, 1941, cover and 34–39.

17   Berenice Abbott, Preface, *Lisette Model* (Millerton, NY: Aperture, 1979), 8–9.

18   *A Way of Seeing: Photographs of New York by Helen Levitt,* essay by James Agee (New York: Viking Press, 1965). The book has been republished in revised forms in 1981 and 1989 with resequencing, recropping, and the addition and subtraction of images. For discussion see Katherine Dieckmann, "Mean Streets," *Art in America* (May 1990), 223–29, 263.

19   James Agee, essay, *A Way of Seeing* (New York: Viking Press, 1965), 4–5, 78.

20   Helen Levitt in Brooks Johnson ed., *Photography Speaks: 66 Photographers on Their Art* (New York: Aperture/The Chrysler Museum, 1989), 64.

21   Morris, 536.

22   Wright Morris, "In Our Image," *The Massachusetts Review,* vol. 19, no. 4 (1978). Reprinted in Vicki Goldberg, ed., *Photography in Print* (1988), 542.

23   Harold E. Edgerton and James R. Killian Jr., *Moments of Vision: The Stroboscopic Revolution in Photography* (Cambridge, MA: The MIT Press, 1979), 10.

24   This series of nonstrobe photographs is in keeping with Edgerton's passion for finding a way to present the unseen. They were made by Edgerton from atop a seventy-five foot tower, seven miles from the blast site, using a ten-foot focal length telescope and a magneto-optic shutter for split-second imaging of the explosion.

CHAPTER FOURTEEN

Photography and the Halftone

Pictures and Printers Ink

The initial success of the daguerreotype was based on its ability to fulfill underlying desire, which was stated during Roman times in Pliny's myth about a young woman who outlines the shadow of her paramour on a wall as a mechanism of remembrance. Its failure was due to its inability to reproduce itself. People not only wanted an automatic way of capturing nature, they also wanted an easy and inexpensive method for sharing their remembrances with as many people as they pleased. It was this human characteristic, the desire to share something of personal importance with others, that led Niépce to first experiment with light to make images that could be printed by a press in ink.

As England and France expanded basic public education laws during the 1830s, publishing grew to meet the needs of a newly literate industrial society. The rapid growth of cities that accompanied industrialization increased the demand for newspapers, illustrated books, and

NICKOLAS MURAY. *Hand and X-Ray Machine*, ca. 1962. 10½ × 11¼ inches. Carbro print. Courtesy George Eastman House.

magazines. In 1842, *The Illustrated London News* became the first weekly magazine to favor images over text. It contained numerous full-page illustrations, including two-page bleeds, becoming a model other publishers would follow. The biggest technical obstacle such publications faced was how to use ink to print pictures and text at the same time. Neither Daguerre's nor Talbot's processes could make high-quality, reproducible, and permanent images to compete with the economy of production and permanence of ink-based lithographs and wood engravings in this thriving picture market.

Intaglio printing methods for reproducing images, such as aquatint, etching, line engraving, and mezzotint, used recessed printing areas and were therefore incompatible with moveable type, which relies on relief printing, in which the raised areas are inked. *Lithography*, a planographic process in which an image is drawn on a flat surface, was also unsuitable for use with moveable type. Illustrations made from either of these two methods had to be printed separately and hand-pasted into a publication, making them costly and time consuming. What was needed was a process that would allow both text and pictures to be printed simultaneously using the same equipment, materials, and skills.

In 1842 the search for a process that would bring photography into the arena of publishing led Hippolyte Fizeau to devise a method for making prints from etched daguerreotypes, but it was impractical. The real breakthrough was in the work Talbot did for what would come to be known as the *halftone process*. The halftone process permits a continuous tone image, such as a photograph, to be printed simultaneously with text. The halftone principle utilizes an optical illusion in which tones are represented by numerous small dots of different sizes having equal optical density and equal spacing between their centers. In printing, the halftone screen divides an image into tiny dots that deposit ink on paper in proportion to the density of the original image tones in the areas they represent. In 1858, Talbot published an article describing how he devised a way for images and text to be printed at the same time through relief methods, by making exposures through a fabric screen to break the image up into tiny sections that when etched would make tolerable prints. By 1856, improvements in Talbot's method, which he called photoglyphic engraving, contained all the data that Karl Klic would need to invent his intaglio *photogravure process* in 1879. Refinements in the halftone process, such as Frederic E. Ives's cross-line screen, which generated images made of dots of varying size and distribution just as we see them in today's newspapers and magazines, and the high-speed relief (letterpress) press, made it economically feasible to print text and images together, ending the era of photographers acting as small independent publishers.

By the 1890s, monochromatic pictures could cheaply and easily be reproduced alongside type, but photography did not immediately replace the previous conventions of newspaper and magazine illustration. Editors were reluctant to change the "artistic" engravings and woodcuts accepted as *pictorial illusion,* the understanding between the viewer's reaction to an image and the reality it represents. People were accustomed to specific styles of depiction and reluctant to accept anything different. As photography was a new medium, there was no backlog of historical photographs for publishers to call upon and use in their illustrations. Photographers had to be present at events to record them; draftsmen could produce pictures of events they had never observed without their credibility being questioned. As photomechanical reproduction improved, however, picture magazines used more photographs for illustration and advertising and their sales rose. The expansion of the audience for photographs changed the subject matter depicted. Previously, photographers could make a living selling postcards of local scenes and people. Now, to reap the economic advantages of the new technology, publishers needed subjects that interested large audiences, leading to the glamorization of people and places from Babe Ruth to the Grand Canyon.

Photomechanical reproduction made pictures ubiquitous and altered concepts of art while raising issues of control and censorship. In "The Work of Art in the Age of Mechanical Reproduction" (1936),[1] Walter Benjamin [1892–1940] stated that even the best reproduction has an imperfect presence, therefore it lacks a unique existence, an authenticity, a state of being and authority he called *aura.* Benjamin wrote that reproduction eliminates aura, shatters tradition, and emancipates a work of art from its dependence on ritual, reducing the distance between artists and viewers and making the work more accessible. The breakdown of aura and its replacement of reality with reproduction smashed conventions, but the loss of contact with the authentic (original) left a spiritual vacuum of "secondhand" experiences. As photographically based reproduction became routine during the twentieth century, the authentic individuality of an art work and, in turn, the personal self suffered from a mounting sense of alienation due to a loss of belief in the power of nature and its replacement by technology. By the close of World War II, American artists who previously portrayed the beauty of the natural world joined their European counterparts in turning inward to find subjective responses to their existential woes. Ironically, as inky reproductions age they become "antique images" with a patina of nostalgia and our culture then reassigns an aura, based on the romantic sentiments about the passage of time. This liberates the reproductions from their primary function, converting them into new ways of seeing the past based on the present.

14.1   JOHN HEARTFIELD.   *Hitler erzählt Märchen II* (*Hitler Tells Fairytales II*). *From AIZ* (March 5, 1936). 14¾ × 10⁷⁄₁₆ inches. Photogravure print.   Courtesy George Eastman House.

The Photo Magazine

A twentieth-century newspaper's dynamic combination of graphic systems, drawing, photography, and type anchored a photograph's free-floating meaning to an instructive mode not chosen by the photographer but by an editor, editorial committee, or paying client. In a technologically based culture that depended on precise definitions, a multiple reading of a news photograph was not considered desirable. The control of meaning for commercial, editorial, and political purposes was refined by German illustrated magazines, such as *Berliner Illustrierte Zeitung (Berlin Illustrated Newspaper)*, founded in 1890; *Münchner Illustrierte Press (Munich Illustrated Press)*, begun in 1923; and *AIZ*, or *Arbeiter Illustrierte Zeitung (Workers' Illustrated Newspaper)*, started in 1921. Their illustrated lessons about how to manipulate meaning were quickly conveyed throughout the world.

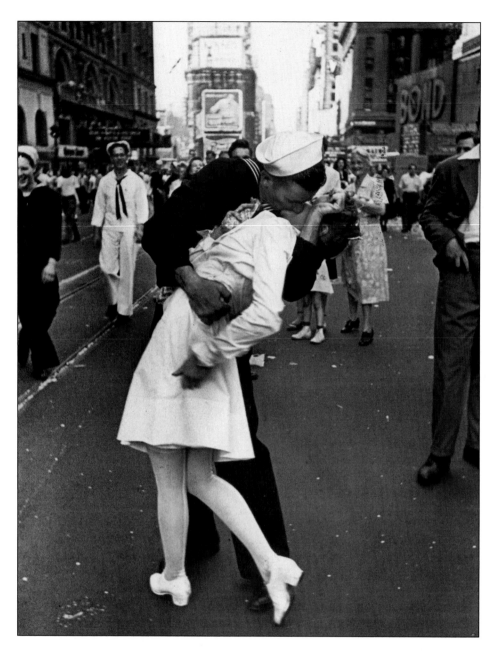

14.2.   ALFRED EISENSTAEDT.   *V.J. Day,* 1945.
Gelatin silver print. One of the original *Life* staff
photographers, **Alfred Eisenstaedt** [1898–1995]
pioneered the use of the 35-mm camera for photo-
reportage in Germany while cementing his reputation
as a photographer capable of making printable images
in almost any time-based, assignment-driven situation.
He produced over 2,000 people-oriented news assignments during his forty years with *Life.*   Courtesy Alfred
Eisenstaedt, *Life Magazine.* © Time Warner, Inc.

The passionate, political photomontages of Helmut
Herzfeld, who later anglicized his name to **John
Heartfield** [1891–1968] as a protest against a German
anti-British campaign in 1916, were specially constructed for ink reproduction. According to fellow
dadaist George Grosz [1893–1959], he and Heartfield
"[re]invented the photomontage in his studio at five
o'clock on a May morning in 1916."[2] Both were probably familiar with the cutting and pasting of images
done by soldiers on the Western front to get reports of
the slaughter of World War I past the censors. Heartfield most often appropriated images that he then
metaphorically reassembled, especially pictures dealing with Nazis, dramatically subverting their original
intent to make scathing social commentary (see Figure
14.1). The photographic nature of montage lends it
credibility. Its photographic exactness makes printed
advertisements successful, and observers are convinced
of its message before they have time to analyze how
they have been persuaded.

Hitler's rise to power ended the flowering period of European photojournalism. In 1933 Hitler suppressed all photography-based publications that questioned his authority. Heartfield and his fellow montagemaker Karl Vanek fled to Prague, where *AIZ* continued to publish, and then to England in 1940, where Heartfield stayed until he returned to the former communist East Germany in 1950. Even now, with the specific propaganda message of the work gone, Heartfield's montages continue to cry against greed and oppression.

Editors Karl Korff and Kurt Safranski of the *Berliner Illustrierte* and many photographers escaped to America. Stefan Lorant of the *Münchner Illustrierte* went to London and founded *Lilliput* (1934) and *Picture Post* (1938) and edited the *Weekly Illustrated* before emigrating to the U.S. All these publications were headed by strong editors who took completed photographic assignments and contextualized them through page layout selections and text. Since photographers still did their own processing and printing, they could exercise limited editorial direction through the choice of images they submitted.

The concepts of these exiled pioneers of photojournalism and of Lucien Vogel, editor of the French picture magazine *Vu (Seen),* made their way to America. Many pictures Erich Salomon took during his visit to America in 1929 impressed publisher Henry Robinson Luce [1898–1967], who had them reproduced in *Time* (founded 1923) and *Fortune* (founded 1930). Luce, the child of Christian missionaries in China, adopted the conservative, paternalistic position that objective reporting was not desirable or even possible. In 1934, Luce envisaged a magazine whose managers would "edit pictures into a coherent story [and] harness the main stream of optical consciousness" with the "mind-guided camera."[3] The first issue of *Life* hit the stands on November 23, 1936 with a cover story about the construction workers on the Fort Peck, MT, dam project by *Fortune* photographer Margaret Bourke-White. Writing in a style reminiscent of nineteenth-century stereoview advertisements, Luce declared *Life's* mission:

> To see life; to see the world; to witness great events . . . to take pleasure in seeing; to see and be amazed; to see and be instructed; thus to see, and to be shown, is now the will and new expectancy of half mankind.[4]

Life was a runaway newsstand hit (*Look,* its competitor, appeared in 1937). Following a corporate model, photographers were expected to be disciplined members of a bureaucratic division of labor (see Figure 14.2). Teams of specialists pieced together a magazine that was overseen and directed by men with definite political and social agendas. *Life* became a fixture in middle-class American living rooms, its circulation peaking at 8.5 million copies a week, its estimated readership 24 million people. Over half the U.S. population read at least one or more issues in any three-month period.[5] *Life* spawned similar magazines like *Ebony* (1945) that catered to the African-American community. Through photo-essays, like **Ernst Haas's** [1921–1986] 24-page *Magic Images of New York* (1953), the interpretive and poetic possibilities of color photography were integrated into daily viewing habits. *Life* preached mainline American values throughout the 1950s, but by the late 1960s, rising costs, a shift in societal beliefs away from a homogeneous viewpoint, and television's ability to instantly reach larger audiences with news bites contributed to *Life's* decline. After 1,864 consecutive issues, *Life* ceased weekly publication in 1972. It was restructured as a smaller format monthly in 1978 until it finally ceased regular publication in 2000.

A powerful, popular photographic press, similar in substance to the mass-circulation magazine phenomenon, also emerged in the 1930s. *Popular Photography* (1937) quickly became the leading photographic journal in America. Two other popular magazines also began at this time: *Minicam* (1937), later called *Modern Photography,* and *U.S. Camera* (1938). Unlike older publications designed for salon photographers, these new magazines concentrated on amateurs who favored small, hand-held cameras. The editors relied on democratic appeal, a fascination with technology, and a bit of cheesecake to "spread the cheerful gospel that photography is a lot of fun."[6] Supported by the photographic industry, they encouraged amateurs to buy expensive equipment with the promise that their easy, how-to-do-it articles would instruct and technically empower them with the means of self-expression. As quality rose and production expenses dropped, more illustrated magazines targeted specific audiences. Photography groups, such as the American Society of Magazine Photographers (ASMP) and the Professional Photographers of America (PPA), started their own journals (*Infinity* and *Professional Photographer*).

National Geographic, designed to educate its audience about the world, first appeared as a monthly scientific journal in 1888. In 1906, it started using photography to "illustrate" its stories, becoming one of the first magazines to regularly reproduce autochromes.[7] *Autochrome* was the first practical color photography system, invented by August and Louis Lumière in 1903 and manufactured beginning in 1907. In this additive screen process, a glass plate was dusted with microscopic grains of potato starch that were dyed with orange, green, and blue-violet. A fine powder of carbon black was used to fill in spaces between the grains. A panchromatic emulsion was applied to the plate and the exposure was made through the back of the plate, so that the dyed potato starch acted as tiny filters. This was developed into a positive transparency and viewed from the emulsion side by light that was colored as it passed through the screen.

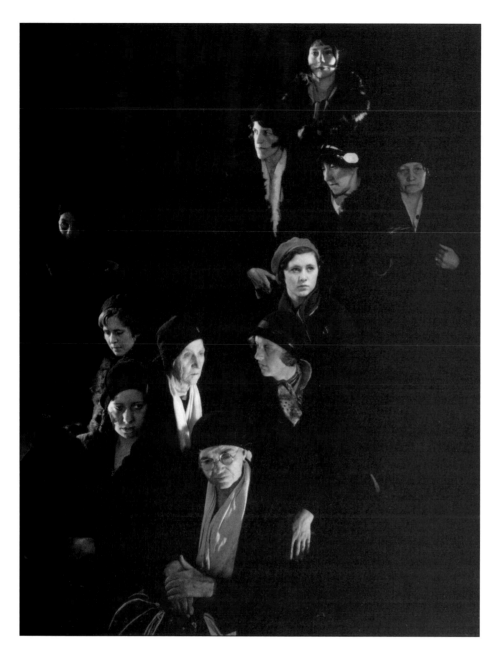

14.3 EDWARD STEICHEN. *Homeless Women,* 1932. 13⅝ × 10⅝ inches. Gelatin silver print. Steichen described how he made this image: "Then there was the story of the homeless women in New York lodging houses during the Depression. It seemed that many women, old and young, jobless or too old to work and contribute to the food supply, left home and came to New York. When the Travelers Aid Society found such people, they put them up in lodging houses for the night. We were to do a brochure for the Travelers Aid Society, and I suggested that the agency bring up the first twenty women who came out of the lodging house in the morning. There was to be no selection. Each woman was to be given ten dollars. . . . To get the rudderless feeling of their story, I instructed each woman to look in a different direction."[8] Reprinted with permission of Joanna T. Steichen.

National Geographic's impact on photographic practice has not been as extensive as *Life*'s because until the 1970s its editors continued to rely on extensive text as the story dynamic, utilizing photographs as story illustrations rather than to drive the narrative. Nevertheless, by the mid-1950s *Geographic* was the reigning exotic picture book for armchair travelers. From its inception in an age of European imperial expansion, *National Geographic* was a *Wunderkammer* (wonder cabinet) of curiosities, collecting, ordering, and summing up knowledge for the pleasure and instruction of educated, upper-class Americans—expanding the territory of the conceivable. Under the guise of scientific pursuit, photography allowed readers to vicariously observe "primitive" customs of *the Other* (see Chapter 7). For young people, *National Geographic* permitted the forbidden viewing of bare-breasted, "native" women. *National Geographic* never aspired to "advocacy journalism," always steering away from hard, unpleasant truths. In commenting about the editorial obsession for "balanced" coverage, a *National Geographic* photographer once joked that "in a story on volcanoes . . . you should balance their destruction with something good about volcanoes."[9] Even critics who question *National Geographic*'s disengagement from its Victorian roots of racial differences, class attributes, and sexual imperatives acknowledge it has nowadays begun to pay attention to the cultural boundaries it depicts for a readership estimated at 40 million.[10]

The Separation of Art and Commerce: Advertising and Fashion

During the nineteenth century, wealthy amateurs discriminated between photographs made for art and those made for commerce; individuals whose livelihood depended on photography seldom made these distinctions. Champions of modernism, such as Stieglitz, required photographers to be commercially untainted, widening the separation between artistic and commercial practice. During the twentieth century, commercial photographers seeking artistic validation led schizophrenic existences. The arts community demanded they create a body of work distinctly different from their commercial activities, reinforcing the notion that making a living through commercial photography and producing art were incompatible and perpetuating the myth of the idealistic, starving artist. Regardless of what the art elite thought, however, commercial photography infiltrated Western consciousness as low-cost and high-quality offset printed images became the major source of visual representation. By the 1960s, a tidal wave of printed color images was eroding the boundaries between these areas.

Fashion magazines were among the first to regularly use editorial photographs. Baron Adolphe de Meyer's elegant pictorial displays of fashion through light and texture began to appear in *Vogue* in 1913. In 1923, **Edward Steichen** replaced de Meyer as chief photographer for the Condé Nast publications of *Vogue* and *Vanity Fair*. Steichen formulated modernistic styles inspired by cubism and art deco for advertising, celebrity, and fashion photography by mastering a new tool in the photographic vocabulary: incandescent light. Steichen's command of artificial lighting enabled him to emphasize or invent the glamour in whatever was before his lens. Steichen stressed the formal aspects of his subject. Relying on a strategy based on class and romance, he helped persuade advertising

agencies that photography was more effective than hand-drawn illustration in reaching the growing market of female consumers.[11] Steichen created bold and dynamic compositions that clearly communicated on a printed page even if the image lost detail or suffered from contrast problems during the printing process. The resulting reproductions appeared more elegant than in reality. Steichen's design sense got him commissions, and he made money not from the direct sale of his prints but through reproduction rights. Photographers like Steichen who worked with publication in mind gave up the trappings of fine art for those of journalism, whose end product is not a photographic print but the printed page. Steichen applied the principle of mechanical repetition to his own seeing, using multiple exposure or repeating shapes to construct images such as his *Homeless Women* (see Figure 14.3), for the Travelers Aid Society. Unlike the FSA photographers who went directly to their subjects, Steichen brought subjects to him and altered their circumstances according to his aesthetic will, raising issues of exploitation that continue to surround the practices of the fashion industry. Advertisers of that time considered it a daring strategy to take a more "naturalistic" approach that associated "real" people, instead of professional models, with their products.

An early successful artistic ad campaign, now considered sexist, was **Lejaren à Hiller's** [1880–1969] *Surgery Through the Ages,* done for Davis & Geck, Inc., makers of surgical sutures. Between 1927 and 1933, Hiller concocted a historic series of over 200 great moments in medical history that appeared in medical journals and hung in hospitals and physician's offices throughout the country. His tableaux, *Etienne Gourmelen* (see Figure 14.4), depicts the sixteenth-century doctor renowned for his heroic treatment of bubonic plague victims. All the men are clothed, while young, beautiful, naked women helplessly die in sexually suggestive positions.

Because advertising fueled profits, advertisers and publishers looked for ways to stimulate sales. Their alchemic formula was to visually represent a dream, spin this dream into desire, and forge the desire into a salable product. Color photography got a big boost as advertisers discovered its added "realism" spurred sales. In 1931, the *Ladies Home Journal* ran the first full-color reproduction of a carbro process print by **Nickolas Muray** [1892–1965]. The *carbro process,* patented in 1855 by Alphonse Poitevin, was designed to make prints from photographic negatives and positives by using an emulsion containing particles of carbon or colored, nonsilver pigment to form an image. Considered the most versatile of the carbon processes, the name carbro was given to an improved version to signify that carbon tissue was used in conjunction with a bromide print (car/bro). Muray's pre–World War II celebrity

14.4 LEJAREN à HILLER. *Etienne Gourmelen,* from the series *Surgery Through the Ages* ca. 1933. 18 × 14¾ inches. Gelatin silver print. Courtesy Visual Studies Workshop. Gift of 3M Company, ex-collection Louis Walton Sipley.

glamour portraits and color advertisements helped formulate an artificial style that communicated not only the needs of the advertiser, but the attitudes and preoccupations of American society as well, ranging from sex to atomic destruction (see chapter opener). By the mid-1930s, American photographer Harold Haliday Costain reported that advertisers were embracing color:

> The most noticeable recent change in advertising tendencies is the widespread use of color photography for all types of illustrations. The American advertisers, realising that over 75 per cent. [sic] of all purchases were made by our women, set about to further appeal to them by means of colour, and the great increase in its general use proves beyond doubt its claim to success.[12]

The desire to convert dreams into dollars was realized on the inky pages of fashion magazines like *Vogue, Harper's Bazaar,* and *Vanity Fair.* The art directors and photographers of these publications absorbed aesthetic trends into their approach that showcased celebrities and juxtaposed fashionable clothing within contemporary settings such as skyscrapers, sports themes, and abstract paintings. Sir **Cecil Walter Hardy Beaton** [1904–1980] was a leading fashion photographer of the 1930s, first for *Vogue* and later for *Harper's Bazaar.* Beaton was one of the first to use actresses as fashion models, importing their fairy-tale mystique to whatever he was photographing. Beaton relied on his flair, wit, and irony to stay in tune with his celebrity and royal subjects, keeping him close to his real interest, fashionability—the manner of being fashionable. Beaton shifted styles to accommodate and reflect those who prided themselves on their ability to outwardly express their inner originality and to serve

14.5   HORST P. HORST.   *From Paris—The New Detolle Corset with Back Lacing,* 1939. $9^{10}/_{16} \times 7^{13}/_{16}$ inches. Gelatin silver print.   The printed ad copy links the city of romance, bondage, and art with the expectations of nighttime pleasures: "Paris puts you back in laced corsets—and here they are. Detolle made the extreme, back-lacing corset . . . to bind you in for the Velasquez silhouette. This corset is specifically for evening."[13]   Courtesy Staley Wise, New York.

Horst P. Horst's [1906–1999] fashion career, spanning almost sixty years with Condé Nast, got underway as a model and assistant for George Hoyningen-Huene, [1900–1968] who brought the functionalism of the New Objectivity into the studio assignments he did for *Vogue* and *Harper's Bazaar* between 1925 and 1945. Horst's mastery of light and use of props is demonstrated in his 1939 *Vogue* corset ad image. Here a faceless corseted torso conveys sexual tension through an object of repression and self-inflicted discomfort, walking the obscure boundary lines of pleasure, pain, eros, and cruelty.

Martin Munkacsi [1896–1963], originally a painter and sportswriter, used the small, hand-held camera with the split-second sensitivity to give a dynamic sense of action to his fashion and sports photographs. Beginning in 1933, Munkacsi adopted the candid technique with athletic models, outside, in

as public tastemakers. People in the fashion business, just like Hollywood moviemakers, learned to visualize American dreams, as in Frank Capra's *It Happened One Night* (1934) and *Mr. Deeds Goes to Town* (1936), and make and distribute these fantasies of idealistic individuals by means of mechanical reproduction at a universally affordable price.

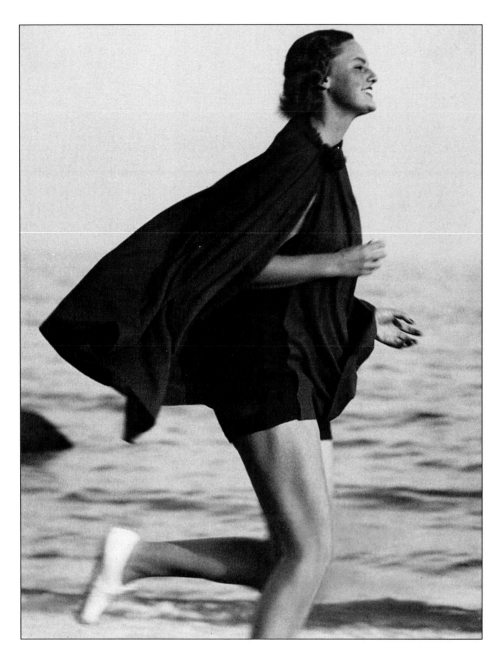

14.6 MARTIN MUNKACSI.   *Lucille Brokaw,* from
Harper's Bazaar, December, 1934. Gelatin silver print.
© Joan Munkacsi. Courtesy Howard Greenberg Gallery, NY

natural light, for *Harper's Bazaar*. His spontaneous approach established the second major fashion magazine working style: naturalism.

In the 1950s **Alexey Brodovitch** [1895–1971], the art director of *Harper's Bazaar* from 1934–58, released fashion from its past genres by devising a new compositional structure for the printed page and challenging photographers to produce daring images for this format. Brodovitch envisioned his layouts as single rectangles that spread over two pages instead of the narrow vertical column of a single page. He experimented with type, illustrations, white space, bleed photographs, and mon-

tage to expand and control the visual pacing of time. Brodovitch's work as a designer and teacher, coupled with his recognition of the abilities of immigrant photographers to find new forms for interpreting the culture of the New World, affected the styles of photographers including Lisette Model, Irving Penn, Richard Avedon, Louise Dahl-Wolfe [1895–1989], Hiro, and Robert Frank. In addition, Brodovitch influenced people in the business who saw his ideas in ink each month on the pages of *Harper's Bazaar* and began to imitate them.

Irving Penn [b. 1917], a student of Alexey Brodovitch, devised an austerely sophisticated graphic form of fashion photography. Working with Alexander Liberman [1912–1999], the art director of *Vogue* for over forty years, Penn dispensed with naturalism and spontaneity in favor of formal studio control, doing away with the cluttered paraphernalia and theatrical lighting of the previous generation of fashion photographers. Whether photographing Peruvian Indians, New Guinea tribesmen, or Hell's Angels, Penn set up a "luminous tent,"[14] a makeshift studio containing a gray or white seamless paper backdrop and artificial lights, to pose his subjects in a blank space. Penn's strategy removed sitters from their normal surrounding, treating all subjects to the same structured composition and elegant lighting fashion models and socialites received. Liberman observed that Penn invented "his space [to give] an immediate reading of character."[15] Penn's method was universally adopted by fashion photographers.

During the 1950s, Penn saw no incongruity between art and commerce, stating: "The fashion magazine is one of the few contemporary media in which commerce success and the highest esthetic standards are not incompatible."[16] Critic Milton Brown disagreed, claiming that countless fashion photographs eroded thoughtful aesthetic explorations and were no more than vacant pastiches of "superficial tricks and attitudes which gives to their pictures an air of sophistication and modernity."[17] By the 1980s, Penn tired of the printed page, redirected his attention to making editioned, platinum-palladium prints of urban detritus, such as cigarette butts, and still lifes of bones and skulls. Regardless of subject matter, Penn's preoccupation with perfection in refined balance and tonal subtlety prunes away the inconsequential, smoothes over established hierarchy, and keeps his subject emotionally detached for contemplation. A believer in the "less is more" theory, Penn said:

> If you had two apples to photograph and could dispense with one, you would have more apple in the remaining one. I know this in terms of communication, though not necessarily in terms of esthetics.[18]

Richard Avedon [b. 1923] studied with Brodovitch after spending World War II making thousands of ID photos for the merchant marine. Under Brodovitch's mentoring eye, and later with art director Marvin Israel [1924–1984], Avedon's work for the printed page was instrumental in casting the look of fashionable post-World War II women. Avedon's control of pose and facial expression depicted women as astute, resourceful, amused, and entertaining. For 20 years his personality portraits, appearing in *Harper's Bazaar,* shaped how America saw public figures from President Eisenhower to Marilyn Monroe.

Although the fine art world continued to reject dual art director/photographer visions for being commercial team operations, photographers often acted as producers whose assistants carried out their plans. This production strategy, common in fashion photography, creates a hierarchical system of patronage for advancement. **Hiro** [b. 1930] (Yasuhiro Wakabayashi), a protégé of Avedon, worked his way through this structure and gained recognition by isolating the glamorous details of fashion and actively using color in a mix that served up material icons to its followers. Such an atelier/studio approach runs contrary to the modernistic sentiment of a single genius whose hand touches every phase of the masterpiece. In seeking the prestige of the "high" culture, photographers run the risk of losing the broader impact that the "low" culture of the printed page affords.

Avedon has actively promoted his work as crossing the imaginary boundaries of the commercial and art worlds. His large format studio practice of isolating people from their environment embraces the detail of facts over idealization. Avedon's visual mapping can be traced to his reading of French novelist Marcel Proust [1871–1922] for insight into societal behavior, manners, and social structure, pursuing a theme that linked external events and internal reality to show how time influences memory.[19] This leads Avedon off the printed page and onto the gallery wall where his productions, such as *In the American West* (1985), use enormous prints that read more like topographic maps than portraits.[20] Avedon, like Proust, is socially resourceful, yet he views individuals as isolated, society as deceptive and governed by snobbery, and artistic enterprise as a theological calling.[21] Avedon delineates and magnifies the smallest detail until it takes on an unsettling sense of importance, existentially isolating and separating people from their surroundings. Whereas Proust was an active participant within the environment he described, Avedon acts as an outside constructionist who locates his subjects, removes them from their surroundings, and brings them to the neutral, floating, white backdrop of his "style" studio. Avedon maintains representational power during these fleeing relationships, shaping the outcome that abstracts subjects from their natural environment. Avedon succeeds in crossing the borders of art and commerce when he sequesters and presents that which makes his subjects exceptional, as in his sequence of his dying father that incorporates personal subject matter with formal studio strategies.[22]

Photography broke down the doors of privacy. Compared with carte-de-visites and lithographs, the halftone and the printed page provided a means to address and expand the public's yearning for celebrity portraits. The public's thirst for images of the famous, as surrogates for their own mingling in a Proustian society for which they had no calling card, encouraged editors to eagerly translate them into ink.

George Hurrell's [1904–1992] studio portraits of Hollywood stars presented the dream of glamour and perfection that provided a fantasy relief from the images of the Great Depression as portrayed by the FSA photographers. Hurrell created beauty and dramatic emotional intensity through his expert lighting and retouching, and his images, distributed by Hollywood fan clubs and magazines, were gobbled up by the public.

14.7 PHILIPPE HALSMAN. *Vice President Richard Nixon, White House,* 1955. Gelatin silver print.   Courtesy Philippe Halsman. © Halsman Estate.

The publishing world's desire to promote and capitalize on the notion of fame can be seen in **Philippe Halsman's** [1906–1979] incisive portraits that appeared on over 100 covers of *Life* as well as in magazines such as *Saturday Evening Post* and *Paris Match*. Halsman believed the portraitist's most important tools were conversation and psychology, not technique. A self-taught photographer, Halsman claimed his greatest influences were the Russian masters of literary psychology Feodor Dostoyevsky [1821–1881] and Leo Tolstoy [1828–1910]. Halsman utilized playful methods, like jumping in the air, to unmask his subjects and divulge their essence. Published as *Philippe Halsman's*

Jump Book (1959), this concept expanded his working repertoire to include multifaceted views designed to simultaneously reveal different aspects of a celebrity's personality.

For over half a century, Canadian **Yousuf Karsh** [b. 1908] made formal environmental portraits not of the merely famous but of world achievers for numerous publications. It is not the stature of his subjects but Karsh's heroic application of incandescent lighting, rendering dramatic highlights and shadows with clarity and textural richness, that appealed to audiences of the printed page. Regardless of a subject's social position, Karsh's lighting fused personality with ability. When applied to a commercial product, his lighting conveyed a sense of competence, making the product appear well-made and worthy of purchase.

14.8   ARNOLD NEWMAN.   *Yaacou Agam #2,*
1966–1972. 12³⁄₁₆ × 12⁵⁄₁₆ inches. Gelatin silver print
collage.   © Arnold Newman.

By means of symbols and arrangement of the figure
within the space of his composition, **Arnold Newman**
[b. 1918] visually orchestrated the interior concerns of
his sitters. Newman's favorite procedure was to bring
his studio to his subjects, integrating their personalities
with their surroundings, thereby affirming the subject's
position, occupation, and status to an audience unfamiliar with the subject. At times Newman's explorations of
the essence of his subject have led him to adopt unconventional means. His collage portrait of pioneer kinetic
artist Agam (Rishon Letzion) broke up the edges of the
frame and destroyed Renaissance perspective, actively
portraying a sense of Agam's work in which the view
metamorphoses as a spectator walks by Agam's sculptural works constructed with air, light, and water.

Michelangelo Antonioni's film *Blow-Up* (1966),
modeled on photographer David Bailey, personified the
pop culture values of "swinging London" during the
1960s and set the fashion photographer up as an unparalleled figure whose self-appointed job was to experi-

ence and photograph every new trend. This made being
a photographer very appealing to the counterculture
generation, who began to take photography and filmmaking courses in record numbers.

By the 1970s fashion was not only covering almost
any topical event but was also representing women in
new ways on the printed page. Helmut Newton's
[b. 1920] highly interpretive images, as in *White
Women* (1976), depict women as aggressive and sexual
but also dangerous and unavailable to intimacy. His
stylish, sadomasochistic portrayals have entered the
mainstream through advertising and fashion, promoting what James G. Ballard, author of *Crash* (1973),
calls the "normalization of the psychopathic."[23] In this
process the media acts as a buffer between viewers and
images, allowing previously aberrant behavior to be
tolerated as long as it is consensual.

The work of more women photographers began to
regularly appear in ink. The ethereal color work of Sarah
Moon [b. 1940], Joyce Tenneson [b. 1945], and Deborah
Turbeville [b. 1937] is subdued, offering a softer sensation of the social and sexual circumstances of women.
Their commercial approach de-emphasizes direct product virtues in favor of a subliminal tack, establishing
a relationship between a product and the promise of

14.9   WEEGEE.   *Drunks,* ca. 1940. 10¼ × 11⁷⁄₁₆
inches. Gelatin silver print. Weegee wrote: "My car became my home. . . . I kept everything there, an extra
camera, cases of flash bulbs, extra loaded holders, a typewriter, fireman's boots, boxes of cigars, salami, infrared
film for shooting in the dark, uniforms, disguises, a
change of underwear, and extra shoes and socks. . . . I
had my wings, I no longer had to wait for crime to
come to me; I could go after it. The police radio was my
life line. My camera . . . my life and my love . . . was my
Aladdin's lamp."[24]   Courtesy Weegee/Liaison International.

achieving the experience depicted in the advertisement.
Rather than portraying a product's virtues, for instance, a
photograph might show two people embracing, suggesting that the product would also deliver extra effects like
fulfillment, happiness, and love. A side effect of this type
of repetitive message has been the public's ability to
make connections from less literal renditions.

The pace quickened and became more fragmentary
during the 1980s, with the rapid and more spontaneous-
looking media productions pioneered by MTV. People's awareness of how fashion photography can influence culture has also increased. Ironically, in 1997
President Clinton criticized the fashion industry for ex-
alting the drug culture with its "heroin chic" pictures of
emaciated young women and tattooed men.

Newspapers

Newspapers were slower than magazines to incorporate
photographs. It took time to discover how photography
could best report the news. Until *telephotography,* the
transmission of images via the telephone, which was
made reliable in the mid-1930s, the delays in getting
photographs back to the home office translated into a
loss of newsworthiness. On a daily basis, editors
learned that photographs could surpass words in con-

14.10 ROBERT CAPA. *Leon Trotsky,* Copenhagen, 1931. 8⅞ × 13⁷⁄₁₆ inches. Gelatin silver print.
© Robert Capa/Magnum Photos.

veying concrete, everyday incidents, such as fires, staged ceremonies, and action-oriented sporting events, as opposed to explaining complex historical issues. News photographs succeeded by letting viewers examine penetrating moments of human behavior at their kitchen tables with coffee cup in hand. Regularly covered events, like meetings, that looked boring when photographed as news could be spiced up with a caption supplied by a reporter.

The golden period of American news photography began in the 1920s and continued through the late 1950s when it was displaced by television news. Newspapers organized their own local staffs and labs and established reliable sources for nonlocal events, as new methods of reproduction convinced management that images and text could be readily printed together. By providing the same format 365 days a year, newspapers create a routine that smoothes over individual stylistic differences among photographers and provides a comforting rhythm of dependability and sameness that people accept as representing the way things are.

Practical and affordable synchronized flashlight expanded the subject possibilities of the photojournalist, not only providing illumination but delineating a spry sense of visual space. The glaring white light froze the

subjects, revealed secrets, and brought them forward out of the darkness to be scrutinized. Whatever a flashlight image lacked in naturalness it made up for in its forceful, graphic simplification, creating a sense of melodrama that was effective in the tabloid press.

Weegee (Arthur Fellig) [1899–1968] represents a resourceful use of flash as a news-gathering tool from this golden period. Weegee, like other notable photojournalists and street photographers, had the gift of "prophecy," a sixth sense enabling him to stay ahead of an unfolding event and know exactly when to release his blazing flash. Named after Ouija, a board game that claims to predict the future, Weegee scooped the competition by monitoring police and fire radio dispatches, sleeping in his clothes, and having a car outfitted with a makeshift office and darkroom in the trunk. Weegee's direct-frontal, synchronized flash assault produced unrefined and titillating images that broke through society's veneer, presenting a raw, spontaneous, pessimistic, and primeval view of humanity.

Dressed in a trenchcoat, wearing a fedora, smoking a cigar, carrying a 4 × 5-inch Speed Graphic with a flashgun, and making sarcastic remarks, Weegee could have been keeping company with the literary characters, Sam Spade and Mike Hammer. His pictures, like those in *Naked City* (1945), speak in the same blunt, uninvolved, and unrefined tone as a Dashiell Hammett or a Mickey Spillane *noir* pulp detective novel. Weegee's working style was classic "f/8 and be there," no fancy

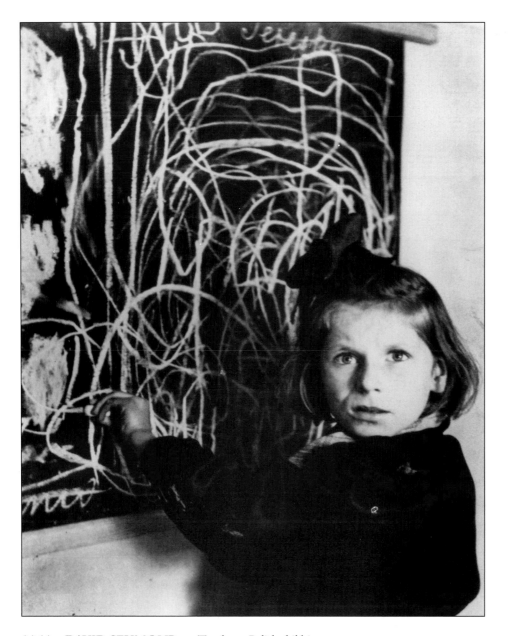

14.11 DAVID SEYMOUR. *Tereska, a Polish child in a home for disturbed children,* 1949. 12½ × 10 inches. Gelatin silver print. "Terezka, a disturbed child in an orphanage. When asked to draw a picture of her home, she produced these scrawls on the blackboard." © David Seymour/Magnum Photos.

techniques, just an instinctive response to the situation, whose structure was later imposed by cropping in the darkroom or by a picture editor. This intuitive method was ideal for tabloid picture news, giving the look and feel of an event the reader was not present to see. The task of interpretation was left to a caption editor, who gave each image an appropriate moral, political, or social accompaniment. Removed from its journalistic bonds, Weegee's work can transcend its news time and take on the distressingly symbolic form of a morality tale by a fabulist whose aggressiveness and antagonism towards his subjects gives his caricatures piercing believability (see Figure 14.9).

War Reportage

As World War II loomed, news gathering organizations and publications shifted their emphasis from features to hard news of the war fronts. As America went to war, so did many of its photographers, including Captain Edward Steichen, who served as Director of Navy Combat Photography. *Life* sent photographers to the fronts and ran a school for army photographers. The country began to rely on picture magazines to stay abreast of events, even after government censorship prevented pictures of Allied "dirty work" or American dead from being published before September 1943.

14.12   LEE MILLER.   *Buchenwald, Germany: Dead Prisoners,* April 30, 1945. Gelatin silver print. Images of concentration camp victims, made by Miller and reproduced in *Life,* provided conclusive evidence that Germany had engaged in the extermination of Jews, gypsies, homosexuals, and other so-called undesirables who they demonized as unalterably dangerous, evil, and unredeemable.[25]   Courtesy Lee Miller Archives.

Reportage-style photography continued to be reshaped by the wars of the twentieth century. Smaller cameras and faster films encouraged war correspondents to risk their lives by getting into the thick of the action and recording what they saw. This new generation was not as concerned with reporting the official story and delivered images that were less inhibited by censorship and the need to make propaganda.

Robert Capa's (André Friedmann) [1913–1954] explosively damaged picture of Russian revolutionary Leon Trotsky ushered in his flamboyant career of covering political movements and war (see Figure 14.10). His image of "a Spanish soldier the instant he is dropped by a bullet through the head"[26] while his shadow still appears to be standing freezes a moment of death. His terse approach, analogous to his writer friend Ernest Hemingway's [1889–1961] war stories, such as *A Farewell to Arms* (1929) and *For Whom the Bell Tolls* (1940), put him actively into the fray. Whether it was China, the beaches of Normandy, Israel, or finally Vietnam, where he was killed by a landmine, Capa's working dictum was: "If your pictures are not good enough, you aren't close enough."[27] A self-declared "gambler," Capa went in on the first wave of the 1944 D-Day invasion, only to have all but eight of his exposures ruined by an excited darkroom assistant, who turned on too much heat while drying the negatives and melted the emulsions before the eyes of the London office.[28] Capa was so animated he often made exposures more rapidly than his camera's fastest shutter speed. These blurry and grainy images give the sense that Capa was capable of recording events that occurred even too quickly for a camera. Capa was instrumental in forming *Magnum Photos* (1946),[29] the first cooperative photographic agency managed by photographers.

David Seymour (David Syzmin) [1911–1956], nicknamed "Chim," shared a darkroom with Robert Capa and Cartier-Bresson in Paris. He was a combat

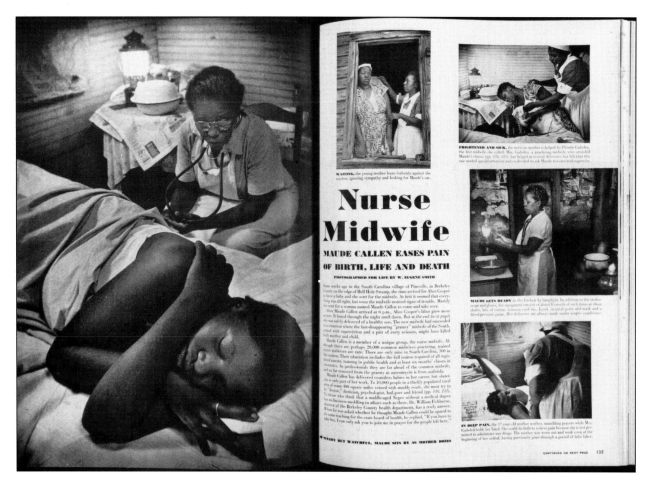

14.13   W. EUGENE SMITH.   *Nurse Midwife: Maude Callen Eases Pain of Birth, Life and Death* (*Life,* December 3, 1951. 13⅝ × 10¹⁄₁₆ inches. *Nurse Midwife* was the first serious essay in a mainline American publication to feature an African-American in a professional context. Smith said: "I was fighting racism without ever making racism the point. I had long crusaded against racism, not by hitting people over the head with a hammer, but by compassionate understanding, presenting something that people could learn from, so they could make up their own minds."[30]   Estate of N. E. Smith/Black Star: Courtesy George Eastman House.

photographer whose documentation of the effects of war in Europe on children for UNESCO resulted in *Children of Europe* (1949) (see Figure 14.11). Cartier-Bresson said: "Chim picked up his camera the way a doctor takes a stethoscope out of this bag, applying his diagnosis to the condition of the heart; his own heart was vulnerable."[31] Chim became president of Magnum upon Capa's death but was killed a few years later by an Egyptian machine-gunner, four days after the Armistice at Suez.

World War II was the first conflict in which photographers expressed empathy with the daily life of the soldiers and the victims of war. The published images of Margaret Bourke-White, **Lee Miller** [1907–1977], and George Rodger [1908–1995] of widespread devastation

and concentration camp victims were visual evidence of the Nazis' indescribable war crimes against civilians (see Figure 14.12). The publication of these images denied the executioners their wish to erase these people from human memory. David Douglas Duncan's [b. 1916] Korean War coverage in *Life* and his book, *This Is War* (1951), showed that war was not full of glory but of the crying and dying of young American soldiers.

William Eugene Smith [1918–1978] was a war correspondent for *Life* who after being seriously wounded at Okinawa in 1945 committed himself to "try and take what voice I have and give it to those who don't have one at all."[32] After recuperating, Smith produced three dramatically heroic photo-essays: *Country Doctor* (September 20, 1948), *The Spanish Village* (April 9, 1951), and *Nurse Midwife* (December 3, 1951) for *Life*.[33]

Smith constantly fought against picture stories put together by an editor. Smith believed that the "photo-essay has to be thought out, with each picture in relationship to the others, the same way you would write an essay."[34] In *Country Doctor* Smith's photographs convey a sense of who this doctor is without editorializing text. Smith's way of working propelled the photo-essay away from *Life*'s imposed format, which led viewers through stories and towards an interpretive explanation discovered by a photographer. Smith claimed he learned how to do this by listening to Beethoven.[35]

14.14 DON MCCULLIN. *Tet Offensive, Hue*
(Fallen North Vietnamese soldier, his personal effects
scattered by body-plundering soldiers), 1968. 16½ ×
11¼ inches. Gelatin silver print. English spy novelist
John Le Carré considers the effect of existential angst
on photographers and viewers: "The dead and nearly
dead, like the mad, are free, but their freedom is no use
to them. I expect that McCullin has committed suicide
through his camera many times. . . . If it is possible—as
Albert Camus insists that it is,—to feel, without romanticism, nostalgia for lost poverty, then perhaps it is
also possible to feel nostalgia for physical suffering as a
form of human nobility from which our good luck too
frequently withholds us."[36]   © Don McCullin/Contact
Press Images.

Smith also went against accepted journalistic practice
by setting up photographs and manipulating his prints to
clarify the feeling he wanted to present. The metrical
Spanish Village was pivotal because it made the entire
village rather than an individual the champion of the
story. Smith's humanitarian concerns are manifested in
his last and most extended work, *Minamata* (1975), about
the effects of industrial pollution on a Japanese fishing
village. The fishing waters of Minamata Bay were being
poisoned by industrial mercury discharge, resulting in
birth defects in a generation of children. While making
these photographs Smith received a terrible beating from

company goons that may have shortened his life. Smith's
position was to affirm that photography can help bring
about social change by stressing that "to cause awareness
is our only strength."[37]

In 1967, **Cornell Capa** [b. 1918], Robert Capa's
brother and a Magnum photojournalist whose work appeared extensively in *Life*, established the Fund for
Concerned Photography at a time when picture magazines were being displaced by electronic media (video)
images. In 1968 Capa stated that "the production demands and controls exercised by the mass communications media on the photographer today are endangering
our artistic, ethical, and professional standards and tend
to obliterate the individuality of the witness-artist."[38]
Initially the fund exhibited and published the work of
Werner Bischof [1916–1954], Robert Capa, David
Seymour (Chim), André Kertész, Leonard Freed
[1929], and Dan Weiner [1919–1959] called *The Concerned Photographer*. This project linked their images
with the "humanitarian-with-a-camera" work of Lewis
Hine that "demands personal commitment and concern
for mankind."[39]

Cornell Capa wrote: "The role of the photographer is
to witness and to be involved with his subject. The role
of the Fund is to encourage and assist such involvement, to preserve and to stress the value of conservation."[40] Cornell Capa widened the activities of this
group to include its own gallery, archive, and teaching

14.15   LARRY BURROWS.   *Reaching Out* (during
the aftermath of taking hill 484, South Vietnam), 1966.
Dye imbibition print.   Larry Burrows/*Life* Magazine
© Time Inc. Print courtesy George Eastman House.

facility. In 1974, Capa opened the International Center
for Photography (ICP) in New York, serving as its director until 1994. During Capa's tenure ICP exhibited
many photographers who practiced his brand of "humanist photography."

Beginning with Shomei Tomatsu's [b. 1930] and Hi-
romi Tsuchida's [b. 1939] documentation of the aftermath of the bombing of Hiroshima and Nagasaki, and
on through the Vietnam War, photographers had an almost continuous series of global war tragedies to
chronicle.[41] The common denominator many of these
photographers shared was an optimistic belief in a humanistic universalism that celebrated the existence of
an eternal human essence, dignified the individuals
photographed, saw the suffering of one as the suffering
of all, and viewed photography as a universal language.

Don McCullin's [b. 1935] horrific images of the
atrocities in the Congo, Londonderry, Vietnam, Biafra,
and Lebanon were published as *Hearts of Darkness*
(1981), a book that presents its deathly verdict through
the images' accumulated effect. The combining of imagery from around the world presents suffering as a
universal experience. The danger for both the photographer and viewer of such an approach is that over time
each individual crisis loses its identity, taking on similar attributes that numb the public to all such situations.
As a habituated traveler into the realm of human an-
guish, McCullin challenges those who want to remain
uninformed about the world and seek shelter in imagi-
native cinematic/video violence that takes visual pleasure in apocalypses (see Figure 14.14).

Henry Frank Leslie "Larry" Burrows [1926–
1971] spent nine years covering the Vietnam War before being killed when his helicopter was shot down
over Laos. Burrow's groundbreaking serial use of color
for *Life* was part of the wave of appalling images that
invaded America's living-rooms. For most people color
added a layer of compelling reality. Unlike in previous
wars, journalists in Vietnam had almost unrestricted access to the action. Debate erupted around whether such
images caused people to question America's right to be
fighting this faraway war and fueled the ranks of pro-
testers demonstrating to end the conflict. Politicians
blamed the media for undermining their authority, but
photographer Philip Jones Griffiths [b. 1936], who did
Vietnam, Inc. (1971), gives a different account:

> I would say 99 percent of all journalists in Vietnam approved
> of the war and 85 percent approved of the way the war was
> being fought. . . . So, the popular conception—*misconcep-
> tion*—by the public at large and the Reagan administration,
> that allowing all the press into Vietnam caused us to lose the
> war [is incorrect]. In fact, for the most part, the press in those
> early years was instrumental in making the war continue be-
> cause most of what was recorded by the press was very, very
> pro the military intervention there.[42]

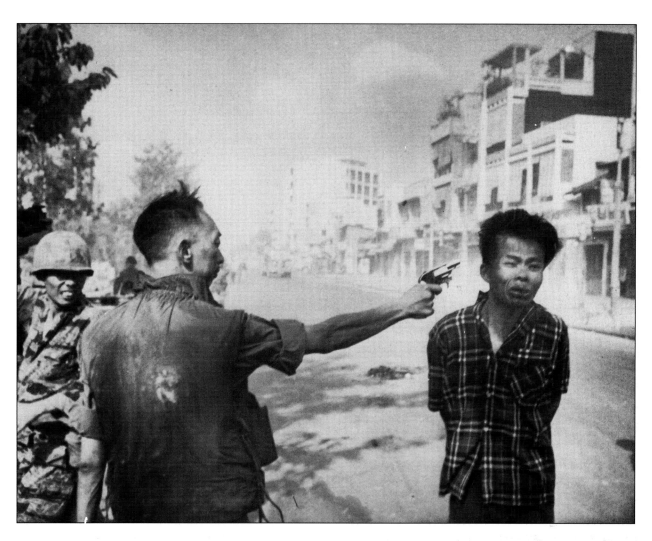

14.16   EDDIE ADAMS.   *Saigon,* 1968. (General
Loan executing prisoner). 10⅝ × 13⅝ inches. Gelatin
silver print.   Associated Press.

Most wars are summed up in public memory by a
few images. From Vietnam, two photographs have held
the public's attention. The first is Huynh Cong "Nick"
Ut's (1951) wrenching image, *Terror of War* (1972),
picturing a hysterical girl who has ripped off her burning clothes, fleeing down the road after an accidental
aerial napalm attack.[43] The other is **Edward T.
Adams's** [b. 1934] photograph of a South Vietnamese
general and chief of police firing a bullet into a sus-
pected Vietcong prisoner's head, without a trial.

This photograph has taken on mythical proportions.
With his hands tied behind his back, the victim's con-
torted face at the instant of death transforms the event
and has become a symbol of the bitter Vietnam legacy.
The picture made Adams famous at the expense of his
other work, making him a one-image photographer.
Adams wrote about the remorse he felt as his image
took on a barbaric meaning that was shaped by people's
disgust for the war: "In taking that picture, I had de-

stroyed his [the South Vietnamese general's] life. For
General Loan had become a man condemned both in
his country and in America because he had killed an enemy in war. People do this all the time in war, but rarely
is a photographer there to record the act." [44] After his
story appeared, the picture took on a different meaning
when Adams received letters from U.S. military officers stating that the victim was a known Vietcong lieutenant who had murdered a South Vietnamese major,
his wife, and their children.[45]

The question of whether the people at home get an
accurate representation of events during wars or misleading dramatic highlights surfaced during the 1994
American invasion of Haiti. David Unger of *The New
York Times* wrote: "Perhaps photojournalism operates
on some variant of the Heisenberg uncertainty principle, which holds that efforts to measure some things
may alter phenomenon they're part of. That is, taking a
picture can change the Big Picture." [46]

Can a picture change the outcome of an event? Images
can effect viewers in different ways, indicating people often see what they want to see when looking at a picture. In
the Rodney King case (1991) four white police officers
stopped a black man for driving drunk and then beat him

14.17   SUSAN MEISELAS.   *Youths Practice Throwing Contact Bombs in Forest Surrounding Monimbo,* 1978. Dye destruction print. Susan Meiselas's work is an example of how life can become art: The hero in Peter Weir's film *The Year of Living Dangerously* (1982) was loosely based on Meiselas's Nicaraguan experiences.   Courtesy Susan Meiselas/Magnum.

for resisting their commands. The incident was captured on videotape which led to indictments of those officers who carried out the violence. Many were convinced that the video evidence guaranteed a conviction. When a jury didn't see it that way and refused to convict, rioting broke out. Others believe that intense television coverage surrounding sensational court cases like the O. J. Simpson murder trial (1995) and President Clinton's impeachment (1998–99), where all the participants play to the truth of the camera can alter the outcome.

The seeming truthfulness of photography overpowers even an adroit viewing public watching CNN cable news. This is important because live television coverage has supplanted photographic coverage. During the 1991 Persian Gulf War CNN featured a video clip (provided by the U.S. military) of a "smart bomb" going down a chimney and blowing up a targeted building. This video clip was replayed over and over until it symbolized the entire sanitized military operation in which death was not pictured. Unger believes that "until viewers come to understand that seeing is not necessarily believing, that *caveat emptor* (let the buyer beware) applies to news as well as commerce."[47]

The New Subjective Journalism

Beginning with the assassination of President John F. Kennedy in 1963 and throughout the civil rights struggle and the Vietnam War of the 1960s, television progressively became the dominant news source for most Americans. To compete, photographers often adopted more subjective, stylized, or satiric approaches like the new British style of reporting associated with Martin Parr [b. 1952]. When *Life's* editorially driven style of photojournalism collapsed in the early 1970s, alternatives developed that were more receptive to new voices, including women and minorities. Publishers began to market books of captioned photographs with condensed text. The new format offered documentary photographers, such as Jill Krementz [b. 1940], the first female staff photographer for the *New York Herald-Tribune* and author of over a dozen books, and **Susan Meiselas** [b. 1948], best known for *The Carnival Strippers* (1976) and *Nicaragua* (1981), the opportunity to edit their own images (see Figure 14.17). This arrangement enabled photographers to have more control over the presentation and perception of an event, putting their work before the public for longer periods of time than a disposable magazine, thereby increasing its potential influence.

As the distinction between what the press considered news and what the museums thought was art blurred, artist-trained photographers, such as **Mary Ellen Mark** [b. 1940], broke the strict confines of journalistic practice to seek a more in-depth and personal interpretation of a subject. Mark's approach, like Avedon's and Newton's, raised the issue of how to delineate between photographic documents and photographic art. Mark not only worked for magazines but received funding from not-for-profit groups for projects that were exhibited in museums and published as books. Her working style did not fit the superficial, drive-by treatment that deadline-driven journalists work against. Mark's treatment required time to develop a relationship between the photographer and the subject, as seen in her books, *Ward 81* (1979), *Falkland Road: Prostitutes of Bombay* (1981), *Streetwise* (1988) (see Figure 14.18), and *Indian Circus* (1993). Counterculture magazines like *Rolling Stone* also hired women photographers such as Annie Leibovitz [b. 1949], to make self-aware, theatrical celebrity portraits that have helped define stardom in a star-struck era.

Sebastião Ribeiro Salgado [b. 1944] first made photographs to supplement his written reports while working as an economic adviser in Africa in 1970. His images, like an endless morality play whose heroic character's suffering knows no end, portray his subjects in the midst of dirty manual work; he presents them simultaneously as themselves and as archetypes of themselves. Salgado's personalized approach, like Avedon's and Mark's, challenges assumptions about the photographic document and art photography. His project, *Workers: An Archaeology of the Industrial Age* (1993), formally interprets the end of large-scale manual labor in mining and other industries due to mechanization. To make his point that the production of goods is global, Salgado has photographed workers using their bodies as machines in Bangladesh, Brazil, Cuba, India, Poland, the Ukraine, and Venezuela. Salgado sees no hierarchy in manual labor, as physical demands equalize workers and give them common ground. Salgado states:

> The form of these pictures must represent the problem, the reality, the basis of what is happening. What I really want to do with these pictures is to produce a kind of homage to the working class and the old ways of producing that are disappearing. . . . I want to portray them as a group. . . . When I put them all together I want to have a family of workers.[48]

Western publishers, who have reaped the benefits of these people's labor while ignoring the effects of the accompanying cultural genocide, have been reluctant to publish Salgado's images. Fred Ritchin, Salgado's collaborator, curator, and editor, complained that magazine editors found his pictures "too disturbing" to use; after five years, Salgado's pictures have only received a fair showing in a museum retrospective of a "famous" photographer. Ritchin describes this as an example of "an unfortunate tendency to elevate the messenger while denying the message."[49] At a time when computer imaging is threatening the trustworthiness of documentary practice, due to what Ritchin calls the "decline of the aura of believability,"[50] Salgado's approach, in which the body of *the Other* becomes a collective manifestation of the human spirit, tries to resuscitate the social-documentary tradition.[51]

Bytes and Halftones

Rising production costs, static growth, and a shifting of resources to electronic media have made the future relationship between photography and the halftone

14.18   MARY ELLEN MARK.   *Lillie, Seattle,* from series *Streetwise* 1983. 9 × 13⁷⁄₁₆ inches. Gelatin silver print.   Mark says: "I'm interested in the guy that doesn't have all the breaks in life and people who live on the edge. . . . I photograph them because they have a certain passion and humanity that really interests me. I would like my pictures to be a voice for them. Photography is about seeing the world in your own peculiar and personal way."[52]   Courtesy George Eastman House.

murky. People can read nonphysical publications made up of bytes instead of atoms, from the *New York Times* to *The Wall Street Journal,* on the Internet. Companies like Bill Gates's Corbis are trying to recast how people think about cultural institutions and the resources they contain. By acquiring the Bettmann Archive[53] in 1995, and by making deals to digitize worldwide museum collections, Corbis hopes to streamline the process of marketing electronic reproductions to communications professionals, make the collections more accessible, and turn a profit. Digitizing collections removes the power of the place and emphasizes the transaction between the viewer and the object in a new way. Dr. Anthony Bannon, director of the George Eastman House, stated: "Instead of museums declaring 'we have the collection and we'll wait for you to come to use them,' we'll wait for you to come to us, and you will, when you need us,' we are now engaging in a reciprocally correcting conversation loop, trying to understand what audiences need, preparing and sending our messages in that format whenever we can, and listening to be sure that our messages were understood."[54]

Another big issue is how such digital advances will affect images printed with ink onto paper. Will the virtual routes inhibit the desire to see the real thing, will people be content to look at pictures on their home computer screen? Or will these changes, as home video has done with films, increase the demand for producing and outputting even more images outside of cyberspace? Another concern is the growing power of computer technology to spread information, whether accurate or not, to a worldwide audience without any checks for accuracy. This is quite different from reading the news in a local or national paper, where readers have some assurance of journalistic standards and can recognize certain biases of reporters and editorial committees. The ability of the World Wide Web to deliver perfect digital copies of false data and propaganda, whether by politicians or hate or paramilitary groups, makes it important to have an audience capable of critically examining the information it is receiving so it does not fall prey to the unquestioning, "we read it, we believe it" syndrome.

As commissions for new journalistic work have steadily fallen, more critics have been questioning the notion of photographic objectivity. This combined with the digital revolution, has produced an ethical and existential identity crisis that has forced journalistic photographers to acknowledge their own subjectivity in reporting the news and helping to define history. The outward illustrative approach has declined in favor of a more inward, exploratory style of photojournalism. Photographers may take a more open and active stance to discovering things they didn't already know and convey that from an editorial point of view. But, most importantly, at the beginning of the twenty-first century the majority of Americans know their world primarily through reproductive media. First, we see the world on the screen of a television or computer; later, the world confirms what we have seen.

Endnotes

1   Walter Benjamin, "The Work of Art in the Age of Mechanical Reproduction," in Walter Benjamin, *Illuminations,* Hannah Arendt, ed., English translation, (New York: Harcourt, Brace, and World, 1968), 219–53. Although published in 1936, this essay did not widely enter into academic discussions of photography until the late 1980s and early 1990s.

2   George Grosz, "Randzeichnungen zum Thema," Blätter der Piscatorbühne (Berlin, 1928); trans. in Peter Selz, "John Heartfield's Photomontages," *The Massachusetts Review,* vol. 4, no. 2 (Winter 1963), unp.

3   From "A Prospectus for a New Magazine," 1934, New York, Time Inc. Archives.

4   Henry Luce in Philip B. Kunhardt Jr., ed., *Life: The First Fifty Years, 1936–1986* (Boston: Little Brown and Co., 1986), 5.

5   Time Inc. Audit Bureau for circulation figures, New York, NY.

6   "We Look Back on a Great Era," *Popular Photography*, vol. 30 (May 1952), 39.

7   Jane Livingston, *Odyssey: The Art of Photography at National Geographic* (Charlottesville, VR: Thomasson-Grant, 1988), p. 27.

8   Edward Steichen, *A Life in Photography* (Garden City, NY: Doubleday and Co., 1981), unp., located in Chapter 9, Introducing Naturalism into Advertising.

9   Catherine A. Lutz and Jane L. Collins, *Reading National Geographic* (Chicago: University of Chicago Press, 1993), 66.

10   Ibid.

11   See Patricia Johnson *Real Fantasies: Edward Steichen's Advertising Photography* (Berkeley University of California Press, 1997).

12   Harold Haliday Costain, "Photography," *Modern Publicity 1935–36* (London, 1936), 20; cited in Robert Sobieszek, *The Art of Persuasion* (New York: Harry Abrams, 1988), 71.

13   *Vogue* (September 15, 1939), 76; cited in Nancy Hall-Duncan, *The History of Fashion Photography* (New York: Alpine, 1979), 64.

14   Alexander Liberman, introduction to Irving Penn, *Passage: A Work Record* (New York: Callaway/Knopf, 1991), 5.

15   Ibid., 6.

16   Jonathan Tichenor, "Irving Penn," *Graphis* vol. 6, no. 33 (1950), 396.

17   Milton Brown, "Badly Out of Focus," *Photo Notes,* January 1948, 5–6.

18   Vicki Goldberg, "Irving Penn Is Difficult. Can't You Tell?" *New York Times* November 24, 1991, Section 2, 40. No Penn image appears as he claimed he would only grant permission for monographs of his work.

19   Jamie James, "Transcending," *ARTnews,* vol. 93, no. 3 (March 1994), 105.

20   For a critique of this project see Richard Bolton, "In the American East: Richard Avedon Incorporated" in Richard Bolton, ed., *The Contest of Meaning: Critical Histories of Photography* (Cambridge: The MIT Press, 1989). 261–282.

21   Based on an extended conversation between Avedon and the author at Toad Hall, the home of Stanley Marsh III, Amarillo, TX, November 1984, while Avedon was photographing *In the American West.* The project was sponsored by the Amon Carter Museum, Fort Worth, TX.

22   A clash between critical thought and commerce has prevented an Avedon image from being reproduced in this project. In a series of telephone calls and faxes during December 1998 and January 1999, Avedon's studio manager, Norma Stevens, requested text and sample designs. Stevens then asked that changes be made to correct "inaccuracies." After this was done, she refused permission to reproduce an Avedon image because she did not like the "tone" of the piece. For the Avedon studio machine all aspects of photographic practice appear to be commodities subject to control, negotiation, and manipulation.

23   "Body Work: Andrew Hultkrans talks with J.G. Ballard and David Cronenberg," *Artforum,* vol. XXXVI, no. 7, March 1997, 117.

24   Weegee, *Weegee by Weegee* (New York: Ziff Davis, 1961), 52.

25   See Daniel Jonah Goldhagen, *Hilter's Willing Executioners: Ordinary Germans and the Holocaust* (New York: Alfred A. Knopf, 1996).

26   Robert Capa, "Death in Spain," 1936. Caption from *Life,* July 12, 1937, vol. 3, no. 2, 19. This image is better known as *Death of a Loyalist Soldier.*

27   Quoted in Cornell Capa, ed. *The Concerned Photographer* (New York: Grossman, 1968), unp.

28   Robert Capa, *Images of War* (New York: Grossman Publishers, 1964), 110.

29   Magnum Photos was founded in Paris in 1946 by Henri Cartier-Bresson, Robert Capa, David (Chim) Seymour, George Rod-Rodger, and Bill Vandivert. The photographers were motivated by exasperation with magazines like *Life* that determined a photographer's assignment, controlled the use of the images, and retained ownership of the negatives.

At Magnum, the photographers select the editors and staff and set policy on how work is represented and sold. Profits are shared in proportion to the sales of the work. Nowadays, younger photographers can become Magnum associates and have their work represented on a commission basis. A New York office was established in 1947.

30   Henri Cartier-Bresson in, *The Concerned Photographer*, unp., 265.

31   Ibid.

32   Paul Hill and Thomas Copper, "W. Eugene Smith," *Dialogue with Photography* (New York: Farrar, Straus and Giroux, 1979), 280.

33   See Glenn G. Willumson, *W. Eugene Smith and the Photographic Essay* (Cambridge: Cambridge Press, 1992).

34   Op. cit., 266.

35   Ibid., 264.

36   John Le Carré, intro. to Don McCullin, *Hearts of Darkness* (New York: Alfred A. Knopf, 1981), 19.

37   W. Eugene Smith and Aileen M. Smith, *Minamata* (New York: Holt, Rinehart and Winston, 1975), 8.

38   Cornell Capa, Introduction, *The Concerned Photographer,* unp.

39   Ibid.

40   Ibid.

41   Photographs of the aftermath of the bombing of Hiroshima and Nagasaki, especially of people, rarely have been published in the West. For an overview see Ryuichi Kaneko et al, *The Half-Life of Awareness: Photographs of Hiroshima and Nagasaki* (Tokyo: Tokyo Metropolitan Museum of Photography, 1995).

42   Marianne Fulton, *Eyes of Time: Photojournalism in America* (Boston: Little Brown, 1988), 208.

43   After making the picture, the 22-year-old Ut drove the girl to a hospital, saving her life. At this writing, the woman in the picture is married, has a child, and lives in Toronto, Canada.

44   Eddie Adams, "The Pictures That Burn in My Memory," *Parade Magazine*, May 15, 1983, 9.

45   Eddie Adams telephone interview with Vicki Goldberg in Vicki Goldberg, *The Power of Photography*, 229.

46   David C. Unger, "Taking Haiti," with photographs by Alex Webb, *The New York Times Magazine* (October 23, 1994/Section 6), 53–54.

47   Ibid., 55.

48   John Bloom, "An Interview with Sebastião Salgado," October 5, 1990, San Francisco in John Bloom, *Photography at Bay: Interviews, Essays, and Reviews* (Albuquerque: University of New Mexico Press, 1993), 151–165.

49   Cited in David Levi Strauss, "Epiphany of the Other," *Artforum* (February 1991), 99.

50   See Fred Ritchin, *In Our Own Image: The Coming Revolution in Photography/How Computer Technology Is Changing Our View of the World* (New York: Aperture, 1990).

51   Ironically, no Salgado photograph appears in this text because his picture use fee was beyond the budget of this production. Salgado's position is that publishers constantly exploit photographers by underpaying them for their work and that he will only allow his images to be reproduced when he is fairly compensated.

52   Mark Edward Harris, "The C & D Interview: Mary Ellen Mark," *Camera and Darkroom* (October 1993), 22–31.

53   The Bettmann Archive was founded in 1930 by Otto Bettmann and contains over 16 million images, making it one of the world's largest and most important photographic archives.

54   Dr. Anthony Bannon, "The Geography of the Collection," a lecture delivered April 27, 1997 for CEPA Gallery at the Anderson Gallery, Buffalo, NY.

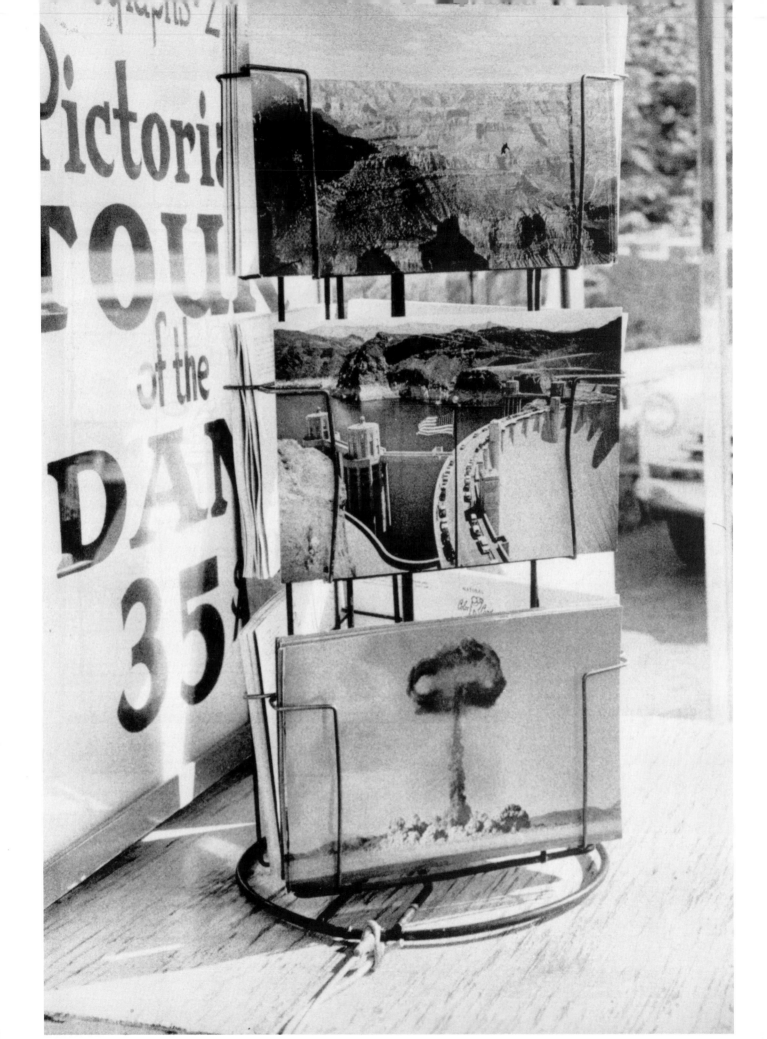

CHAPTER FIFTEEN

The Atomic Age

The 1945 decision by President Harry S. Truman [1884–1972] to drop atomic bombs on the Japanese cities of Hiroshima and Nagasaki ended World War II and began the Atomic Age. Despite the forming of the United Nations Charter (1945), world peace was elusive. Initial postwar exhilaration rapidly gave way to apprehension and tension as the Soviet Union exploded its first atomic weapon (1949). Americans realized that "the bomb" could now be used against them. As practice blasts escalated, the arms race of the Cold War commenced. The physical and psychological fallout from these scientific events altered the American transcendental belief in nature. The incredible economic benefits scientists promised from the "Atoms for Peace" program, such as plutonium nuclear reactors that did not make suitable bomb material and electric power so inexpensive that meters would not be needed, never materialized. Instead, technology seemed on the verge of overwhelming nature, bringing with it a loss of firm moral ground and the possibility of outright extermination. Even Robert Oppenheimer, the head of the Manhattan

ROBERT FRANK. *Hoover Dam,* 1955. 18³⁄₁₆ × 12³⁄₁₆ inches. Gelatin silver print.   © Robert Frank. Courtesy PaceWildensteinMacGill, New York. Print Courtesy of National Gallery of Art, Washington. Robert Frank Collection, Gift of the Evelyn and Walter Haas, Jr., Fund.

Under a blazing Nevada sun, Robert Frank's amalgam of pictures brought together the natural, rough, wild canyons of the Colorado River, the smooth, artificial, restraining container of the Hoover Dam, and the terror of an atomic mushroom cloud, producing a 1950s allegory of the past, present, and future. Frank's vision of the atomic era can be understood in the statement: "Black and white is the vision of hope and despair. This is what I want in my photographs."[1]

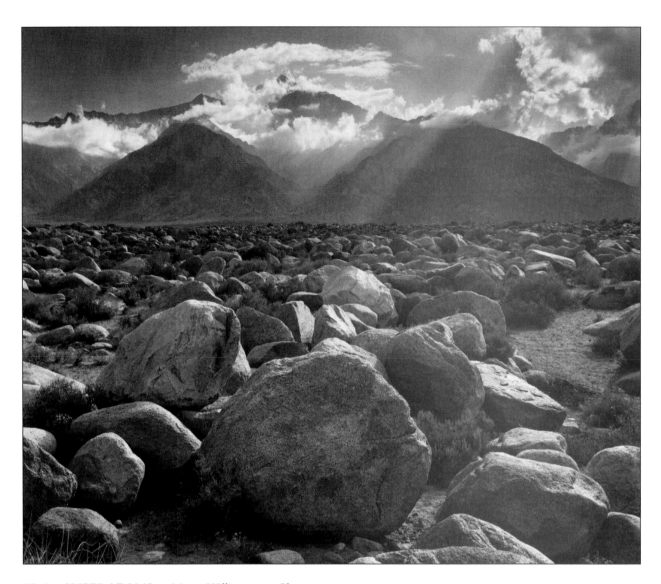

15.1   ANSEL ADAMS.   *Mount Williamson—Clearing Storm*, 1944. Size varies. Gelatin silver print.   Courtesy Corbis/Ansel Adams Publishing Rights Trust.

Project that developed America's first atomic weapon at the Los Alamos laboratory, had so many doubts about what they had unleashed upon the world that he resigned his position.[2] The atomic bomb changed the world, and post–World War II artists started to reflect its destabilizing consequences. A small group of American photographers shifted their modern and naturalistic outlook to a more abstract, surreal, and existential stance.

Until World War II the modernist concept of the naturalistic/documentary photograph, the previsualized, full-frame aesthetic of the individual photographer, reigned supreme. It was reinforced by magazines, such as *Popular Photography* and *U.S. Camera,* that gave national exposure to work produced by the FSA and the Photo League. The modernist agenda was advanced by

Beaumont Newhall [1908–1993], the curator of the recently established Department of Photography at the Museum of Modern Art (1940), the first at a major art museum. Newhall's *The History of Photography: 1939 to the Present Day,* originally published as a catalogue accompanying the MOMA exhibition of the same name in 1937, defined the modernist approach and introduced its artists to the public.[3] Another watershed event was the establishment of the George Eastman House International Museum of Photography and Film in 1949 and the appointment of Newhall as its first curator and, later, its director (1958–1971). From these positions Newhall, often assisted by his wife, Nancy Parker Newhall [1908–1974],[4] championed a select group of photographers, many of whom were personal friends, through exhibitions, publications, and lectures.

Before the atomic bomb **Ansel Adams** made images, such as *Mount Williamson—Clearing Winter Storm, Yosemite National Park (1944),* that embodied Newhall's modern, naturalistic vision. Adams's compositions visualized the essence of nineteenth-century

American transcendentalism: ethereal light illuminating the solid enduring earth. Here the sharp focus of reason co-existed with the timeless beauty of nature. Not far from Mount Williamson, Adams also photographed the human landscape at Manzanar, CA, the site of a "relocation center" where West Coast second-generation Japanese-Americans were interned during World War II by the U.S. government (the resulting images were published as *Born Free and Equal,* 1944). Although removed from the battlefields, Adams made shrewd antiwar images that encouraged people to scrutinize the mountains and heavens for a higher moral authority to replace the one that seemed to be crumbling.

After the detonation of the first test bomb at Trinity Site on July 16, 1945 the earth and the heavens no longer seemed to possess the same degree of lasting spiritual strength that Adams's photographs personified. Even the light was different now. I. I. Rabi, a Nobel laureate physicist who observed the explosion, reported it was "the brightest light I have ever seen or that I think anyone has ever seen. It blasted; it pounced; it bored its way right through you. It was a vision which was seen with more than the eye. It was seen to last forever. You would wish it would stop; altogether it lasted about two seconds."[5] This new world could not be contained by the old transcendental ways that saw the camera as the eye of nature. This new light demanded fresh methods of representing the visions of the world that went beyond what the eye could see.

The increased emigration of artists forced by World War II gave European cultural and intellectual theories wider currency in America and provided photographers with alternative approaches to Newhall's modernist program. The American painters Arshile Gorky [1904–1948] and Adolph Gottlieb [1903–1974] adopted the surrealist ideas of Max Ernst and André Breton into paintings devoid of rational intent or utilitarian representation, forming the basis of *abstract expressionism.* Abstract expressionism was representative of an attitude of intense allegiance to psychic self-expression that paralleled post–World War II's atomic existential philosophy's belief in individual action as the key to salvation. Surrealism also gave expressionist photographers who did not fit the modernist mode the means to rebel against the empirical, realistic outlook that dominated American practice. The infusion of new ideas helped break the domination of the assignment-driven photo-reportage of the literal moment, allowing photographers to make more timeless and intangible representations of the allegorical, the psychological, and the spiritual.

Commercial magazines did not believe that private symbolic imagery was suitable for a popular audience, leaving expressive practitioners to face solitary lives of offering images to tiny audiences with little hope of financial compensation. Still, some found straight realism too restrictive and wanted more mental space for cerebral interpretation and personal enlightenment. The search to find alternatives to *social realism,* representational images with a social purpose, was underway. Photographers sought to extend their practice beyond the commercial and functional to explore internal intellectual and philosophical quests. Their search for a new form of spiritualism in an atomic age shifted from the modernistic approach that favored strongly defined, tangible subject matter and the structuring role of light, to compositions that embraced the subjectivity of inner self-expression, the metaphor, and the manipulation of materials and processes. In a world now controlled by invisible atoms, there was a growing interest by photographers in psychoanalytic theory and surrealist dream imagery that promoted nonrational aspects of being.

The Surrealistic Metaphor

The use of photographic metaphor—a photograph that intends to transcend its exterior appearance—seemed at odds with the presumably objective nature of photography, which is secured to such appearances. Yet it was this metaphorical approach, combined with surrealism, that allowed photographers like **Clarence John Laughlin** [1905–1985] to suggest connections and create new analogies about time and place.

Laughlin was a self-taught New Orleans photographer, with no sphere of like-minded artists, who by the late 1930s was using surrealist strategies, such as blurring, double exposure, light manipulation, and coded poses, to disrupt photographic realism. A devotee of the French symbolist poets Charles Baudelaire and Arthur Rimbaud, Laughlin depended on enigma and fantasy to evoke a disturbing dreamlike quality rich in mysterious allegories and melancholic sexual undertones. His romantic images, filled with the sultry legends of a pretechnological South that wanted to ignore the coming atomic age, incorporate and yet move in a different direction from the modernist aesthetic of Weston and Adams. Laughlin was not interested in representing an outer object as a-thing-in-itself but in its "psychic [content] in terms of inner perceptions and compulsions, in terms of intuition and symbolism (the treating of the object as a-thing-beyond-itself)."[6] His work protested a rational and technical society that denied emotions. Laughlin was after a spiritual resurrection, uniting body and intellect, instinct and reason, poetry and utility. His series, *Poems of the Inner World,* wrestles with the psychology of anxiety, confusion, desire, death, fear, guilt, and renewal. Laughlin's studies of Southern antebellum architecture, published as *Ghosts Along the Mississippi* (1948), concentrate on what he referred to as their "psycho-physical environment." Laughlin said:

15.2   CLARENCE JOHN LAUGHLIN.   *The Head in the Wall*, 1945. 11 × 14 inches. Gelatin silver print. Laughlin wrote: "This broken opening in a shattered building, by a process of natural magic, becomes the head of Havoc, the horrible head of devastation itself symbolizing the ruin which faces a society which cannot control its own destructive impulses—which cannot control war. Visually, space becomes reversed, the opening becoming more solid than the wall itself."[7] Courtesy The Historic New Orleans Collection.

"It is a strange fusion of psychological factors with physical factors that most excites me. . . . All buildings, all cities that have been greatly lived, that have been greatly dreamed on, and that extend far through time—have this secret life."[8]

This combination of cultural and physical ingredients, topography, and *Zeitgeist* (spirit of the time) share similar preoccupations with the Southern gothic literature of William Faulkner, Carson McCullers, and Flannery O'Connor. Laughlin's titles—"We Reached for Our Lost Hearts," "The Eye that Never Sleeps"—made a verbal-visual link, encouraging a metaphorical/poetic interpretation that foils the authority of a photograph to

act as a literal representation of what it depicts. Laughlin's theatrically staged scenes stymie realism with montage and multiple exposure, destroying the accepted continuum of time. Laughlin's belief that "the limitations of photography are nothing more than the limitations of photographers"[9] informs a generation of magical Southern photographic thinking in the work of Jerry Uelsmann, Van Deren Coke [b. 1921], Robert Fitcher, and Ralph Eugene Meatyard.

Frederick Sommer [1905–1999], raised in Brazil and trained as a landscape architect, seriously pursued photography after meeting with Stieglitz in 1935. Charles Sheeler and Max Ernst encouraged his systematic explorations with "the sensitized surface, rather than photography itself" that included cameraless negatives, clichés-verre, smoke-on-glass, paint-on-cellophane, cut-paper images, and musical notation as art. Although Sommer cares for the accurate illustration of how things are and studies their shapes in the manner of a Renaissance anatomist, surrealist underpinnings add a phantasmagoric quality to his imagery. Sommer's early photographs step into a realm of the grotesque and nightmarish to question temporal existence while func-

15.3 FREDERICK SOMMER.   *Eight Young Roost-ers*, 1938. 7⅝ × 9½ inches. Gelatin silver print. His search for order led Sommer to conclude that, "Nature respects only evidence. . . . I think this takes us to the very nature of photography. Perhaps the most peculiar and most distinguishing characteristic is that you can never photograph a thing. What you're essentially pho-tographing is how it related to a great many other things. So it seems like photography was environmental long before the word got to be a fetish. And it can't be anything else."[10]   Courtesy Frederick Sommer Archive.

tioning as metaphors for war and foreshadowing the mass destruction that would leave Europe in ruin. Im-ages like *Eight Young Roosters* demonstrate an aware-ness of positivistic typology, the scientific recording of specific genres that uses repetition to encourage view-ers to ponder the essence of the subject. Sommer ap-plied his typological thinking, stressing the relationship between similar subjects, to his landscapes.

Sommer struggled with how to depict the landscape of the American West. Finding the Arizona desert im-mune to traditional rendition, Sommer looked at nature to suggest its own order. By eliminating the sky and the foreground, Sommer made images that defy gravity and occupy their own dreamlike space. The harsh land-scape seems to float in its own endless and enigmatic space (see Figure 15.4). The lack of classical associa-tions for measurement and placement in the Arizona desert give his pictures a disorienting sense of being in a foreign world where one's position in time and space is uncertain. Its topography reflects Sommer's conclu-sion that the landscape "exists for itself." Sommer's de-tailed, horizonless views in the 1940s shaped his topo-logical response to the desert landscape and anticipated the more obscure imagery he would make twenty years later using smoke on cellophane. Jam-packed, edge to edge, they express and foreshadow the same set of con-cerns as Jackson Pollock's [1912–1956] skein painting. Sommer's observation—"What is the importance of Duchamp, if not to tell us that the things that go on in painting can be done without painting"[11]—reveals his desire to push the envelope of photography.

The desire for a metaphoric resonance can be seen in the work of **Val Telberg** [b. 1910], who became in-terested in surrealism and experimental filmmaking

15.4   FREDERICK SOMMER.   *Arizona Landscape,*
1943. 7⅝ × 9⁹⁄₁₆ inches. Gelatin silver print. "For years
I looked at the Arizona landscape and it seemed almost
a hopeless task. . . . There wasn't anything worth featuring, nothing worth making a to-do about. All those
plants were dry and dead and dying. And, if they
weren't, you could take them as a whole, in their total-
ity. . . . What was the difference between the top of the
picture and the bottom of it? It was all the same. But
there was a difference. The only thing is that it was
more subtle . . . there's a great deal going on. Maybe
this helped me to realize that I was looking at details.
These were enormous areas, but still there were no
details. . . . There's nothing happening in the sky and I
decided, 'No skies for me.' Finally there was no foreground, there was no middle distance, there was nothing. And there was very little distinction between the
plants and the rocks. Even the rocks were struggling."[12]
Courtesy Frederick Sommer Archive.

while studying painting at the Art Students League in
New York. He learned photography in order to support
himself by making "quickie" photos of nightclub patrons. Impressed by the films of Maya Deren and
Frances Lee, Telberg adapted cinematic techniques,
such as the dissolve and jump cut, to still photography, distorting its narrative content. Telberg challenged "previsualization" by using the darkroom as a
workshop for his imagination. Working on a light
table, Telberg arranged negatives, often hand-altering
them, into mental images that were sandwiched between glass and printed. As in a dream narrative, the
action jump cuts from one element to another. The
overlapping negatives can offer the illusion that the
viewer is watching a cinematic projection that flattens
space, shifts scale, and compresses time. Telberg's
mental cross-cutting of these reality fragments provides a hallucinatory, time-based stream-of-con-
sciousness, offering a multivisual forum for exploring
the normally unseeable relationships among his fantasies, feelings, and memories, often with tragic undertones (see Figure 15.5).

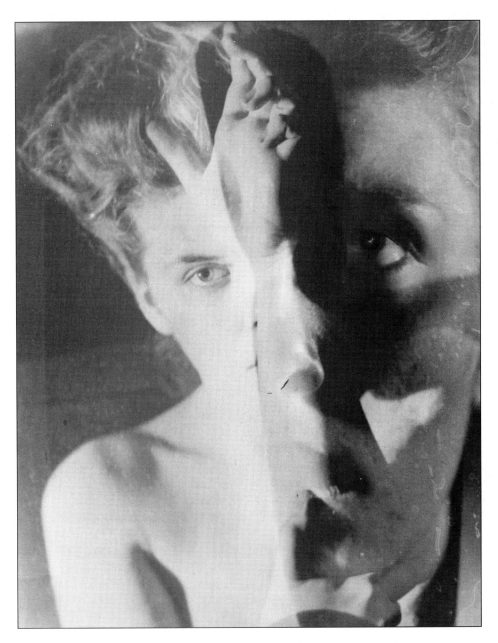

15.5 VAL TELBERG. *Unmasking at Midnight*, 1948.
11⅛ × 9⅜ inches. Gelatin silver print. "What interests
me most is not what one can see, but what goes on unseen in one's mind," Telberg said.[13] And "I try and invent
a completely unreal world, new free and truthful, so that
the real world can be seen in perspective and in comparison."[14]   Courtesy Los Angeles County Museum of Art, Ralph
M. Parsons Fund.

The Photograph as Spirit

Upon his return from active military duty in the Philippines during World War II, **Minor White** [1908–1976]
sought visual metaphors in order to access the hidden
mythical nature within reality. His first attempt was a
portfolio, *Amputations* (1947), of portraits of soldiers
juxtaposed with images of nature and with verse:

> If battle gives me time
> It is my will
> To cut away all dear insanities
> I get in War
> Or if I live
> To amputate the pain
> I've seen endured

For decades, White continued to reedit and alter
this metaphoric sequence of images, reaching back
before Nazism, Stalinism, the Holocaust, and the
atomic bomb to find an aesthetic order that made
sense. During the politically oppressive Cold War era
of communist witch hunts and blacklists, artists and
intellectuals turned away from activist social encoun-
ters. They searched for an inward path of myth and
transcendence from suffering that would lead to personal contentment and wholeness. White returned to

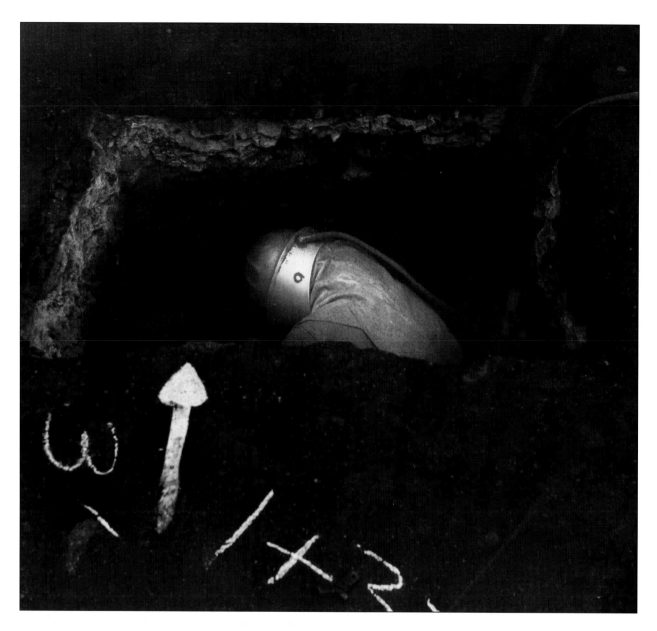

15.6   MINOR WHITE.   *Sand Blaster, San Francisco,*
1949. 10⁷⁄₁₆ × 11⁷⁄₁₆ inches. Gelatin silver print. The wall
statement for a White exhibition curated for the Eastman
House by Walter Chappell said: "This photographer releases the shutter while looking at things for what else they
are, and later reflects on the photographic image for what
else it is. Why? Because this is the way to use camera work
to mirror inner life. This is the way of what Alfred Stieglitz
called *Equivalents.* Because this is the liberating discipline
by which photographs become turning points between
man and nature and looking glasses that can be walked into.
Only half the story is given in photographs and words. The
other half, as 11th century Chinese painters believed, is
given by the viewer as he completes the images in his
mind. What he remembers later is his own. . . . In payment
of promises made to Walt Whitman and acknowledgments
of invoices from Donne, Emily Dickinson and Blake;
Freud, Ansel Adams, Edward Weston and *I Ching.*"[15]
Courtesy The Minor White Archive, Princeton University. © 1982
by the Trustees of Princeton University. All rights reserved.

Stieglitz's *Equivalents* of the 1920s, photographs that
function metaphorically by subordinating their literal
subject matter, not to explore photography but himself. He would later state: "I photograph not that
which is, but that which I AM."[16] During World War
II White converted to Catholicism. The unshakable
existential angst instilled by the war led him to study
aesthetics with modernist art historian Meyer
Schapiro (1946) and explore mysticism, Zen Bud-
dhism, Gestalt psychology, and the teachings of
George Ivanovich Gurdjieff [ca. 1877–1949]. White
achieved the same sense of mystical naturalism that
abstract painters, such as Mark Tobey, sought, not by
inventing subjects to be photographed but by editing

and sequencing reality-based images into a framework that liberated them from their original meaning. Once the photographic image was freed from its burden of representation, White believed that viewers could subjectively "read" an image for personal meaning. In a process referred to as *mirroring,* White postulated that we "invent a subject . . . out of the stuff and substance of ourselves . . . [and] turn the photo into a mirror of some part of ourselves."[17] By the 1960s, White was convinced that photographs do not contain their own meaning, that a photograph may contain numerous meanings, and that viewers are the source of these meanings. Thus "the audience can be as creative as the photographer . . ."[18]

White's major contribution to photography was his ability to share his ideas with the field. White taught at the California School of Fine Arts (1946–53) with Ansel Adams, at the Rochester Institute of Technology (1955–65), and at Massachusetts Institute of Technology (1965–74); conducted workshops throughout the country; and was the assistant curator of exhibitions and editor of *Image* at the George Eastman House (1953–57). White's *Zone System Manual* (1953) helped introduce and expand Adams's concepts. His biggest impact on the fine art of photography was helping found *Aperture* magazine in 1952 and acting as editor from 1952 until 1975. *Aperture,* with roots in the San Francisco renaissance of Eastern philosophy and religion, manifested its photographers' concerns for the contemplative, the intuitive, the mystical, and the universal. White used *Aperture* to champion his reinterpretation of Stieglitz's photographic equivalents as a form of Zen meditation "akin to the mystic and to ecstasy. . . . One feels, one sees on the ground glass into a world beyond surfaces. The square becomes like the words of a prayer or a poem, like fingers or rockets into two infinities—one into the subconscious and the other into the visual-tactile universe."[19]

Photo Education as Self-Expression

America, left economically and physically whole after World War II, became the world leader of visual culture. President Truman's GI Bill provided federal funding to educate some eight million returning veterans. To take advantage of thriving enrollments, college and university art departments offered photography courses stressing personal expression. Despite the death of Moholy-Nagy in 1946, the new Chicago Bauhaus School of Design, renamed the Institute of Design, became a center for "New Vision." Here students were encouraged to think of photography's foundation in terms of light instead of equipment, to work with unconventional methods, and to cross boundaries by mixing media. Self-expression and experimentation, rather than documentation, became the photographic destination. These concepts informed a generation of teachers who would oversee the explosive growth of photographic education beginning in the late 1960s and running through the early 1980s. Two of the most influential photographers/educators associated with the Institute of Design were Harry Callahan and Aaron Siskind.

Harry Callahan [b. 1912–1999], with Arthur Siegel [1913–1978] and Aaron Siskind, developed the expressive photography program at Chicago's Institute of Design (which in 1950 became part of the Illinois Institute of Technology), where he taught from 1946–61. In 1961, he moved to the Rhode Island School of Design (RISD) to head its photography department and taught there until 1977. Callahan saw photography not in terms of a camera but as a process through which one could see the self. Photography was about learning to control the visual *gestalt* of the picture, the photographer's mental organization that determines the image's construction and cognitive meaning. Callahan wrote: "I am interested in relating the problems that affect me to some set of values that I am trying to discover and establish as being my life. I want to discover and establish them through photography. . . . This reason, whether it be good or bad, is the only reason I can give for these photographs."[20]

Using a thematic approach that can be arranged under the headings of Eleanor (Eleanor Knapp, Callahan's wife), the City, and Landscape, Callahan worked intuitively to infuse his pictures with feeling and selfhood. Spare, highly abstracted winter scenes, such as *Detroit,* 1948, hearken back to Moholy's prenuclear reductionist impulses in which nature is seen as design and form. In one series, Callahan diminishes nature by projecting outdoor scenes onto Eleanor's bare back. The image suggests that simply reproducing the natural world will not answer existential questions and that such knowledge can only be found by examining one's private emotions and thoughts. The expression of this detached consciousness, the desire to withdraw into the self, became an early nuclear motif: the artist as an island. The confusion, disorientation, and growing isolation of the early nuclear era can be seen in Callahan's early street images, in which he uses a telephoto lens to fill the frame with heads of isolated people, cut away from their environment, alienated in their own inner reality.

Callahan's experiments with double exposure and collage are visual signs of the fragmenting self and the lost spiritual values that were rapidly being replaced by a booming consumer economy. As Akira Kurosawa's postnuclear film, *Rashomon* (1950), affirmed in its tale of rape and murder told from four different perspectives, a uniform approach to life and history is not possible. Truth is a patchwork resulting from a multitude of personal inquiries and positions (see Figure 15.8).

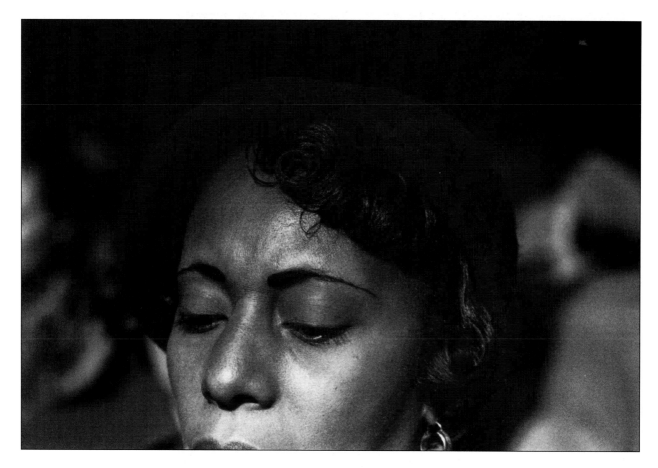

15.7   HARRY CALLAHAN.   *Untitled,* Chicago, 1950. 8 × 11¹³⁄₁₆ inches. Gelatin silver print.   © Harry Callahan. Courtesy PaceWildensteinMacGill, New York.

Callahan was an archetypal modernist who saw form as a path to the spirit. His vision of an artist was patterned after Somerset Maugham's *The Moon and Six-pence* (1919), a fictionalized account of Paul Gauguin [1848–1903], in which the artist is a solitary hero with a sacred calling, beyond the comprehension of his fellow mortals.[21] Callahan, known for being tongue-tied when discussing his work, stated: "Photography seems so simple to me that there doesn't seem to be much to say."[22] After an almost complete 25-year silence concerning the meaning of his work, Callahan wrote a short statement about what was important for him and his struggle to keep working:

It's the subject matter that counts. I'm interested in revealing the subject in a new way to intensify it. A photo is able to capture a moment that people can't always see. Wanting to see more makes you grow as a person and growing makes you want to show more of life around you. I photograph continuously, often without a good idea or strong feelings. During this time the photos are nearly all poor but I believe they develop my seeing and help later on in other photos. I do believe strongly in photography and hope by following it intuitively that when the photographs are looked at they will touch the spirit in people.[23]

The other major figure to come from the Institute of Design was **Aaron Siskind** [1903–1991]. After producing documentary projects, such as the *Harlem Document* and *The Most Crowded Block in the World,* during the late 1930s, Siskind dropped the Film and Photo League's social documentary stance to pursue the abstract and personal. Siskind's aesthetic switch led him to become friends with painter Franz Kline and his coterie during the emergence of abstract expressionism.

Siskind brought the concepts of abstract expressionism to photography by using the straight photographic style (no unusual manipulation of materials) to make a visual analogy that transcended the literalness of the subject and promoted a subjective interpretation. Through controlling the tension between representation and the independent image, Siskind balanced photography's descriptive capacity with allusion, converting direct photographic observations into visual metaphors. In 1951, after meeting Callahan at Black Mountain College, Siskind was invited to teach at the Institute of Design, and in 1971 he joined Callahan at RISD.

Siskind's sharp, highly detailed, large-format abstract images of dripped paint, graffiti, and peeling walls symbolize the disintegration of nuclear life and the search for a self-centered spiritual core that does not compromise reality. Siskind's ordered work is difficult, as he does not rely on the literal, sexual, or spiritual devices of his contemporaries to delve into the symbolic

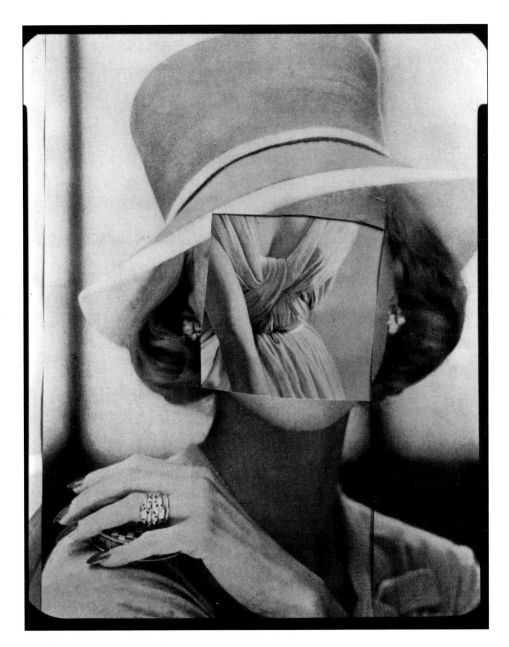

15.8 HARRY CALLAHAN.   *Cutouts,* ca. 1956.
4¾ × 3¾ inches. Gelatin silver print. Callahan's description of his collage process is ambiguous and intuitive: "I had seen an article in *Life* magazine on slavery
and wanted to express my view in some way. I started
cutting out the photographs, pinning them up and
photographing them. Unfortunately I didn't get very
far with that idea, because I ran out of slave pictures.
Instead I got hold of a lot of fashion magazines, such as
Harper's Bazaar, and cut out pictures of beautiful models. I have no idea what my motivation was. I just did
it."[24]   © Harry Callahan. Courtesy PaceWildensteinMacGill,
New York.

character of communication. Bypassing the photo-essay's interchangeability of words and pictures,
Siskind's calligraphic/hieroglyphic images converge at
the juncture where pictures and words become one (see
Figure 15.9). Through a process of renewal and self-
discovery, similar in concept to Stieglitz's *Equivalents,*
Siskind not only internalized photography but liberated
his thinking from pictorial subject matter. Siskind assembled an experience by transforming the outer wrap-
per of a subject into an inner reality through the camera's ability to isolate and alter scale, generating drama
by disclosing the relationship of one object to another.

The desire to invent fresh forms that expressed the
new psychological needs of the atomic era could also
be seen in the work of the German group **fotoform**.
Fotoform was founded in 1949 to explore photographic
abstraction and to challenge the belief that photography

15.9   AARON SISKIND.   *Chicago 22,* 1960. 10⁷⁄₁₆
× 13⁵⁄₁₆ inches. Gelatin silver print. Siskind discussed
the needs he sought to satisfy in his work: "For the first
time in my life, subject matter, as such, had ceased to be
of primary importance. . . . Essentially then, these photographs are psychological in character. . . . this kind of
picture satisfies a need. I may be wrong, but the essentially illustrative nature of most documentary photography, and the worship of the object "per se" in our best
nature photography is not enough to satisfy the man of
today, compounded as he is of Christ, Freud, and Marx.
The interior drama is the meaning of the exterior
event. And each man is an essence and a symbol."[25]
© Aaron Siskind Foundation/Courtesy Robert Mann Gallery.

was objective. Their effect on mainstream German photography at the time was said to have been like "an
atomic bomb in the compost heap." One of the group's
members, Otto Steinert [1915–1978], promoted *Sub-
jektive Fotografie* (subjective photography), a new
international movement designed to encompass "all
domains of personal photography" that advanced "conscious subjectivism."

Family of Man

Introducing this metaphorical style to the public was a
curatorial challenge. Steichen thought **Wynn Bullock's**
[1902–1975] image, *Child in the Forest* (see Figure
15.10), symbolized the mythical first woman and selected it as the opening piece to his exhibition, *The
Family of Man* (1955), a celebration of universal hu-
manism. Steichen picked Bullock because he believed
Bullock's visual language joined the natural environment with the abstract symbolism of the inner world in
an accessible manner. Although the composition of
Bullock's work is highly structured, the authority of his
images lies in their ambiguous temperament that expresses his belief that reality is constructed through personal experience.

The Family of Man exhibition and book was the major American photographic event of the 1950s.[26] Organized by Steichen, the director of the Department of
Photography at MOMA (1947–1962), "as a mirror of
the essential oneness of mankind,"[27] it was enthusiastically received in 1955. Working on the premise that
photography was a universal language, Steichen assem-

15.10 WYNN BULLOCK. *Child in the Forest,*
1951. 7⁷⁄₁₆ × 9⁷⁄₁₆ inches. Gelatin silver print. Bullock
said: "I think everything is mysterious. . . . To me everything in art is a symbol, it's never the thing. . . . I believe
that symbols are more important than the people. They
have more power to influence the world than the people who create the symbols. Why is it that all the great
philosophers, scientists, painters, and so forth still have
this great influence? It's because of the symbols they've
left us."[28]   Courtesy Bullock Photography Trust.

bled 508 images, from 68 countries, by 273 photographers, into a giant three-dimensional magazine layout.
To match its democratic premise that people were the
same, Steichen did not treat the photographs as individual works but as pieces of a larger tapestry. Just as in
magazine practice, photographers gave up control over
image quality, size, placement, and context. Jacob Deschin, the photography critic for *The New York Times,*
called it "essentially a pictured story to support a concept . . . an editorial achievement [for Steichen] rather
than an exhibition of photography."[29] The public, weary of the Korean War and Senator Joseph

McCarthy's House Un-American Activities Committee
investigations, was ready to affirm the goodness of humankind. The show traveled for years, to over thirty
countries, and was seen by a reported nine million people. Despite its unquestioned commercial success, the
show had little impact on furthering the thinking of
American photographers because it ignored the
changes and traumas that the first nuclear decade had
brought about. But the silent 50s heard no public outcry
from photographers rejecting Steichen's controlled,
sentimental approach. The real problem was the lack of
exhibition and publication alternatives that might offer
a different viewpoint. Photographers who did not share
Steichen's rosy outlook and believed humanity was
staring into an atomic void, who wanted to address issues that threatened their artistic and intellectual freedom, found reaching the public extremely difficult.

Photography and Alienation

During the same year *The Family of Man* opened,
Robert Frank [b. 1924], a Jewish émigré photographer
who was included in the show, used the money he

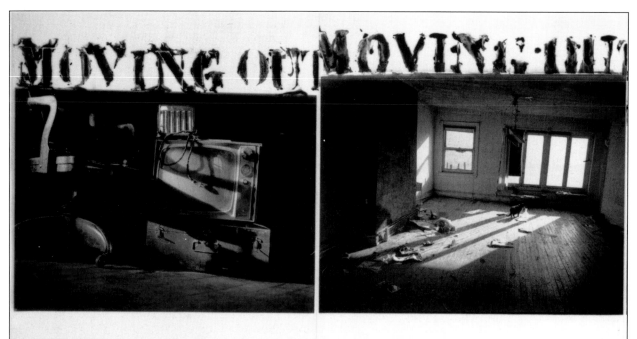

FORGOTTEN POSESSIONS IN JOHN TURNERS FINAL ROOM LONG GONE SHADOW OF MARRIAGE ON THIRD AVE LOFT

15.11   ROBERT FRANK.   *Moving Out,*
1962/1984. 19¹⁵⁄₁₆ × 47¹³⁄₁₆ inches. Gelatin silver
prints with acrylic paint. Frank said: "I'm not interested
in taking a beautiful photograph. . . . I don't believe in
it anymore—beauty, aesthetics. I think it is crazy if you
are a photographer, and the only idea that you have is
that you want to be an artist. . . . To me photography
is life. It has to deal with life."[30]   © Robert Frank. Courtesy PaceWildensteinMacGill, New York. Print Courtesy National Gallery of Art, Washington. Robert Frank Collection,
anonymous gift.

received from a Guggenheim fellowship[31] to undertake
what has become America's most photographically influential and mimicked cross-country road trip. Frank
came from Switzerland to New York in 1947, where he
met Alexey Brodovitch, a conduit of European photographers into the U.S. market, and worked as a fashion
photographer for *Harper's Bazaar.* By 1953, Frank was
part of New York's restless "Beat" scene, in contact with
the poet Allen Ginsberg [1926–1997] and the writer Jack
Kerouac [1922–1969]. Frank's intensely personal vision
of the culture of the Eisenhower years was not an optimistic Steichenist celebration of togetherness; instead it
reflected the alienation, loneliness, and spiritual desola-
tion he felt while reading Jean-Paul Sartre's trilogy, *Four
Roads to Freedom.*[32] By exposing some 800 rolls of 35-
mm film during his meandering journey that crisscrossed
the United States, Frank was actively searching for a new
structure with which to comprehend the nuclear world

(see Chapter opener). Frank intuitively used a small
35mm Leica in available light situations as an extension
of his body, disregarding the photojournalistic standards
of construction and content matter. Frank's stealthful,
disjointed form, his use of the blur, grain, movement, and
off-kilter compositions, became the emotional, unpicturesque, and gestural carrier of what would be the new
35-mm message: the freedom to discover new content
and formal methods of making photographs. Frank said:
"I was very free with the camera. I didn't think of what
would be the correct thing to do; I did what I felt good
doing. I was like an action painter."[33]

Frank absorbed and transformed the aesthetics of
abstract expressionism into his photographs, creating
a constant tension within his picture frame. He applied
a type of photographic description to his driving
odyssey that was not interested in salable public images. These were nervous, private, unglamorous images that did not always deliver a clear, single narrative message or give way to social or visual clichés.
Frank responded to the American cultural landscape
as seen from an automobile elliptically, like the existential authors and philosophers who stated that
everything was tentative and relative, giving his images of the American road an unstable sense of am-
bivalence and ennui. It was a way out of the prewar
contemplative aesthetics of his close supporter Walker
Evans, providing no sense of security, no decisive moments, and no independent masterpieces. Standard
practice taught photographers to discard all exposures
except "The One." Frank's accomplishment was in us-

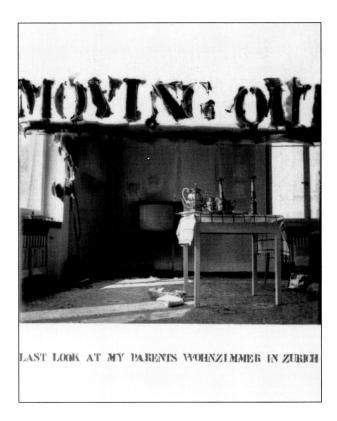

LAST LOOK AT MY PARENTS WOHNZIMMER IN ZURICH

ing the succession of 35-mm images to arrange sequences that have a completeness and makeup that no single image possessed.

Frank assembled the results of his road trip into a symbolic montage to make *The Americans,* in which he let the camera discover its own way of telling. Frank photographed people in states of boredom and emptiness. The incidental details themes of power, privilege, race, and religion to circulate, generating meaning by a complex layering of relationships between images. Frank avoided signs of the "good life" and newsworthy topics. He hated "Those god-damned [*Life*] stories with a beginning and an end."[34] He concentrated on marginalized groups that the media often left out: African-Americans, senior citizens, teenagers. Frank's portrayal of businessmen, cowboys, movie stars, and politicians simultaneously invoked and critiqued familiar American myths. In *The Americans* meaning is built up from each preceding image, like a jazz piece, where even the blank soundless spaces are necessary for flow and interpretation. The visual motifs that hold *The Americans* together—automobiles, diners, flags, jukeboxes, televisions—created a new iconography for "the road." In his introduction to *The Americans* Jack Kerouac, author of *On the Road* (1957), recognized Frank as a modern Ulysses who critically conveyed the paradoxical feelings of stimulation and isolation that accompany a voyage through popular culture:

Anybody doesnt like these pitchers dont like potry, see? Anybody dont like potry go home see Television shots of big hatted cowboys being tolerated by kind horses . . . Robert Frank,

Swiss unobtrusive, nice, with that little camera that he raises and snaps with one hand he sucked a sad poem right out of America onto film, taking rank among the tragic poets of the world [sic].[35]

Frank was unable to find a U.S. publisher and *The Americans* was first released in France in 1958. The initial responses to the 1959 American Grove Press version were negative. The editors of *Popular Photography* took the unusual step of collectively reviewing it. Almost without exception they condemned Frank's approach: It showed "contempt for any standards of quality or discipline in technique." His point of view was "an attack on the United States" and "a sad poem for sick people."[36] Frank knew that his photographs that did not embrace the values of the family of man, that violated the canons of documentary methods and techniques, that ignored the country's natural beauty, technological achievements, and virtues of hard work would be controversial. He believed "that life for a photographer cannot be a matter of indifference and it is important to see what is invisible to others." But the criticisms of *The Americans* increased Frank's disgust with the state of professional practice. He wrote:

Photography is a solitary journey. That is the only course open to the creative photographer. There is no compromise: Only a few photographers accept this fact. That is probably the reason why we have only a few really great photographers. In recent years camera journalism has become many people's definition of good photography. For me camera journalism means taste dictated by the magazines.[37]

By the early 1960s, Frank's talent for sequencing images led him into filmmaking, and he made *Pull My Daisy* (1959–60), *Me and My Brother* (1965–68), the infamous *Cocksucker Blues* (1972) (which was suppressed by Mick Jagger of the Rolling Stones), and a video, *Home Improvements* (1985). His film editing experience suggested and led to his later inclusion of words with his still pictures, which appeared in *The Lines of My Hand* (1972). Frank also experimented with mixed media—glue, tape, and nails—and still photographs to demonstrate the impossibility of "securing" a fixed meaning. Frank's most accessible and forceful still and motion picture work created a structure that portrayed its subjects without the hierarchy of a master narrative, directly from life's ordinary nonevents that nobody had bothered to depict. The disjunctions between the figures and objects express a sense of urgency about mundane things while retaining a sly sense of humor. These unidealized commonplace pleasures purposely abandon the merchandising context of commercial publishing and the constraints of photojournalistic time. Instead, they are pictures of existential doubt that make observers examine their own values. Frank's joining of the documentary mode with the subjective metaphor along with his resistance to

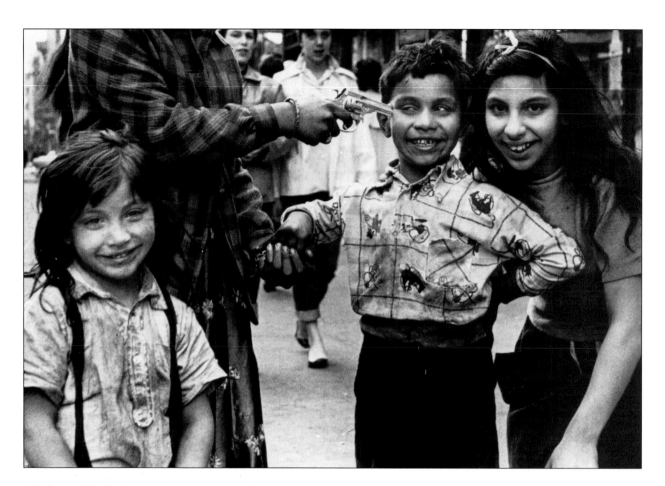

15.12   WILLIAM KLEIN.   *Gun 2, near the Bowery,
NY*, 1955. 9³⁄₁₆ × 13⁵⁄₈ inches. Gelatin silver print. Klein
recalled that he was "very consciously trying to do the
opposite of what Cartier-Bresson was doing. . . . I
wanted to be visible in the biggest way possible. My aesthetics was the New York *Daily News.* I saw the book I
wanted to do as a tabloid gone berserk, gross, grainy,
over-inked, with a brutal layout, bull-horn headlines.
This is what New York deserved and would get."³⁸
© William Klein. Courtesy Howard Greenberg Gallery, New York.

structure, his demand for authorial control, and his
willingness to learn how to present what the camera
sees are his strongest attributes.

The union of moody subjectivity and the documentary style was also being perfected by **William Klein** [b.
1928]. Klein, an ex-patriot American fashion photographer, filmmaker, designer, and painter, has made Paris
his home. While recognized in Europe, his nonfashion
work was largely ignored in the United States during the
1950s because his images did not fit into the social realist working mode.³⁹ Klein enlarged the syntax of photography by combining the in-your-face action approach of Weegee with the sensibility of a satirical
Sartre. Using a Leica with a wide-angle lens to satisfy
what he called "a gluttonous rage . . . to see all the contradictions and confusion"⁴⁰ of big cities like New York,

Rome, and Tokyo, Klein courted accident, blur, contrast, distortion, cockeyed framing, graininess, and
movement. Klein encouraged chance by making long
exposures in dim light and shooting without looking
into the viewfinder. Klein rebelled against the 1950s notions of the *decisive moment*, which included not intervening into a scene, making good compositions, and
producing normal looking prints. His images are not
those of a detached observer but those of a provocateur.
Klein referred to his *Life is Good for You in New York—
William Klein Trance Witness Revels* (1956) as "a crash
course in what was not to be done in photography."⁴¹
His dynamically unconventional framing and printing
techniques, which wooed the luminous light-scattering
qualities of photographic halation (or lens flare), emphasize the vaporization of preatomic values and a rising
sense of anarchy, chaos, and dread that most people
wished to ignore. His use of black tones challenged traditional photographic print values and accentuated the
sense of the city as *théâtre noir*. According to Klein,
"everyone I showed them to said, 'Ech! This isn't New
York—too ugly, too seedy, too one-sided.' They said,
'This isn't photography. This is shit!'"⁴²

The direct eye contact between subject and photographer often found in Klein's compositions clues viewers that Klein's presence has caused a response. Despite Klein's confrontational strategy, which captures
or elicits overt social hostility, his attitude toward his

15.13.   MARIO GIACOMELLI.   *La Gente del Sud: Scanno,* 1959. 11 × 14⁷⁄₁₆ inches. Gelatin silver print.
Courtesy George Eastman House.

subjects remains ambiguous. His practice of getting too close and violating the conventions of proximal space flew in the face of the modernist reliance on formal pictorial organization that deemphasized and distanced photographers from their subjects. Klein's city books, *Rome* (1958), *Moscow,* and *Tokyo* (1964), revolve around aggression. Regardless of the culture, polite values are nonexistent. What Klein pictures is a subject's animosity toward the whole process: the camera, the photographer, and the viewer. His catalogue of irreverent "mistakes" as masterstrokes helped codify a new way of seeing. Klein's incorporation of text, billboards, and signs, along with his book's aggressive layout, assaults viewers with innovative montage that combines images and words to recreate the same sense of action that he and other filmgoers experienced in Paris's Cinemathèque.

Between 1955 and 1965, Klein worked with Alexander Liberman at *Vogue,* taking models out of the studio and into the street, pioneering a new use of space with his wide-angle and telephoto lenses. In 1958,

Klein took up filmmaking. Among his works are a problematic trilogy on African-Americans: *Eldridge Cleaver, Black Panther* (1970); *Muhammad Ali the Greatest* (1964–74); and *The Little Richard Story* (1979). The films address the role of language: who controls it in the media and how words and images are used to formulate identity.[43] Recent fashion work, *In and Out of Fashion: William Klein* (1994), reflects Klein's interest in motion and time. Some prints from this body of work appear to have been made directly from a grease-pencil-marked 35-mm contact sheet.[44] Here the enlarged image contains a central frame that has been circled along with parts of the preceding and following frames. When exhibited the images look like pieces of movie film stock and are read chronologically from left to right. Klein also presents contact sheets in his exhibitions to provide a visual record of how he sees his way through situations.

Klein's audacious framing and image cropping combined with radical darkroom techniques represent the spirit to transcend the traditions of the media that were also displayed by **Mario Giacomelli** [1925–2000]. Giacomelli was a landscape painter who operated a typography shop in his agricultural village of Senigallia, Italy before taking up poetry and then photography. The

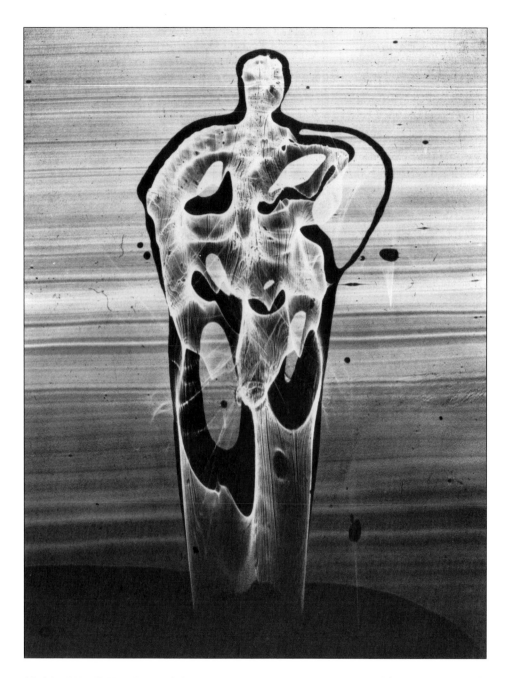

15.14   HENRY HOLMES SMITH.   *Giant,* 1949.
11⅞ × 9¹⁄₁₆ inches. Gelatin silver print.   Courtesy
Smith Family Trust.

neo-realist films of Vittorio DeSica, Roberto
Rossellini, and Luchino Visconti, frankly depicting the
loss of direction facing war-ravaged Italy, made Giacomelli aware of the camera image's power. The neo-
realist aesthetic is characterized in Rossellini's film
Open City (1945). Shot on newsreel stock, the images
convey a sense of authenticity and journalistic immediacy. The film was made on location with available light
and with mainly nonprofessional actors. Its structure
was a series of episodic vignettes that did not idealize
the characters but showed ordinary people in heroic
moments. Rossellini stated the neo-realist motto after
his film opened: "This is the way things are."

Working with these values, Giacomelli dealt with his
community's partnership with the land. He photographed the same piece of earth, from the same vantage point, throughout the year, usually altering the perspective by excluding the horizon line to deprive
onlookers of any visual anchor. Giacomelli foreshortened space by stacking up forms as if they were on a
vertical plane. In 1956, Giacomelli wrote:

> I have taken from the conscience of nature; the work of man, the
> marks, the ground, and here the chance instants of recording be-
> fore the losses are gone for the relative duration of time.[45]

By 1960, Giacomelli's response to his sense that nature had been overrun by humans was to cut patterns
into the landscape with a tractor. In 1970, he was photographing the plowed fields from the air. The sensation
of violent upheaval can be seen in the physical appear-

ance of Giacomelli's work. People were agitated by his high-contrast prints, which often had only three tones, a departure from the fine-print aesthetic. Giacomelli did not see a negative as a fixed, sacred entity but as a flexible starting place for inner expression. Giacomelli executed darkroom techniques to intensify and/or eliminate information. He was not content to stick with what the camera delivered but was determined to shape the medium to his vision.

In 1956, Giacomelli embarked on a long-term project based on the title of a poem, "Death will come and it will have your eyes," about old age. The series has been called bleak and pessimistic, but it accurately conveys the passionate sense of enclosing darkness that his elderly subjects were experiencing. He distorted some of his prints by letting one corner of the paper curl up and float while it was being exposed under the enlarger. This project was followed by others on butchered animals, gypsies, and war victims at Lourdes. Giacomelli's dynamic urgency and lack of concern for proper use of materials found a following in the United States during the 1960s and can also be seen in the work of Robert Frank and Josef Koudelka [1938].

Making a Big Jump

The ideas of Moholy-Nagy and the images of Francis Bruguière, Lotte Jacobi, and Frederick Sommer opened the doors of subjective realities to the abstract experiments of **Henry Holmes Smith** [1909–1986] of the late 1940s.[46] Smith supported the metaphorical mode while working to establish art photography in academia using a scientific model. In "XI Zero in Photography" (the title refers to the name of an atomic particle), Smith wrote that photographers should follow the example of nuclear physicists and create their own community to control photographic discourse without concern for popular opinion. Smith's semiscientific position is indicative of the confusion during the early atomic era, when science appeared to have flattened all natural avenues for connecting with life forces. Smith was not interested in pursuing the seen world of facts but in searching for ways to visualize myth. Smith was absorbed in how light formed images. He wrote: "Photographers know something special about light: the photographic mark of light is dark, the brightest light makes the blackest mark."[47] Smith demonstrated his ideas using Karo corn syrup in place of a lens. "As the syrup runs down the sheet of glass it causes light falling on it to refract making marks that celebrate light itself."[48] The light came from a 50-year-old, 100-watt theater spotlight with a clear lens, set up 15 to 20 feet from the syrup and enlarging paper (which was placed behind the syrup) and turned on and off with a foot switch. "The shapes . . . tell me things . . . how a child might imagine a giant in a horrid ancient tale, the mystery of all that I shall never see and the wonder of a good many things I shall never understand. There may be more than I know in the pictures and I am content to know that."[49]

This process of combining cliché-verre with the photogram used drawing and painting methods to create symbolic images that Smith claimed allowed "intangible characters from the ancient mythological world" to appear (see Figure 15.14). The technique was an "automatic" photographic process of poetic picturemaking similar to the gestural methods of abstract expressionists. Smith's color experiments, begun in 1936, followed a similar course of not being limited by the rules of color representation that relied on filters or colored lights to achieve their color balances. Smith dismissed the relationship of the subject's color to his results by picking monochromatic subjects and introducing color through a color printing process.[50] Such experiments in printmaking methods set the stage to the investigation of alternatives to straight photography that would characterize the 1960s. At the invitation of Moholy-Nagy, Smith began teaching at the New Bauhaus in 1937. Between 1947 and 1977, Smith taught at Indiana University, where he developed one of the first college-level courses in the history of photography.

A hallmark of the atomic age was the knowledge that science could change things irrevocably in a flash. Edward H. Land's [1909–1991] Polaroid process satisfied the desire to make one's own images in a moment. Land got the idea while taking snapshots of his daughter, who wanted to know why she could not see the pictures instantly. The result was the 1948 Christmastime introduction of a self-contained camera system that delivered a browntone print in one minute. Today a wide range of Polaroid films, including color, are routinely used by amateurs and professionals. Polaroid encouraged artistic exploration by employing Ansel Adams as a consultant from 1948 until his death in 1984. The company also had a unique policy of collecting images for exhibition and publication by artists working with Polaroid products.[51] Land refined and speeded up Eastman's underlying concept, that one did not have to be a photographer to make photographs. Polaroid products and the Kodak Instamatic camera (1963) continued to democratize the practice, encouraging people who knew nothing about photography to become their own photomakers.

The smashing of atoms to produce nuclear fission produced transformations in other aspects of society that had been taken for granted. The phenomenon of a camera-free photographer taking preexisting photo-based images, removing them from their original circumstances, and through juxtaposition giving them new meaning, is indicative of how picturemaking criteria were changing in the nuclear age. **Richard Hamilton's** [b. 1922] collage, *Just What Is It That Makes Today's Homes So Different, So Appealing?* (see Figure 15.15), in which the word "Pop" makes its artistic debut, contains the key visual ingredients of *pop art*.

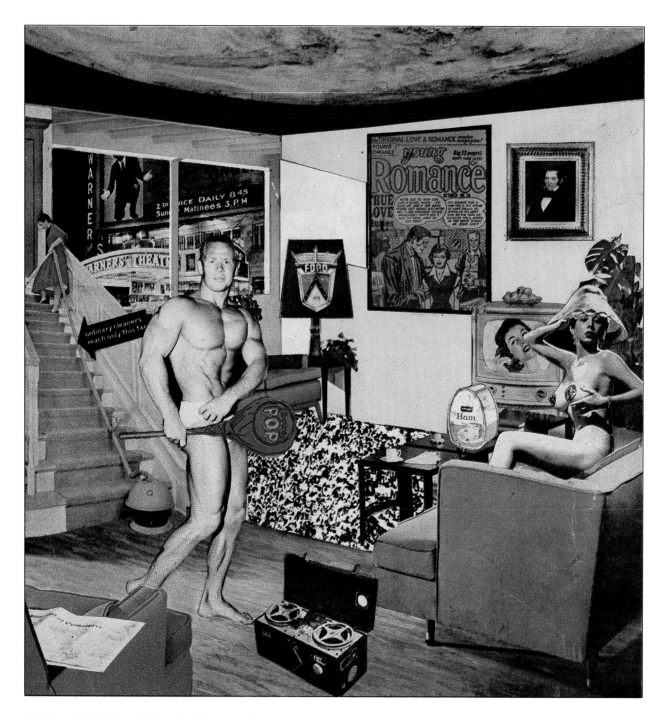

15.15   RICHARD HAMILTON.   *Just What Is It
That Makes Today's Homes So Different, So Appealing?*
1956. 10¼ × 9¾ inches. Collage.   © Kunsthalle,
Tübingen, Germany.

Pop art came out of what Hamilton called a "landscape of secondary, filtered material." Hamilton
wrote that "Pop should be: Popular (designed for a
mass audience), Transient (short-term solution), Ex-
pendable (easily forgotten), Low-cost, Mass-produced, Young (aimed at youth), Witty, Sexy, Gim-
micky, Glamorous, Big Business. . . ."[52] In an era
when television and radio were replacing books and

painting as the social carriers of culture, Lawrence
Alloway, the English critic who in 1958 coined the
term "pop art," had this to say:

> Mass production techniques, applied to accurately repeatable
> words, pictures, and music, have resulted in an expendable mul-
> titude of signs and symbols. To approach this exploding field
> with Renaissance-based ideas of the uniqueness of art is crip-
> pling. Acceptance of the mass media entails a shift in our notion
> of what culture is. Instead of reserving the word for the highest
> artifacts and the noblest thoughts of history's top ten, it needs to
> be used more widely as a description of "what society does."[53]

Under an ironic guise, pop art took hold in America,
celebrating the postwar-nuclear era—mass consumer
theater of desire and illusion while rejecting the heroic

15.16   WALLACE BERMAN.   *Untitled.* 12³⁄₁₆ ×
13⅛ inches. Verifax matrix prints.   Courtesy Wallace
Berman Estate and L. A. Louver Gallery, Venice, California.

personal, spiritual stance and psychological content of
the abstract expressionists. It provided the foundation
for the silk-screened celebrities of Andy Warhol, the
comic strip look of Roy Lichtenstein's [1923–1997]
paintings, and the transformation of commonplace objects into monumental sculpture by Claes Oldenburg [b.
1929]. This technically rooted work asserted that American culture was about the multiple—the assembly line
that made identical products that everyone could buy.

As the nuclear age challenged the belief in nature as
the source of creation, artists turned to the inventive
possibilities of the machine for inspiration. In 1957,
California assemblage artist **Wallace Berman**
[1926–1976] made collages with a new technology—

the Verifax machine.[54] Using a constant motif, such as a
hand holding a transistor radio, Berman replaced the radio with commonplace images, like a football player or
a Master lock, to form a repeating cinematic structure.
Hebrew letters were featured in many images as Berman
strived to incorporate sociological and spiritual meaning
through the mysticism of the Cabala.[55] Berman often
turned the process itself around by using the negative
matrices as the images. This reversal simplifies a subject
and heightens the emblematic power of an image by removing it from the documentary arena. These dark,
gritty, and streaked prints were generally presented in a
grid series, suggesting a cosmic oracle or force (atomic)
that transforms energy into visible symbols.

Berman is characteristic of those nonphotographers,
knowing nothing of photographic convention, who
burst onto the scene in the 1960s. These artists used
copying machines not to duplicate text-based documents but to record a new set of materialistic values

drawn from popular mass-media sources to make new works. These isolated experiments, made during an era that would only accept the "straight" documentary approach, displayed the ease by which any image could be appropriated and made a part of another work. One could now be a cameraless photographer, making compositions of the pyramids on a copy-machine glass instead of on a camera's ground glass and using the new-found technology to push a button and instantaneously print the results.

The Subjective Documentary

During the early years of the atomic age, most Americans did not see the work of cloistered artists but experienced photography through a humanistic reporting style brought over by exiled European practitioners. This subjective-documentary approach gained popularity in the late 1940s and was typified in the lyrical photography of Marc Riboud [b. 1923] and the sympathetic authenticity of **Robert Doisneau** [1912–1994]. The popularity of Doisneau's bistro and street scenes hinged on presenting a disappearing lifestyle, a respite from nuclear angst. Doisneau's image, *Le Baiser de l'Hotel de Ville*, 1950, a.k.a. *The Kiss*, became a poster icon of street photography and young love. The photograph appears to have "caught" a woman and a man spontaneously kissing in front of an outdoor café on a busy Parisian street. The man's right hand on the woman's right shoulder draws her to his lips and they kiss, all in perfect view of the camera. Shortly before Doisneau's death troubling questions surrounding this image were raised by a French couple, claiming to be the kissers, who unsuccessfully sued for royalties. Doisneau's lawyers disproved their claim by producing contact sheets of the couple in the photograph in locations around Paris and contracts showing that they had been hired for a project commissioned by *Life*. The text accompanying the original piece in *Life* said the photographs were "unposed," a claim Doisneau never denied. In an interview Doisneau stated: "Photography is not a document on which a report can be made. It is a 'subjective' document. Photography is a false witness, a lie. People want to prove the universe is there. It is a physical image that contains a certain amount of documentation, which is fine, but it isn't evidence, a testimony upon which a general philosophy can be based."[56]

These revelations broke an unspoken contract governing what viewers call reality. The strength and weakness of documentary photography is based on the collective trust between the photographer and the viewer. By accepting Doisneau's "unposed" picture his audience agreed to believe they were witnessing a scene from "real" life. Instead they were taken in by a docu-drama.

Doisneau's work is emblematic of the changing ground rules of the 1950s that revealed the contradictions and incongruities in prenuclear assumptions. Relativism, what conservatives would call the great disease of modernity, reshaped relationships. Agreements between photographers and viewers were called off as the age of viewing innocence ended. The concept of a photograph as a nonfictional transcription of reality had to be rethought and seen instead as constructed fiction. A new public viewing motto could have been: "Seeing is not believing." During a time when artists were questioning the idea of proof and reality, people still wanted pictures that confirmed their ideas about the universe, widening the gap between public expectation and how artists were now presenting the world. The process of renegotiating what constituted reality in the atomic age was underway.

The atomic age broke the stranglehold of the "big" picture magazines. Readership diminished as a generation brought up on the immediacy of television and airplane travel found the photo-essay an inadequate and worn-out experience. This loss of purpose and vitality plus rising production costs led to *Colliers'* folding in 1957, followed by *Coronet* in 1961, *The American Weekly* in 1963, *Look* in 1971, and *Life* in 1972.

A transition in viewing habits began as a small audience developed an interest in photographer-artists. In New York, Helen Gee opened Limelight, a gallery devoted to photography that was supported by profits from its coffeehouse. Between 1954 and 1961, the Limelight presented 61 exhibitions, including Robert Frank and Lisette Model.[57] Coffeehouses became sites for Beat poets, folk singers, jazz musicians, and the counterculture of social protest. Allen Ginsberg's "hydrogen jukebox" attack on American values, *Howl* (1956) expressed the sentiments of the era: "I saw the best minds of my generation, destroyed by madness starving, mystical, naked, who dragged themselves thru the angry streets at dawn looking for a negro fix . . ." His poem stirred up so much anger that it was seized.[58] During the same year, African-American photographer Roy DeCarava opened A Photographer's Gallery (1955–57) in New York, where artists like Harry Callahan and Minor White could be seen by appointment.[59] However, aside from small irregularly operating galleries, MOMA was the only regular source of photography exhibitions in New York.

The atomic era fissures open in the area of race relations in America. In 1947 Jackie Robinson [1919–1972] became the first black man to play major league baseball, part of a larger trend that would eventually lead the Supreme Court to strike down "Jim Crow" segregation laws that controlled how and where blacks could interact with white society.[60] The desire to show these changing parameters of the atomic world can be seen in the work of **Roy DeCarava** [b. 1919], for which he became the first African-American to receive a Guggenheim fellowship. De-Carava's work expressed a fundamental paradox that

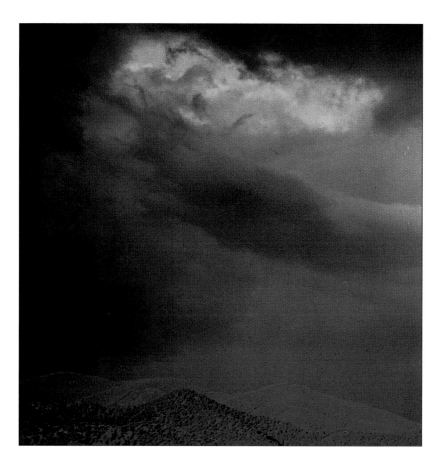

15.17   ELIOT PORTER. *Sangre de Christo,* Mountains at Sunset, Tesuque, NM, 1958. 8⅝ × 8⁷⁄₁₆ inches. Dye transfer print.   Porter believed that "to put the world, and yourself at the same time, in a valid perspective you must remove yourself from the demands of both. The world's demands fade the faster, but nonetheless surely your own will shrink to acceptable proportions and cannot sally forth to attack you. In the wilderness of Glen Canyon you do not assail yourself. You glide on into the day unpursued, living, as all good river travelers should, in the present."[61]   © 1990 Amon Carter Museum, Fort Worth, TX. Bequest of Eliot Porter.

African-Americans faced in the materialistically expanding nuclear culture of the 1950s; being surrounded by white dreams that blacks were often denied the means to attain. DeCarava came into the public eye for collaborating on a book about life in Harlem, *The Sweet Flypaper of Life* (1955), with writer Langston Hughes. His moody prints, often dark and with a glowing area of light, whether of jazz musicians or urban street life, show the competing dynamism of darkness and light. His wife, art historian Sherry Turner DeCarava, wrote:

> Such forces in DeCarava's pictures are both visible and invisible; they may manifest themselves as a psychological valent of terror or fear, as a social valent of abandonment or as a human form. Yet there is no "nature morte" in the images. The

pictures display an atomic life-energy as both positive and negative elements occur in relation to each other; an interpenetration and exchange of vital forces occurs on all levels. In the midst of these illusions, however, the photographs express not struggle but a sense of stillness.[62]

While African-American life and culture are central to DeCarava, his most resolute work transcends the literalness of situations and penetrates their binary meaning. In *Hallway New York* (1953), a claustrophobic tenement hallway, illuminated by a dim overhead light, whose walls seem almost a mirror reflection of each other, propel the viewer to a barely visible doorway.[63] DeCarava's psychological involvement, traveling down the hallway of the present to the door (escape) of the future, transforms the subject into a metaphor. Although DeCarava emphatically states that his "work is about beauty and caring,"[64] this interaction of reality and illusion and its accompanying contradictions provides context, tension, and shared ground for meaning within a moment of stillness, revealing that racism has excluded the majority of African-Americans from the post-nuclear boom. This adoption of an autobiographical approach, the incorporating of oneself into the visual structure, widely filtered into the practice of the 1960s. As the demand for photographic education increased, DeCarava ran the Kamoinge Workshop for young black photographers (1963–66) and later taught at New York's Hunter College.

Running on a parallel track of opposite aesthetics was **Eliot Porter** [1901–1990], a Harvard Medical School graduate, teacher and researcher in bacteriology and biochemistry, and amateur photographer, who was profoundly impressed by Ansel Adams's work. After Stieglitz showed Porter's images at An American Place in 1938–39, Porter devoted himself to photography, developing new methods for photographing wild animals, birds, and insects by using telephoto lenses, flash, and special shutters. To Porter, nature was "an undiluted source of pleasure and a reservoir of mysteries" about life, and he wanted to use science to understand and protect it. In 1940, Porter started making his *dye transfer process* prints in order to achieve more accurate and permanent colors. The dye transfer process was a subtractive *imbibition* assembly method that relied on the selective absorption of dyes for making color prints from color negatives or positives. Gelatin relief matrices were produced from three separation negatives made through red, green, and blue filters, soaked in yellow, magenta, and cyan dyes, and transferred in register to a support (paper). The system can be traced back to 1875 and remained commercially accessible until Kodak discontinued its product line in 1993. The process was complex, but it offered incredible latitude in manipulating a print and was more stable than a chromogenic color print.

Porter became well-known through his publications, such as *The Place No One Knew: Glen Canyon on the Colorado* (1963), showing what was lost when technology was used to flood Glen Canyon to create Lake Powell and dam the Colorado River to generate electricity. This was a belated lesson for the Sierra Club as it discovered the effectiveness of harnessing *beauty*, that which makes the content of art powerful to the beholder,[65] to promote environmental causes. Porter's "beautiful" color images helped awaken consciousness about ecological issues and the dangers of uncontrolled technology. They assisted the newly forming environmental movement by getting people to join the Sierra Club and also had a side effect of helping color photography gain entry into the art world. In the forward of *The Place No One Knew*, editor David Brower asked:

> But where will the chance to know wildness be a generation from now? How much of the magic of this, the American earth, will have been dozed and paved into oblivion by the great feats of engineering that seem to come so much more readily to hand than the knack of saving something for what it is?. . . Again and again the challenge to explore has been met, handled, and relished by one generation—and precluded to any other.[66]

But as much as artists like Porter and Paul Caponigro [b. 1932], a student of Minor White, continued to celebrate Thoreau's "tonic of wildness," the world was pushing the limits of nature. Some of Caponigro's early east coast work incorporated urban distress, but his move to the southwest, allowing him to stay within his internal universe, typified the division in photographic practice between these two philosophies. Most of Caponigro's high modernist work deals with uniting people's relationship to nature, revealing "the landscape behind the landscape."[67] But there was a division forming between the artists born in preatomic and postatomic times, as it became harder to believe in past truths in the face of the atomic reality. Those capable of maintaining a preatomic outlook kept their faith in the mysteries of nature; those who dissented against the scientific atomic outlook became existentialists.

The Terror of Riches

The automobile, as Frank had observed, symbolized a machine of personal power. The American love affair with the automobile was demonstrated by President Eisenhower's Federal-Aid Highway Act of 1956, authorizing the construction of over 40,000 miles of interstate superhighways without much thought to carnage, congestion, destruction of core city neighborhoods, suburban sprawl, or petroleum dependence. The 1950s saw the American family's disposable income rise by 49 percent. A baby boom began in the United States after World War II; more babies were born between 1948 and 1953 than in all the previous thirty years. But what was the price of this new affluence? Between 1940 and 1964, the number of psychiatrists increased almost sixfold. Americans believed they needed the Bomb to protect their newfound material wealth, and test bombs were regularly set off. H-bomb tests annihilated atolls in the South Pacific; A-bombs charred the Nevada desert. Cold War East-West relations deteriorated with the Soviet downing of an American U-2 spy plane in 1960. The politics of brinkmanship was brought to a climax by President John F. Kennedy [1917–1963] and Soviet Premier Nikita Khrushchev [1894–1971] during the 1962 Cuban missile crisis that took the world to the edge of nuclear destruction. (Time as given Nikita Khrushchev's famous provocation to the West, "We will bury you," a previously unimaginable twist to history as his son and cold war scholar, Sergei N. Khrushchev, became a United States citizen in 1999.) Beneath the material riches lay terror. Social activist/critic Todd Gitlin wrote:

> We grew up taking cover in school drills—the first American generation compelled from infancy to fear not only war but the end of days. Every so often, out of the blue, a teacher would pause in the middle of class and call out, "Take cover!". . . . Under the desks and crouched in the hallways, terrors were ignited, existentialists were made. . . . Several observers have reported what my own impressions and interviews confirm: Children who grew up in the Fifties often dreamed, vividly, terrifyingly, about nuclear war.[68]

While middle-class Americans indulged in the contradictory aspirations of creativity and security, painting pictures by numbers with John Negy on TV, a fringe subculture of alienated antiheroes began to rebel against what J. D. Salinger's Holden Caulfield called "phoniness" in *Catcher in the Rye* (1951). For this affluent and educated minority, who felt caught in a restrictive world, science had failed, and reliance on the Bomb meant there was no future. "Alternative" directions and solutions were necessary if humankind was to continue to evolve.

Endnotes

1   Robert Frank quoted in Sarah Greenough, Philip Brookman, et al, *Robert Frank: Moving Out* (Washington, D.C.: National Gallery of Art, 1994), 54.

2   See Richard Rhodes, *Dark Sun: The Making of the Hydrogen Bomb* (New York: Simon & Schuster, 1995), 203–5.

3   Newhall rewrote the catalogue as a book in 1949. Its narrative strategy was planned with the assistance of a storyteller, Hollywood scriptwriter and novelist Ferdinand Reyher. See Paul Hill and Thomas Copper, *Dialogue with Photography* (New York: Farrar, Straus, and Gioux, 1979), 407–8.

4   Nancy Newhall was a writer and worked with Ansel Adams on eight books, including *This Is the American Earth* (1960) and her biography of Adams, *The Eloquent Light*, 1963. While Beaumont was in the military service she was acting photography curator at MOMA. She wrote the poetic text for Paul Strand's *Time in New England* (1950), edited *The Daybooks of Edward Weston* (1957 and 1961), and authored *P. H. Emerson: The Fight for Photography as a Fine Art* (1975),

5   See Rhodes, 175.

6   Clarence John Laughlin, "Beyond Documentation and Purism," text accompanying slide set distributed by Light Impressions, Rochester, NY, "Clarence John Laughlin," produced by Focal Point Press, 1977, 1.

7   Clarence John Laughlin in Jonathan Williams Introduction, *Clarence John Laughlin: The Personal Eye* (Millerton: Aperture, 1973), 13.

8   Clarence John Laughlin, *Lost Louisiana: An Essay in the Poetry of Remembrance,* unpublished manuscript, begun ca. 1973, 27. Manuscripts Division, Historical New Orleans Collection. Quoted in Nancy C. Barrett, "Brick and Wood and Spirit: The Architectural Photographs of Clarence John Laughlin," in Keith F. Davis, *Clarence John Laughlin: Visionary Photographer* (Kansas City: Hallmark Cards, Inc., 1990), 36.

9   Laughlin in Williams Introduction, 12.

10   Frederick Sommer, "Extemporaneous Talk," *Aperture* (1971), unp., cited in Leland Rice, "Introduction," in *Frederick Sommer at Seventy-Five: A Retrospective* (Long Beach: The Art Museum and Galleries, California State University, 1980), 13.

11   Ibid.

12   Ibid., 9 and 13.

13   "Art and the Subconscious: The Multi-Negative Photography of Vladimir Telberg-von-Teleheim," *American Artist,* vol. 13, no. 1 (January 1949), 60.

14   "Composite Photography by Val Telberg," *American Artist,* vol. 18, no. 2 (February 1954), 47.

15   Wall label from *Sequence 13—Return to the Bud*, curated by Walter Chappell during the spring of 1959 at the Eastman House, Minor White Archive, Eastman House, Rochester, NY.

16   Minor White, *Mirrors, Messages, Manifestations* (Millerton, NY: Aperture, 1969), 186.

17   Minor White, "Equivalence: The Perennial Trend," [1963], *Photographers on Photography*, Nathan Lyons, ed. (Englewood Cliffs, NJ: Prentice Hall, Inc., 1966), 173.

18   Minor White, "Extended Perception through Photography and Suggestion," *Ways of Growth*, Herbert Otto and John Mann, eds. (New York: Grossman, 1968), 35.

19   Minor White, "The Camera Mind and Eye," [1952] *Photographers on Photography*, 166.

20   Harry Callahan, "An Adventure in Photography," *Minicam Photography*, vol. 9, no. 6, 28–29. Reprinted in *Photographers on Photography,* Nathan Lyons, ed., (Englewood Cliffs, NJ: Prentice Hall, Inc., 1966), 40–41.

21   From a taped conversation between Callahan and John Szarkowski (April 1975, Providence). Tapes are in MOMA's Department of Photography. Cited in John Szarkowski, *Callahan* (Millerton: Aperture, 1976). 16–17.

22   Letter from Harry Callahan to Ann Armstrong (February 19, 1947). Files of the Department of Photography, MOMA. Cited in ibid., 17.

23   Harry Callahan, statement on *Photographs: Harry Callahan* (Santa Barbara: El Mochuelo Gallery, 1964).

24   Pat Booth, ed., *Master Photographers: The World's Great Photographers on their Art and Technique* (New York: Clarkson N. Potter, 1983), 64

25   Aaron Siskind, "The Drama of Objects," *Minicam Photography*, vol. 8, no. 9 (1945), 20–23, 93–94. Reprinted in Nathan Lyons, ed., *Photographers On Photography*, 96–98.

26   *The Family of Man* created by Edward Steichen, prologue by Carl Sandburg (New York, The Museum of Modern Art, 1955). Steichen claimed that he, Wayne Miller (photographer), and Paul Rudolph (architect) looked at more than two million images before designing the exhibition.

27   Ibid. Edward Steichen, introduction, 4.

28   Interview with Wynn Bullock, in Paul Hill and Thomas Copper, *Dialogue with Photography*, 331.

29   Jacob Deschin, "Panoramic Show at The Museum of Modern Art," *The New York Times,* January 30, 1955. Cited in

John Szarkowski, *Mirrors and Windows: American Photography since 1960* (New York: The Museum of Modern Art, 1978), 16.

30   "Robert Frank," in *Photography Within the Humanities*, eds., Eugenia Parry Janis and Wendy MacNeil (Danbury, NH: Addison House Publishers and the Art Department, Jewett Arts Center, Wellesley College, Wellesley, MA, 1977), 61.

31   Steichen, along with Walker Evans, Alexey Brodovitch, Alexander Liberman of Condé Nast, and art historian, Meyer Shapiro: all were listed on his application as supporting his project.

32   Jean-Paul Sartre, *The Age of Reason* (1945), *The Reprieve* (1945), and *Troubled Sleep* (1949). Frank said: "I read all the early books by Sartre, the *Roads to Freedom* novels. It helped me, it strengthened my determination." In William S. Johnson, "The Pictures are a Necessity: Robert Frank in Rochester, NY, November 1988" *Rochester Film & Photo Consortium Occasional Papers, No. 2*, January 1989 (Rochester, NY: George Eastman House), 27.

33   Ibid., 30.

34   Janis and MacNeil, 56.

35   Jack Kerouac, "Introduction," *The Americans*: *Photographs by Robert Frank*. (New York: Grove Press, 1959), unp.

36   "An Off-Beat View of the U.S.A.," *Popular Photography*, vol. 46, no. 5 (May 1960), 104–6.

37   *Du*, vol. 22, no. 1 (January 1962), unp.

38   William Klein, in Jane Livingston, *The New York School Photographs 1936–1963* (New York: Stewart, Tabori & Chang, 1992), 314.

39   A jury at *Photokina 1963*, an international photographic exhibition and trade fair held about every two years in Cologne, Germany, voted Klein one of the 30 most important photographers in the medium's history, yet he was not even listed in the index of Newhall's final edition of *The History of Photography*.

40   Klein, in Livingston, *The New York School*, 314.

41   Cited in Jerry Mason, ed., *The International Center of Photography Encyclopedia of Photography* (New York: Crown Publishers, 1984), 282.

42   Cited by Jonathan Green, *American Photography: A Critical History 1945 to the Present* (New York: Harry Abrams Publishers, 1984), 216.

43   For more information on these and other Klein films, see Katherine Dieckmann, "Raging Bill," *Art in America* (December 1990), 71, 73, 75, 77, 79.

44   See William Klein, *In and Out of Fashion: William Klein* (New York: Random House, 1994).

45   Cited by Stephen Brigidi and Claire V. C. Peeps, Introduction, "Mario Giacomelli," *Untitled 32* (Carmel, CA: The Friends of Photography, 1983), 9.

46   See Henry Holmes Smith interview in Hill & Cooper, *Dialogue with Photography*, 132–59.

47   Henry Holmes Smith, *Portfolio #2, Henry Holmes Smith* (Louisville, KY: Center for Photographic Studies, 1972), unp.

48   Ibid.

49   Ibid.

50   See Henry Holmes Smith interview in John Bloom, *Photography At Bay*, 207–8.

51   For additional information about how artists use Polaroid materials see Robert Hirsch, *Exploring Color Photography*, 3rd ed. (New York, McGraw-Hill, 1997).

52   Richard Hamilton, 1957, cited Robert Hughes, *The Shock of the New* (New York: Alfred A. Knopf, 1981), 344.

53   Cited ibid., 342.

54   Verifax was a wet-print process developed at Kodak during the 1940s. A disposable paper negative formed a matrix from which a print was made on a specially treated paper. See Marilyn McCray, *Electroworks* (Rochester: George Eastman House, 1979), for information about these machine processes.

55   Cabala is based on the belief that every accent, letter, number, and word of the Scriptures contains mysteries. Cabalistic signs and writing are used as amulets and in magical practice.

56   Robert Doisneau in Hill & Cooper, *Dialogue with Photography*, 108. Also note that *The Kiss* does not appear because the Doisneau estate, concerned that this image was being overexposed, raised its reproduction fee well beyond the means of this project.

57   See Helen Gee, *Limelight: A Greenwich Village Photography Gallery and Coffeehouse in the Fifties* (Albuquerque: University of New Mexico Press, 1997).

58   In 1956, poet/publisher Lawrence Ferlinghetti's Beat City Lights Bookstore in San Francisco was raided and Allen Ginsberg's *Howl* was seized and declared obscene. A trial exonerated *Howl* and its accompanying publicity gave the Beat writers national attention, resulting in the publication of Jack Kerouac's *On the Road*. For details, see Barry Miles, *Ginsberg: A Biography* (New York: Simon & Schuster, 1989).

59   See Peter Galassi, *Roy DeCarava: A Retrospective* (New York: The Museum of Modern Art, 1996), 22–23 & 269–70.

60   In Brown *v*. Board of Education of Topeka Kansas (1954) Chief Justice Earl Warren moved to protect the rights of minorities by outlawing public school segregation.

61   Eliot Porter, *The Place No One Knew: Glen Canyon on the Colorado*, abridged, David Brower (ed.) (San Francisco: Sierra Club and New York: Ballantine Books, 1968), 14.

62   Sherry Turner DeCarava, Introduction, *Roy DeCarava: Photographs*, James Alinder, ed., *Untitled 27* (Carmel: The Friends of Photography, 1981), 7.

63   In a telephone conversation with the author on March 4, 1999, DeCarava denied permission to reproduce this work. He stated: "I want to control the context of my work . . . . I keep it from getting abused."

64   Ibid.

65   See Dave Hickey, *The Invisible Dragon: Four Essays on Beauty* (Los Angeles: Art Issues Press, 1993).

66   Porter, 8.

67   Paul Caponigro, *Landscape* (New York: McGraw-Hill, 1975), unp.

68   Todd Gitlin, *The Sixties: Years of Hope, Days of Rage* (New York: Bantam Doubleday Dell Publishing, 1987), 22–23.

CHAPTER SIXTEEN

New Frontiers

Expanding Boundaries

Structuralism: Reading a Photograph

The 1960s was a decade of cultural, economic, and political upheaval that challenged American societal values. At age 43, John F. Kennedy was the youngest president ever, and he invited artists and poets to White House events. After Eisenhower, Kennedy brought a new sense of vitality to the nation as he declared a "New Frontier" of social reform that included aid to education, medical care for the aged, the extension of civil rights, the formation of the Peace Corps, and a physical fitness program. This progressive social agenda was juxtaposed with an aggressive foreign policy that included the abortive Bay of Pigs invasion of Cuba in 1961, the Cuban Missile Crisis of 1962 that brought the United States and the former Soviet Union to the brink of nuclear war, and increased the number of U.S. military advisors in South Vietnam. When astronaut Neil Armstrong walked on the moon (1969), there were those who claimed that

Duane Michals. *Things Are Queer,* 1973. 3$\frac{5}{16}$ × 5$\frac{1}{16}$-inch each image. Gelatin silver prints. © Duane Michals.

Michals believes that diversity of practice is essential, as "... everything is a subject for photography including your own fantasies, your own truth, your own desires, your own fears. That's where you live. You don't live on the streets looking at people's faces or looking at sunsets. You live in your mind. And you know your fears more intimately. What I want from you is your secrets. That's the only thing you can give me: your secrets."[1]

the entire event was staged by NASA in a secret airplane hangar in Houston. The bottom line was: Surface appearances could not be trusted.

In the arts people were discarding the idea that photographs were direct pictures of the world and replaced it with the concept that photography had its own morphology that intervened between reality and the viewer. In the 1950s, French semiotician and structuralist (see Structuralism below) Roland Barthes [1915–1980] decoded the formal relations of signs (syntax) to one another and the symbolic logic of photography for the purpose of cultural analysis. *Semiotics* is based on the work of American philosopher Charles Sanders Pierce [1838–1914] and Swiss linguist Ferdinand de Saussure [1857–1913]. Semioticians state that the relation of words to things is not natural but assigned by society. They believe that language is basically a self-contained system of signs made up of two components, the "signifier" and the "signified." The signifier is the word itself that people use to define the material world around them. The signified represents the mental associations we have with that word, which may or may not be conscious and which are affected by our culture. Semioticians analyze these mental associations to understand how a society creates meaning and to find hidden meaning(s). Semioticians do not limit their practice to language and stress that any aspect of a culture, such as a photograph, can communicate meaning and thus function and be analyzed as a sign. Semiotics has provided the historical foundation for modern structuralism.

Barthes wrote that "photography crushes all other images by its tyranny."[2] In the United States, he wrote, "everything is transformed into images: Only images exist and are produced and consumed . . . and [this] de-realizes the human world of conflicts and desires under cover of illustrating it."[3] This was a revelation compared to Vance Packard's *Hidden Persuaders* (1957), an exposé about concealed advertising practices, which never discussed the persuasive role of photography in a consumer society. Surveying the scene Henry Holmes Smith wrote: "Before I can make any estimate of photography's present state and future prospects, I need to know what a photograph should look like and I am not at all certain that I do."[4] What had been sanctioned was now under scrutiny. Against a Stieglitzian framework of straight photographers canonized by Newhall in his *The History of Photography,* debate opened over craftsmanship (the fine-print aesthetic and proper use of materials), formal concerns (compositional construction), social duty (the depiction of beautiful and spiritually ennobling subjects), and just what it was that a photograph could mean. Was a photograph a witness to history or an equivalent to inner vision? Was its meaning determined by its maker, or by an editor, or was its meaning free floating? And lastly, could two individuals read the same photograph and ascribe different meanings to it?

The notion that one could read a photograph was given currency by Henry Holmes Smith and Robert Forth and endorsed by Minor White. Its foundations can be traced to Ferdinand de Saussure, who established a structural study of language that emphasized the arbitrary relationship of the linguistic sign or code to what it signifies and how meaning is determined. *Structuralism* analyzes society by looking at cultural phenomena as signs that have hidden underlying meaning(s) that can be decoded. These signs can be compared to the basic grammatical components of language that together create linguistic meaning, or the essential elements of myths that reveal how a society creates a framework for understanding the world. Structuralism states that no single element has meaning in itself but must be understood as an integrated part of a society's fundamental organization. Structuralists think that meaning is derived by seeing how one sign relates to another. For structuralists photographs do not exist in isolation but are a part of a complex cultural structure of signs, filled with hidden messages, that must be analyzed for their meaning based on the experiences of the photographer and the viewer. Structural theory gave hope for understanding a seemingly chaotic atomic world that saw Newton's unified mechanical universe crumble into the physics of Einstein's invisible particles. Coupled with existentialism, structuralism offered tactics for refitting the pieces of the world and making it whole again.

In the late 1950s, Noam Chomsky [b. 1928], an American linguist, revolutionized the study of language with his theory that innate structures, not sounds, are the basis for speech. This idea that inherent, unconscious structures might serve as the foundation of understanding started philosophers and artists searching for the hidden structures that shaped meaning. In photography, such doctrines questioned the trustworthiness of the singular, modernist construct of the "thing itself." Photographers began to pay attention to the overall context of their work. The result was a loss of belief in the approach of Blossfeldt and Weston that isolated subjects from their surroundings.

During the 1960s, Chomsky accused the media of conspiring to suppress information vital to the understanding of the Vietnam War and massage it into a misleading and consumable format. Chomsky believed in the ideal of an informed, democratic society freely arriving at decisions, and he pointed out that images are not neutral containers and that people must actively ferret out their meaning. If the thing itself could no longer be trusted to supply an accurate and complete meaning then photographers had to devise new ways of making images that offered insight into the world. In turn, viewers were asked not to passively accept any image or statement about the image on face value but to take responsibility and extrapolate their own meaning.

Throughout the 1950s, exhibitions like Steichen's *The Family of Man* (see Chapter 15) reinforced the general belief that photography was exempt from these "hidden persuaders" that shaped meaning. By the early

16.1   ROBERT RAUSCHENBERG AND SUE
WEIL.   Cyanotypes in *Life*, April 9, 1951. 13⅝ ×
10¹⁄₁₆ inches. The April 9, 1951 issue of *Life* opened with
a mini-story about life-sized blueprints being made by
the "young painters" Robert and Sue (Weil) Rauschenberg in their New York apartment. Their blueprints
used photograms to directly quote from the presence of
bodies rather than optically depicting them by means
of a lens. The work was kindred to the abstract expressionists as it possessed exact traces of the physical activity, prefiguring the attraction to the body performance
artists would pursue in the 1960s and 1970s.   © Robert
Rauschenberg. Courtesy PaceWildensteinMacGill, New York.

1960s photographers began to question whether photography was a universal language, or whether outside
influences, like its surrounding context and viewer subjectivity, determined reality and hence photographic
meaning. Curator/photographer Nathan Lyons wrote:

> If we are to confront the meaning of contemporary photo-
> graphic expression . . . then let us establish a working premise
> by asking: Was a pepper to Edward Weston or a photogram to
> Moholy-Nagy less real than a breadline to Dorothea
> Lange? . . . Our discourse concerning this matter has frag-
> mented the photographic community into reverently biased
> schools of thought, and by doing so has retarded a much
> needed dialogue concerning ideas which are essential to an
> understanding of photographic expression.[5]

The Found Image: The Beginnings of Postmodernism

Walter Benjamin observed that one consequence of
photomechanical reproduction was the disturbance of
authenticity and originality, which diminished the aura
of an original work. As a result of the growing domination of the photographic image, many modernistic
twentieth-century artists expanded the definitions of
their media. The new definition toppled the established
importance of the subject matter itself and the "correct"
use of materials for making pictures. Although artists
like Picasso often were silent concerning their direct
use of photographs, both the detailed information and
the way it was "automatically given" by photography
was now invading the artistic vocabulary.[6]

In 1955, **Robert Rauschenberg** [b. 1925] began to
exhibit "combines" of painting and sculpture that incorporated seemingly discordant and incompatible
items, such as stuffed animals, photographs, and photomechanical reproductions. In what the critic Lawrence
Alloway labeled "an aesthetic of heterogeneity,"[7]
Rauschenberg constructed work of dissimilar parts, ex-
cerpted directly from popular culture and filled with
contradictions that left the origins of his source materials open and available for public inspection.

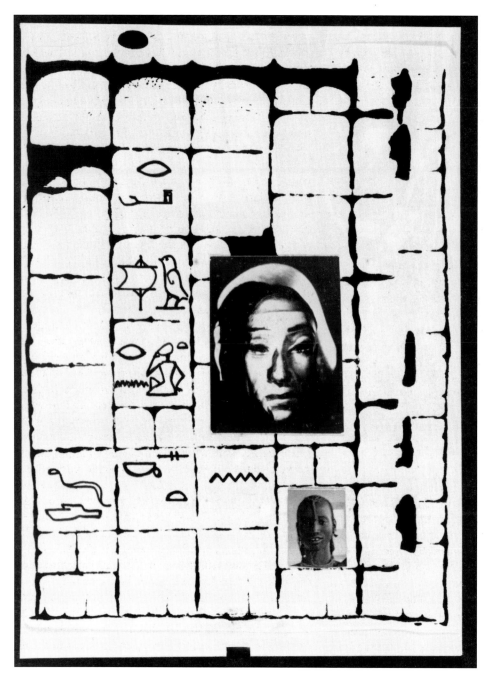

16.2   WILLIAM S. BURROUGHS AND BRION
GYSIN.   *Untitled* [Projection Performance], ca. 1965.
9⅞ × 7⅛ inches. Gelatin silver prints and ink on
paper. The hieroglyph exemplifies Burroughs's
challenge to the classical narrative structure. Burroughs
insists that "The study of hieroglyphic languages shows
us that a word is an image . . . [and] written work is an
image."[9] Burroughs and Gysin were fascinated by the
capacity of images to mutate and replicate, like viruses
within the "social body," and how this phenomenon
could be used to defy society's authority and
conventions.   Courtesy Los Angeles County Museum of Art.
Purchased with funds provided by the Hiro Yamagata
Foundation.

Rauschenberg had been making photographs since
his student days at the Bauhaus-émigré outpost of
Black Mountain College in North Carolina, where he
worked with color abstractionist Josef Albers
[1888–1976] and chance operations composer John
Cage [1912-1992].[8] By the early 1960s, Rauschenberg
had abandoned abstract expressionism and was using
transfer processes to overlap found images and/or his
own photographs onto his canvases, which also united
lithography and silkscreen. This new use of materials
and subject matter reflected his belief that "Painting relates to both art and life. Neither can be made. (I try to
act in that gap between the two)."[10]

Rauschenberg, like Robert Frank, used existing readymade vernacular sources, like tires and diners from the

automobile culture, to create motifs and push the content of high art to include mass communication, politics, and technology. Rauschenberg's embrace of the photographic sensibility, in terms of content, style, and technique, and as a photographer meant his painting had to be reconsidered in terms of printing. The critic Douglas Crimp wrote:

> Rauschenberg had moved definitively from techniques of production (combines, assemblages) to techniques of reproduction (silkscreens, transfer drawings). And it is this move that requires us to think of Rauschenberg's art as postmodernist. Through reproductive technology postmodernist art dispenses with aura. The fantasy of the created subject gives way to the frank confiscation, quotation, excerptation, accumulation, and repetition of already existing images. Notions of originality, authenticity, and presence, essential to the ordered discourse of the museum are undermined.[11]

This way of working was antithetical to the accepted definition of photography as the supplier of an ordered, unbroken view of reality, one comprised of single moments. Rauschenberg saw the world as a camera saw it, selecting, extracting, and assembling the visual information that was already there. This method of thinking exemplified Duchamp's belief that creation is about decision making, that a photographer is not simply one who makes photographs but is one who thinks and works with photographs.

The Rise of Pop Art

During the 1960s, assemblage, conceptual art, environmental art, minimalism, op art, pop art, and photo-realism explored form, syntax, and style, demonstrating the struggle in the art world between the painterly and the photographic. The ubiquitous nature of photography and its ability to deliver fresh forms of representation provoked new attitudes, forms, iconographies, and strategies that affected aesthetics. Artists incorporated photographic mannerisms and processes into their projects, and they directly placed photographs into their work. Pop art rejected the conventions of painting and turned to photography for its images and process. Artists like Andy Warhol, James Rosenquist, and Tom Wesselmann used consumer-based images, including advertising photographs, pictures of celebrities, news photos, and postcards, to destroy artists' handwork and make recognizable subject matter from soup cans to comic strips supreme.

The rage produced by race riots, the Vietnam War, and the assassinations of John F. Kennedy (1963), Malcolm X (1965), Martin Luther King, Jr. (1968), and Robert F. Kennedy (1968) resurrected the myth of the doomed outsider. Yet within the alternative community there remained a sense that anything was possible. At the suggestion of the British-Canadian artist Brion Gysin [1916–1986], the experimental beat writer **William S. Burroughs** [1914–1997], whose *Naked Lunch* (1959/65) was ruled obscene in Massachusetts

for its open depiction of homosexuality and drugs, applied dadaist montage methods to his writings. In *The Ticket That Exploded* (1962), Burroughs cut-up and rearranged texts to free himself from cognitive processes and linear time. Cut-ups allowed Burroughs to fantasize a hallucinatory universe made up of a mosaic of voices in which society's familiar rules no longer applied, a universe in which anything could happen because "Nothing is True" and "Everything is Permitted."[12]

Around 1965, Burroughs and Gysin collaborated on collages of hieroglyphs and photographs placed over an irregular grid (see Figure 16.2), presenting their view that reality was not singular or holistic but a dynamic system of local, interdependent perceptions.[13] The duo forced the narrative construct by overloading the page with text and images that multiplied to the borders of the irrational. This procedure also denoted the way an image cannot be commanded or its course foretold once it gets into circulation.

Andy Warhol's [1928–1987] acceptance and use of commodity images from advertising, magazines, and newspapers came to symbolize pop art. Warhol's *Campbell's Soup Cans* (1962) was hand-painted, but by the end of 1962 he had switched to photo-silkscreen. His *Disaster Paintings* (1963), covering tragedies like a plane crash and President Kennedy's assassination, offered an alternative to the romantic modernism of abstract expressionism, aligning Warhol with photography by appropriating sensational news photos, enlarging them, repeating them, and adding flat fields of color.[14] Warhol destroyed the photographs' original context and distanced viewers from any sense of loss or horror, leaving them uninvolved spectators. The technique reflects on psychiatrist R. D. Laing's observations in *The Divided Self* (1959) in which he portrayed the schizophrenic (the "mad" person) as an outsider, estranged from himself, in a society that he or she could not accept as real. As Charlie Chaplin had done in *Modern Times* (1936), Warhol announced that he wanted "to be a machine," declared his own estrangement from society, and proceeded to use photography to extract repetitious images from popular culture. Whether it was soup cans, a car crash, or the electric chair (see Figure 16.3), Warhol was devoted, like an intensely neurotic person who repeats an act over and over, to the static sameness and banality of a mass-produced commodity, and his work sparked debate on the effects of technology on society. His early plotless, single-action films—such as *Sleep* and *Empire* (1963)—were interminable exercises in camera passivity. In *Sleep* the camera remained fixed on a sleeping man for eight hours. *Empire* consisted of a seemingly endless shot of the Empire State Building. Warhol's studio, aptly named The Factory, did not create fine art in the tradition that stretches back to Renaissance Florence as much as it manufactured products. Warhol celebrated capitalism and commerce, making fashion and promotion the means to their own ends, granting greater importance to perception than to the means of artistic production. Art

16.3   ANDY WARHOL.   *Orange Disaster #5*, 1963.
106 × 82 inches. Acrylic and silkscreen enamel.   © 1999
Andy Warhol Foundation for the Visual Arts/ARS New York.
Photo © The Solomon R. Guggenheim Foundation, New York.

was commerce and the artist a businessman who with the right spin could sell anything. The avant-garde stance of the new was replaced with a stance based on novelty. Everybody, every work of art, would be "famous for fifteen minutes," in Warhol's words. A Warhol piece could be glanced at like a television screen, as authenticity was replaced by artifice. Second-handedness became a virtue. Warhol treated Mao Tse-tung and Mickey Mouse with the same reverence, demonstrating how meaning can reside in the eyes of the beholder. Such restless trend-surfing was evidence that the cultural scales balancing the past and present, guided by what T. S. Eliot called the "pres-

ence of the past," had shifted, making the past only a burden to be rid of rather than a provider of cultural context. The avant-garde prophecy that tradition would kill conventional subjects and materials of fine high-brow art making and viewing became self-fulfilling in a way quite different than the avant-garde founders had intended. Warhol's use of photographic repetition reinforced his position of not placing himself above his audience. He stated:

> "What's great about America is that it started the tradition where the richest consumers buy essentially the same things as the poorest. You can be watching TV and see Coca-Cola, and you know that the president drinks Coke, Liz Taylor drinks Coke, and just think, you can drink Coke, too. A Coke is Coke and no amount of money is going to get you a better Coke than the one the bum on the corner is drinking. All the Cokes are the same and all the Cokes are good. Liz Taylor knows it, the president knows it, the bum knows it, and you know it."[15]

16.4   ART SINSABAUGH.   *Chicago #29,* 1964.
7 × 19⁷⁄₁₆ inches. Gelatin silver print.   Courtesy Estate
of Art Sinsabaugh.

Canadian media analyst **Marshall McLuhan** [1911–1980] provided a philosophical base for discussing the pivotal themes facing photography in the 1960s with his book, *Understanding Media* (1964). In a chapter called "The Medium Is the Message," McLuhan stressed that new technology gradually creates a dynamic environment grounded in process. He wrote:

> The electric light is pure information. It is a medium without a message. . . .This fact, characteristic of all media, means that the "content" of any medium is always another medium. The content of writing is speech, just as the written word is the content of print, and print the content of the telegraph . . . the message of any medium or technology is the change of scale or pace or pattern it introduces into human affairs . . . . Whether the light is being used for brain surgery or night baseball is a matter of indifference . . ."the medium is the message" because it controls the scale and form of human association and action.[16]

McLuhan noted that "camera[s] tend to turn people into things, and the photograph extends and multiplies the human image to the proportions of mass-produced merchandise."[17] The quantity (repetition) of information being delivered became more important than its quality. The contemplation of this overload of electric information was replacing creativity. The pop artists mesmerization with this sensibility sent a message to the public that art and artists no longer shared any responsibility for explaining the incomprehensible, for unmasking frauds, or for acting as a gyroscope for morals or taste, because it made no difference what art said. Numerous artists and critics felt that understanding could only be achieved through verbal narration. McLuhan did not share this view.

> Education is ideally civil defense against media fall-out. Yet Western man has had, so far, no education or equipment for meeting any of the new media on their own terms. Literate man is not only numb and vague in the presence of film or photo, but he intensifies his ineptness by a defensive arrogance and condescension to "pop kulch" and "mass entertainment". . . But the logic of the photograph is neither verbal nor syntactical, a condition which renders literary culture quite helpless to cope with the photograph.[18]

Rather than evaluating a photograph by a literary standard, McLuhan wanted a photograph to be understood on its own characteristics. McLuhan recognized the fundamental confrontations between literary and visual culture and the flaws inherent in imposing a verbal and/or ideological framework on visual information. Cultural critics, whether political or religious, often project their "correct" views of an image, denying the possibility of understanding an image on other levels. Such critical filters tend to distrust photography's democracy and assume positions that value a work in terms of ideology and language, placing a literary model above a visual one. This removes the prospect of the average person formulating his or her own understanding without guidance from the experts. It also denies the pleasure of approximation, even though it may result in a failure to apprehend.

Challenging the Code

In the 1960s photographers began to contest the code of direct optical and chemical imaging. **Art Sinsabaugh** [1924–1983], a student of the Chicago Institute of Design, did a series in the early 1960s using a 12 × 20-inch banquet camera to make long horizontal landscapes. Although he still relied on an archaeological approach, making highly detailed, exquisitely seen, frieze-like compositions, Sinsabaugh discovered a somber way of looking at the landscape.

As a boy, Sinsabaugh had photographed with an 8mm movie camera, and his later panoramic images retain a cinematic sense of extending time and the field of view. The empty spaces in many of these unsentimental compositions foreshadow the "new topographics" landscape photography of the 1970s and 1980s, as we will

16.5   SYL LABROT.   *Untitled*, 1972. 18³⁄₁₆ × 22⁵⁄₁₆
inches. Portfolio: *Ten Synthetic Landscapes*. Color seri-
graph.   © Syl Labrot/Visual Studies Workshop.

see. Sinsabaugh's detached and unromantic images
describe the low ground of the American prairie,
revealing its sparseness and the severity of its beauty.
They also reveal an abrupt and discordant human presence against an empty sky and endless horizon. As a
teacher on the cusp of a shift in photographic practice,
Sinsabaugh foreshadowed the coming changes: "Today
can and should be the time for those interested in the visual images possible through photography to advance
the quality of this imagery by turning back to the techniques of the past. . . . I appeal for a critical reevaluation
of the discarded techniques of photography to enhance
the images of the future."[19]

Syl Labrot [1929–1977] investigated ways of
cracking the codes of representation at the crossroads
of painting, printmaking, and photography to uncover
opportunities for joining these three medias. Labrot's
purpose was to explore subjects in a manner that
would not be possible with photography alone. Labrot

was interested in picturing a subjective, inner world of
emotional states as opposed to replicating the exterior
world. Labrot's immersion in abstract expressionism
and *color field* painting, whose large, abstract areas of
unmodulated color rejected illusions of visual depth
and expressive gestural brushwork, led him in the late
1950s to investigate the dye transfer process. These
experiments reveal the inclination of photographers to
expand the monochromatic palette and break color
free from its negative commercial associations. Labrot
used the graphic qualities of printmaking to transform
his images. His method of extracting details, simplify-
ing a subject down to just color and texture, and layering striking hues that do not resemble the effects of
the paintbrush, demonstrates how photography can
also address an inner spirit. The sensuous, colored,
photo-based surface of Labrot's fictionalized *Synthetic Landscape* series, as seen in his artist's book
Pleasure Beach (1976), visually evokes territory similar, metaphysically, to that of the Argentine writer
Jorge Luis Borges [1899–1986], whose work intrigued Labrot. Labrot's imaginary landscapes blend
fantasy, myth, and symbolism to question destiny and

time. If Labrot saw life as a Borgian labyrinth, he also, unlike Warhol, saw art as his way of overcoming the chaos of life.

The Social Landscape

By the late 1950s, many photographers felt a passionate discontent with a variety of sources. There still lingered a generally unspoken spiritual void, a vast unexplainable emptiness, caused by the Holocaust. The aftershocks of this event, even on those it did not directly effect, would cause a group of photographers with Jewish backgrounds to question the rules that make society function. Other artists began to examine what economist John Kenneth Galbraith labeled the *Affluent Society* (1958), an atomic culture where "wealth is the relentless enemy of understanding."[20] This questioning led to a rejection of many photographic conventions: photography's aesthetics, definitions, subject matter, and the role of the photographer. The rising interest in popular culture vis-à-vis the snapshot encouraged imagemakers to work with vernacular subjects found in family albums, magazines, and newspapers, and stylistically extend them, as Robert Frank had done, into new aesthetic and communicative purposes.

In 1960 and 1961, Nathan Lyons's lecture series, "Photography and the Picture Experience," opened a discussion on the influence of the snapshot on the syntax of photography that would continue throughout the 1960s. At a conference at the George Eastman House in 1964, John Szarkowski [b. 1925], director of MOMA's department of photography from 1962 to 1991, made a presentation on vernacular imagery. It was informed by John A. Kouwenhoven's *Made in America* (1948), which examines the conflict between the "cultivated" effect of European art and the "vernacular" style of American technological design. Lyons made a presentation on the role of the snapshot in contemporary imagemaking.[21] The conference resulted in three important exhibitions, Lyons's *Toward A Social Landscape* (1966) at the George Eastman House, Szarkowski's *New Documents* (1967) at MOMA, and *12 Photographers of the American Social Landscape*, curated by Thomas H. Garver with assistance from Szarkowski at Brandeis University. These shows introduced a number of imagemakers who were repudiating formal, modernistic expectations about how photographs should look and helped launch a movement based on the casual and unconventional characteristics of the snapshot. Lyons stated:

> I wanted to deal with photographers who were questioning the issue of picture content and how pictures were formulated. It was an early investigation into the work of Lee Friedlander, Garry Winogrand, Danny Lyon, Duane Michals, and Bruce Davidson[22] to show that the vocabulary of the medium was shifting, if not expanding.[23]

Lyons observed that a number of younger photographers were refining a gut-level response to their subjects that would clarify, but not define, life as it is found. Lyons believed that these photographers who directly questioned the genuine relevance of daily events and objects worked out "authentic photographic forms,"[24] based on the snapshot, that encouraged direct commentary on "people and people things." Their approach, which incorporated the diverse traditions of art and documentary photography, was coined the *snapshot aesthetic,* referring to the *cinema vérité,* or direct cinema, filmmaking method that dispensed with directorial control and previsualization techniques. It was a label most photographers considered a contradiction in terms, since snapshooters did not pay attention to aesthetics; thus it was the aesthetic of nonaesthetics. Most photographers preferred the term *social landscape,* which referred to scenes based on the instantaneity and interconnectedness of people to their environment. In his introduction to *Toward A Social Landscape,* Lyons wondered if photographs of natural landscapes should be more highly prized, aesthetically, than man-made landscapes. He suggested that our classical notions of landscape should be reevaluated and expanded to include a greater "interrelatedness" with the environment, forming "the context of a more total landscape."

A photographer whose work radically redefined the social landscape was **Garry Winogrand** [1928–1984]. Too young to fight the Nazis, Winogrand, a gruff New York Jew, worked out of a manic desire to purge himself of trauma by balancing chaos and impending disaster. Winogrand accomplished this by challenging assumptions of order, sorting out relationships through the act of photographing. Winogrand used a 35mm camera and a wide-angle lens not to show more of a subject but to get closer and more involved in the forces propelling a situation. His statement, "I photograph to find out what something will look like photographed"[25] blasts the system of previsualization. He turned familiar incidental occurrences into complex and unsettling environments capable of subverting suppositions about his subjects. Winogrand's tilted framing was a radical reimaging of the straight aesthetic. It destroyed a viewer's sense of order: His subjects often appeared to be on the verge of falling out of the frame, infuriating people who accused him of not being able to hold his camera steady. According to Szarkowski, Winogrand "discovered that he could compose his pictures with a freedom that he had not utilized before, and that the tilted frame could not only maintain a kind of discipline over the flamboyant tendencies of the wide-angle lens, but could also intensify his intuitive sense of his picture's meanings."[26]

Winogrand's compulsive machine-gun, cinematic approach, always on the verge of anarchy, was a way of discovering what the subject actually was. Between 1978 and 1984, Szarkowski estimated that Winogrand

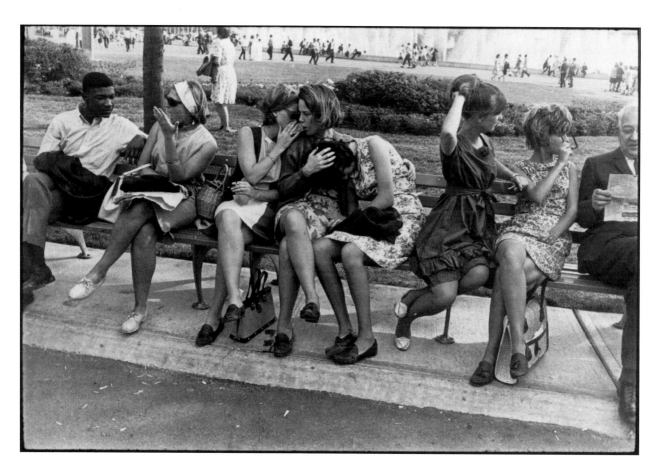

16.6   GARRY WINOGRAND.   *World's Fair, New York*, 1964. 8¹³⁄₁₆ × 13⅛ inches. Gelatin silver print. Winogrand positioned himself not as a critic looking for closure but as an artist who was actively discovering life forces that transform situations. In his *Women Are Beautiful Portfolio* he stated: "I suspect that I respond to their energies, how they stand and move their bodies and faces. In the end, the photographs are descriptions of poses or attitudes that give an idea, a hint of their energies."[27]   © The Estate of Garry Winogrand. Courtesy Fraenkel Gallery, San Francisco.

made more than 300,000 exposures he never looked at.[28] Szarkowski speculated that Winogrand "photographed whether or not he had anything to photograph, and that he photographed most when he had no subject, in the hope that the act of photographing might lead him to one."[29] This is consistent with Winogrand's conviction that "there was no special way a photograph should look," that the compositional components of any photograph were forged by framing a point of view that best described the photographer's sense of a subject.

Szarkowski championed Winogrand's images as demonstrating his own belief that photography's power lay in its descriptive and formal characteristics and not in its cerebral reasoning possibilities. In *The Photographer's Eye* (1966), Szarkowski named five elements that form a vocabulary and a critical perspective for photography: "The Thing Itself (the actual world), The

Detail, The Frame, Time, and Vantage Point."[30] His theoretical construct provided a system for reevaluating photography. Through his MOMA bully-pulpit of curation, collecting, and writing, Szarkowski functioned as tastemaker for a movement of photographers and educators including William Eggleston, Nicholas Nixon, Stephen Shore, Lewis Baltz, Tod Papageorge, and Robert Adams. He favored work that emphasized topographical description and had a minimum of emotional attachment. For Szarkowski, a consummate modernist, form rather than historical context made pictures interesting. Szarkowski's influence was felt for three decades, creating a methodic and sanitary mechanistic climate of straight camera vision that insisted that order and meaning could be imposed on the messiness and unpredictability of life.

Another Szarkowski favorite who could organize and convey the visual chaos and complexity of the urban environment was **Lee Friedlander** [b. 1934]. Friedlander worked to privatize public subjects, pushing the narrative dialogue into a discussion of description and observation. Friedlander's spiritual explorations questioned God's silence during the Holocaust and led him to favor individual redemption through personal grace and hard work. Friedlander constructed an interior world that was not apparent until it was organized through his camera. The discontinuous urban landscape became raw material for a hybrid, formalized, personalized aesthetic that reshaped American

16.7   LEE FRIEDLANDER.   *Philadelphia*, 1965.
7⁵⁄₁₆ × 11⅛ inches. Gelatin silver print.   Courtesy
Fraenkel Gallery, New York.

street photography.[31] With sardonic humor, Friedlander ordered fragmented chaos to define not society but his place within society. Like jazz musicians John Coltrane, Miles Davis, Bill Evans, and Thelonius Monk, who used their music to help forge new identities for themselves, Friedlander's solipsism, his belief that the self is the only object of verifiable knowledge, became the benchmark for photographers examining the inner landscape. Friedlander's inquiry is summed up in his introduction to the first of his numerous books, *Self Portrait* (1970):

> I suspect it is for one's self-interest that one looks at one's surroundings and one's self. This search is personally born and is indeed my reason and motive for making photographs. The camera is not merely a reflecting pool and the photographs are not exactly the mirror, mirror on the wall that speaks with a twisted tongue. . . . The mind-finger presses the release on the silly machine and it stops time and holds what its jaw can encompass and what the light will stain. That moment when the landscape speaks to the observer.[32]

The urban landscape becomes a framing device, like the camera, that sets the stage for an investigation of the human presence within its enclosures, juxtapositions, and overlapping realities. The conceptual basis for Friedlander's metropolis can be linked to Duchamp

as his visual radar leads him to readymade sites that contain images of images. Friedlander's structuralist approach involves an often extremely complex piecing together, a reading of all the interconnected parts and signs to determine meaning. Friedlander uses the reproducibility of the photograph to dismantle the conventional documentary mode of labeling the specifics. People are no longer individuals but are metamorphosed into reproducible forms. Favoring the ordinary, Friedlander does away with hierarchical ordering and makes objects, people, places, and time interchangeable. He forces viewers to search for a lone, human presence, often Friedlander's shadow, which could be anyone's shadow, in a desolate landscape from which God has vanished.

The people and ideas that aroused the intense curiosity of **Diane Nemerov Arbus** [1923–1971] were not to be found in the *Family of Man* but on the outer fringe of society that tyrants like Hitler wanted to eradicate. Arbus grew up in an upper-middle-class Jewish family in New York and was educated at the progressive Ethical Culture school. She did advertising photographs with her husband, Allen Arbus, for her father's store, which led to their being hired to take fashion pictures for *Harper's Bazaar*. Between 1955 and 1957 Arbus studied privately with Lisette Model, who stressed that "the most mysterious thing is a fact clearly stated."[33]

An emerging feminist awareness in the 1960s

expanded opportunities for women photographers.[34] Arbus's interest shifted from the studio fashion work to a confrontational style that relied on frontal light, often a flash, to sharply depict people who seemed willing to reveal their hidden selves for the camera. What Arbus pictured often seemed sensational because she unrelentingly broke down public personas. Arbus unblinkingly pictured people in the margins of society so that their images were no longer about them as individuals but about them as archetypes of human circumstances. People found her pictures, like the cover of *New Documents*, *Triplets in Their Bedroom, N.J.* (1963), distressing because the subjects did not fit into the American dream, even if they were outwardly trying to do so. For Arbus living one's private life was not enough. A public morality was needed to avoid ending up like those "good Germans" who had made a clear distinction between who was acceptable and who was not. Arbus pushed the boundaries of what was permissible by heroically visualizing her subjects and then recording them within a snapshot framework. After her suicide in 1971, Arbus's work developed a cult following, though some critics, such as Allan Sekula, said that her "fetishistic cultivation" of freaks had cruelly sacrificed their humanity.

However, such critiques miss the force of her work, which is underscored by Arbus's favorite Goethe quote: "Every form correctly seen is beautiful."[35] Arbus was known to wear her camera everywhere: "I never take it off."[36] For Arbus the process of photographing was the paramount experience and through it she expressed the ambiguities and contradictions of herself and life. Arbus often got to know her subjects, such as Eddie Carmel, the 495-pound, eight-foot tall "Jewish Giant," who she photographed for years before making the images she was after.

Arbus believed that "a photograph is a secret about a secret. The more it tells you the less you know."[37] Arbus said that "photographing is not about being comfortable, either for the photographer or the subject" and that "you've got to learn not to be careful."[38] Her portraits are the result of her process of collecting and exchanging secrets that nobody wanted to share. Arbus knew that people did not want to look at what they perceived as a horror, barely covered by a thin layer of human skin. She understood that "Most people go through life dreading they'll have a traumatic experience. Freaks were born with their trauma. They've passed their test in life. They're aristocrats."[39]

Arbus's final series dealt with retardates, whose being and identity take us to an edge of human experience. These images challenge the definition of self and confront viewers with the secret fact that nobody is "normal." The pathos in Arbus's photographs is not that of her subjects but that of the viewer. Arbus's pictures are not about types of freaks but a cataloging of that communal secret of wanting to be "normal" and wanting to be accepted for who we are. The pain that makes

viewers avert their eyes is due to the internal violence Arbus pictures between the void of our inner self-perception and that of outer public reality.[40]

New Journalism

Arbus's photographs, which often appeared in *Esquire*,[41] were part of a trend towards personal journalism that used the guise of reportage to present a highly subjective view of the world. **Bruce Davidson's** [b. 1933] images, like the "new journalism" of Tom Wolfe, Hunter Thompson, and Norman Mailer, contain authentic details of people and their situations. Davidson's early photo-essays about an old French widow and a circus midget are indicative of his sympathetic representations of those who are not part of mainstream culture. During 1958, Davidson photographed a New York City gang and their rituals—hanging out under the boardwalk, drinking beer, dancing, or combing their hair in the mirror of a cigarette machine (see Figure 16.8). He recalled:

> I took the finished photographs to the editors at *Life* who looked at them and gave them back to me. . . . I became more aware of the photographs of Robert Frank, who had just published *The Americans*. In it I saw an America that diminished the dream and replaced it with a piercing truth. It was hard for me to endure those bitter, beautiful photographs, for I had still within me the dream of hope and sympathy. . . .[42]

Davidson's personal involvement with gangs drove him in 1974 to look for the girl he had photographed combing her hair in the Coney Island mirror, to see what had happened to her dream since 1958. Davidson wrote:

> She had married the gang leader. . . . Their daughter was fifteen, the same age she was then. She said: "We all had a dream, but we lost it. Most of the kids we knew are on drugs, in crime, or dead. You meant a lot to us because you were someone from the outside who had a camera and was taking pictures of us." I told her that her picture was hanging in museums around the world. When her teenage daughter came into the room, she turned to her daughter and said, "Look, this is a picture of your momma when she was your age." Then she turned to me and smiled. "Maybe my dream isn't quite lost."[43]

Davidson's photo essays, whether of the Los Angeles ghettos (1966), or of Spanish Harlem (*East 100th Street*, 1970), and of the *Garden Cafeteria* (1976), where many of his subjects were Holocaust survivors, are about perseverance and holding on to dreams. They are the result of an extended involvement that depends on the complicity and trust of his subjects. Like Walker Evans's sharecropper images, Davidson shows the face of human dignity in the midst of tribulation. But unlike Evans, Davidson's empathy with many of his subjects provides an intimate sense of what it takes to endure in a hostile world. His photographs are not radical in form, but they are compelling in their social conscience. In the humanitarian spirit of the 1960s, in an era before many subcultures were publicly pursuing

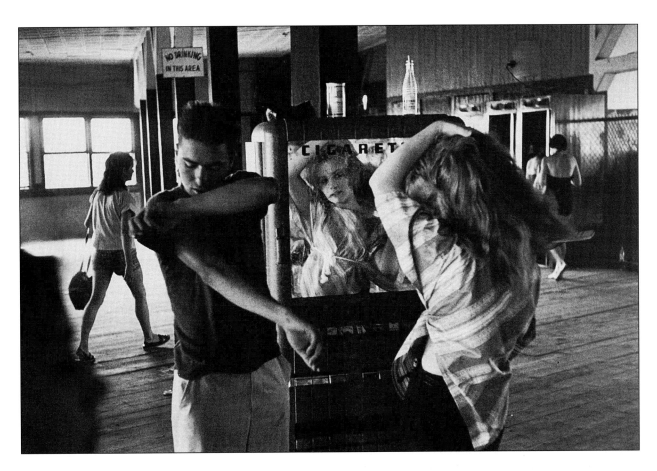

16.8   BRUCE DAVIDSON.   *Two Youths, Coney Island*, 1959. Gelatin silver print.   © Bruce Davidson/Magnum Photos.

self-representation, Davidson gave photographic validation to the everyday effects of disenfranchisement and loneliness within the urban landscape. Davidson has been criticized as an outsider exploiting marginalized people, but his full tonal range, view-camera prints convey a sense that he honestly respects his subjects and amidst despair seeks to affirm the diversity of life. The activities of photographers like Davidson demonstrate that the lives of ordinary people are worthy of preservation. They provide an opportunity for an initial dialogue, bridging the gap between Them and Us, and they foretell the fact that numerous cultural groups would actively begin to represent their own identities in the closing decades of the twentieth century.

In the early 1960s the active desire to directly change the world led to political actions like the Freedom Rides, marches, and sit-ins to end segregation. **Danny Lyon** [b. 1942] was one of the new journalism photographers in the 1960s who rebelled against the status quo, the values of measured material success, and the passive role of the documentary photographer. Lyon was radicalized by the civil rights movement of the early 1960s and became an official photographer for the Student Nonviolent Coordinating Committee. In 1965, half of Americans over 65 still had no medical insurance; one-third of Americans lived below the poverty line; more than 90 percent of the black adults in many southern counties were not registered to vote; nationwide, only 200 blacks held elected office; and only a third of 3–5-year-old children attended nursery school or kindergarten.[44] Believing they could change the world, photographers like Lyon did not heed psychedelic guru Dr. Timothy Leary's call to "tune in, turn-on, and drop-out" but instead gave up being observers and actively immersed themselves within the situations they were photographing. Their viewpoint shifted from outsider to adopted guest member of a community. They were granted the privilege of making images from a vantage point in which the traditional subject/photographer relationship was jettisoned in favor of a more personal approach. Such relationships set the groundwork for imagemakers from within the groups themselves to take over the task of self-representation that would be the hallmark of politically motivated photography in the 1980s and 1990s.

Lyon's photographs of the early civil rights confrontations and marches resulted in *The Movement* (1964). Some of the conditions Lyon photographed were improved by President Lyndon B. Johnson's "Great Society" laws dealing with Medicaid benefits, the Voting Rights Act, and Federal aid to education. Lyon continued to be a participatory photographer who saw his function as giving form to a subject's own story. Lyon's next

16.9   DANNY LYON.   *Hoe Sharpener and the Line,*
1969. 7⅝ × 11⁷⁄₁₆ inches. Gelatin silver print.
Courtesy George Eastman House.

experience was as "staff photographer" for the Chicago
Outlaws motorcycle gang, where he provided form to the
subject's own story that concluded with the publication of
Bikeriders (1968). The authenticity of the photographs
was evidenced by over forty text pages of the bikers
telling their own stories. This active immersion methodology climaxed in *Conversations with the Dead: Photographs of Prison Life with the Letters and Drawing of
Billy McCune # 122054* (1971), the result of fourteen
months spent photographing inside six Texas prisons. The
book focused on one prisoner's story, incorporating his
letters and drawings "to explain to the free world what life
in prison is like."[45]

Multiple Points of View

By the mid-1960s people in many levels of society were
exploring options to the business as usual, we have done
it this way for years, why change approach to life now.
Consumer activist Ralph Nader's [b. 1934] exposé of
General Motors, *Unsafe at Any Speed* (1965), had shown
that what was good for GM was not necessarily good for
America. Nader's citizen action groups lobbied for consumer, financial, and legal rights and demonstrated that

there were alternatives to established practices. At the
same time, photographers challenged the cherished notions of photographic veracity and time by using the blur,
double exposures, high-contrast print tonal values, and
multiple images (sequences).

During the mid-1960s, **Duane Michals** [b. 1932]
shifted from photographing single enigmatic moments,
as in his unpeopled sites of *Empty New York,* to invented sequential images that wrestle with inner dramas. His evolution reflects a shift from public to private
concerns as well as a changed view of photographic
time. The theatrical, time-lapse reality of Michals's images, informed by the work of surrealistic artists René
Magritte and Georgio De Chirico, the visionary poet
William Blake, and the magical realist Borges, represents another way of knowing the world. Where Minor
White used photographic sequencing metaphorically,
Michals's photo-fables and passion plays are narrative
(see chapter opener).

Initially working with a simple Argus C-3 camera and
natural light, Michals's cinematic *mise-en-scène* sequences, the arrangement of visual forms and movement
within a given space, blend the implausible with the mundane. Inherently photographic means, including lens
flare, multiple exposures, and the snapshot, are used to
suggest an unseen, ethereal spirit world. Michals said:
"What I cannot see is infinitely more important than what
I can see."[46] In 1974, Michals added handwritten text,
sometimes in the first person and other times from an om-

16.10   NATHAN LYONS.   *Untitled,* 1997. 4⅜ ×
6⅝ inches. Gelatin silver print.   Courtesy Visual Studies
Workshop, Rochester, NY.

niscient point of view, to direct the viewer's response
while maintaining a balance and distinction between the
words and images he tethered to make a distinct impression (see chapter opener). By the early 1980s, Michals
was painting directly onto his prints. Michals's blending
of mediums and methods enabled him to make visible
what would have been invisible in a straight photograph.
These experiments in photography, language, and painting allowed him to expand his investigations and their
metaphysical themes of the psychic, spiritual, and sexual,
exemplifying his own dictum: "Either you are defined by
your medium or you must redefine it."[47] Even when
Michals deals with his homosexuality, as in *Salute, Walt
Whitman* (1996), his characterization remains the universal exploration and discovery of the self.

The transformation in Michals's work was denotative
of the mood of the 1960s: questioning how things were
done, trying new procedures, and eliciting fresh out-
comes. The accuracy of what the American government
was telling people was being disputed on numerous
fronts. Many people were convinced the Warren Commission Report (1964) about President Kennedy's assassination was a cover-up, that other creditable points
of view that could explain the event were not being presented. Visually these concerns, asking for alternative

viewpoints rather than a single fixed perspective, were
expressed by Nathan Lyons in the 1966 exhibition, *The
Persistence of Vision.* The show of the work of Donald
Blumberg [b. 1935], Charles Gill [b. 1933], Robert Heinecken, Ray K. Metzker, Jerry N. Uelsmann, and John
Wood [b. 1922] challenged the assumption that a photograph's worth should be based on its ability to convey
knowledge directly from nature. Wood's cross-
disciplinary approach influenced artists such as Nathan
Lyons, Robert Heinecken, Robert Fichter, Thomas Barrow, and Betty Hahn to jump in and break down barriers
between mediums. Lyons wrote:

> One factor which appears to have conditioned our attitude to-
> ward the acceptable nature of the photograph as a picture ex-
> perience has been the degree to which the object or situation
> pictured is presented unaltered in relation to its physical coun-
> terpart. . . . If we consider man's visualizing activities in rela-
> tion to the photographic picture, then we may readily under-
> stand how the nature of sequential concerns, or the multiple
> exposure, might be considered more naturalistic perceptually
> than our traditionally held concept of the straight photograph.[48]

Nathan Lyons [b. 1930], like Michals, is a maker
whose images emphasize the subjective nature of photographic vision. Lyons believes that meaning has no archetypal arrangement and that photographers do not
find meaning but have to construct it through a combination of verbal and visual thinking. Lyons thinks that
meaning arises from a group of images rather than one
isolated one and that the ordering of a group (that is, in

16.11 RAY K. METZKER. *Untitled, 1966–67.*
32¼ × 34¾ inches. Gelatin silver prints. Metzker
wrote: "Discontented with the single, fixed frame image
. . . my work has moved into something of the composite, of collected and related moments. . . . I employ
methods of combination, repetition and superimposition. Where photography has been primarily a process
of selection and extraction, I wish to investigate the
possibilities of synthesis."[49]   © Ray K. Metzker, Courtesy
Laurence Miller Gallery, New York. Copy Print © The Museum
of Modern Art, New York.

a sequence) does not have to have an apparent rational
or thematic foundation. In books of his own work, *Notations in Passing* (1974), *Verbal Landscape, Dinosaur
Sat Down* (1987), and *Riding First Class on the Titanic*
(2000), Lyons pursues sequential ordering, suggesting
that meaning is determined by the "combinatory play,"
as he calls it, of the images. Often using diptychs, Lyons
depends on the space and time between the images to
bring out associations in the viewer, allowing his mindfully observed world to awaken. For Lyons, meaning
can be conveyed without written or spoken symbols.
Lyons is distrustful of attempts to translate images into
words, insisting that the way to deal with the content of
nonliteral photographs is to experience the images.

Ray K. Metzker's [b. 1931] sequential, multiframe,
mosaic images brought the New Bauhaus design approach, through his studies with Callahan and Siskind
at the Institute of Design, to bear on the integrity of the

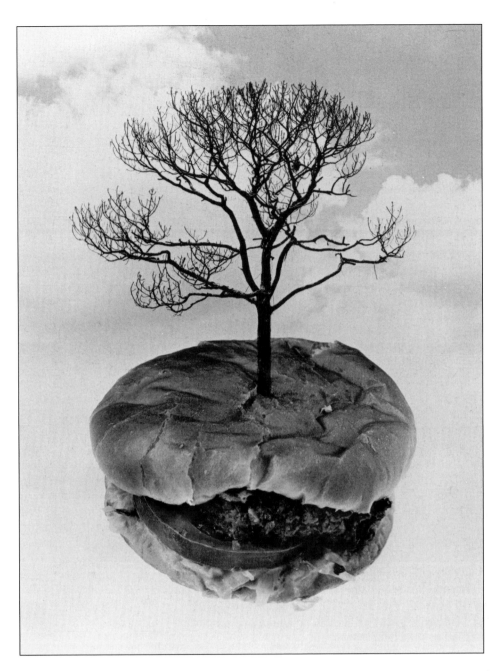

16.12   JERRY UELSMANN.   *Little Hamburger Tree,*
1970. Gelatin silver print. Uelsmann is a darkroom en-
chanter who makes people wonder. Uelsmann writes:
"For me the darkroom (containing eight enlargers)
functions as a visual research laboratory. . . . I believe
that almost anything you can think of is worth trying.
It is difficult to make a qualitative judgment in the initial stages of the creative process."[50]

photographic process. Metzker presents the idea of a
contact sheet, with its multiple views and tonal variations in the prints, as a way to understand a subject
rather than a means of distilling the one answer. Metzker utilizes a calligraphic tension, a visual script that
weaves the black photographic frame line into a rhythm
that produces a gridlike ordering of the subject. Metzker builds meaning by taking individual visual units,
representing time and space and light and dark pictorial
values, and arranges them into a formal visual matrix
that gives his subject the impression of interruption; of
simultaneously being whole and fractured. His composites of many small images depart from the usual
photographs made for reproduction in book form, functioning instead as a large single image to be displayed
on a gallery wall. The composites work well both from
a distance, as scenes take on rhythmic, abstract qualities, and close up where attentive viewers can see the
crisp photographic particulars.

During the 1960s photographers explored the strain
between the belief in the fundamental realism of the
photograph and the subjectivity of the artist's vision.
Jerry Uelsmann [b. 1934] did this by making complex

multi-image allegories with sophisticated multiple-printing techniques. Uelsmann, who studied with Minor White and Henry Holmes Smith in the late 1950s, was the first of a new breed of university-trained imagemakers whose support comes from teaching and grants. Thus freed from commercial restraints, Uelsmann challenged the mindset that photography's place was to deal with the rational and that printing a negative was a rote process. Uelsmann reintroduced Rejlander's idea that a single camera image did not have to yield up the final image but could act as part of a larger, constructed representation. Uelsmann collects and combines components directly from his own experience to realize a formal pictorial configuration whose meaning lies outside of the everyday world. Unlike Rejlander, Uelsmann does not tell narrative stories but uses his virtuosic combination printing technique to confront the incomprehensible. The process itself is an interactive performance that can be seen in the music of Jimi Hendrix (*Purple Haze*), the Beatles (*Sgt. Pepper's Lonely Hearts Club Band*), the Paul Butterfield Blues Band (*East/West*) and The Doors (*Light My Fire*), for discovering what lies beyond the logical, offering evidence of the independence of the imagination.

Uelsmann's seamless multi-image productions are like dreams freed from the anchors of reason. In the predigital age, they offered objective optical records of impossible situations—trees floating in air, faces coming out of rocks, radical contrasts in scale, positive and negative imagery—expanding photographic discourse and ambiguous enough to contain both multiple meanings and no meaning. His iconography paradoxically combines popular culture with playfully fabricated mythological settings, often using humor. His intuitive methods can communicate complex emotions and contain ingredients similar to the romantic Southern magical realism of John Laughlin. Uelsmann's fantastical juxtapositions of the seemingly unrelated form seamless "psychic landscapes," becoming so wondrously believable as to question the supposedly self-evident empirical nature of photographs. It is a transcendental approach that synthesizes discordant parts to reconcile the suitable and inappropriate, the natural and the artificial, the physical and the spiritual.

In response to the social upheavals of the 1960s, photographers like **Robert Heinecken** [b. 1931] searched for new artistic and technical options that not only relied on multiple images but saw any photographically based activity as source material for picturemaking. In the anything-can-go spirit of the *happening*,[51] in which the audience became part of the event and was responsible for its interpretation, Heinecken suggested how the boundaries of photographic content and form could be expanded. Rarely using a camera himself, Heinecken worked with direct processes, such as the photogram. Using a printed magazine page as a negative, he foiled the conventions of previsualization in favor of chance and free association. These reformulated combinations of images and sometimes text can generate new meanings from the original materials by destroying their original context. Heinecken experimented with photographic emulsion on canvas, metal, and plastic and presented his work in the form of pictures on cubes, picture puzzles, and stacked blocks.

Heinecken's work departed from the customary appearance and form of photographs. Heinecken was not interested in photography as a means of taking pictures but for its ability to reproduce images. As far as Heinecken was concerned the world already had all the images he needed. Any image was raw information containing the "residual of actuality," a fragment of truth that could be synthesized to show the culture that produced it. His methods visualize Marshall McLuhan's ideas of how advertising and news photographs seduce consumer/ viewers by generating a false reality whose foundation is based on clichés and stereotypes. Using a magazine page as a contact negative and printing both sides of the page together, as in his *Are You Rea* series, confirms how meaning can be buried inside the image and must be excavated. Former George Eastman House curator William Jenkins observed: "Fashion, sports, home decorating and sex inexplicably melt into a consistent magma of contemporary culture."[52] Trained as a printmaker, Heinecken used offset printing to alter pornographic and war atrocity images and rebound his altered materials into existing magazines, which were then replaced at newsstands. In the same way that comedian Lenny Bruce's sardonic social critiques surfaced via the media, Heinecken's combined pages of popular and pornographic magazines confronted the similarities rather than the differences between the two. Photographer/historian Carl Chiarenza explains:

> Indeed, one is hard put to name anything that has not been replaced by a photographically derived image. His recycling of these images makes this astounding point before making any other. Heinecken knows the photograph is not real. He also knows that most of us still believe it is. Photography can be the perfect voyeur for a mechanical age. The camera eye is lusty and insatiable, a perfect match for Heinecken's eye.[53]

This lusty match has meant Heinecken's work has been attacked by those who object to the sexual subject matter and by others who feel it represents women in a subservient manner. Heinecken is often a humorous disrupter of the notions about how things are, who incorporates cultural images to examine issues concerning gender, imaging, power, sex, and violence from a male point of view. The work also reflects the undercurrent of violence—race riots and the Vietnam War— that the media brought nightly into peoples living rooms. Like the nameless photographer in Michelangelo Antonioni's

16.13   ROBERT HEINECKEN.   *Cliche Vary/ Fetishism,* 1974. 42 × 42 inches. Photographic emulsion on canvas, pastel chalk.   Courtesy Robert Heinecken and George Eastman House.

film *Blow-Up* (1966), Heinecken uses the reproducibility of photographic processes to question and reveal the subsurface truths that the photograph delivers and the culture that has produced them. Interested in a media-oriented approach to photography that could offer a critical process for collecting, reorienting, and transforming images and their meaning from popular culture, Heinecken's working methods of montage and mixed media pointed out ways to extend the expressive possibilities of the medium.

The Rapid Growth of Photographic Education

The forces driving social change in the 1960s affected how photographic issues were analyzed. The growing interest in photographic education shifted the dialogue from the professional sector and the pages of *Popular Photography* to the university. In 1962, Nathan Lyons sponsored an invitational teaching conference at George Eastman House that sparked the concept for the Society for Photographic Education (SPE), whose purpose was to create a forum for people involved in the teaching of photography.[54] The group was formalized in Chicago in 1963 with Lyons as SPE's first president;

16.14   CHUCK CLOSE.   *Working grid photograph of Phil,* 1969. 13¾ × 10¾ inches. Gelatin silver print with ink and masking tape. Chuck Close was considered an artistic anti-Christ by some art critics because he worked from photographs instead of directly from life. Close admired the camera's ability to level hierarchy, to see all of a subject equally and not to place more importance on one area than another. Close took that lack of hierarchy, as used by Abstract Expressionistic painters like Frank Stella, and applied it to representational painting so that every square inch was made the same way and had the same visual attitude. Close stated: "I wanted to make something that was impersonal and personal, arm's-length and intimate, minimal and maximal, using the least amount of paint possible but providing the greatest amount of information . . . . I always thought the best art was extreme whatever it was."[55]   © Chuck Close. Courtesy PaceWildensteinMacGill, New York.

Aaron Siskind, Art Sinsabaugh, Henry Holmes Smith, Clarence White, Jr., and Minor White were installed as members of the first board of directors.[56] In 1969, Lyons resigned as Curator of Photography at the George Eastman House and founded the Visual Studies Workshop (VSW) in Rochester, N.Y. VSW became a widely copied model whose interdisciplinary approach to photography and visual culture influenced the next generation of photographers. Photography, now based in art departments, received a pronounced injection of academic aesthetic discourse through the influence of SPE. This growth burst open during the 1970s, offering teaching, gallery, and museum jobs for graduates who came out of the university photography programs that sprang up across the United States. The mixing of photography with other visual mediums had an invigorating, cross-pollinating effect on the visual arts.

During the mid-1960s, painters like **Chuck Close** [b. 1940], Robert Cottingham, Richard Estes, Audrey Flack, and Ralph Going developed *photorealism,* whose subject matter was how the objective and descriptive qualities of photographic vision affected the interpretation of reality. The photorealists were entranced by the lenticular and spectral effects of photographs—background blurring, depth of field, perspective distortion, selective focus, spatial flattening. Their skillfully executed paintings were conceived from photographs rather than directly from life, and in Close's methodology the photograph acted as a small-scale grid template (see Figure 16.14) for his descriptive painting that converted the human face into unfamiliar landscape. Ironically, in spite of their reliance on photographic appearances, most of the photorealists rejected the direct photograph as an inferior art. Only Close, who used the large-format Polaroid studio camera to make bigger-than-life, multi-image portraits, welcomed photographic syntax in its fundamental form. Close is not so much a photorealist, but rather an artist concerned with using photographic detail as a building block. By thinking with photography Close takes what appears to be a chaotic system and shows how it can make sense.

The 1960s did not see a single stylistic approach like Group *f*/64 or an individual like Stieglitz dominating the medium but rather a loose democratic assemblage whose experiments, rebellions, and social critiques expanded the ranks of people involved with photography. Technical innovations like the introduction of the Nikon F in 1959 which ushered in fully interchangeable high-quality 35-mm cameras, and the Kodak Instamatic in 1963, with its drop-in film cartridge, made it easier for both professionals and amateurs to photograph. The teaching of photography at the university swelled the ranks of practitioners and introduced fresh ideas to developing imagemakers, broadening the practice, breaking away from standardized mass-produced materials, and widening its critical audience. The new and different ways that people used photographs ignored the tradition of the fine print and spiritually elevating subjects. The desire for reform actively affected people's social and artistic lives and a tiny, dynamic group of imagemakers rethought the definitions and content of the nature of the photograph and applied their counterculture ideas to revamp what a photograph was supposed to look like; who a photographer was; what a photographer did; and how an audience might respond. This discussion soon extended to a larger audience one concerning how photographs could be conceived conceptually and technically, viewed, and evaluated. In this expansive framework of individualism photography did not have to confine itself to views of the external world but could fabricate a new aesthetic that interacted with other media, explore subjective inner realities, and transcend its previous limits.

Endnotes

1   Quoted in A. D. Coleman, "Duane Michals," *Camera & Darkroom,* vol. 15, no. 11, (November 1993), 30.

2   Roland Barthes, *Camera Lucida: Reflections on Photography,* translated by Richard Howard (New York: Hill and Wang, 1981), 118.

3   Ibid, 118.

4   Henry Holmes Smith, "Photography in Our Time: A Note on Some Prospects for the Seventh Decade," *Henry Holmes Smith: Collected Writing, 1935–1985* (Tucson: Center for Creative Photography, 1986), 68.

5   Nathan Lyons, *Toward A Social Landscape* (New York: Horizon Press, 1966), 5.

6   See Van Deren Coke, *The Painter and the Photograph, from Delacroix to Warhol* (Albuquerque: University of New Mexico Press, 1964). Revised and enlarged edition, 1972.

7   Lawrence Alloway, Introduction, *Robert Rauschenberg* (Washington, D.C.: Smithsonian Institution, 1976), 5.

8   During the 1940s, artist Joseph Cornell [1903–1972] began using photographic images in combination with found objects in his theatrical box constructions, but these were not widely seen and had little immediate impact on other artists' working methods.

9   Daniel Odier, *The Job: Interviews with William S. Burroughs* (Harmondsworth, Penguin Books, 1989), 59.

10   In Lucy R. Lippard, *Pop Art* (New York: Frederick A. Praeger, 1966), 6.

11   Douglas Crimp, "Appropriating Appropriation," *Image Scavengers* (Philadelphia: Institute of Contemporary Art, 1983), 33.

12   William S. Burroughs, *Nova Express* (New York: Grove Press, Evergreen Edition, 1992), 147–49.

13   For details about their collaborations, see Robert A. Sobieszek, *Ports of Entry: William S. Burroughs and the Arts* (Los Angeles County Museum of Art, 1996).

14   Warhol's appropriation of such materials has raised legal and ethical issues surrounding copyright violation. In 1996, Time Inc. and photographer Henri Dauman sued his estate, claiming Warhol had used a *Life* magazine photo of Jacqueline Kennedy at her husband's funeral to make silkscreen prints without getting permission, paying, or crediting Dauman or Time/Life. See "Warhol Estate Sued for Using Kennedy Photo," *New York Times,* Sunday, December 8, 1996, 52.

15   Kynaston McShine, *Andy Warhol: A Retrospective* (New York: Museum of Modern Art, 1989), 458.

16   Marshall McLuhan, *Understanding Media: The Extensions of Man* (New York: McGraw-Hill, 1964), 8–9.

17   Ibid., 189.

18   Ibid., 195 and 197.

19   Art Sinsabaugh, *Six Photographers* (Urbana: University of Illinois, 1963), unp.

20   John Kenneth Galbraith, *The Affluent Society* (Boston: Houghton Mifflin, 1958), 1.

21   For details on these events see Robert Hirsch, "Nathan Lyons on the Snapshot," *CEPA Journal,* Winter 1992–1993, 6–7.

22   Lyons planned to include Diane Arbus, but she declined, deciding to debut in the smaller *New Documents* show at MOMA. Nathan Lyons, in phone conversation with author on December 20, 1994.

23   Hirsch, 7.

24   All quotes in this paragraph from: Nathan Lyons, Introduction, *Towards A Social Landscape,* 6–7.

25   Quoted by Janet Malcolm, "Photography: Certainties and Possibilities," *The New Yorker,* vol. 51, no. 24 (August 4, 1975), 56–59.

26   John Szarkowski, *Winogrand: Figments From the Real World* (New York: Museum of Modern Art, 1988), 23.

27   Garry Winogrand, "Women Are Beautiful Portfolio," (Austin, TX: RFG Publishing, 1981), unp.

28   Szarkowski, *Winogrand: Figments From the Real World,* 36.

29   Ibid., 39.

30   John Szarkowski, *The Photographer's Eye* (New York: Museum of Modern Art, 1966), 8.

31   For information about street photography see Colin Westerbeck & Joel Meyerowitz, *Bystander: A History of Street Photography* (Boston: Little Brown, 1994).

32   Lee Friedlander, Introduction, *Self Portrait* (New York: Haywire Press, 1970).

33   Quoted in Patricia Bosworth, *Diane Arbus: A Biography* (New York: Alfred A. Knopf, 1984), 187.

34   During this time social reformers like Betty Friedan (1921), author of *The Feminine Mystique* (1963) and founder of the National Organization for Women (1966), questioned the notion that a woman could only achieve fulfillment by being a wife, having children, and managing the home.

35   Bosworth, 41.

36   Ibid., 132.

37   Ibid., Preface, xi.

38   Ibid., 249 and 303.

39   Ibid., 177.

40   Initially, the lawyer for the Arbus Estate, John Pelosi, said: "Sorry to disappoint you but your request is denied." Eventually he forwarded the text to Doon Arbus. On April 26, 1999, Mr. Pelosi called the author's permission editor and said, "She didn't understand the points the author was making and failed to see a reason why a photo was needed."

41   See *Diane Arbus: Magazine Work* Doon Arbus and Marvin Israel, (eds.) (Millerton, NY: Aperture, 1984).

42   Bruce Davidson, Introduction, *Bruce Davidson Photographs* (New York: Agrinde Publications Ltd., 1978), 10.

43   Ibid., 14.

44   Cited by David E. Rosenbaum, "Time Wrap: Republicans Like Both Previews and Reruns," *The New York Times,* Sunday, December 11, 1994, Section 4, 16.

45   Danny Lyon, *Conversations with the Dead: Photographs of Prison Life with the Letters and Drawing of Billy McCune # 122054* (Holt, Rinehart and Winston, 1971), 13.

46   Quoted in Shelley Rice, "Duane Michals's 'Real Dreams,'" *Afterimage,* vol. 4 (December 1976), 6.

47   Quoted in A. D. Coleman, "Duane Michals," *Camera & Darkroom,* vol. 15, no. 11, (November 1993), 27.

48   Nathan Lyons, Introduction, *The Persistence of Vision* (New York: Horizon Press, 1967), 5.

49   Ray K. Metzker, [Statement], *Aperture,* vol. XIII, no. 2 (1967), unp.

50   Jerry Uelsmann, *Uelsmann: Process and Perception* (Gainesville, FL: University of Florida Press, 1985), 3.

51   A Happening was part of the 1960s Pop Art scene. Its name derived from Allan Kaprow's 1959 New York show *18 Happenings in 6 Parts,* in which a rehearsed, multimedia event unfolded. The audience moved on cue from room to room, becoming part of the performance, and it was their job to unravel the disjointed events. Kaprow said a happening was an "assemblage of events performed or perceived in more than one time and place."

52   William Jenkins, "Introduction," James Enyeart, ed., *Heinecken* (Carmel, CA: Friends of Photography, 1980), 15.

53   Carl Chiarenza, from an unpublished article, September, 1976 in *Heinecken,* 29.

54   See "Invitational Teaching Conference at the George Eastman House 1962," (Rochester: George Eastman House, 1963).

55   Robert Shorr, et al, *Chuck Close* (New York: The Museum of Modern Art, 1998), 89.

56   See "The Society for Photographic Education, Chairman's Report 1962–65 with Appendixes A–H and Membership List (November 1966)." Available at Visual Studies Workshop Resource Center, Rochester, NY.

CHAPTER SEVENTEEN

Changing Realities:
Alternative Visions

The Vietnam War (1946–75) ended with a cease-fire agreement in 1973 and American troops withdrew. Before divisions in the country could heal, the Watergate affair caused many people to abandon the notion of government integrity and forced Richard M. Nixon to resign in 1974, the first president to do so. People were worn out from a decade of internal dissension and were looking toward quieter and more peaceful times. The raw, screaming guitars of the 1960s gave way to the canned disco sounds of the Bee Gees. This distinctive split could be seen in photography. The first half of the decade saw a settling of the emotionally charged frontiers of the 1960s, while the second half was a dry, formal, cooling-down period. Photographic practice, like the conservative "Silent Majority" that ushered in the "Reagan Revolution" of the 1980s, moved from the idealistic, community-based search for open form experiments to the restrained stance of the straight gelatin silver print and a pessimistic philosophy of diminished possibilities that questioned the foundations of originality and quality.

ROBERT FLICK. *SV(Sequential Views),* 035/81, Near Live Oak, Joshua Tree National Monument, CA, 1981. 20 × 24 inches. Gelatin silver prints. Courtesy Craig Krull Gallery, Santa Monica, CA.

Flick's *Sequential Views* combines the characteristic photographic trends of the 1970s. Relying on the verisimilitude of the gelatin silver print, Flick creates a formal repetitious structure that is paradoxical to what the images appear to conceptually divulge. His continuum of views, merging into one, challenge presumptions about photographic process, space, and time. By shifting location, extending or negating forms through perspective, or using different focal length lenses, Flick disrupts the borders between indexical documentary practice that offers a cataloging of subjects and artistic interpretation. Besides questioning the physical makeup of any place and the notion of the single photograph, these views provide alternative explanations to the difference(s) between appearance and reality.

17.1   ROBERT FICHTER.   *Geronimo (Apache: Southwest)* with fold mark, 1970.   12¾ × 19¹³⁄₁₆ inches. Gum bichromate with oil and crayon.   Courtesy George Eastman House.

Alternative Visions

In the 1960s the democratic-based social movements— which extended into photographic practice—had their basis in doubt. Many believed that any problem-solving process had to allow for the possibility that one might not get it precisely right. The American appreciation of uncertainty finds its lineage in the thinking that created the U.S. Constitution, whereby new ideas, in the form of Amendments, could be developed, implemented, and discarded—providing a structure open to change.

During the 1960s, photographers challenged accepted chemical and optical methods of photographic presentation. The philosophies of Cartier-Bresson's "decisive moment" and Szarkowski's "photographer's eye" were put in the backseat by a new group of image-makers. **Robert Fichter** [b. 1939] pushed the boundaries of conventional practice in his explorations of the Sabattier effect (a.k.a., solarization) and by exposing the same roll of film numerous times in a cheap plastic toy *Diana* camera. Fichter, a painter and printmaker who studied with Jerry Uelsmann and Henry Holmes

Smith, experimented with alternative imagemaking methods, including collage, cyanotype, gum bichromate, hand-coloring, and an old Verifax copy machine. Fichter's work and especially his teaching, at UCLA (where Heinecken taught) and later at Florida State, gave students the support to conduct their own investigations into the expressive form and the symbolic content of the photographic image.

As the 1970s opened, photographers were seriously examining their medium's roots. Universities added courses in photographic and film history to their curriculums. Photographers reexamined anonymous vernacular images, such as snapshots and postcards, which gave legitimacy to collecting photography and fueled its acceptance in art galleries, museums, and publishing houses. As part of a movement that was rediscovering historical processes, photoeducators like Betty Hahn, [b. 1940] who also studied with H. H. Smith, used the cyanotype and gum processes to make loose, roughly detailed, impressionistic images, with flat fields of color that disputed the ideals and content of the glossy print. Hahn and photoeducator Bea Nettles [b. 1946] looked into the sculptural properties of scale, space, and volume by making images on fabric and then stuffing and stitching them. Nettles then spread the concepts in her own alternative process book, *Breaking the Rules* (1977), and in artists' books, such as *Flamingo in the Dark* (1979).

17.2 DOUG PRINCE. *Floating Fan,* 1972. 8 × 8 × 3½ inches. Acrylic plastic and gelatin silver print on graphic arts film.   Courtesy George Eastman House.

In curating *Photography into Sculpture* (1970) for MOMA, photo-historian Peter Bunnell [b. 1937] gave credibility to twenty artists, including Ellen Brooks [b. 1946], Darryl Curran [b. 1935], Robert Heinecken, Bea Nettles, and **Doug Prince** [b. 1943], who were broadening the flat photographic playing field into the third dimension. Prince's small Plexiglas boxes house a series of transparent images, one in front of the other, whose multilayering and sense of depth resist the opacity of the photographic image by allowing a solitary viewer to look through time and space. **Naomi Savage** [b. 1927], who had worked with Man Ray, combined photographic methods such as multiple exposure, neg-

ative printing, and toning with collage, engraving, and intaglio. Her most intriguing work involves metal photographic etchings in which the plate itself becomes the final object rather than a part of the process, transforming her subject's appearance and a viewer's expectations (see Figure 17.3).

Interest in how imagery could be formulated got a boost from photographs produced for scientific purposes. NASA's intricate composite photographs taken by the Surveyor landing craft in 1966 and 1968 were of interest to artists and the public. Uses of such technology encouraged photographers to explore the possibilities of new imaging systems like the photocopy machine. **Sonia Landy Sheridan** [b. 1925] operated the copy machine as a camera. Often using her own body as source material, Sheridan's electrostatic prints demonstrated the immediacy of the process and the interactive connection that was possible between artist

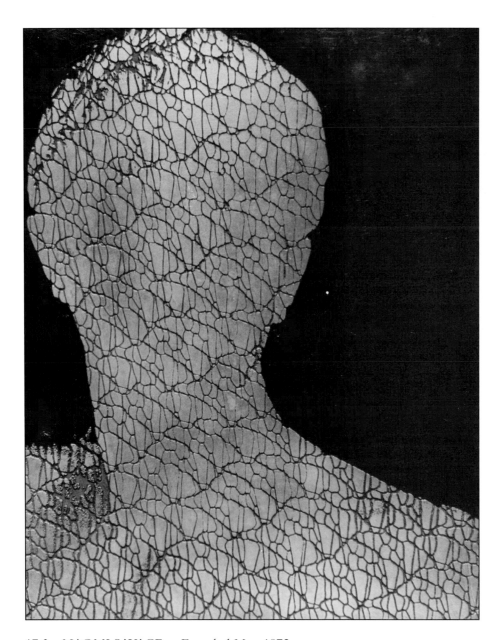

17.3   NAOMI SAVAGE.   *Enmeshed Man,* 1972.
70 × 55½ inches. Paint and tempera on copper-plated
magnesium.   Courtesy Naomi Savage.

and machine. This concept was furthered by Ellen
Land-Weber [b. 1943], who placed three-dimensional
objects on the copymachine's document glass and
printed the resulting images on Arches watercolor paper, which produced a soft, muted, lithograph-like rendering. Sheridan founded the Generative Systems Department at the School of the Art Institute of Chicago in
1970 to offer a forum for artists and scientists to investigate new methods of image production, including
copiers, video, and computer-generated images.

   Thomas Barrow [b. 1938], who studied at the Institute of Design, experimented with found mass-media sources on an outmoded Verifax photocopier to
create quick, densely packed montages that comment
on America's intense level of consumerism. The direct, cameraless images led Barrow to his Man Ray-
like spray-painted photograms of the late 1970s and
early 1980s. Here he investigated concepts concerning abstraction, language, representation, and the cultural thinking process that ties them together. For
Barrow photographic data is a jumping-off spot, as
the immaculate print is discarded in the conviction
that artistic response lies beyond the pictorial vision
of the lens.

   Barrow continued to work with these issues in his
Cancellation series (1974–78), bridging the two seemingly incompatible photographic trends of the
1970s—of highly charged personal experimentation
and emotionally minimal formalism. Barrow photographed the southwestern, social landscape in the lit-

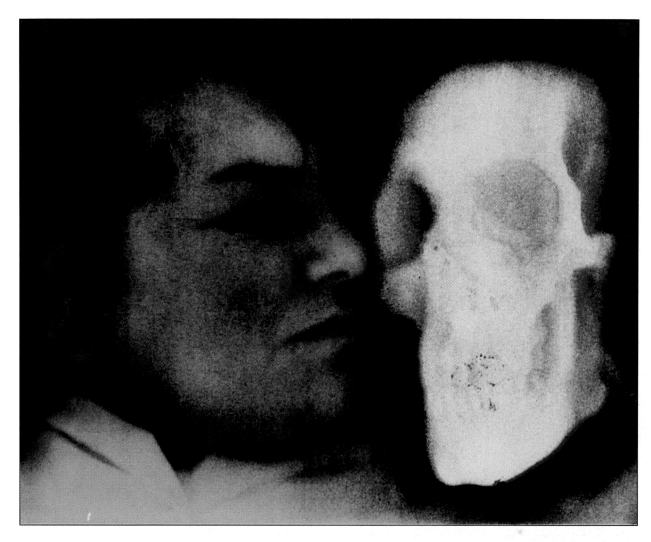

17.4   SONIA LANDY SHERIDAN.   *Sonia with Skull*, 1971. 8⅞ × 11 inches. 3M Color-in Color print. Courtesy Sonia Landy Sheridan, Visual Studies Workshop, Rochester, NY.

eral, deadpan style known as New Topographics that had become popular with photographers in the West. Barrow breaks the neutrality of the images with an explosive hand gesture, slashing an "X" onto the hallowed surface of the negative. This physical alteration separates the subject from its image, demanding that we recognize that the picture is a facsimile of reality. It also, according to curator McCarthy Gauss, lodges a protest against the inhumanity, insensitivity, and unaesthetic nature of the landscape:

> The obvious marking, the attempted destruction of the negative carries a veiled humorous allusion to the historical tension between craft and machine. The mechanically derived landscapes are highly rational and formal, rendered with a dispassionate approach that contrasts with the slash marks. The primitive defacing introduces an element of intellectual discord aimed against the refined mechanistic photographic image. The marks are akin to graffiti and suggest a repudiation, a tweaking of the subject that recalls Marcel Duchamp's alteration of the Mona Lisa.[1]

At the end of the 1970s Barrow took the *Cancellations* a step further by vandalizing the print. In the *Caulked Reconstructions* Barrow dismantles the flat, fine print and then reassembles it into a three-dimensional patchwork that is joined together with silicone caulk, staples, and spray paint (see Figure 17.5). Barrow's direct intervention signals his dissatisfaction with the straight print and the machinelike, spiritual detachment of the photographic process. By extending his physical presence into the picturemaking process, Barrow asks viewers to spend more time with the work than they would with a conventionally made camera image. This recycling of imagery and materials, with references to contemporary culture and art history, into concentrated multilayered formats reminds viewers about the complexity of modern existence and how difficult it can be to decipher what is really happening in any image.

William Larson [b. 1942], who also attended the Institute of Design, was interested in the interactive nature of the photographic process and in finding methods to transcend the limitations of the modernist print aesthetic. Working with a Graphic Sciences Teleprinter that converted an image into audio signals which were

17.5   THOMAS BARROW.   *Teepees,* 1979. 18 × 19 inches (irregular). Reconstructed gelatin silver print with caulking, staples, and spray paint.   © Tom Barrow. Photo courtesy Washington Art Consortium, Western Washington University.

transmitted via telephone and reassembled to produce a facsimile, Larson built up an image over time through multiple transmissions. The collaged data, based on snapshots, snippets of text, and marks made by sounds, suggested ambiguous messages and the kinds of memories that are experienced when trying to recall a dream. These electro-carbon renditions, made between 1970 and 1976, were called *Fireflies* because of the recurring image of a firefly and the allusion to the ephemeral flight of information. The low-resolution images use open space to impart a sense of the alienation, distance, and uncertainty that surrounds new technology (see Figure 17.6).

Turning the Straight Photograph on Itself

Other photographers turned the straight photograph inside-out to remind viewers that photography is simultaneously a trace of the real and an inherent abstraction. **Ken Josephson** [b. 1932], who studied at Rochester Institute of Technology and the Institute of Design, investigated the truthfulness of the silver print. Josephson's approach is conceptual, de-emphasizing subject matter and stressing the relationship between a photograph of a subject and the subject itself. Josephson makes photographs about photographs that reveal "the process of creating pictures as ideas rather than as representations."[2] In one series, Josephson holds a postcard of each scene into his photographic frame, playfully interjecting himself as a performer who is

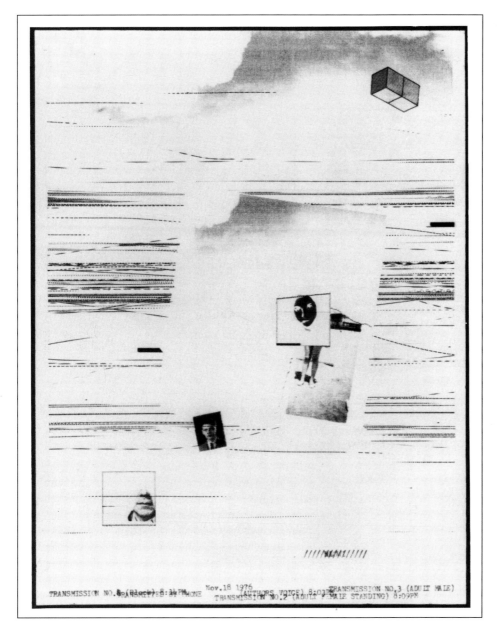

17.6   WILLIAM LARSON. *Transmission 0035,* 1974. 11 × 8½ inches. Electro-carbon print. Larson states: "The early fax technology, although slow in transmitting (6 minutes per 8½ × 11 inch paper) produced relatively high resolution for reproduction of visual materials. Since it translated everything into an audio signal to be sent via telephone, it read everything from images to classical music as a simple digital code which was then converted into corresponding voltage levels to literally burn the image(s) into their special paper at the receiving end. It was also possible to manipulate the image, while it was printing, by simply moving the stylus as it burned the image into paper."[3]
© William Larson. Courtesy George Eastman House.

formally distorting reality while mocking the idea of photographic duplication, demonstrating the absurdity of attempting to reoccupy the same space (see Figure 17.7). In some cases Josephson goes beyond the issues of how the photographic frame functions and gets into what the frame includes and excludes and how the photograph conveys data. In *Honolulu,* 1968, Josephson printed the image of three people so dark that its specific informational value was lost; you knew they were people but could not identify them as individuals. He then printed the same image with the details present, tore away parts of the images he didn't want, and collaged the remaining pieces on top of the full dark image so you could now see their faces and know who they were. Through collage methods that create intersections between black-and-white and color, Josephson examines what takes place along the borders of

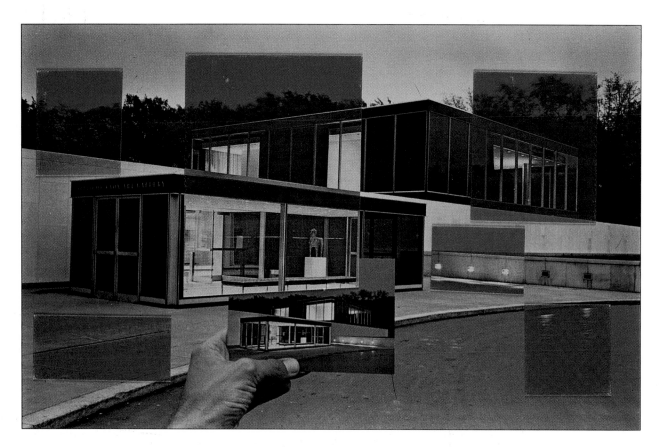

17.7   KENNETH JOSEPHSON.   *Postcard Visit, Buffalo,* 1970. 4¹⁄₁₆ × 6¼ inches. Gelatin silver print and postcard.   © Kenneth Josephson. Transparancy © 1999 The Art Institute of Chicago. All Rights Reserved.

photographic reality. His work stresses the ambiguity of representation and the effect of time on the realization of the subject. Josephson reshapes the photograph to discover a new vantage point that disrupts Renaissance concepts of how the world is and what a picture is supposed to look like.

The notion of photographic veracity was likewise examined by **Joseph Jachna** [b. 1935], who also went to the Institute of Design. Jachna constructed formal landscapes around handheld mirrors he introduced into his frame to make his audience aware of the differences between natural and photographic space (see Figure 17.8). By self-consciously revealing the image and the procedures of its creation, Jachna held up the manipulative power of the photograph for examination. By layering a number of images into a single photograph Jachna fooled the viewer's sense of time and space. The intensely printed blacks and glowing highlights lend a spiritual quality and reverence to an ambiguous space that has been distorted and flattened by the mirrored reflections. These personal mediations disturb the boundaries between optical fact and optical illusion.

The authority and dominance of the single, straight gelatin silver print aesthetic was questioned through other innovative approaches that encouraged individual expression. The concept, championed by Szarkowski, that the frame was singular and all-inclusive was questioned by artists such as Barbara Blondeau [1938–1974], Barbara Crane, and **Robert Flick** [b. 1939] (see chapter opener), who worked with multiple, extended framing and serial repetition. Paradoxically, they used the straight print to challenge its own aesthetic and its accompanying assumptions about time and how it relates to picture-making and viewing. **Barbara Crane** [b. 1928] examined these ideas often on a large scale, building up temporal relationships between objects that cannot be comprehended all at once but disclose themselves over time. It is this "extra" time that allows complex interrelationships to be discovered (see Figure 17.9).

Personal Accounts: Documentary Fiction

The attention Diane Arbus's work received in the 1960s encouraged other photographers to personalize photographs made as social documents. Beginning in the 1960s, some photographers like Ralph Eugene Meatyard, Les Krims, Arthur Tress [b. 1940], and Lucas

17.8.   JOSEPH JACHNA.   Iceland South Coast, facing Ljomagnupur, 1976. 8¹⁵⁄₁₆ × 13⁵⁄₁₆ inches. Gelatin silver print.

Samaras used a narrative, neosurrealist approach to map interior landscapes. They dealt with the irrational by ordering an environment they could control. These fictions, made up of ordinary objects and set in commonplace environments, were intentionally organized to reveal underlying psychological conditions in a documentary style. The effect of this direct intervention by artists with their subjects was to stimulate tension between the fundamental formalism of the photograph and the subjectivity of the artist's personal vision, creating a hybrid form—documentary fiction.

Ralph Eugene Meatyard [1925–1972], who studied with photographic curator/historian Van Deren Coke, was an optician from Lexington, Ky. Working in the Southern Gothic tradition, Meatyard used family and friends as models to generate enigmatic, hauntingly impenetrable dramas filled with surprise and fear. In his series of surreal "Romances," Meatyard had his models wear cheap Halloween masks as a symbolic device for diving below the surface of outer reality (see Figure 17.10). Meatyard turned the regular confines of his square 2¹⁄₄-inch camera format askew, portraying the precarious voyage of life. His often darkly printed and sometimes ghostly blurred images reinforced the idea of the world as frightening, unseeable, and unknowable. Like Clarence John Laughlin before him, Meatyard's combination of real environments and phantasmal effects created ambiguous documents about identity, remembrance, and the continuance of time. Although Meatyard worked throughout the 1960s, his images did not receive attention until the posthumous publication of *The Family Album of Lucybelle Crater* (1974), which used the family snapshot genre to present the dark side of Steichen's *Family of Man*. It was built around a fictional character based on a Gertrude Stein story.[4]

Les Krims [b. 1943] staged preposterous situations from his internal theater of the absurd and grotesque that were calculated to disturb and shock Main Street's sense of decency and propriety.[5] His images from the late 1960s and early 1970s were printed on Kodak Kodalith paper, a graphic arts material not intended for pictorial use, to deliver dramatically grainy, high-contrast, brown-toned effects that defied conventions of print quality. Provocative, self-published, boxed folios on dwarfs, deer hunters, murder scenes of nude young women, and his topless mother making chicken soup, received wide notice, encouraging young photographers to visualize their inner fictions and explore forbidden subjects. There is no neutrality or compassion in

17.9   BARBARA CRANE.   *Just Married*, 1975.
From the Baxter/Travenol Laboratories series. 16 × 20
inches; mural size 9 × 7 feet. Gelatin silver prints.

Krims's intent; the absurd is given full rein. His vexing image of a screaming, legless man on a pedestal leaves viewers no place to go except to confront the affliction (see Figure 17.11). When some of his photographs were shown in Memphis, TN, an enraged viewer kidnapped the son of the gallery director and held him hostage, demanding that Krims' pictures be removed.

At his best, Krims was a court jester who tested viewers' tolerance by photographing taboo subjects. But Krims's aggressive attitude was condescending,

and he often mocked his subjects. The harsh flashlight and wide-angle lens he used to photograph dwarfs in *The Little People of America* (1972) sensationalized their differences in a comic manner. Many considered his work such as *Making Chicken Soup* (1972) which mocks Jewish mothers and family albums, to be buffoonery and socially unenlightened. His book of manipulated Polaroid SX-70 charades, *Fictcrytokrimsographs* (1975), contained women whose distorted nude bodies were under attack by bananas, meat grinders, and toy airplanes. During a time of rising feminist consciousness and the era of the Vietnam War, it was considered a prime example of adolescent, machismo misogyny. This led Krims to largely withdraw his

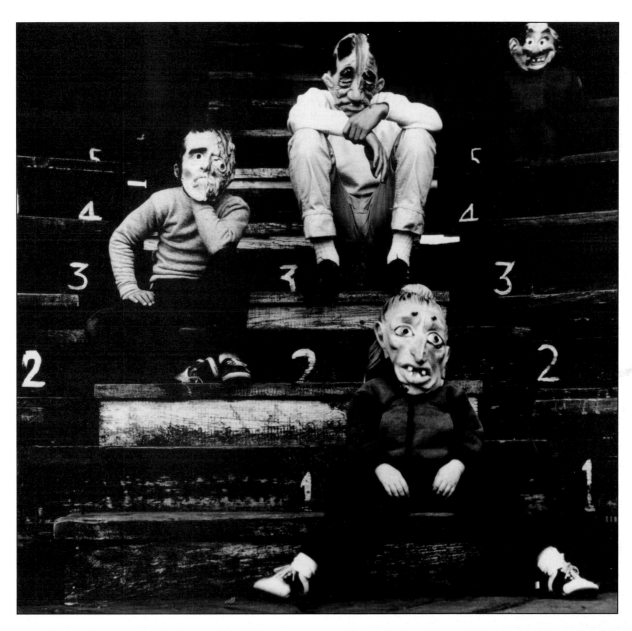

17.10   RALPH EUGENE MEATYARD.   *Romance (N) from Ambrose Bierce, No. 3,* 1962. 7 × 7⁵⁄₁₆ inches. Gelatin silver print.   Courtesy Estate of Ralph Meatyard.

work and himself from the the U.S. photography scene, but continued to show in countries like Germany and Japan.

The interaction between art and photography can be seen in the fictional creations of **Lucas Samaras** [b. 1936]. Samaras is a painter, sculptor, and performance artist who in the late 1960s did a series called *Auto-Polaroids* in which he manipulated his face and body, altering his appearance to visualize a psychological autobiography. In 1973, Samaras started his *Photo-Transformations,* a body of work in which he photographed himself with colored lights and a Polaroid SX-70 camera to confront the theme of the modern self

that Samaras sees as being open to constant reinvention. Designed as the definitive snapshot system, the SX-70, introduced in 1972, was ideal for experimentation because it did not have an established aesthetic, the results were immediate and private, and it freed makers from having to know anything about photographic process. Vernacular imagemakers, such as Walker Evans, took up the SX-70 for its ability to directly collect and present data. Unhappy with the confines of the gelatin silver print, Samaras used the SX-70 to relocate his manipulative impulses directly into the medium. Samaras interacted with the process by using a stylus to move the dye layers of the film before they hardened, achieving the same raw, gestural effect and extravagant, unnatural color within the rococo motif he favored in his painting and sculptures. Within the mundane setting of a cramped New York City apartment, Samaras's body erupts, spreads, stretches, as if

17.11   LES KRIMS. *Legless Man on Pedestal,* 1970.
4⅝ × 6⅞ inches. Gelatin silver (Kodalith) print.
© 1970 Les Krims.

possessed by demonic forces, revealing a hidden monster lurking below the surface. Samaras's self-obsessed, surreal tableaux dispense with romantic and sentimental ideals of the self, and like a psychedelic drug experience, they engage the viewer in a dynamic hallucinatory state of psychic transformation (see Figure 17.12). The instant Polaroid print, having no negative to be tinkered with, lends a sense of authenticity to his visions. Critic Peter Schjeldahl called Samaras "the artist laureate of narcissism."[6] Samaras's favorite subject is himself, which he organizes to show viewers how multinatured the self can be. Samaras stated, "When I say 'I,' more than one person stands up to be counted."[7]

The counterculture of the 1960s developed its own brand of American existentialism, stressing that there were no single answers and that people were free to discover their own meaning of life. Many artists thus pursued their understanding of the world through the filter of the self and tracked their observations through a personal journal. For photographers, this diaristic impulse, the desire to make a visual record about a subject based on one's own experiences, reached its widest audience in book form. The nonviability of publishing controversial material for small audiences

forced photographers to return to self-publishing. The content and form of these biographical narratives were often a personal mix of images and text, having roots in the snapshot and the family album. This flexible form allowed for individual freedom, self-definition, and the expression of alternative lifestyles. The format departed from the photo-essay, giving a sense of looking at an anecdotal scrapbook. These young photographers were working with the one subject they knew best: their own lives. The books did not rely on single decisive moments but spun their tales through a collage of sequences that often alternated between black-and-white and color images, contact sheets, film clips, found images, newspaper stories, handwritten notes, drawings, paintings, and informally written accounts.

This biographical approach formed the basis for the publishing experiments of **Ralph Gibson** [b. 1939]. In 1969 Gibson, a former assistant to Dorothea Lange and Robert Frank, founded Lustrum Press, which during the 1970s published an unconventional collection of books.[8] Gibson's tightly composed, high-contrast 35mm work reflects the *minimalist* impulse to eliminate extraneous detail and get down to the essentials of producing a nonliteral, but visually complex, symbolic system that evokes an oracular, dreamlike state. Gibson's use of the close-up, visually editing-out detail (that is, the world), strengthens the fleeting, transient quality of his enigmatic settings (see Figure 17.13).

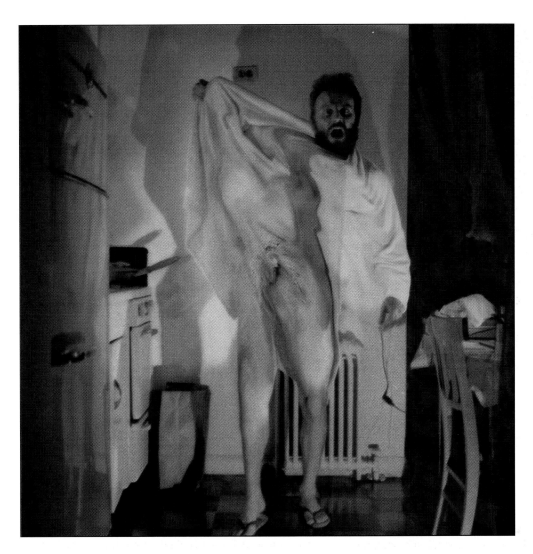

17.12   LUCAS SAMARAS.   *Photo-Transformation, #39.* June 13, 1974. 3⅛ × 3¹⁄₁₆ inches. Diffusion-transfer print.   © Lucas Samaras. Courtesy of Pace Wildenstein MacGill, New York.

Gibson demonstrates that the gelatin silver print is capable of revealing a separate and distinct realm beyond empirical thinking, as his introduction to The *Somnambulist* states: "Clarity is all any man seeks, this somnambulist merely finds his on the Other Side."[9]

The publication of **Larry Clark's** [b. 1943] *Tulsa* (1971) was an insider's look into the nether world of drugs, guns, and sex without excuses or righteous statements (see Figure 17.14). Working from his personal observation that "once the needle goes in it never comes out,"[10] Clark indulges a viewer's appetite for voyeurism. Dispensing with conventional artifice and interjecting his own presence, Clark visually steers people through the ritualized but abjectly unromantic working-class underside of the permissive 1960s' "Free Love Generation." Clark continued to use photography as a form of erotic and metaphysical rescue from the brutality and hopelessness of the low-life drug and gun world, making the book *Teenage Lust* (1983) and a film, *Kids* (1996). *Vagabond* (1975), a self-published book by another Tulsa artist, Gaylord Oscar Herron [1942], expanded the autobiographical form by presenting the artist as an outsider in search of metaphysical understanding. In a 1992 interview Clark discussed how he came to his autobiographical approach. "I know a story that no one's ever told, never seen, and I've lived it. I would go back to Oklahoma and start photographing my friends. That's when it snapped—I wanted to be a storyteller, tell a story. Which I hate even to admit to now, because I hate photojournalism so badly."[11]

Michael Lesy [b. 1945] revealed the subjective nature of historical investigations by showing viewers how historians are montagemakers who assemble, edit, and juxtapose images and text to impose order and meaning on the chaos of human and natural events. The extension of this line of reasoning denies that the facts of any photo-essay can been seen as the Truth. Lesy appropriated turn-of-the-nineteenth-century images of small town America by a Wisconsin photographer, Charles Van Schaick [active 1890–1910], and

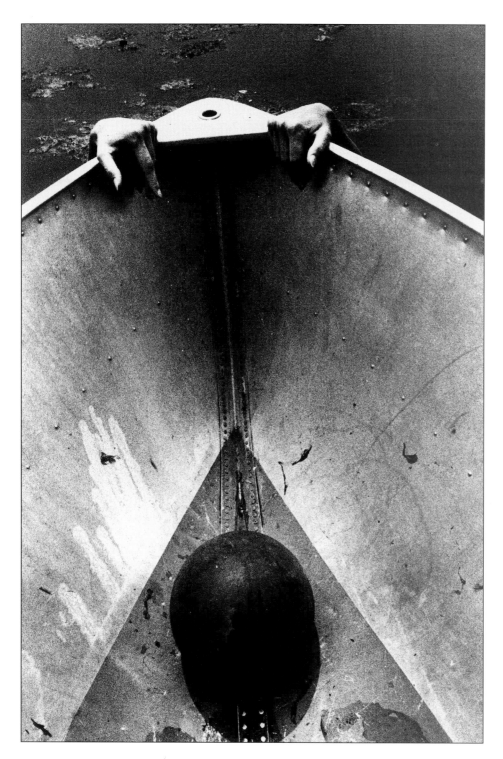

17.13   RALPH GIBSON.   *Untitled*, N. D. (Cover image of *The Somnambulist*, 1970.) Size varies. Gelatin silver print.   © Ralph Gibson.

combined them with bizarre news items from a local weekly newspaper of the time to create *Wisconsin Death Trip* (1973). Lesy's montage, which received an enthusiastic reading, was structured entirely of quotations, unconcerned with the logic of observation, description, systematic analysis, or original intent. At a time when myth killing was a growing academic preoccupation in American Studies, Lesy fashioned a surrealistic psychohistory of a midwestern American Dream revolving around pathological patterns of death, fear, and decline. Dwelling in the underworld of mental breakdowns, murder, sex, and suicide, Lesy undermined the notion that small town America was an ideal, anxiety free place.

At times the demarcation point between what is documentary and what is fiction can be very difficult to distinguish for both the photographer and the viewer.

17.14   LARRY CLARK.   *Untitled*, N. D. (Cover image of *Tulsa*, 1971). Size varies. Gelatin silver print. Inside the book this image appears with text under the image that reads: "dead 1970" and on opposite page text that reads: "death is more perfect than life." Courtesy of the artist and Luhring Augustine Gallery, New York.

Eugene Richards [b. 1944], a former Vista worker, made the photographs for his book *Dorchester Days* (1978) throughout the 1970s. They are a dark, fragmented, diaristic chronicling of a poverty-stricken Boston neighborhood, whose residents show the consequences of being out of reach of the American dream. His documentary approach measured authenticity by how deeply he felt about the subjects he was involved with and photographed. Richards's *Knife and Gun Club: Scenes From an Emergency Room* (1989) led to

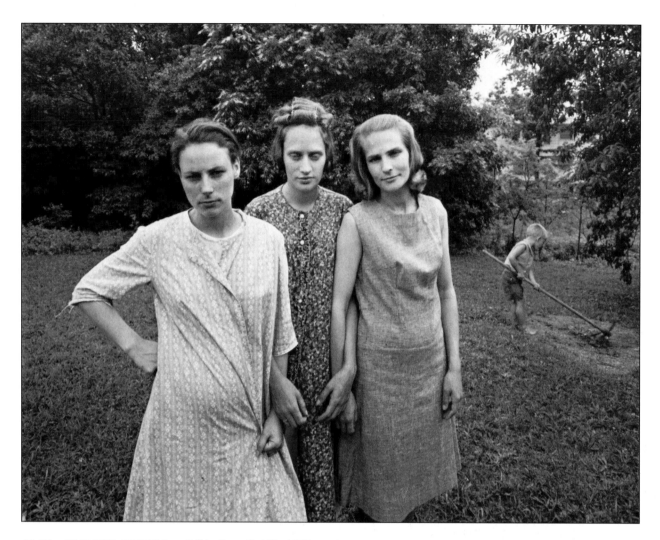

17.15   EMMET GOWIN.   *Edith, Danville, VA*, 1971.
5½ × 7 inches. Gelatin silver print. Gowin says: "My
pictures are made as part of everyday life . . . with a
camera on a tripod. In this situation, both the sitter and
photographer become part of the picture. Sometimes
my photographs resemble home snapshots, . . . but I always want to make a picture that is more than a family
record. I feel that the clearest pictures were at first
strange to me; yet whatever picture an artist makes, it is
in part a picture of himself—a matter of identity."[12]
Courtesy of the artist and Pace WildensteinMacGill, New York.

accusations that he was a ghastly voyeur hooked on
misery. In *Cocaine True Cocaine Blue* (1993) Richards
coupled his images with the narrative voices of addicts
and their families to provide a chilling account of how
addiction has scorched their lives. Brent Staples, author
of *Parallel Time: Growing Up in Black and White*
(1994), accused Richards of prolonging myths of
"black depravity," asking "why are nearly all of the
people in these photographs black? [when] The vast
majority of drug addicts in America are white."[13] Sta-

ples raises the issue of the inherent inequality between
subjects and photographers in such undertakings. Staples makes the larger point that "When the culture focuses on black addiction alone, we miss the breadth of
the danger and confine the problem to 'those people'
over there."[14] This can be one of the difficulties of personal journalism, fueled as it is by the obsessions of
even the most socially conscious photographers who
bring their private concerns and prejudices to a project.
When asked by reporter Lisa Redd if people of color
are too often used to demonstrate pathology in the media, Richards said:

> If you are going to go out and do something about the way
> drugs are hurting people, you've got to say how it's hurting
> people. If you're going to do a book on the worst drug addic-
> tion, then you go to areas not unlike the ones I went to. The
> drugs are coming in and devastating these communities. You
> asked me if I understood the pain people are feeling from
> looking at those pictures? Of course I do. But you have to
> look at what the book is about. If I had done a book repre-
> senting black America, then I should have been shot. . . . Jour-
> nalism isn't journalism by consensus; it is by a person doing
> the best he or she can to find the truth."[15]

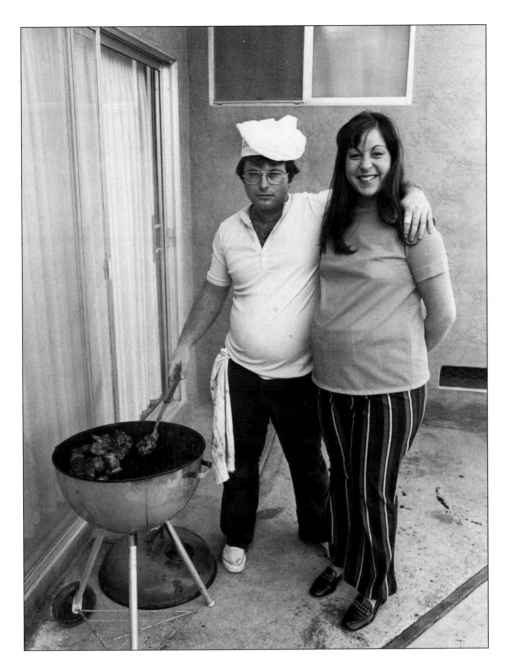

17.16   BILL OWENS.   *Sunday afternoon we get it together. I cook the steaks and my wife makes the salad,* ca. 1970. 14 × 11 inches. Gelatin silver print. Owens wrote of his suburban experience: "The people I met enjoy the lifestyle of the suburbs. They have realized the American Dream. They are proud to be home owners and to have achieved material success. To me nothing seemed familiar, yet everything was very, very familiar. At first I suffered from culture shock."[16]

The Snapshot

Many photographers thought the experiments of the 1960s had taken photography away from its vernacular roots and wanted to return to what Nathan Lyons referred to as "photography's most authentic form"—the snapshot.[17] The attraction was the snapshot's artless ability to directly communicate the vitality of our ordinary, personal, and communal affairs. A snapshot is not a manufactured episode but a record that can reveal the essence of a situation. Through a series of articles, interviews, and portfolios, Jonathan Green's *The Snapshot* (1974) examines the nature of the snapshot and its relationship to contemporary photographic practice.[18] Green declared:

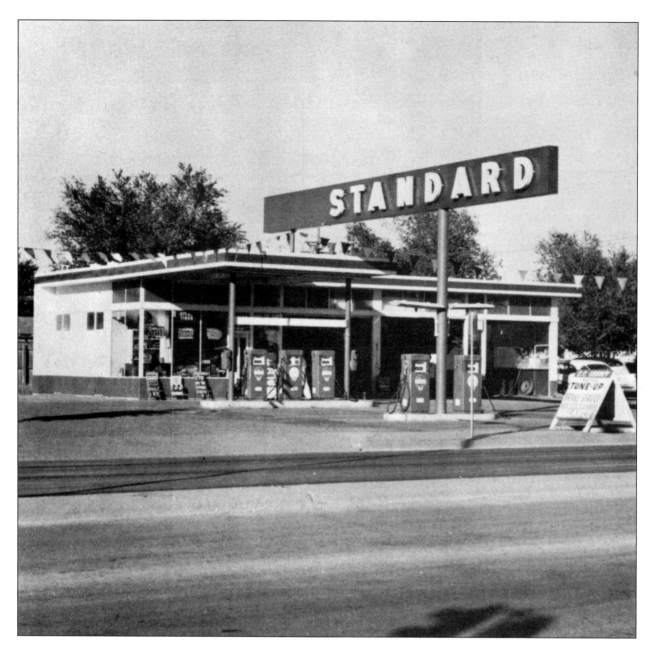

17.17   EDWARD RUSCHA.   *Amarillo, TX*, from *Twenty-Six Gasoline Stations*, 1962. 7 × 5½ inches. Photo off set.   Courtesy Edward Ruscha.

The word snapshot is the most ambiguous, controversial word in photography since the word art. It has been bandied about as both praise and condemnation. It has been discussed as both process and product. A snapshot may imply the hurried, passing glimpse or the treasured keepsake; its purpose may be casual observation or deliberate preservation. The snapshot may look forward in time to a chaotic, radically photographic structure, the appropriate equivalent of modern experience; or it may look backward to the frontal formal family portrait of a bygone age.[19]

Emmet Gowin [b. 1941], one of the photographers featured in *The Snapshot*, consciously incorporated the personal iconography of his life in the rural South with the "snapshot aesthetic." Gowin concentrated on his immediate family and surroundings, doing extended portraits of his subjects, especially his wife in allegorical roles, like Madonna, mother, odalisque, prankster, and Venus and tableaus of family groups (see Figure 17.15). The actions of daily life take on a quixotic identity, while the injection of sensuality helps avoid sentimentality. Gowin considered this work, influenced by Cartier-Bresson and Robert Frank, to be his apprenticeship, a necessary preparation that would help him find his own photographic voice documenting the dramatic contest between the powers of nature and culture.[20] His search to "discover the inherent value that's hidden in things that you haven't yet seen"[21] led Gowin into aerial landscapes that seek a balance between the real and the surreal, to reestablish his spiritual connectedness with nature.

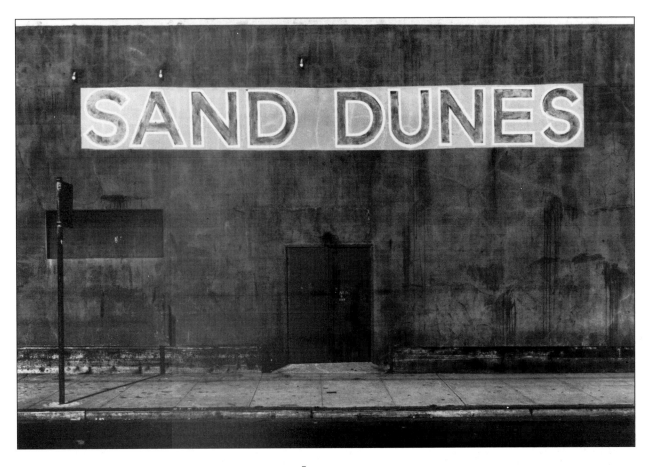

17.18   LEWIS BALTZ.   *San Francisco,* 1973. 6 × 8⅞ inches. Gelatin silver print.   Courtesy George Eastman House.

Judy Dater [b. 1941] combined the intimacy of the snapshot with the formal structure of large-format interpretive portraiture. Dater's involvement in the developing women's movement manifested itself in a group of theatrical, urban portraits whose premise was that a woman, rather than a man, looking at women would bring fresh insights and display a different range of attitudes and styles. Dater's work rebelled against fashion's exploitation of women through expensive, superficial accessories that encourage unrealistic standards of appearance. Dater's nudes did not exploit women's sexuality but presented the women as being more at ease with their bodies. Dater often photographed her subjects in their own surroundings and gave them leeway in determining the choice of costume and pose. In her work women were not defined by their outfits but by the strength of their physical presence.

One element of the snapshot, often lacking in serious imagemaking, is the recording of humorous events.[22] The acceptance of the spontaneous, life as you find it, 35mm aesthetic and its ordinary subject matter paved the way for humor-based photographers like **Eliot Erwitt** [b. 1928] and **Burk Uzzle** [b. 1938] to express their visual wit as a legitimate component of thoughtful imagemaking. **Bill Owens** [b. 1938] *Suburbia* (1973), based on his work as a newspaper photographer for the Livermore, CA *Independent,* satirizes the suburban experience of abundance. Owens's environmental portraits of Livermore residents (Owens lived there, too) were allegedly neutral, but his process of selection and the juxtaposing of these images with comments on "what the people feel about themselves"[23] deliver a devastating look at a place lacking a collective focus and a historic identity (see Figure 17.16).

Post-Structuralism/ New Topographics

Post-structuralism, based on the work of three French structural theorists, Jacques Derrida, Jacques Lacan, and Michel Foucault, formed the minimal and conceptual art movements of the 1970s. Its premise was that words, and by inference photographs are unstable and cannot be trusted, that everything is a momentary construction that contains no ultimate meaning or truth. Post-structuralism's elitist, jargon-filled texts countered the personal, emotion-filled work of the 1960s and rejected Western values as pointless and transparent. It also served notice

17.19   ROBERT ADAMS.   *Mobile homes, Jefferson County, Colorado,* 1973. 5^{15}⁄₁₆ × 7½ inches. Gelatin silver print.   Courtesy Fraenkel Gallery, San Francisco.

to historians that they must become aware of how their strategies effect the outcome of their research. The post-structuralists favored work that was emotionally detached and concerned with illusions and constructed reality. The "new topographics" approach expressed some of these concerns in photographic practice.

"New topographics" refers to the human-altered landscape that became a theme for photographers who sought a return to the landscape aesthetic without the romantic notions of the picturesque or the sublime. These photographers saw the once abundant landscape as physically and spiritually depleted, with only finite potentialities left.[24] To portray the drastic changes that had occurred to the landscape since the end of World War II and to dispute the monumental myths of the enduring and lyrical American landscape, these image-makers photographed the intersection where nature and culture collided, such as the development of subdivi-

sions near the mountains in Park City, UT. Their strategy was to take the direct nineteenth century view and use it to conduct a clinically detached examination of a painful subject. They looked for banal, little, minimal things along the road, avoiding the dramatic, heroic, and transcendental displays of Ansel Adams, to convey a sense of loss. They rebuked the sublime as an insupportable ghost of the past and embraced the ordinary iconography of urban modernity. New topographics practitioner Robert Adams (not related to Ansel) explained his position:

> To the extent that life is a process in which everything seems to be taken away, minimal landscapes are inevitably more, I think, than playgrounds for aesthetics. They are one of the extreme places where we live out with greater than usual awareness our search for an exception, for what is not taken away.[25]

The new topographics ambivalent, highly structured, masculine approach also distanced their work from the poetic, pictorial expressionism of the 1960s. The viewers, like jurors in a courtroom, were expected to review the evidence and pass judgment.[26] The difficulty was that ordinary onlookers had no understanding of the premises informing the work. The minimalist

17.20   TIMOTHY O'SULLIVAN.   *Green River Buttes, Green River WY*, 1872. 6¼ × 8½ inches. (plate 130) Albumen silver print.   U.S. Geological Survey. Print courtesy Mark Klett.

stance of the new topographics photographers made many images interchangeable with commercial commissions, further confusing the public. The exhibition *New Topographics: Photographs of a Man-altered Landscape,* curated by William Jenkins at the Eastman House in 1975, featured Robert Adams, Lewis Baltz, Bernd and Hilla Becher, Joe Deal, Frank Gohlke, Nicholas Nixon, John Schott, Stephen Shore, and Henry Wessel, Jr. [b. 1942]. Jenkins linked their "stylistic anonymity" to conceptual artist **Edward Ruscha's** [b. 1937] sardonic, stripped-down, topographic books, such as *Twenty-Six Gasoline Stations* (1962), *Some Los Angeles Apartments* (1965), and *Every Building on the Sunset Strip* (1966), that shun beauty, emotion, Mother Nature, and sentiment (see Figure 17.17). As John Schott [b. 1944], who did a series conceptually linked to Ruscha entitled *Route 66 Motels,* said: "They are not statements about the world through art, they are statements about art through the world."[27] This subtle approach pictures the inconspicuous nuances of the human constructions within the nat-

ural landscape, maintaining what Gohlke [b. 1942] refers to as a "passive frame," where "there is a sense of the frame having been laid on an existing scene without interpreting it very much."[28]

Lewis Baltz's [b. 1945] *The New Industrial Parks near Irvine, California* (1974) is a dispassionate, minimalist social critique of the desolate sites of the new urban/suburban landscape. Baltz claimed that "The ideal photographic document would appear to be without author or art."[29] Through the act of precise "Flaubertian" description, of finding just the right vantage point, Baltz used the discipline of formalism to order and repossess a bland, desolate subject. His sophisticated and unemotional disinterest symbolically presented the dehumanized, placeless corporate warehouse space of the late twentieth century (see Figure 17.18).

Robert Adams [b. 1937], a former English professor, takes a literary approach to the "New West," as site of diverse interaction between nature and culture. This approach was based on the personalized New Journalistic critiques of American society, such as Truman Capote's *In Cold Blood* (1966) and Norman Mailer's *The Executioners Song* (1979), where tales of heroic deeds were replaced with a senseless lack of

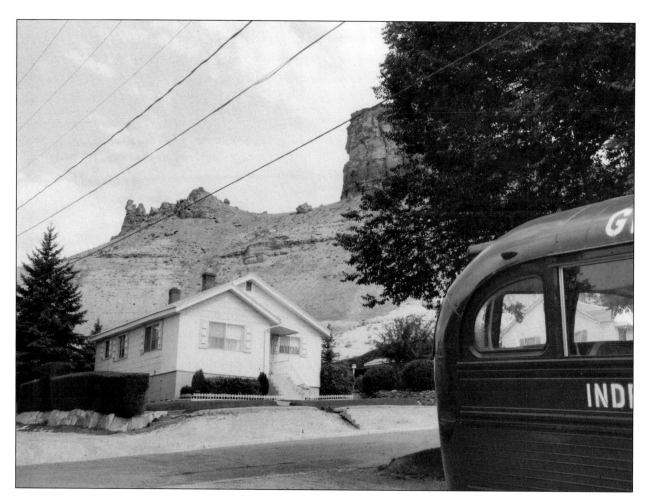

17.21   MARK KLETT AND GORDON BUSHAW.
Castle Rock, Green River, WY, 1979. 6¼ × 8½ inches.
Gelatin silver print.   © 1979 Mark Klett and Gordon
Bushaw for the Rephotographic Survey Project.

respect for life. In *The New West* (1974) Adams recognizes that the grace, beauty, and order of the open American West has been obscured by the confusing commercial upheaval of freeways, strip malls, tract and trailer homes (see Figure 17.19), and road signs. Adams uses a Western roadside scene as an analogy to explain what he is after:

> By Interstate 70: a dog skeleton, a vacuum cleaner, TV dinners, a doll, a pie, rolls of carpet. . . . Later, next to the South Platte River: algae, broken concrete, jet contrails, the smell of crude oil. . . . What I hope to document, though not at the expense of surface detail, is the Form that underlies this apparent chaos.[30]

Eastman House curator William Jenkins claimed that the purpose of his *New Topographics* exhibition was "not to validate one category of pictures to the exclusion of others,"[31] but the ease with which the style could be feigned brought out an army of imitators. *New Topographics* also neatly dovetailed with MOMA's John Szarkowski's opinions about what a

photograph should do and how a photograph was supposed to look, which he summed up in *Mirrors and Windows: American Photography since 1960* (1978). Szarkowski acknowledged "a fundamental dichotomy between those who think of photography as a means of private, self-expression and those who think of it as a method of exploration relating to public concerns."[32] Szarkowski's allegiance was with the latter who acted "as a trustworthy interpreter of events and issues he was privileged to witness."[33]

The Rephotographic Survey Project/Time Changes

Between 1977 and 1979, the Rephotographic Survey Project (RSP), formed by Mark Klett [b. 1952], Ellen Manchester, JoAnn Verburg [b. 1950], Gordon Bushaw, and Rick Dingus [b. 1951], precisely rephotographed 122 nineteenth-century western survey sites, like Mountain of the Holy Cross, CO, and Canyon de Chelly, AZ, that had been pictured a century before by Western. After the coolness of the New Topographics, the RSP pointed out how nineteenth-century photographers saw the landscape and the unfolding interaction of human development and natural transformations over time. The project's act of pairing old and new images showed how photography can display and measure time (see Figures 17.20 and 17.21). This method established a dualistic meaning of time and space, putting spectators into a time machine that permits them to glance between then and now. The group effort of doing "a survey of a survey" led RSP participant Verburg to reflect:

> Our representation of the West is less the result of what we noticed or preferred then [sic] of what we found—changed or not,—at predetermined vantage points. So, ironically our survey did what theirs [the original survey photographers] purported to do: to show the West without shaping it to our own artistic purposes.[34]

The RSP was indicative of a larger cultural interest in reseeing and reassessing American values. Other photographers during this time took a different approach to re-entering the past. Bill Ganzel [1949] did not replicate FSA pictures in his *Dust Bowl Descent* (1984), but he revisited many of the same people and scenes that had been photographed during the original project, examining cultural changes and ways in which meaning is transformed by new contexts. Nicholas Nixon's [b. 1947] yearly ritual of taking the same pose of his wife and her sisters, allows small physical changes to take on larger psychological importance. This serial approach to time elevates private subjects into symbols of aging and change. In the early 1970s, **Milton Rogovin** [b. 1909] made a series of working-class people's portraits near his neighborhood. He returned to photograph the same people in the early 1980s and again in the 1990s. The results were published as *Triptychs: Buffalo's Lower West Side Revisited* (1994) so that viewers could compare the photographs to see how the people aged, changed, and endured over time (see Figure 17.22).

Color Rising

The experimental characteristic of the 1960s and 1970s saw the emergence of color from the commercial world into the realm of art. Previously only a few photographers, such as Ernst Haas, Helen Levitt, Eliot Porter, and Arthur Siegel [1913–1978], could claim significant bodies of work in color. Color was associated with garish and decorative ways of advertising and was deemed inappropriate for art photographers. As magazines ran more color and as color materials became less expensive, easier to use, and more permanent, an increasing number of photographers ignored the commercial stigma and ventured into this sphere.

The small fine art aesthetic of photography had been built around black-and-white images. After World War II Kodak tried to encourage the artistic use of color materials by giving boxes of 8 × 10-inch Kodachrome to

photographers like Edward Weston and Walker Evans who were extremely suspicious of color; they believed it exaggerated realism while diminishing expressiveness. Most remained unconvinced. As late as 1969 Walker Evans said: "These are four simple words which must be whispered: color photography is vulgar."[35]

By 1965 color, through movies and television, was omnipresent in American life, and for the first time both amateur and commercial photographers bought more color film than black and white. Color's former drawbacks now became sought-after characteristics. In the spirit of the 1960s, color was seen as shattering photography's traditions and meshing with the here and now on its own terms. The 1966 MOMA exhibition of 4 × 5-inch Polaroid images by Marie Cosindas [b. 1925] signaled Szarkowski's willingness to open the door of high art to color. It paved the way for others like **Stephen Shore** [b. 1947] to reconsider the worthiness of working in color. Shore's 8 × 10-inch color view camera images formally described familiar but peopleless scenes within the human-altered landscape of the new topographics style. Shore's passive yet circumspect work found acceptance in Szarkowski's schema by setting up a distilled atmosphere and spatial arrangement for contemplating this secular world with the utmost clarity and detail. Shore's restraint subdues the easy, sensuous nature of the color palette and concentrates on the nuance of light and color upon the artifacts of street life without human presence.

In 1976 Szarkowski mounted a major exhibition of **William Eggleston's** [b. 1939] work at MOMA that touched off arguments over color photography's status in the art world. In the catalogue, *William Eggleston's Guide* (1976), Szarkowski claimed the works were "perfect: irreducible surrogates"[36] of understated, vernacular views about the social landscape of the New South. Often verging on the trivial, the enlarging of Eggleston's personal "snapshots" into lush dye-transfer prints, making them valuable art objects, exaggerated the mundane and confronted onlookers with the insipid emptiness of the contemporary American environment (see Figure 17.23). Eggleston's openness to the most insignificant subject matter, like a dog lapping water from a puddle or an inside view of a home oven, gave the idea that anything could be photographed. This approach was criticized as one of diminishing expectations, an epiphany of the banal, a declaration that there was nothing left to photograph. Many viewers were unwilling to elevate a mundane color snapshot to High Art. Art critic Hilton Kramer responded to Szarkowski's claims by writing, "Perfect? Perfectly banal, perhaps. Perfectly boring, certainly."[37]

In the afterword of *The Democratic Forest* (1989), Eggleston laments that the public only looks at his subject matter and not at how he has "seen" it. Critics raise the point that people might not care for such nihilistic

17.22   MILTON ROGOVIN.   *Untitled Triptychs*, 1974/1986/1992. From series *Buffalo's Lower West Side*. 5⅞ × 6⅞ inches. 6¾ × 6½ inches. 7 × 6¼ inches. Gelatin silver prints.

work because it affirms nothing but one individual's idiosyncratic way of seeing. Photographers tend to conclude that such shortcomings of understanding are those of the audience and not the makers. Indirectly, Eggleston raises questions about the interpretation and response to images. Are these issues strictly problems for viewers or are they a shared concern, an interaction between makers and viewers, and what, if any, responsibility do photographers have for educating their audience? The controversy surrounding Eggleston's work became part of a full-scale discussion about color practice and its dramatic emergence in the 1970s as an acceptable artistic form.

The rethinking of color as a viable option for serious photography is evident in the work of **Joel Meyerowitz** [b. 1938]. Meyerowitz left his career in advertising to become a black-and-white style street photographer after watching Robert Frank work and realizing the gestural potential of the small camera. By the late 1960s Meyerowitz used color for its additional descriptive qualities. In 1976 Meyerowitz began to photograph with an 8 × 10-inch view camera around Cape Cod, MA, concerning himself with the polymorphous aspects of sand, sky, and water. The publication of Meyerowitz's popular *Cape Light* (1978) announced the shift from the split-second, jazzy black-and-white improvisations of 35mm street photography to the formal, contemplative, and descriptive qualities of a view camera and an orchestral color palette. Meyerowitz now lingered around a scene, waiting to record the subtle passages of light and time that slowly transformed the subject (see Figure 17.24). His color prints stress a slower, more distant, romantic, sensuous response to

luminous effect, the pure beauty of light, rather than the close, edgy, instantaneous reaction of the black-and-white street moment. Meyerowitz recalled the descriptive and suggestive qualities that led him to pursue color photography.

> When I committed myself to color exclusively, it was a response to a greater need for description . . . color plays itself out along a richer band of feeling—more wavelengths, more radiance, more sensation. . . . Color suggests more things to look at [and] it tells us more. There's more content [and] the form for the content is more complex.[38]

Following her dictum that "formalism is everything,"[39] **Jan Groover's** [b. 1943] still-life arrangements proved popular with institutions, such as MOMA, that held on to formalism because it was familiar and understandable to their audiences and staffs. In reaction to the societal looseness of the 1960s, Groover empirically exercised control over color, form, light, and space in her studio. "For me, the rules are how things go together,"[40] she stated. The isolated spatial readability of the large format enabled her to create perceptual illusions that suspend normal photographic time. Groover's staged events impart an impression of being in the present rather than in the past. Through her use of reflection and transparency, Groover fabricates a sensation of spatial ambiguity in which depth becomes inaccessible and observers experience a disruption of *figure-ground*, the relationship between the subject and the background. The enlarging process further distorts reality by making commonplace objects, like kitchenware, slightly larger than life, giving them a sculptural personality that makes viewers reconsider the prosaic.

John Pfahl's [b. 1939] *Altered Landscapes: The Photographs of John Pfahl* (1981), playfully uses the cyclopean vision of a view camera to reveal the synthetic nature of Renaissance pictorial theories of distance, perspective, and scale. Pfahl maintains an intellectual distance by combining the picturesque, nineteenth-century landscape with his own formal manipulation of scenes, from the exact vantage point of the camera, delivering a conflicting message in a single image. Pfahl gives ironic colorful evidence of that which we believe cannot be so, humorously informing onlookers that all facts are conceptual and that visual truth is a matter of consensual agreement (see Figure 17.25).

Joel Sternfeld's [b. 1944] cross-country pilgrimages through America in a Volkswagen camper are about reconciling issues of appearance and myth with the landscape. Sternfeld uses a 8 × 10-inch camera to load his color documents with a tension caused by the intrusion of mundane human objects and the invasiveness of technology on the beautiful and sublime landscape. Sternfeld often relies on humor to confront intriguing contradictions and incongruities that unmask the superficial and call attention to ordinary life (see Figure 17.26).

Mark Cohen's [b. 1943] aggressive, close-up, flash 35mm images extend the formal sense of how a color photograph can look. Cohen's physical intrusiveness violates society's comfortable proximal distance to document private portions of a subject's personal space. His images deliver undefended views that disrupt the rules about how photographs are made and how they appear. Cohen is not looking for detached observations but active engagements with strangers that are brazenly uncivil and can produce social embarrassment and confrontation. Cohen's encroachments get to

the crux of the struggle, that began with the small handheld camera, between photographers who pursue images without permission and the subject's right to privacy and ability to respond to an intrusion. These situations are about the power to control visual representation, the photographer's ability to stealthily make pictures by surprise and the subject's chance to reply (see Figure 17.27).

Artists' Books

At the same time the formal physical concerns of photographic practice were being addressed by many photographers, other artists were examining photography's cultural context. Lew Thomas's *Photography and Language* (1976) used the work of over 30 artists to investigate the interrelationships of images and text. During the 1960s, members of the Fluxus group worked to break down the barriers between art and the public. Their activities can be linked with a new interest in the book format. During the 1970s, artists' books became a way for imagemakers to control production and costs, deliver their work to an audience in context, and express concepts too complex for a single image. Artists' books used autobiography, narrative, and humor to deal with the new pluralistic concerns of women and minorities that surfaced in the 1960s.[41] Artists set up independent presses, like **Joan Lyons's** [b. 1937] Visual Studies Workshop Press in Rochester, N.Y. to publish works by artists (see Figure 17.28).[42] Keith Smith [b. 1938], who studied at the Institute of Design and made work at VSW, produced over a hundred artists' books, featuring an interactive use of materials that took the medium beyond its factual realm. Scott Hyde [b. 1926] worked directly from color separations so that every image in his offset, photolithograph books and journals was an "original." Michael Snow's [b. 1929] *Cover to Cover* (1975) investigated the nature of the book, the concept of the sequence, the act of picturing, and the process of perception. In a world that has witnessed a steady decline in the role of animals, Peter H. Beard's [b. 1938] *African Diaries* (1978) juxtaposed a tapestry of collaged newspaper clippings, Polaroid SX-70s, snake skins, and hand-prints made from his own blood with images of fashion, "primitive" culture, and wild animals to tell "secrets" about his adopted home in Kenya. Beard's foot-high memento scrapbooks reveal the diversity of the book form in terms of object, image, and its ability to transform the personal into a shared experience that reminds us of the important connections between the animal and human kingdoms. Combined with his earlier photo-essay, *The End of the Game* (1965), Beard's work helped replace the high-powered firearms safaris with high-tech camera safaris to the world's wildlife meccas.

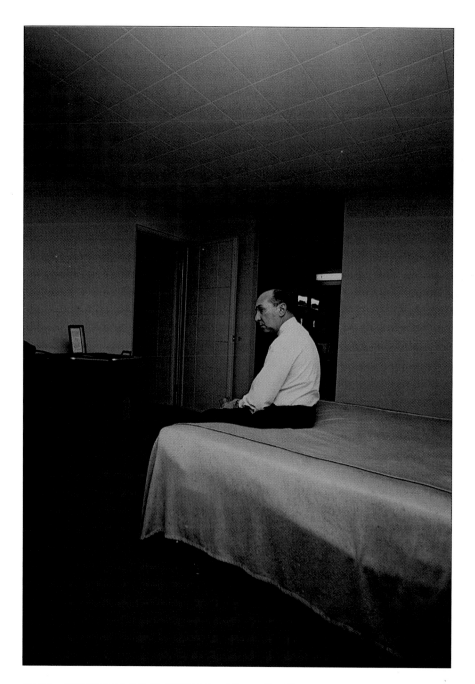

17.23 WILLIAM EGGLESTON. *Huntsville, AL. (Man in a Motel Room)*, ca. 1969–70. 18⅝₆ × 12¾ inches. Dye-transfer print.   Courtesy Art and Commerce Anthology, New York. Copy print © 1999 The Museum of Modern Art, New York.

Reconfiguring Information

Nancy Rexroth's [b. 1946] non-linear memory book, *Iowa* (1977), made with a Diana Camera,[43] and Eric Renner's [b. 1941] use of pinhole cameras dispute the modernist presumption that equates image sharpness with quality of information. The toy Diana Camera achieved cult status among photographers for being noncommercial. Its cheap plastic construction made it notorious for producing light leaks and guaranteed low image resolution. *The Less Than Sharp Show* (1977) demonstrated how variety of practice could "relax the veracity issue of a photographic image." The exhibition featured an array of approaches that disassembled image clarity, including Gary Hallman's [b. 1940] use of flash during long exposures, Bea Nettles's Kodak Instamatic camera work, and Linda Connor's [b. 1944] old 8 × 10-inch view camera with a soft-focus lens. Curator Howard Kaplan wrote:

> The less than sharp image facilitates the viewing of the photograph for its intrinsic value as a photograph, as opposed to a document of what once existed. . . . Being spared much of the hard edge content associations, the viewer can now focus

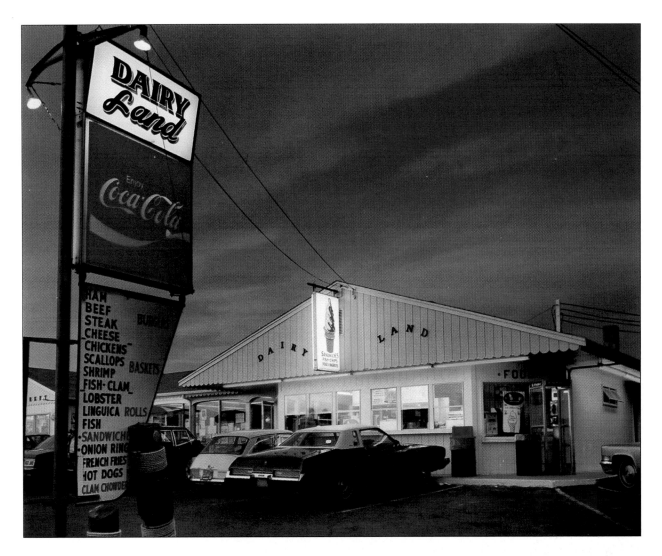

17.24   JOEL MEYEROWITZ.   *Provincetown* (Dairy-land), 1976. 16 × 20 inches. Chromogenic color print. © Joel Meyerowitz. Courtesy Bonni Benrubi Gallery, New York.

on other aspects of the photographic image. . . . The *new* content may now be quite *loaded* so as to provoke quite different associations/experiences from it.[44]

Ruth Thorne-Thomsen's [b. 1943] poetic *Expeditions* combine collage aesthetic expectations based on nineteenth-century travel pictures and pinhole images to construct false historical landscapes. The softness of the pinhole distorts one's perception of time and scale, allowing viewers to become dreamlike voyagers into the personal archetypes of their subconscious (see Figure 17.29).

Historic landscape traditions were also overturned by photographers taking camera equipment into the night. Roger Mertin [b. 1942] and Richard Misrach [b. 1949] applied flash to distort and prolong time. Steve Fitch's [b. 1949] night images in *Diesels and Dinosaurs* (1976) string together a progression of nocturnal illuminations, adding mystery to banal American

road culture. **Robert Hirsch's** [b. 1949] outdoor, nighttime flashes incorporated postvisualization methods that added time and movement into the frame. This was part of a *haptic,* or kinesthetic, approach that actively incorporated the photographer into the entire picture-making process. Hirsch's series, *The Underground City* (1974–78) encompassed numerous alternative approaches, hand-coloring, enlarger movement, appropriated images, and toning to disturb the landscape and inject a feeling of loneliness. The effect was to dismantle the decisive moment and conventional print values while expanding the boundaries of the frame (see Figure 17.30).

David Levinthal [b. 1949] and cartoonist Garry Trudeau collaborated to produce *Hitler Moves East: A Graphic Chronicle, 1941–43* (1977), rerepresenting World War II battle scenes from the eastern front using miniature studio sets and selected archival materials. These small tableaux, based on actual visual models, utilize the historical illusionism of documentary war images to narrate and make the past accessible (see Figure 17.31). Levinthal has continued to mine these fabricated tabletop landscapes in projects that look at the

17.25 JOHN PFAHL. *Six Oranges, Buffalo, N.Y.,* 1975. 8 × 10 inches. Chromogenic color print. © John Pfahl. Courtesy Janet Borden, Inc.

West and romance, that strike at the genuineness of photographic meaning while remaining believable, enabling viewers to criss-cross between their imagination and reality. Levinthal said that his tiny scenes "were mirrors of society's image of itself, much like Norman Rockwell paintings for the *Saturday Evening Post*. Playsets reinforced the popular culture and beliefs and stereotypes of America."[45]

Expanding Markets

Government funding from the National Endowment for the Arts (NEA) sparked artistic growth in the 1970s. The NEA, established in 1965 as a tiny part of President Johnson's Great Society program, made its first grant to an individual photographer, Bruce Davidson, in 1968. The NEA set up a special category for Photog-

rapher's Fellowships in 1971 (discontinued in 1996), giving recognition to photography as an independent art form. In 1972, the NEA established its Workshop Program to fund the first generation of "artist-run" spaces, which led to the organizing of other not-for-profit spaces like Friends of Photography, established in 1967, which evolved into a large membership organization devoted to exhibitions, publishing, and workshops. Another alternative organization, Visual Studies Workshop (1969), became an important training ground for people seeking an MFA degree in visual culture that featured an interdisciplinary approach to photographic education and alternative publications.

In 1973, the NEA established grant categories for Photography Exhibitions and Publications, enabling museums and alternative spaces to produce their own projects and literature. NEA funding encouraged the formation of state art councils and the giving of private matching donations, which helped artist-run spaces expand and achieve a limited degree of stability.[46] These spaces became creation and presentation sites for new artists and their ideas, eventually influencing the com-

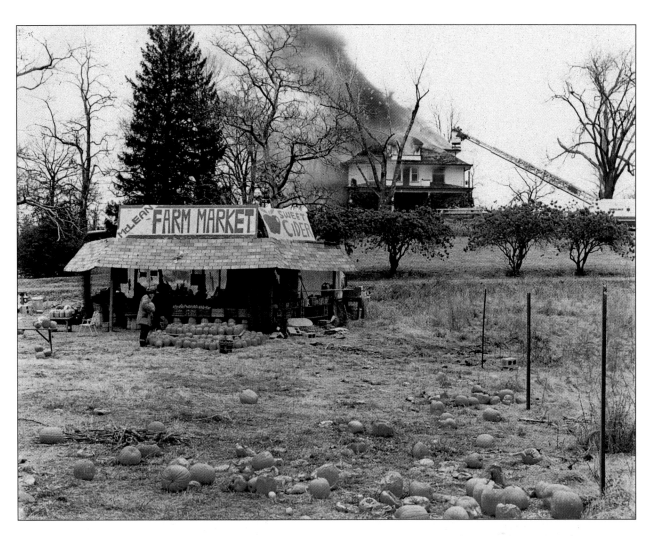

17.26   JOEL STERNFELD.   *McLean, Virginia,* December 4, 1978. 18 × 22 inches. Chromogenic color print.   © Joel Sternfeld. Courtesy PaceWildensteinMacGill, New York.

mercial galleries and museums. The spaces movement continues to play a pivotal role in maintaining the vital and experimental outlook of American photographic practice. They provide a flexible and meaningful alternative to the rigid framework of commercial galleries and large museums. The spaces provide outlets that have championed diversity and broadened the scope of artistic and critical practice. The success of such initiatives can be seen along Interstate 90 in western and central New York. This photographic corridor has been a focus of alternative activities and currently is home to The Center for Exploratory and Perceptual Art (CEPA Gallery) in Buffalo (1974), Light Work in Syracuse (1973), and Visual Studies Workshop in Rochester.[47]

The expansion of photographic practice in the early 1970s resulted in the establishment of a new generation of commercial galleries, such as Lee D. Witkin's Witkin Gallery (1969–1999) and Light Gallery (1971) in New York, and museum programs, including the

California Museum of Photography (1973), the International Center of Photography (1974), the Center for Creative Photography (1975), and the Chicago Center for Contemporary Photography, later the Museum of Contemporary Photography (1977), all dispensing photography to a wider audience. High school, college, and university photography courses continued to expand, giving rise to record numbers of people earning Master of Fine Arts degrees in photography. The university scene connected photography to the art gallery world, enabling a few imagemakers to support themselves by selling their work. New York gallery interest led photography into the art auction market, which intensely raised the price of historical photographs. The recession of 1979–82 drastically cooled down the market, but by then photography had established a place in the commercial side of the art world.

Critical Writing

The 1970s witnessed a wave of republished works, such as *The Literature of Photography: An Arno Press Collection* (1973), which included 62 classic volumes on aesthetic, historical, scientific, and technical

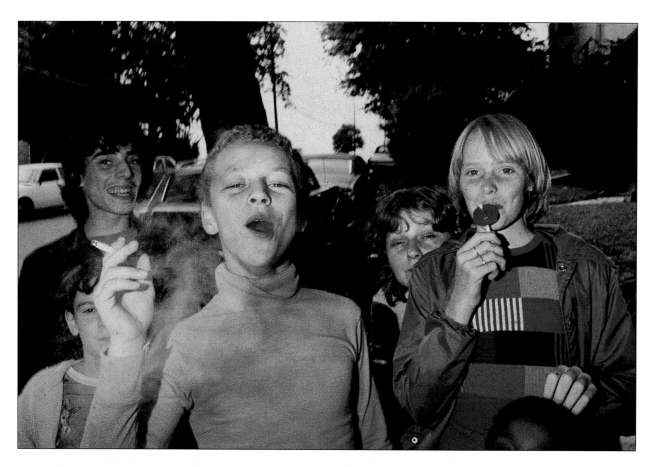

17.27   MARK COHEN.   *Untitled*, ca. 1977–78.
13 × 19⁵⁄₁₆ inches. Chromogenic color print.
Courtesy George Eastman House.

17.28   JOAN LYONS.   *My Mother's Book,* 1993.
6 × 9 inches. Offset lithography.
Courtesy Visual Studies Workshop, Rochester, NY.

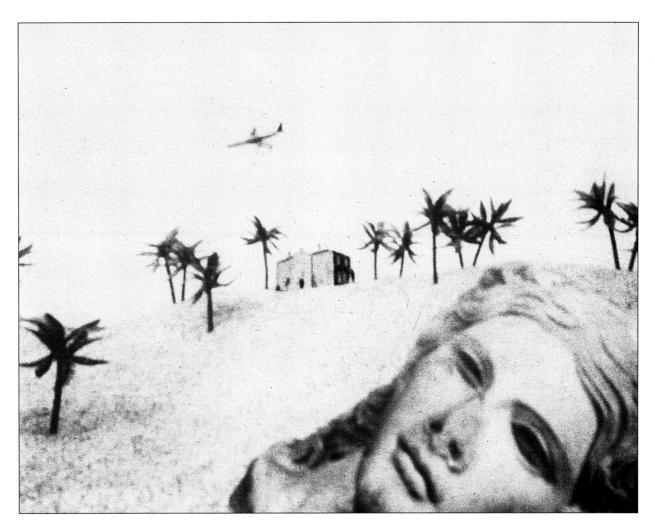

17.29 RUTH THORNE-THOMSEN. *Head with Plane, IL,* 1979. 4 × 5 inches. Toned gelatin silver print. © Ruth Thorne-Thomsen. Courtesy Laurence Miller Gallery, Inc.

aspects of photography. Barbara London and John Upton's *Photography* (1976), based on the *Life Library of Photography* (1970–72), provided an opportunity for teachers to break out of the mechanic, manual mentality of instruction by linking ideas to technique and providing readers with stimulating visual examples. The 1970s saw a widening of photography's intellectual base with the founding of publications such as Visual Studies Workshop's *Afterimage* (1972) and Friends of Photography's *Untitled* quarterly series (1972) and the evolution of SPE's *Exposure* into a critical journal (ca. 1973). The editorial policies of *Afterimage* and *Exposure* gave voice to feminist and lesbian theorists, such as Catherine Lord, Jan Zita Groover, and Deborah Bright.[48] A. D. Coleman began to write serious photography reviews for the general public in the *Village Voice* (1968–73) and the *New York Times* (1970–74).[49] Additional voices included Marxist critic John Berger's *Ways of Seeing* (1972), which critiqued West-

ern capitalist art as a symbol of ownership and a demonstration of male power. Allan Sekula and Martha Rosler also wrote Marxist and feminist political critiques for *ARTFORUM*[50] and *exposure*.[51]

The 1973 publication by the *New York Review of Books* of Susan Sontag's critical essay about the nature of photography, later expanded and revised as *On Photography* (1977), initiated a serious intellectual dialogue from within the practice and the community of arts and letters. Sontag related how her own life was changed by viewing photographs of Nazi concentration camps:

> Nothing I have seen—in photographs or in real life—ever cut me as sharply, instantaneously. Indeed, it seems plausible to me to divide my life into two parts, before I saw those photographs (I was twelve) and after . . . something broke. . . . I felt irrevocably grieved, wounded, but a part of my feelings started to tighten; something went dead; something is still crying.[52]

The experience shaped her belief that the "camera is sold as a predatory weapon. . . . To photograph people is to violate them, by seeing them as they never see themselves, by having knowledge of them they can never have; it turns people into objects that can be symbolically possessed. Just as the camera is a sublimation of the gun, to photograph someone is a sublimated

17.30   ROBERT HIRSCH.   *The Illuminated Man,*
1973. 16 × 20 inches. Toned gelatin silver (Kodalith)
print.   Courtesy Visual Studies Workshop, Rochester, New York.

murder—a soft murder."[53] Although numerous photographers were upset with Sontag's claims about the inauthenticity of photographs, based on an educated sensibility from outside the field rather than a research methodology, her writing raised fundamental philosophical questions facing the practice.

There was renewed interest in the writing of Walter Benjamin, to whom Sontag paid homage in the last chapter of *On Photography,* and to Barthes's and Derrida's concept of *deconstruction,* that is, the exposing and tearing down of any arbitrary construction of reality, which began to appear in a photographic context in works by John Baldessari, Sherrie Levine, and Richard Prince. These writings forecast the rise of *postmodern criticism,* the rejection of the notion of originality in a society that ceaselessly recycles ideas and images, as espoused by Craig Owens and Douglas Crimp in the late 1970s in the journal *October.* The effect of these endeavors was a broadening of the practice to include a greater diversity of approaches and voices, particularly those of women, gay, and minority imagemakers, or *the Other,* challenging power relationships between photographers and subjects and how viewers see and understand these associations.

17.31   DAVID LEVENTHAL.   *Untitled*, from *Hitler
Moves East*, 1976. 8 × 10 inches. Gelatin silver (Kodalith) print.   Courtesy David Levinthal.

Endnotes

1   Kathleen McCarthy Gauss, *Inventories and Transformations: The Photographs of Thomas Barrow* (Albuquerque: University of New Mexico Press, 1986), 120.

2   Carl Chiarenza, "Eye and Mind: The Seriousness of Wit," in Lynne Warren, *Kenneth Josephson* (Chicago: Museum of Contemporary Art, 1983), 7.

3   William Larson, letter to author, February 12, 1999.

4   Ralph Eugene Meatyard, with texts by Jonathan Greene, et al, *The Family Album of Lucybelle Crater* (Millerton, NY: Jargon Society, 1974), 73.

5   See A. D. Coleman, *The Grotesque in Photography* (New York: Ridge Press/Summit Books, 1975).

6   Peter Schjeldahl, "The Wizard in the Tower," in *Lucas Samaras* (NY: Pace/MacGill Gallery, 1991), unp.

7   Lucas Samaras, Samaras Album (NY: Whitney Museum/Pace Editions, 1971), 9.

8   The Lustrum line featured Danny Seymour's *A Loud Song* (1971), Robert Frank's *The Lines of My Hand* (1972), Larry Clark's *Tulsa* (1971), as well as instructional books such as *Darkroom, Darkroom II, SX-70, Contact Theory, Landscape Theory*, and *Nude: Theory*. In addition, Lustrum published Gibson's dreamlike trilogy of photo-novels *The Somnambulist* (1970), *Deja-Vu* (1973), and *Days at Sea* (1974).

9   Ralph Gibson, *The Somnambulist* (New York: Lustrum Press, 1970), unp.

10   Larry Clark, preface, *Tulsa* (New York: Lustrum Press, 1971), unp.

11   Larry Clark, *Flash Art*, May/June, 1992 quoted in Brooks Johnson, *Photography Speaks II* (NY: Aperture/The Chrysler Museum of Art, 1995), 106.

12   Emmet Gowin, *Emmet Gowin: Photographs* (New York: Alfred A. Knopf, 1976), 100.

13   Brent Staples, "Coke Wars," *The New York Times Book Review*, Sunday, February 6, 1994, 11–12.

14   Ibid.

15   Eugene Richards, *ReView,* vol. 17 no. 3 (May/June 1994), 13. Unhappy with the context of how his work was being discussed, Richards declined to give permission to reproduce an image.

16   Bill Owens, *Suburbia* (San Francisco: Straight Arrow Books, 1973), unp.

17   See Robert Hirsch, "Nathan Lyons on the Snapshot," *CEPA Journal*, Winter 1992–93, 6–9.

18   *The Snapshot* included work by Emmet Gowin, Henry Wessel, Jr., Tod Papageorge, Joel Meyerowitz, Nancy Rexroth, Garry Winogrand, Lee Friedlander, and Robert Frank.

19   Jonathan Green, Introduction, *The Snapshot* (Millerton, NY: Aperture, 1974), 3.

20   See Sally Gall, "Emmet Gowin," *Bomb 58*, Winter 1997, 21.

21   Ibid.

22   For an early history of this genre see Heinz K. Henisch and Bridget A. Henisch, *Positive Pleasures: Early Photography and Humor* (University Park: The Pennsylvania State University Press, 1998).

23   Owens, unp.

24   The photographers of the "New Topographics" were working in the same arena as eclectic postmodern architect Robert Venturi, whose book *Learning from Las Vegas* (1972) emphasizes the validity of American roadside strip building and advertising.

25   Robert Adams, "In the Nineteenth-Century West," in *Why People Photograph* (New York: Aperture, 1994), 148–49.

26   In terms of popular culture, the New Topographics mission can be summed up by the *Dragnet* TV character, Joe Friday, played by the deadpan Jack Webb, who was always instructing witnesses to deliver "just the facts."

27   John Schott quoted by William Jenkins, Introduction, *New Topographics: Photographs of a Man-altered Landscape* (Rochester, NY: George Eastman House, 1975), 5.

28   William Jenkins, *New Topographics*, 5.

29   Lewis Baltz quoted in *New Topographics*, p. 6, from review of *The New West* by Robert Adams, in *Art in America*, vol. 63, no. 2 (March/April 1975), 41.

30   Robert Adams, *New Topographics*, 7.

31   William Jenkins, *New Topographics*, 7.

32   John Szarkowski, *Mirrors and Windows: American Photography since 1960* (New York: The Museum of Modern Art, 1978), 11.

33   Ibid.

34   JoAnn Verburg, "Between Exposures," Mark Klett, et al *Second View: The Rephotographic Survey Project* (Albuquerque: The University of New Mexico Press, 1984), 10.

35   Quoted in Louis Kronenberger, *Quality: Its Image in the Arts* (New York: Atheneum, 1969), 208.

36   John Szarkowski, *William Eggleston's Guide* (New York: The Museum of Modern Art, 1976), 14.

37   Hilton Kramer, "Art: Focus on Photo Shows," *New York Times* (May 28, 1976) Section C, 18.

38   Joel Meyerowitz, *Cape Light: Color Photographs by Joel Meyerowitz* (Boston: New York Graphic Society, 1978), unp.

39   Jan Groover, Renato Danese, ed., *American Images* (New York: McGraw-Hill, 1979), 140.

40   Jan Groover, *Outside the City Limits: Landscape by New York City Artists*, exhibition catalogue (Sparkill, NY: Thorpe Intermedia Gallery, 1977), 22.

41   Pluralists oppose the notion of having a single mainstream of thought in favor of a multitude of approaches that present diverse points of view.

42   See Joan Lyons, ed., *Artists' Books: A Critical Anthology and Sourcebook* (Rochester: Visual Studies Workshop, 1985).

43   See David Featherstone, *The Diana Show: Pictures Through a Plastic Lens*, *Untitled 21*, (Carmel, CA: Friends of Photography, 1980).

44   Howard N. Kaplan, *The Less Than Sharp Show* (Chicago: The Chicago Photographic Gallery of Columbia College, 1977), 4.

45   David Levinthal, *Small Wonder: Worlds in a Box* (Washington: National Museum of American Art, 1996). Front interior dustjacket.

46   For a critical article about the NEA and artist-spaces, see Grant Kester, "Rhetorical Questions: The Alternative Arts Sector and the Imaginary Public," *Afterimage* (January 1993), 10–16.

47   Some of the other important alternative spaces that continue to operate include Light Factory (Charlotte, NC); Camerawork (San Francisco, CA); Los Angeles Center for Photographic Studies (Los Angles, CA); Nexus (Atlanta, GA); Photographic Resource Center (Boston, MA); Houston Center for Photography (Houston, TX); The Center for Photography at Woodstock (Woodstock, NY); Blue Sky (Portland, OR) and pArts Photographic Arts (Minneapolis). The NEA ended general operating support to all of these organizations in 1996. In 1998 the Supreme Court ruled that "decency" standards could be considered in awarding federal art grants. Information about each of these organizations can be found by visiting their website.

48   See Deborah Bright, ed., *The Passionate Camera: Photography and Bodies of Desire* (London and New York: Routledge, 1998).

49   See A. D. Coleman, *Light Readings: A Photography Critics Writing 1968–1978* (New York: Oxford University Press, 1979).

50   See Allan Sekula, "On the Invention of Photographic Meaning," *Artforum*, vol. 13 (January 1975), 36–45; "The Instrumental Image: Steichen at War," *Artforum*, vol. 14 (December 1975), 26–35.

51   See Martha Rosler, "Lookers, Buyers, Dealers, and Makers: Thoughts on Audience," *exposure*, vol. 17, no. 1 (1979), 10–25.

52   Susan Sontag, *On Photography* (New York: Farrar, Straus and Giroux, 1977), 20.

53   Ibid., 14–15.

CHAPTER EIGHTEEN

Thinking About Photography

Conceptual Art: The Act of Choosing

During the socially turbulent 1960s, artists rethought the roles of photographers, photographs, and viewers. Photographic practice shifted from modernistic formalism that emphasized compositional and tonal elements of the straight print to a conceptual approach in which ideas took precedence over how subjects were depicted. *Conceptual art* offered a way to circumvent commercialization and formalism and supply a concrete framework for cerebral works of art. Conceptual artists adopted photographs, undervalued by the art establishment, as organizing mechanisms for transmitting cultural messages. Applying aspects of semiotics, feminism, and popular culture, conceptual artists used the camera as an alleged neutral recording device. They made deadpan-prints that appeared to be aesthetically artless and that bore little resemblance to traditional fine art objects.

ARNULF RAINER. *Bundle in Face,* 1974. 20⅟₁₆ × 23¹³⁄₁₆ inches. Gelatin silver print with ink and oil crayon. Courtesy San Francisco Museum of Modern Art.

Arnulf Rainer photographed himself grimacing to access a preverbal body language, but he felt the resulting images did not capture the psychic reality of his self-transformation. By uniting his photography and drawing Rainer created a tension between the comic and the tragic in which "all sorts of new personages suddenly appeared to me who, all being ME, were not capable of manifesting themselves solely by the movement of my muscles."[1]

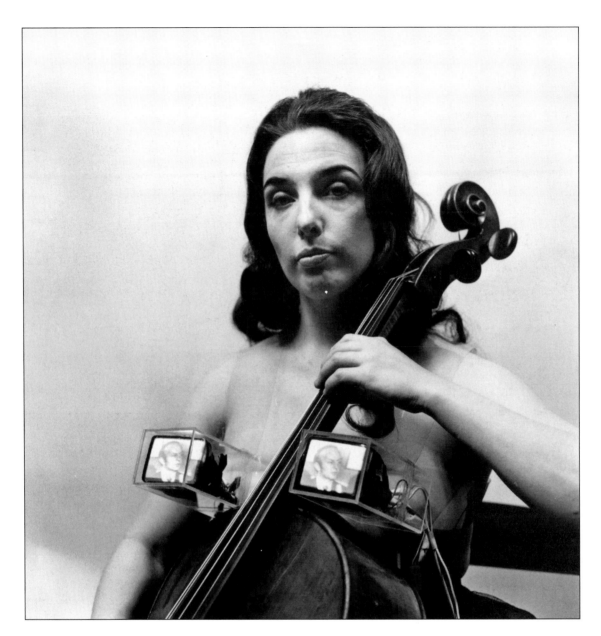

18.1   NAM JUNE PAIK.   *TV Bra for Living Sculpture*, 1969. Television sets and cello (worn by cellist Charlotte Moorman). Gelatin silver print.   Photo © Estate of Peter Moore/Licensed by VAGA, New York, NY.

Conceptual artistic collaborations like Fluxus, which included Joseph Beuys [1921–1986], Nam June Paik [b. 1932], and Yoko Ono [b. 1933], upset bourgeois expectations by choosing invisible intellectual/social concerns over tangible aesthetic/visual ones. Although Fluxus had a foothold in mainstream culture, their agenda was to revamp it. Mixed media events, such as the Charlotte Moorman and Nam June Paik collaboration featuring Moorman playing her cello while wearing miniature television sets fashioned into a brassiere, were their forte. Mail art and rubber stamp art were other nonconformist, low-cost

Fluxus activities. In mail art the pieces were addressed, stamped, and mailed to the exhibition. Shows were often loosely organized around a theme and all work that was received was displayed. In rubber stamp art an image and/or text was made into cheap rubber stamps to be quickly reproduced endlessly, anytime, anywhere. Both were open democratic approaches that did not require high levels of technical skill. These approaches rejected the notions that expert curatorial judgment was necessary to organize a show and that art was something original, precious, and irreplaceable.

Along with the practitioners of pop art, artists and critics explored *semiotics*, the study of the signs that make up the basis for all forms of communication (see Chapter 17).[2] During the 1970s, certain artists used the analytical tools of semiotics to examine clichés,

18.2 JOHN BALDESSARI. *An Eight-Sided Tale,*
1980. 3⅝ × 6 inches (irregular shape). Photo offset.
© John Baldessari. Courtesy CEPA Gallery, Buffalo, NY.

myths, and stereotypes about gender and power that
were communicated and reinforced through mass-
media sign systems. They used semiotics-based analysis to try and reveal the multitude of possible meanings
produced by the variations between the apparent, professed content of a work of art (that semoticians call
the "text") and the cultural assumptions of the viewer.
This approach disclosed the social context for the production, reception, and dissemination of images
and how this shapes the underlying message of all
representations.

John Baldessari's [b. 1931] work of the late 1960s
reconstituted the text from his readings of John Barthes
onto canvas to invest Barthes ideas about images and
mythologies with new meaning. Baldessari playfully
commingled mediums to court ambiguity and the dual-
ities of chaos and order and to free himself from doing
what artists had previously been expected to do: Organize the world and give it a defined, narrative meaning.
During the 1970s, Baldessari asked himself "why photographers do one thing and painters another."
Baldessari stated:

> The real reason I got deeply interested in photography was
> my sense of dissatisfaction with what I was seeing. I wanted
> to break down the rules of photography—the conventions. I
> began to say photographs are simply nothing but silver

deposit on paper and paintings are nothing more than paint
deposited on canvas, so what's the big deal? Why should
there be a separate kind of imagery for each?[3]

Baldessari appropriated images from popular culture, especially Hollywood film stills, taking the existential position that choice making is what makes both
your life and art authentic. His work is not grounded in
formal issues but "is about the moment of decision and
about fate intervening and chance eroding and disrupt-
ing our powers to make a decision."[4] In *Close Crop
Tales* (1981), Baldessari rejected the rectangular picture format and broke away from formalistic confines
of the edge by cutting his content-loaded images (film
and publicity stills) into dynamic shapes with between
three to eight sides.[5] The book tells six "tales," from "A
Three-Sided Tale" to "An Eight-Sided Tale." Baldessari explained: "All the images are the different
sides dictated by the internal composition, so there was
a three-sided shape triangle, then there's something in
there that dictates those three sides. . . . All of the framing is dictated by what is inside."[6]

In *Blasted Allegories* (1978), Baldessari invited
friends to ascribe a single word to black-and-white images randomly taken from television, which were then
arbitrarily colored or shaded with a hue whose first letter started with the same first letter of the chosen word.
Algebraic messages were then added to the pieces to
form verbal and visual "sentences." This mutual
exchange of visual and verbal groupings encouraged
an open, multiple "reading" of the work. The dense,

18.3 BRUCE NAUMAN. *Portrait of the Artist as a Fountain,* 1966. 19⅞ × 23¾ inches. Chromogenic color print. In *Portrait of the Artist as a Fountain,* the half-naked Bruce Nauman first elevated his body to the status of a traditional sculptural motif (this work references Marcel Duchamp's *Fountain* (1917), a urinal signed and exhibited as art). By spewing liquid, Nauman mimics ejaculation and urination, demoting the functions of his mouth from the intellectual process of speech to the physical process of elimination.   © 1999 Bruce Nauman/Artist Right's Society (ARS), New York. Photo courtesy Sperone Westwater, New York.

layered meaning of allegory replaced the homogeneity of the metaphoric modernist approach. *Allegory,* the reliance on symbols to represent meanings other than those indicated on the surface, was resurrected in the late 1950s by the French *situationists.* The situationists proposed that transient experiences, like walking through a city, furnished fleeting sights and sounds that were themselves art. Their stance implied an end of art objects, but it was based on a society so attuned to the aesthetic qualities of its everyday surroundings that the people no longer required art. Allegory permits artists to deal with appropriation, fragmentation, transience, the disintegration of tangible means of measurement, and the uncertainty of meaning and time while emphasizing content over pictorial concerns. Questioning a work's source, purpose, context, audience, and meaning disturbs the importance typically given to an artist as a shaman who can see and explain the world, suggesting a more equal and open-ended exchange between artists and audiences.

As approaches to photography became more cerebral, photographers searched for fresh models. Conceptual work dispensed with the modernist physical standards of the fine print—the thoughtful use of light, material, process, and technique—dismissing the bedrock upon which photography had gained its artistic acceptance. Sharing the character and outlook of Marcel Duchamp's readymades (see Chapter 10),

18.4   ANSELM KIEFER.   *Your Age and Mine and the Age of the World,* 1997. 129⅞ × 220½ inches. Emulsion, acrylic, shellac, burnt clay, and sand on canvas.
Courtesy Gagosian Gallery, New York, NY.

conceptual images blatantly ignore past aesthetics and heroic subject matter in favor of blandly describing mundane facts. Unlike documentary artists, conceptual artists recorded arranged events with a minimal severity that abolished any visual components included for the sake of beauty. This reductionist outlook shaved subjects down to fundamental abstract ideas, often too complex to be understood within the confines of a single photograph, further challenging the reportorial mode of photography. Artists not absorbed in the observation of outer reality or their own personal lives abandoned the photographic method of making selections from the external world. These artists gave up acting as spectators and editors and instead took directorial responsibility for constructing images in their studios and darkrooms. The studio, instead of the street, became a creation site, recasting the nineteenth-century compositional syntax of Oscar Rejlander and Henry Peach Robinson, which had been exiled by modernism. This way of thinking put photographers on equal footing with other artists who had the authority to fashion images based on their internal directives. A photographer no longer had to take what was visible, to be a reliable witness of outer reality, a reporter subject to the whims of available light, a presenter of physical evidence. A photographer now took the privileged position of creating what had formerly been considered an "unphotographable" internal event.

Performance Art

The conceptual artist **Bruce Nauman** [b. 1941] used the supposed objectivity of the photograph to give a documentary look to his contrived situations, known as *performance art.* This term has been retroactively applied to early live-art forms, such as body art and happenings. The progressive disintegration of conventional artist materials and presentation forms led to the engagement of the real body as a forum for cultural critiques. Performance art is an open-ended classification for art activities that include elements of dance, music, poetry, theater, and video, presented before a live audience and usually "saved" by photographic methods and shown to larger audiences. One of its purposes is to provide a more interactive experience between artists and audiences.

Robert Smithson's [1938–1973] constructed Earth Work projects, like *Spiral Jetty* (1970), a 1,500-foot long spiral of earth and rock that jutted out into Great Salt Lake, and Christo's [b. 1935] temporary projects, such as wrapping a building, or his *Running Fence* (1976), a 24½-mile fence of fabric, rely on photography to reach larger audiences. Initially, many conceptual artists resisted being documented, claiming that photographs would convert their art into marketable objects, violating their basic concept that such work

18.5   GILBERT AND GEORGE.   *Down to Earth,*
1989. 88½ × 125 inches. Chromogenic color print.
Courtesy Sonnabend Gallery, New York.

was supposed to be experienced in person. But soon,
Smithson was exhibiting his photographs and Christo
was selling his. Artists like Smithson, who created transitory situations that he extracted from nature or left for
nature to decompose, fixed his work with photography,
stating: "Photography makes nature obsolete."[7] Such
strategies helped to dissolve the boundaries that divided photography from other media.

German artist **Arnulf Rainer's** [b. 1929] body became a site for merging the historical pain of World War
II with the fierce gestural marking or defacing of the
print surface, violating modernist tenets about the separation of art and photography (see chapter opener).
Anselm Kiefer [b. 1945], whose thickly painted can-
vasses dealing with the seductive and violent German
mythos of "blood and soil" often contain a mural-sized
photograph beneath the paint, confronted the historical
reality of German militarist authoritarianism.[8] Kiefer's
enormous paintings, based on photographs of architectural subject matter, meditate on the linkage of history,
time, and memory. What appears to be a landscape
painting of a pyramid is actually a creation based on a

photograph Kiefer made in India of a building where
bricks are hand-made. Kiefer utilizes photography to
create an obscured image of the world based on the debris of history that emphasizes the ambiguity and para-
doxes of reality and the intrinsic suffering that is an in-
escapeable component of human affairs (see Figure
18.4). Considering Kiefer's absorption with Nazi Germany, is it mere chance that these brick factories are in
essence ovens?

Some say only those who have directly experienced
the Holocaust have the ability to truly represent it. Others disagree claiming that the aftershocks of this calum-
nious event, and by extension other such occurrences,
that continue to vibrate so intensely give the right to
anyone who feels its effects to try and find new ways of
representing and understanding such trauma. Such conceptual interpretations can be seen in Art Spiegelman's
comic books *Maus: A Survivor's Tale: My Father
Bleeds History* (1986) and *Maus II: A Survivors Tale:
And Here My Troubles Began* (1991) and in the work of
Christian Boltanski [b. 1944]. Though the first-hand
presentation of a historical event that does not rely on
the traditional documentary formula of being a witness,
narrator, or photographer on the spot, each artist
demonstrates what Ernst van Alphen calls the "Holocaust effect".[9] Boltanski uses postmodern methods that

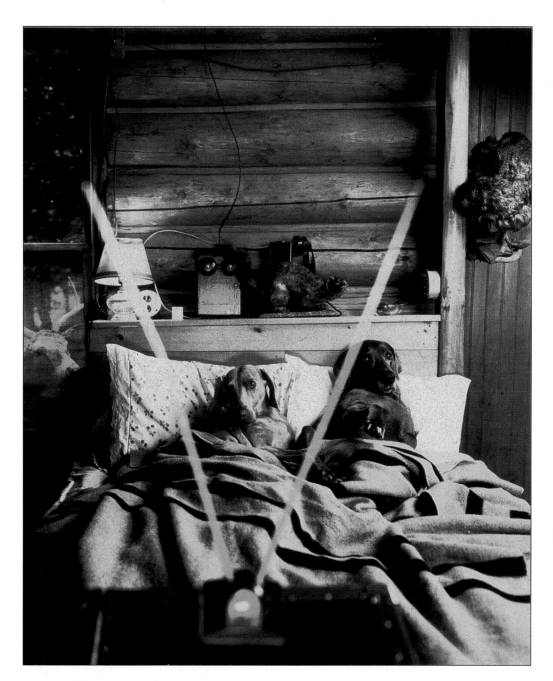

18.6   WILLIAM WEGMAN.   *Ray and Mrs. Lubner in Bed Watching TV* (second version), 1981. 24 × 20 inches. Diffusion transfer print.   © 1981 William Wegman. Courtesy PaceWildensteinMacGill Gallery, New York.

engage the past through indirect references to the Holocaust that enlist its signifiers like archival boxes, deteriorated snapshots, and piles of clothes. These items establish an environment that encourages viewers to reflect on how this tragic event continues to haunt Western culture and its political policies in places like the former Yugoslavia, and reminds us to be on guard against what Holocaust survivor Elie Wiesel calls the "Perils of Indifference."

Former performance artists **Gilbert and George** (Gilbert Dolomites [b. 1943] and George Totnes [b. 1942]), who played on their sense of photographic time as they posed for hours as living sculpture, manipulated themselves as the content in their series of photographs presented in a grid formation. Photography became their vehicle for suspending movement and memorializing their daily lives. These monumental pieces, having much in common with sculpture, confronted an audience with "modern fears" involving British social attitudes and homosexuality. Appearing in their work as respectable, contemporary dandies, their persnickety, conservative sartorial style concealed their irreverence, pederasty, and voyeurism (see Figure 18.5).

18.7   BERNHARD AND HILLA BECHER. *Tipples From Small Mines, East Pennsylvania,* 1991. 67 × 92 inches. Gelatin silver prints.   Courtesy Sonnabend Gallery, New York.

William Wegman [b. 1943] wittily incorporated his dog, Man Ray (1970–1982), into real-time videos that built on repetition to observe and record numerous staged situations. In 1978, Wegman shifted his modus operandi from these spare studio video performances (a stream of moments) to the large-format Polaroid camera (a formalized controlled moment). This transformed the way Wegman worked and led to *Man's Best Friend* (1982), the first of numerous publishing ventures in which his dogs appeared (see Figure 18.6).

Wegman's dogs (Fay Ray followed Man Ray and Wegman now works with her offspring) became "blackboards of living art materials" that Wegman nursed "into engagements not of their own thinking that are disturbing and funny . . . [while] being careful not to make them ridiculous."[10] By combining body and performance art, substituting a canine for familiar people and situations, Wegman systematically explored the metamorphosis of a single subject. Mixing detachment and love, Wegman cultivated his fantasies with a patient, "neutral" companion that takes all the transformations seriously.

A Return to Typologies

Bernhard [b. 1931] and **Hilla** [b. 1934] **Becher** have collaborated since the late 1950s to document industrial structures as *archetypes,* the paradigm of a class of subjects that represents the essential elements shared by all varieties of that class. Their dispassionate scrutiny favors a centered, frontal confrontation, utilizing a high point of view. Backgrounds are minimized, eliminating the surroundings and diminishing perspective. The light is direct, flat, and lacking in luminosity. There are no shadows, clouds, or traces of other human activity; absolute stillness prevails. The Bechers refer to these artifacts as "anonymous sculpture," based on an industrial archeology whose topology can be studied in a new setting without nostalgia and in whose configuration lies the microcosm of the ideal universe. The Bechers' stated purpose is "to collect the information in the simplest form, to disregard unimportant differences and to give a clearer understanding of the structures."[11]

Their images are a form of comparative anatomy, which they claim provides a system of understanding the world that cannot be achieved in a natural setting.

The Bechers' posed photographs are generally presented in a grid format (often about 3 × 3 feet), where the image clarity allows the nuances of these functionalist sculptural compositions, about to be destroyed as obsolete, to be comprehended and appreciated. By objectively "naming" the subjects, the Bechers' hope to convey their historical condition within an industrialized culture. As a teacher, Bernhard Becher's conceptual approach, treading between order and disorder, shaped the austere work of his students Thomas Ruff [b. 1958] and Thomas Struth [b. 1954]. Ruff and Struth's images emphasize an empirical formula of amassing facts to study in a judicious and systematic fashion. Ruff's larger-than-life-size head-shots serve as archetypes, presenting a human head as a summary of the universe.

The Bechers' methodology renews the positivist, encyclopedic compulsion to catalog the world in the belief that to know something is to subdivide it, quantify it, and recombine it. Their work asks the "how" question without getting entangled in the thorny thicket of "why?" The work ignores the issue of whether compiling more information always leads to a greater understanding. What is important is observing, measuring, and making conclusions based on the data, even if the subject of the data-gathering cannot be explained. It is a way of distancing oneself through the act of presenting nature as an abstraction, moving observers towards the Elizabethan philosopher Francis Bacon's proclaimed goal of science: mastery over the natural world. Bacon's Cartesian model equates truth with utility and the intentional manipulation of the environment. It considers the *neoplatonist* outlook that sees the universe as a holistic, living, interconnected organism, as mystical fluff, and directs a course towards the domination of nature through a rational, technologically based thought process.[12] This level of detachment may prompt viewers to examine the relationship of these photographs to the amoral historical events of World War II that affected artists of the Bechers' generation. Does the Bechers' stance come from a minimalist disposition or is it indicative of a consciousness defined by its refusal to examine its own authoritarian history?

Robert Cumming's [b. 1943] analytical photographs came out of scientific procedures for gathering evidence that stress objective measurement, controlled procedure, and technological methods. Cumming's images run contrary to fine art expectations of personal expression and seem to rely on the photographic process to gather, organize, and document data into logical information. However, Cumming's work does not really do this. The images are pseudo-events,

astutely staged, droll fictions that distort assumptions surrounding photographic veracity. Cumming's meticulous "anti-documents" parody scientific correctness. Their purpose is not to dupe people—Cumming provides clues—but to challenge observers to find the defects in the visual logic. In the series *Three Sides of a Small House, the Fourth Being Obscured by a Low Wall and Some Foliage* (see Figure 18.8), an attentive onlooker will notice that the side walls of the house are identical. Cumming's visual record of this event is so minimal that it steers viewers into considering the ideas that constitute the event; in this case, the fictional nature of the subject becomes apparent, revealing how a photographer can contrive information. Cumming points out how the act of observing alters what is being observed, while he also questions photography's impartiality and the role of the camera as a recorder and formulator of reality. Cumming's tableaux, reflecting his interest in Hollywood movie-making, caution us to beware of messages delivered on a screen, whether TV, film, or computer.

The obsession with cataloging pushes its conceptual limits with Douglas Huebler's [1924–1997] proposal to photograph "the existence of everyone alive in order to produce the most authentic and inclusive representation of the human species . . ."[13] Instead of aesthetically pleasing objects, Huebler used the objective repeatability of photography as a thinking aid to call attention to his larger conceptual goals. In this case Huebler wanted to show the notion of impossibility. The purpose of his utterly banal images was to challenge the idea that a single picture could explain any subject, and therefore deny the significance of visual documents, which in turn pointed out the deceptive rationalism that went into the making of an archive.

Postmodernism

Postmodernism refers to the dissolving of traditional boundaries between art, architecture, popular culture, and the media that has been accomplished by an open-ended process of borrowing ideas, art forms, and representations from the past and the present. As differences between mediums become less distinct, their unique concepts and processes commingle. This has led to the formation of ambiguous and contrary hybrids that pay no attention to the modernist concept of trying to achieve "pure" articulated ways of thinking, making, and understanding the arts. Postmodernist theoreticians borrow heavily from structuralist and poststructuralist theory. They believe meaning cannot be determined by surface appearances since everything from a photograph to a television program is a text that must be decoded.[14] The act of deciphering the "text" and

18.8   ROBERT CUMMING.   *Three Sides of a Small House, the Fourth Being Obscured by a Low Wall and Some Foliage,* 1974. 6¼ × 8 inches each. Gelatin silver prints. Cumming sums up the underlying themes of his images as "out-and-out illusionism and magic tricks, satires on the misreading of natural phenomena, and sardonic commentaries on the history of art and photography."[15]   © Robert Cumming.

unveiling the hidden assumptions behind it is what Jacques Derrida calls *deconstruction.* However, Derrida believes that all meaning is fluid and temporary and there is no such thing as an absolute meaning. Derrida and other poststructuralists conclude that finding true meaning is like trying to find your true reflection in a hall of mirrors. Everything is distorted. The notion that there is not a single truth of experience is at the core of postmodern thinking. This is in direct opposition to the modernist view of trying to discover the "essence" or essential meaning in the world. Postmodernism has disallowed the notion of artistic intention, reference, and meaning and has lead some critics to say it has cut off art from its political and social moorings. It has also encouraged artists to explore divergent ways of representing reality and reintroduced issues from the 1960s like feminism, racism, and sexual orientation, and brought them to the forefront.

For postmodern thinkers photography is not the stimulus for theory but the consequence of it. Jean Baudrillard [b. 1929] states that we are a media-saturated society of the *simulacrum,* a 'copy' of which there is no original. From his viewpoint, we are a culture not just of the image, but one in which the image has replaced that which it was supposed to represent. These phantom images, or *simulacra,* supplant reality and curtail our ability to make genuine responses to life.[16] Originality, a building block of modernism, is no longer viable, since everyone in the industrialized West is contaminated by mass culture. Its indiscriminate effects render us incapable of originality, making recycled, second-hand imagery the clear choice.

Bart Parker [b. 1934] used photographs and text to examine the separation between reality and the image of that reality. Parker asserted the primacy of the image by showing how a subject can be confused with its representation. Parker's *Tomatoe Picture* (1977) evokes semiotic theory by directly comparing a subject with its sign: Two images, one made of an actual tomato and the second taken from a color photograph of a tomato, seem identical. However, the captions tell us that one image is of a "real" tomato while the other is a flat representation, making visible the postmodernist belief that representation misconstrues the original.

Over the course of a year, **Paul Berger** [b. 1948] photographed diagrams and formulas on classroom blackboards, only partially advancing the film after each exposure. The developed film was cut into thirds and contact printed, and the continuously overlapping sequence of image strips was made into an abstracted progressive grid. The repetition of chalk lines in this series, *Mathematics* (see Figure 18.9), takes on calligraphic flow, using photographic accuracy to transform scientific information into a study about photographic representation, scale, space, and time. The fact that Berger spent a year making photographs of chalk lines reveals the growing artistic disenchantment with "the subject." If one accepts the postmodern notion that there is no "original," it is easy to believe that the subject of one's work is of little consequence. This acceptance of secondhand experience that denied the possibility of an original parallels the ideas in Barthes's essay "Death of the Author" and scholar Frederic Jameson's pronouncements about the "death of the subject." Poststructuralists would say that this position is an indication that the construct of the self never has existed and never can exist.[17] Berger's *Seattle Subtext* (1984) draws on these semiotic studies, using electronically transmitted imagery to comment on the mechanisms from which we obtain knowledge by reading photographs. Berger examines the collision between reality and illusion that occurs in viewer expectations when the changeable, electronic, digital mentality confronts that of the fixed, mechanical Gutenberg press. Berger wrote:

> *Seattle Subtext* is an imaginary and reordered magazine, a hypothetical alteration of the context and composition of all the "information" that pours into ones [sic] home. By drawing on the conventions of "layout," it becomes possible to construct relationships among still photographs and television imagery, typeset captions and computer text. These relationships posit a personalized environment of great density and simultaneity in a format usually thought of as fixed when received—the magazine.[18]

In *Driftworks* (1984), postmodern philosopher Jean-Francois Lyotard pursues the position of "active nihilism"—"pushing decadence [of capitalist society] to destroy the belief in truth under all its forms"—where the artist hopes for nothing and admits art is insignificant and powerless to change anything. Ronald Jones, deconstructionist artist and critic, says:

> Instead of creating anything new, we move into slow motion where nothing seems to change. We create a "hover" culture. . . . Throwing things into neutral becomes the most radically charged gesture of the moment.[19]

In this position an artist forsakes an activist approach to fulfilling heroic cultural ideals, conceding that an individual no longer possesses the ability to rectify much that is wrong with reality. Instead the artist "hovers" over existing cultural models, in a paradoxically passive approach, hoping that the act of "hovering" will somehow fatigue the structure and cause it to fail. Such a belief implies that we are victims of our preconceived thoughts; an artist's work and a viewer's response can only affirm these predispositions. The assertion concludes that a source of single truth is impossible, as meaning depends upon its context. Opposing

critics say that such an embrace of "received ideas" accepts a dangerous and tyrannical form of mental conformity, the type that gives rise to totalitarianism.

The artistic collaboration known as **MANUAL** was formed in 1974 by Suzanne Bloom [b. 1943] and Ed Hill [b. 1935]. Their choice of name implies a guiding handbook as well as the sense of touch, reflecting their concerns about the *phenomenological* aspects of artmaking: observable facts and occurrences. MANUAL has used electronic methods to merge images/identities of the past with those of the present, atomizing time and space, leaving its audience with only the now. Its strategy suggests that originality is a myth and that there can be no creativity or true self because everything inside a person's mind has been imprinted by culture and language. MANUAL's digital work is often based on the premise that there can be no author or artist since all works and texts are simply reworkings of existing texts. Artists make copies of what is already a copy and not even a photographer has a chance of being able to reveal anything.[20] MANUAL's recent work combines analog and digital photography to focus on the destructive effects of the mythic Arcadian image of nature.[21] This combination provides a platform for the issue of ecology (clear cutting) while referencing the history of the Western ideology toward nature that allows humans to think in terms of possession, consumption, and idealization (see Figure 18.10).

Deconstructing Myths

Richard Prince [b. 1943] claims to be unmasking the schema of advertising imagery by rephotographing and cropping found magazine images (see Figure 18.11). Prince's position is one of exhaustion: The world has all the photographs it requires, he says, and there is no need to make new ones; consequently Prince is satisfied to cull material from the existing stockpile. Prince makes it clear that, "These pictures are more than available, and unless you've been living in an alley, inside an ash-can, wrapped up in a trash liner (with the cover closed), chances are better than even, you've seen them too."[22] The postmodernists call this practice of using existing images *appropriation*; critics refer to it as pirating. Prince describes the postmodern condition in his writing, which features nameless characters (who serve as surrogates for the artist):

> Magazines, movies, TV, and records. . . . It wasn't everybody's condition but to him it sometimes seemed like it was, and if it really wasn't, that was alright, but it was going to be hard for him to connect with someone who passed themselves off as an example or a version of a life put together from reasonable matter. . . . His own desires had very little to do with what came from himself because what he put out (at least in part) had already been out. His way to make it new was *make*

18.9   PAUL BERGER.   *Mathematics #57*, from the series, *Mathematics*, 1977. 16 × 20 inches. Gelatin silver print.   Courtesy Paul Berger.

it again, and making it again was enough for him and certainly, personally speaking, *almost* him.[23]

Prince's postmodern stance is that most people only know the world through secondhand experience, through copies. Prince says:

The photographs of [Jackson] Pollock were what they [the media and through them the public] thought Pollock was about. And this kind of take wasn't as much a position as an attitude, a feeling that an abstract expressionist, a TV star, a Hollywood celebrity, a president of a country, a baseball great, could easily mix and associate together.[24]

As the original disappears so does its mythic value, emphasizing the act of choosing as the artistic feat. Prince asks: "What measurements or speculations that used to separate their value could now be done away with."[25] His radical cropping and enlargement of detail provide an avenue of inquiry into the media's presentation of gender through posing and stereotype, although Prince never comes out and condemns such practices.

Sherrie Levine [b. 1947] took Prince's concept further by rephotographing a reproduction of Edward Weston's *Torso of Neil* and exhibiting it as her own work, *Untitled (After Edward Weston)*, in 1979. Levine also did this with Walker Evans's photographs and later with reproductions of well-known paintings. Her action bluntly criticizes what Levine and other feminist artists consider a competitive, male-dominated, capitalist culture's insistence on the importance of originality—on who did it first. After doing commercial art earlier in her career, Levine states she "was really interested in how they [the commercial art field] dealt with the idea of originality. If they wanted an image, they'd just take it. It was never an issue of morality; it was always an issue of utility."[26] Others argue

18.10 MANUAL (Suzanne Bloom and Ed Hill). *Quinault,* from *A Contructed Forest,* 1993. 24 × 36 inches. Chromogenic color print.

that culture cannot be divorced from morality, that culture is selective, and that selection involves choice. These choices form the basics of our ethics. Levine's renouncing of the traditional meaning of authorship, creativity, and originality was a rejection of the modernist belief in progressive change, which infuriated most viewers and foreshadowed ethical issues surrounding the digital appropriation of work. Levine's copies of copies, functioning as stand-ins for the originals without the original artists' agreement, amplify the inherent defects of the mechanical reproductions process. Levine's "ghosts" reinforce Baudrillard's position that power can be exercised through control of the means of representation. By understanding the code in which the originals support cultural assumptions and stereotype, and reusing the images critically, one can deplete their power. Levine says:

> The pictures I make are really ghosts of ghosts; their relationship to the original images is tertiary, i.e., three or four times removed. . . . I wanted to make a picture which contradicted itself.[27]

The team of **Michael Mandel** [b. 1950] and **Larry Sultan** [b. 1946] satirized and deconstructed expectations surrounding the American myth of fame. Their photo-offset series, *Baseball Photographer Trading Cards* (1975), took a group of "photo stars" like Ansel Adams, dressed them up like baseball players, and anointed them with the visual status accorded to sports idols who are collected as bubble gum trading cards. While normal baseball cards give a player's batting statistics, these cards listed items like the photographer's favorite film and developer. These "clubby" cards pay ironic homage to a photo-elite unknown to the public at large. Indirectly they ask why top artists do not receive the same status and financial rewards as celebrity sports figures, pointing out the lack of respect, understanding, and value placed on artmaking.

Barbara Kruger [b. 1945] spent ten years working as a graphic designer for various women's magazines that extolled beauty, fashion, and heterosexual relationships before she began to produce photomontages, resembling billboards, with text that questioned capitalism's relationship to patriarchal oppression and the role consumption plays within this social structure (see Figure 18.12). In *Remote Control: Power, Culture, and the World of Appearance* (1994), Kruger deconstructs consumerism, the power of the media, and stereotypes of women to show how images and words manipulate and obscure meaning. Kruger says: "I work with pictures and words because they have the ability to determine who we are, what we want to be, and what we become."[28] Her work concisely asks: Who speaks? Who

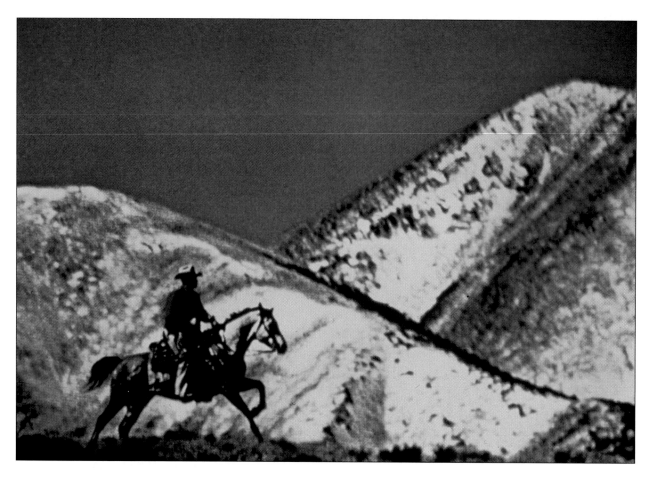

18.11   RICHARD PRINCE.   *Untitled,* 1987. 27 ×
40 inches. Chromogenic color print.   Courtesy Barbara
Gladstone Gallery, New York.

is silent? Who is seen? Kruger visualizes what Roland
Barthes called "the rhetoric of the image," showing
viewers the tactics by which photographs impose their
messages, revealing the hidden ideological agendas of
power. Kruger sees stereotypes of women as instruments of social power, determining who is in and who
is out. Her curt phrases—"Who is bought and sold?"
"Your manias become science," "Your gaze hits the
side of my face"—go to the core of male demonstrations of financial, physical, and sexual power.

Drawing on the seductive strategies of advertising,
Kruger reuses anonymous commercial, studio-type
images of purposely orchestrated movements. Kruger,
like Prince, is not interested in action per se but in "the
stereotype's transformation of action into gesture."[29]
Kruger's use of personal pronouns—I/my, you/
your—builds attraction, emphasis, and significance
by simultaneously connecting the addressee and the
speaker. Since pronouns do not carry gender, they allow female observers to enter into Kruger's work and
illuminate the mechanisms of involuntary subjection.
Kruger also recognizes the changing usage and reality

of a photographic message and designs her work to
function in numerous situations, including books,
gallery walls, installation environments, and billboards. Kruger states:

> But to me the real power of photography is based in death:
> The fact that somehow it can enliven that which is not there
> in a kind of stultifyingly frightened way, because it seems to
> me that part of one's life is made up of a constant confronta-
> tion with one's own death. And I think that photography has
> really met its viewers with that reminder.[30]

Victor Burgin's [b. 1941] work takes on the photographically fragmented nature of the postmodern environment that deals with all events and images as being
equally encoded with meaning, readable, and woven
into one seamless reality. Along with conceptual artist
Hans Haacke [b. 1936], Burgin created forums to address political consciousness in order to upset the modernist belief in making aesthetic considerations a prior-
ity. In *The End of Art Theory* (1986), Burgin places the
visual arts in the context of contemporary cultural theory that embraces language and socio-economic issues.
Burgin's combinations of images and text cut across
advertising, film, painting, and photography to deconstruct the modes and means of symbolic representation
(see Figure 18.13).

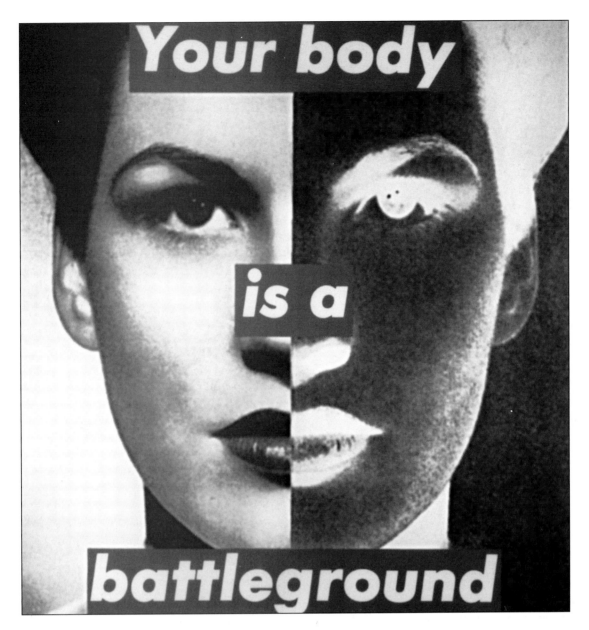

18.12   BARBARA KRUGER.   *Untitled*, 1989.
112 × 112 inches. Photographic silkscreen on vinyl.
Kruger said: "The thing that's happening with photography today vis-à-vis computer imaging, vis-à-vis alteration, is that it no longer needs to be based on the real
at all. I don't want to get into jargon—let's just say that
photography to me no longer pertains to the rhetoric
of realism; it pertains more perhaps to the rhetoric of
the unreal rather than the real or of course the hyper-
real."[31]   Eli Broad Family Foundation, Santa Monica. Courtesy Mary Boone Gallery, New York.

Gender Issues

The tableau became a locale where artists deconstructed the underlying assumptions that define the
practice of photography. **Judith Golden's** [b. 1934]
work represents the burgeoning feminist expression of
the 1970s movement that rejected modernism's values
of ideal beauty. Golden's decade-long investigation of
female personas and roles examines the ways photography can transform a subject. By humorously hand-ma-
nipulating the picture surface, Golden disregards traditional aesthetic values and emotional responses. Her
approach was part of a penchant among artists who
used handwork and appropriation to blur the distinction
between the beautiful chemically produced image and the
image that was graphically generated. Golden assumes
authority and control over her public representation,

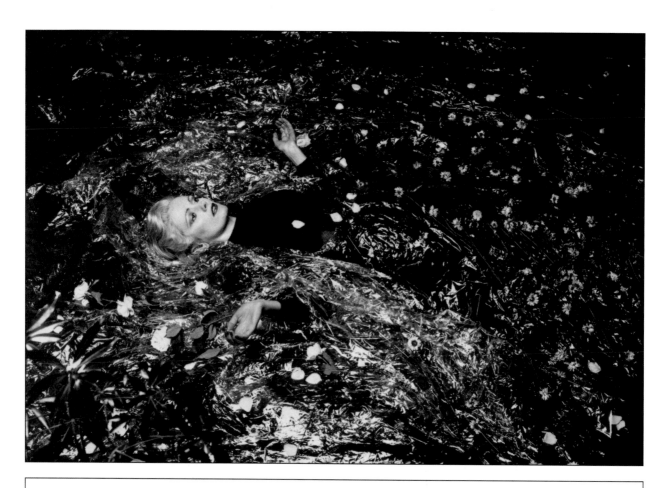

SILENTLY	LIE
VIOLENTLY	ACROSS THE POOL
THE WATERS BREAK	FALLING
AROUND THE EMERGING FORM	UPON THE GLASS WALLS
OF A WOMAN	OF THE CORRIDOR
HER TANNED FLANKS	I TOOK MY LAST CASE
STREAMING WATER	FROM THE ROOM
SHE FOLDS A TOWEL	AND CLOSED THE DOOR
AROUND HER NEW-BORN BODY	LEAVING
LONG SHADOWS OF PALMS	CALIFORNIA

18.13   VICTOR BURGIN.   *The Bridge—Venus Perdica*, 1984. 44¼ × 30³⁄₁₆ inches. Gelatin silver print with separately framed text panel.   Courtesy Victor Burgin.

creating a groundwork that other artists, such as Cindy Sherman (see next section), would build upon. Her incorporation and subversion of pictures of women from popular magazines questions the media's presentation of women and reveals how a magazine cover acts as a facade to conceal the real individual; she encourages viewers to look beneath the surface of an image to see what is really occurring (see Figure 18.14).

In *Untitled Film Stills* (1978–79) **Cindy Sherman** [b. 1954] appropriates the 1950s black-and-white movie publicity format, assuming female roles that unmask the Hollywood conventions of *film noir* and its objectification of women. Although technically self-portraits, Sherman's photographs question the stereotypical representation of all female "types" in the media and raise issues about personal and social identity for

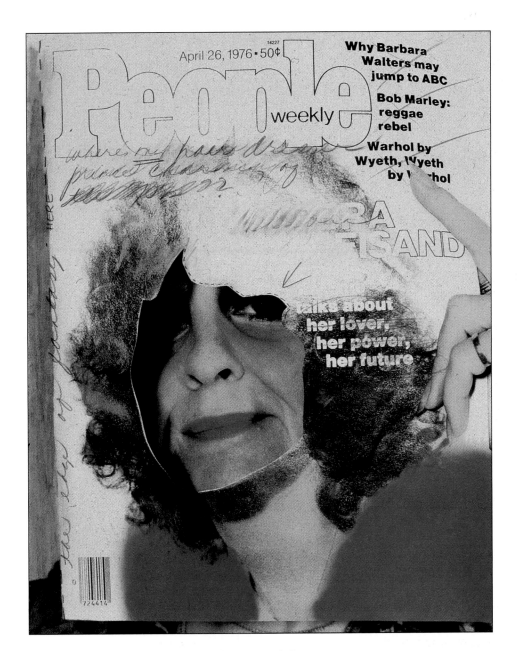

18.14   JUDITH GOLDEN.   *Barbra Streisand,* from the *Self-Portrait Series,* 1976–78. 14 × 11 inches. Gelatin silver print with oil paint.   Courtesy Judith Golden.

both sexes. The veracity of the photograph is turned upon itself in compositions that call attention to the duality that exists between the performance and the artist. Sherman's equivocal images do not show a single true self but a series of discontinuous representations, fictionalized copies, of the self that blend artifice and authenticity. This amalgam of mutable self-identities, without an original, created by bouncing off of cultural portrayals is representative of Douglas Crimp's theories on what would later be called postmodernism. According to Crimp:

We only experience reality through the pictures we make of it. To an even greater extent our experience is governed by pictures, pictures in newspapers and magazines, on television and in the cinema. Next to these pictures, firsthand experience begins to retreat, to seem more and more trivial. While it once seemed that pictures had the function of interpreting reality, it now seems that they have usurped it.[32]

Even though Sherman made her own images, Crimp considered her a postmodernist, because her pictures duplicate existing representations of women whose author is our cultural consciousness. Meaning is achieved not by what is represented, but in relation to already available images. Sherman agrees:

I didn't actually lift the image. . . . I would rehash it and spit it out, which was a different sort of process. Watching a lot of movies, looking at a lot of movie books, I absorbed as much information about the "look" of movies as possible. No one

18.15   CINDY SHERMAN.   *Untitled, #119*, 1983.
45½ × 94 inches. Chromogenic color print. Sherman
stated that: "The role-playing was intended to make
people become aware of how stupid roles are, a lot of
roles, but since it's not all that serious, perhaps that's the
moral to it, not to take anything too seriously."[33] By
purposely saying little about her work, Sherman encourages viewers to see whatever they want to see.
Courtesy Cindy Sherman and Metro Pictures.

had ever literally seen any of my images until they were produced, and yet one felt the gnawing of recognition upon
viewing them.[34]

Sherman's next project was staged large-scale
tableaux of distracted women, played by herself, in
ambiguous, often angst-ridden situations, utilizing
color to maintain a sensual edge. Sherman's self-conscious work actually possesses the qualities of formal
composition, control of light, and sense of play that
deliver aesthetic pleasure, an element that has been either discredited or denied by other postmodernists.
Sherman's psychological images of the masking of
self-identity and her subsequent movement into the
realm of myth and fairy tale, through reenacting well-
known paintings and sometimes changing the gender
of the protagonist from male to female, were popular
because audiences understood the work and did not
view her as an ideologue. When asked if she agreed
with Crimp's analysis of her work, Sherman replied:

The only way it makes sense to me now is because you've
paraphrased the core of what was in those articles. Even
though I read them at the time and understood the general
concept, I couldn't have repeated it to someone else if my life

depended on it. I've only been interested in making the work
and leaving the analysis to the critics, I could agree with
many different theories in terms of their formal concepts but
none of it really had any basis in my motivation for making
the work.[35]

By the late 1980s, Sherman had reduced the female
body to vulgar fragmented physical by-products: men-
strual blood, internal organs, vomit. In the early 1990s
she armored herself with fabricated body parts. Finally
her own body disappeared and was completely replaced by plastic prostheses, a comment on the disintegration of her own body that also stridently attacked the
fetishism of the male gaze. By the close of the 1990s,
Sherman had returned to making small black-and-white
prints that tightly depict dolls from popular culture
whose mangled appearance convey a sense of sexual
rage with an undercurrent of revenge.

Artists like **Eileen Cowin** [b. 1947] examined the
unstable dynamics of the postmodern family instead of
the individual. Cowin's *Family Docu-dramas* came out
of television soap operas and characterize the anxiety
and tension within the American family structure (see
Figure 18.16). The lack of text makes these stylized
scenes elusive. The gestures of participants tell onlookers that a dramatic confrontation is taking place, but the
details remain purposely vague so that viewers can fill
in their own details. Cowin used herself, her family, and
often her twin sister as players in these tableaux. When
the Cowin twins appeared in the same scene, viewers
could get the strange sensation that there was only one
woman instead of two. This combination entity could
simultaneously take on the roles of participant and observer, allowing viewers to indulge their voyeuristic
impulses without having to admit to them. By breach-

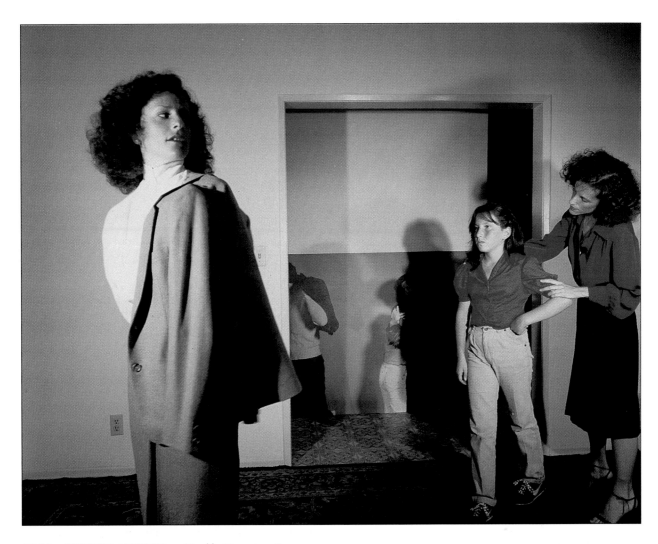

18.16   EILEEN COWIN.   *Double Departure Scene,* 1981. From the series *Family Docu-drama.* 18¾ × 23⅝ inches. Chromogenic color print.   Courtesy Eileen Cowin.

ing the conventions of familial representation and displacing their normal cultural context, Cowin both unveils and deconstructs the differences between how we think we act and how others see us.

Laurie Simmons [b. 1949] stages miniature figures and environments as stand-ins for suburban middle-class cultural models. Her strategy, surrounding *In and Around the House* (1983),[36] often included the use of a dollhouse, symbolizing the loss of childhood innocence, where small-scale figures reenact scenes of how society teaches women to behave. The toy figures provide the distancing necessary for Simmons to scrutinize and disclose the patriarchal customs that express and teach her cultural behavior models (see Figure 18.17). Dealing with similar themes, Ellen Brooks's [b. 1946] tableaux also use miniature substitutes that displace the sentimental nostalgia of the dollhouse with a disquieting and trenchant milieu of sexual anxiety.

Fabrication

Instead of reusing existing images, James Welling [b.1951] photographically converts household items into familiar, archetypal images: Crumpled aluminum foil becomes what viewers think is an abstract landscape. Expectations related to what viewers think they have seen and felt are left unfulfilled, setting up a contradictory mental state that promises emotion and insight, but only reveals the materials from which the scene was manufactured. Welling's synthetic landscapes personify the circumstances of postmodern representation that are simultaneously about something specific, everything in general, and nothing whatsoever. The work embodies the postmodern concept that all representations only refer to other representations in a process of circular meaning.

Carl Chiarenza [b.1935], working in his studio, makes collages out of scrap materials specifically to be photographed. The collages are means to an end which is the photograph. In the tradition of Alfred Stieglitz,

18.17   LAURIE SIMMONS.   *Woman Opening Re-frigerator,* 1979. 6⅛ × 9½ inches. Chromogenic color print.   Courtesy Cindy Sherman and Metro Pictures.

Minor White, and Aaron Siskind, Chiarenza's pensive symbols formulate a connection between the mind and nature that elicit inner emotional states. This work, that often references the landscape, deconstructs the formal media boundary lines and allows photography to merge with sculpture, graphic design, and painting. For Chiarenza photography is a process of transformation and as such Chiarenza utilizes photography's illusional qualities to remind viewers about the difference between a photograph and reality and that they are looking at a picture and not a concrete reality (see Figure 18.18). Chiarenza states: "The problem is to get the viewer to release the commonly but falsely held belief in the photograph as a window; to get the viewer to go through the window in a state of openness to a new experience, not a representation of one that has already occurred."[37]

Artists such as Sarah Charlesworth [b. 1947] and **James Casebere** [b. 1953], manufacture stylized "signs" to present archetypal situations. In *In The Second Half of the Twentieth Century,*[38] Casebere deploys his handcrafted miniatures along with text to examine the way society uses toys to encode cultural messages to children. The practice of building and photographing models allows artists to contemplate subjects for longer periods of time than would be possible working directly from an actual subject. The models serve as abstract stand-ins for previous ways of representing the subject, prompting viewers to question how images are loaded with intentions and how this affects their own thoughts about the subject. Synthetic archetypes also permit artists to combine or use subjects that do not physically exist, as in Casebere's moody recreation of the prison of the Bastille (see Figure 18.19). Such recreations play with notions of traditional photographic time by permitting prephotography subject matter to be fixed in photographic form.

Sandy Skoglund [b. 1946] made room-sized installations in supersaturated and contrasting colors, impossible situations, often portraying adult anxieties in childlike models and surreal confrontations between nature and culture; then she photographed them (see Figure 18.20). The final results are both temporary installations and permanent photographs. The crossing of sculpture and photography humorously expresses the continuing need artists have to be physically involved in the process of making objects. "Instead of taking everything out, like Minimalism did, I turned around and started to put everything back in,"[39] Skoglund said. The emphasis remains on controlling

18.18   CARL CHIARENZA.   *Untitled Triptych,*
56/55/54, 1996. 5 × 11 feet. Gelatin silver prints.
Courtesy of the artist.

the subject while creating juxtapositions that reveal the tension between the external and the internal worlds that is normally not visible in the natural world. Skoglund uses photography as a unifying container of meaning. She does not want to be caught up in making things look "natural" for the camera. Skoglund does not see fabrication as being cynical or out of touch with reality but as a place where "the world of ideas and the world of appearances come together"[40] so that viewers may contemplate the connection between nature and the man-made environment.

Olivia Parker's [b. 1941] enigmatic still-life assemblages, featuring organic (as in flowers) and inorganic (as in maps) subject matter, rely on a process of recontextualization to achieve their "human implications." Her juxtapositions, based on the legacy of cubism and constructivism, describe a realm of interior spaces and inner states. Parker elegantly suggests themes, such as death, sensuality, and physical and spiritual travel, but she does not provide definitive meanings. A major focus of her work has been on how our understanding of the world has shifted from alchemy and magic, to an empirical mechanical model, to a realm of theoretical mathematics (or chaos theory).[41] Parker believes that part of being creative is the ability to dive off into the unknown. Parker says: "It's not just the willingness to go off the edge; it's the ability to move and act without knowing exactly what's going to happen."[42]

The studio tableaux is combined with the legacy of surrealism in the work of **Joel-Peter Witkin** [b. 1939] to upset photography's associations with the real. Witkin blends the erotic and the macabre to examine ar-

eas that are considered off-limits by society. His morbid Hieronymus Bosch-like scenes, replete with corpses, fetuses, and hermaphrodites, suggest that hell is a current state of being. Witkin compares his work with the last trial of St. Francis of Assisi, who confronted the demise of his own flesh by kissing a leper's pus-filled lips and saw the leper turn into Christ. As with the writings of the Marquis de Sade, Witkin's grotesque permutations of bestiality, crucifixion, and sadomasochism have a commanding physical appearance that allows us to see that beauty and evil are not mutually exclusive. Witkin tells us:

> The Grotesque derives from grotto, the caverns and subterranean darkness. Saints loved the darkness because that's where you go to bring out the people who are drowning. When I, as an individual, continue my journey into perception and better realities, I have to engage the person in darkness because I'm in darkness. . . . We all have to make a decision as to what we've basically serving. If your life and work are about despair, there's no resolution, no redemption.[43]

Witkin uses the darkroom to tamper with expectations about the imagery a photograph delivers and how a photograph looks. Witkin often reinforces the brutality of his scenes by scratching the negative and staining and vignetting the print, giving us the feeling that his prints "were to be punished for the vision they carried."[44] Witkin also exposes areas of the print through tissue—flat, wrinkled, wet or dry—for a selective visual softening and uses toners to produce a warm effect. These methods, which some consider heretical for their unorthodox craftsmanship, build in an atmosphere of age, giving his prints the authority and believability of daguerreotypes. Within the studio, Witkin conjures up artifice and reality, using historical art references to speculate on allegorical, conceptual, religious, and sexual potentialities (see Figure 18.21).

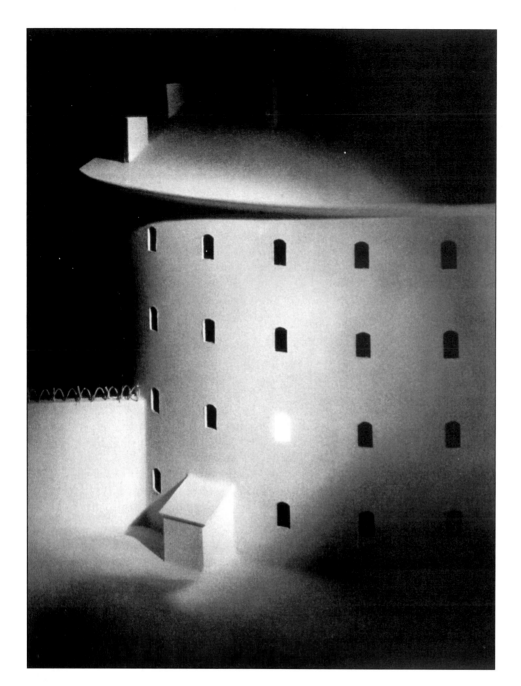

18.19   JAMES CASEBERE.   *Prison*, 1993. 22¾ × 25¾ inches. Waterless lithograph.   Courtesy CEPA Gallery, Buffalo, NY.

Fabricating environments for the camera allowed the team of **Patrick Nagatani** [b. 1945] and **Andrée Tracey** [b. 1948] to densely pack symbols from popular culture into a controlled situation. The influence of movie special effects is evident in their extensive sets and painted backdrops, which also recall Nagatani's work as a Hollywood set painter. Their images contradict our expectations as the outer logic of photographic truth commingles with modern anxieties, allowing an interior landscape to come into view (see Figure 18.22).

Nagatani's book *Nuclear Enchantment* (1991) employs similar strategies to metaphorically examine the history and social issues surrounding America's nuclear culture and the events that have shaped it, such as the internment of Japanese-Americans during World War II.

Philip Lorca diCorcia [b. 1951] and **Jeff Wall** [b. 1946] continue to use conventional means but take a similar conceptual approach to scripting out their photographs. In staging his images for the camera, diCorcia has models perform familiar domestic scenes, like a man staring into an open refrigerator at night, to convey existential dread. Wall deals with metaphysical panic by orchestrating elaborate and obsessive scenes, like *Dead Troops Talk (A Vision After an Ambush of a Red Army*

18.20   SANDY SKOGLUND.   *Revenge of the Goldfish*, 1981. 30 × 40 inches. Dye–destruction print. © 1981 Sandy Skoglund.

Patrol, near Moqor, Afghanistan, Winter 1986), 1992, that meditate on anxiety, fear, and violence. Both assemble ambiguous facts and fictions camouflaged as truth to describe real situations that defy the traditional photographic approach of grabbing the scene out of the flow of real time. By skating the edge between life and theater these imagemakers reveal certain veiled stories, mythic forms, and perplex situations in what we call life.

Altering Time and Space

Imagemakers like Jan Dibbets [b. 1941], Eve Sonneman [b. 1946], and **Lew Thomas** [b. 1932] investigated the cultural functions of photography as it was influenced by the sequential nature of film, by serial forms of minimal art, and by the use of language in conceptual art. Working with multiple images that often used the stability of the grid to ground their compositions, they expressed conceptualist concerns with real time, information systems, and theories of knowledge and process and challenged the notion that there was a singular, stable existence. Thomas would expose thirty-six frames of black-and-white 35mm film of a mundane subject, making only slight compositional changes in each frame. The result was ordered into large grids, which further diminished the subject and forced a viewer's attention to issues of time and space to examine the underlying structure of how an image is experienced. The structuralist filmmaker **Hollis Frampton** [1936–1984] and **Marion Faller** [b. 1941] utilized adjoining 35-mm frames to humorously explore real-time activity and pay homage to Eadweard Muybridge.[45] In their *Vegetable Locomotion* series (see Figure 18.23) the grid is deployed to lend the empirical appearance of science. Painter Chuck Close adopted a modified grid to assemble extreme close-ups and highly detailed photographic sections into intensely intimate canvas-sized portraits (see Chapter 17). Mike Mandel carries on a satirical critique in *Making Good Time* (1989),

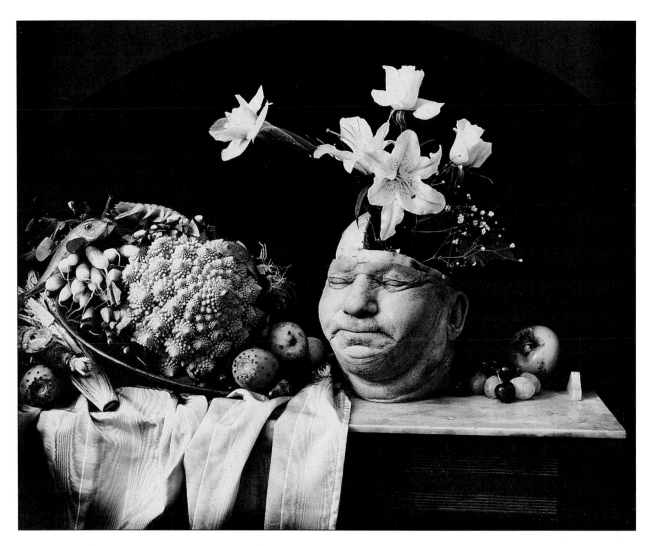

18.21 JOEL-PETER WITKIN. *Still Life, Marseilles,*
1992. 26 x 32 inches. Toned gelatin silver print. Witkin
says that: "When I'm working with a severed head, I'm
engaged in very direct spiritual dialogue. . . . My job,
given the opportunity, is to put flowers into the remain-
der of his brain, as if it were the well of *my existence*."[46]
© Joel Peter Witkin, Courtesy PaceWildensteinMacGill, New
York, and Fraenkel Gallery, San Francisco.

applying early twentieth-century beliefs about how to
scientifically manage time/space reality to the domestic
middle-class culture of southern California. Mandel's
tableaux, based on the Gilbreths' work (see Chapter
10), reveal the limited nature of photographically portrayed time and deconstruct the supposed model of reality that it assembles (see Figure 18.24). Although
their approaches were diverse these artists shared the
desire to transform and expand the photographic experience predicated on the supremacy of the single image
of a moment in time. Their efforts at reimaging time
and space helped to widen the discussion concerning
the nature of photography.

Barbara Kasten's [b. 1936] constructivist studio
assemblages formally intermix color, line, perspective,
texture, and volume to deconstruct hypothetically designed spaces into separate sectors. Her work was so in
tune with postmodern architecture that Kasten left her
studio to use actual buildings as sites to "reorganize the
visual environment."[47] Her large-scale productions, requiring a crew to handle the lights and mirrors, alter
perception by disorienting our customary sense of how
things appear (see Figure 18.25). By recording everything in a single moment, with no multiple exposures
or postcamera manipulations, Kasten asserts that there
is an unexplored realm beyond the familiar photographic reality.

The sanctity of the individual image was attacked by
artist **David Hockney** [b. 1937] as he explored multifaceted representations of a subject. Hockney was dissatisfied with the way photography rendered depth and
represented time and space. Hockney believed that people only looked at conventional photographs very
briefly because they lack "lived time." "Life is precisely what they don't have . . . photography is all right

18.22 PATRICK NAGATANI AND ANDRÉE TRACEY. *Alamogordo Blues,* 1986. 20 × 31 inches. Diffusion transfer print.

if you don't mind looking at the world from the point of view of a paralysed cyclops—*for a split second.*"[48] Hockney expresses philosopher Henri Bergson's idea that matter is in constant movement. One way to convey this reality is through a synthetic view of a subjective experience, an artist's projection of self-awareness onto the external world. Hockney did this by making numerous photographs of a scene and arranging the resulting prints into a cubistlike collage. Hockney's canvas-sized visions bring together an expanded collection of components observed over time and fabricated into a grand, extended, constantly changing entirety. By interrupting space and displacing time, Hockney breaks the perspective of the Renaissance window, carrying his swaying synthetic images beyond the edges of the frame, dissolving the rectangle (see Figure 18.26). Joyce Neimanas [b.1944] did similar work, arranging Polaroid SX-70 prints, not to reproduce the scene as the camera sees it, but according to her own internal rules of perspective.

Michael Spano [b. 1949] used a Graph-Check sequence camera to make a two-tiered grid of eight separate exposures on a single piece of 4 × 5-inch film as he actively moved the camera into and through a scene (see Figure 18.27). The motion in his work dynamically visualizes the chaotic and frenzied nature of postmodern city life: Subjects appear, disappear, reappear, and move about within a scene; Renaissance time and space collapses; ordinary transactions dissolve into uncommon incidents. The juxtaposing of images invites viewers to make fresh associations. As the narrative format dematerializes, a new perception comes into being, presenting the world in a state of multiplicity.

Holly Roberts [b. 1951] obliterates the mechanical photographic image with paint, allowing visceral feeling to dominate subject matter. Real world time is left behind as observers are engaged by the visual presence of an altered dreamlike state and the physicality of the pictures themselves, which meditate on cultural history, human emotions, the landscape, and interpersonal relationships. In addition to single images, Roberts also cut out portions of her photographs and mounted them on canvas, permitting her to work on a larger scale, combine parts of different images, and obtain a richer intricacy of surface quality and texture.

Doug and **Mike Starn** [b. 1961], the Starn Twins, have cultivated ideas of replication and the possibility of identical doubles. Often basing their work on self-conscious, historical paintings, the Starns were noticed in the 1987 Whitney Museum of American Art Biennial, a notable exhibition of contemporary art, for splattering chemicals, tearing prints, and putting pictures together with transparent tape. A pseudo-antique patina of cracked emulsions, creases, and torn edges gives their images a sense of time and decay, making their often familiar content seem like a retelling of

18.23   HOLLIS FRAMPTON AND MARION FALLER.   *Apple Advancing* from the series *Sixteen Studies from Vegetable Locomotion,* 1975. 11 × 14 inches. Gelatin silver print.   © Marion Faller.

Western history. Their hand-based studio method is not so much a postmodern deconstruction as it is a romantic reconstruction, recalling the building of Western civilization. The borrowing of figures and compositional schema from past artistic movements places them in these earlier traditions. Their complex sculptural approach, relying on glass, Plexiglas, wood, silicone, and pipe-clamps, yields seductive, fetishist objects that mock the efforts of collectors and curators to preserve original works. The Starns, rather than neutralizing the physical carrier of the photographic message, make the carrier as aesthetically consequential as the image (see Figure 18.28).

Against the widening backdrop of digital technology artists like **Adam Fuss** [b. 1961] and **Abelardo Morell** [b. 1948] alter conventional photographic notions of time and space by returning to the most direct and fundamental principles of photography. Fuss dispenses with the camera to produce large color photograms that remove the mechanical obstacles between himself and his subjects. Fuss says "I like the idea of things being as they are. A photogram can be two things at the same time. It's light passing through the egg yolk [referencing one of his photograms that incorporates egg yolk]; the fact that it looks like the sun is wonderful, but it *is* an egg yolk. It's the perfect metaphor.[49]

Morell was a street photographer who now converts rooms into pinhole camera obscuras. He then uses a view camera to make extended (eight hours and longer) exposures that record the composite image produced by the pinhole projection of what is outside the space upon what is in the room itself (see Figure 18.29). This dualistic engagement transforms the subjects into alternative visions of themselves.

Investigating the Body

The explosive growth of photography slowed and was forced to consolidate and downsize during the late 1980s and since as government funding first leveled off and then diminished. Galleries and alternative spaces closed. Auction prices dropped. Student enrollment and full-time academic teaching appointments declined. One growth area was the Internet. Today's digital imagemakers use the Internet not only as a source of information but as an exhibition forum. The Internet has become a site of expanded photographic dialogue with *"zines,"* Web site pages, discussion groups, and chat rooms offering email alternatives to standard practice. As avenues of support dropped, due to a conservative reluctance to fund art, imagemakers turned from introspective self-portraits to more public and often raw confrontations of cultural, sexual, spiritual, and social identity.

Andres Serrano's [b. 1950] tableau, *Piss Christ* (see Figure 18.30), became a cause célèbre when it was attacked by U.S. congressmen and religious leaders.[50]

18.24 MIKE MANDEL. *Emptying the Fridge,* 1985. From *Making Good Time,* 1989. 20 × 24 inches. Dye-destruction print.

Serrano integrates spiritual aspirations and the human body into his art-making, not to malign religion but to return sacred concerns to the creative process. Serrano's work is informed by "unresolved feeling about [his] own Catholic upbringing which helped [him] redefine and personalize [his] relationship with God. For [Serrano], art is a moral and spiritual obligation that cuts across all manner of pretense and speaks directly to the soul."[51] Serrano titles his work so that viewers will know the bodily source of his materials: blood, milk, menses, semen, urine. Serrano's large-scale photographs of bodily fluids opens a discourse around society's anxiety surrounding the drug- and sex-related situations by which the HIV virus is transmitted. His title, "Piss Christ," recasts a solemn cultural symbol—a crucifix—into a representation of rebellion. The use of text to alter a viewer's perception also becomes a way for Serrano to connect the corporeality of his body with the spiritual nature of Christ.

Serrano's work is postmodern; he disrupts the pleasure one expects to receive from an icon of spiritual solace. Some multicultural critics have stated that North American artists of color, like Serrano, are forced to learn the ways of the dominant culture alongside their own, often mixed cultures and live perilously between the two. Only these outsiders, like Serrano, are capable of provoking real change in how encoded cultural messages are read. Critic Lucy Lippard stated that "Serrano's work is part of the polyphonous discourse many Third World scholars have been calling for; he challenges the boundaries formed by class and race, and between abstraction and representation, photography and painting, belief and disbelief."[52] Whether photographing Ku Klux Klan members in full regalia or bodies in a morgue, Serrano attempts to "take a formal tradition and subvert it by inverting the images, abstracting that which we take for granted, in an attempt to question not only photography, but [his] own experience and social reality."[53]

During the politically conservative 1980s, the Christian right wing started a culture war as a conspicuous way for people to express their political beliefs

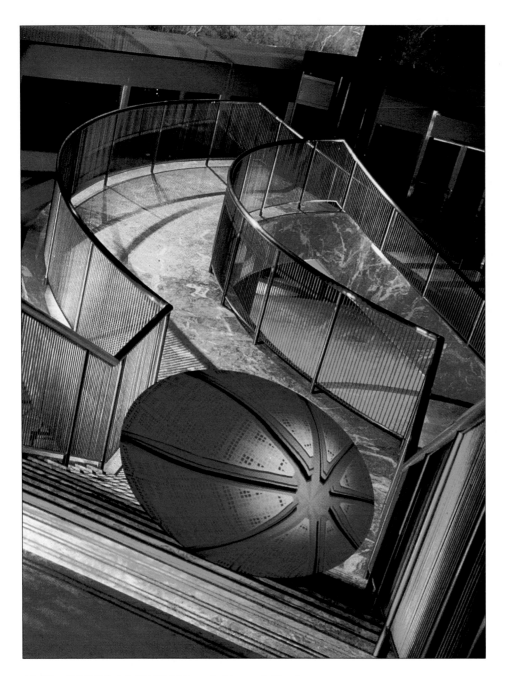

18.25   BARBARA KASTEN. *Architectural Site 6,*
July 14, 1986. 30 × 40 inches. Dye-destruction print.
Courtesy John Weber Gallery.

concerning the type of society America should be.[54]
Robert Mapplethorpe's [1946–1989] homoerotic and
sadomasochistic images became a flash point for conservative members of Congress, who found these explicit images so disturbing that they called for their
censorship.[55] Mapplethorpe's flawlessly ordered and
crafted images are built, like our own society, on conflict and contradiction. Filmmaker/author Michael Gill
calls them "calculating and intense; cold and intimate;
abstract and erotic; cruel and witty; classical and
pornographic; clinical yet human."[56] Mapplethorpe's
highly formalized yet intimate portraits push taboo areas of sexuality, especially male homosexuality in the
time of AIDS, into the mainstream gaze. Erotic work of
women, like bodybuilder Lisa Lyon, and of male
African-Americans straddle a line between formal
beauty and sexual objectification. Mapplethorpe's often classically inspired headless pictures, featuring
close looks at genitalia, represent the postmodern condition that has broken everything down into fragments
of specialized interest, signifying a cultural split between emotion and reason. *Man in Polyester Suit*
(1980) is a close-up of a black man's penis sticking out
of his pants. Mapplethorpe said: "I zero in on the part

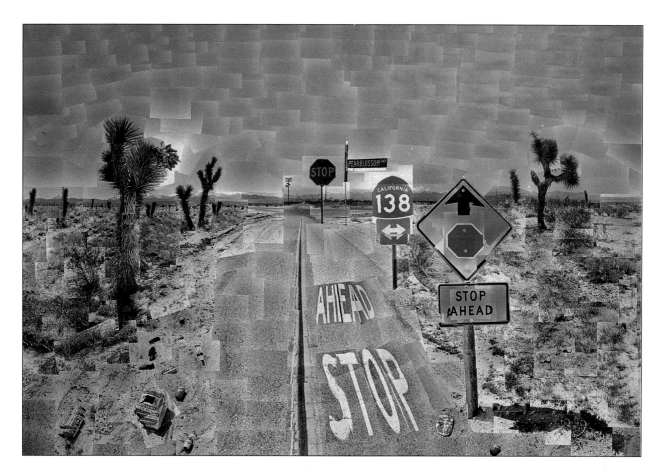

18.26   DAVID HOCKNEY.   *Pearblossom Hwy.*, April 11–18, 1986 (2nd version). 72 × 107 inches. Chromogenic color prints.   Courtesy David Hockney No. 1 U.S. Trust, Santa Monica. © David Hockney.

that I consider the perfect part in that particular model."[57]   Critics labeled the image racially obscene, presenting an African-American man as civilized on the outside while reinforcing the stereotype that underneath it all he is a wild sexual monster. By presenting highly sexualized imagery without the normal contextual framework of advertising or art, Mapplethorpe defied the constraints upon which the use of sex in the media depends, opening a national discourse on the boundaries of art, pornography, and censorship. Mapplethorpe's most haunting works are metaphors of his life and death (Mapplethorpe died of AIDS) that present the beckoning illusion of physical beauty and its erotic power, like a pristine poison mushroom that invites one to take a bite and die a horrible death (see Figure 18.31).

During an era when the privileged cultural position of straight white men continued to be assailed by women and minority groups, **John Coplans** [b. 1920] broke another taboo. When he was sixty-four, Coplans started a 15-year project that depicted details of his own aging body—hands, feet, back, thighs—in a direct, un-

flatteringly monumental manner. His formal, faceless close-ups are unrelenting and unsentimental reminders of diminishing capacity and mortality, visualizing unidealized conventions that a media-driven "youth culture" has repressed (see Figure 18.32). These looming, highly detailed images, in which the body becomes landscape, possess a sculptural quality and point out how the male body has been largely excluded from the modernist aesthetic. In forming this series Coplans asked himself:

"Why are you doing what everyone else does? Why don't you go back to that moment when you began to photograph . . . and see what happens? That's when I took my clothes off and asked my assistant to photograph me. And I was simply entranced with the process. The result was me there, but it wasn't me, it was some archaic figure, I didn't have any icongraphy, because it was all done intuitively."[58]

Nan Goldin's [b. 1953] garish, vérité-style slide and music diary, *The Ballad of Sexual Dependency* (published as a book in 1986), used 700–800 images and popular songs to spin a tale of abuse, drugs, and sex. Her images have been criticized as voyeuristic, but Goldin is a member of the group she photographs. For Goldin her camera and photographs become part of her intimate relationships, recording her subjective internal feelings rather than objective external experiences. The camera joins and clarifies what is going on between

18.27   MICHAEL SPANO.   *Untitled*, 1984. 46 × 55 inches. Gelatin silver print. Spano builds postmodern associations by juxtaposing his subject(s) in space and time. The sequence camera allows Spano to physically move through a scene as each of the eight lenses exposes a different section of the film, creating an interval of time that is longer than a single instantaneous moment.

Goldin and her subjects (see Figure 18.33). Goldin explores how sexual addiction is a motivating factor in coupling, maintaining that certain people are unable to leave destructive relationships because they are addicted to the physical gratification of sex. Goldin believes that the estrangement people bring to their relationships derives from society's expectations about gender roles. Her images are intended to confront viewers with behaviors society has wanted to keep unseen.

While postmodernism has offered photographers more self-conscious and taboo-breaking ways of depicting the body, the depiction of nude children remains a very controversial topic. The child's age and the surrounding circumstances—whether a child has the ability to decide whether or not to be photographed nude—has been a contentious issue. Jock Sturges's [b. 1947] nude portraits of prepubescent teenage girls led to the confiscation of his equipment and photographs by the FBI and $100,000 in legal fees (a grand jury refused to indict him).[59] Images of nude children have shifted from Gertrude Käsebier's nineteenth-century symbols of optimism and ideal beauty to metaphors for adult desires. The issue has been complicated by society's debate on how children should be educated and how much freedom an individual can have in a pluralistic society.

Sally Mann's [b. 1951] chronicle of her children's growing up in *Immediate Family* (1992) has raised questions concerning the boundaries of art and the responsibilities of being a parent: Can young children truly give consent to be in sensual pictures made by their parent? Do these sensual images spring from the children, or are they shaped by an adult? What are the private boundaries of a child's body? Is it courageous or is it solicitation to confront what others have turned

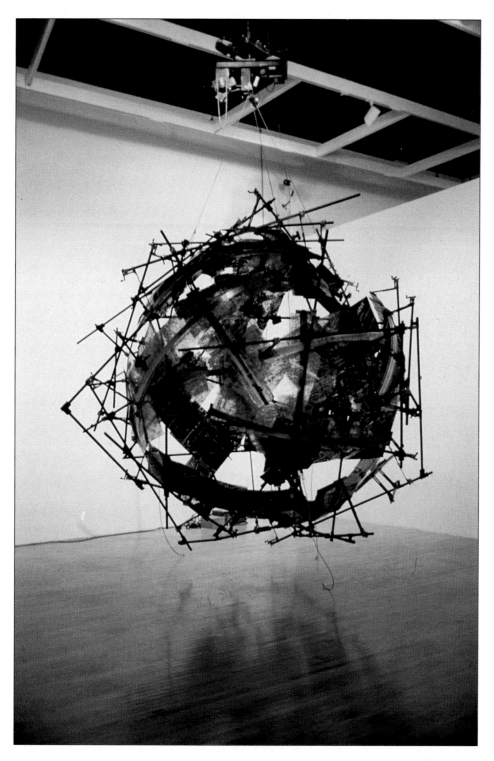

18.28   DOUG AND MIKE STARN.   *Sphere of Influence*, 1990–92. 23 × 14 × 14 feet. Toned gelatin silver film, silicone, tar, steel, Plexiglas, pipe clamps. Courtesy Mike and Doug Starn.

away from? Mann's finely crafted, self-conscious tableaux, which she asserts were made with her children's cooperation, create a web of confessional documentary and contrived fiction. Their power depends on photography's descriptive ability to evoke forgotten and/or repressed childhood feelings and memories of innocence and sexuality. Mann says that she would stop making these images if she thought they would hurt her children, and she defends her position by stating:

18.29 ABELARDO MORELL. *Camera Obscura Image of Manhattan View Looking South in Large Room,* 1996. 20 × 24 inches. Gelatin silver print.   © Abelardo Morell, courtesy Bonni Benrubi Gallery, New York, NY.

I'm responding with the only vocabulary I have to ordinary and extraordinary situations that I see around me. . . . But the more I look at the life of the children, the more enigmatic and fraught with danger and loss their lives become. That's what taking any picture is about. At some point, you just weigh the risks.[60]

Multiculturalism: Exploring Identity

For most of the twentieth century, America maintained the optimistic belief that it was a pluralistic culture, a "melting pot," that assimilated each new group that arrived into a single larger society. In the last decades of the twentieth century, numerous cultural communities have come to consider assimilation a bogus ethnocentric concept and have sought to replace it with *multiculturalism*. Multiculturalism emphasizes group identity and building self-esteem through learning about the achievements of one's own group. It decries the elevation of European cultural traditions over those of Asia, Africa, and the indigenous nonwhite populations of the Americas. It rejects remnants of colonialism and its tendency to view "other" cultures as primitive or exotic. It demands that the non-European concepts of art, family, and concepts of time be considered on their own terms.

Artists became aware of how society-at-large construct concepts of identity and reacted by making portraits of their group that countered this often stereotypical view. Imagemakers from specific cultural groups provide readings from an internal point of view to reveal how each group saw itself. They bring with them an understanding of their own cultural group's social rituals that allows them to deliver intimate, first-hand accounts of their group's values. They offer a view from within, rather than a gaze from without. For ex-

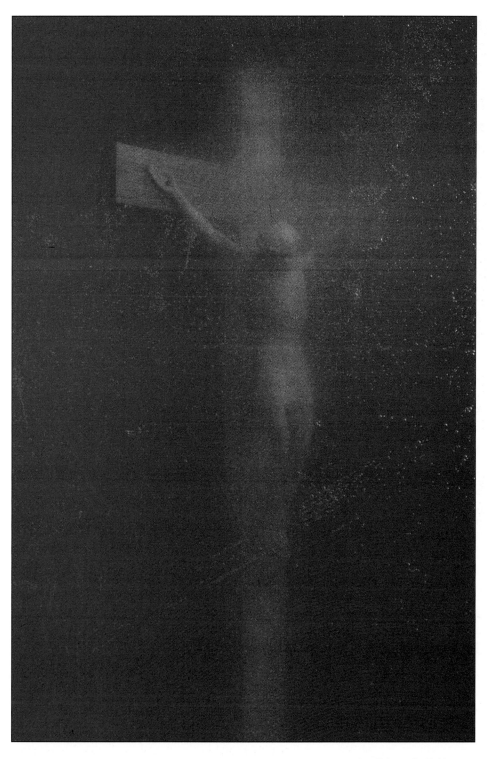

18.30   ANDRES SERRANO.   *Piss Christ*, 1987.
60 × 40 inches. Dye-destruction print. Serrano walks
the line between the sacred and the sensational in images such as *Piss Christ* and his recent *The History of
Sex*. Serrano has stated that: "I think God created the
body for a reason and we were meant to exploit it."[61]
Courtesy Paula Cooper Gallery, New York.

ample, **Dinh Q Lê's** [b. 1968] woven color images
from his series *Portraying White God* are indicative of
work by artists from subcultures struggling to establish
their identity in relation to the predominate culture (see
Figure 18.35). **Jeffrey Henson Scales** [b. 1954] and
Stephen Marc [b. 1954] present accounts from the
male African-American experience that examine urban
racial, social, and family issues with aesthetic flare
(see Figure 18.36). **The Guerrilla Girls** (formed

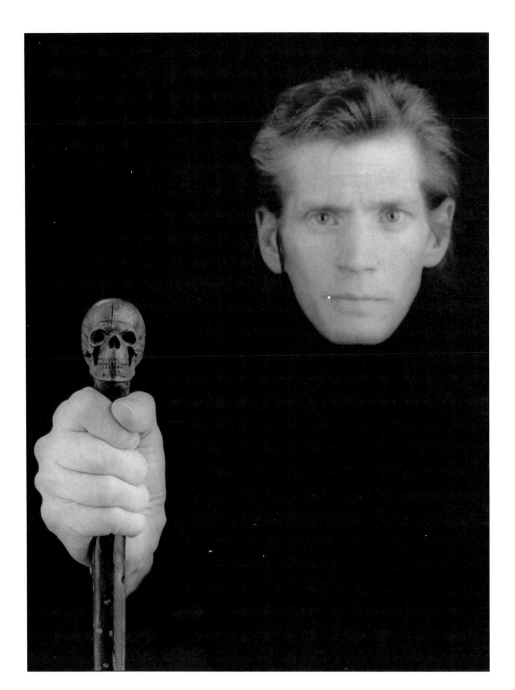

18.31   ROBERT MAPPLETHORPE.   Self-Portrait, 1988. 20 × 24 inches. Gelatin silver print.   Copyright © The Estate of Robert Mapplethorpe. Used by permission.

1985), an anonymous, feminist collaborative that protects its members' identities with gorilla masks, use photo-based images and processes in the production of street posters that criticize racism and sexism.[62] The Guerrilla Girls scrutinize the traditional role of women within visual culture as objects, rather than as makers of art (see Figure 18.37). Also working collaboratively, **Jo Spence** [1934–1992] and **Terry Dennett** [b. 1938] did a series, *Remodeling Photo-History* (1982), juxtaposing the unidealized female body with mundane landscapes featuring power transmission lines to call attention to contradictions and myths about women and nature. After Spence was diagnosed with breast cancer in 1982, the two investigated the significance society has given to women's breasts. In 1986 Spence and Rosy Martin did *Photo Therapy,* in which Spence, a former wedding photographer, explored issues surrounding women including beauty, marriage, and powerlessness. **Annette Messager's** (1943) mixed media productions that extract body details—eyes, feet, hands, mouth, nipples, nose, pubic area—rely on fragmentation and isolation to facilitate the suspension of modernist beliefs concerning identity and the body (see Figure 18.38).

18.32   JOHN COPLANS.   *Self-Portrait (Legs, Hands and Thumbs Together)*, 1985. Gelatin silver print.

Multiculturalism has increased access to education for women of color, who have been able to combine ethnic and feminist concerns in their work. Tuscarora Native American **Jolene Rickard** [b. 1956] uses photography to empower one of the oldest continually surviving aboriginal communities with a knowledge of its symbols and relationships. Rickard allows the photograph to function as a survival strategy, just as traditional storytelling or bead work was used to propagate and extend cultural meaning to the next generation. For Rickard the photograph serves to merge the material and spiritual worlds while also pointing out the lack of harmony in these worlds (see Figure 18.39).

Family stories have been the basis of the work of many people of color, especially women.[63] Family therapist Alan D. Entin believes snapshots can reveal the power structure of family existence. Entin discusses how the "background [of a photograph] can be read as information about social-cultural values, traditions, and ideals [of the family]. Photographs tell not only about what is photographed but about who is doing the photographing. Photographs are biographical as well as autobiographical."[64]

Clarissa Sligh [b. 1939] reexamines her past by looking at family snapshots to discover the differences between the pictures and her memories. Joining together the African-American storytelling tradition with a postmodern strategy of combining family snapshots with collage, cyanotype, Vandyke brownprint process, and handwritten text, Sligh underscores how difficult it can be to obtain the information one needs (see Figure 18.40). Sligh's visual connections empower her to explore the factors that have made up her African-American identity and move her beyond the characterizations that society has tagged her with. Sligh adopted an autobiographical image, Skookie, in her reworking of the universal reading primer, *Dick and Jane,* to confront class values and racial exclusions.

Holding advanced degrees in folklore and art, **Carrie Mae Weems** [b. 1953] examines the narrative systems, steeped in myth and religion, that make up a variety of African-American voices based on the historic catastrophe of slavery. In *Then What? Photographs*

18.33   NAN GOLDIN.   *Nan and Brian in Bed,
NYC,* 1983. 20 × 24 inches. Dye-destruction print.
Courtesy Nan Goldin.

and Folklore (1990), Weems uses a photo-narrative of
staged events and text to perform a cultural analysis
and meditation on the issues surrounding power. She
does this by showing the development and collapse of
a romantic relationship around a kitchen table and the
emergence of a sense of self that transcends the individual and speaks as a collective autobiography (see
Figure 18.41). Her methodology has a persistent political resonance without being didactic. Weems' work
focuses on the shared theme of what society has
deemed normal by addressing issues of race, gender,
class inequities, and stereotypes from her perspective
as an African-American woman. In the *Africa* series,
Weems explores the mythic quest for origins by sub-
versively retelling the Adam and Eve story in an
African Garden of Eden (see front cover). Weems's
work demonstrates that beauty and the pursuit for
change are not necessarily antithetical. She states: "I
want to make things that are beautiful, seductive, formally challenging and culturally meaningful. I'm also
committed to radical social change . . . . Any form of
human injustice moves me deeply . . . the battle against

all forms of oppression keeps me going and keeps me
focused."[65] Her image and sound installation, *Ritual
and Revolution* (1998), gave voice to numerous failed
revolutions of the past 200 years, and aroused more
than difficult thoughts when it was vandalized while
on display in a museum.[66]

Lorna Simpson [b. 1960] is another African-American artist whose postmodern sectioned constructions,
combining image and text, give evidence that relates to
falsehoods about class, gender, and race. Her faceless
portraits are generic emblems; they resist racist conjec-
tures about black physicality by defying the power of a
photographer to capture and impose a context on an image (see Figure 18.42). They are part of Simpson's
strategy of "not giving up everything, not giving up
your face, completely who you are and everything to
the camera."[67] By shifting the power of the gaze, Simpson disrupts the voyeuristic relationship of the observer
and the observed, asserting her identity rather than having it imposed on her.

The form of public address empowers and gives
space for others to tell their stories. Artist and industrial designer **Krzysztof Wodiczko** [b. 1943] believes
art and design should engender postmodern debate. As
an exile from Poland, Wodiczko identifies with the
voiceless *Other* in a strange land who feels boxed in by

18.34 DAVID WOJNAROWICZ. *Where I'll Go After I'm Gone,* 1988–89. 45 × 64 inches. Gelatin silver prints, acrylic, spray paint, and collage on Masonite.
David Wojnarowicz [1954–1992], who died of AIDS in 1992, interwove his life and work to wrestle with issues of identity, sexuality, and the fragility of life. In opposition to Mapplethorpe, Wojnarowicz delivered a dark vision of physical decline and death. Entirely self-taught, Wojnarowicz relied on collage, paint, and text to challenge what he called the "pre-invented existence" that discriminates and imposes a power structure on people based on ethnicity, gender, race, and sexual preference.   Courtesy P.P.O.W., New York.

preconceived categories. Wodiczko dramatizes political and social dilemmas, including colonialism, consumerism, homelessness, and slavery, through slide projections on the facades of public buildings (see Figure 18.43). Using on-site trucks with projectors and generators, Wodiczko's guerrillalike critiques take control of public places away from the dominating class and its ideology. His actions convert public spaces into theaters that confront problems many people wish to ignore.[68]

A Personal Cultural Landscape

Although much activity has been focused on power issues relating to gender, identity, and sexuality, image-makers have been re-examining how socioeconomic forces shape and define the landscape. During the nineteenth century the vast majority of landscape photographs were made by commercial photographers whose content and style were dictated by the market place. More recently, the lens of environmental organizations, whose mission is to preserve the wilderness, has formed people's perception of nature. These groups often visually establish the boundaries of nature through romantic color reproductions of pristine wilderness, which this gives people the misleading concept that anything that is not wild is not natural. The current generation of progressive landscape photographers has repudiated this point of view. Their position is that the landscape is a more complex artificial perception: A human construct that blends the artifice of civilization with natural forms. Working from the premise that anything that can be photographed can be a landscape, these photographers have personalized the ingredients of their landscapes to reflect a broader range of societal issues. This has allowed them to bring

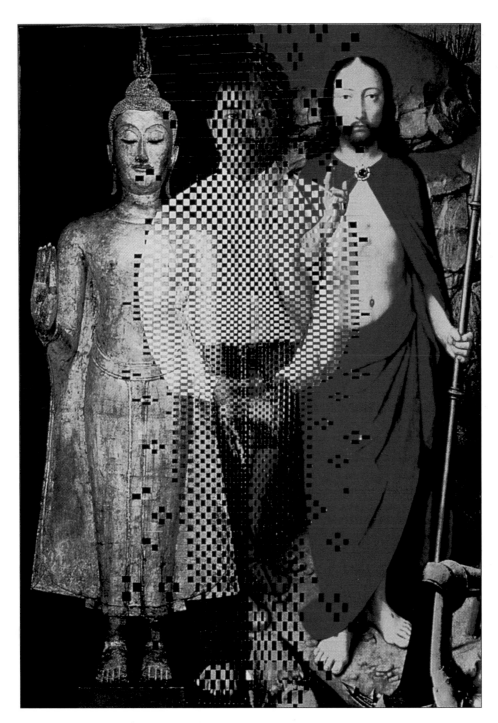

18.35 DINH Q. LÊ. *Between,* 1994. 65 × 40 inches. Chromogenic color prints with tape. Lê says: "As a Vietnamese living in a western society, educated in western institutions and surrounded by western popular culture, I am a product of both East and West. Through my work, I explore the exchange and interweaving of cultures and identities from a bicultural perspective."[69] Courtesy CEPA Gallery, Buffalo, NY.

forward environmental issues that have been produced through the collision of culture and nature. Their work announces that there is "trouble in paradise" and that we can no longer afford an attitude that segregates nature into a discrete category of wilderness. By adopting a strategy of publishing the results of their inquiries, they are able to reach a broader audience than would see such work in a gallery setting.

In his book, *Waste Land: Meditations on a Ravaged Landscape* (1997), **David T. Hanson** [b. 1948] presents beautiful yet disturbing color images (many of them

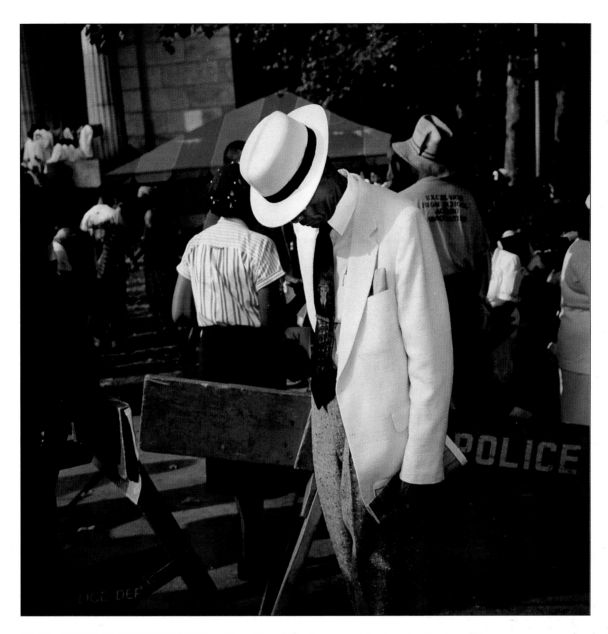

18.36   JEFFREY HENSON SCALES.   *Grant's Tomb,*
NYC, 1993. From the series *America*. 30 × 30 inches.
Iris print. Scales considers this series a work in progress
and states that "The rapidly changing appearance of the
American landscape, as well as the people who are
themselves challenging the very dated concept of na-
tionality, renders any attempt at a visual description a
work in progress. Perhaps it is my optimism that enables me to see America herself as still a work in
progress, despite our government's recent, punitive, re-
gressive policies . . . . My work can be understood as
moments and experiences, both vivid and hideous, that
can allude to the dramatic melange of possibilities that
in themselves are America."[70]   © Jeffrey Henson Scales.
Courtesy Visual Studies Workshop, Rochester, NY.

aerial views) of an American topography wounded by
the assault of industrial and military economic forces.
Hanson's images also remind us that the notion of landscape is never fixed, but is a creation of human perception and boundaries that is constantly shifting.

Richard Misrach [b. 1949] brought together 20
years of categorizing and probing society's relationship
to the desert in *Crimes and Splendors: The Desert Cantos of Richard Misrach* (1996). His use of an 8 × 10-inch
view camera allows him to create formal, lush, color
prints of the mythical Western terrain that delight viewers visually. However, Misrach fashions a jarring duality
by juxtaposing these photographs with others that show
the presence of human occupation of the desert with its
accompanying gas-powered vehicles, man-made floods,
dead animal pits, and remnants of violent and radioactive
military activity.

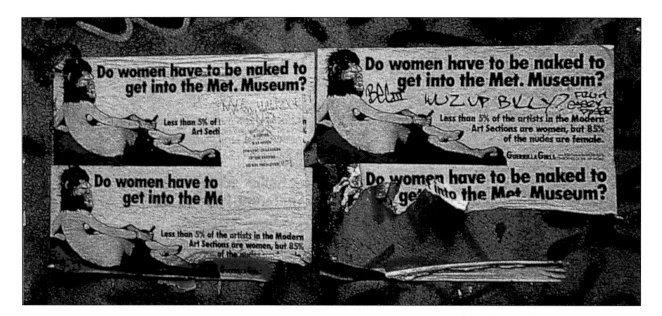

18.37   GUERRILLA GIRLS.   *Do women have to be naked to get into the Met. Museum?* 11 × 28 inches. Photo-lithograph. The Guerrilla Girls would paste posters like this around New York City to focus attention on how society has defined gender differences based on women's bodies. Such work examines how women's roles have been reinforced by images throughout the history of Western art. Obscuring the identity of individual guerrilla girls allows the group to represent all female artists who feel opposed by patriarchal systems while protecting them from retribution. Their masquerade reinforces the concept of *the Other* as it deflects the power of the male gaze.

Peter Goin [b. 1951] has produced books like *Nuclear Landscapes* (1992) that depict the contaminated and uninhabitable ruins of the scientific, technological, and military infrastructure that spawned the nuclear age. In *Humanature* (1996), Goin looks at how people have purposely re-shaped the natural world. These views reveal that the transcendental concepts of nature as power spots have been overturned as humans attempt to control the natural world by managing natural resources through engineering and biotechnology.

In *Farewell, Promised Land: Waking From the California Dream* (1999), photographer **Robert Dawson** [b. 1950] and writer Gray Brechin present their five-year study of the historic and social forces that have altered this legendary region. Although they present an often tragic view of how the land has been cynically developed, they also look to the future by representing those committed to safeguarding the state from its course of exploitation.

What these artists share is an outlook that calls for action by challenging viewers to think about the human impact on the natural world, to learn more about their relationship to their environment, and to consider changes that could offer hope for the coming generations (see Figure 18.44). Their point is that we make the landscape and it is therefore our responsibility to craft its future. Robert Dawson sums up this attitude with his statement that:

> It quickly became clear to us that depicting only devastation would invite cynicism and detachment. I felt it was essential to go beyond showing our failures by calling attention to individual and collective efforts to restore and sustain our home. People involved in preserving California are engaged in a struggle that agriculturist Wes Jackson once described as 'becoming native' to a place. Jackson argues that our culture has settled on the American landscape but that we have yet to become native to that place we call home. That process of becoming native motivates many of the people and organizations in our book. In undertaking this project, we too were searching for a way to come home.[71]

The Digital Future

Photography's fundamental concept has been about light imprinting an image at a specific juncture in space and time. Digital imaging breaks the customary prescription by giving imagemakers authority not only to determine place and time, but to control space and time. This is possible because images are formed into a binary numerical code that is electronically stored and available for future retrieval. The seamless ease with which digital technology allows photographs to be combined and manipulated suggests that future photographs might be a hybrid of mixed media based not on an observable reality of actual events, but on the inner workings of imagination. Digital imaging, like fairy tales and structuralism, offers the possibility of dreaming out loud about ourselves.

18.38 ANNETTE MESSAGER. *Mes Voeux* (*My Wishes*), 1989. 78 × 55 inches. 250 framed gelatin silver prints and string.   Courtesy Musée National D'Art Moderne Centre Georges Pomidou, Paris.

Digitalization has made the geography of the world smaller and moved our dreams inward. Before computers, ambitious people dreamed of vast empires and of making great works now they dream about computer chips. This shift not only alters notions about the nature of photography but conceptions about art and reality as well.

A major cultural issue is who gets to play in this new digital arena? In 1999 the United Nations Development Program issued a report stating that the digital gap between the wealthy nations that have logged on and those countries that have not yet plugged into the new information age is widening at a fast pace. The report said that 26 percent of Americans were using the World Wide Web, compared to 3 percent of Russians, and a small fraction of a percent of the population of South Asia. The report also stated that the United States has more computers than the rest of the world combined.[72]

This disparity is also apparent within the United States. While computer costs have plummeted, the constant need for new training, equipment, and software upgrades favors those who already have over those who do not. This exacerbates the divide between people who have integrated computers into their daily lives and people who have not, which calls attention to a pre- and post-computer generation gap. Those left behind tend to be older or young and poor. This situation is compounded by a lack of access to quality education. In 1999 about 25 percent of American youth did

18.39   JOLENE RICKARD.   *Buffalo's Smoke: Buf-falo's Breath*, 1992 . 8 × 10 inches. Gelatin silver print.

not graduate from high school and are not likely to have daily access to up-to-date equipment and software.

Those people who are not able or comfortable in keeping up with these rapid changes are in danger of becoming a technological underclass. A small but telling example can be found in how technology is transforming the tradition of the snapshot and the family album. In 1999 Kodak introduced its Picture CD service that "gives you everything you need: your full roll of pictures, organized and safely stored, plus fun interactive software (Kodak PhotoNet) [that] makes it easy to email a picture, even share a whole roll with family and friends around the world and (Kodak Pic-tureDisk) [that] lets you view your pictures on screen and more."[73] On a larger scale, the future measure between riches and poverty for countries may be gauged in terms of how financial, military, and technological power are integrated.

In the past philosophers like Immanuel Kant [1724–1804] devised categorical imperatives, which acted as preconditions for prognosticating the ultimate reality—the causes and principles that make up Western thinking. Now images define behavior, shape identities, set fashions, and permeate our memories.

Photo-based images are so interwoven into daily existence that life has become a collection of images, producing confusion between the artifice and the real.[74] As a result, entertainment and mass-media are the primary frames of reference through which we filter experience. As a bloody, botched bank robbery televised live in Los Angeles on February 28, 1997, graphically demonstrated, the authority of images goes further than framing reality. The events so paralleled director Michael Mann's noir thriller, *Heat* (1995), that the press and audience experienced a sense of déjà vu, as old style turned the news into entertainment.

Digitalization gives new meaning to Kant's belief that we should behave as if the maxims on which we act and define society become, through our will, universal laws. Digitalization converts the static into the dynamic, turning completed, unalterable ideas and works into things of the past by permitting the process to be part of the product. Professions like photojournalism, rooted in the authenticity of photographic appearance and their circulation via the halftone process, must be radically retailored in the digital age. As the public becomes more aware that it is no longer possible to discern a "legitimate" image from one that has been manipulated, it will regard news pictures as illustrations instead of reportage. Instead of knowing images through the maze of halftone dots, people will ex-

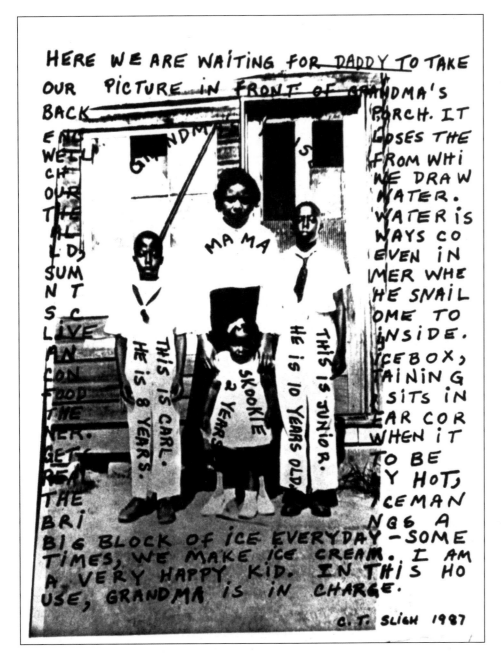

18.40 CLARISSA SLIGH. *Waiting for Daddy,* 1987. 14 × 11 inches. Vandyke print. Jeffrey Hoone, director of Light Work, observed: "Sligh invites us to look closer at the posed facades and readymade ideals in the pictures that make up the memories of our lives. Her work tells us that we often see who we are told to see, feel what we are told to feel, and know what we are told to know. She also tells us that when we are told these things often enough, we become convinced that they are true. In this process of false fulfillment the substance of our memories is disengaged and we are restricted by the images we are forced to accept."[75]

perience images primarily through a universe of electronic pixels.[76] Western society's compact with the photograph as an empirical catalog of the real is being appropriated. Digital imaging has placed the photograph in the same position the invention of photography put painting: The photograph's metamorphosis into fiction is the end of an era that has dominated photographic history to date. Since the storage disks in electronic cameras are designed to be erased and reused, the concept of a permanent master negative also disappears. If a photographer records over an original image and an editor alters the image before it is printed, we cannot even know how the image was changed. The loss of the original could affect all forms

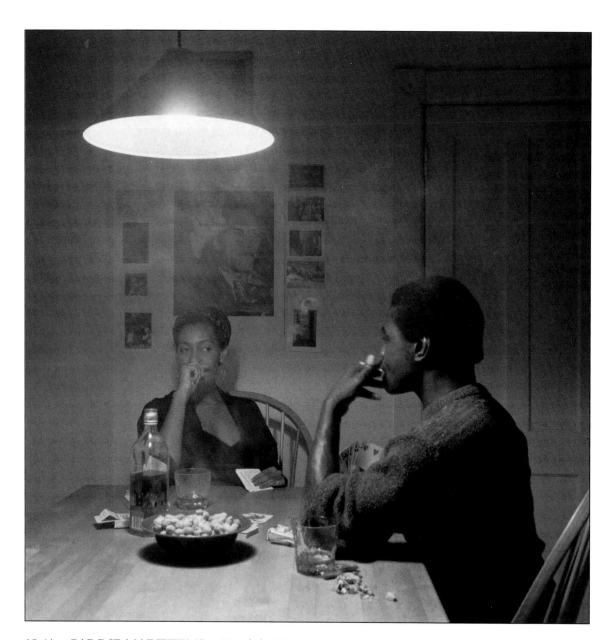

18.41   CARRIE MAE WEEMS.   *Untitled,* 1990.
28¼ × 28¼ inches. Gelatin silver print.   Courtesy
P.P.O.W., New York.

of photography, making the truthfulness of cultural history, political events, and even personal memories suspect. The fear of losing the original has surfaced in debates surrounding the ethics of genetic cloning. Even in postmodern society where the camera is part of life, there is an apprehension that a more advanced form of photographic cloning might steal our identities—that we would cease being individuals.[77]

The meaning of photographs depends on what viewers decide to believe about them. By disputing the medium's claims of objectivity through the use of photographic strategies that embrace artifice and sim-

ulation, conceptual and postmodern artists anticipated the digital message that photographs are not neutral containers of reality. Digital imaging tools have made it possible to easily improvise the content of reality, spawning artists who are accustomed to inventing worlds rather than presenting them, and viewers who are willing to accept the inventions. At the end of the twentieth century, artists are taking advantage of this expanded ability to express what makes up the "truth" of our world, and the signs that once were meant to refer to reality now point to individualized versions of that reality. Digital imaging allows truth to be made up by whatever people deem to be important and whatever they choose to subvert. Digitalization permits artists to convey the sensational and emotional weight of a subject without being bound by its physiis

�%₁₀ths

of

the

law

18.42 LORNA SIMPSON. *Self-Possession,* 1992. 25 × 20½ inches. Diffusion transfer print with engraved Plexiglas.   Courtesy Sean Kelly Gallery, New York.

cal conventions, giving imagemakers new ways to think about truth and beauty.

Nancy Burson [b. 1948] takes advantage of digital technology to create computer images of people who never existed. *Mankind* is a composite of Caucasian, Negroid, and Oriental features (see Figure 18.45). The computerized result, having no original body but only a mechanical reproduction, is emblematic of our media-based society where the image (the perception of reality) is more important than reality itself. Like a magician, Burson shows us that appearances are nothing. Along these same lines, **Tyrone Georgiou's** [b. 1947] "computer-affected" images adopt an archaeological model to illustrate the malleability of fact and information. Georgiou's fabricated archaeology uses the scientific forms and symbols, like artifacts, fossils, monoliths, mound sites, and petroglyphs, to develop ironical relationships and present a distorted sense of prehistory that consciously reminds observers

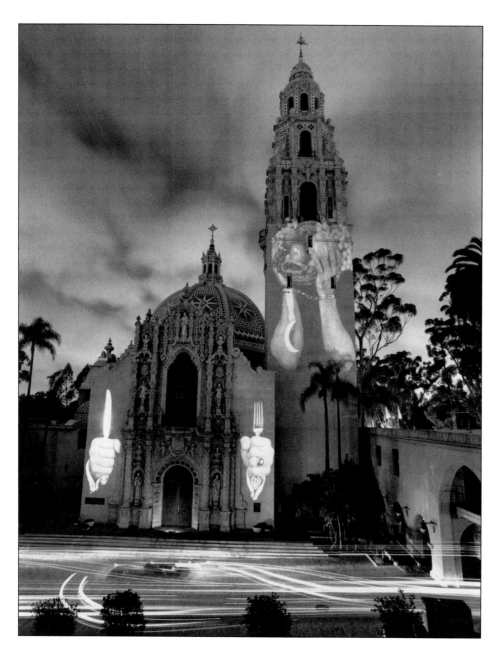

18.43   KRZYSZTOF WODICZKO.   *In The Border Projection* (part one), San Diego Museum of Man, 1988. Installation view.   *Courtesy of the artist and Galerie Lelong, New York.*

of the ease with which digital information can be distorted (see Figure 18.46). By inference, any kind of information—voice, film, video—that can be digitized can become real. This means digital truth, truth without the authority of the original, can be used to perpetrate dangerous fallacies. For instance, how will digital tools affect our cultural and private memories? People always like to "improve" on the past. Will we in our sophistication delete people and events that fall out of favor?[78] Will we convincingly rewrite a mem-

ory to alter the outcome of an event or exaggerate our strengths and play down our weaknesses? How will these new abilities change the future?

The marketing of digital image manipulation programs like PhotoShop®, introduced in 1989, coupled with new delivery formats—CD-ROMs, DVDs and the Internet—have given digitalmakers cheaper, easier, faster, and more reliable methods of making and distributing their work. **Pedro Meyer** [b. 1935] has taken advantage of these new ways of working to explore how these shifts in visual truth alter our relationship to photographic representation in his bilingual CD-ROM, *Truths & Fiction: A Journey from Documentary to Digital Photography* (1995). By combining images, Quick Time video, and narration, Meyer asks:

18.44 ROBERT DAWSON. *Private Property, Lake Tahoe,* 1988. 16 × 20 inches. Gelatin silver print.

"What should we expect or trust from an image during this time of transition between the analog and digital eras?" Meyer challenges assumptions about where photographic "truth" ends and "fiction" begins (see Figure 18.47). In the "Digital Studio" section of his CD, Meyer takes viewers through the process of making completed images. The "Correspondence" section contains a discussion by people from various countries about the aesthetic and cultural ramifications of working digitally and the struggle with the uncertain nature of the photographic image.

Another significant difference between analog and digital imagemaking tools is the scanner and how it differs from a film camera in the method it collects and records visual information. The shutter of a conventional camera exposes an entire piece of film at one time. A scanner, be it the frame in a digital camera or the platen of a flatbed scanner, only records one line at a time as it moves across its recording area. Activity occurring elsewhere in the field of view is not perceived, and motion is not recorded as a blur like it is with film, but as a series of distinct pixels, displaced in a predictable manner based on the speed and direction of motion. For instance, in the scanned animal work of **Carol Selter** [b. 1944], when the organism she places on the scanner moves in the same direction as the scanner, at about the same pace, its body is elongated because parts of it are imaged repeatedly. If it moves in the opposite direction, its body will be shortened as it moves away from the imaging line. When the animal moves at an angle to the scanner, a curved or angled, jagged track is formed because the organism is moving both obliquely and forward. These patterns are complicated by the way a particular scanner stops to send information to the computer, because then there are breaks in the pattern as the animal moves while the scanner is not recording. Nevertheless, the dynamic patterns of the process of movement are recognizable and broadly predictable as part of the final product. Renaissance perspective is destroyed and a different way of seeing a subject is presented for viewer contemplation (see Figure 18.48).

A key element of postmodern discourse can be understood in terms of photography's relinquishing its role as society's authoritative chronicler, in favor of a position that acknowledges that reality is a constantly evolving construction of our culture. As we have learned, Baudrillard does not see photography, in the words of Oliver Wendell Holmes, as a "mirror with a memory," but instead as an endless passageway of mirrors. The photo-based arts, including film, television, and video, serve as cultural agents that provide representational images that society sanctions as simulacrum of the real.[79] The decline in the documentary authority of photography has much to do with American life, where an abundance of images has led to a devaluation of a photograph's inherent believability. Two important questions

18.45   NANCY BURSON with **RICHARD CAR-LING** and **DAVID KRAMLICH.** *Mankind,* 1983–85. 7¾ × 7½ inches. Gelatin silver print.

facing the arts are: Can digital replication, the twin who offers comforting fellowship at the expense of individuality, escape the aura of the original and provide insight into reality? And can this release be effected by making a reproduction that is not only trustworthy, but at times even better than the original? The Las Vegas casino complex *New York, New York,* is an example of architectural playacting that creates a hybrid form. Here the surrogate is not only acceptable but becomes for many a preferred way of visiting New York without the per-

18.46   TYRONE GEORGIOU.   *Socket Ruins, Oregon,* 1992. From the series *Unexplained Archaeology of North America.* Digital file. Chromogenic color print.
Courtesy Tyrone Georgiou.

ceived risk of a trip to the real city.[80] This reflects the postmodern mind that believes reality doesn't exist until it is analyzed by the viewer. Another important question is: Will digitalization inspire a metaphysical meditation about the one (the original) and the many (the copies), about appearance and reality? By accepting the enigma of doubleness, it is possible to acknowledge the creative tension between the original and what the original needs to firmly fix and flourish: the copy. Like presenting ourself to ourself in a mirror, the quest for authenticity inevitably involves a doubling back, so that ultimately it takes a multiple view to know the one. The previous value of an image based on the aura of originality may be replaced by the authenticity circulation. Digital copying and Web site hits boost an image's currency and make it more widely known. This may provide the copy with an importance not available to the original: the sense of being part of an extended collective memory. A critique of this digital fabric of uniformity can be seen in Peter Weir's film *The Truman Show* (1998). It calls at-

tention to a bourgeois aesthetic that dispenses with idiosyncrasy and spontaneity in favor of sameness: A place in which everything is controlled and repeated, like the numerical values that make up a computer screen, and where nothing is permitted to be itself.

As electronic media become more enmeshed in Western culture, imagemakers inevitably ask, Will digital imaging be the death of analog photography? One answer is that it does not matter. Although the digital image has cracked the photograph's role as picturer of nature (the real world), the numerous personal Websites in cyberspace have brought photography closer to Henry Fox Talbot's *Pencil of Nature* (1844) dream, that everyone would be his "own printer and publisher." The primary issue should be what is being said, not how it is made. What continues to be astonishing is how often photographs do succeed in communicating meaning, not that they are unfailing containers of an agreed upon reality. Digital imaging is another evolutionary step in photographic imagemaking. What is important is how it will transform our thinking. In the 1970s holography was heralded as a revolutionary form of imagemaking, but at present it is used primarily as a security device on credit cards and the bar-codes in supermarkets. If electronic imagery is going to radically affect our consciousness and perception of reality,

18.47   PEDRO MEYER.   *Truths & Fiction: A Journey From Documentary to Digital Photography,* 1995. CD-ROM. This screen shot shows the original images Meyer used to digitally fashion his final representation. In the introduction to the print version of *Truths & Fiction* Joan Fontcuberta stated: "Today more than ever the artists should reestablish the role of a demiurge and sow doubts, destroy certainties, annihilate convictions so that, at the other end of confusion, a new sense and sensibility can be created."

artists and scientists need to go beyond using computers as convenient means for mimicking visions of the past and discover their native diction. The promise of digital technologies and cyberspace provides an exciting arena for the creation of something new. It not only changes the present and shifts the future, but also alters everything that went before it. With its emphasis on nonlinearity, intertextuality, and the development of multimedia, digitalization encourages the hybridization of artistic practice, which in turn actively challenges the traditional divides between mediums and their

18.48   CAROL SELTER.   *Ducklings*, 1995. 28½ × 39 inches. Chromogenic color print. Selter says: "The scanner records movement differently from the conventional camera. A filmed, one-frame analog image of my work would be straightforward tracks left in sand or some other substrate. The pixeled traces of the animal movements I record are only possible using a scanner. Most remarkable is despite the highly mediated imaging technology, each animal still creates a pattern typical of its mode of locomotion—in effect, a signature of that animal."[81]   © 1995 Carol Selter.

attendant cultural spaces. Digitalization heralds a rethinking of ideas surrounding cultural identity, nationhood, race, and our sense of place and position. What digital imaging does not change is photography's identity as a visual sign whose strength is its ability to represent the space between the constructs of the artificial and the "natural." Here at the beginning of the twenty-first century, as the first generation of imagemakers who have grown up with computers initiates its course and seeks to discover its own syntax, photography is poised for a conceptual shift from a medium that records reality to one that transforms it.

Endnotes

1   Arnulf Rainer, *Arnulf Rainer: Face-fareces, Bodyposes 1968–1975*, exhibition catalogue (Paris: Galerie Stadler, 1975), unp.

2   Chapter 17, "Changing Realities," discusses this topic in more detail.

3   John Baldessari in Jeanne Siegel ed., "John Baldessari: Recalling Ideas," *Art Talk: The Early 80s* (New York: Da Capo, 1988), unabridged reprint of *Artwords 2* (Ann Arbor, MI: UMI Research Press, 1988), 40.

4   Ibid., 38.

5   This book was part of the third project of *Four By Three*, a series of four exhibitions and concurrent artists' residencies in 1980–81, jointly sponsored by the Albright-Knox Art Gallery, CEPA Gallery (The Center for Exploratory and Perceptual Art), and Hallwalls in Buffalo, NY.

6   Ibid., 42.

7   Guglielmo Bargellesi-Severi, ed., *Robert Smithson Slideworks* (Verona, Italy: Carlo Frua, 1997), 13.

8   See Simon Schama, *Landscape and Memory* (New York: Vintage Books, 1996), 122–134. Also see Rafael López-Pedraza, Anselm Kiefer: The Psychology of "After the Catastrophe" (New York: George Braziller, 1996).

9   See Ernst van Alphen, *Caught by History: Holocaust Effects in Contemporary Art, Literature, and Theory* (Stanford, CA: Stanford University Press, 1997).

10   William Wegman, National Public Radio interview on WBFO, Buffalo, NY, January 15, 1995.

11   Interview with Lynda Morris in *Bernd* [sic] *& Hilla Becher* (London: Arts Council of Great Britain, 1974), unp. Cited in Marc Freidus, et al, *Typologies: Nine Contemporary Photographers* (Newport Beach, CA: Newport Harbor Art Museum, 1991), 15.

12   For details on the role of neoplatonism in the formation of photographic practice, see Kathleen Campbell, "Nature and the Cosmic Circle: A Philosophical Study of Conflicts in Western Culture and Their Relation To Nineteenth Century Photography," unpublished M.F.A. dissertation, University of New Mexico, Albuquerque, 1994.

13   Douglas Huebler, Title page, *Crocodile Tears* (Brief fictions re-sounding from the proposal in Variable Piece #70:1971 "to photographically document the . . . existence of everyone alive.") (Buffalo, NY: The Albright-Knox Art Gallery and CEPA Gallery, 1985), unp.

14   See Roland Barthes, "From Work to Text," in Brian Wallis, ed. *Art After Modernism: Rethinking Representation*, (Boston: Godine, 1984), 169–174.

15   James Alinder, *Cumming Photographs* (Carmel, CA: Friends of Photography, 1979), 5–6.

16   See Jean Baudrillard, "The Precession of the Simulacra," in *Simulations*, translated by Paul Foss, Paul Patton, & Philip Beitchman (New York: Semiotext(e) 1983).

17   Fredric Jameson, "Postmodernism and Consumer Society," in *The Anti-Aesthetic* (Port Townsend, WA: Bay Press, 1983), 114–15.

18   Paul Berger, "Introduction," *Seattle Subtext* (Rochester, NY: Visual Studies Workshop Press; Seattle: Real Comet Press, 1984), unp.

19   Quoted in Suzi Gablik, *The Reenchantment of Art* (New York: Thames and Hudson, 1991), 16.

20   Douglas Crimp, "Pictures," *October 8* (Spring 1979) and "The Photographic Activity of Postmodernism," *October 15* (Winter 1980).

21   See Ed Hill and Suzanne Bloom, "The Trouble with Arcadia," in *Ruins in Reverse: Time and Progress in Contemporary Art* Grant Kester (ed) CEPA Gallery Exhibition Journal, September 1998 – March 1999, Buffalo NY, 16.

22   Richard Prince, "The Perfect Tense," in Brian Wallis ed., *Blasted Allegories*, Blasted Allegories: An Anthology of Writing by Contemporary Artists (New York: The New Museum of Contemporary Art and Cambridge: The MIT Press, 1987), 416.

23   Richard Prince, *Why I go to the Movies Alone* (New York: Tantam Press, 1983), 63.

24   Ibid., 69.

25   Ibid., 70.

26   "After Sherrie Levine," Jeanne Siegel, ed., in *Art Talk: The Early 80s*, (New York: De Capo Press, 1988), 246.

27   Ibid., 247.

28   Barbara Kruger in Jeanne Siegel, ed., "Barbara Kruger: Pictures and Words, *Art Talk: The Early 80s*, 303.

29   Ibid.

30   Ibid., 307–8.

31   Kruger in Siegel, 307–8.

32   Douglas Crimp, *Pictures*, catalogue essay, (New York: Committee for the Visual Arts, Inc., 1977) 3. This show took place in New York at Artist Space in the fall of 1977 and included the work of Jack Goldstein, Sherrie Levine, and Robert Longo.

33   Cindy Sherman in Jeanne Siegel, ed., *Art Talk: The Early 80s*, 272.

34   Sherman, 283.

35   Ibid, 275.

36   See Laurie Simmons, *In and Around The House, Photographs 1976–1979* (Buffalo, NY: CEPA Gallery, 1983).

37   Email correspondence between Carl Chiarenza and the author, March 6, 1999.

38   James Casebere, *In The Second Half of the Twentieth Century* (Buffalo, NY: CEPA Gallery, 1982).

39   Nan Richardson, "Sandy Skoglund: Wild at Heart," *ARTnews* (April 1991), 115.

40 Ibid., 118.

41 See: James Gleick, *Chaos: Making a New Science* (New York: Viking Penguin, 1987).

42 Donna Conrad, "Olivia Parker: Constructions," *Camera & Darkroom*, vol. 17, No. 2 (February 1995), 38.

43 R. H. Cravens, "Joel-Peter Witkin," *Aperture: On Location*, Fall 1993, 58.

44 Kathleen McCarthy Gauss in: Andy Grundberg & Kathleen McCarthy Gauss, *Photography and Art: Interactions Since 1946* (New York: Abbeville Press, 1987), 65.

45 See Hollis Frampton, *Circles of Confusion: Film, Photography, Video Texts 1968–1980* (Rochester, NY: Visual Studies Press, 1983).

46 Gauss in Gauss, 57.

47 Barbara London, "Public Spaces and Private Places," *American Photographer* (September 1988), 48.

48 Lawrence Weschler, *Cameraworks: David Hockney* (New York: Alfred A. Knopf, 1984), 9.

49 Jamie James, "Adam Fuss: Photographer without a Camera," ARTnews vol. 94 no. 2 (February 1995), 98.

50 The work of Andres Serrano and Robert Mapplethorpe led Congress in 1989 to approve restrictions on federal aid for "obscene" art or art lacking "serious literary, artistic, political or scientific value," restrictions that were first struck down and then reinstated by the courts. Conservative members of Congress have attempted numerous times to eliminate the National Endowment for the Arts (NEA) and end federal funding of the arts entirely. In 1994, in an attempt to rescue the NEA from funding cuts, the National Council on the Arts voted to reject Serrano and two other artists, Merry Alpern and Barbara DeGenevieve, who had been recommended by the Photography Fellowship Peer Panel of the Visual Artists Program of the NEA to receive fellowships Funding was cut anyway. Individual visual arts fellowships have since been curtailed by the NEA.

51 Serrano, unpublished statement, 1989 in Lucy R. Lippard, "Andres Serrano: The Spirit and The Letter," *Art in America* (April 1990), 239.

52 Lucy R. Lippard, "Andres Serrano: The Spirit and The Letter," *Art in America* (April 1990), 239.

53 Serrano, unpublished statement, 1989, Ibid., 240.

54 See Richard Bolton, ed., *Culture Wars: Documents from the Recent Controversies in the Arts* (New York: New Press, 1992).

55 For an accessible account of the controversy surrounding Mapplethorpe's work see Terry Barrett, *Criticizing Photographs: An Introduction to Understanding Images* (Mountain View, CA: Mayfield Publishing, 1990), 110–118.

56 Michael Gill, *Image of the Body: Aspects of the Nude* (New York: Doubleday, 1989), 17.

57 Ibid., 20.

58 John Coplans in Chris Townsend, *Vile Bodies: Photography and the Crisis of Looking* (Munich & New York: Prestel-Verlag, 1998), 99.

59 See Doreen Carvajal, "Pornography Meets Paranoia," *The New York Times*, Sunday, February 19, 1995, 4-E.

60 Richard B. Woodward, "The Disturbing Photography of Sally Mann," *The New York Times Magazine* (September 27, 1992), 36. Mann denied permission to reproduce one of her images because she did not like the text. On February 26, 1999, Mann's gallery, Houk Friedman, NYC said "It would be better if Sally were portrayed as championing a certain venue rather than appearing as if she really might be doing something illicit."

61 Andres Serrano in Richard Goldstein, "The Taboo Artist," *The Village Voice*, vol. XLII, no. 10 (March 11, 1997), 51.

62 The Guerrilla Girls, dressed in gorilla masks, fishnet stockings, and black leather jackets, were formed on the streets of New York in front of the Museum of Modern Art during the exhibition *An International Survey of Recent Painting and Sculpture* (Spring 1985) to protest that of the 166 artists only 15 were women. To protect their identities, individual Guerrilla Girls use the names of dead women artists as pseudonyms. The group publishes a quarterly tabloid, *HotFlashes*.

63 For more on this theme see: Deborah Willis, *Imagining Families: Images and Voices* (Washington, D.C.: National African American Museum, Smithsonian Institution, 1994).

64 Alan D. Entin, "Family Icons: Photographs in Family Psychotherapy," *The Newer Therapies: A Sourcebook*, L. Abt and I. Stuart, eds. (New York: Van Nostrand, 1982), 209.

65 Wall statement by the artist from *Carrie Mae Weems: Recent Work, 1992–1998* at the Everson Museum, Syracuse, NY [September 26, 1998–February 14, 1999] that brought together five of Weems's installations works.

66 This incident occurred at the Everson Museum of Art, Syracuse, NY for organized the exhibition. See Erin Duggan, "Thoughtful Art, Thoughtless Act," *The Post-Standard* (Syracuse, NY), Tuesday, November 3, 1998, B1.

67 Lorna Simpson, interview with Fatimah Tobing Rony, January 11, 1992, as quoted in "We Must first See Ourselves," *Personal Narratives: Women Photographers of Color* (Winston-Salem, NC: Southeastern Center for Contemporary Art, 1993), 12. This was an exhibition catalogue, October 23, 1993–January 2, 1994, featuring the work of Lorraine O'Grady, Coreen Simpson, Lorna Simpson, Clarissa T. Sligh, Carrie Mae Weems, Pat Ward Williams, and Deborah Willis.

68 For more on public art see *The Citizen Artist: 20 years of Art in the public Arena, An Anthology from High Performance Magazine, 1978–1998,* Linda Frye Burnham and Steven Durland, eds. (Gardiner, NY: Critical Press, 1998).

69 Dinh Lê in Robert Hirsch, "Ritual: Social Identity/A View From Within," *CEPA Journal* (Spring/Summer 1994), 4.

70 Artist statement from *Pictures From America*, a Visual Studies Workshop Traveling Exhibition, Rochester, NY.

71 Robert Dawson, Preface, Robert Dawson and Gray Brechin, *Farewell, Promised Land: Waking from the California Dream* (Berkeley and Los Angeles: University of California Press, 1999), xvi.

72   See David E. Sanger, "Agony of Victory: America Finds It's Lonely At the Top" in *The New York Times,* Sunday, July 18, 1999, section 4, 1 & 4.

73   "Put Your Pictures on Your PC," *The Buffalo News,* Sunday, July 18, 1999, Wegman's grocery store supplement, 23.

74   A seemingly alluring juncture of the camera and the computer is the proliferation of 24-hour live camera Web sites where people encourage strangers to view, even ask questions, about the most intimate and generally banal details of their lives.

75   Jeffrey Hoone, *Clarissa Sligh: The Presence of Memory*, Robert B. Menschel Photography Gallery, 24, (Syracuse: Light Work, 1991), unp.

76   See Robert Hirsch and AnJanette Brush, "From Dots to Pixels: Tracing Truth & Desire," *U-Turn E-zine* 1:1 (1998) @ http://www.uturn.org (Chicago, IL).

77   George Johnson, "Soul Searching, Don't Worry. A Brain Still Can't Be Cloned," *The New York Times*, Sunday, March 2, 1997, Section 4, 1, 16.

78   See David King, *The Commissar Vanishes: The Falsification of Photographs and Art in Stalin's Russia* (New York: Metropolitan, 1997).

79   See Jean Baudrillard, *America*, "Utopia Achieved," trans. by Chris Turner (London: Verso, 1988).

80   Ada Louise Huxtable, "Living With the Fake, and Liking It," *The New York Times*, vol. CXLVI, no. 50,747 (Sunday, March 30, 1997, Section 2), 1, 40.

81   Email with Carol Selter and author, February 25, 1999.

A

Ades, Dawn. *Photomontage.* New York: Pantheon Books, 1976.

After Daguerre: Masterworks of French Photography (1848–1900) from the Bibliothèque Nationale. New York: Metropolitan Museum of Art; Paris: Berger-Levrault, 1980.

B

Baldwin, Gordon. *Looking at Photographs: A Guide to Technical Terms.* Malibu, CA: J. Paul Getty Museum; London: British Museum Press, 1991.

Bannon, Anthony. *The Photo-Pictorialists of Buffalo.* Buffalo, NY: Media Study, 1981.

Barrow, Thomas F., et al. *Reading into Photography: Selected Essays, 1959–1980.* Albuquerque: University of New Mexico Press, 1982.

Barthes, Roland. *Camera Lucida, Reflections on Photography.* New York: Hill and Wang/A division of Farrar, Straus, Giroux, 1981.

Bates, Lowry and Isabel Barrett. *The Silver Canvas: Daguerreotype Masterpieces from the J. Paul Getty Museum.* Los Angeles: J. Paul Getty Museum, 1998.

Batchen, Geoffrey. *Burning with Desire: The Conception of Photography.* Cambridge and London: The MIT Press, 1997.

Bayer, Jonathan, et al. *Reading Photographs: Understanding the Aesthetics of Photography.* New York: Pantheon Books, 1977.

Beaton, Cecil, and Gail Buckland. *The Magic Image: The Genius of Photography from 1839 to the Present Day.* Boston and Toronto: Little, Brown and Company.

Benjamin, Walter. "The Work of Art in the Age of Mechanical Reproduction," *Illuminations.* Hannah Arendt, ed. Translated by Harry Zohn. New York: Schocken Books, 1969.

Berger, John. *About Looking.* New York: Pantheon Books, 1980.

Bertell, Richard, with Roy Flukinger, Nancy Keeler and Sydney Kilgore. *Paper and Light: The Calotype in Great Britain and France, 1839–1870.* Boston: David R. Godine, 1984.

The Black Photographers Annual. 4 vols. Brooklyn, NY: Black Photographers Annual, Inc. 1973–1976.

Bloom, John. *Photography at Bay: Interviews, Essays and Reviews.* Albuquerque: University of New Mexico Press, 1993.

Bolton, Richard, ed. *The Contest of Meaning: Critical Histories of Photography.* Cambridge and London: MIT Press, 1989.

Bolton, Richard, ed. *Culture Wars: Documents from the Recent Controversies in the Arts.* New York: New Press, 1992.

Booth, Pat, ed. *Master Photographers: The World's Greatest Photographers on Their Art and Technique.* New York: Clarkson N. Potter, Inc., 1983.

Borcoman, James. *Magicians of Light: Photographs from the Collection of the National Gallery of Canada.* Ottawa: National Gallery of Canada, 1993.

Braun, Marta. *Picturing Time: The Work of Etienne-Jules Marey (1830–1904).* Chicago and London: The University of Chicago Press, 1992.

Brewster, Sir David. *The Stereoscope, Its History, Theory and Construction.* Facsimile ed. Dobbs Ferry, NY: Morgan & Morgan, 1971.

Bright, Deborah, ed. *The Passionate Camera: Photography and Bodies of Desire.* London and New York: Routledge, 1998.

Browne, Turner, and Elaine Partnow. *Macmillan Biographical Encyclopedia of Photographic Artists and Innovators.* New York: Macmillan Publishing Company, 1983.

Buerger, Janet E. *The Era of the French Calotype.* Rochester: International Museum of Photography at George Eastman House, 1982.

Buerger, Janet E. *French Daguerreotypes.* Chicago: University of Chicago Press, 1980.

Buerger, Janet E. *The Last Decade: The Emergence of Art Photography in the 1890s.* Rochester: International Museum of Photography at George Eastman House, 1984.

Bunnell, Peter C. *Degrees of Guidance: Essays on 20th-Century American Photography.* Cambridge: Cambridge University Press, 1993.

Bunnell, Peter, ed. *A Photographic Vision: Pictorial Photography, 1889–1923.* Salt Lake City, UT: Peregrine Smith, 1980.

Burgin, Victor, ed. *Thinking Photography.* London: Macmillan Press, 1982.

Burnham, Linda Frye and Durland, Steven. *The Citizen Artist: 20 Years of Art in the Public Arena,* Vol. 1. Gardiner, NY: Critical Press, 1998.

C

Caffin, Charles H. *Photography as a Fine Art.* Facsimile edition. Hastings-on-Hudson, NY: Morgan & Morgan, Inc., 1971.

Camera Work: The Complete Illustrations 1903–1917. "Alfred Stieglitz, 291 Gallery and Camera Work" by Pam Roberts. Köln: Taschen, 1997.

Capa, Cornell, ed. *The Concerned Photographer.* New York: Grossman Publishers in cooperation with The International Fund for Concerned Photography, 1968, 1972.

A Century of Japanese Photography. Intro. by John Dower. New York: Random House, Pantheon Press, 1980.

Coar, Valencia Hollins, ed. *A Century of Black Photographers, 1840–1960*. Providence: Rhode Island School of Design, 1983.

Coe, Brian. *Colour Photography: The First Hundred Years, 1840–1940*. London: Ash & Grant, 1978.

Coe, Brian, and Paul Gates. *The Snapshot Photograph*. London: Ash & Grant, 1977.

Coke, Van Deren. *Avant-Garde Photography in Germany, 1919– 1939*. New York: Pantheon Books, 1982.

Coke, Van Deren. *The Painter and the Photographer, from Delacroix to Warhol*. Albuquerque: University of New Mexico Press, 1964. Revised and enlarged edition, 1972.

Coke, Van Deren, with Diana C. Du Pont. *Photography: A Facet of Modernism*. New York: Hudson Hills Press, 1986.

Coke, Van Deren, ed. *One Hundred Years of Photographic History: Essays in Honor of Beaumont Newhall*. Albuquerque: University of New Mexico Press, 1975.

Coleman, A. D. *The Digital Evolution: Visual Communication in the Electronic Age. Essays, Lectures and Interviews 1967–1998*. Tucson: Nazraeli Press, 1999.

Coleman, A. D. *Critical Focus: Photography in the International Image Community*. Tucson, AZ: Nazraeli Press, 1995.

Coleman, A. D. *The Grotesque in Photography*. New York: Ridge Press/Summit Books, 1977.

Coleman, A. D. *Light Readings: A Photography Critic's Writings, 1968–1978*. New York: Oxford University Press, 1979.

Collins, Kathleen, ed. *Shadows and Substance: Essays on the History of Photography*. Bloomfield Hills, MI: The Amorphous Institute Press, 1990.

Coote, Jack H. *The Illustrated History of Colour Photography.*

Surrey, England: Fountain Press, 1993.

Crary, Jonathan. *Techniques of the Observer: On Vision and Modernity in the Nineteenth Century*. Cambridge and London: The MIT Press, 1990.

Crimp, Douglas with photographs by Louise Lawler. *On the Museum's Ruins*. Cambridge: The MIT Press, 1993.

D

Daniel, Pete, Merry A. Foresta, Maren Stange and Sally Stein. *Official Images: New Deal Photography*. Washington D.C.: Smithsonian Institution, 1987.

Darrah, William Culp. *Stereo Views: A History of Stereographs in America and Their Collection*. Gettysburg, PA: Times and News Publishing Co., 1964.

Daval, Jean-Luc. *Photography: History of an Art*. Translated by R. F. M. Dexter. New York: Rizzoli International Publications, Inc., 1982.

Davis, Keith F. *An American Century of Photography: From Dry-Plate to Digital.*

The Hallmark Photographic Collection, Second Edition, Revised and Enlarged. Kansas City, MO: Hallmark Cards in Association with Harry N. Abrams, 1999.

Deribere, M., ed. *Encyclopedia of Colour Photography*. Watford, England: Fountain Press, 1962.

Diamonstein, Barbaralee, et al. *Visions and Images: American Photographers on Photography*. New York: Rizzoli, 1981.

Doty, Robert. *Photo-Secession: Stieglitz and the Fine-Art Movement in Photography*. Foreword by Beaumont Newhall. New York: Dover Publications, Inc., 1978.

Druckery, Timothy, ed. *Electronic Culture: Technology and Visual*

Representation. New York: Aperture, 1996.

Dugan, Thomas. *Photography Between Covers*. Rochester: Light Impressions, 1979.

E

Earle, Edward W., ed. *Points of View: The Stereograph in America—A Cultural History*. Rochester, NY: The Visual Studies Workshop Press in collaboration with the Gallery Association of New York State, 1979.

Easter, Eric, et al., eds. *Songs of My People. African-Americans: A Self-Portrait*. Boston: Little, Brown and Company, 1992.

Eauclaire, Sally. *American Independents: Eighteen Color Photographers*. New York: Abbeville Press, Inc., 1987.

Eauclaire, Sally. *The New Color Photography*. New York: Abbeville Press, Inc. 1981.

Eder, Josef Maria. Edward Epstean (trans.). *History of Photography*. 4th ed. New York: Columbia University Press, 1945. Reprint. Dover Publications, Inc., 1978.

Edgerton, Harold E., and James R. Killian, Jr. *Moments of Vision: The Stroboscopic Revolution in Photography*. Cambridge, MA: MIT Press, 1979.

Eisinger, Joel. *Trace and Transformation: American Criticism of Photography in the Modernist Period*. Albuquerque: University of New Mexico Press, 1995.

Emerson, Peter Henry. *Naturalistic Photography for Students of the Art*. 1889; 3rd ed., 1899. Reprint. New York: Arno Press, 1973.

Enyeart, James, ed. *Decade by Decade: Twentieth Century American Photography from the Collection of the Center for Creative Photography*. Boston, Toronto, London: Bullfinch Press, Little, Brown and Company, 1989.

Eskind, Andrew H., and Greg Drake, eds. *Index to American Photographic Collections.* 2nd ed. Boston: G.K. Hall and Co., 1990.

Evans, Jessica, ed. *The Camerawork Essays: Context and Meaning in Photography.* London: Rivers Oram Press, 1997.

Ewing, William A. *The Body: Photographs of the Human Body.* San Francisco: Chronicle Books, 1994.

Experimental Vision: The Evolution of the Photogram Since 1919. Denver: Roberts Rinehart, Denver Art Museum, 1994.

F

Fiedler, Jeannine, ed. *Photography at the Bauhaus.* London: Dirk Nishen Publishing, 1990.

Fleming, Paula Richardson, and Judith Lynn Luskey. *Grand Endeavors of American Indian Photography.* Washington, D.C.: Smithsonian Institution Press, 1993.

Flukinger, Roy. *The Formative Decades: Photography in Great Britain, 1839–1920.* Austin: University of Texas Press, 1985.

The Founding and Development of Modern Photography in Japan. Tokyo: Tokyo Metropolitan Museum of Photography, 1995.

Frampton, Hollis. *Circles of Confusion: Film, Photography, Video Texts 1968–1980.* Rochester: Visual Studies Workshop, 1983.

Freidus, Marc, et al. *Typologies: Nine Contemporary Photographers.* New York: Rizzoli, 1991.

Freund, Gisèle. *Photography and Society.* Boston: David R. Godine, Publisher, 1980.

Friedman, Joseph S. *History of Color Photography.* Boston: American Photographic, 1944. Reprint. London and New York: Focal Press, 1968.

Frizot, Michel, ed. *A New History of Photography.* English language edition. New York: Könemann, 1998.

Fulton, Marianne. *Eyes of Time: Photojournalism in America.* Boston, Toronto, London: New York Graphic Society, 1988.

Fulton, Marianne, ed. *Pictorialism into Modernism: The Clarence H. White School of Photography.* New York: Rizzoli, in association with George Eastman House and the Detroit Institute of Arts, 1996.

G

Galassi, Peter. *American Photography, 1890–1965.* New York: Harry N. Abrams, Inc., Museum of Modern Art, 1995.

Galassi, Peter. *Before Photography: Painting and the Invention of Photography.* New York: Museum of Modern Art, 1981.

Gernsheim, Helmut, and Alison Gernsheim. *The History of Photography: From the Camera Obscura to the Beginning of the Modern Era.* New York, St. Louis, San Francisco: McGraw-Hill Book Company, 1969.

Gernsheim, Helmut, and Alison Gernsheim. *L. J. M. Daguerre: The History of the Diorama and the Daguerreotype.* New York: Dover Publications, Inc., 1968.

Gernsheim, Helmut, and Alison Gernsheim. *The Origins of Photography.* Vol. 1 of *The History of Photography.* New York: Thames and Hudson, 1982.

Gernsheim, Helmut, and Alison Gernsheim. *The Rise of Photography, 1850–1880: The Age of Collodion.* Vol. 2 of *The History of Photography.* New York: Thames and Hudson, 1988.

Glassman, Elizabeth, and Marilyn F. Symmes. *Cliché-verre: Hand-Drawn, Light-Printed, A Survey of the Medium from 1839 to the Present.* Detroit: The Detroit Institute of Arts, 1980.

Goldberg, Vicki. *Photography in Print: Writings from 1816 to the Present.* New York: Simon and Schuster, 1981.

Goldberg, Vicki. *The Power of Photography: How Photographs Changed Our Lives.* New York: Abbeville Press, 1991.

Goldschmidt, Lucien, and Weston J. Naef. *The Truthful Lens: A Survey of the Photographically Illustrated Book, 1844–1914.* New York: The Grolier Club, 1980.

Gover, C. Jan. *The Positive Image: Women Photographers in Turn-of-the-Century America.* Albany: The State University of New York Press, 1988.

Green, Jonathan. *American Photography: A Critical History, 1945 to the Present.* New York: Harry N. Abrams, Inc., 1984.

Green, Jonathan, ed. *Camera Work: A Critical Anthology.* Millerton, NY: Aperture, 1973.

Green, Jonathan, ed. *The Snapshot.* Millerton, NY: Aperture, 1974.

Greenough, Sarah, et al. *On the Art of Fixing a Shadow: One Hundred Fifty Years of Photography.* Washington, D.C.: National Gallery of Art; Chicago: The Art Institute of Chicago, 1989.

Grundberg, Andy. *Crisis of the Real: Writings on Photography, 1974–1989.* New York: Aperture, 1990.

Grundberg, Andy, and Kathleen Gauss. *Photography and Art: Interactions Since 1946.* New York: Abbeville Press, Inc., 1987.

Guimond, James. *American Photography and the American Dream.* Chapel Hill: University of North Carolina Press, 1991.

H

Hales, Peter Bacon. *Silver Cities: The Photography of American Urbanization, 1839–1915.* Philadelphia: Temple University Press, 1984.

Hambourg, Maria Morris, and Christopher Phillips. *The New Vision: Photography Between the World Wars: The Ford Motor Company Collection at the Metropolitan Museum of Art.* New York: Harry N. Abrams, 1989.

Hambourg, Maria Morris, et al. *The Walking Dream: The Gilman Collection of Photography.* New York: Harry N. Abrams, Metropolitan Museum of Art, 1993.

Handy, Ellen. Pictorial Effect, *Naturalistic Vision: The Photographs and Theories of Henry Peach Robinson and Peter Henry Emerson.* Norfolk, VA: Chrysler Museum, 1994.

Harker, Margaret. *The Linked Ring: The Secession Movement in Photography in Britain, 1892–1910.* London: Heineman, 1979.

Haworth-Booth, Mark. *The Golden Age of British Photography, 1839–1900.* Millerton, NY: Aperture, 1984.

Haworth-Booth, Mark. *Photography: An Independent Art: Photographs from the Victoria and Albert Museum 1839–1996.* Princeton: Princeton University Press, 1997.

Henisch, Heinz K., and Bridget A. Henisch. *The Photographic Experience.* University Park: The Palmer Museum of Art and Pennsylvania State University Press, 1988.

Henisch, Heinz K., and Bridget A. Henisch. *The Photographic Experience.* University Park: The Palmer Museum of Art and Pennsylvania State University Press, 1988.

Heron, Liz, and Val Williams, eds. *Illuminations: Women Writing on Photography from the 1850's to the Present.* Durham: Duke University Press, 1996.

Heyman, Therese Thau, ed. *Seeing Straight: The f.64 Revolution in Photography.* Oakland, CA: Oakland Museum, 1992.

Hill, Paul, and Thomas Cooper, eds. *Dialogue with Photography.* New York: Farrar/Straus/Giroux, 1979.

Homer, William Innes. *Alfred Stieglitz and the American Avant-Garde.* Boston: New York Graphic Society, 1977.

Homer, William Innes. *Alfred Stieglitz and the Photo-Secession.* Boston: A New York Graphic Society Book, Little, Brown and Company, 1983.

Hoy, Anne H. *Fabrications: Staged, Altered and Appropriated Photographs.* New York: Abbeville Press, 1987.

Hurley, F. Jack. *Portrait of a Decade: Roy Stryker and the Development of Documentary Photography in the Thirties.* Baton Rouge: Louisiana State University Press, 1972.

I

In/sight: African Photographers, 1940 to the Present. Introduction by Clare Bell. New York: Guggenheim Museum and Abrams, 1996.

Italy: One Hundred Years of Photography. Texts by Cesare Colombo and Susan Sontag. Florence: Fratelli Alinari, 1988.

Ivins, William Jr. *Prints and Visual Communication.* Cambridge: Harvard University Press, 1953.

J

Jammes, André, and Eugenia Parry Janis. *The Art of French Calotype.* Princeton, NJ: Princeton University Press, 1983.

Jammes, André, and Robert Sobieszek. *French Primitive Photography.* Millerton, NY: Aperture, 1970.

Janus, Eugenia Parry and Max Kozloff, et al. *Vanishing Presence.* Minneapolis: Walker Art Center, 1989.

Jay, Bill, and Margaret Moore, eds. *Bernard Shaw on Photography.* Salt Lake City: Peregrine Smith Books, 1989.

Jay, Bill. *Cyanide and Spirits: An Inside-Out View of Early Photography.* Munich: Nazraeli Press, 1992.

Jay, Bill. *Occam's Razor: An Outside-In View of Contemporary Photography.* Munich: Nazraeli Press, 1992.

Jeffrey, Ian. *Photography: A Concise History.* New York and Toronto: Oxford University Press, 1981.

Johnson, Brooks, ed. *Photography Speaks: 66 Photographers on Their Art.* New York: Aperture, The Chrysler Museum, 1989.

Johnson, Brooks, ed. *Photography Speaks II: 70 Photographers on Their Art.* New York: Aperture, The Chrysler Museum of Art, 1995.

Jones, John. *Wonders of Stereoscope.* New York: Alfred A. Knopf, 1976.

Jussim, Estelle. *The Eternal Moment: Essays on the Photographic Image.* New York: Aperture, 1989.

Jussim, Estelle, and Elizabeth Lindquist-Cock. *Landscape as Photograph.* New Haven and London: Yale University Press, 1985.

K

Kemp, Martin. *The Science of Art: Optical Themes in Western Art from Brunelleschi to Seurat.* New Haven and London: Yale University Press, 1990.

Kozloff, Max. *The Privileged Eye: Essays on Photography.* Albuquerque: University of New Mexico Press, 1987.

Krauss, Rosalind, et al. *L'Amour Fou: Photography & Surrealism.* Washington, D.C.: The Corcoran Gallery of Art; New York: Abbeville, Press, 1985.

L

Lemagny, Jean-Claude, and André Rouillé, eds. *A History of Photography: Social and Cultural Perspectives.* English edition transl. by Janet Lloyd. Cambridge, New York, New Rochelle, Melbourne, Sydney: Cambridge University Press, 1987.

Lippard, Lucy R., ed. *Partial Recall.* New York: The New Press, 1992.

Livingston, Jane. *The New York School Photographs, 1936–1963.* New York: Stewart, Tabori & Chang, 1992.

Lowary, Bates and Isabel Barrett. *The Silver Canvas: Daguerreotype Masterpieces from the J. Paul Getty Museum.* Los Angeles: J. Paul Getty Museum, 1998.

Lyons, Nathan ed. *Photographers on Photography: A Critical Anthology.* Englewood Cliffs, NJ: Prentice-Hall, 1966.

Margolis, Marianne Fulton, ed. *Camera Work: A Pictorial Guide.* New York: Dover Publications, 1978.

M

Malcolm, Janet. *Diana & Nikon: Essays on the Aesthetic of Photography.* Boston: David R. Godine, 1980.

Mathews, Oliver. *The Album of Carte-de-visite and Cabinet Portrait Photographs 1854–1914.* London: Reedminster Publications, Ltd., 1974.

McCauley, Elizabeth Anne. *Likenesses: Portrait Photography in Europe 1850–1870.* Albuquerque: Art Museum, University of New Mexico Press, 1980.

McLuhan, Marshall. *Understanding Media: The Extension of Man.*

New York, Toronto, London: McGraw-Hill Book Company, 1964.

Mitchell, William J. *The Reconfigured Eye: Visual Truth in the Post-Photographic Era.* Cambridge, MA: MIT Press, 1992.

Moholy, Lucia. *100 Years of Photography: 1839–1939.* Hammondsworth, Middlesex: Penguin Books, Ltd. 1939.

Mora, Gilles. *Photo Speak: A Guide to the Ideas, Movements, and Techniques of Photography, 1839 to the Present.* New York: Abbeville Press, 1998.

Morgan, Hal, and Andreas Brown. *Prairie Fires and Paper Moons, the American Photographic Postcard: 1900–1920.* Boston: David R. Godine, 1981.

Morgan, Willard D., ed. *The Encyclopedia of Photography.* 20 vols. New York: Greystone Press, 1963–64.

Moutoussamy-Ashe, Jeanne. *Viewfinders: Black Women Photographers.* New York: Dodd, Mead, 1986. Reprint. New York: Writers and Readers Publishing, 1993.

Mrazkova, Daniela. *Masters of Photography: A Thematic History.* London: Hamlyn, 1987.

N

Naef, Weston J., and James N. Wood. *Era of Exploration: The Rise of Landscape Photography in the American West, 1860–1885.* Buffalo: Albright-Knox Art Gallery; New York: The Metropolitan Museum of Art, 1975.

Naef, Weston. *Fifty Pioneers of Modern Photography: The Collection of Alfred Stieglitz.* New York: The Metropolitan Museum of Art and Viking Press, 1978.

Naef, Weston. *The J. Paul Getty Museum Handbook of the Photographs Collection.* Malibu, CA: The J. Paul Getty Museum, 1995.

Negroponte, Nicholas. *Being Digital.* New York: Alfred A. Knopf, 1995.

Newhall, Beaumont. *The Daguerreotype in America.* 3rd revised edition. New York: Dover Publications, Inc., 1976.

Newhall, Beaumont. *Focus: Memoirs of a Life in Photography.* Boston: Little, Brown, Bulfinch Press, 1993.

Newhall, Beaumont. *The History of Photography: From 1839 to the Present.* 5th ed. New York: Museum of Modern Art, 1982.

Newhall, Beaumont. *Latent Image: The Discovery of Photography.* Garden City, NY: Anchor Books, Doubleday & Co., Inc., 1967.

Newhall, Beaumont, ed. *Photography: Essays & Images.* New York: The Museum of Modern Art, 1980.

New Topographics: Photographs of a Man-altered Landscape. Intro. by William Jenkins. Rochester: The International Museum of Photography at George Eastman House, 1975.

O

Ostroff, Eugene, ed. *Pioneers of Photography: Their Achievements in Science and Technology.* Springfield, VA: The Society for Imaging Science and Technology, 1987.

P

Palmquist, Peter E., ed. *A Bibliography of Writings by and about Women in Photography, 1850–1990.* 2nd ed. Arcata, CA: Peter E. Palmquist, 1994.

Palmquist, Peter E., ed. *Camera Friends & Kodak Girls II: 60 Selections by and about Women in Photography, 1855–1965.* New York: Midmarch Arts Press, 1995.

Pantheon Photo Library. *Early Color Photography.* New York: Pantheon Books, 1986.

Parker, William E., ed. *Art and Photography: Forerunners and Influences.* Layton, UT: Peregrine Smith Books, 1985.

Petro, Patrice, ed. *Fugitive Images: From Photography to Video.* Bloomington and Indianapolis: Indiana University Press, 1995.

Petruck, Peninah, ed. *The Camera Viewed: Writings on Twentieth Century Photography,* 2 vols. New York: E. P. Dutton, 1979.

Phillips, Christopher, ed. *Photography in the Modern Era: European Documents and Critical Writings, 1913–1940.* New York: Metropolitan Museum of Art; Aperture, 1989.

Pictorialism in California: Photographs 1900–1940. Malibu, CA: J. Paul Getty Museum; San Marino, CA: Henry E. Huntington Library and Art Gallery, 1994.

Points of Entry. A series of three books: *A Nation of Strangers.* Essays by Vicki Goldberg. San Diego: Museum of Photographic Arts, 1995. *Reframing America.* Essay by Andrei Codrescu. Tucson: Center for Creative Photography, University of Arizona, 1995. *Tracing Cultures.* Essays by Rebecca Solnit and Ronald Takai. San Francisco: Friends of Photography, 1995.

Pollack, Peter. *Picture History of Photography.* New York: Harry N. Abrams, Inc., 1969.

Pultz, John. *The Body and the Lens: Photography 1839 to the Present.* New York: Harry N. Abrams, Inc., 1995.

Pultz, John, and Catherine B. Scallen. *Cubism and American Photography, 1910–1930.* Williamstown, MA: Sterling and Francine Clark Art Institute, 1981.

R

Rabb, Jane M., ed. *Literature & Photography: Interactions 1840–1990.* Albuquerque: University of New Mexico Press, 1995.

Rinhart, Floyd and Marion. *The American Daguerreotype.* Athens: University of Georgia Press, 1981.

Ritchin, Fred. *In Our Own Image: The Coming Revolution in Photography.* New York: Aperture, 1990.

Rosenblum, Naomi. *A History of Women Photographers.* New York: Abbeville Press, 1994.

Rosenblum, Naomi. *A World History of Photography.* Revised edition. New York: Abbeville Press, 1989.

Rudisill, Richard. *Mirror Image: The Influence of the Daguerreotype on American Society.* Albuquerque: University of New Mexico Press, 1971.

S

Sandweiss, M. A., ed. *Photography in 19th-Century America.* Fort Worth: Amon Carter Museum; New York: Harry N. Abrams, 1991.

Schaaf, Larry J. *Out of the Shadows: Herschel, Talbot and the Invention of Photography.* New Haven, CT: Yale University Press, 1992.

Scharf, Aaron. *Art and Photography.* London: Allen Lane, 1968, and Baltimore: The Penguin Press, 1969.

Scharf, Aaron. *Pioneers of Photography.* New York: Harry N. Abrams, Inc., 1975.

Schwartz, Henrich.: *Art and Photography: Forerunners and Influences.* Layton, UT: Peregrine M. Smith Books, 1985.

Sipley, Louis Walton. *A Half Century of Color.* New York: The Macmillan Company, 1951.

Sobieszek, Robert A. *The Art of Persuasion: A History of Advertising Photography.* New York: Harry N. Abrams, Inc., 1988.

Sobieszek, Robert A. *Masterpieces of Photography from the George Eastman House Collections.* New York: Abbeville Press, 1985.

Solomon-Godeau, Abigail. *Photography at the Dock: Essays on Photographic History, Institutions and Practices.* Minneapolis: University of Minnesota Press, 1991.

Sontag, Susan. *On Photography.* New York: Farrar, Straus, and Giroux, 1973.

Sullivan, Constance, ed. *Women Photographers.* New York: Harry N. Abrams, Inc., 1990.

Squiers, Carol, ed. *The Critical Image: Essays on Contemporary Photography.* Seattle: Bay Press, 1990.

Stott, William. *Documentary Expression and Thirties America.* New York: Oxford University Press, 1973.

Strong Hearts: Native American Voices and Visions. New York: Aperture, 1995.

Stryker, Roy, and Nancy Wood. *In This Proud Land: America 1935–1943 as Seen in FSA Photographs.* Greenwich, CT: New York Graphic Society, 1974.

Szarkowski, John. *Looking at Photographs: 100 Pictures from the Collection of the Museum of Modern Art.* Boston: New York Graphic Society; New York: The Museum of Modern Art, 1973.

Szarkowski, John. *Mirrors and Windows: American Photography Since 1960.* New York: The Museum of Modern Art, 1978.

Szarkowski, John. *The Photographer's Eye.* New York: The Museum of Modern Art and Doubleday & Co., 1966.

Szarkowski, John. *Photography Until Now.* New York: The Museum of Modern Art; Boston, Toronto: Bulfinch Press, Little, Brown and Company, 1989.

T

Taft, Robert. *Photography and the American Scene: A Social History, 1839–1889* (1938). Reprint ed. New York: Dover Publications, Inc., 1964.

Tagg, John. *The Burden of Representation: Essays on Photographies and Histories.* Minneapolis: University of Minnesota Press, 1993.

Tausk, Peter. *Photography in the 20th Century.* London: Focal Press, 1980.

Teitelbaum, Matthew, ed. *Montage and Modern Life, 1919–1942.* Cambridge and London: MIT Press; Boston: The Institute of Contemporary Art, 1992.

Thomas, Lew, ed. *Photography and Language.* San Francisco: NFS Press, 1979.

Townsend, Chris. *Vile Bodies: Photography and the Crisis of Looking.* Munich and New York: Prestel-Verlag, 1998.

Trachtenberg, Alan, ed. *Classic Essays on Photography.* New Haven, CT: Leete's Island Books, 1980.

Trachtenberg, Alan, and Lawrence W. Levine. *Documenting America, 1935–1943.* Berkeley: University of California Press, 1988.

Tucker, Ann, ed. *The Woman's Eye.* New York: Alfred A. Knoft, 1973.

20th Century Photography: Museum Ludwig Cologne. Introduction by Marc Scheps. Koln: Taschen, 1996.

W

Wade, John. *The Camera from the 11th Century to the Present Day.* Leicester, England: Jessop, 1990.

Walch, Peter, ed. *Perspectives on Photography: Essays in Honor of Beaumont Newhall.* Albuquerque: University of New Mexico Press, 1986.

Waldsmith, John S. *Stereo Views: An Illustrated History and Price Guide.* Radnor, PA: Wallace-Homestead Book Co., 1991.

Wall, E. J. *The History of Three Color Photography.* Boston: American Photographic Publishing Company, 1925. Reprint. London and New York: Focal Press, 1970.

Wallis, Brian, ed. *Art After Modernism: Rethinking Representation.* New York: The New Museum of Contemporary Art & Boston: David R. Godine, Publisher, 1984.

Wallis, Brian, ed. *Blasted Allegories: An Anthology of Writings by Contemporary Artists.* New York: The New Museum of Contemporary Art & Cambridge: MIT Press, 1987.

Weaver, Mike. *The Art of Photography.* New Haven: Yale University Press, 1989.

Weaver, Mike, ed. *British Photography in the 19th Century: The Fine Art Tradition.* Cambridge: Cambridge University Press, 1989.

Welling, William. *Photography in America: The Formative Years, 1839–1900.* New York: Thomas Y. Crowell Company, 1978. Reprint. Albuquerque: University of New Mexico Press, 1987.

Westerbeck, Colin, and Joel Meyerowitz. *Bystander: A History of Street Photography.* Boston: Little, Brown, Bulfinch Press, 1994.

Williams, Val. *Women Photographers: The Other Observers, 1900 to the Present.* London: Virago Press Ltd., 1986.

Willis-Thomas, Deborah. *An Illustrated Bio-Bibliography of Black Photographers, 1940–1988.* New York: Garland, 1989.

Willis, Deborah, ed. *Picturing Us: African American Identity in Photography.* New York: The New Press, 1994.

Witkin, Joel-Peter, ed. *Harms Way: Lust & Madness, Murder & Mayhem.* Santa Fe: Twin Palms Publishers, 1994.

Witkin, Lee D., and Barbara London. *The Photograph Collector's Guide.* Boston: New York Graphic Society, 1979.

Wood, John. *The Art of the Autochrome: The Birth of Color Photography.* Iowa City: University of Iowa Press, 1993.

Wood, John, ed. *The Daguerreotype: A Sesquicentennial Celebration.* Iowa City: University of Iowa Press, 1989.

Y

Yochelson, Bonnie and Erwin, Kathleen A., Fulton, Marianne, ed. *Pictorialism into Modernism: The Clarence H. White School of Photography.* New York: Rizzoli, 1996.

INDIVIDUAL ARTISTS

A

BERENICE ABBOTT

McCausland, Elizabeth, and Berenice Abbott. *Changing New York*. New York: E. P. Dutton, 1939. Revised and reprinted as *New York in the Thirties, as Photographed by Berenice Abbott*. New York: Dover Publications, 1973.

Van Haaften, Julia, ed. *Berenice Abbott, Photographer: A Modern Vision*. New York: New York Public Library, 1989.

Yochelson, Bonnie. *Berenice Abbott: Changing New York*. New York: New York Press: Museum of the City of New York, 1997.

ANSEL ADAMS

Ansel Adams: An Autobiography. Boston: Little, Brown, 1985; paperback ed., 1996.

Ansel Adams: Images, 1923–1974. Boston: New York Graphic Society, 1974.

Newhall, Nancy. *Ansel Adams: The Eloquent Light*. San Fancisco: Sierra Club, 1963.

ROBERT ADAMS

Adams, Robert. *The New West: Landscapes Along the Colorado Front Range*. Colorado: Colorado Associated University Press, 1974.

Adams, Robert. *Why People Photograph: Selected Essays and Reviews*. New York: Aperture, 1994.

ALINARI BROTHERS (COMPANY)

Fratelli Alinari: Florence "1852–1992". Bologna, Italy: Graftche Zanini, 1993.

Zevi, Filippo. *Alinari-Photographers of Florence, 1852–1920*. Edinburgh and Florence: Idea Editions and Edizioni Alinari in association with the Scottish Arts Council, 1978.

THOMAS ANNAN

Annan, Thomas. *Photographs of the Old Closes and Streets of Glasgow, 1868–1877*. Introduction by Anita Ventura Mozeley. Reprint. New York: Dover Publications, 1977.

Stevenson, Sara. *Thomas Annan, 1829–1887*. Edinburgh: National Galleries of Scotland, 1990.

DIANE ARBUS

Arbus, Doon, and Marvin Israel, eds. *Diane Arbus*. Millerton, NY: Aperture; Museum of Modern Art, 1972.

Arbus, Doon, and Marvin Israel, eds. *Diane Arbus: Magazine Work*. Millerton, NY: Aperture, 1984.

Bosworth, Patricia. *Diane Arbus: A Biography*. New York: Alfred A. Knopf, 1984.

Arbus, Doon, and Yolanda Cuomo, eds. *Untitled: Diane Arbus*. New York: Aperture, 1995.

EUGÈNE ATGET

Nesbit, Molly, ed. *Atget's Seven Albums*. New Haven, CT: Yale University Press, 1992.

Szarkowski, John, and Maria Morris Hambourg. *The Work of Atget*. Vol. 1: *Old France*; Vol. 2: *The Art of Old Paris*; Vol. 3: *The Ancien Régime*; Vol. 4: *Modern Times*. New York: Museum of Modern Art, 1981, 1982, 1984, 1985.

ANNA ATKINS

Schaaf, Larry J. *Sun Gardens: Victorian Photograms by Anna Atkins*. Millerton, NY: Aperture, 1985.

RICHARD AVEDON

Avedon, Richard. *In the American West, 1979–1984*. New York: Harry N. Abrams, 1985.

ÉDOUARD BALDUS

Daniel, Malcolm R. *The Photographs of Édouard Baldus*. New York: Metropolitan Museum of Art; Montreal: Canadian Centre for Architecture, 1994.

B

GEORGE N. BARNARD

Barnard, George N. *Photographic Views of Sherman's Campaign*. Preface by Beaumont Newhall. New York: Dover Publications, 1977.

Davis, Keith F., ed. *George N. Barnard: Photographer of Sherman's Campaign*. Kansas City, MO: Hallmark Cards, 1990.

THOMAS BARROW

McCarthy Gauss, Kathleen. *Inventories and Transformations: The Photographs of Thomas Barrow*. Albuquerque: University of New Mexico Press, 1986.

HERBERT BAYER

Cohen, Arthur A. *Herbert Bayer: The Complete Work*. Cambridge, MA: MIT Press, 1988.

Herbert Bayer: Photographic Works. Essay by Beaumont Newhall. Los Angeles: Arco Center for Visual Art, 1977.

E. J. BELLOCQ

Bellocq: Photographs from Storyville. The Red-Light District of New Orleans. Introduction by Susan Sontag. Interviews by John Szarkowski. Preface by Lee Friedlander. New York: Random House, 1996.

KARL BLOSSFELDT

Blossfeldt, Karl. *Urformen der Kunst*. Tübingen, Germany: Ernst Wasmuth Verlag, 1928.

Blossfeldt, Karl. *Natural Art Forms: 120 Classic Photographs*. Mineola: Dover, 1998.

ERWIN BLUMENFELD

Teicher, Hendel, ed. *Blumenfeld: My One Hundred Best Photographs*. New York: Rizzoli, 1981.

MARGARET BOURKE-WHITE

Callahan, Sean, ed. *The Photographs of Margaret Bourke-White.* New York: Bonanza; Greenwich, CT: New York Graphic Society, 1972.

Goldberg, Vicki. *Margaret Bourke-White: A Biography.* New York: Harper and Row, 1986.

SAMUEL BOURNE

Ollman, Arthur. *Samuel Bourne: Images of India.* Carmel, CA: Friends of Photography, 1983.

MATTHEW BRADY

Meredith, Roy. *Matthew Brady's Portrait of an Era.* New York and London: W. W. Norton, 1982.

BILL BRANDT

Bill Brandt Behind the Camera: Photographs, 1928–1983. Introduction by Mark Haworth-Booth. Essay by David Mellor. Millerton, NY: Aperture, 1985.

Warburton, Nigel. *Bill Brandt: Selected Texts and Bibliography.* World Photographers Reference Series, vol. 5. Boston: G. K. Hall, 1993.

BRASSAÏ (GYULA HALÁSZ)

Brassaï. Intro. by Lawrence Durrell. New York: Museum of Modern Art, 1968.

Brassaï. *Paris de Nuit.* Paris: Arts et Métiers Graphiques, 1933.

Brassaï. *The Secret Paris of the 1930s.* Published in Paris as *Le Paris Secret des Années 30.* New York: Random House, Pantheon Books, 1976.

Warehime, Marja. *Brassaï. Images of Culture and the Surrealist Observer.* Baton Rouge and London: Louisiana State University Press, 1996.

MANUEL ALVAREZ BRAVO

Livingston, Jane. *M. Alvarez Bravo.* Boston: David R. Godine;
Washington D.C.: The Corcoran Gallery of Art, 1978.

FRANCIS BRUGUIÈRE

Enyeart, James. *Bruguière: His Photographs and His Life.* New York: Alfred A. Knopf, 1977.

WYNN BULLOCK

de Cock, Liliane, ed. *Wynn Bullock, Photography: A Way of Life.* Dobbs Ferry, NY: Morgan and Morgan, 1973.

WILLIAM S. BURROUGHS

Sobieszek, Robert A. Afterword by William S. Burroughs. *Ports of Entry: William S. Burroughs and the Arts.* Los Angeles: Los Angeles County Museum of Art, 1996.

C

HARRY CALLAHAN

Davis, Keith F. *Harry Callahan: New Color, 1978–1987.* Kansas City, MO: Hallmark Cards, 1988.

Davis, Keith F., ed. *Harry Callahan: Photographs.* Kansas City, MO: Hallmark Cards, 1988.

JULIA MARGARET CAMERON

Cameron, Julia Margaret. *Victorian Photographs of Famous Men and Fair Women.* New York: Harcourt, Brace, 1926. Expanded and reprinted, with an introduction by Virginia Woolf and Roger Fry; preface and notes by Tristam Powell, London: Hogarth Press, Boston: David R. Godine, 1973.

Ford, Colin. *The Cameron Collection: An Album of Photographs by Julia Margaret Cameron Presented to Sir John Herschel.* New York: Van Nostrand Reinhold; London: National Portrait Gallery, 1975.

Gernsheim, Helmut. *Julia Margaret Cameron, Her Life and Photographic Work.* New York: Aperture, 1975.

Weaver, Mike. *Julia Margaret Cameron: 1815–1879.* Boston:
Little, Brown, New York Graphic Society, 1984.

Wolf, Sylvia. *Julia Margaret Cameron's Women.* Chicago: Art Institute of Chicago & New Haven: Yale University Press, 1998.

CORNELL CAPA

Cornell Capa: Photographer. Boston: Little, Brown, Bulfinch Press, 1992.

ROBERT CAPA

Robert Capa. New York: Random House, Pantheon Books, 1989.

Whelan, Richard. *Robert Capa: A Biography.* New York: Alfred A. Knopf, 1985.

PAUL CAPONIGRO

Paul Caponigro: Masterworks from Forty Years. Carmel, CA: Photography West Graphics, 1993.

LEWIS CARROLL

Cohen, Morton N. *Lewis Carroll: A Biography.* New York: Alfred A. Knopf, 1995.

Gernsheim, Helmut. *Lewis Carroll, Photographer.* 1949. Rev. ed. New York: Dover Publications, 1979.

HENRI CARTIER-BRESSON

Cartier-Bresson, Henri. *The Decisive Moment.* New York: Simon and Schuster, 1952.

Galassi, Peter. *Henri Cartier-Bresson: The Early Work.* New York: Museum of Modern Art, 1987.

Henri Cartier-Bresson: Photographer. Boston: Little, Brown, 1992.

CLEMENTINA, LADY HAWARDEN

Clementina, Viscountess Hawarden, Photographer. London: Victoria and Albert Museum, 1989.

CHUCK CLOSE

Shorr, Robert, et al. *Chuck Close.* New York: Museum of Modern Art, 1998.

ALVIN LANGDON COBURN

Weaver, Mike. *Alvin Langdon Coburn: Symbolist Photographer.* New York: Aperture, 1986.

IMOGEN CUNNINGHAM

Dater, Judy. *Imogen Cunningham: A Portrait.* Boston: New York Graphic Society, 1979.

Lorenz, Roland. *Imogen Cunningham: Ideas Without End: A Life and Photographs.* San Francisco: Chronicle Books, 1993.

Rule, Amy, ed. *Imogen Cunningham: Selected Texts and Bibliography.* World Photographers Reference Series, vol. 2. Boston: G. K. Hall, 1992.

EDWARD S. CURTIS

Davis, Barbara A. *Edward S. Curtis: The Life and Times of a Shadow Catcher.* San Francisco: Chronicle Books, 1985.

Lyman, Christopher M. *The Vanishing Race and Other Illusions: Photographs of Indians by Edward S. Curtis.* New York: Random House, Pantheon Books, 1982.

Native Nations: First Americans as Seen by Edward Curtis. Boston: Little, Brown, Bulfinch Press, 1993.

D

LOUIS JACQUES MANDÉ DAGUERRE

Daguerre, Louis Jacques Mandé. *An Historical and Descriptive Account of the Various Processes of the Daguerreotype and the Diorama.* 1839. Reprint, with an introduction by Beaumont Newhall, New York: Winter House, 1971.

Gernsheim, Helmut, and Alison Gernsheim. *L. J. M. Daguerre: The History of the Diorama and the Daguerreotype.* 2nd ed. New York: Dover Publications, 1968.

BRUCE DAVIDSON

Bruce Davidson Photographs. Intro. by Henry Geldzahler. New York: Agrinde Publications LTD., 1978.

ROBERT DAWSON

Dawson, Robert and Gray Brechin. *Farewell, Promised Land: Waking From the California Dream.* Berkeley and Los Angeles: University of California Press, 1999.

F. HOLLAND DAY

F. Holland Day: Suffering the Ideal. Essay by James Crump. Santa Fe: Twin Palms Publishers, 1995.

Jussim, Estelle. *Slave to Beauty: The Eccentric Life and Controversial Career of F. Holland Day.* Boston: David R. Godine, 1981.

RAJA LALA DEEN DAYAL

Worswick, Clark. *Princely India: Photographs by Raja Lala Deen Dayal, Court Photographer (1884–1910) to the Premier Prince of India.* New York: Alfred A. Knopf, Pennwick/Agrinde, 1980.

ROY DECARAVA

Alinder, James, ed. *Roy DeCarava, Photographs.* Introduction by Sherry Turner DeCarava. Carmel, CA: Friends of Photography, 1981.

DeCarava, Roy, and Langston Hughes. *The Sweet Flypaper of Life.* New York: Simon and Schuster, 1955.

Galassi, Peter. *Roy DeCarava: A Retrospective.* New York: Museum of Modern Art, 1996.

ROBERT DEMACHY

Robert Demachy—Pictorialist. Paris: Bookking International, 1990.

ADOLF DE MEYER

Ehrekranz, Anne. *A Singular Elegance: The Photographs of Baron Adolph de Meyer.* San Francisco: Chronicle Books; New York: International Center of Photography, 1994.

ROBERT DOISNEAU

Hamilton, Peter. *Robert Doisneau: A Photographer's Life.* New York: Abbeville Press, 1995.

Three Seconds from Eternity: Photographs by Robert Doisneau. Boston: New York Graphic Society, 1979.

E

THOMAS EAKINS

Danly, Susan, and Cheryl Leibold. *Eakins and the Photograph: Works by Thomas Eakins and His Circle in the Collection of the Pennsylvania Academy of the Fine Arts.* Washington D.C.: Smithsonian Institution Press; Philadelphia: Pennsylvania Academy of the Fine Arts, 1994.

Hendricks, Gordon. *The Photographs of Thomas Eakins.* New York: Grossman, Publishers, 1972.

HAROLD EDGERTON

Bruce, Roger, ed. *Seeing the Unseen: Dr. Harold Edgerton and the Wonders of Strobe Alley.* Rochester, NY: George Eastman House; Cambridge, MA: MIT Press, 1994.

ALFRED EISENSTAEDT

Eisenstaedt, Alfred. *Eisenstaedt on Eisenstaedt.* Introduction by Peter Adam. New York: Abbeville Press, 1985.

PETER HENRY EMERSON

Newhall, Nancy. *P. H. Emerson: The Fight for Photography as a Fine Art.* Millerton, NY: Aperture, 1975.

FREDERICK H. EVANS

Hammond, Anne, ed. *Frederick H. Evans: Selected Texts and Bibliography.* World Photographers Reference Series, vol. 1. Boston: G. K. Hall, 1992.

WALKER EVANS

Agee, James, and Walker Evans. *Let Us Now Praise Famous Men*. Boston: Houghton Mifflin Company; Cambridge: Riverside Press, 1960.

Greenough, Sarah. *Walker Evans: Subways and Streets*. Washington, D.C.: National Gallery of Art, 1991.

Keller, Judith. *Walker Evans: The Getty Museum Collection*. Malibu, CA: J. Paul Getty Museum, 1995.

Mora, Gilles. *Walker Evans: The Hungry Eye*. New York: Harry N. Abrams, 1993.

Rathbone, Belinda. *Walker Evans: A Biography*. Boston and New York: Houghton Mifflin Co., 1995.

Walker Evans: American Photographs. New York: Museum of Modern Art, 1938.

F

HOLLIS FRAMPTON

Jenkins, Bruce and Susan Krane. *Hollis Frampton: Recollections/ Recreations*. Cambridge: The MIT Press, 1984.

ROGER FENTON

Hannavy, John. *Fenton of Crimble Hall*. Boston: David R. Godine, 1975.

Lloyd, Valeri. *Roger Fenton: Photographer of the 1850s*. London: South Bank Board, 1988.

ROBERT FRANK

Frank, Robert. *Les Américains*. Paris: Delpire, 1958. Published in English as *The Americans*. Introduction by Jack Kerouac. New York: Grove Press, 1959. Rev. eds. Millerton, NY: Aperture, 1969, 1978.

Frank, Robert. *The Lines of My Hand*, revised edition. New York: Lustrum Press, 1972.

Greenough, Sarah, and Philip Brookman, et al. *Robert Frank: Moving Out*. Washington, D.C.: National Gallery of Art, 1994.

LEE FRIEDLANDER

Letters from the People: Photographs by Lee Friedlander. New York: Museum of Modern Art, 1993.

FRANCIS FIRTH

Firth, Francis. *Egypt and the Holy Land in Historic Photographs*. C. 1860s. Reprint. New York: Dover Publications, 1980.

G

ALEXANDER GARDNER

Gardner, Alexander. *Gardner's Photographic Sketchbook of the Civil War*. New York: Dover Publications, 1959.

Johnson, Brooks. *An Enduring Interest: The Photographs of Alexander Gardner*. Norfolk, VA: Chrysler Museum, 1991.

PETER GOIN

Nuclear Landscapes. Baltimore: The Johns Hopkins University Press, 1991.

Humanature. Austin: University of Texas Press, 1996.

H

DAVID T. HANSON

Waste Land: Meditations on a Ravaged Landscape. Preface by Wendell Berry. New York: Aperture, 1997.

RAOUL HAUSMANN

Hausmann, Raoul. *Photographies, 1927–1957*. Paris: Editions Crétis, 1979.

JOHN HEARTFIELD

Heartfield, John. *Photomontages of the Nazi Period*. New York: Universe Books, 1977.

Pachnicke, Peter, and Klaus Honnef, eds. *John Heartfield*. New York: Harry N. Abrams, 1993.

FLORENCE HENRI

du Pont, Diana C. *Florence Henri: Artist-Photographer of the Avant-Garde*. San Francisco: San Francisco Museum of Modern Art, 1990.

DAVID OCTAVIUS HILL AND ROBERT ADAMSON

Ford, Colin, ed. *An Early Victorian Album: The Photographic Masterpieces (1843–47) of David Octavius Hill and Robert Adamson*. Introduction by Colin Ford. Essay by Roy Strong. New York: Alfred A. Knopf, 1976.

Schwarz, Heinrich. *David Octavius Hill: Master of Photography*. London: George C. Harrap, 1932.

LEWIS W. HINE

Gutman, Judith Mara. *Lewis W. Hine and the American Social Conscience*. New York: Walker, 1967.

Kaplan, Daile, ed. *Photo Story: Selected Letters and Photographs of Lewis Hine*. Washington, D.C.: Smithsonian Institution Press, 1992.

Rosenblum, Walter, Naomi Rosenblum, and Alan Trachtenberg. *America and Lewis Hine: Photographs, 1904–1940*. Millerton, NY: Aperture, 1977.

HANNAH HÖCH

Lavin, Maud. *Cut With the Kitchen Knife: The Weimar Photomontages of Hannah Höch*. New Haven and London: Yale University Press, 1993.

J

WILLIAM HENRY JACKSON

Hales, Peter B. *William Henry Jackson and the Transformation of the American Landscape*. Philadelphia: Temple University Press, 1988.

Jackson, William Henry. *Time Exposure: The Autobiography of William Henry Jackson.* Intro. by Ferenc M. Szasz. Albuquerque: University of New Mexico Press, 1986.

FRANCES B. JOHNSTON

Johnston, Frances Benjamin. *The Hampton Album.* New York: Museum of Modern Art, 1966.

K

GERTRUDE KÄSEBIER

Michaels, Barbara. *Gertrude Käsebier: The Photographer and Her Photographs.* New York: Harry N. Abrams, 1992.

ANDRÉ KERTÉSZ

Ducrot, Nicholas, ed. *André Kertész: Sixty Years of Photography, 1912–1972.* New York: Viking Press, Grossman Publishers, 1972.

Kertész, André. *J'aime Paris,* New York: Viking Press, Grossman Publishers, 1974.

Phillips, Sandra S., David Travis, and Weston Naef. *André Kertész: Of Paris and New York.* Chicago: Art Institute of Chicago, 1985.

ANSELM KIEFER

Rafael López-Pedraza Anselm Kiefer: *The Psychology of "After The Catastrophe."* New York: George Braziller, 1996.

WILLIAM KLEIN

Close-up: Photographs and Texts by William Klein. London: Thames and Hudson, 1990.

William Klein: New York, 1954–1955. Paris: Editions de Seuil, 1956. Manchester, England: Dewi Lewis Publishing, 1995.

William Klein: Photographs. Profile by John Heilpern. Millerton, NY: Aperture, 1981.

JOSEF KOUDELKA

Koudelka, Josef. *Gypsies.* Millerton, NY: Aperture, 1975.

L

DORTHEA LANGE

Dorthea Lange: American Photographs. San Francisco: San Francisco Museum of Modern Art; Chronicle Books, 1994.

Dorthea Lange: Photographs of a Lifetime. Millerton, NY: Aperture, 1982.

Elliot, George P. *Dorthea Lange.* New York: Museum of Modern Art, 1966.

Lange, Dorthea, and Paul S. Taylor. *An American Exodus.* Oakland, CA: Oakland Museum; New Haven, CT: Yale University Press, 1969.

Meltzer, Milton. *Dorthea Lange: A Photographer's Life.* New York: Farrar, Straus and Giroux, 1978.

Partridge, Elizabeth, ed. *Dorthea Lange: A Visual Life.* Washington, D.C.: Smithsonian Institution Press, 1994.

L

JACQUES HENRI LARTIGUE

Lartigue, Jacques Henri. *Boyhood Photos of J. H. Lartigue: The Family Album of a Gilded Age.* Lausanne, Switzerland: Ami Guichard, 1966.

Goldberg, Vicki, introduction. *Jacques Henry Lartigue, Photographer.* Boston: Bulfinch Press, 1998.

CLARENCE J. LAUGHLIN

Davis, Keith F., ed. *Clarence J. Laughlin: Visionary Photographer.* Albuquerque: University of New Mexico Press, 1990.

Laughlin, Clarence J. *Ghosts Along the Mississippi.* New York: Bonanza Books, 1961.

RUSSELL LEE

Hurley, F. Jack. *Russell Lee, Photographer.* Dobbs Ferry, NY: Morgan and Morgan, 1978.

GUSTAVE LE GRAY

Janis, Eugenia Parry. *The Photography of Gustave Le Gray.* Chicago: Art Institute of Chicago; University of Chicago Press, 1987.

HELEN LEVITT

Levitt, Helen. *A Way of Seeing.* 3rd ed., with additional photographs. Durham, NC: Duke University Press, 1989.

Phillips, Sandra S., and Maria Morris Hambourg. *Helen Levitt.* San Francisco: San Francisco Museum of Modern Art, 1991.

DANNY LYON

Danny Lyon: Photo-Film. Tucson: Center for Creative Photography, University of Arizona; Essen, Germany: Museum Folkwang, 1992.

Lyon, Danny. *Conversations with the Dead.* New York: Rinehart and Winston, 1971.

NATHAN LYONS

Notations in Passing, Visualized by Nathan Lyons. Cambridge: The MIT Press in collaboration with Light Impressions Corporation, 1974.

Verbal Landscape/Dinosaur Sat Down. Buffalo: CEPA Gallery & Albright-Knox Art Gallery, 1987.

Riding First Class on the Titanic. Andover, MA: Addison Gallery of American Art, 2000.

M

MAN RAY

Foresta, Merry A., et al. *Perpetual Motif: The Art of Man Ray.* New York: Abbeville Press, 1988.

Man Ray. *Self-Portrait.* Boston: Little, Brown, 1963.

ETIENNE–JULES MAREY

Braun, Marta. *Picturing Time: The Work of Etienne-Jules Marey (1830–1904)*. Chicago: The University of Chicago Press, 1992.

E. J. Marey: 1830–1904, La Photographie du Movement. Paris: Centre Georges Pompidou, 1977.

MARY ELLEN MARK

Fulton, Marianne. *Mary Ellen Mark: 25 Years*. Boston: Little, Brown, Bulfinch Press, 1991.

DON MCCULLIN

Hearts of Darkness: Photographs by Don McCullin. Intro. By John Le Carré. New York: Alfred A. Knopf, 1981.

RALPH EUGENE MEATYARD

Hall, James Baker, ed. *Ralph Eugene Meatyard*. Millerton, NY: Aperture, 1974.

Meatyard, Ralph Eugene. *The Family Album of Lucybelle Crater*. Millerton, NY: The Jargon Society, 1974.

PEDRO MEYER

Meyer, Pedro. *Truths and Fictions: A Journey from Documentary to Digital Photography*. New York: Aperture, 1995.

JOEL MEYEROWITZ

Meyerowitz, Joel. *Cape Light*. Boston: Museum of Fine Arts/New York Graphic Society, 1978.

DUANE MICHALS

Livingstone, Marco. *The Essential Duane Michals*. Boston: Little, Brown, Bulfinch Press, 1997

LEE MILLER

Miller, Lee. *Lee Miller's War*. Edited by Anthony Penrose. Boston: Little, Brown, Bulfinch Press, 1992.

RICHARD MISRACH

Wilkes Tucker, Anne with an essay by Rebecca Sonit. *Crimes and Splendors: The Desert Cantos of Richard Misrach*. Boston: Little, Brown, Bulfinch Press, 1996.

LISETTE MODEL

Lisette Model. Preface by Berenice Abbott. Millerton, NY: Aperture, 1979.

Thomas, Ann. *Lisette Model*. Ottawa: National Gallery of Canada; Chicago: University of Chicago Press, 1990.

TINA MODOTTI

Constantine, Mildred. *Tina Modotti: A Fragile Life*. New York: Rizzoli, 1983. Reprint. San Francisco: Chronicle Books, 1993.

LÁSZLÓ MOHOLY-NAGY

Haus, Andreas. *Moholy-Nagy: Photographs and Photograms*. New York: Random House, Pantheon Books, 1980.

Moholy-Nagy, László. *Malerei, Photographie, Film, Bauhausbook 8*. Munich: Albert Langen Verlag, 1925; rev. ed., 1927. English ed., *Painting Photography Film*. Cambridge, MA: MIT Press, 1969.

Moholy-Nagy, László. *Vision in Motion*. Chicago: Paul Theobold and Co., 1947.

BARBARA MORGAN

Barbara Morgan: Photomontage. Dobbs Ferry, NY: Morgan and Morgan, 1980.

WRIGHT MORRIS

James Alinder, ed. *Wright Morris: Photographs and Words*. Carmel, CA: The Friends of Photography, 1982.

Morris, Wright. *Time Pieces: Photographs, Writing, and Memory*. New York: Aperture, 1989.

MARTIN MUNKACSI

Morgan, Susan. *Martin Munkacsi*. New York: Aperture, 1992.

White, Nancy, and John Esten. *Style in Motion: Munkacsi Photographs '20s, '30s, '40s*. New York: Clarkson N. Potter, Inc., 1979.

EADWEARD MUYBRIDGE

Eadweard Muybridge: The Stanford Years, 1872–1882. Intro. by Anita Ventura Mozley. Palo Alto, CA: Stanford University Museum of Art, 1972.

Haas, Robert Bartlett. *Muybridge: Man in Motion*. Berkeley, Los Angeles, London: University of California Press, 1976.

Muybridge's Complete Human and Animal Locomotion. 3 vols. Intro. by Anita Ventura Mozley. New York: Dover Publications, 1979.

N

NADAR

Gosling, Nigel. *Nadar*. New York: Alfred A. Knopf, 1976.

Hambourg, Maria Morris, Francoise Heilburn, and Philippe Neagu. *Nadar*. New York: Metropolitan Museum of Art, 1995.

Prinet, Jean, and Antoinette Dilasser. *Nadar*. Paris: Armand Colin, 1966.

Nadar. *Quand J'étais Photographe*. Preface by Leon Daudet (1900). Reprint. New York: Arno Press, 1979.

CHARLES NÈGRE

Borcorman, James. *Charles Nègre, 1820–1880*. Ottawa: National Gallery of Canada, 1976.

ARNOLD NEWMAN

Fern, Alan, and Arnold Newman. *Arnold Newman's Americans*. Boston: Little, Brown, Bulfinch Press, 1992.

One Mind's Eye: The Portraits and Other Photographs of Arnold Newman. Boston: David R. Godine, 1974.

O

TIMOTHY O'SULLIVAN

Dingus, Rick. *The Photographic Artifacts of Timothy O'Sullivan.* Albuquerque: University of New Mexico Press, 1982.

Snyder, Joel. *American Frontiers: The Photographs of Timothy H. O'Sullivan, 1867–1874.* Millerton, NY: Aperture, 1981.

PAUL OUTERBRIDGE

Dines, Elaine, ed. *Paul Outerbridge: A Singular Aesthetic; Photographs and Drawings, 1921–1941. A Catalogue Raisonné.* Santa Barbara, CA: Arabesque, 1981.

Howe, Graham, and G. Ray Hawkins, eds. *Paul Outerbridge, Jr.: Photographs.* New York: Rizzoli, 1980.

P

GORDON PARKS

Parks, Gordon. *Voices in the Mirror: An Autobiography.* New York: Doubleday, Nan A. Talese, 1990.

IRVING PENN

Foresta, Merry A., and William F. Stapp. *Irving Penn: Master Images—The Collections of the National Museum of American Art and the National Portrait Gallery.* Washington, D.C.: Smithsonian Institution Press, 1990.

Penn, Irving. *Worlds in a Small Room.* New York: Grossman/Viking Press, 1974.

PABLO PICASSO

Baldassari, Anne. *Picasso and Photography: The Dark Mirror.* Translated by Deke Dusinberre.

Paris: Flammarion & The Museum of Fine Arts, Houston, 1997.

ELIOT PORTER

Intimate Landscapes: Photographs by Eliot Porter. Essay by Weston J. Naef. New York: Metropolitan Museum of Art; E.P. Dutton, 1979.

Porter, Eliot. *The Place No One Knew: Glen Canyon on the Colorado.* Edited by David Brower. New York: Sierra Club & Ballantine Books, 1968.

MARION POST WOLCOTT

Hurley, F. Jack. *Marion Post Wolcott: A Photographic Journey.* Albuquerque: University of New Mexico Press, 1989.

Hendrickson, Paul. *Looking for the Light: The Hidden Life and Art of Marion Post Wolcott.* New York: Alfred A. Knopf, 1992.

R

ROBERT RAUSCHENBERG

Hopps, Walter, and Susan Davidson, et al. *Robert Rauschenberg: A Retrospective.* New York: Guggenheim Museum, 1997.

OSCAR GUSTAV REJLANDER

Spencer, Stephanie. *O. G. Rejlander: Photography as Art.* Ann Arbor, MI: UMI Press, 1985.

ALBERT RENGER-PATZSCH

Albert Renger-Patzsch: 100 Photographs, 1928. Essays in English, German, and French. Cologne, Germany, and Boston: Schurmann and Kicken; Paris: Créatis, 1979.

Renger-Patzsch, Albert. *Die Welt ist schön: Ein Hundert photographische Aufnahme.* Published in English as *The World Is Beautiful.* Munich: Kurt Wolff Verlag, 1928.

JACOB A. RIIS

Alland, Alexander, Sr. *Jacob A. Riis: Photographer and Citizen.* Millerton, NY: Aperture, 1974.

Riis, Jacob A. *How the Other Half Lives: Studies Among the Tenements of New York.* New York: Charles Scribner's Sons, 1890. Reprint, with added photographs, New York: Dover Publications, 1971.

HENRY PEACH ROBINSON

Harker, Margaret F. *Henry Peach Robinson: Master Photographic Art, 1830–1901.* Oxford, England: Basil Blackwell, 1988.

Robinson, Henry Peach. *Pictorial Effect in Photography.* Intro. By Robert Sobieszek. Reprint. Pawlet, VT: Helios, 1972.

ALEXANDER RODCHENKO

Elliot, David, ed. *Alexander Rodchenko, 1891–1956.* Oxford, England: Museum of Modern Art, 1979.

Khan-Magomedov, S. O. *Rodchenko: The Complete Work.* Cambridge, MA: MIT Press, 1986.

Lavrentiev, Alexander. *Alexander Rodchenko: Photography 1924–1954.* Edison, NJ: Knickerbocker Press, 1995.

MILTON ROGOVIN

Wypijewski, Joann. *Triptychs: Buffalo's Lower West Side Revisited.* Photographs by Milton Rogovin. New York: W. W. Norton, 1994.

ARTHUR ROTHSTEIN

Rothstein, Arthur. *The Depression Years as Photographed by Arthur Rothstein.* New York: Dover Publications, 1978.

S

SEBASTIÃO SALGADO

Salgado, Sebastião. *Workers: An Archeology of the Industrial Age.* New York: Aperture, 1993.

ERICH SALOMON

Hunter-Salomon, Peter. *Erich Salomon: Portrait of an Age.* New York: The Macmillan Co., 1967.

Salomon, Erich. *Porträt einer Epoch.* Frankfurt and Berlin: Verlag Ullstein, 1963. Published in English as *Portrait of an Age.* New York: Macmillan Company, 1967.

AUGUST SANDER

August Sander: Photographs of an Epoch. 1904–1959. Preface by Beaumont Newhall; historical commentary by Robert Kramer. Millerton, NY: Aperture, 1980.

Heiting, Manfred ed., *August Sander 1876–1964.* Cologne: Taschen, 1999.

Sander, August. *Antlitz der Zeit.* Munich: Kurt Wolff/Transmare Verlag, 1929.

Sander, August. *Men Without Masks: Faces of Germany, 1910–1938.* Greenwich, CT: New York Graphic Society, 1971.

BEN SHAHN

Pratt, Davis, ed. *The Photographic Eye of Ben Shahn.* Cambridge: Harvard University Press, 1975.

CHARLES SHEELER

Millard, Charles W., III. "Charles Sheeler, American Photographer," *Contemporary Photographer,* vol. 6, no. 1 (1967): entire issue.

Stebbins, Theodore E., Jr., and Norman Keyes, Jr. *Charles Sheeler: The Photographs.* Boston: Little, Brown, 1987.

CINDY SHERMAN

Cruz, Amada, and Elizabeth A. T. Smith and Amelia Jones. *Cindy Sherman: Retrospective.* New York: Thames and Hudson, Inc. and the Museum of Contemporary Art, Chicago, and The Museum of Contemporary Art, Los Angeles, 1997.

Krauss, Rosalind, and Norman Bryson. *Cindy Sherman, 1975–1993.* New York: Rizzoli, 1993.

CAMILLE SILVY

Haworth-Booth, Mark. *Camille Silvy: River Scene, France.* Getty Museum Studies on Art, Malibu, CA: J. Paul Getty Museum, 1992.

AARON SISKIND

Chiarenza, Carl. *Aaron Siskind: Pleasures and Terror.* Boston: New York Graphic Society, 1982.

Siskind, Aaron. *Road Trip: Photographs 1980–1988.* Albuquerque: University of New Mexico Press; Carmel, CA: Friends of Photography, 1993.

W. EUGENE SMITH

Hughes, Jim. *W. Eugene Smith: Shadow and Substance. The Life and Work of an American Photographer.* New York: McGraw-Hill 1989.

Johnson, William S., ed. *W. Eugene Smith: Master of the Photographic Essay.* Millerton, NY: Aperture, 1981.

Smith, W. Eugene, and Aileen M. Smith. *Minamata.* New York: Holt, Rinehart and Winston, 1975.

W. Eugene Smith: His Photographs and Notes. Millerton, NY: Aperture, 1969.

Willumson, Glenn G. *W. Eugene Smith and the Photographic Essay.* New York: Cambridge University Press, 1992.

FREDERICK SOMMER

Weiss, John, ed. *Venus, Jupiter and Mars: Frederick Sommer.* Wilmington: Delaware Art Museum, 1980.

ALBERT SANDS SOUTHWORTH AND JOSIAH JOHNSON HAWES

Sobieszek, Robert, and Odette M. Appel. *The Spirit of Fact: The Daguerreotypes of Southworth and Hawes.* Boston: David R. Godine; Rochester, NY: International Museum of Photography, 1976.

EDWARD STEICHEN

Longwell, Dennis. *Steichen: The Master Prints. 1895–1914.* New York: Museum of Modern Art; Boston: New York Graphic Society, 1978.

Steichen, Edward. *A Life In Photography.* Garden City, NY: Doubleday, 1963.

RALPH STEINER

Steiner, Ralph. *A Point of View.* Middletown, CT: Wesleyan University Press, 1978.

JOEL STERNFELD

American Prospects: Photographs by Joel Sternfeld. Preface to the new edition and introduction by Andy Grundberg, afterword by Anne W. Tucker. San Francisco: Friends of Photography in association with Chronicle Books, 1994.

ALFRED STIEGLITZ

Doty, Robert C. *Photo-Secession: Stieglitz and the Fine Art Movement in Photography.* New York: Dover Press, 1978.

Greenough, Sarah, and Juan Hamilton. *Alfred Stieglitz, Photographs & Writings.* Washington, D.C.: National Gallery of Art and New York: Callaway Editions, 1983.

Homer, William Innes. *Alfred Stieglitz and the Photo-Secession.* Boston: A New York Graphic Society Book, Little, Brown and Company, 1983.

Norman, Dorothy. *Alfred Stieglitz: An American Seer.* Millerton, NY: Aperture; New York: Random House, 1973.

Peterson, Christian A. *Alfred Stieglitz's "Camera Notes."* New York: W. W. Norton, 1993.

Waldo, Frank, et al. *America and Alfred Stieglitz: A Collective Portrait*. 1934. Rev. ed. Millerton, NY: Aperture, 1979.

PAUL STRAND

Hambourg, Maria Morris. *Paul Strand, Circa 1916*. New York: Metropolitan Museum of Art & New York: Abrams, 1998.

Paul Strand: Sixty Years of Photographs. Profile by Calvin Tompkins. Millerton, NY: Aperture, 1976.

Paul Strand: A Retrospective Monograph, the Years 1915–1968, 2 vols. Millerton, NY: Aperture, 1976.

Stange, Maren, ed. *Paul Strand: Essays on His Life and Work*. New York: Aperture, 1990.

Strand, Paul, and Nancy Newhall. *Time in New England*. New York: Oxford University Press, 1950. Rev. ed. Millerton, NY: Aperture, 1982.

T

WILLIAM HENRY FOX TALBOT

Arnold, H. J. P. *William Henry Fox Talbot: Pioneer of Photography and Man of Science*. London: Hutchinson Benham, 1977.

Buckland, Gail. *Fox Talbot and the Invention of Photography*. Boston: David R. Godine, 1980.

Talbot, William Henry Fox. *The Pencil of Nature*. Facsimile ed. New York: Da Capo Press, 1961.

Weaver, Mike. *Henry Fox Talbot: Selected Texts and Bibliography*. World Photographers Reference Series, vol. 3. Boston: G. K. Hall, 1993.

JOHN THOMSON

Thompson [sic], John, and Adolphe Smith. *Street Life in London*. Facsimile ed. Bronx, NY: Bernard Blom, 1969.

White, Stephen. *John Thomson: Life and Photographs*. Albuquerque: University of New Mexico Press, 1989.

U

JERRY N. UELSMANN

Jerry N. Uelsmann. Essay by Peter Bunnell. Millerton, NY: Aperture, 1970.

Photo-Synthesis: Photographs by Jerry Uelsmann. Gainesville: University of Florida Press, 1992.

Uelsmann, Jerry N. *Silver Meditations*. Dobbs Ferry, NY: Morgan and Morgan, 1975.

V

JAMES VAN DER ZEE

James Van Der Zee. Dobbs Ferry, NY: Morgan and Morgan, 1973.

Willis-Braithwaite, Deborah. *Van Der Zee: Photographer, 1886–1983*. New York: Harry N. Abrams; Washington D.C.: National Portrait Gallery, Smithsonian Institution, 1993.

ROMAN VISHNIAC

To Give Them Light: The Legacy of Roman Vishniac. New York: Simon and Schuster, 1993.

ADAM CLARK VROMAN

Webb, William and Robert A. Weinstein. *Dwellers at the Source: Southwestern Indian Photographs by A. C. Vroman, 1895–1904*. New York: Viking Press, Grossman Publishers, 1973.

W

CARLETON E. WATKINS

Carleton E. Watkins, Photographs, 1861–1874. San Francisco: Bedford Arts Publishers, 1989.

Palmquist, Peter E. *Carleton E. Watkins: Photographer of the American West*. Albuquerque: University of New Mexico Press, 1983.

Rule, Amy, ed. *Carleton Watkins: Selected Texts and Bibliography*. Oxford, England: Clio Press, 1993.

WEEGEE (ARTHUR FELIG)

Stettner, Louis, ed. *Weegee*. New York: Alfred A. Knopf, 1977.

Weegee. *Naked City*. New York: Essential Books, 1946.

Weegee's New York: Photographs, 1935–1960. Munich: Schirmer Art Books, 1982, 1996.

CARRIE MAE WEEMS

Carrie Mae Weems: Recent Work, 1992–1998. Essays by Thomas Piché Jr. and Thelma Golden. New York: George Braziller Publisher in association with Everson Museum of Art, 1998.

WILLIAM WEGMAN

Man's Best Friend: Photographs and Drawings by William Wegman. New York: Harry N. Abrams, 1982.

EDWARD WESTON

Conger, Amy. *Edward Weston: Photographs*. Tucson: Center for Creative Photography, University of Arizona, 1992.

Maddow, Ben. *Edward Weston: Fifty Years*. Millerton, NY: Aperture, 1973.

Newhall, Nancy, ed. *The Daybooks of Edward Weston: Volume 1, Mexico*. Millerton, NY: Aperture, 1961, 1973.

Newhall, Nancy, ed. *The Daybooks of Edward Weston: Volume 2, California*. Millerton, NY: Aperture, 1961, 1973.

Weston, Edward. *My Camera at Point Lobos*. Yosemite National Park, CA: Virginia Adams; Boston: Houghton Mifflin Co., 1950.

Wilson, Charis, and Edward Weston. *California and the West*. 1940. Reprint, Millerton, NY: Aperture, 1978.

CLARENCE H. WHITE

Homer, William Innes. *Symbolism of Light: The Photographs of Clarence H. White*. Wilmington: Delaware Art Museum, 1977.

MINOR WHITE

Bunnell, Peter. *Minor White: The Eye That Shapes*. Boston: Little, Brown, Bulfinch Press, 1989.

GARRY WINOGRAND

Szarkowski, John. *Winogrand: Figments from the Real World*. New York: Museum of Modern Art, 1988.

JOEL-PETER WITKIN

Witkin, Joel-Peter. *Gods of Earth and Heaven*. Altadena, CA: Twelvetrees, 1989.

TECHNOLOGY

A

Auer, Michael. *The Illustrated History of the Camera, from 1839 to the Present*. Boston: New York Graphic Society, 1975.

B

Broecker, William L., ed. *Encyclopedia of Photography*. New York: Crown Publishers, Inc., 1984.

C

Crawford, William. *The Keepers of the Light: A History and Working Guide to Early Photographic Processes*. Dobbs Ferry, NY: Morgan and Morgan, 1979.

G

Golding, Stephen. *Photomontage: A Step-by-Step Guide to Building Pictures*. Rockport, MA: Rockport Publishers, 1997.

H

Haworth-Booth, Mark, and Brian Coe. *A Guide to Early Photographic Processes*. London: Victoria & Albert Museum, 1983.

Hirsch, Robert. *Exploring Color Photography*. Third Edition. New York: McGraw-Hill, 1997.

Hirsch, Robert. *Photographic Possibilities: The Expressive Use of Ideas, Materials, and Processes*. Boston and London: Focal Press, 1991.

J

Jussim, Estelle. *Visual Communication and the Graphic Arts: Photographic Technologies in the Nineteenth Century*. New York: R. R. Bowker Company, 1974.

K

Keefe, Laurence E., Jr., and Dennis Inch. *The Life of a Photograph*. Second edition. Boston and London: Focal Press, 1990.

L

Life Library of Photography, 17 vols. New York: Time-Life Books, 1970–72.

London, Barbara, and John Upton. *Photography*, Fifth Edition. NY: Harper Collins College Publishers, 1994.

Lothrop, Eaton S., Jr. *A Century of Cameras from the Collection of the International Museum at George Eastman House*. Dobbs Ferry, NY: Morgan & Morgan, 1973.

M

Mees, C. E. Kenneth. *From Dry Plates to Ektachrome Film*. New York: Ziff-Davis, 1961.

N

Nadeau, Luis. *Encyclopedia of Printing, Photographic and Photomechanical Processes*. Revised combined edition, vols. 1 and 2—A–Z. Fredericton, New Brunswick, Canada: Atelier, 1997.

S

Seeley, J. *High Contrast*, second edition. Boston: Focal Press, 1992.

Shaw, Susan D., and Monona Rossol. *Overexposure: Health Hazards in Photography*. New York: Allworth Press, 1991.

Stone, Jim. *Darkroom Dynamics: A Guide to Creative Darkroom Techniques*. Marblehead, MA and New York: Curtain and London and Van Nostrand Reinhold, 1979.

Stone, Jim. *A User's Guide to the View Camera*, 2nd edition. New York: Addison Wesley Longman, 1997.

Stroebel, Leslie, and Richard Zakia, eds. *The Focal Encyclopedia of Photography*, 3rd edition. Boston and London: Focal Press, 1993.

Stroebel, Leslie, et al. *Basic Photographic Materials and Processes*. Boston: Focal Press, 1990.

W

Wall, E. J. and Franklin I. Jordan. *Photographic Facts and Formulas*. Boston: American Photographic Publishing Co., 1940.

Wilhelm, Henry, with Carol Bower. *The Permanence and Care of Color Photographs*. Grinnell, IA: Preservations Publishing Co., 1993.

Wilson, Edward L. *Wilson's Photographics: A Series of Lessons . . . on all Processes which are Needful in the Art of Photography (1881)*. Reprint. New York: Arno Press, 1973.

A

Aperture, 20 East 23rd Street, New York, NY 10010

A.R.T. Press, 5820 Wilshire Blvd., Suite 402, Los Angeles, CA 90036

C

Center for Book Arts, 626 Broadway, 5th Floor, New York, NY 10012

Center for Exploratory & Perceptual Art (CEPA Gallery), 617 Main Street, Suite 201, Buffalo, NY 14203

D

D.A.P., 636 Broadway, 12th Floor, New York, NY 10012

H

Hacker Art Books, Inc. 45 West 57th Street, New York, NY 10019

L

Light Work, 316 Waverly Avenue, Syracuse, NY 13244

N

Nexus Press, 535 Means St., Atlanta, GA 30318

P

A Photographer's Place, P.O. Box 274, Prince Street Station, New York, NY 10012

Photo-Eye Books, 376 Garcia Street, Santa Fe, NM 87501

Printed Matter Bookstore at Dia, 77 Wooster Street, New York, NY 10012

U

University of New Mexico Press, 1720 Lomas Boulevard, Albuquerque, NM 87131

V

Visual Studies Workshop, 31 Prince Street, Rochester, NY 14607

W

World Wide Web. Numerous Web sites offer photography books. Use your search engine for current addresses.

SOURCES OF ARTISTS BOOKS

ABOUT THE AUTHOR

Robert Hirsch is an imagemaker, curator, professor, and writer. He is on the Art Faculty of the State University of New York at Buffalo. He is the author of *Exploring Color Photography* (McGraw-Hill) and *Photographic Possibilities: The Expressive Use of Ideas, Materials, and Processes* (Focal Press). With many one-person and group shows to his credit, he has also curated numerous photography exhibitions during his tenure as Executive Director of the CEPA Gallery (Center for Exploratory and Perceptual Art) in Buffalo, New York. Hirsch is a columnist for *Photovision* magazine and teaches the history of photography online. For details visit: www.enmu.edu/photohistory.